SOCIAL DEMOCRACY IN THE MAKING

BOOKS BY GARY DORRIEN

Logic and Consciousness

The Democratic Socialist Vision

Reconstructing the Common Good

The Neoconservative Mind: Politics, Culture, and the War of Ideology

Soul in Society: The Making and Renewal of Social Christianity

The Word as True Myth: Interpreting Modern Theology

The Remaking of Evangelical Theology

The Barthian Revolt in Modern Theology

The Making of American Liberal Theology:
Imagining Progressive Religion, 1805–1900

The Making of American Liberal Theology:
Idealism, Realism, and Modernity, 1900–1950

Imperial Designs: Neoconservatism and the New Pax Americana

The Making of American Liberal Theology:
Crisis, Irony, and Postmodernity, 1950–2005

Social Ethics in the Making: Interpreting an American Tradition

Economy, Difference, Empire: Social Ethics for Social Justice

The Obama Question: A Progressive Perspective

Kantian Reason and Hegelian Spirit: The Idealistic Logic of Modern Theology

The New Abolition: W. E. B. Du Bois and the Black Social Gospel

Breaking White Supremacy: Martin Luther King Jr.
and the Black Social Gospel

Social Democracy in the Making: Political and Religious Roots of
European Socialism

SOCIAL DEMOCRACY IN THE MAKING

Political and Religious Roots of European Socialism

Gary Dorrien

Yale
UNIVERSITY
PRESS
New Haven & London

Yale University Press books may be purchased in quantity for educational, business, or promotional use. For information, please e-mail sales.press@yale.edu (U.S. office) or sales@yaleup.co.uk (U.K. office).

Set in PostScript Electra type by IDS Infotech, Ltd.
Printed in the United States of America.

Library of Congress Control Number: 2018945481
ISBN 978-0-300-23602-6 (hardcover : alk. paper)

A catalogue record for this book is available from the British Library.

This paper meets the requirements of ANSI/NISO Z39.48-1992 (Permanence of Paper).

10 9 8 7 6 5 4 3 2 1

*To my doctoral advisees, past and present,
with gratitude and affection:*

*Malinda Berry, Chloe Breyer, Ian Doescher,
Babydoll Kennedy, David Orr, Keun-Joo Christine Pae,
Dan Rohrer, Charlene Sinclair, Joe Strife, Eboni Marshall Turman,
Rima Vesely-Flad, Colleen Wessel-McCoy, Demian Wheeler,
Jason Wyman, and Tracy Riggle Young;
Nkosi Anderson, Jeremy Kirk, Kelly Maeshiro,
Anthony Jermaine Ross-Allam, Isaac Sharp,
Aaron Stauffer, and Todd Willison*

CONTENTS

PREFACE

This book combines my longtime work in political history and political economics, modern theology and post-Kantian philosophy, and social theory and social ethics, focusing on the intertwined history of Christian socialism and Social Democratic politics in Britain and Germany. It also draws upon my forty-plus years of social justice activism, most recently in the Bernie Sanders electoral campaign. It thus has a long personal backstory, while registering the hopes and traumas of the 2016 U.S. American presidential election.

Two presidential candidates drew enormous crowds in 2015 and 2016 — Democratic primary contender Sanders and Republican winner Donald Trump. Both made strong appeals to working-class and middle-class voters who felt left behind by corporate capitalism and the power of Wall Street over both political parties. Sanders and Trump, however, waged so-called populist campaigns of dramatically contrasting kinds. Sanders advocated a democratic socialist politics of freedom, equality, and universal human solidarity. Trump achieved political prominence by leading the "birther" movement, which had no basis besides racism; formally launched his candidacy by demonizing Mexican immigrants, which lifted him above all other Republican candidates; and called for a ban on all Muslim immigrants, which made him unbeatable in the Republican Party. Trump's narcissistic amorality carried him to the presidency, a spectacle that haunted me as I wrote this book. But this book came out of the other campaign story of 2016.

Today the Social Democratic idea of social decency is embattled across Europe, and the few victories it ever achieved in the United States are under assault. In Europe, Social Democratic parties are struggling to counter the dominating power of finance capitalism, restrain the explosion of inequality wrought by economic globalization and technology, sustain generous systems of social

insurance, combat the rise of anti-immigrant nationalism, and distinguish themselves from center-right parties. Many are so integrated into the establishment
that their socialist pasts are invisible. In Germany the Social Democratic Party
(SPD) joined Chancellor Angela Merkel's Conservative government for her
third term in December 2013, subsequently confirming that the hollowing out
had run its course. The SPD ran a desultory election campaign in 2017, failed to
distinguish itself from Merkel, and tried to stay out of her fourth government,
hoping to thwart the far-right Alternative for Germany from becoming the official opposition. But Merkel could not form a governing coalition with other
parties, so the SPD resigned itself to propping up another Conservative government. In Britain the Labour Party similarly refashioned itself as a center-left
bastion of neoliberalism under Labour prime ministers Tony Blair and Gordon
Brown, fell out of power, turned to old-style leftist Jeremy Corbyn, and coped
with an anti-immigrant upsurge that pulled Britain out of the European Union.
In the United States, where the lack of a Social Democratic tradition ensured
that social insurance was never generous, even minimal social decency is now
in jeopardy. The Sanders campaign was a protest against the assault on virtually
all progressive gains and a demand for something unprecedented in U.S.
American history: a Social Democratic standard of social decency.

Forty years of letting Wall Street and big corporations do whatever they want
have yielded belated protests against the predatory logic of global finance capitalism. Occupy Wall Street, a sensational moment of rebellion, signaled that
something had changed. Occupy was not geared to forge alliances, scale up, or
construct anything, but it changed movement politics. Sanders seized on this
turn in his campaign for the Democratic nomination. He stunned the political
class of party professionals in Washington, DC, by drawing huge crowds and
winning primaries. Sanders did not create the upsurge against inequality and
exclusion; he simply spoke to it, realizing it was there. He did not fudge his
democratic socialist beliefs; he straightforwardly espoused the worldview of the
Socialist International enunciated at its 1962 conference in Oslo, Norway: "We
democratic Socialists proclaim our conviction that the ultimate aim of political
activity is the fullest development of every human personality, that liberty and
democratic self-government are precious rights which must not be surrendered;
that every individual is entitled to equal status, consideration and opportunity;
that discrimination on grounds of race, color, nationality, creed or sex must be
opposed; that the community must ensure that material resources are used for
the common good rather than the enrichment of the few; above all, that freedom and equality and prosperity are not alternatives between which the people
must choose but ideals which can be achieved and enjoyed together."[1]

For twelve years before I became an academic I served as a solidarity organizer, national board member, and chapter president in two Social Democratic organizations, a foundational experience for what became my academic work. Two historic figures inspired and shaped my thinking and feeling: Martin Luther King Jr. and Norman Thomas. Both were mediated to me partly through my mentor and friend Michael Harrington. The influence of King in my life was and is spiritual and political, the bedrock of my lifework. Thomas was the leading American exponent of democratic socialism for forty years and the six-time Socialist Party candidate for president. In my twenties I absorbed Harrington's stories about his friendships with King and Thomas, and his perspective on how their causes should be renewed.

Thomas worked tirelessly for racial justice, civil liberties, peace, and economic justice, imploring Americans that a strong dose of European Social Democracy would be good for America. In 1932 he ran on the usual Socialist platform, sharing no positions with Democratic candidate Franklin Roosevelt. Then Thomas watched Roosevelt carry out 90 percent of the Socialist platform, ruefully protesting that he carried it out on a stretcher. Socialists got no political credit for the New Deal, as Thomas won fewer votes in 1936 than in 1932, despite being called the conscience of the nation. Thomas showed that one could win respectability in American politics as a Socialist as long as one opposed Communism and did not seem dangerous. He wore three-piece suits and sounded like the Princeton graduate and former Presbyterian minister that he was. He dreamed of a farmer–labor Social Democratic party modeled on the Cooperative Commonwealth Federation in Canada, which morphed into the New Democratic Party in 1961. King called Thomas the most courageous man he ever met. Thomas, however, never won more than 2.2 percent of the national vote.[2]

I was schooled in the bitter lessons of the Norman Thomas era by Old Left socialists who had lived through the humiliation and futility of the Thomas campaigns. In the 1970s and 1980s the Social Democratic organizations in which I worked periodically raised the Norman Thomas question, which in our context meant, "Should we run Mike Harrington for president?" If we didn't run Harrington for president, how were Americans to learn there was such a thing as democratic socialism? Harrington cofounded the organizations that succeeded the Socialist Party—the Democratic Socialist Organizing Committee and Democratic Socialists of America. He persuaded them to work in the left wing of the Democratic Party, which he called "the left wing of possibility." Every election season many of us youthful types, having come of age in the civil rights and antiwar movements of the 1960s, chafed at Harrington's strategy. Why should we join campaigns in which we were silenced? How did that move the needle toward economic democracy and a universalized Medicare? How were we to advance Social Democratic politics in a party that opposed socializing anything? Always the old-timers invoked the bitter lessons of the Thomas era: Liberal victories cleared room for Social Democratic gains, now as then. There was no other way, lacking an eruption that changed the lessons of history.

In the United States that was a plausible judgment. In Britain and Germany significant movements for Social Democracy—broadly conceived in the British case—coalesced in the nineteenth century and won their first flings at national power after World War I, in contrasting circumstances made similar by the ravages of the war. The core ideas of what progressive Christian socialism should be were very similar in England, Germany, the United States, Canada, and the Germanic regions of Switzerland. But Christian socialism had very different legacies in these places. The story of Christian socialist theology, Marxist theory, and Social Democratic politics in Britain and Germany cannot be told without ranging into France, Switzerland, Austria, Sweden, and Russia because Socialist movements in these nations spilled into the story. This is not true of Christian socialism and Social Democracy in the United States and Canada, so I have fixed on the two nations with the richest traditions of my twofold subject. Thus I have left aside North American traditions that inform much of my previous work; holding together two sprawling traditions of political theology and socialist politics in two national contexts is enough for one book.

I have resisted the nearly constant impulse to comment upon current Social Democratic debates and electoral fortunes, a project for a later book. Today the democratic socialist streams in every European Social Democratic party are outnumbered by mainstreams that relinquished the goal of economic democracy long ago. In Germany Marxists in the Rosa Luxemburg–Antonio Gramsci tradition—some with Euro-Communist backgrounds—have claimed the language of democratic socialism despite spurning the Social Democratic traditions that created it, reasoning that Social Democrats abandoned it anyway. I do not dispute the right of Luxemburg–Gramsci Marxists to call themselves democratic socialists because, as this book documents, democratic socialism has never been one thing only. For much of its history it has been a theory of Social Democratic governance, yet most democratic socialist traditions have in their DNA the dream of a socialist state that votes itself out of existence. The contradictions in the idea of a "socialist state" alone have yielded different kinds of democratic socialism. Other factors multiplied the possibilities.

This book describes and interprets the Social Democratic and Christian socialist backstory to where we are today. I have long believed, before Barnard political scientist Sheri Berman superbly documented the argument, that the achievements of Social Democracy are seriously and routinely underestimated. It is factually wrong, plus bad for us, to believe the regnant propaganda that the twentieth century ended with the triumph of free market capitalism. Like Berman, I shall argue that Social Democracy is an ideology in its own right, distinct from orthodox Marxism and free market capitalism. Unlike her, I hold Social Democracy to a democratic socialist standard, believing that Social Democracy loses its soul when it does not fight for economic democracy.[3]

In 1982 Sweden made a historic breakthrough by enacting a program to substantially democratize ownership of major firms and, potentially, the process of investment, the Meidner Plan for Economic Democracy. It was backed by Swedish unions and the base of the Social Democratic Party and fiercely opposed by the nation's investor class and conservatives. It also got tepid, reluctant, halfway support from Social Democratic leaders, which killed it after an eight-year run. The intraparty battle that occurred over the Meidner Plan reflected the gap between the democratic socialist idea and the fallback to welfare state capitalism that exists in every Social Democratic party. I am a proponent of narrowing the gap. But I believe that politics, not a political ideal, must be primary in politics *and* that the historic achievements of Social Democracy are seriously underestimated. We must understand what Social Democracy achieved and what it took to create modern standards of social decency if we are to avoid squandering these achievements. We cannot build upon the lessons of the past if we do not know the past. On occasion I have peeked ahead of the book's mid-1960s endpoint to indicate how an argument or trend played out. Codetermination, the Meidner Plan, and the social movements of the 1970s get brief mentions of that sort. But this book holds to its subject and historical period, always with an implied judgment about which parts of the history still matter.

Harrington tried to make Marx more democratic than he was, a problem I was compelled to sort out many years ago. I greatly respect the contributions of Marxists to democratic socialism and Social Democracy and to the neverending work of adjudicating the relationships between them. Any attempt to interpret the democratic socialist tradition has to wrangle with difficult questions about the role of Marxism in it. To me it is not as important as it was to Harrington to say that Marx was a democratic socialist. On the other hand, I do not read Marx or Marxism out of democratic socialism or Social Democracy, as both would have been greatly impoverished lacking Marxist criticism—and that is putting it as mildly as possible.

In previous books I thanked numerous academics with whom I am linked by friendship and mutual scholarly engagement. This book is like the others in drawing upon ongoing conversations with academic friends, but this time I cite longtime friends from solidarity and peace activism. A few happen to be academics, but I befriended all in the activist trenches: Wade Adams, Larry Alcoff, Linda Martín Alcoff, Lynwood Bartley, April Brumson, Joan Brown Campbell, Ignacio Castuera, Paul Clements, the late William Sloane Coffin Jr., Henry Cohen, John Collins, Sheila Collins, Danny Collum, Don Cooney, the late John C. Cort, Ernesto Cortes, Kim Cummings, Gene Damm, the late Bogdan Denitch, Judith Deutsch, Frank Fitzgerald, James Forbes, Otha Gilyard, Gertrude Goldberg, the late Vincent Harding, Richard Healey, Chris Iosso, Maggie Kirwin, Ron Kramer, Becca Kutz-Marks, Chuck Kutz-Marks, Peter Laarman, Michael Lerner, Felipe Luciano, the late Manning Marable, Bob Massie, Lillie McLaughlin, Liz Nolan, Brian O'Shaughnessy, Darby Penney, Al Pennybacker, Stephen Phelps, Maxine Phillips, Bob Redlo, George F. Regas, Ronnie Steinberg, Francie Traschen, Dorothy Tristman, Jim Wallace, Jim Wallis, Cornel West, Jim Wilson-Garrison, and Larry Wittner.

I am equally grateful to friends who read parts of this book on its way from conferences and seminars to production: Sheri Berman, Luke Bretherton, Katrina Forman, Obery Hendricks Jr., Brigitte Kahl, Catherine Keller, Michael Lerner, Kelly Maeshiro, Maxine Phillips, Jan Rehmann, Joerg Rieger, Anthony Jermaine Ross-Allam, Isaac Sharp, Aaron Stauffer, Stanley Talbert, Gotlind Ulshöfer, Benjamin Van Dyne, Gerhard Wegner, and Andrea White. Jan reminds me, justly, that the Luxemburg–Gramsci line is ideologically purer than the sprawling traditions I hold together. Luke and I share the same belief in the importance of the ethical socialist, Christian socialist, and social unionist streams of the Labour Party, even if I dwell too much on the Fabians who dominated the party for decades. Joerg's voice is in my head from the conference platforms we have shared and his books. The same is true of Obery and Michael, with longer historical arcs. Catherine prodded me to remember that wading this deeply into a historical subject has to be justified. Blessings and thanks to all.

I am grateful for permission to adapt material from my books *The Barthian Revolt in Modern Theology* (Louisville: Westminster John Knox Press, 2000) and *The Making of American Liberal Theology: Idealism, Realism, and Modernity* (Louisville: Westminster John Knox Press, 2001). Many thanks to my editors Heather Gold and Susan Laity for their superb work, and especially to executive editor Jennifer Banks and copyeditor Lawrence Kenney. And thanks to my longtime indexer Diana Witt for another excellent index.

Social Democracy in the Making

CHRISTIAN SOCIALISM IN THE MAKING OF SOCIAL DEMOCRACY

Every Social Democratic party in the world is a reminder of the nineteenth-century dream of democratic socialism—a fully democratized society in which the people control the economy and government, no group dominates any other, and every citizen is free, equal, and included. The founders of Social Democracy believed that capitalism is antagonistic toward democracy and only socialism is truly democratic. Many claimed that a proletarian victory had to be achieved before democracy would be possible; others countered that socialists had to be resolutely democratic and supportive of liberal rights on the way to achieving socialism; and others said the sequence depended on circumstances. The emphasis on democracy helped many socialists cope with the fact that no socialist revolution occurred in an advanced capitalist society. But when democratic socialists founded the Socialist International in 1889, they believed that socialist revolutions were inevitable. "Democratic socialism" and "Social Democracy" came to mean different things because democratic socialists were wrong about socialist revolutions occurring in many capitalist nations, or any at all. Meanwhile they competed for votes in capitalist societies.

Social Democracy became synonymous with its record, something less daring and interesting than democratic socialism—unless revisionists were right that democratic socialism should not be defined by an idealistic or Marxist goal. The revisionist impulse in Social Democracy is always about revising the ideal to fit the achievements and goals of a real-world political tradition. Every Social Democratic party is a pale reflection of a founding vision and an obstacle to remembering that democratic socialism is a radical idea. Today Social Democratic parties are struggling to sustain the welfare states they built after World War II and to hold off reactionary movements based on nationalism and racism. Economic globalization has battered the social contracts that Social

Democracy constructed during its heyday. Moreover, "socialist" names a tradition of ethical and economic criticism more than a particular idea of an alternative system. But the greatest democratic socialist achievements occur through organizations that begin with the everyday praxis of unions and social movements; dismantle structures of racial, gender, sex, class, and imperial domination; welcome religious allies; renew the struggles for freedom, equality, and cooperative community; and care for the planet's ecological health.

This book describes the differently intertwined legacies of Christian socialism and Social Democratic politics in Britain and Germany, with a constructive purpose. It argues that distinctly British cultural and historical factors enabled Christian socialists to be deeply involved in the making of British Social Democracy. It argues that the embedding of British socialism in a labor movement party, not a Continental-style Social Democratic party, allowed Christian socialists to continue to play this role even after the Labour Party adopted a Fabian socialist constitution. It argues that early Christian socialism was much less compelling and accomplished in Germany, even though Germany had the richest traditions of modern theology and Social Democracy and even though Germany and Germanic Switzerland produced leading socialist theologians. The book tracks the making of Social Democracy in Britain and Germany to the mid-1960s, when revisionist versions of both traditions gained power. It construes the British tradition as a form of Social Democracy while stressing Labour Party distinctiveness. It makes arguments for decentralized economic democracy and anti-imperial internationalism while emphasizing that socialism in the foremost bastions of empire was usually statist, plus wobbly on anti-imperialism. It favors, among the theologians discussed in this book, Leonhard Ragaz, Paul Tillich, and William Temple, and it argues that the Christian socialist tradition offers a better backstory for political theology than the usual one.

Political theology needs a better genealogy than the Carl Schmitt story it usually tells. It has an incomparably better one in the religious and ethical socialists who imagined a democratic socialist society and contributed to the making of Social Democracy. Many theologians and religion scholars, however, are somehow content to say that modern political theology began with a Nazi legal theorist, Schmitt, who despised liberal democracy in standard Nazi fashion. Schmitt taught, cynically but interestingly, that the distinction between friends and enemies is the key to politics. He reasoned, provocatively, that all forms of political thinking are ways of renaming theological categories. His scholarly bandwagon, which got rolling in the political theologies of the 1960s, sprawled to multiple fields in the 1980s, and is now a cottage industry, gave theologians an opening to reverse his program: All theology is political, especially when it claims otherwise.[1]

This reverse-Schmitt procedure undergirds much creative work in contemporary religious thought, especially in neo-Marxist, Whiteheadian, Deleuzian, and liberationist forms of political theology. It tracks the displacement of God by the sovereignty of the modern state, which in some renderings gave way to the godly sovereignty of corporate neocolonialism, capitalist Empire. It importantly counters the isolation of the political from the theological and religious that defined the soulless subjectivity of Enlightenment rationality, which uprooted transcendence from the materiality of life. But Christian socialists were doing explicit political theology long before Schmitt, Emanuel Hirsch, and Paul Althaus championed the atrocious idea of fascist theology. Early Christian socialism in England, Germany, Switzerland, the United States, and Canada was a creative response to the social ravages of unfettered nineteenth-century capitalism. In England and North America it was predominantly cooperative, progressive, social ethical, and pragmatic, usually fusing liberal and democratic elements, with less opposition from ecclesiastical establishments than Christian socialists experienced elsewhere. In Germany Christian socialism had a stronger ideological and statist character as a consequence of yearning for, and then defending, a unified state. Here, Christian socialists had to fight off a Social Democratic movement that was hostile to religion and established churches that were hostile to trade unions and socialism.

Early Christian socialism in Britain and Germany shared similar understandings of Christian social ethics and dreams of replacing capitalism with a political economy geared to the common good. It differed sharply by virtue of developing in profoundly diverse cultural, political, religious, and economic contexts and by playing dissimilar roles in national politics. Christian socialism paved the way for all liberation theologies that make the struggles of oppressed peoples the subject of redemption. Yet a great deal of contemporary religious thought proceeds as though Christian socialism never happened and Carl Schmitt invented political theology.

My dual focus on Christian socialism and Social Democracy in two national contexts yields some sections that are wholly devoted to socialist theory and history, some that are extensively theological, and some that hold these discourses together, reflecting actual convergences. In England socialism was pragmatic, nonideological, commonwealth-minded, open to clerics, sometimes romantic, and often middle class. Socialist clerics assumed they should be involved in public contentions over liberal politics, state funding for cooperatives, the merits of Marxism and Fabianism, whether England needed a party of workers, and how to oppose British imperialism. In Germany, where Social Democracy was ideological, anticlerical, and overwhelmingly proletarian, British assumptions were hard to fathom.

Charles Fourier, in France, and Robert Owen, in England, propounded the original idea of socialism in the 1820s. It was to achieve the unrealized demands of the French Revolution, which never reached the working class. Instead of pitting workers against each other, a cooperative mode of production and exchange would allow them to work for each other. Socialism was about reorganizing society as a cooperative community. Soon there were many kinds of socialism conceived by Louis Jean Joseph Blanc, Pierre-Joseph Proudhon, Mikhail Bakunin, Karl Marx, Ferdinand Lassalle, Wilhelm Liebknecht, Georgi Plekhanov, Karl Kautsky, William Morris, Sidney Webb, Rosa Luxemburg, V. I. Lenin, and G. D. H. Cole. The founders blamed capitalism for all of society's ills, but religious socialists did not, so there were Christian and Jewish versions of nearly every kind of socialism, notably by Philippe-Joseph-Benjamin Buchez, Frederick Denison Maurice, John Ludlow, Moses Hess, George Herron, Stewart Headlam, Theodor Herzl, Abraham Cahan, Charles Marson, Conrad Noel, Hermann Kutter, Walter Rauschenbusch, Vida Scudder, and Martin Buber.

Every kind of socialism retains the original idea of reorganizing society as a cooperative community, yet there is no core that unites the many schools of socialism and democratic socialism, and democracy is as complex and variable as socialism. The many schools of democratic socialism alone do not reduce to a unifying essence, and certain Communist thinkers such as Rosa Luxemburg and Karl Korsch might arguably be included in democratic socialism, even as the Communist traditions are excluded from it. I believe that the best candidate for an essential "something" in democratic socialism is the ethical passion for social justice and radical democratic community. This ethical impulse retains the original socialist idea in multiple forms, playing out in struggles for freedom, equality, recognition, and democratic commonwealth, conceiving democracy in terms of the character of relationships in a society, not mere voting rights.

Many socialist traditions have denigrated moral-anything as mere idealism, usually in favor of a collective determinist claim along Marxian or Fabian lines. But no definition of socialism as economic collectivism or state control of the economy or any particular ownership scheme is common to the many traditions of socialist thought. Various schools of democratic socialism hold ample right to the name without agreeing on its defining meaning or goal. Historically, Marxism played the leading role in reducing, for many, the idea of socialism to collective ownership. Karl Marx taught that the structure of economic ownership determines the character of an entire society, and socialism is the collective ownership of the means of production—a sufficient condition for fulfilling the essential aspirations of human beings. He developed the most powerful and illuminating critique of the capitalist system ever conceived, inspiring numerous traditions of Marxian criticism. His focus on the factors of production and the structural capitalist tendency to generate crises of overproduction and crash made permanent contributions to socialist thought. His achievement was so great that even non-Marxian traditions of socialism have to be understood in relationship to his thought. But Marx's dogmatic determinism, catastrophe mentality, and doctrine of proletarian dictatorship wrecked colossal harm. He developed his theory during an era in which democracy was merely a form of government and thus of low importance to him. His denigration of moral-everything obscured his own ethical wellspring. And his fixation on collective ownership wrongly identified socialism with a totalizing goal.

England had rich traditions of cooperative ethical socialism and Christian socialism long before it produced a Marxist group of any kind and very long before it had a significant Marxist thinker or tradition. Germany had two Social Democratic parties that were radically democratic, broadly socialist, and not very Marxist, until Marx himself intervened in 1875. In England Christian socialism began in 1848 with a fabled trio of Anglicans led by Frederick Denison Maurice, just in time to be ridiculed by young Marx for trying to co-opt a revolutionary upsurge. Maurice was a moral theologian and Anglican priest who said that Christianity and socialism belong together because they espouse the same defining principles of cooperation and fellowship. There is a divine moral order, cooperation is the moral law of the universe, and socialism embodies the divine order by creating a cooperative society. Maurice's lawyer friend John Ludlow, schooled in cooperative socialism in France, helped him launch a movement for Christian socialism in England, along with Charles Kingsley, an Anglican priest and author of popular novels.

Early Christian socialism was a tame affair, a counterword to unruly socialisms and to Christianities lacking a social conscience. The first Christian socialists, to put it slightly anachronistically, were Broad Church Anglicans with Anglo-Catholic leanings, though Maurice loathed the party system in the Church of England, aspiring to float above partisan fighting. Politically, the founders were exponents of different kinds of cooperative activism. Theologically, they adhered to Maurice's progressive sacramental ecumenism. Ideologically, they were descendants of the cooperative movement founded by the first British socialist, Robert Owen, sometimes with a French inflection. Owen's legacy was mostly cooperative-communal, although he tried to build a socialist union movement. Maurice taught that Christian socialism was a unifying alternative to partisan conflict, not a new form of it. His socialism was strongly theological and minimally political—an argument about recognizing an already existing divine order.

From the beginning, however, Maurice's band of Christian socialists clashed over what cooperative activism should be. Ludlow wanted to organize aggressive producer cooperatives like the labor organizations in France. Edward Neale and Lloyd Jones wanted to organize networks of producer and consumer cooperatives. Why should consumers be regarded as less important than producers? There were bruising arguments over state-financed producer cooperatives, a divisive issue in Britain, France, and eventually Germany. Maurice lamented that socialist politics was as divisive as ordinary politics. He and Ludlow agreed to oppose consumer cooperatives, but Maurice shuddered at the politicking that came with Ludlow's ambition to build labor societies. To Maurice, labor societies smacked too much of French radicalism. He had company in his wariness of France because French radicalism was stridently antireligious and very French, with syndical tendencies. It was hard to imagine a wholesome Christian socialism coming out of France, where a republican revolution had quickly morphed into a reign of terror. Ludlow, however, worked hard to pass the Industrial and Provident Societies' Act of 1852, a breakthrough for cooperative societies in Britain. Maurice pulled back to something equally novel but less political, worker education, a sequel to his pioneering work in founding England's first college open to women. Many Christian socialists later wished that Ludlow or Neale had played the Maurice role in defining what Christian socialism should be.

But Maurice's theology was distinctly enabling for British Christian socialism, usually in tandem with cooperative network activism. In the 1860s and 1870s, as capitalism grew and reigned triumphant in England, Maurice's progressive sacramental theology kept alive the vision of a cooperative order. Then his spiritual disciples renewed Christian socialism in the 1880s, showing that some churches cared about the poor and the newly unemployed. The new generation of Christian socialists railed against the novel phenomenon of mass unemployment. They fused the kingdom of God with the Commonwealth consciousness of British culture, conceiving the universal church as the corporate body of Christ and Britain as an ethical Commonwealth. In the academy it helped that a Hegel vogue overtook British philosophy. Multiple versions of G. W. F. Hegel's post-Kantian idealism were proffered, notably Anglo-Catholic socialist versions in which Hegelian idealism improved upon classic Neoplatonist Christianity by adapting it to the modern world of process.

One scrappy Anglo-Catholic organization, the Guild of Saint Matthew (GSM), and one radical paper, the ecumenical *Christian Socialist*, played the trailblazing roles in renewing Christian socialism. Anglo-Catholic cleric Stewart Headlam founded the GSM as a spirit-of-Maurice enterprise shorn of Maurice's Broad Church sensibility. It was stringently High Church but allied with atheistic humanists and artists and focused politically on socializing land and opposing imperialism. The *Christian Socialist*, brilliantly edited by Anglo-Catholic cleric Charles L. Marson, seeded ecumenical and denominational offshoots with its fiery anti-imperialism and its call for public control of land, capital, and all means of production, distribution, and exchange. Both of these vehicles had friendly relationships with the Fabian Society, a mostly secular powerhouse founded in 1884 to promote gradual progress toward state socialism. In 1889 two Anglo-Catholic clerics headed for eminent careers in the Church of England, Henry Scott Holland and Charles Gore, founded another spirit-of-Maurice enterprise, the Christian Social Union (CSU). It was basically Anglo-Catholic too but closer than GSM to Maurice's inclusive spirit and long on Oxford dons determined not to miss out on Christian socialism. Like the Fabian Society, the CSU permeated British centers of power with a vision of progressive centralized governance. It mushroomed to six thousand members, including many bishops, and sixty chapters.

There were tiny socialist fellowships in the Congregational, Baptist, Quaker, and Unitarian denominations; there were two interdenominational socialist organizations that rose and fell, plus a Free Church version; and one organization — the Labour Church — built a successful post-Christian movement conceiving socialism as a new religion. Tellingly, the denominations with significant percentages of trade unionists — the Primitive Methodists, Bible Christians, and Roman Catholics — produced almost no avowed socialists, and neither did the Wesleyan Methodist and United Methodist traditions. To British Methodists and Catholics, socialism was alien, threatening, and anti-Christian, exactly as the papal encyclical *Rerum Novarum* (1891) powerfully asserted, even as Pope Leo XIII and many Methodist union leaders stoutly defended trade unions. The Nonconforming traditions made their chief contributions to British Christian socialism by giving individual leaders to it. Labor leader Keir Hardie was vaguely Methodist before he joined the (Congregational) Evangelical Union Church; the short-lived Christian Socialist League was led by a Baptist, John Clifford; guild socialist leader and onetime Fabian S. G. Hobson was the most radical Quaker of his time; Unitarian minister Philip Wicksteed introduced the neoclassical economic focus on marginal utility to the Fabian Society and the Labour Church; and for ten years preceding World War I, England's most famous preacher, R. J. Campbell, was a Congregational socialist before he converted to Anglo-Catholicism.

Anglo-Catholics dominated British Christian socialism, even in the leadership of the ecumenical socialist organizations. Headlam and GSM won influence despite antagonizing the church establishment; Holland, Gore, and CSU made deep inroads in the ecclesiastical and political establishments; and ecumenical organizations came and went, never breaking the power of denominational loyalties and financial structures. British Christian socialism, like British socialism generally, had significant middle-class organizations well before it broke through to unions and working-class communities. It did not break through until a band of radical Anglo-Catholic socialists led by clerics G. Algernon West, Conrad Noel, and P. E. T. Widdrington founded the Church Socialist League in 1906. This was the third major Anglican vehicle of social Christianity, and the most radical. It was belatedly possible because British socialism belatedly acquired a workers' party in 1893, which morphed into something bigger in 1900, which morphed into the Labour Party in 1906.

Keir Hardie was the key founder of the three parties that became the Labour Party. A Scottish Christian socialist and union leader, he endured so hardpressed an upbringing that he began working full-time at the age of eight. The greatest of his many achievements, founding the Independent Labour Party (ILP) in 1893, forced Christian socialists and Fabians to decide whether they still belonged in the radical wing of the Liberal Party or were willing to support the party of actual workers. For many it was an excruciating question. Some preferred middle-class company, and many shared Holland's fear that a workers' party would be a disaster for anti-imperialism, destroying the Liberal Party's left wing and perhaps the Liberal Party altogether. Even if the ILP opposed imperial wars—something nobody knew for sure until the ILP opposed the Boer War—splitting the progressive vote would hand the government to the Tories. Holland grieved at the prospect of Tory imperialists taking power and doing whatever they wanted. To radical socialists such as Noel and S. G. Hobson, however, not siding with the workers was a ridiculous option for any socialist.

Hobson and ILP up-and-comer Ramsay MacDonald, while belonging to the Fabian Society in the 1890s, railed against it for denigrating workers *and* for being soft on imperialism. They blistered the Fabian Society for the same reasons that Noel and Marson disliked middle-class Christian socialism. Socialism was supposed to be radical, anti-imperialist, antimilitarist, slightly dangerous, allied with the working class, and unconcerned about how it smelled. If the workers' party didn't see the importance of anti-imperialism, it had to be persuaded by anti-imperialists *in* the party. Staying in the Liberal Party was anathema to real socialists, now that a workers' party existed. Nesting in the Conservative Party, which Fabian leaders Sidney Webb and Beatrice Webb did during the Balfour administration of 1902–1905, was worse yet. Christian socialists urged genteel comrades to overcome their qualms about aligning with politicized trade unions and angling for power in Parliament. Many of them did so after the ILP cofounded the Labour Representation Committee (LRC) in 1900, which became the British Labour Party six years later.

The idea of a respectable, ethical, reformist, evolutionary socialism was second nature to many Christian socialists, and it defined Fabian socialism until Sidney Webb replaced ethical idealism with a doctrine of bureaucratic collectivism. Christian socialism and Fabian socialism were both predisposed to middle-class reforms, averting class warfare. Both were suited for a nation lacking revolutionary traditions of ideological class war and hostility to the state. The Fabian Society was an industrious band of pamphleteers, lecturers, and researchers led by Webb and upcoming literary star George Bernard Shaw. It said British socialism did not need Marx's glorification of revolutionary violence or his exotic doctrines; all it needed was to proceed on its present course. Fabian socialism under Webb and his savvy partner Beatrice Webb became an ideology of centralized government collectivism, a vision of bureaucratic deliverance for decades before the Webbs disastrously idealized Communist deliverance in Russia. Sidney Webb, a pioneering labor researcher and institution builder, stressed that the reach of government in every industrial society grew every year. This process was relentless, beneficial, and civilizing, taming the predatory and anarchic impulses of capitalism. Getting the best possible outcome would not require class warfare or even anything disruptive. It only needed the process of rationalizing society to continue on its existing course. The flow of Progress would carry Britain and the entire world to a civilized order.

All good liberals, progressives, ethical socialists, radical democrats, and radical Tories of the late Victorian era believed the world was progressing toward unity and freedom. Even Marxists held a version of the belief in Progress, one that inverted Hegel's idea of dialectical unfolding. The Fabians were distinct mainly for building a socialist movement on a progressive bureaucratic version of the Progress idea. True Fabians felt no tension in the idea of state socialism, for only a socialist state would achieve socialism. Many Christian socialists became state socialists on more or less Fabian terms, accepting the ideology of progressive socialization. Some joined the Fabian Society and more stuck to their own organizations.

But Christian socialists did not believe the progressive logic of history trumped the ethical struggle for social justice. Therefore they did not defend imperialism, racism, and eugenics, unlike certain leading Fabians, and some did not believe that state socialism was the best option. At best, state socialism was a fallback. The idea of socialism as ethically based, decentralized, economic democracy has deep roots in Britain through the cooperative traditions associated with Owen and Maurice, and the aesthetic-ethical visions of two

Victorian literary icons, John Ruskin and William Morris. Ruskin, an art critic and Oxford don, wrote monthly letters to workers imagining a cooperative society. The book version was an eight-volume series titled *Fors Clavigera* (1884), a play on the human powers of force, fortitude, and fortune. Morris, an epic poet and novelist, founded the Socialist League in 1884 and wrote brilliant propaganda for it until quitting in 1890, despairing of sectarian dogmatists. He died in 1896, leaving a romantic legacy centered on novels in which people found happiness by building an egalitarian society. Ethical socialists and religious socialists bonded over their devotion to Ruskin and Morris, especially Morris. Both represented the idea that a good society was conceivable and achievable. The offshoots of the Owen, Maurice, and Morris traditions were determined to get as much as possible out of cooperative societies and other decentralized forms of working-class self-determination. These traditions, in my telling, were the heart and soul of the British socialism worth renewing today.[2]

One offshoot was settlement ministry, a form of community social work originating at Toynbee Hall. Samuel Barnett, an Anglican socialist cleric, and his wife, Henrietta Barnett, a forceful personality and manager, founded Toynbee Hall in 1884. Both were close to the Webbs and prone to Fabian technocracy, but their ministry practiced the evangelism of friendship, education, and social services, inspiring a settlement movement that had more in common with Maurice than with Fabian technocracy. Albert Mansbridge founded another offshoot in 1903, the Workers' Educational Association (WEA). A victim of England's suffocating class system in education, Mansbridge was a cooperative society official and Christian progressive who befriended Christian socialists on the Oxford faculty. He enlisted his friends to help him do something about class suffocation, building an organization for worker education that sprawled across the nation. Formal partnerships with universities were established, students and teachers worked together as equals, and the WEA became a training school for socialist thinkers, notably William Temple, R. H. Tawney, and G. D. H. Cole.

From the beginning, British socialism differed from Continental socialisms in being religion-friendly and ideologically porous. Then these differences were institutionalized in the British Labour Party—a labor movement vehicle, not a socialist party in the Continental sense. The First International (the International Workingmen's Association, 1864–1876) clashed and crashed over Marxism versus Anarchism, but Britain had only a handful of Marxists, and its tiny anarchist tradition was mostly libertarian, not revolutionary. In Britain Fabian gradualism swept the field, and Christian socialists were deeply involved in socialist politics. Working-class organizing was long delayed by the fearsome spectacle of 1834, when the government crushed Owen's fledgling union movement. In

1906 the LRC created the British Labour Party, a stockpot of reform, socialist, and union groups uniting on the idea that workers should have their own party; the ILP became a socialist ginger group in the Labour Party. Shortly after the Labour Party stumbled at the starting gate, Britain got a burst of syndical activism that morphed into a national movement for guild socialism, challenging the Fabian Society and Labour Party, very much in the manner of Continental radicalism.

Syndicalism, the idea that unions should run the economy and whatever government might exist in a revolutionary society, had a rich history in French labor unions. In the early twentieth century syndical movements arose in Italy, Spain, and the United States and, to a lesser degree, Britain. Socialist Labour Party founder James Connolly and union firebrand Tom Mann led the British versions in Scotland and England, respectively. Both, however, had marginal status in British unionism, as British workers did not endorse the syndical rhetoric of violent overthrow. Guild socialism played out differently by playing down the syndical fantasy of One Big Strike. Guild socialism was a blend of syndicalism, Fabian theory, Christian socialism, and medieval guild nostalgia, usually without citing Marx, although it had key affinities with Marxism. Its founders included former Fabians S. G. Hobson and Arthur Penty, dissident Fabians A. R. Orage, G. D. H. Cole, Holbrook Jackson, and William Mellor, and Christian socialists Maurice B. Reckitt, Conrad Noel, P. E. T. Widdrington, and R. H. Tawney. Socialism, they said, should be about worker self-determination, not building a collectivist government. The productive life of the nation should be organized and operated by self-governing democratic organizations embracing all workers in every industry and service. These National Guilds will emerge from the existing union movement. The guilds will organize industry but not own it. They will be owned by the state, which provides the capital, while the guilds produce the goods.

Guild socialism was attractive to Christian socialists from the Maurice tradition, ethical socialists from the Morris tradition, and followers of Roman Catholic author Hilaire Belloc, who wanted to re-create the medieval guild economy. *Rerum Novarum* blasted capitalism for destroying the guild system and condemned socialism as an anti-Christian menace bent on destroying private property. Guild socialists recognized Belloc and his followers as allies of their movement, while accepting that socialism was anathema to them. There was a significant cross section of Roman Catholics and Anglo-Catholics who favored the guild pluralism of Anglo-Catholic political theorist J. N. Figgis. For a decade the guild socialist movement fired the radical wing of the Labour Party and made Britain seem less exceptional. It founded a National Guilds League and was funded by the Labour Party, albeit while antagonizing Labour officials. Now even British socialists fought over worker self-government versus state socialism. Then the economy crashed in the early 1920s, the guild movement lost its financial basis in the party, and the season for exotic experiments ended. Normal Labour politics, as defined by Sidney Webb's constitution, prevailed.[3]

Sidney Webb, joining the Labour Party in 1914, established its official ideology in 1918. The British Labour Party, according to the constitution that Webb wrote for it, stood for pure Fabian Collectivism — full employment and a living wage, common ownership of industry, progressive taxation, and surplus spending for the common good. Clause Four, demanding common ownership of the means of production, distribution, and exchange, defined the party until 1959, ostensibly until 1995, and rhetorically after that. It did not say that socialization meant nationalization. Clause Four was also consistent with guild socialism, worker ownership, consumer cooperatives, municipal ownership, competitive public enterprises, and mixed forms of these strategies. Tawney, having advised Webb on Clause Four, had strong feelings on this point. But nationalization was popular in 1918 and demanded for the coal mines and railways. To some, nationalization was the preferred mode of socialization. To many, including Webb, it was the only one that mattered. In common usage "socialism" came to mean nationalization, notwithstanding that state socialism was the latecomer in the history of socialism. British Social Democracy grew powerful on the proposition that workers needed (Fabian) state socialism, not worker ownership or neo-syndical guilds. Always there were multiple kinds of socialists and nonsocialists in the Labour Party, contesting differences — especially in the 1930s — that exploded into factional battles in the 1950s. But the Fabian Collectivists held the upper hand until they achieved most of their agenda in the late 1940s, after which a powerful revisionist trend redefined democratic socialism as pluralistic, mostly realized Social Democracy.[4]

German Social Democracy reached a similar outcome by a very different route. Originally, German Social Democracy was statist and only slightly Marxist; then it acquired a Marxist character that made it very distinct from British socialism. My discussion of British socialism emphasizes that Marxism played a small role in it until the 1930s, even though Britain gave Marxism to the world by providing safe harbor to Karl Marx and Friedrich Engels. In Germany, by contrast, and in the smaller half of the First International, Marxist criticism played a significant role in creating a Social Democratic movement and subsequently defining socialist orthodoxy. From the beginning, Marxism had an ironic and conflicted influence. Young Marx was a radical humanist who spent his early intellectual career thrashing out his relationship to Hegel.

Eventually Marx settled on an inverted Hegelianism retaining Hegel's logic and key concepts, especially that dialectical conflict impels history to move forward as the struggle for freedom. Much of Marx's early work, however, was unknown to the early Marxists. Marx stepped into history as the coauthor of the *Communist Manifesto* of 1848. Capitalism, he said, stood for the rule of human products over human communities. It gained power, grew out of control, constrained human expectations, and blighted the lives of the overwhelming majority, the working-class proletariat. Communism was precisely the abolition of capitalist tyranny and liberation from it.

The *Manifesto* was shot through with motivational language, and it came at the outset of Marx's ultraleft phase. Thus it conveyed only one side of his complex, scholarly, radically democratic vision, with fateful consequences. Marx said the "bourgeoisie" of middle-class business owners and professionals was corrupt, hostile to workers, and dying, but proletarians should help bring it to power. Once the bourgeois revolution took place, the proletarian revolution would sweep it aside, apparently with no intervening period of bourgeois government, instituting a "dictatorship of the proletariat." Every part of this catastrophe-vision of deliverance was rife with danger if taken literally, yielding fateful debates about revolutionary violence, proletarian dictatorship, vanguard centralism, and anarchist expectations. To Marx, a Communist state was a contradiction in terms, but he fought with anarchists over the enormous difference between vowing to abolish the state (Anarchism) and believing the state would die out after the proletarian revolution (Marxism). Meanwhile Marx tried not to fight with his first disciples—German socialists who accepted only the parts of Marxism they liked or dubiously understood.[5]

Ferdinand Lassalle was the first and foremost German proto-Marxist. A legal scholar who was imprisoned for supporting the Republican revolution of 1848, he launched Germany's first socialist party almost single-handedly in Leipzig in 1863—the General German Workers Association (ADAV). Lassalle was brilliant, eccentric, Jewish, a democratic socialist, and, above all, Prussian. He achieved financial independence by waging thirty-five lawsuits on behalf of an unhappily married countess, winning a divorce for her in 1854. He embraced much of Marx's critique of capitalism but contended that the revolutionary phase of the proletarian struggle ended by 1862, when the Italian revolution sputtered inconclusively and did not spread to other nations. According to Lassalle, the road to socialism was legal, democratic, and parliamentary. It relied on the organized power of human will, not inevitable laws of history. Socialism was democracy realized, and the state had a vital role to play in it, especially in Germany. Lassalle colluded secretly with Prussian minister president Otto von Bismarck over their mutual aversion to bourgeois liberals and their dream of a united German Empire. Lassalle's fiery speeches inspired a proletarian movement featuring a cult of personality tinged with Hegel's cult of the state. He called for state-financed producer cooperatives and played up his affinities with Marx, who struggled to be cordial to him. Lassalle's vanity was hard to take, and Marx resented that Lassalle helped himself to Marx's ideas selectively. But Marx was in no position to antagonize the only person to get something started in Germany. He and Engels wrote for the ADAV newspaper, *Der Sozial-Demokrat*, trying to steer the party toward real Marxism, but gave up after it stuck with Lassalle.

Lassalle had a mutually respectful relationship with Wilhelm Emmanuel von Ketteler, the Roman Catholic archbishop of Mainz. Briefly there was a chance that German Social Democracy and part of the Catholic working class might achieve a decent working relationship. In 1864, however, Lassalle got himself killed at the age of thirty-nine in a duel over a brief romantic entanglement, and the chance was lost. Lassalle's party ran through seven successors in three years, finally settling on an ironhanded authoritarian, Johann Baptist von Schweitzer, in 1867. Two years later it acquired a rival, the Social Democratic Workers Party (SDAP). Wilhelm Liebknecht and August Bebel founded the new party in Eisenach as a protest against von Schweitzer's autocratic rule, the ADAV's coziness with Bismarck, its Prussian base, and its claim to be Marxist. The Lassalle group's reputed alliance with Bismarck was anathema to the SDAP—shameful and repugnant. Now there were two German Social Democratic parties. Each claimed to be redder than the other and blasted each other for selling out Marxism. Each wore its hostility to religion as a badge of honor and grew impressively. Both parties won breakthrough vote tallies in 1874 but split the socialist vote, compelling bitter antagonists to merge. The merger occurred in 1875 in Gotha, forming the Socialist Workers Party of Germany (*Sozialistische Arbeiterpartei Deutschlands*, SAPD); originality in nomenclature was not a strong point in these circles.

Both parties were less Marxist than they claimed, and both had radical-democratic leaders with socialist tendencies. The chief cause of their rivalry was pro-Prussia versus anti-Prussia, not Marxist doctrine. Everything concerning the united party's basis of existence was at stake at Gotha. Marx felt he was overdue to correct what both parties called Socialism and Marxism. His blistering polemic against the Lassalle group shrewdly masked that the other party in the merger wasn't very Marxist either. The united Social Democrats went on to establish the gold standard socialist party in Europe, heroically enduring government repression and a hostile Protestant establishment that denounced Social Democracy as anti-German, anti-God, anti-Civilization, too Jewish, and too Marxist. After it survived a storied drama of persecution, the party renamed itself in 1890, *Sozialdemokratische Partei Deutschlands* (the Social Democratic Party of Germany, SPD).

Any rendering of true versus false Marxism has to sort out Marx's tour de force at Gotha, *Critique of the Gotha Program* (1875). My rendering focuses on this text, plus the first and third volumes of Marx's *Capital* (1867, 1894), his *Contribution to the Critique of Political Economy* (1859), and his political writings, headed by *The Communist Manifesto* and *The Civil War in France* (1871). Engels emphasized the same texts in his classic exposition of orthodox Marxism, *Socialism: Utopian and Scientific* (1892), as did Eduard Bernstein, Karl Kautsky, and Rosa Luxemburg in their debates on orthodox and revisionist Marxism. My rendering of Marxism and German Social Democracy in chapter 3 builds upon my discussion of early Marxism and the First International in chapter 2, which naturally draws upon Marxian texts that Bernstein, Kautsky, and Luxemburg did not know when they fought over Bernstein's challenge to Marxism. But I am careful not to distort this historic debate by appealing to a humanistic early Marx they knew little about. I take a strong view of Bernstein's importance and his essential correctness, while appreciating that Luxemburg, a spectacular figure, scored against him, brilliantly defending a possibility that was not to be—a freedom-loving revolutionary Marxism that abolished capitalism, state domination, and alienation by creating a classless society.

Bernstein rightly identified the aspects of Marxism that were problematic for democratic socialism. He established that democratic socialism could draw deeply from Marx's economic analysis without accepting Marx's apocalyptic vision of deliverance. Bernstein showed that the SPD's ethical-reformist and union factions had a real basis in socialist and even Marxist theory; he and his allies were not mere opportunists. Socialists needed to grasp that capitalist economies were more complex than Marx said. Control of the economy was not inevitably destined by the process of industrial concentration to fall into the hands of a few monopolistic firms. Desperate to prevent World War I, Bernstein railed against the anti-French and anti-British fearmongering that paved the way to it. Like all SPD officials, he wanted to believe that socialism was the antidote to capitalist wars. Still, he shared the customary German dread of Russia, plus the SPD's fear of being trampled by prowar patriots, so he voted for war on August 4, 1914.

Shortly afterward he judged that Germany was chiefly responsible for causing the war. Bernstein allied with SPD center leftists who tried to stop the war without opposing Germany's war aims or government, but that was impossible in every way, including intraparty politics. Bernstein's antiwar faction was expelled from the Reichstag and regrouped as a new party, the Independent Social Democratic Party (USPD), which opposed the prowar SPD and Germany's imperialist war aims. Afterward, during the German Revolution of November 1918–February 1919, Bernstein tried to unite the SPD and USPD— another hopeless impossibility and equally fateful. The USPD conceived the worker and military councils of the November Revolution as foundations of a new society, advocating pure council-Marxism in opposition to parliamentary democracy. It prohibited dual memberships with the SPD because the SPD was twice discredited—once for the war and once for killing radical socialists in the November Revolution. Then the majority half of the USPD, in 1920, joined the Communist International, shattering Bernstein's dream of what should have been.

Subsequently he played a mostly commendable role in trying to create a decent republic. Bernstein saw the demon coming in his beloved nation before it fell for hypernationalism and stab-in-the-back mythology. He inveighed against Germany's refusal to accept responsibility for the war, which made him a pariah in his own party, the SPD, albeit with a seat in the Reichstag. When Bernstein died in 1932 nobody in Germany treated him as an esteemed founder of Social Democracy. His death passed without notice. Not only had capitalism failed to evolve into socialism; the chasm between his vision and the reality made him obsolete. His ethical-evolutionary brand of socialism seemed completely irrelevant and discredited. He got his due only long after he was gone, at the same time that German Social Democrats reclaimed Lassalle.[6]

In the 1920s a postwar generation of more or less orthodox Marxists revived Marxian theory by taking for granted some of Bernstein's criticisms. Georg Lukács, Karl Korsch, Antonio Gramsci, Friedrich Pollock, and Max Horkheimer relinquished just enough of Kautsky's base-superstructure orthodoxy to reopen the debate about what was essential to Marxism. Some were personally impacted by the Leninist dogmatism imposed on all Communist parties, and others steered clear of Communism. Lukács and Gramsci renewed the conception of Marxism as a radical critique of ideology, in both cases while they were enmeshed in complicating allegiances to Communist parties. All felt the necessity of rethinking Marxist theory. This generational phenomenon—a renaissance in Marxian theory—helped Paul Tillich find his way to a neo-Marxian form of religious socialism and a band of Jewish and Christian allies in Germany. Tillich espoused conventional German nationalism as a military chaplain during the war, moved swiftly to democratic socialism after the war, and tried to renew the best parts of a battered, reeling, marginal, and defective tradition in Germany, Christian socialism. This tradition had roots in the social activism of court chaplain Adolf Stöcker and author Friedrich Naumann. It had an exemplar of progressive social Christianity in Lutheran pastor Christoph Blumhardt, who served during World War I as a state government SPD official. It had allies of a sort in a prominent venue, the Evangelical Social Congress, led by eminent historical theologian Adolf von Harnack.

But Christian socialism in Germany was a patsy for nationalism, militarism, cultural chauvinism, and slurs against the too-Jewish, too-Marxian, too-atheistic, and too-threatening SPD. The coming of a proletarian movement in Germany terrified officials of the Lutheran, Reformed, Lutheran/Reformed Union, and Catholic churches. The world of the working class was a foreign country to German Protestant churches, and the Catholic working class had to create its own party to be involved in politics. Catholics were squeezed between hostile state governments on one side, especially in Prussia, and a hostile Social Democratic movement on the other. Lassalle's early death ended what might have been between Social Democrats and the (Catholic) Centre Party. After the socialist parties merged, Stöcker and Naumann tried to persuade working-class people that Protestant churches cared about them. But German Protestant socialism was late, flawed, and then toxically flawed.

Stöcker won a following for a right-wing populist form of Christian socialism, at first without featuring his anti-Semitic asides, until he realized that nothing revved up his crowds like a run of Jew bashing. Naumann was a smoother, more intellectual version of Stöcker, building a middle-class following for a mildly progressive Christian socialism before he morphed into a flaming militarist and imperialist. German social Christianity, as represented by Stöcker, Naumann, and Harnack, offered no check on escalating hypernationalism. Naumann perfected the aggrieved tone and feeling of a newfangled genre, national existentialism. Nationalism was distinctly legitimizing and unifying. Even the SPD had a right flank that cheered for war and empire after the nation went to war in August 1914. Germany had a trickle of progressive Christian socialists before, during, and after World War I. Many of them showed up at a conference in Tambach in September 1919 to regroup.

But there were never enough of them to rectify a failed beginning. Theologian Karl Barth, while remaining a Social Democrat on his quirky personal terms, ridiculed the idea of Christian socialism just after the war ended. Barth was Swiss but trained in German theology and identified with it, like other theologians from Germanic areas of Switzerland. His powerful rendering of a neo-Reformation approach to theology stoked an explosion of dialectical theologies that overtook Continental theology. Barth and Tillich were briefly allied as contributors to dialectical rethinking, as both were Pauline radicals about faith and grace, and both condemned Germany's liberal Protestant theological establishment. They also shared a commitment to radical democratic socialism, outflanking the SPD to the left, though both belonged to the SPD just before the Nazis took over. Otherwise they were profoundly different kinds of theologians.

My chapter on how theologians conceived Social Democracy and reacted to World War I dwells extensively on Barth and Tillich, explaining their highly influential theories, legacies, and mutual criticism. Barth is often caricatured in this area, and the only way to avert this outcome is to carefully explicate his tangle of arguments and self-understanding. Thus I have gone to some length to explain his perspective. Tillich integrated Christian theology and Social Democratic politics more profoundly and creatively than any theologian, with the possible exception of Anglican theologian William Temple. But Tillich's anti-ethical idealism gave him an excuse to change the subject after he fled to a capitalist colossus lacking a socialist tradition.

Swiss Reformed theologians Hermann Kutter and Leonhard Ragaz are important figures in my discussion of how theologians rendered Christian socialism as political theology. Both influenced Barth, but not enough. Kutter and Ragaz differently focused on what God was doing in the world, pointing to Social Democratic activism that lifted up the poor and oppressed, in contrast to the churches. A contrasting form of political theology arose in Germany just as Barth and Tillich began their academic careers; during the Nazi era it was called "German Christianity." Its major theologians were Emanuel Hirsch, an illustrious Lutheran scholar and close friend of Tillich who became an outright Nazi apologist, and Paul Althaus, an eminent Lutheran scholar who cheered for Adolf Hitler and supported German Christianity without formally signing up for either one. Barth and Tillich had a close-up view of the coming German Christian catastrophe, partly as a consequence of being closely acquainted with Hirsch. Much of Barth's legacy is directly attributable to his revulsion for German Christianity before it got organized. However, when Hitler came to power it was Tillich who was immediately branded as an enemy of the regime. Twelve years of espousing interreligious religious socialism, culminating in his prophetic book *The Socialist Decision* (1932), provided plenty of evidence to convict Tillich of being too Marxist, friendly to Jews, and opposed to fascism.[7]

To American readers familiar with American theology, the fates of liberal theology in Britain and Germany tend to be puzzling, so a prefatory word is needed. Six planks defined the liberal approach to theology wherever it sprouted. Liberals refused to establish or compel religious beliefs on the basis of a bare authority claim, carved a third way between orthodox over-belief and secular disbelief, accepted the historical critical approach to the Bible, allowed science to explain the physical world, looked beyond the church for answers, and sought to make faith relevant to the modern world.

During the Progressive Era there was a seventh plank that played a fatefully implosive role in German liberal theology, very little role in British liberal theology, and a permanently redefining role in American liberal theology: social Christianity. In Germany, liberal theology became wholly identified with Culture Protestantism, the bourgeois civil religion of an expanding German Empire, which set up liberal theology for a devastating crash. In England, Broad Church Anglicanism was only vaguely liberalizing for decades, there was no full-fledged liberal theology movement until the end of the nineteenth century, and it took very little interest in Christian socialism. In the United States, liberal theology surged into the established churches through the social gospel, a cultural earthquake that should be called the Third Great Awakening. American liberal theology originated in the eighteenth century among latter-day Puritans in the Congregational Church and became a field-changing movement in the late nineteenth century as the theology underlying the social gospel.

The American social gospel had a deeper, wider, and more lasting impact on established churches than was true anywhere in Europe, owing to its abolitionist and evangelical Puritan roots, plus America's lack of a state church. It was politically activist and progressive, supporting cooperatives, the nationalization of monopolies, and a doctrine of social salvation. In America the movements for liberal theology and the social gospel fused together as one movement. It was possible to be one without the other, and there were a few notable examples on each side. But the leaders of the social gospel said it made no sense to be one without the other. They conceived of the liberalizing impulse in theology and the social conscience of the social gospel as complementary aspects of the same struggle for freedom and progress.[8]

In Britain and Germany liberal theology had a stronger elitist character. British and German theological liberals took pride in belonging to a cultural elite, having been trained in highly prestigious universities. German theology was far more creative and profound than British theology, partly because Britain had no tradition of treating theology as a university discipline. For most of the nineteenth century, British liberals had to fight for the right to accept modern criticism. In both contexts, socialism was more serious and looming than in the United States, not a foreign idea, and liberalism retained its original character as the individualistic ideology of the middle class.

Liberal theology and Christian socialism were decidedly separate enterprises in Britain, with very few overlapping figures. Britain had no formal liberal movement in theology until the end of the nineteenth century because liberal theology was perceived as threatening, blasphemous, atheistic, and German. In the early eighteenth century British Anglicanism absorbed the mild rationalism of Anglican divines Joseph Butler and Samuel Clarke, which inoculated it from dreaded German novelties. The mid-nineteenth-century forerunners of liberal theology in Britain—disciples of Samuel Taylor Coleridge at Cambridge and Oxford—had to play down their Broad Church liberalism and their affinities with Kantian criticism. Anglican theology, despite its traditions of Renaissance humanism and Enlightenment rationalism, and despite its doctrine that reason is an authority in theology alongside tradition and below scripture, was powerfully constrained by ecclesiastical authority and creedal orthodoxy. In 1860 a mildly liberal book, *Essays and Reviews*, caused a firestorm of condemnation that raged across England, Scotland, and Wales for months. It killed the possibility of liberal theology in Britain for the next generation. In Britain only a handful of Anglicans, Unitarians, Congregationalists, and Presbyterians espoused liberal theology, and they tended toward humanistic deism, a fateful specter. British Anglicanism produced no explicitly liberal organization until 1898, when a group of low-church rationalists founded the Churchmen's Union for the Advancement of Liberal Religious Thought. These founders naturally fixed on intellectual freedom, especially the right of Anglican clergy to be theologically liberal. Otherwise, they warned, the church would be discredited and theology was sure to be expelled from the academy.

In Germany liberal theology had a long and storied background that reflected the strengths of a German invention, the modern research university. The founders of liberal theology in Germany were mid-eighteenth-century founders of the historical critical approach to the Bible: Johann S. Semler, Johann Gottfried Eichhorn, Johann Jakob Griesbach, and Johann David Michaelis. They surpassed the rationalist scholarship of the early Enlightenment by deconstructing the literary history of the scriptural text. They called themselves "neologians" or liberals until Immanuel Kant emerged as a commanding thinker in the 1780s, after which they called themselves Kantians. For the next century the Kantians claimed to own the liberal designation in theology, notwithstanding that post-Kantian disciples of Hegel and Friedrich Schleiermacher formed rival schools that were no less liberal, usually under the name "Mediating Theology," which variously fused Kant, Hegel, and/or Schleiermacher. In the 1870s a fourth major type of German liberal theology arose, Ritschlian historicism. Theologian Albrecht Ritschl contended that Kant, Hegel, Schleiermacher, and the Mediating tradition variously evaded or minimized historical consciousness. Ritschl said Christianity is irreducibly a sociohistorical movement with a particular ethical character, as expressed in the doctrine of the kingdom of God. The Ritschlian School emphasized the role of religion in cultivating a strong German society, and it dominated German theology in the late nineteenth and early twentieth centuries. One preeminent scholar, Harnack, epitomized the ethos of the Ritschlian School: learned, disciplined, pious, respectable, mannered, prolific, culturally refined, nationalistic, statist, and socially conservative.

In England the foremost theological liberal was an Oxford religious philosopher, Hastings Rashdall. Philosophically, he was a post-Kantian subjective idealist and the originator of ideal utilitarian moral theory. Theologically, he was a powerful critic of traditional atonement theories, an eloquent advocate of moral influence theory, and a prolific exponent of idealistic religious philosophy. Rashdall was by far the leading intellectual in the early Churchmen's Union. He managed to join the Christian Social Union (CSU), demonstrating a stronger social conscience than many of his liberal colleagues. But Rashdall was an unabashed elitist who wavered between CSU progressivism and Social Darwinism, fearing that Social Democracy would reduce Europe to the cultural level of a Moravian revival camp. He joined the CSU mostly to thwart more radical versions of social Christianity. In this respect Rashdall was like the German Ritschlian liberals who created the Evangelical Social Congress.[9]

The Ritschlian School signed up for opposing Social Democracy, defending Bismarck's welfare state, boosting the German army, and thwarting radical Christian socialism. It provided a theological basis for bourgeois civil religion, usually called Culture Protestantism. Its socialist flank was nearly always conservative and nationalist, and its political leaders, notably Harnack and Naumann, were conservative liberals. At the turn of the twentieth century the Ritschlian School suffered a bruising theological schism that created the history of religions approach to religion; theologically, the Ritschlians were still at the cutting edge of modern theology. But the leading exponents of Ritschlian theology—Harnack, Naumann, Wilhelm Herrmann, Theodore Häring, and Ernst Troeltsch— assured their readers that good religion backstopped the cultural and political establishment. German social Christianity existed primarily to thwart the SPD. It was a grimly serious business because the SPD surged as a political force, and the churches feared the SPD as a mortal threat to their existence.

Nationalistic feeling soared in Germany during the period that Ritschlian liberals secured their privileged standing in Germany's government and elite academic culture. These factors came to define liberal theology in Germany, notwithstanding that its founders were Kant, Hegel, and Schleiermacher.

To the dialectical theologians who toppled Germany's liberal establishment after World War I, "liberal theology" meant, above all, the latter-day, Culture Protestant, statist Ritschlian School liberalism that helped to destroy the nation. It retained the major chairs of theology in German universities, especially in Berlin, but had no credibility.

American liberal theology went through nothing like that until the Great Depression of the 1930s. Many American social gospel leaders were influenced by the social-ethical historicism of the Ritschlian School, but in the United States one kind of left-progressivism led to another, logically and historically. The socialist wing of the American social gospel, led by Rauschenbusch, assumed that theological liberals should be socialists and Christian socialists should be theologically liberal. Some European theologians agreed, notably Ragaz in Switzerland and Charles E. Raven in England. But the three greatest socialist theologians of the early twentieth century—Tillich, Barth, and Temple—exemplify the point that mostly there was disagreement in Europe.

Tillich was a liberal in the sense of belonging to the tradition of Kant, Hegel, and Schleiermacher, but he condemned liberal theology almost as stridently as Barth, sometimes remembering to explain that he referred only to its Ritschlian corruption. To Barth, the problem in theology began with Ritschlian Culture Protestantism, until he later decided it began with Kant and Schleiermacher. To Temple, the emphasis of liberal theology on what it disbelieved was the wrong approach. Temple insisted that one could be fully modern and more or less orthodox simultaneously because Mother Church accommodated the best of modern knowledge, contrary to what deracinated liberals said. A great deal of progressive Anglican theology took Temple's tack, with or without his politics. Politically and theologically, Temple exemplified the tension felt by many socialist theologians between the rationalistic individualism of the liberal tradition and the solidarity consciousness of socialism and Christian ecclesiology.

The relationship between democratic socialism and Social Democracy is equally complex, yet it bent toward a similar outcome in Britain, Germany, and most of Europe. For much of the story told in this book, "democratic socialism" and "Social Democracy" were interchangeable terms, since Social Democrats had little or no record in power to defend. Bernstein's critique of orthodox Marxism contained the germ of the distinction that later became conventional. Bernstein said Marx's mechanistic catastrophe thinking made democracy dispensable in revolutionary Marxism, a very serious defect. Socialism had to be thoroughly democratic to be authentically socialist, and socialists had to practice parliamentary politics on its own terms, not as a way station to abolishing it. These arguments magnified already existing tensions in the SPD over its unwieldy fusion of revolutionary rhetoric and reformist politics. The tensions mounted as Social Democrats made political gains and Bernsteinian revisionism won influence in the SPD. Bernstein's legacy was ironic inasmuch as he had no intention of settling for something less than democratic socialism. Defending the inherently democratic idea of socialism was the whole point for him. Fifty years later a similar party-dividing rift occurred in Britain, where the reform party was also tagged as revisionist. In between these two controversies, the rise of Communism compelled socialists to explain why they were not Communists, an imperative that pressed in Bernstein's direction.

Nearly every European Social Democratic party of the early 1920s debated revolutionary insurrection versus parliamentary politics, usually favoring the latter without renouncing the dramatic language of the former. The Swedish Social Democrats became exceptions by definitely opting for nonrevolutionary politicking, replete with a homey language of community and caring. Wherever Social Democrats ran for office and won power, or a share of it, Social Democracy morphed into the name for what they did when they gained power. They did not achieve democratic socialism, but they made significant advances toward it that had to be named and defended. The logic of Social Democracy yielded this conceptual adjustment, for Social Democracy originated as a political ideology advocating a peaceful evolutionary transition from capitalism to socialism via parliamentary politics. The gains of Social Democratic parties created something new—mixed economies in which socialists fought for socialist objectives within the framework of capitalism. "Social Democracy," as the name of an ascending party movement and ideology, no longer had to be imagined. It gained power, respectability, and accountability. Always it negotiated the tricky politics of contending for democratic socialism on capitalist terms, never reaching its ostensible goal, which yielded compromised forms of Social Democracy, plus denials that socialists wanted to socialize everything, or everything big. The latter acknowledgment compelled socialists to rethink the idea of democratic socialism itself. It was one thing to acknowledge that Social Democratic politics was inevitably complex, messy, and pluralistic. What if the same thing was true of democratic socialism?

The three British socialists featured in chapter 5—William Temple, R. H. Tawney, and G. D. H. Cole—grappled differently with the latter question. Did acting in a Social Democratic fashion change the goal of democratic socialism? This question simmered at a low level through most of their careers and became a fighting, party-dividing, realigning issue in the 1950s, which Tawney and Cole lived to see. All three were born to cultural privilege, graduated from Balliol College, Oxford, and joined the socialist movement before graduating. Temple developed a modern Anglican theology, a creative Whiteheadian form of neo-Hegelian metaphysics, and a novel argument for a scaled-back guild social- ism, all on his way to serving as archbishop of Canterbury. His closest friend, Tawney, a Christian socialist and celebrated economic historian, gave decades of quiet service to Labour and the trade unions. Tawney's books *The Acquisitive Society* (1920) and *Equality* (1931) had veritable scriptural status for many British socialists. Cole, a fiery William Morris socialist and atheist, led the fight for guild socialism before retreating to state socialism. He achieved academic eminence as an Oxford don but gave even more service than Tawney to the Labour Party.[10]

The Labour Party claimed through the 1920s to believe its ideological iden- tity was clear. Labour was a socialist party, as defined by Sidney Webb's constitu- tion. To be sure, there was an important difference between serving the interests of the working class and serving the nation as a whole. Every Labour confer- ence wrestled with various aspects of the difference, including the relationship between being a labor movement and a parliamentary Labour Party. Ramsay MacDonald's first Labour government (1922–1924) conveyed the mentality of a self-interested workers' party, but by 1929, when Labour and MacDonald returned to power, Labour was adept at saying that socialism was best for almost everyone and for the nation as a whole. Labour officials did not ask, as yet, whether they were true socialists if they did not expect to enact the Labour platform. Socialism was the goal, and they would enact as much of it as possi- ble. That was the point of running for office.

The second Labour government, however, much like SPD leader Hermann Müller's "Great Coalition" government of the same period in Germany, dith- ered confusedly over how it should respond to the economic crisis of 1929–1930. Being in power prevented socialists from merely waiting for capitalism to die, but they had no solution to the crisis. Some Labour officials bonded with Liberal economist John Maynard Keynes, imploring MacDonald to pump a Keynesian stimulus into the economy. Others said that was the worst possible solution. In Britain and Germany the leading socialist experts on finance were true believers in balanced budgets. Philip Snowden, as chancellor of the exche- quer under MacDonald, and SPD economist Rudolf Hilferding, as minister of finance in Müller's government, feared inflation more than the misery and anger of ordinary citizens. This fear contributed to fateful endings in both cases. The last genuinely democratic government of the Weimar Republic folded in 1930, yielding elections that failed to create a majority government. Meanwhile MacDonald's government crumbled, and he cut a face-saving deal with the Conservative Party that left Labour wrecked and enraged. Many said that

MacDonald was a traitor and nothing was wrong with Labour. Some were more reflective. What was the meaning of the MacDonald debacle? What was the point of Clause Four if socialists had only Keynesian answers, or no answer at all to the Great Depression?

Temple, Tawney, and Cole confronted this crisis with characteristic humility. They knew they lacked an answer and that Labour needed better answers. Temple absorbed the new economic theories of his friend Keynes, scaled the hierarchy of Anglican bishoprics, and became a global figure as an ecumenical leader and the voice of the Church of England. Although he seemed comfortable with Fabian socialism, near the end of his life Temple reformulated the guild idea along lines that proved to be thirty years ahead of his time. Cole was a union of contrasting things—radical and conservative, Fabian and anarchist, romantic and rationalist, and practical and utopian. The memory of his frustration while advising MacDonald helped Cole be honest, probing, and creative about rethinking socialist politics. Tawney, after the MacDonald debacle, excoriated Labour for not believing in socialism and not having thought seriously about what it was. He said the party relied in a shallow manner on Webb's constitution, and thus it was flummoxed when it came into power, lacking deep convictions about what it should do.

Then the question changed to what Labour should do about Germany. Hitler seized absolute power, abolished the Weimar Republic, built up a racist war machine, and threatened to devour Europe. Tawney came early, by supporting Labour stalwart Clement Attlee, to the reluctant conclusion that Britain would have to fight again. Labour played a significant role in Winston Churchill's wartime coalition government, which set up Attlee to become prime minister after the war ended.

The Attlee governments of 1945–1951 transformed Britain into a British version of Social Democracy. Labour made health care a fundamental right for all citizens, nationalized one-fifth of the economy, significantly increased the incomes of wage earners, sustained the full employment economy that the war created, instituted a steeply progressive income tax and a pension system, abolished antiunion laws, abolished restrictions on the rights of women to own property, established a minimum wage for agricultural workers, and got colonial Britain out of India, Pakistan, Burma (Myanmar), Ceylon (Sri Lanka), and Palestine. Soon the question shifted: Should Labour push for full-orbed democratic socialism, getting rid of capitalism? Was it a socialist party, as party leaders claimed it was, if it stuck with a Social Democratic agenda of reforming capitalism? Even for Labour unionists who didn't care about the socialist name, was welfare capitalism something to be settled for?

The Labour mainstream, led by Fabian stalwart Herbert Morrison, settled for defending Labour's historic achievements. The Labour left wing, led by Aneurin Bevan, pressed for more nationalization. An ascending revisionist right flank led by Hugh Gaitskell said Morrison versus Bevan was the wrong debate, being backward looking. Industrial ownership no longer mattered very much because the "New Class" of corporate managers and government bureaucrats ran the world anyway. The new task of socialism was to transform an increasingly managerial order into a society defined by democratic socialist values. Labour socialism had to become more pluralistic, accepting of the mixed economy, and explicitly fired by ethical socialist ideals. Democratic socialism had to be redefined in a way that fit Social Democratic politics.

Germany reached a remarkably similar outcome by a dramatically different route. In West Germany Social Democracy had to be Marxist to be resurrected from the ashes of Nazi fascism, but it could not succeed as a Marxist movement. Nearly every SPD leader fled Germany after the Nazi takeover. One SPD leader, Kurt Schumacher, endured ten years of Nazi concentration camps before resurrecting the party as an orthodox Marxian force. He fully expected in 1949 to win the first election of the German Federal Republic. Normal politicking would be unnecessary because the logic of history and German guilt about fascism would carry the SPD to victory. Under Schumacher's commanding, fiercely patriotic, anti-Communist, anti–Cold War, anticapitalist leadership, the SPD built an impressive party operation that vied for national power. It felt entitled to middle-class votes, denigrated churches, and was slow to fathom what was politically awry in both cases; thus it posed no electoral threat to the ruling Conservatives. Schumacher and his successor Erich Ollenhauer led the SPD to three successive second-place finishes behind the Christian Democratic Union (CDU) and far ahead of other parties.

It took until 1959 for the SPD to accept that West Germany was not an exception to the revisionist logic of Social Democracy. The class basis of Marxian politics was too small and shrinking, and the SPD had a missing generation, the children of the 1950s. Belatedly the SPD dropped its language of proletarian conflict, identified socialism with socialist values, embraced economic pluralism, touted its role in creating German codetermination, and disavowed antireligious prejudices. Swiftly the party stopped its downward slide. The SPD grew powerful and respectable on its message that Germany needed a progressive party with socialist values. It became so respectable that its commitment to economic democracy became hard to see. Still later it became not merely hard to see. It was left behind—except for the stubborn types in the back rows.

2

BRITISH ORIGINS: ANGLICAN SOCIALISM, EARLY MARXISM, AND FABIAN COLLECTIVISM

The first Christian socialists were British Anglicans who claimed during the year of revolutionary convulsion—1848—that the Christian idea of cooperation trumped other values. They were not theologically liberal or politically radical and did not conceive of socialism as an economic ideology. They did not urge Christians to take the side of oppressed workers, for they were averse to class struggle rhetoric and had no intention of deferring to workers. In the early going most Christian socialists were not even democrats, although they learned to say that socialism had to be democratic. They said socialism was a modern name for the unifying and cooperative divine order that already exists.

The founders of Christian socialism were Church of England cleric Frederick Denison Maurice, his lawyer friend John Ludlow, their clerical friend Charles Kingsley, and the school of Mauricites who joined them. Ludlow embraced socialism first, having absorbed the cooperative socialism of Philippe-Joseph-Benjamin Buchez and Louis Jean Joseph Blanc while growing up in France. He converted Maurice to it, after which Ludlow and Kingsley became Maurice's disciples in things socialist. Christian socialism got only a brief run under Maurice, aborted by his aversion to factions and fighting, but it revived dramatically in the 1880s, reverberating with appeals to the spirit of Maurice.

In France socialism resounded with revolutionary feeling and rhetoric. Buchez converted to Catholicism in 1829 after many years of cooperative activism, and Blanc was vaguely theistic, so Ludlow did not lack examples of how cooperative socialism could be friendly to religion. But French socialism was mostly antireligious and radical, a legacy of the French Revolution *and* its bitter aftermath. The French Revolution was so radical it tried to abolish churches and universities; then it yielded hardly anything for workers. Antiunion laws were enacted as soon as the Republic existed, and the commercial and manufacturing classes took control of the government. French socialism acquired a decidedly defiant spirit in response, taking root in organizations that were bitterly antigovernment, antipolitical, usually antireligious, devoted to direct action and the general strike, and fixed on the syndicalist dream of a new social order based on radical worker organizations. France contributed mightily to the idea that socialism got rid of God.

In England the customary hostility between socialist movements and established religion was much less pronounced. England had no peasant class, English law and political liberalism injected just enough freedom into English society to make a difference, and England's anarchist tradition was slight and mostly nonrevolutionary. English culture was tempered and deferential, and Anglican clerics panned individualism and hypercapitalism as Protestant heresies. These factors made British socialism middle class, idealistic, and communal before it had a Marxist tradition or even a workers party. Maurice and his progeny played a role in diminishing the usual hostility between socialism and religion. Maurice was highly respected, pious, peaceable, and a disciple of Samuel Taylor Coleridge. He established that Christians could be socialists, whether or not socialists wanted Christian allies. Britain had important Christian socialist and ethical socialist traditions before it spawned a third non-Marxian socialism, Fabian Collectivism. All were iterations of an English dream, a commonwealth led by good-spirited progressives. Christian socialists, ethical socialists, Fabian socialists, and those who combined these identities boasted that England was too civilized to need Marxism. England was so civilized it provided refuge and opportunity to Karl Marx himself.

MAURICE AND THE KINGDOM OF CHRIST

Maurice came by family drama to his vocation as a muddling advocate of generous Anglican orthodoxy and a believer in the unifying divine order of all things. His Presbyterian father, Michael Maurice, lost his family inheritance when he converted to Unitarianism and became a Unitarian minister. Michael Maurice married a Unitarian, Priscilla Hurry, moved to Yarmouth, and raised a family of four daughters and one son, plus an orphaned cousin whose death triggered a prolonged family religious crisis. The Maurice family wrote letters to each other to express their deepest feelings. In Maurice's youth his sister Anne joined the Society of Baptist Dissenters; his three eldest sisters became Baptists too, with strict Calvinist theologies; and his mother joined them in

Baptist Calvinism. Maurice spent his adolescence caught between the rival theologies of his parents and siblings. Michael Maurice grieved as his wife and daughters repudiated Unitarian humanism. He was not anti-Christian, but it was hard to bear that his loved ones embraced a dogmatic, authoritarian religion. He forbade religious discussions at home, so his wife and daughters wrote long, impassioned letters to each other defending their theological positions. Eventually Michael Maurice was left alone in the Unitarian Fellowship. F. D. Maurice, near the end of his life, tried to write an account of his family's religious experience and was still so pained by it he could not complete the story. As a teenager he was confused and depressed by religion. Later he recoiled at conflict, while respecting theological honesty and the right to dissent.[1]

Maurice felt his sisters and mother made compelling points against Unitarianism, but he stayed, more or less, in his father's religious community, enduring a home life marked by long verbal silences interrupted by the cross-fire of credos masked as letters. In 1823 he entered Trinity College, Cambridge, where Coleridge had just acquired his first academic disciples. Coleridge's stew of Romantic poetry and literary criticism, post-Kantian metaphysics, and Anglican theological liberalism had no following among British academics until the early 1820s, when Julius Hare and Connop Thirlwall assigned his writings at Trinity College. Hare and Thirlwall converted two students, Maurice and John Sterling, to Coleridge's spiritual vision, which yielded a Romantic literary society called "the Apostles' Club." The Cambridge Apostles lauded Lord Byron, William Wordsworth, Robert Southey, and John Keats; some liked Percy Bysshe Shelley, who was too radical for others; and all favored Coleridge. Coleridge, besides epitomizing the Romantic imagination, imported post-Kantian metaphysics to England virtually by himself. Maurice appreciated that Coleridge did both things with a distinctly Anglican, liberal, theological sensibility. Coleridge's late-career pastiche of spiritual commentary and apologetics, *Aids to Reflection* (1825), was a bellwether text for Maurice that set him on the road to Anglicanism. Charles Merivale, Maurice's classmate, later recalled that "Coleridge and Wordsworth were our principal divinities, and Hare and Thirlwall were regarded as their prophets."[2]

Intellectually, Maurice bloomed under Hare's teaching of Plato, Kant, and various post-Kantians and Romantics, especially Coleridge. Personally, Maurice overcame his depressed shyness; it helped that his friend Sterling was extroverted, devoted to him, and enthusiastic about Coleridge. Maurice had atheistic friends and no atheistic inclinations—"Coleridge had done much to preserve me from that." On the other hand, since Maurice was not an Anglican he was barred from receiving a degree. In 1827 he and Sterling launched a literary journal, *Athenaeum*, in London, where Maurice pondered the Trinity, Anglicanism, and Coleridge's arguments for both. Finally he joined the Church of England in 1831, telling his father tenderly he would not have left the Unitarians if he did not believe in the Trinity. Enrolling at Exeter College, Oxford, to prepare for ordination, Maurice gave pro-Coleridge lectures and was ordained to the Anglican priesthood in 1834, one year after Oxford don John Keble launched the Oxford Movement, also called the Tractarian Movement, in a blistering sermon against national apostasy.[3]

Two rival parties dominated the Church of England—Evangelical Protestants and High Church Catholics. The Tractarian Movement was a High Church phenomenon charging that Protestants and a plague of liberals were ruining English Christianity. A smattering of liberals called for a more inclusive and modernized party in the Church of England. They were forerunners of what became a third party, the Broad Church—a handful of Coleridge disciples at Cambridge led by Hare; an equally tiny group at Oxford led by mathematician/scientist Baden Powell and Oxford Fellow Henry Bristow Wilson; and a few others. From the beginning of Maurice's career as a cleric and theologian, his theme was the unity and Catholic foundation of the Christian Church. He was against partisan divisiveness of every kind, including liberal divisiveness. Had Maurice believed that Cambridge wronged him by refusing him a degree, he could not have become an Anglican. His first book, *Subscription No Bondage* (1835), defended the subscription requirement at English universities, contending that the Anglican Thirty-nine Articles offered an exemplary approach to theology. Admittedly, Maurice said, the Thirty-nine Articles were usually associated with "large wigs, afternoon slumber and hatred of all youthful eagerness and hope." But the divines who founded Anglicanism knew what they were doing. They did not try to write a creed, they were specific without getting too specific, and they began from above, with the ecumenical doctrines of the Trinity and the Son of God.[4]

Subscription No Bondage lauded the Christian foundations of English culture and the wisdom of the Anglican way. Maurice won the attention of Tractarians by defending subscription and the Catholic basis of Anglicanism. The Tractarians got their tag from their trademark publication series, *Tracts for the Times*, published from 1833 to 1841, although some preferred the prestige of another name, "the Oxford Movement." Led by Keble, John Henry Newman, Edward Bouverie Pusey, and Richard H. Froude, the Oxford Movement was an aggressive version of High Church Catholicism later called Anglo-Catholicism. To the Tractarians, liberal theology was a species of apostasy, Protestantism was a modern individualistic disaster, and "Germanism" was the worst of both.

There was one Catholic Church, which had three branches: Roman Catholicism, Orthodoxy, and Anglicanism. Until 1845, when Newman gave up on the branch theory and converted to Roman Catholicism, the Tractarians were often called "Newmanites." After 1845 they were called "Puseyites."[5]

Maurice welcomed the Tractarian appeal to Catholic feeling but recoiled at its attacks on Protestantism in general and Martin Luther in particular. The Tractarians refused to see the gospel spirit in Luther's Reformation. They had a baleful tendency, Maurice said, to minimize the tyranny and corruption of the Roman church, both of which were worse than Luther's exaggerations. Had there been no Reformation to restore the principle of a national church, the Church of England would still be a captive of Rome. Maurice added that Tractarians betrayed and damaged the very thing they prized—Catholic feeling—by constantly making "disparaging and insulting" statements about the Reformers. Had he felt compelled to attack Protestants in Tractarian fashion, "instead of being able the better to reverence the early fathers of the church, I should lose the sense of reverence altogether."[6]

Maurice yearned for a peaceable, rational Anglican Catholic orthodoxy that carried no grudge against the Reformation or modern learning. In 1838 he published a three-volume work on the unity and universality of the Christian church, *The Kingdom of Christ*. Originating as letters addressed to Quakers and expanded in its second edition of 1842, *The Kingdom of Christ* ranged over Quakerism, "pure Protestantism" (Lutheranism, Calvinism, Zwinglianism, and Arminianism), Unitarianism, and Roman Catholicism, plus various philosophical and political movements; Methodism was a special case for having broken away from Anglicanism. At each turn Maurice said that religious movements tend to go wrong at the point of negation, not affirmation. Party thinking reduced the magnificent splendor of the divine order to self-enclosed systems. Each Christian tradition had a compelling religious truth contributing something to the vitality and spiritual richness of the church catholic. But each tended to settle for an impoverished embodiment of its truth, excluding aspects of the catholic faith it needed for its own sustenance.[7]

The Society of Friends, for example, upheld a "grand and fundamental truth," the Quaker inner light, a great evangelical and mystical reality. But over time, Maurice said, the Quakers lost their robust evangelical character, minimized their theological identity, discarded the incarnation and atonement, and settled for being a mere sect. The great Quaker emphasis on the necessity of a vibrant personal faith degenerated into something "narrow and contradictory" because the Society of Friends had no ordinance that embodied its principle and made it universal. All they had was the assertion of the universal Spirit within. In England, Maurice acknowledged, the Friends movement retained a stronger evangelical character than in America, where it drifted in the opposite direction, toward Unitarianism. But in both cases the fix was in for Quakerism: "All its grand pretensions are at an end; its greatest defenders speak of it now not as the Church or Kingdom of God, but as the best of the sects which compose the religious world." This was a far cry from "the old Quaker spirit" and the spirit of vibrant, catholic, evangelical, world-changing Christianity. Anyone who had either spirit had to believe "that there is a spiritual kingdom some- where," perhaps in Lutheranism or Calvinism or somewhere else.[8]

The Kingdom of Christ was simultaneously depressing and hopeful. Its first edition coincided with the Chartist eruption demanding the political enfran- chisement of workers. The Reform Bill of 1826 excluded the working class from voting, it became law in 1832, and the excluded struck back in 1838, brandishing the People's Charter. Maurice did not write about the great seething below. He revered the monarchy as divinely ordained and feared the unruly vengeance of populist movements. But he took seriously the biblical teaching about seeing Christ in the poor and oppressed, and he had an overarching conviction that all things fold together. *The Kingdom of Christ* was not merely about theology or ecclesiology. It was about the divine order of all things that already existed but remained to be realized.

To Maurice, the theocratic principle was the key to fulfilling the mission of Christianity. A good society would reflect the goodness and beauty of the divine order. Every denominational tradition had serious problems, Maurice argued. English Anglicanism was the most ecumenical and catholic tradition, but it was fractured theologically and tended to reduce baptismal regeneration to a mere ceremony. Maurice wanted Anglicanism to recover, for the sake of the entire church, the spiritual and universalistic import of the ancient doctrines of cre- ation, incarnation, the cosmic Christ, redemption, and the Trinity. The funda- mental principle of the Bible and creeds is the creation and redemption of the entire human race through God in Christ. Ancient orthodoxy, Maurice argued, began with the biblical story of divine acting and ruling, not an account of human fallenness. The Bible tells a story of God's covenantal relationships with humanity through the institutions of the family, the nation, and the church as the kingdom of Christ.[9]

The church has six signs—baptism, the creeds, worship, the Eucharist, ordained ministry, and, underlying and interpreting all signs, the Bible. Maurice gleaned the normative meaning of each sign from the Bible and ancient tradi- tion, and he stressed that every sign has a history of embattlement with unbelief and truncated systems of thought. Persistently he defended the biblical story against all sects and systems of thought, contending that Christianity stands or falls on its story of a creating and redeeming cosmic Christ, the divine Logos eternally begotten of the Father. Divine reason created and rules a sacramental universe. Every system, Maurice warned, including every system of orthodoxy, militates against the flourishing of the kingdom. On most issues that divided Evangelical, High Church, and liberal Anglicans, Maurice took the liberal side, as every party noticed. But he did not say he was a liberal. He said he was for unity and rising above parties.[10]

It did not matter that the liberal party was tiny and beleaguered. Maurice said liberals had the same will to dominate as other parties, so they deserved no moral credit for being small. All three parties had good points and terrible deficiencies. Maurice agreed with liberals that the church had to "breathe and move," profiting from new experiences and pushing for greater inclusiveness. Like Coleridge, Maurice loathed bibliolatry, the Evangelical worship of the Bible. But liberals wrongly dispensed with indispensable aspects of the church's tradition. Some prayers, derided by liberals as outdated, were the very means by which "we have been preserved from the bondage to particular modes and habits of feeling." Some doctrines, rejected by liberals as obsolete, "kept us from sinking into a particular theological system, and have compelled us to feel that there were two sides of truth, neither of which could be asserted to the exclusion of the other." Maurice said it was better to keep the entire biblical story and ancient tradition in play than to adopt a factional worldview, which always involved losing something precious. It was better to draw universality out of the biblical witness than to justify it on independent grounds.[11]

And it was better to treat each party generously, as he boasted of doing, than to skewer each other with exaggerations. This was the proper catholic approach. Maurice did not claim that liberals substituted rationalism for orthodoxy or that Evangelicals were purely negative, always standing for dissent or that High Church types were really Romanists in disguise. He acknowledged that partisans of all three parties were often better than their worldviews and their critiques of each other. Then he took it back, charging that all three parties were self-defeating because each lived down to its stereotype when it developed its defining principles into a system. Liberalism cast aside orthodox teaching, evangelicalism eliminated "the very idea of church fellowship or unity," and the logic of High Church Catholicism led to Rome. Better manners would not solve the problem, for the problem was party-line thinking itself: "I do not see how anything can be done towards the formation of the system, without introducing a seed of evil which must germinate till it produces all its natural fruits." Each party represented a "miserable, partial, human substitute" for the kingdom of Christ, the already-existing divine order that remained to be recognized.[12]

The theological problem and the social problem had the same solution: to embrace the freedom of Christ's kingdom, throwing off all ideologies and prejudices that prevented Christians from obeying God's will. Maurice boasted about English Anglicanism and grieved over it. Happily, it had less party spirit than Lutheranism, Calvinism, the radical Protestant sects, and Roman Catholicism: "It seems to me that in England we have a clearer witness than there is anywhere of our right to this emancipation, and of the way in which it may be effected. This system-building is not natural to us." Anglicans mediated between Protestantism and Catholicism, had a history of muddling through their conflicts, and held together. They realized the best systems were the worst ones for Christ's kingdom "because in them there are the fewest crannies and crevices through which the light and air of heaven may enter." Rome, in this telling, had the strongest system of thought and organization. Rome was monolithic, coherent, dogmatic, self-enclosed, and self-idolatrous. Hence it was farther from the kingdom than all Protestant groups. All parties were bad, and the strongest ones did the most harm: "If his faith be in the doctrines of men and not in the wisdom of God, the sooner it falls the better."[13]

But English Anglicanism featured a distinctly noxious form of party politics. To Maurice, this was the bitter irony of the most catholic form of Christianity. English Anglicans, being English, were quick to politicize everything. German theologians prized their schools of thought, but the English inclined to politics, not theory. Thus they formed new parties: "The moment we have adopted a peculiar theory, we begin to organize. We have our flags and our watchwords, our chiefs and our subordinates. All the generous feelings of sympathy and courage, of readiness to support a friend, of unwillingness to desert him when he has done some unpopular act, bind us to one and another maxim which our leaders or allies have put forth, even though there is nothing in our minds which answers to it."[14]

This proclivity to get political was not completely bad, Maurice allowed. It was better than being politically apathetic or intellectually elitist. At least the party ideologues got involved with ordinary people, refusing to hang their heads in "stupid indolence." If one cared about ordinary people, a certain amount of party activism was unavoidable. But Maurice implored party-line types to ask what they did *with* the people they recruited to their cause. Did they seek unity in Christ or further divide the body of Christ by seeking political advantage? Maurice supported the National Church *and* he criticized its arrogance, agreeing with critics of its haughty, bullying, selfish complacency. The National

Church was supposed to be a catholic kingdom serving all nations as a vehicle of universal grace. Instead it was an English Church that imposed itself on all British subjects whether they liked it or not. The Church of England lacked any will to reach the hearts of the poor and downtrodden because it was a tool of the aristocracy. Thus it was no match for Bible Christian and Primitive Methodist preaching to the poor; even Wesleyan Methodists, though stamped with the taint of the employer class, did better. Maurice said if the National Church had tried and failed to fulfill its catholic mission, he would lapse into defeated despair. As it was, the church had never tried, so he hoped it might still become what it was supposed to be.[15]

English Christianity had begun with great promise—Anselm leaving his Norman convent in 1093 to become archbishop of Canterbury. Anselm offended the Normans by refusing to favor them over the conquered Saxons, insisting his vocation was to be a friend of the poor and downtrodden of all peoples, making no distinction of race. The moral of the story: It was possible for the conquerors and the conquered to become one people, the English nation. But Maurice acknowledged that the English did not behave that way in Ireland. Always they favored the English interest, which turned the Irish implacably against the English Church. Maurice wanted the Church of England to be known for other things, even if it was too late to redeem the church's reputation in Ireland. He declared that all English Church members, especially him, were complicit in the sins of the English Church. He wanted the English Church to say, "God has cared for you, his Spirit is striving with you; there is a fellowship larger, more irrespective of outward distinctions, more democratical, than any which you can create; but it is a fellowship of mutual love, not mutual selfishness, in which the chief of all is the servant of all."[16]

This irenic, paternalistic, theocratic, social ethical, mildly liberal rendering of good religion had a long run in Victorian England. When Maurice published the first edition of *The Kingdom of Christ*, in 1838, he was a hospital chaplain and only recently ordained. When he published the second edition in 1842 he was a professor of English history and literature at King's College, London, and a symbol of Coleridge-style inclusivity. Many English Anglicans wanted a slightly modernized faith that claimed continuity with the church's orthodox tradition, eschewed factionalism, adjusted to social trends, and kept the peace. Maurice's gibes at the rival parties provoked backlashes from them, boosting his stature. Anglo-Catholics constantly found him disappointing, wishing he would grow a backbone. Evangelicals realized he was not a candidate for their side. Liberals tried to claim him, usually at their expense, since he blasted them for watering down the faith. Maurice was for generous orthodoxy,

Christian unity, godly rationalism, and Christianizing the world. The idea of an inclusive party was absurd to him, smacking of another absurdity, dogmatic liberalism. Theologically he never changed, sticking to his imagined catholic universalism and eschewing biblical criticism. Politically, however, the Chartist movement inadvertently lured Maurice into socialist activism.

OWENITE SOCIALISM

Socialism was amenable to Christian appropriation in England because it already had an amenable history. "Socialism" became an English word in 1827, when *Cooperative Magazine* described Welsh reformer Robert Owen (1771–1858) as a socialist—an advocate of the view that industrial wealth should be owned in common, on a cooperative basis. Owen was the first Briton to grasp the meaning of the Industrial Revolution. Born in North Wales to a saddler, he was apprenticed at the age of ten to a prosperous Stamford clothier, where he toiled for three years and read assiduously on the side, enjoying his employer's ample library. Young Owen was appalled that other Stamford employers forced their employees to work seven days per week, violating the Sabbath. He also puzzled about religion, reading books that compounded his confusion. If there were so many religions and even multiple versions of Christianity, how was one to decide which one was right? It seemed to Owen the various religions refuted each other, leaving him dubious about all of them.[17]

As a teenager he worked for a London retailer, enduring sixteen-hour workdays for six days per week, which left a mark on Owen's psyche. At nineteen he landed a job running a cotton mill in Manchester, England. The Industrial Revolution had transformed Manchester and other English towns, enriching a new class of manufacturers. The mill prospered, and Owen climbed into the capitalist class. He married the daughter of a mill owner in New Lanark, Scotland, and in 1799 he bought the New Lanark mill (with partners) for $300,000. New Lanark had the usual problems of mill towns—rampant crime and illiteracy, alcoholic mill hands, and hundreds of pauper children. Owen had an unusual conscience about child laborers, having been one, albeit spared from the worst of the factory system. He improved conditions for workers, built decent houses and a school system, established affordable stores, and enforced a code of good behavior.

He got a chilly welcome from local Scots but won them over by stunningly paying workers when exports were down or embargoed. Owen paid his workers even when the War of 1812 shut down textile exports to the United States. He made a fortune in New Lanark, showing that labor reforms were good for business, although his partners protested that he was too generous. In 1813, backed by Quaker reformer William Allen and utilitarian philosopher Jeremy Bentham, Owen launched a new firm offering a maximum 5 percent return on capital to investors. This enterprise succeeded, and Owen was lauded across Europe for prospering at business while treating workers commendably. Streams of reform pilgrims and dignitaries came to New Lanark to see how he did it; the future Russian tsar, Nicholas, was among them.

Owen was happy to dispense advice; plus, he got increasingly radical, prompting him to expound his developing views. He taught that the proper aim of human society is the greatest happiness attainable for the greatest number of people, as Bentham said, and human character is completely determined by social conditions over which children lack any control, a truism of Owen's experience. Every individual should strive for as much happiness as possible, both individual and collective. Education is the key to developing a healthy, moral, and proficient character. People become good or bad depending on whether they are bred by good conditions, especially good schooling. In 1813 Owen took his first pass at expounding this philosophy, in a book titled *A New View of Society: Essays on the Principle of the Formation of Human Character*. He argued that free will is an illusion, plus a useful myth by which the strong kept poor people down. Reason is the prime mover in human action. Bad conditions breed bad people, and nothing causes greater misery than the false belief that human beings forge their own character. Owen warned that the industrial system made nearly everyone more selfish, hypocritical, crass, and violent than before, but it could be reformed to produce generous, productive people.[18]

For a while Owen sustained his favorable image as a visionary reformer and humanitarian. From 1815 to 1818 he pushed hard for workplace reforms, blasting England for enslaving children in the cotton mills. He implored Parliament to limit the mill workday to twelve hours, limit the workday of eleven- and twelve-year-olds to six hours per day, and prohibit the employment of children under the age of ten. He lost every legislative battle except repealing the import duty on cotton. He also lost his rich friends, which cut him deeply as manufacturers denounced him. Owen got more radical, charging that the system itself was indefensible and corrupting. He already had the idea that cooperative villages might solve the problem of pauperism. Owenism, at its root, was a cooperative solution to unemployment and homelessness. But during the bitter political crossfire over labor legislation in 1817, Owen decided that cooperatives were the solution to the industrial problem itself, not merely a remedy for its poorest victims.

The system pitted human labor against machines in a fight that workers had no chance of winning. The solution was to create a system based on human unity and cooperation that subordinated machines to the needs of human beings. Villages of approximately twelve hundred people—the size of New Lanark—should be organized on a cooperative basis, spread over one thousand acres. Communities would raise the produce needed for their own consumption, exchanging different kinds of surplus products with each other. Members would live together in quadrangular buildings containing dining rooms, libraries, reading rooms, and schools and located at the center of each village. All members except children would be compelled to perform productive work, and an expert technician would supervise each community. Gardens would be plentiful, and buildings containing laundries and factories would border the outside gardens. Families would have their own apartments, caring for their children until the age of three, after which the community assumed primary responsibility for the nurture and education of children. Owen had not read his French forerunners, Francis Noel Babeuf and Comte Henri de Saint-Simon, but he shared their passion for a communal system that disallowed anybody from living off the labor of others, and his scheme influenced the next notable utopian in the French line, François-Marie-Charles Fourier, the founder of French anarchism (1772–1837).[19]

Owen's scheme was widely dismissed as paternalistic, confining, and unworkable, even by workers who liked him. Editorialists chided that his antipauperism crusade drove him crazy. Owen judged that Britons were too corrupted by church religion and too brainwashed by economists to try something better. He ran for Parliament twice in Scotland but lost. By 1821, when he wrote the first version of another book destined for many editions, *The Book of the New Moral World*, Owen was a pure utopian communalist, and bitter. Political economics, a deductive enterprise invented in England by Adam Smith and David Ricardo, had great prestige in polite society and the academy. Owen charged that it degraded workers by celebrating individualism and competition. Society should enable all citizens to be happy, but the Smith–Ricardo tradition of economic theory didn't even try to solve the problem of distribution. Chagrined at losing his rich friends and disillusioned that workers did not support him, Owen fell back on the only group he had left—idealistic reformers. To them he was a realized impossibility—rich, famous, revered in reform circles, and totally committed to the cause of cooperative idealism.[20]

Many of them launched experiments in Owen-style cooperation. Owen threw himself headlong into two such ventures. One took him to Harmony, Indiana, a German Lutheran town unsullied by English industrial corruption. Owen bought the town for $135,000, renamed it New Harmony, struggled for three years to build a cooperative village of eight hundred members, and failed, losing 80 percent of his fortune. Later he tried again in England, in Queenwood, Hampshire, which also failed, as did two Owenite communities in Scotland. Owen underestimated the obstacles to creating cooperative communities from scratch—especially that it took many years to develop the requisite skills and ethos. Religion was always a divisive issue, as the Owenites battled over Owen's creed and spurning of Christian churches.

In between his failures in New Harmony (1825–1828) and Queenwood (1839–1845) Owen tried to build the Grand National Consolidated Trades Union. This was the first national union movement in England, a reaction to the exclusion of workers from the Reform Bill. Owen proposed to unite the cooperative societies and trade unions, turning the unions into cooperative societies that bartered their goods through labor exchanges. Workers surged into the union, at first with impressive commitment to Owen's vision. He told a vast throng in London in May 1833 that they represented the dawning of a new order. The old order of competition and division had passed away. He exhorted the workers to renounce every vestige of envy, jealousy, and vengeance, showing that they stood for cooperation and sympathy—the hallmarks of the new order. For a while it seemed to be happening, as up to eight hundred thousand workers joined the union. But a bitter fight ensued between Owenite proponents of peaceful cooperation and syndicalist demands for class war and a general strike. Factionalism weakened the union, manufacturers vilified the union, government forces repressed the union, and courts supported the manufacturers and government. Unionism was excoriated as socialism by another name, which eviscerated socialism as a force in the British labor movement for four decades.[21]

Karl Marx and Friedrich Engels, assessing the European situation in 1848, wrote off Owen as the best of the British reformers. Owen, they said, grasped much of the problem with capitalism, but he was a product of the "early undeveloped period" and had interests to protect in bourgeois society. More important, Owen and his kin did not recognize the proletariat as a revolutionary class holding its own political independence and historical initiative. Owen got no credit from Marx and Engels for trying to build a national union because, they claimed, he had a bourgeois concept of the problem, and not much came of Owenism. The Owenites worked harder at founding quaint little communes than at forging alliances with proletarians. They failed even to be political, much less revolutionary, holding themselves above the proletariat, painting "fantastic pictures" of an ideal society removed from the real world. These "castles in the air," Marx and Engels said, besides being ridiculous, compelled the Owenites to "[appeal] to the feelings and purses of the bourgeois." That was pathetic. Marx and Engels piled on, wrongly claiming that the Owenites opposed Chartism. "Socialism," before Marx and Engels and before Maurice came out for Christian socialism, smacked of Owen-style, anticlerical, utopian communal failure.[22]

MAURICE AND CHRISTIAN SOCIALISM

Then the Chartist explosion yielded a mass movement for political rights. Chartism was the democratic revolution trying to happen, an eruption of the masses excluded from the Reform Act of 1832, which granted seats in the House of Commons to new industrial cities and curtailed the power of borough fief-doms but left 80 percent of adult males unable to vote. The People's Charter of 1838 demanded that working-class males deserved the right to vote by a secret ballot, whether or not they owned property, paid taxes, or could read, and to run for election in the House of Commons. Mass meetings in Birmingham and Glasgow ignited a sprawling movement that shook the nation, threatening a social revolution. The movement scared Maurice and evoked his sympathy. He was never sufficiently political to care about politics, but Maurice cared very much about imbuing society with a peaceful, Christian, unifying spirit. He urged fellow clergy not to scorn the Chartists. Charles Kingsley, a rural pastor and author of preachy novels, was Maurice's first clerical ally.

On a fateful day—April 10, 1848—the Chartists marched on Kennington Common in London, demanding that Parliament take up their petition for a democratic electoral law. Government troops brutally dispersed the demonstrators, and the House of Commons dismissed the petition. Maurice huddled with Kingsley and Maurice's new friend, John M. Ludlow, to formulate a response.

Ludlow was born in India, where his father, a colonel, died during Ludlow's infancy. He grew up in Paris, excelled at the Collège Bourbon, and moved to London in 1838 to study law. He joined the bar in 1843 and wrote books on the side, beginning with two books on joint stock companies in 1849. Unlike his English friends, Ludlow understood democratic aspiration. He was schooled in the early French socialisms of Babeuf, Saint-Simon, and Fourier, which were paternalistic, and cut his teeth intellectually on the cooperative socialism of Philippe Buchez and Louis Blanc, which reflected the deeper democracy of the late 1830s. Buchez (1796–1865) was a physician, a follower of Saint-Simon, and the leading French advocate of state-supported producer cooperatives. He served as president of the National Assembly in 1848. Blanc (1811–1882) was a revolutionary socialist and historian, a member of the provisional government in 1848, and Buchez's leading opponent on state-supported cooperatives. His book *L'Organisation du Travail* (1840) advocated producer cooperatives administered by self-governing agencies independent of the state. Blanc fled to London in 1848, where he lived in exile until 1871; then he served in the National Assembly upon returning to France.[23]

Ludlow absorbed the fractious debate between Buchez and Blanc over state-supported cooperatives, a flashpoint issue because it gave the state a central role in building a socialist society. He favored Blanc, but Blanc versus Buchez was academic in England. Ludlow came to England imbued with the promise of cooperative socialism, lacking Maurice's reverence for the monarchy. In 1846 Ludlow reached out to Maurice, hoping to find a social work ally, but Maurice was busy founding Queen's College—the first college in England open to women. When Paris erupted in February 1848, Ludlow rushed there to protect his two sisters from revolutionary carnage, only to find that his sisters and friends rejoiced at their new freedom. Ludlow wrote a letter to Maurice urging him not to fear the revolution; this was a momentous opportunity for Christianity to get on the right side of the democratic eruption.

Maurice was deeply moved by the letter. The following Sunday he preached a sermon on it, as a convert. When Ludlow returned from Paris, Maurice embraced him as a treasured friend, which overwhelmed Ludlow with gratitude and admiration. He looked up to Maurice, rejoiced at Maurice's reaction to him, and pledged his utter loyalty to Maurice. Ludlow was fatherless and uprooted, plus deeply religious. He later recalled that Maurice was "the only man for whom I have ever felt a sense of reverence." Ludlow agreed with Maurice and Kingsley that allowing nontaxpayers and nonreaders to vote would be going too far; otherwise he pulled them toward the Chartists' demands, in a perilous moment. Maurice embraced Ludlow's plea that the church's moment had come. April 1848 was a precious opportunity to befriend a battered workers' movement that despised the church. The threesome started with a leaflet to "the Workmen of England," authored by Kingsley. Exuding Kingsley's catchy, patronizing style, it told the defeated Chartists they were not ready to get their rights but had unexpected friends in a respected place, the Church of England. Kingsley described the trio as "men who are drudging and sacrificing themselves to get you your rights, men who know what your rights are better than you know yourselves, who are trying to get you something nobler than charters and dozens of Acts of Parliament."[24]

Maurice had aristocratic self-regard to overcome, and Kingsley routinely talked to workers in the same admonishing, self-righteous tone he used with his rural congregation. Both were hard to chasten on this theme, although Ludlow tried to restrain Maurice, who let him try. The trio founded a weekly newspaper, *Politics for the People*, which expounded on moral uplift. Maurice and

Kingsley said workers had to make themselves sufficiently respectable to win self-respect and the respect of the upper class. Maurice said the equality of the divine order was spiritual and communal, not fixed on grubby things like property, income, or status. Workers needed to feel their fraternity with aristocrats and shop owners, and aristocrats and shop owners needed to feel their fraternity with workers. England would become equal and good to the extent that it grew in Christian fellowship and love. Socialism was a divine religious ideal, an expression of the kingdom of God already existing on earth. Political parties, unions, and strikes got in the way of creating a good society. Education and Christian virtue were the keys to a better life, for individuals and society. Politics was for the people, but the people had to work up to it.[25]

Politics for the People ran for three months and seventeen issues. Kingsley wrote snappy, personal, edgy prose, confessing that Anglican clerics usually ignored what the Bible said about justice and poverty. Ludlow had a similarly vigorous style without Kingsley's glibness and with less of a patronizing tone. Ludlow wrote prolifically for the paper, twice as much as Kingsley and Maurice. He made a case for the Blanc version of cooperative socialism, a precursor of guild socialism: The state should own essential industries but self-governing worker associations should manage them. The trio and their half dozen collaborators sparked little reaction, most of it negative, but at least they tried—showing that a few Anglican clergy cared about the working class. Meanwhile Ludlow worked on Maurice, urging him to come out for socialism. Ludlow said he was a socialist because industrial society pitted individuals against each other, defying the Christian principle that all human beings are partners. Socialism was a strategy to attain partnership in the economic sphere. Maurice, in the same issue, called readers and himself to study what was false in socialism and what was true and divine in it.[26]

The paper drew newcomers to Maurice's circle, notably author Tom Hughes. The group launched a weekly Bible study at Maurice's home in Queen Square and a workers' night school in London and won a burst of attention from Kingsley's sudden renown. Kingsley's early novels put Christian socialism on the map. His first novel, *Yeast*, began as a series in *Fraser's Magazine* in 1848. It inveighed against the degraded housing conditions forced upon agricultural workers, blasted Roman Catholicism and the Tractarian Movement for shuttering England's social conscience about poverty, destitution, and urban decay, and caused an outcry against Kingsley before the book version appeared. The book was published in 1851; the outcry was so bad that Ludlow asked Kingsley to stop writing. But Kingsley had already finished two more novels, both surging with vitriolic anger. *Alton Locke*, the best of Kingsley's early novels, was about an impoverished tailor boy with poetic ambitions who joined the Chartist movement, was devastated by its crushing, moved to the United States in desperation, and died shortly after arriving. It was published in two volumes in 1849 and 1850. *Cheap Clothes and Nasty*, overflowing with quotable zingers about the horrors of clothing trade sweatshops, also came out in 1850. Kingsley said capitalism degraded workers and owners alike. If allowed to continue, the predatory capitalist system "will weaken and undermine more and more the masters, who are already many of them speculating on borrowed capital, while it will depress the workmen to a point at which life will become utterly intolerable."[27]

Many readers first encountered London's slums through Kingsley or Charles Dickens, who wrote *David Copperfield*, *Bleak House*, and *Hard Times* during the same period. Kingsley's renown ended any possibility that Ludlow or Maurice might restrain his penchant for exaggeration and glibness. Who were they to instruct him? But Kingsley revered Maurice, like all Mauricites. Maurice secured a job for Kingsley at Queen's College, until he didn't need it, and Maurice tried to get one for Ludlow at King's College, unsuccessfully. Maurice had the gifts of magnetism and persuasive sincerity, however one rated him as a thinker, on which estimates differed wildly among outsiders. Among insiders, admiration was uniform. Everyone in Maurice's circle deferred to him as the founder of Christian socialism, which won a following on Kingsley's novels and the group's next project, *Tracts on Christian Socialism*.

The Christian socialists realized that working on socialism involved reaching out to people beyond their group. Maurice found himself working with others more than ever. Ludlow told Maurice a clash was coming between unsocial Christians and unchristian socialists. Their mission was to head off the clash. Maurice embraced this maxim, declaring in the group's first *Tract on Christian Socialism* (1850), "I seriously believe that Christianity is the only foundation of Socialism, and that a true Socialism is the necessary result of a sound Christianity."[28]

Maurice feared the rising tide of revolutionary socialists bent on smashing the capitalist state and bourgeoisie. Christianity had to be fused with the right kind of socialism before the wrong kind of socialists set off colossal violence. Maurice was both specific and ecumenical in describing good socialism. It was defined by the principle that cooperation is "a stronger and truer principle than that of competition," and it included all who held fast to this principle, whatever their disagreements about other things. Every strong defender of the cooperative principle "has a right to the honor or the disgrace of being called a Socialist." In England the entire Owen school qualified. In France Maurice commended Fourier, who appealed to the privileged classes, but he also commended Blanc, who appealed to workers and employed the political machinery of the state. Maurice took no interest in debating Fourier versus Blanc, since this contention reminded him of the party rivalries in theology. What mattered was that social- ists rebelled against societies in which competition was said to be the law of life. This rebellion put them in conflict with churches that sanctified the competi- tive principle. Maurice lauded the socialists for embracing the "godly doctrine" of cooperation that Christians were supposed to practice. As it was, it was not too late for the churches to rediscover Christian cooperation.[29]

Maurice felt the urgency of saying it in 1850, one year after the revolutions of 1848 flopped across Europe. The first revolutionary outbreak occurred in January 1848 against Bourbon rule in the Italian states. In February the nationalist/ republican revolution in France overthrew the constitutional monarchy of Louis-Philippe and briefly installed radical communism in Paris. In Germany the "March Revolution" swept across the southern and western states, demand- ing German national unity and political rights. Democratic revolutions surged through most of Europe, especially in Poland, the Netherlands, and the Habsburg Austrian Empire. Maurice shuddered at the carnage of 1848. He was grateful that England escaped it, as the Reform Act of 1832 and the repeal of protectionist agricultural tariffs in 1846 defused proletarian sentiment. The year of revolutions produced much bad fruit, Maurice observed, but the year of reac- tions yielded nothing better. The moment had come to lift the cooperative prin- ciple above predatory competition: "If the supporters of cooperation made some strange plunges and some tremendous downfalls, I believe the progress to perdi- tion under your competitive system is sufficiently steady and rapid to gratify the most fervent wishes of those who seek for the destruction of order, and above all, of those who would make England a by-word among the nations."[30]

Maurice advocated producer cooperatives, conducted classes in a poor sec- tion of London, and tried to erase the oxymoronic connotations of "Christian socialism." True socialism had nothing to do with overthrowing the capitalist class or abolishing the capitalist state, and it was not a movement for radical democracy. Never a radical, Maurice disliked unions, which he viewed as class- war organizations, and he opposed universal suffrage, believing that workers and the poor could not be trusted with the vote. Maurice's socialism grew out of his kingdom theology and the Neoplatonist idealism he took from early Christianity and Coleridge. There is a divine order, which is ethical, coopera- tive, harmonious, and ultimately ruled by love divine. Everything was at stake for Christianity in opposing the capitalist lie that competition is the law of the universe. The mission of Christian socialism was to regenerate English society by reasserting its Christian foundation, lifting the laboring classes to their rightful place of co-ownership and dignity in society, in accord with the divine order of things.

Maurice emphatically did not believe that Christian socialism required a new kind of Christianity. Christianity, he said, did not teach the world to worship power and competition. Medieval Europe would have gone to hell, consumed by selfishness and greed, if not for the spiritual power of Christianity. Christianity saved Europeans from the social ravages of their own sin. Rightly understood, Christianity was a gospel from heaven "concerning the relation in which God stands to His creatures, concerning the true law under which He has constituted them, and concerning the false, selfish tendency in you and me, which is ever rebelling against that law." Industrialism changed the equation by celebrating greed and prospering from it, to which modern churches capitulated, becoming "mingled with that maxim of selfish rivalry which is its deadly opponent." Therefore, in the modern context, it was imperative to say that true Christianity was socialist. Christian socialism was the modern church being faithful to the gospel. It was also what French socialists were actually seeking when they tried to make a religion out of utopian anticlerical socialism.[31]

Maurice's spiritual sincerity and forthright advocacy of cooperatives made him a hero to Christian socialists in England, even as they debated his moralistic and aristocratic opposition to unions, strikes, and radical democracy. Ludlow and Kingsley called Maurice "Master" with no hint of irony. To reform activists, it was astonishing to hear a respected priest implore that opposing capitalism was imperative. Altogether the group published seven tracts on Christian socialism in 1850, while Kingsley poured out novels. Hughes wrote about the tailors' association; Maurice wrote about baptismal regeneration and the ethics of associating with radicals; and Ludlow wrote about political economics and the worker organizations in Paris. Ludlow enthused that these tracts were circulated "to the extent of thousands, and have been favorably noticed in the most unforeseen quarters by men perhaps whose candor their authors were presumptuous enough to distrust." This was a glass-half-full reaction, in the face of severe criticism. Conservatives vilified the Maurice group, blasting its publications as "tracts full of disreputable rant . . . mouthpieces of class selfishness . . . ravings of blasphemy . . . mischievous provocations clothed in oily phrases of peace and charity."[32]

Maurice puzzled that critics worked up so much disgust for the obviously commendable idea of a producer cooperative. He grieved at seeing his motives impugned. To him, Christian socialism stood, exactly, for Christian peace and charity. Ludlow and Kingsley wanted something like the French *associations ouvrières*, worker associations providing financial, legal, and technical assistance to producer cooperatives. Edward Neale and Lloyd Jones went farther, calling for networks of producer and consumer cooperatives because consumers were no less important than producers. The Christian socialists fell into fractious arguing about it. Maurice accepted Ludlow's opposition to consumer cooperatives but disliked his politicking for the Industrial and Provident Societies' Act of 1852, a breakthrough for cooperative societies when it passed. To Maurice, Christian socialism was becoming dreadfully political. Ludlow's producer organizations smacked of unionism and radicalism, which led to class warfare, the very things Maurice was trying to prevent. Strikes gave workers an exaggerated and dangerous sense of their power, yielding hateful polemics against employers. Maurice said Christian socialism should be something else entirely: "Christian socialism is the assertion of God's order. Every attempt to bring it forth I honor and desire to assist. Every attempt to hide it under a great machinery, call it Organization of Labor, Central Board, or what you like, I must protest against as hindering the gradual development of what I regard as a divine purpose, as an attempt to create a new constitution of society, when what we want is that the old constitution should exhibit its true function and energies."[33]

Christian England did not need a revolution or anything radical; it needed only to fulfill its Christian character. This concept of cooperative activism long outlasted Maurice through a hardy cooperative movement that traced its origins to Owen and physician William King and included many Christian socialists. In 1828 King founded *The Co-operator*, an influential movement journal. In 1844 weavers and skilled trade workers in Rochdale, Lancashire, founded the Rochdale Society of Equitable Pioneers, a breakthrough that yielded the Rochdale Principles—open membership, democratic control, distribution of surplus in proportion to trade, limited interest on capital, political and religious neutrality, cash trading, and support of education. Within a decade there were nearly one thousand new cooperatives in England. In the early 1850s the Amalgamated Society of Engineers, Machinists, Smiths, Millwrights and Patternmakers (ASE) forged the nation's most powerful union, which was friendly to producer and consumer cooperatives. Ludlow enthused that Christian socialism was getting somewhere, but Maurice wanted nothing to do with unions, so his group missed its chance—in February 1852—to ally with the ASE. That was the downward turning point for early Christian socialism. Ludlow bitterly regretted that Maurice was too moralistic and aristocratic to bond with unionists wanting to bond with him. Meanwhile the pure cooperatives that Maurice liked kept growing. In 1864 more than three hundred cooperative enterprises across Yorkshire and Lancashire banded together to form the North of England Co-operative Society. In 1872 this society morphed into a powerhouse, the Co-operative Wholesale Society.[34]

Christian socialism itself, apart from its cooperative version, faded to near extinction in the mid-1850s, as Maurice disbanded the movement in 1854. Fired from King's College in 1853 for rejecting the doctrine of eternal punishment, the following year Maurice rallied his group to a new venture, the Workingmen's College in London, which suited him better. This was the first center for adult education in Europe. Maurice's cofounders were his Christian socialist comrades: Ludlow, Kingsley, Hughes, John Llewelyn Davies, Lowes Dickinson, Frederick James Furnivall, Richard Buckley Litchfield, and John Westlake. His treasurers, besides Hughes and Furnivall, included a wealthy supporter of cooperatives, Edward Vansittart Neale. The college had eminent supporters, notably philosopher John Stuart Mill, and two artistic luminaries on the faculty, John Ruskin and Dante Gabriel Rossetti. It had Maurice as president and Ludlow as his loyal, dutiful assistant, but Ludlow seethed inwardly at missing his chance at something great. He later reflected that Maurice apparently did not feel "the crushing nature of the blow he was giving me." Christian socialism, Ludlow said, was big, broad, and historic, but Maurice settled for "narrow channel" reform work: "To me the very bond of our friendship lay in the work to Christianize Socialism. But I saw that I was myself at fault; that I had willfully blinded myself; that the Maurice I had devoted myself to was a Maurice of my own imagination."[35]

The real Maurice was a paternalistic and magnetic reformer with a comfortable perch in polite society and a powerful intellect that favored abstractions. He recoiled at the thought of seeming threatening to anyone, preaching peaceable Christian charity. When Maurice had a clear position he was capable of writing clear sentences, but he subjected his readers to opaque, lumbering, disjointed excurses that left his position in doubt. Reviewers complained that his writing was obscure and convoluted, featuring circuitous comments on topics he failed to properly introduce. Sometimes it was hard to tell what, exactly, he was writing about. Critics suggested that either Maurice couldn't think straight or he lacked the capacity to communicate whatever thoughts he held. His sermons yielded similar reviews. One critic, Aubrey de Vere, famously quipped, "Listening to Maurice is like eating pea soup with a fork." Another reviewer, after hearing Maurice speak more than thirty times, claimed he never heard Maurice expound a single clear idea or even convey "the impression that he had more than the faintest conception of what he himself meant."[36]

Much of Maurice's notorious obscurity reflected his determination to float above party lines, but he was clear enough about everlasting punishment to be fired from King's College. Uncharacteristically, Maurice cut to the heart of the matter, observing that everlasting punishment could not be a minor issue in

Christianity: "If it is anything, it is fundamental. Theologians and popular preachers treat it as such. They start from it; they put it forth as the ground of their exhortations." If Christian orthodoxy compelled Christians to believe that God condemns most people to burn in hell forever, it was pointless to pretend that something else, such as atonement or regeneration, is the central thing in Christianity. No one could be blamed for concluding that Christianity is about avoiding endless torment.[37]

Maurice acknowledged that the New Testament often speaks of eternal life and eternal punishment and denied that either has anything to do with time or duration. Eternal life is the state of knowing God through Christ, and eternal punishment is the state of not knowing God through Christ. "Eternal" in Christianity, he explained, does not mean "endless" or "forever." It is a state of being, either of righteousness or unrighteousness, referring to the reconciliation between God and human beings achieved by Christ (eternal life) or the continued alienation between God and an individual (eternal death): "What is Perdition but a loss? What is eternal damnation, but the loss of a good which God had revealed to His creatures, of which He had put them in possession?" If divine love is the root of all things, to lose it is to lose everything. This is the gospel understanding of damnation, Maurice argued, which the Church Fathers and better medieval theologians usually grasped, but which the medieval papacy utterly distorted, teaching that salvation is deliverance from punishment, not deliverance from sin. Martin Luther, grasping the difference, recovered the gospel faith by proclaiming that redemption is salvation from sin, and no pope or church functionary had the power to grant exemptions from punishment.[38]

Maurice stressed that Luther had to throw off Aristotle before he fastened on Paul's teaching that God wills the salvation of all and John's teaching that God is love. Medieval theology had a practical, Aristotelian, commonsense idea of the gospel as deliverance from endless punishment. Luther struggled with Paul for years before Paul's message of salvation by grace broke through to him. Maurice said modern English Christians had to throw off John Locke to achieve a similar breakthrough. Locke, to be sure, was a great thinker who courageously stripped away layers of mystification, and he spoke wisely "to the love of the simple and practical, in which lies the strength of the English character." But simple, practical, Lockean common sense was so imbedded in English culture that English Christians could not fathom the biblical concept of salvation. Maurice lamented, "When any one ventures to say to an English audience, that Eternity is not a mere negation of time, that it denotes something real, substantial, before all time, he is told at once that he is departing from the simple intelligible meaning of words; that he is introducing novelties; that he is talking abstractions."[39]

English Christians were sincere and wrong in believing their understanding of divine punishment was biblical: "They did not get it from the Bible. They got it from Locke." The old Unitarians, being Lockeans, had good reason to drop orthodox Christianity on their way to becoming universalists. But the real problem was simpleminded literalism, Maurice contended, not anything in orthodox Christianity. The idea of endless punishment turned God into a "destroyer," subjecting sinners to infinite torment far exceeding any conceivable offense. This picture was unbelievable to "cultivated men of any class," although they usually were too polite to say it to clergy. Eternal life is already lived in the present, and separation from God—homeless alienation—is a terrible enough punishment for rejecting Christ. Maurice did not say the gospel teaches universal salvation, but he stopped just short of saying it: "I am obliged to believe in an abyss of love which is deeper than the abyss of death: I dare not lose faith in that love. I sink into death, eternal death, if I do. I must feel that this love is compassing the universe. More about it I cannot know. But God knows. I leave myself and all to Him."[40]

That got him fired, whereupon he turned Christian socialism into an educational reform project. In 1866 he won the Knightbridge chair in moral philosophy at Cambridge. Maurice settled for small-scale reformism but not because he made his peace with capitalism. Witnessing the triumph of commercial society, he felt more repulsed than ever by its predatory and debasing spirit. In his telling, nothing came close to capitalism as a corrupting force in society and human souls. It made nearly everyone more selfish, grasping, and superficial. Maurice had almost nothing in common with his fellow Londoner Karl Marx, except a very similar perception that capitalism contained within itself the seeds of its own undoing. Marx published his dense, searing version of this indictment, the first volume of *Capital*, in 1867. Three years later, shortly before his death, Maurice wrote to his son, "It seems to me sometimes as if the slow disease of money-getting and money-worship, by which we have been so long tormented, must end in death, and though I do believe inwardly and heartily in a regenerative power for Societies as well as individuals, the signs of its active presence here are not yet manifest to me. Neither in Conservatism nor Liberalism as I find them here, can I see what is to make the dead bones stir and live."[41]

With Maurice there was always an irony. He pleaded against party thinking but was repeatedly an object of controversy. He did not quite belong to the Broad Church, although he did more than anyone to further it. He tried to make socialism as tame as a middle-class sermon, which made him notorious. Afterward his fling with socialist activism sealed his legacy as a prophet with honor. Eminent figures described him as a world historical genius and a provincial sluggard. Julius Hare said Maurice had "the greatest mind since Plato." Poetic icon Alfred, Lord Tennyson, perhaps forgetting Plato, said Maurice had "the greatest mind of them all." Positivist historian Frederic Harrison begged to differ: "A more utterly muddle-headed and impotent mind I have never known." Three observers split the difference. Liberal Party titan and four-time prime minister William Gladstone said he respected Maurice but never got solid food for thought from him. John Henry Newman said the same thing: "That Maurice is a man of great powers as well as great earnestness is proved, but for myself I ever thought him hazy, and thus lost interest in his writings." Mill, though Maurice's friend, was similarly frustrated: "More intellectual power is wasted in Maurice than in any other of my contemporaries." Charles E. Raven, a leading twentieth-century Anglican theologian, made a case for Maurice's greatness, while acknowledging that many did not see it. To Raven, as for most Anglican socialists, it mattered greatly that the founder had a noble and charitable spirit, though they wished the radicalizing spirit of democracy had gotten deeper into him.[42]

MARXISM AND THE FIRST INTERNATIONAL

England in the 1860s and 1870s was overwhelmingly averse to critiques of its fantastic commercial expansion, a fact that Karl Marx absorbed while living there as an émigré journalist, scholar, and revolutionary. Marx was born in 1818 in Trier, in the German Rhineland, to a Jewish family that converted to Protestantism so his father could keep his job as a lawyer in city and county courts. Jews in the Rhineland won new rights under Napoleon, which were mostly sustained after Napoleon fell, except for employees of the state. Heinrich Marx, a liberal Enlightenment deist devoted to Voltaire, Rousseau, and Lessing, readily chose his job and cultural Protestantism over Judaism the year before his son Karl was born. The family lived comfortably, with two maids and a vineyard. Marx studied law at Bonn for a year and partied riotously. He transferred to the University of Berlin in 1836, switched to philosophy, and fell hard for Hegel, enthralled by Hegel's system. He befriended a radical atheist theologian, Bruno Bauer, who told Marx that theory was becoming more practical than any practical career. Marx and Bauer confirmed each other in believing that religion was backward and suffocating, and Hegel's ostensibly Christian philosophy was actually a cunning form of atheistic humanism. Writing a doctoral dissertation on ancient Greek philosophies of nature, Marx returned to Bonn in 1841 in hopes of teaching there, but his academic career never began.[43]

Marx and Bauer bonded with a fellow anti-Christian left-Hegelian, Ludwig Feuerbach. They wrote articles for a "Young Hegelian" journal, *Deutsche Jahrbücher,* mostly about religion and philosophy, as politics was a dangerous topic in autocratic Prussia; plus, Marx was unsure of his politics. Writing about religion from Feuerbach's humanistic standpoint was a cunning way of writing about politics. In December 1841 Prussian king Frederick William II issued a paternalistic censorship instruction forbidding attacks on the Christian religion. Marx seethed and radicalized, abandoning any hope of an academic career. He protested that modern Prussia would have silenced Kant and Fichte on religion and morality. He wrote slashing articles for a liberal paper, *Rheinische Zeitung,* newly founded to defend the interests of Rhineland industrialists against the Prussian central government.

Marx honed his scathing writing style, featuring contrasts, polemical caricatures, slogans, insults, sneers, italicized declamations, chiasms, and antitheses. He took over the paper in October 1842 and met Friedrich Engels the following month at its office in Cologne. Born in Barmen, Prussia, in 1820, Engels was the son of a wealthy cotton textile manufacturer and Pietistic Protestant. He became an atheist, dropped out of high school, worked as an office clerk, and wrote radical articles under a pseudonym, protecting the family name and his anticipated business career. Engels served in the Prussian army and read a lot of Hegel, attending lectures at Berlin. He fell in with Marx's crowd of radical Hegelians at Hippel's bar, but Marx had just turned against them. Marx was done with bourgeois graduate school conceits about being free and knowing the secret of Hegel. That made him skittish about Engels; plus, Engels was on his way to a business career in Manchester, England. In Manchester Engels partnered with a radical woman, Mary Burns, who shared his opposition to marriage, an instrument of class oppression. Meanwhile Marx battled censors on a weekly basis until the government shut down his paper in March 1843. He fled to Paris and married his cultured childhood sweetheart, Jenny von Westphalen, who called him, adoringly, "my dark little savage."[44]

Marx got a job editing the Franco-Prussian Yearbook (*Deutsch-Französische Jahrbücher*) in Paris, through which he befriended Engels. Engels said the working class suffered all the problems of capitalism without receiving any of its benefits. Thus socialism had to be achieved by a revolution of the working class against the bourgeoisie; there was no parliamentary road to socialism. Marx bonded with Engels over this contention, later explaining that Engels "arrived by another road at the same result as I." Marx began his rethinking by grappling with Hegel. Left Hegelians battled over Hegel's defense of Prussia's constitutional monarchy; this issue, linked with religion, had given rise to left-

Hegelianism in the first place. Now Marx judged that Hegel's political theory had a fatal defect, not merely an unfortunate outcome. The problem was Hegel's endorsement of the liberal idea of an autonomous political sphere. States and the legal regimes of states, Marx reasoned, are rooted in the material conditions of life. Hegel wrongly split off the state from civil society, which underwrote his disastrous attempt to preserve the medieval system of estates in a modern legal framework. Hegel began with the state and rendered the human subject as a subject state, the opposite of real democracy, which began with particular human subjects. His pretentious theorizing about civil (*bügerlich*) society abstracted from its class character as *bourgeois* society, masking what mattered. Marx put it epigrammatically: "Just as it is not religion which creates man, but man who creates religion, so it is not the constitution which creates the people, but the people which creates the constitution."[45]

This critique insightfully cut to something deeper than the usual claim that Hegel deified the Prussian state. Marx pioneered the argument that the real problem with Hegel's political philosophy was his mythology of civil society. Hegelian "civil society," in this telling, veiled the terribly real divisions of bourgeois society, which Hegel backstopped by lauding the unifying role of the state. Marx pointed to an archaic foible in Hegel's *Philosophy of Right* and his unabashed defense of government bureaucracy. The foible was Hegel's strained defense of limited primogeniture rooted in landed property and family tradition. Hegel said that modern government bureaucracy retained and refashioned the social value in ancient primogeniture. A decent society needs a class of officials that devotes itself to public service and is free from the pressures and corrupting temptations of politics. Marx countered that ancient primogeniture was based on private property, both were indefensible, and the modern state rests on both. This critique became a pillar of neo-Marxist theory after Marx was gone, but Marx never published it—the germ of his subsequent verdict that true democracy has no state at all.

From there Marx moved to Feuerbach, still enthralled by Feuerbach's humanistic materialism. Feuerbach said Hegel's idealism was the last refuge of theology, a rationalistic mystification of the Absolute. Philosophy, to get real, had to begin with finite realities perceived by the senses. Marx lauded Feuerbach for proving "that philosophy is nothing but religion conceptualized and rationally developed; and thus that it is equally to be condemned as another form and mode of existence of human alienation." In that spirit Marx dramatically told his friend Arnold Ruge, "I am speaking of a *ruthless criticism of everything existing*, ruthless in two senses: The criticism must not be afraid of its own conclusions, nor of conflict with the powers that be." He did not grope for a new dogma, he told Ruge. Marx proposed to interrogate all dogmatisms. For example, the communism of German writer Wilhelm Weitling was a "dogmatic abstraction." The French anarchist tradition from Charles Fourier to Pierre-Joseph Proudhon similarly offered a "one-sided realization of the socialist principle." Marx scoffed that imagining utopias did not change the world. To do that, philosophy had to ruthlessly criticize everything, beginning with religion and politics, which were terribly important because they stirred human passions, interpreted the world, and got people in trouble. Weitling and Proudhon commanded the world to bow down to their truth. Marx proposed to unveil "new principles to the world out of its own principles." Like Feuerbach, he sought to change human consciousness, waking the world "from its dream about itself." That required "putting religious and political questions into self-conscious human form," showing that the real sins of individuals and societies were not what people confessed in church. Marx published his letter to Ruge in *Jahrbücker*, where he also published Engels's article on the English working class, soon expanded in a book version: *The Condition of the Working Class in England* (1845).[46]

In April 1844 the Prussian government accused Marx of high treason for his offensive articles in *Jahrbücker*, calling for his arrest if he crossed the Prussian border. The following January he was banished from Paris by order of the French government, under Prussian instigation. Meeting with Proudhon and other anarchists counted against him. Marx took exile in Brussels, where he remained until Europe erupted in revolutions. That spring he decided that Feuerbach's invaluable critique of philosophy applied to Feuerbach. It was one thing to demythologize the self-alienated consciousness of all religious projection, showing how religion creates an imaginary world as an escape from the real world. Feuerbach deserved unstinting praise for that. However, Feuerbach overlooked "that after completing this work, the chief thing still remains to be done." Feuerbach's humanism was not very deep, and it never left his head. Marx reasoned that religious consciousness is a *social* product, religious individuals belong to specific societies, and all social life is essentially practical. The antidote to religion is not a superior theory about the religious consciousness of an abstract individual. It is to transform society at the level of social practice: "The philosophers have only *interpreted* the world, in various ways; the point, however, is to *change* it."[47]

To care about the human ravages of religion is to struggle for a society purged of religion. Marx and Engels agreed that "Critical Criticism" had to begin there. Their first two collaborations sought to get German idealism out of their heads by developing a materialist theory of history. *The Holy Family* (1845, *Die heilige Familie*, a dig at the Bauer brothers) took aim at Bruno and Edgar Bauer, who ran a journal, *Allgemeine Literatur-Zeitung*. Marx blasted his former friend for sticking with Hegelian idealism, turning politically conservative, and skewering Proudhon. The Bauer brothers said the Spirit of freedom moves history forward. Marx and Engels countered that the movement of the masses, not some idealized "Spirit," moves history forward. Edgar Bauer had recently attacked Proudhon's rejection of private property as a showcase example of radical idiocy. Marx and Engels said Proudhon's book, *What Is Property?* (1840), commendably criticized the presupposition of "all treatises on political economy," private property. Deconstructing private property was fundamental for critical criticism. However, Proudhon hammered on only one thing, failing to consider wages, trade, value, price, and money as forms of private property, a project already begun by Engels in *Jahrbücker* and *The Condition of the Working Class in England.*[48]

The Holy Family was discursive, winding, and tedious, a running commentary on obscure articles. Marx and Engels, especially Marx, worked harder on their next book, *The German Ideology* (1845). All of Marx's left-Hegelian intellectualizing led to this book's argument for materialism. Hegelian enlightenment, he and Engels argued, was still religious. It was the last rationalistic resort of a spiritualizing project, "the rule of thoughts." Germans regarded Hegelian philosophy with "horror and awe," in both cases not perceiving that it glorified the German middle class and obscured "the wretchedness of the real conditions in Germany." Marx and Engels said they began with the premise of human history—concrete individuals who distinguished themselves from animals as soon as they produced their means of subsistence and thus indirectly produced their material life. The mode of production, whatever it is, is always crucial, expressing the specific mode of life of a people: "As individuals express their life, so they are. What they are, therefore, coincides with their production, both with *what* they produce and with *how* they produce."[49]

Every division of labor through human history marks a specific form of ownership. Tribal ownership came first, a form of extended family structure tied to hunting, fishing, and farming production. Ancient communal and state ownership models came next, where citizens held power over slaves only in their community, and town and country antagonism appeared. In more developed forms states were pro-town or anti-town, and towns fought internally over industry versus maritime commerce. The third form of ownership, feudalism, replaced the town focus of antiquity with the vaster expanse of the country. The Roman conquests made feudalism, still a form of communal ownership, possible, with peasant serfs replacing the slaves. Feudalism gave rise to corporate property—the feudal organization of trades—and it had very little division of labor, since every country contained within itself the town and country polarity.

All of this mattered far more than any idealistic theory of ideas, Marx and Engels insisted. The production of ideas is always interwoven with the material activities of human agents. Human beings produce their ideas within and through particular forms of production and material life. They put it epigrammatically: "Life is not determined by consciousness, but consciousness by life." They turned political, taking aim at typical bourgeois debates about democracy, voting, aristocracy, and the like. These debates were a distraction from what mattered. To rattle on about democracy and the extent of the franchise was to ignore the real struggle of the laboring masses not to starve or freeze: "Of this the German theoreticians have not the faintest inkling, although they have received a sufficient introduction to the subject in the *Deutsch-Französische Jahrbücher* and *Die heilige Familie*." For a moment Marx and Engels turned lyrical, writing a fanciful passage that stood out in Marx's entire subsequent corpus. In all societies preceding the coming communist society, one was a hunter, a fisher, a shepherd, or even a cultural critic—pointedly they left out slaves, serfs, and factory workers. But to not starve, one had to stick with hunting, fishing, shepherding, or criticizing. Losing your livelihood was life threatening in all heretofore-existing forms of life. Marx and Engels declared that in a communist society no one would be consigned to one thing or forced to stick with it: "Each can become accomplished in any branch he wishes, society regulates the general production and thus makes it possible for me to do one thing today and another tomorrow, to hunt in the morning, fish in the afternoon, rear cattle in the evening, criticize after dinner, just as I have a mind, without ever becoming hunter, fisherman, cowherd, or critic."[50]

Communism was precisely the abolition of and liberation from the rule of human products that gains power over human communities, grows out of control, constrains human expectations, and blights the lives of many. In 1836 German workers living abroad founded the League of the Just, a radical organization with multiple outlets and headquartered in London. Engels joined the renamed League of Communists in the summer of 1847. The following November Marx and Engels participated in its Second Congress, and in December Marx joined. The league commissioned Marx and Engels to draft a new program. Thus *The Communist Manifesto* was perfectly timed when Europe erupted in revolutions. Marx returned to Germany flush with revolutionary excitement, having renounced his Prussian citizenship in 1845. He believed the revolutionary upheaval of 1847 would far exceed what happened in France in 1789. In June 1848 he launched a paper, *Neue Rheinische Zeitung*, which supported radical liberals in the early going before tacking toward proletarian radicalism at the end of the year. Not until April 1849 did Marx abandon his strategy of linking arms with liberal democrats, imploring that workers needed their own party. Yet his strongest flirtation with conspiratorial insurrection coincided with the year of revolutionary ferment for liberal democracy, 1848. After the revolution failed and Marx's paper was suppressed, he briefly returned to Paris and then took exile in London, where he lived for the rest of his life.

Marxist theory from the beginning was ambiguous, ironic, and variously interpreted. *The Communist Manifesto* flushed with motivational language, it came at the outset of Marx's ultraleft phase, and it conveyed only one side of his brilliantly complex thought. But it was by far his most famous work, and it defined true Marxism for many. Its opening sentence declared that Europe was haunted by the "specter of communism." Marx and Engels knew that was absurd. Europe in 1848 was at war over bourgeois freedoms, not communism. Europe had very few communists, and Marx was just beginning to meet them. In section 2 he and Engels announced the funeral of the bourgeoisie, but in the final section they urged proletarians to make alliances with it. The bourgeoisie was corrupt, inevitably hostile to workers, and dying, yet proletarians should help bring it to power, working with Chartists in England, petit bourgeois radicals in France, agrarian reformers in the United States, and the bourgeoisie itself in Germany.[51]

Once the bourgeois revolution took place, the proletarian revolution would replace it. Marx and Engels said the bourgeois revolution in Germany would be the prelude to an immediate proletarian revolution. That sounded like an immediate transition to a communist revolution, skipping an intervening period of bourgeois government. Over the next two years Marx seemed to confirm this reading by urging workers to form secret armed organizations prepared for class war and set up revolutionary regimes alongside the victorious bourgeois governments. He also used the fateful phrase, "dictatorship of the proletariat." In April 1850 he and Engels signed the declaration of the World Society of Revolutionary Communists: "The aim of the association is the overthrow of all privileged classes, their subjugation by the dictatorship of the proletariat which will maintain the revolution in permanence until communism, the last organizational form of the human family, will be constructed."[52]

For at least two years Marx was an ultraleftist who envisioned the proletarian revolution as a popular explosion or insurrection from below. He flirted with conspiratorial fantasies in the fashion of Louis-Auguste Blanqui, a French communist revolutionary who played a role in every Paris uprising from 1830 to 1871 and was a leading member of the 1871 Paris Commune. Marx implored a pitifully fragmented industrial proletarian movement to take up revolutionary violence. Then for a year after the stormy drama of 1848 and 1849 had passed, he spoke of the dictatorship of the proletariat (*Diktatur*), not the rule of the proletariat (*Herrschaft*), his usual formulation. Subsequent Marxist schools clashed fatefully over what that meant. German Social Democratic doyen Karl Kautsky, a father of orthodox Marxism, said Marx got sloppy for a while, carelessly using a term he never meant, since Marx was a radical democrat to his core. Vladimir Lenin said *Diktatur* was exactly what Marx meant; Marx was the commanding theorist of Lenin-style vanguard manipulation, violence, and dictatorship.[53]

Leninists had a battery of proof texts on their side, plus Marx's vituperative relationships with allies, enemies, and, especially, hapless comrades who failed to keep up with him. But Social Democrats had the stronger case, since Marx cared about civil liberties and was committed to democratic self-determination. The fact that Marx, between 1872 and 1875, went back to saying *Diktatur* instead of *Herrschaft* was a problem for democratic Marxists, and the later Engels spoke of dictatorship too. The effusions of Marx's ultraleft period and his occasional lapses afterward had horrible consequences, buttressing Communist tyranny.

Marx did not mean what his Anarchist opponents, Leninist usurpers, and bourgeois enemies said he meant by "dictatorship of the proletariat," especially after 1850. To him, "dictatorship" referred to the class basis of precommunist parties, not revolutionary repression. Every state was a dictatorship because the purpose of the state was to maintain the ruling class. Marx believed the state was necessary only in class societies, to uphold and defend class privileges. Once the proletarian revolution achieved a definitive victory by overthrowing capitalism and the capitalist state, the state would be unnecessary. Revolutionary states, though necessary in transitions, were still dictatorships. A communist state was a contradiction in terms. Marx described the Paris Commune of 1871 as a dictatorship because its property forms organized a proletarian version of class rule. This was a transition to the real thing, a revolution that abolished class rule and the state. On the very things that destroyed the First International, Marx was closer to the anarchists than they acknowledged. But Marx did not exude their hatred of the state, and to them Marxism smacked of German state socialism. So the International crashed.[54]

All of that lay far ahead when Marx holed up in the British Museum. In the 1850s he developed his critique of capitalism, publishing *A Contribution to the Critique of Political Economy* in 1859. The preface had a fateful legacy as the master text of "vulgar Marxism," a simplistic, mechanistic theory of economic determinism: "It is not the consciousness of men that determines their existence but, on the contrary, their social existence determines their consciousness."

Marx, a thinker of enormous power who absorbed Hegel during his coming of age, was not a vulgar Marxist. His unpublished *Grundrisse*, a prolegomena to his masterwork, *Capital*, described the economic, political, and cultural dimensions of society as interacting with and mutually determining one another. But Marx made a mighty contribution to vulgar Marxism by publishing the preface to the *Critique of Political Economy*, standing by it, and repeating it in other contexts. In 1852 he told Joseph Weydemeyer that his central discovery was the structural development of the class struggle, "which necessarily leads to the dictatorship of the proletariat," and that "this dictatorship itself only constitutes the transition to the abolition of all classes and to a classless society."[55]

This formulation combined the three planks of what came to be called "vulgar Marxism": economic determinism, the dictatorship of the proletariat, and utopianism. Marx did not mind that his followers adopted a simplistic doctrine of determinism because this doctrine supported his concept of class, what really mattered to him. Marx believed the mode of production determined the organization of slave, feudal, and capitalist economies. To him, a class was defined precisely by its function in the mode of production, as he declared in the *Communist Manifesto*: "The history of all hitherto existing society is the history of class struggles."[56]

These ideas defined the Marxist tradition in Germany after the nation's two socialist parties merged in 1875 and Marx repudiated the program of the new party, which he said smacked too much of Ferdinand Lassalle, not Marx. Lassalle was born to wealthy Jewish parents in Breslau in 1825, studied philosophy at Breslau and Berlin, and served a six-month prison sentence for supporting the Republican revolution of 1848. The postrevolutionary backlash in Prussia was harsh and devastatingly effective. Labor organizing was ruthlessly repressed by the police, many workers were deported from Berlin and other cities, democratic newspapers were shut down, and King Frederick Wilhelm IV issued a Constitution mocking "The Fundamental Rights of the German People," the declaration of the 1848 German National Assembly at Frankfurt. For a while Lassalle tried to stay out of trouble. He wrote books on Heraclitus and legal theory and read Marx. He corresponded with Marx and Engels and visited them in 1862, making a poor impression. Lassalle's flagrant vanity and devotion to Prussia put off Marx. Marx bristled that Lassalle helped himself to Marx's ideas *and* that Lassalle was a state socialist. To his face, Marx managed to be cordial toward Lassalle; he was in a poor position to alienate any ostensible German follower. To Engels, he made racist cracks about Lassalle's dark complexion. Later that year Lassalle ignited Germany's first socialist movement.[57]

Lassalle lit up mass meetings across Prussia and broke through to Catholic working-class audiences in the Rhineland. In 1863 he organized the world's first socialist party, the General German Workers' Association, winning the canny attention of Otto von Bismarck just after Bismarck became minister president of Prussia. Lassalle's movement was a German socialist form of Chartism. The party's platform proposed to build a socialist order by winning elections; its first plank was universal suffrage; it was democratic, reformist, and friendly toward religion; it gave a strong role to the state; and it called for state-supported producer cooperatives. All of this, to Marx, was pitifully bourgeois, undermining the proletarian revolution. Lassalle created his struggling party out of nothing. It barely topped one thousand members, and then it lost Lassalle, who was killed in a duel in 1864. The same year a ray of hope appeared in London, as an unwieldy smattering of English Owenites, Chartists, and unionists, French socialist followers of Proudhon and Blanqui, Italian republicans, Irish and Polish nationalists, and German socialists convened in St. Martin's Hall to found the International Workingmen's Association—the First International. Edward Spencer Beesly, a history professor at London University, chaired the founding meeting. Marx represented himself and did not speak, although he soon became a leader in the General Council in London. This was his first plunge into sustained activism, sixteen years after the *Communist Manifesto.* At last there was a real workers' organization to join.[58]

Now Marx had an opportunity to apply his theorizing to a proletarian organization sprawling across national borders. He gave a skillful speech to the General Council in 1864, tamping down the revolutionary ardor of the manifesto, mindful that this group was not very radical. Marx believed in working with actually existing unions. He tried not to alienate the English unionists sitting before him, although he said Owen-style cooperatives and unionism would never free the masses from industrial slavery. Proletarians of all nations had to band together to do that.[59]

From the beginning the International battled over rival ideologies, especially Anarchism. In the early going Marx clashed with Proudhon; then the battle escalated after Michael Bakunin, a Russian revolutionary and exile, joined the International in 1868. French Proudhonists advocated a federation of communes, Blanqui's followers advocated violent insurrection, and Bakunin was steeped in the communal antistatism of the Proudhon tradition. In 1870 the French government of Louis Napoleon fell after France lost the Franco-Prussian War. The following year Marx heralded the insurrection of radicals in Paris against the provisional French government and defended the Paris Commune, which instituted most of the Proudhon/Bakunin program. Marx's influence in the International soared after he scathingly attacked the provisional government and defended the Paris Commune. His notoriety in antisocialist circles also soared, as newspapers charged that the International somehow plotted the uprising in Paris. Behind this conspiracy, supposedly, stood Karl Marx, hereafter a menacing figure. The Paris uprising marked the high point of Marx's career as a revolutionary activist. He boosted his reputation among radicals by acting nothing like a stodgy German socialist. But he used his new influence to ridicule the antistate ideology of his short-lived admirers. The majority of Continental Internationalists were Anarchists, not Marxists. This difference was the root of nearly everything that wrecked the International.[60]

Marx contended that socialism was impossible until capitalism fully matured. Strategically, this was a matter of utmost importance, not a negligible debating point. Capitalism would create the necessary conditions of socialist revolution and was unable to avoid doing so. Meanwhile the state had a role to play in bringing about socialism. The proletarian movement needed to use the state to help bring about the bourgeois revolution and the socialist revolution. There were furious debates about that, notwithstanding that Marx had his own version of no-state utopianism.

Bakunin charged that Marxism was an authoritarian ideology that colluded with bourgeois governments and would institute a new form of class rule wherever it took over. In Germany, Bakunin said, Marxism was the basis of so-called democratic socialism, which had no trouble bonding with Bismarck to build a German Empire—the obsession of all Germans. "Every German," Bakunin charged, yearned for an empire sprawling across Sweden, Denmark, Holland, part of Belgium, all of Austria except Hungary, part of France, and all of Switzerland up to the Alps. Since this was what all Germans cared about, only a statist socialism got anywhere in Germany. According to Bakunin, the difference between Lassalle and his hero-theorist, Marx, was that Lassalle was honest and a power broker whereas Marx was dishonest and a failure. Bakunin declared, "They say that this state yoke, this dictatorship, is a necessary transitional device for achieving the total liberation of the people. Anarchy, or freedom, is the goal, and the state, or dictatorship, the means. Thus, for the masses to be liberated they must first be enslaved." He countered, "No dictatorship can have any other objective than to perpetuate itself." Anyone who doubted it was unfamiliar with human nature. To the extent that any state succeeded, even a socialist one, it deepened the slavery of the people it ruled. The idea of a people's state, Bakunin charged, was the root of everything wrong in Marxism: "If there is a state, then necessarily there is domination and consequently slavery. A state without slavery, open or camouflaged, is inconceivable—that is why we are enemies of the state."[61]

Bakunin advocated federations of self-governing enterprises and communes—pure anarcho-syndicalism. He had some hope for Britons and Americans because the freedom principle meant something in England and the United States. There, in his telling, when someone said, "I am an Englishman" or "I am an American," it really meant, "I am a free man." But when a German said, "I am a German," it always meant, "I am a slave, but my emperor is stronger than all other princes, and the German soldier who is strangling me will strangle all of you." Upon clashing with German Marxists in the International, Bakunin gave up on Germans, not just Prussians. All Germans were infatuated with their story of how they overcame a sprawling multiplicity of kingdoms, princedoms, states, estates, and municipalities to become an almost-mighty nation. All Germans lusted for a powerful unitary state, and socialism had not helped them to yearn for freedom. Bakunin countered with colorful defiance: "On the social-revolutionary banner, our banner, in letters of fire and blood, is inscribed: *Abolish all states, destroy bourgeois civilization, organize freely from below upward, by means of free associations—organize the unshackled laboring hordes, the whole of liberated humanity, create a new world for all mankind.*"[62]

Marx blasted Bakunin with comparable fury, accusing him of "schoolboy asininity. . . . He does not understand a thing about social revolution, only the political phrases about it; its economic conditions do not exist for him." To Bakunin's dogmatic mind, Marx said, the colossal differences between Germany and Russia meant nothing. Bakunin applied his dogma wherever he landed, learning nothing, and distorted what it meant to say that the proletariat organized as a ruling class. It meant that instead of fighting piecemeal against the privileged classes, the proletariat achieved enough strength and organization to express itself forcibly in the class struggle. But when the proletariat used economic means toward this end, it abolished its own character as the wage-laboring class: "With its complete victory, therefore, its domination is at an end because its character as a class has disappeared." Self-government meant precisely that all people governed and thus no one was governed. In other words, Marx said, when a man ruled himself, he did not rule himself since he was only himself and no one else. Marx fantasized that if Bakunin were to acquire some experience managing a single cooperative, the Bakunin utopians might enter the real world and thus grasp the concept of self-governance. As it was, too many revolutionaries wallowed in utopian fantasies while the exploited masses suffered and died.[63]

In Germany the First International stood for patchy versions of Marxian socialism and radical democracy, variously understood, as Lassalle's party merged in 1875 with the Social Democratic Workers Party of Wilhelm

Liebknecht and August Bebel to form the Socialist Workers Party, later called the Social Democratic Party (SPD). In southern Europe the International stood for Anarchism, swayed partly by Bakunin's hero stature as a Russian exile. In France and Belgium the International oscillated between Marxism and Anarchism, with radical democratic varieties of both. In England the movement stood for mere international trade unionism; thus the English party was not a player in the blowout between Marx and Bakunin that destroyed the International. Marxists got the upper hand at the Hague Congress in 1872, repudiating Bakunin. Anarchists struck back the same year at a separate congress in St. Imier, Switzerland, gaining control of the International. Afterward the organization splintered and shriveled, dying in 1877. To Continental socialists, the self-destruction of the First International felt catastrophic. In England it barely mattered because the International barely existed in England, and the nation lacked a socialist organization of any kind beyond the cooperative societies.

STEWART HEADLAM, HENRY GEORGE, AND THE NEW CHRISTIAN SOCIALISMS

The plucky clerics who revived Christian socialism in the 1880s had almost nothing going for them except a bitter economic downturn. English religion was severely segmented by class and had almost no heritage of caring about the poor, aside from aristocrats congratulating themselves on their charitableness. Anglicanism catered to the upper class and the universities, worshipping with an archaic formality that reinforced the church's indifference to the poor. The Protestant Nonconforming churches catered to middle-class strivers, looking down on the poor and lowly. The poor felt more or less welcome only at Bible Christian and Primitive Methodist congregations. They were foreigners in their own country, unmistakably unwelcome in established English churches. This was not just a failing of late Victorian religion. The urban poor had never gone to church in England and never been welcome. The idea that the gospel commends seeing Christ in the poor was a novelty in England, aside from a trickle of reformers and a sprinkling of Methodist street preachers and Quakers. The Bible Christians and Primitive Methodists produced labor leaders but no socialists. The Wesleyan Methodists produced a few labor leaders but mostly produced believers in middle-class capitalism and respectability. Then a nervy band of Maurice admirers revived Christian socialism.[64]

In England the Christian socialist upsurge was mostly Anglo-Catholic, sometimes with friendly connections to Congregational, Unitarian, and Quaker socialists who tried and failed to build Nonconforming socialist organizations. Christian socialism and liberal theology, in England, were decidedly different things. English Anglicans had a spectacular controversy in 1860 over liberal theology, biblical criticism, and Darwinism. The stormy reaction to a single multiauthor book, *Essays and Reviews*, killed theological liberalism in England for thirty years, as church leaders furiously defended traditional doctrine. Liberal theology in England was restricted to a handful of upper-middle-class Congregational and Presbyterian congregations and a quiet smattering of academics. In 1867 a major new Reform Bill gave the vote to urban workers, which gave heartburn to prominent Anglican clerics; even Maurice said he would not be guided by the will of the majority. When the Church of England belatedly acquired a liberal theology movement in the 1890s, it did not talk about fulfilling the gospel mission to the poor. Only Christian socialists and their political allies talked like that; in England they were mostly Anglo-Catholics serving hurting congregations.[65]

The clerics who revived Christian socialism in the 1880s were admirers of Maurice who stressed their theological reasons for being socialists, not their ideas about worker guilds or the like. They responded as clerics to a crisis in English society: The supposed ever-upward climb of the world's first industrial power had stopped. Prices began falling in England in the mid-1870s and kept falling into the early 1890s. Railway construction ran out of territory, and shipbuilding passed through an overproduction phase. Absolute output kept expanding in England, but growth decelerated just as the German and U.S. economies rapidly industrialized. Germany and the United States had newer equipment and technology and did better at developing human capital. Both nations raced past England in making steel, the key to the next great wave of industrialization. Economic historians subsequently debated whether England had a "Great Depression" in the 1880s or merely a bad recession. To the late Victorians who lived through it, the depression seemed fully great, and crushing. They had never experienced structural unemployment. Previously, if one could not find a job one simply moved to where jobs existed. Now "unemployment" became an everyday concept, something integral to the economic order. Liberal politicians had no answer for it. Moreover, the unemployed no longer waited quietly at home for better times. They protested in the streets and sometimes the churches, demanding the right to a job.[66]

Prominent liberals began to apologize in public. Churchgoing readers of Henry George's blockbuster *Progress and Poverty* (1879) organized meetings to discuss what should be done about poverty. British imperialism staved off some of the economic pain, but left-Liberals recognized that that was a morally disastrous solution. The issue of Irish Home Rule roiled Parliament, earnest radicals in the Liberal Party opposed Gladstone's punitive treatment of Ireland, and they recoiled at English imperialism in Egypt. Fabian luminary Beatrice Webb, explaining the ferment of the 1880s, said, "Men of intellect and property" acquired a "consciousness of sin," a guilty recognition that they lived off the labor and suffering of others. This was partly self-descriptive. Beatrice Webb, born Martha Beatrice Potter in 1858, also known as Baroness Passfield, was the daughter of a wealthy timber merchant and granddaughter of a prominent Liberal politician. In the mid-1880s she had a crippling romantic entanglement with Radical politician Joseph Chamberlain before he found his third wife. Her friend Herbert Spencer sparked her interest in social research, which Potter took up with pioneering sociologist Charles Booth, studying the poor of London's docklands and East End. Upper-middle-class guilt was her daily bread. Oxford economist Arnold Toynbee expressed it poignantly in a lecture shortly before his death in 1883: "We—the middle classes, I mean, not merely the very rich—we have neglected you; instead of justice we have offered you charity, and instead of sympathy we have offered you hard and unreal advice; but I think we are changing. If you would only believe it and trust us, I think that many of us would spend our lives in your service. You have—I say it clearly and advisedly—you have to forgive us, for we have wronged you; we have sinned against you grievously—not knowingly always, but still we have sinned, and let us confess it; but if you will forgive us—nay, whether you will forgive us or not—we will serve you, we will devote our lives to your service, and we cannot do more."[67]

These contrite words rang in the heart of Samuel Barnett when he founded the first settlement house in 1884, Toynbee Hall. Barnett was a kindly, humble, affable Anglican cleric who typified the renewal of social Christianity. His wife, Henrietta, was hard charging, not so affable, and definitely not humble. Together they created a settlement ministry in London's East End featuring seminars, concerts, community services, and conversation. It was a tremendous success, spawning settlements across England and North America. At Toynbee House the mission included solidarity work with unions, which surprised U.S. American visitor Jane Addams, who had been raised to believe that unions were bad. The Barnetts were radical and conservative at the same time, like many Christian socialists who leavened socialist radicalism with a churchly ethos. They called themselves "Practicable Socialists" dedicated to social reform. Their success was cheered by every new Christian socialist organization.[68]

The Guild of Saint Matthew (GSM) was the first to arise. Maurice protégé Stewart Duckworth Headlam founded it in 1877, originally as a congregational vehicle for Holy Communion and social activism. In 1884 he turned it into a national vehicle of socialist activism. In 1883 a band of Mauricites active in the Land Reform Union launched a spunky, ecumenical, radical magazine, the *Christian Socialist*, which got more radical the following year after Anglo-Catholic cleric Charles L. Marson took over as editor. Marson and Headlam had a similar outrage and a willingness to confront, though the Anglo-Catholic factor played out differently between them, as Headlam catered to Anglo-Catholics and atheists, and Marson wrote for the interdenominational movement his magazine tried to create. A flock of other socialist and religious socialist organizations arose during the same period. Businessman Henry M. Hyndman founded the Democratic Federation in 1881, which morphed into the proto-Marxist Social Democratic Federation in 1884, the same year that a band of mostly secular progressives launched the Fabian Society. The following year a schism in the federation produced another radical socialist organization, William Morris's Socialist League, which was ethical socialist like Morris but fatefully long on anarchists. In 1886 Marson's brilliant journalism in the *Christian Socialist* yielded a new ecumenical organization, the Christian Socialist Society. He wrote the platforms for both groups, calling for public control of land, capital, and all means of production, and production for use. Three years later a group of Oxford dons, needing a socialist-like organization they could join, founded the Christian Social Union, soon a major enterprise.

The gusher of new organizations continued. In 1891 a group of union activists in North England founded the Labour Church, a post-Christian outfit founded by John Trevor, for whom socialism was a new religion. In 1894 an ecumenical group of North Englanders led by Baptist minister John Clifford and Anglican cleric Henry Cary Shuttleworth founded the union-oriented Christian Socialist League, which morphed four years later into the mostly Nonconforming Christian Social Brotherhood. Small socialist fellowships arose within the Congregational, Baptist, Unitarian, and Society of Friends denominations, and in 1906 a group of radical northern Anglican clerics led by G. Algernon West and Conrad Noel founded the Church Socialist League, soon a bastion of guild socialism. One group changed the political landscape for all these groups after it was founded in 1893—the Independent Labour Party (ILP), founded by Keir Hardie. All the interdenominational religious groups were chronically strapped for money, loyalty, and institutional outlets, while Headlam's group held the advantages of being Anglican, theologically definite, early, and confidently led. But in the early going the *Christian Socialist* and the vehicle it created, the Christian Socialist Society, were distinctly catalyzing for the gusher of Christian socialisms.

The *Christian Socialist* went through two editors in its first year before turning to Marson, who ramped up the rhetorical fire, giving the paper its three best years. Marson wrote searing editorials against the ravages of capitalism and the dependence of British capitalism on British imperialism. He blasted British conceits about spreading Anglo-Saxon civilization, calling out the racism in it. He ripped the organizers of antilabor clubs as pampered, cowardly, gutter-level scoundrels, and the Church of England as a racket lacking minimal moral health. He said that women should be priests and anything else they wanted to be; otherwise the world would keep going to hell. Marson had a slew of epithets for Anglican bishops centered on the imagery of aged, creepy, dim-witted, readily herded sheep. He welcomed the new socialist and Christian socialist organizations, with a sharp eye for their flaws. The Social Democratic Federation, he judged, blathered too much about guns and fighting. The Socialist League had commendable politics and an ethical spirit, except for its disastrous spurning of Christians. The Fabian Society was too bourgeois and respectable, the same thing Marson later said about its Anglican version, the Christian Social Union. As for Headlam's group, Marson said it was fine for Anglican socialists who loved church drapery and creeds, but that excluded too many people. What British Christianity really needed was an interdenominational, radically socialist, radically anti-imperialist organization dedicated to "the good of the commonwealth and of mankind" and standing unequivocally for "public control of Land, Capital, and all means of production, distribution, and exchange, involving the abolition of all Interest."[69]

Marson took for granted that Christian socialism had to rip the bark off churchly decorum, an assumption his successors tamped down in pursuit of milder folk who joined the Fabian Society and Christian Social Union. W. Howard Paul Campbell, a Fabian and Congregationalist who took over the *Christian Socialist* in 1887, said that a bit of tamping down was in order. Campbell's widely read tract of 1884, *The Robbery of the Poor*, featured sermonic appeals to Jesus and the claim that Christian socialism was the abolitionist movement updated. Alfred Howard, a lay Anglican and Fabian who headed the Christian Socialist Society, agreed that finding the right tone was crucial, since socialism was radical enough on its own. Howard explained in 1888: "We hold that the underlying principles of Christianity, though laid down ages before Socialism had found a name, were actually and designedly intended as the foundation for the essential economic principles of the superstructure which Socialism has erected upon them without knowing it. This being so, we, in advocating Socialism, appeal to the heart, to the deepest and strongest human passions and emotions—to which Christianity also appeals, as well as to the head and reasoning faculties." Lay Congregationalist George W. Johnson, taking over the *Christian Socialist* in 1891, heightened the paper's Christian identity, contending that antireligious socialisms were "doomed to decay." Johnson inveighed against the idea that socialism was a form of rebellion against "all faith and all that makes society possible." The Socialist League, he protested, tied the living body of socialism to the corpse of atheistic materialism, a terrible mistake that violated the religious wellspring of socialism itself: "Without an ideal faith Socialism will have no power over men." All great movements of human history exude idealism and spiritual feeling: "We aim at the effectual purifying of the *whole* man—body, mind, spirit. No aim can be higher than that."[70]

The *Christian Socialist* made this case with verve, eloquence, and conviction, convincing many that Christian socialism was a good thing that crossed denominational boundaries. It had a rich legacy at the propaganda level, creating Christian socialists who would never have joined the Guild of Saint Matthew (GSM). In that sense it outlasted the GSM, which eventually suffered the consequences of its insularity. But the *Christian Socialist* was far more successful at lifting up Christian socialism than at changing England's religious market. The market ran through denominations; ecumenical socialist activism was a novelty ahead of its time. Thus, for a while, Headlam's weird insularity was rewarded. Headlam bonded readily with atheists and skeptics but spurned Christians who were not Anglo-Catholics. GSM was decidedly his group, notwithstanding that Shuttleworth, a jovial ecumenist, and Thomas Hancock, a sensational Anglo-Catholic writer and speaker, were prominent in it. Headlam was a contrarian. He followed Maurice into sacramental Christian socialism, after which he acquired his own opinions and imposed them on GSM. He championed music hall gaiety, secular education, and Maurice's vision of the kingdom of Christ, embracing everything that late Victorian church conservatives loathed—liberalism, Catholicism, low-end theaters, ballet, political radicalism, disestablishment, and atheists. He did it in the name of true Anglican Christianity, galling his church audiences. Like Maurice, Headlam endured career setbacks for preaching a sacramental socialist theology of divine order. Unlike Maurice, he was a fervent Anglo-Catholic *and* a fervent advocate of disestablishment—an eccentric pairing that endeared him to atheists.

Born in Wavertree, near Liverpool, in 1847, Headlam grew up comfortably middle class. His father, Thomas Headlam, worked in a family firm of underwriters that clashed over Tractarianism versus evangelicalism, always a debate about which party should control the church establishment. Spiritually, it was a low period in the Church of England. Worship was dry and formulaic and Holy Communion rare. Kingsley acidly remarked that the Church of England

was notable only for its "ghastly dullness." As a youth Headlam endured contentious debates between his father, an aggressive Evangelical, and his uncle, an
old school High Church cleric. He wilted under Thomas Headlam's proselytiz-
ing and caught a break at the age of thirteen by enrolling at Eton, a prestigious
boarding school. Headlam's housemaster was J. L. Joynes, a Christian socialist
friend of Maurice and Kingsley. His favorite teacher, William Johnson, was a
skeptical-leaning Whig and admirer of Maurice. Eton loosened Headlam's
Evangelical anxiety and introduced him to Anglo-Catholic ritual, which he
liked. Then he studied moral theology under Maurice at Cambridge University
and embraced Maurice's teaching. Thomas Headlam resisted for a while before
accepting that his son had become a dreaded Anglo-Catholic, albeit a liberal
one. Had Thomas Headlam taken a less generous attitude, Stewart Headlam
would not have been able to afford blowing up his clerical career.[71]

Graduating in 1868, Headlam found a curacy at a humble congregation at
Drury Lane, London. His vicar, Richard Graham Maul, admired Maurice, and
Headlam found a local mentor in Thomas Wodehouse, a veteran Christian
socialist with a gut-level passion for the downtrodden. Headlam developed his
sacramental socialism: Baptism reasserts the Christian doctrine of human
equality before God, and the Mass supremely expresses the Incarnation of
Christ and the divine consecration of all life. But Headlam got in trouble for
preaching Maurice's theology about eternal life. Maul cringed whenever
Headlam warmed to this subject, wishing he would drop it and avoid trouble.
John Jackson, the bishop of London, told Headlam to stop preaching against
everlasting punishment because half the human race was destined for hell.
Headlam could not do that; he could not say God-anything if people thought
he was referring to a tormenter of souls. He lasted three years at Drury Lane and
narrowly averted not being ordained to the priesthood in 1871.

His next curacy went better, in a desperately poor congregation and parish,
Saint Matthew's Church in Bethnal Green. Bethnal Green was filled with tenements packing twenty to thirty families. There were no sanitary facilities, tenants defecated in open ditches in front of the buildings, and hardly anyone went
to church. Typhus was rampant, and the smell was overwhelming. Headlam's
socialist rector Septimus Hansard was a legendary figure in the East End for his
ministry to the poor, but even Hansard did not reside in Bethnal Green.
Headlam vowed to live where he served, where the miserable suffering of his
neighbors radicalized him. Headlam preached that the poor did not go to
church because the Church did not care about the poor. He hung out in music
halls and low-end theaters, befriending performers. He attracted the theater
crowd to church, a startling spectacle to churchgoers, and bonded with union

organizers, especially Emma Patterson, founder of the Women's Trade Union League. He befriended two notorious atheistic advocates of birth control, Charles Bradlaugh and Annie Besant, and three curates at the Junior Clergy Society who shared his socialist politics—George Sarson, Thomas Hancock, and Henry Cary Shuttleworth. Three other Anglo-Catholic clerics—Charles Lowder in London Docks, A. H. Mackonochie in Holborn, and H. D. Hill in Shoreditch—influenced Headlam, all by emphasizing ritual beauty while ministering to the poor in harsh conditions.[72]

Headlam's devotion to ritual deepened, creating problems with Hansard, who also became jealous of Headlam's growing notoriety. Being a bohemian aesthete predisposed Headlam to Anglo-Catholicism, but now he had religious reasons for believing in it, preaching that Catholic ceremony distinctly expressed Maurice's theology. English Anglicanism, Headlam said, was appallingly depressing most of the time. With grim mediocrity it worshipped a gloomy Calvinist God. The Mass was so much better, notwithstanding that most Britons were averse to anything smacking of Roman Catholicism. Headlam founded the GSM to promote early morning communion services, contending that the beauty of the Mass reflects the beauty of God and the world. For that matter, the joyful frivolity of theaters, bars, music halls, and ballet was more Christian than the repressive severity of churchgoers. The church had the right theology—Maurice's theology of incarnation, sacrament, and divine order—but most of the church gave a cramped and stuffy witness to it that repelled all but the privileged churchy types.

Headlam said that bad theology and ugly worship go together. Protestant worship was harsh and forbidding because so was the Calvinist God. He told the East London Secular Society in 1876 that eternal punishment was "a horrid doctrine," adding in a sermon it was "a monstrous libel upon God." Headlam refused to be shamed about his party lifestyle, insisting that the Church of England was too starchy to practice its gospel of incarnation. It needed more priests who drank and danced and befriended showgirls. Ritualistic religion and radical socialism were the faith and politics of oppressed people yearning for a better life. The same Christians who carried on against ritual and socialism railed against music halls, theaters, and beautiful ballerinas. Headlam said it was his priestly duty to battle against the bad name they gave to Christianity. Nothing was more anti-Christian than the dreadful contention "Beautiful things are evil." He told church prudes to stop looking down on his friends, especially the actresses and ballerinas, who made wonderful role models for repressed church girls: "I should make it my duty to send every 'young woman whose name was Dull' to see these young women, who are so full of life and mirth." Jesus Christ, Headlam said, was a revolutionary. Not to get that about Jesus was not to get him at all.[73]

That incurred the wrath of Bishop Jackson, who summoned Headlam to Fulham Palace, chastising him for bringing shame on the church. Obviously a Christian could not be a theatergoer; every decent person knew that. A crossfire of letters ensued. Headlam said good Catholic theology sanctified all human things, something Jackson somehow failed to grasp. If only the bishop would do what the gospel commanded—devoting himself to the poor—he would not waste time fretting about coarse people in music halls. Headlam published the back-and-forth, Jackson was offended, and Hansard fired Headlam from Saint Matthew's, a blow Headlam never overcame.[74]

For a while it seemed he would never get another job. In the winter of 1878–1879 Headlam stewed over his vocational crisis and aborted marriage, as his wife turned out to be a lesbian. Finally he got a curacy at St. Thomas, Charterhouse, in East London, where vicar John Rogers welcomed and supported him. Headlam preached about trade unions, contending that female workers deserved a share of industry profits. In 1880 he defended Bradlaugh's right to be seated in Parliament after Bradlaugh became the first atheist to win a House of Commons election. After the House refused to seat Bradlaugh, Headlam lauded him as a Christian martyr, enraging Jackson. This time Headlam had a boss who protected him, but Rogers died a few months later, leaving Headlam out of work again. An ultraritualist friend, Henry David Nihill, long accustomed to battling Jackson, gave Headlam a curacy at Shoreditch. Nihill regarded Headlam as an Anglo-Catholic brother, underestimating how hard it would be to cope with Headlam's politics. It was very hard, with constant complaints. In December 1882 Headlam was fired. He asked Jackson for a general license so he could apply for a new position; Jackson said his diocese had no place for a priest that scandalized the faithful. Headlam never got another official cure in the Church of England.[75]

Building a Christian socialist organization became Headlam's ministry. He turned the GSM into a national organization after he got fired from Saint Matthew's, telling lecture audiences that Anglo-Catholic sacramentalism and radical politics went together. In his early ministry Headlam puzzled over political economy, since Maurice and the slum priests were not helpful in this area, and Headlam spurned Marx. Then Henry George published *Progress and Poverty*, and Headlam knew what to say about economics. In 1884 he committed the GSM to a four-plank political program. One, restore to the people all increments in the value of land. Two, redistribute the wealth created by labor. Three, demand a voice for all people in their own government. Four, abolish "false standards of worth and dignity." Number four was the most radical, and unusual for any British Socialist platform of the time. For years afterward

Headlam admonished Fabian allies and clerical colleagues that class snobbery was something to overcome, not to boast about. He claimed to be a democrat first and a collectivist second, although his sermons were sprinkled with patronizing snorts, and he shared the aversion of his friends to deferring to workers in a solidarity struggle. As for GSM's first plank, it was a page from George—the rocket fuel for the entire Christian socialist movement during its takeoff.[76]

Henry George was a high school dropout whose Damascus-road moment occurred at the age of thirty. Walking the streets of New York in 1869, he was overwhelmed by the contrast between the comforts of the city's upper class and the degradation of the poor. He resolved to devote his life to reforming the system that produced such extremes of wealth and poverty. Ten years later, in *Progress and Poverty*, he argued that landownership is the root of all social evil. As long as land values increase, those who work the land are forced to pay more for the right to work.

George had nothing against Adam Smith–David Ricardo economic theory. He accepted that economics is a deductive science expounding laws of nature and that Ricardo's law of rent was one of them. George was against monopoly, not capitalism. He argued that land cannot be reproduced, its value varies with demand, and charging rent for the mere possession of land is unjust. Deriving earnings from the application of labor or capital is legitimate, but extracting wealth as rent is not. Rent unjustly charges producers for the right to produce. It is a toll levied by monopoly, expropriating wealth for something—mere possession—that performs no useful function. Since God created the land for everyone, and society creates the increment in the value of land, the increment should go to society. George did not want the state to buy the land, since landlords did not deserve any compensation except for whatever capital improvements they made. Neither did he want the state to nationalize the land, since he was not a socialist. The answer was to impose a "Single Tax" on the increment of land values, appropriating the unearned value. Sufficiently taxing the land was the key to creating a morally healthy society. If landowners persisted in calling it their land, let them: "We may safely leave them the shell, if we take the kernel. It is not necessary to confiscate land; it is only necessary to confiscate rent."[77]

This book electrified an enormous reading public as soon as it was published in the United States (1879) and England (1880). Within a few years it sold seven million copies in ten languages, an astounding achievement for a bulky tome on economics. George said abolishing land oppression would change everything: "From this fundamental injustice flow all the injustices which distort and endanger modern development." The Single Tax would free up land held for speculation, stimulate construction, create new housing and jobs, drive down rent, and fund government programs for the needy. In the 1880s George visited the British Isles six times and conducted three extensive lecture tours. He reaped a huge windfall of publicity, winning converts everywhere he went, and intervened in Ireland, where he was arrested twice. In Ireland he provided ballast for Michael Davitt's land reformers against a parliamentary faction led by C. S. Parnell. George influenced every socialist and Christian socialist leader in Britain, notably William Morris, George Bernard Shaw, Beatrice Webb, Keir Hardie, H. M. Hyndman, and Headlam, even as they chided him for going halfway, and some confused the public by describing George as a proponent of land nationalization.[78]

George's simplicity was crucial to his impact. Private property in land was incompatible with the right of individuals to live and to own the product of their labor. The Single Tax changed everything without making heroic demands on the political system. It did not require sweeping transformations of human consciousness or society. It did not rest on a theory or strategy of class war. All it needed was movement advocacy and a few good electoral outcomes. George said so, vibrantly, on his lecture tours. He urged his socialist friends not to overreach by calling for land nationalization or a tax on the unearned interest on capital, but he remained friendly with most of them after they spurned his pleas on these issues. In 1884 Headlam organized a farewell banquet for George, declaring that owning private property in land violated biblical theology. Headlam came out for the nationalization of land, identified the GSM with it, and bought a newspaper to publicize the proposal and the guild, *The Church Reformer: An Organ of Christian Socialism and Church Reform.* The new Christian socialism was like the new socialism more broadly in featuring the land issue, mostly on George's extraordinary impact.

THE SOCIAL DEMOCRATIC FEDERATION AND THE FABIAN SOCIETY

Meanwhile Hyndman founded the Democratic Federation in 1881, and the Fabian Society was founded in 1884. Hyndman had begun as a radical Tory advocate of land nationalization, espousing land reform ten years before George made his splash. He served in Davitt's Land League, began to wonder if he was becoming some kind of socialist, and read Lassalle, which led him to Marx. Hyndman read Marx's *Capital* in French while crossing to America, resolving to look up Marx when he got back to London, where he told Marx he was wrong about the inevitability of revolution. That gave Hyndman the idea of reviving the Chartist movement. With two of his radical Tory friends, H. Butler Johnstone and John Morrison Davidson, he recruited former Chartists, neo-Chartist followers of Bronterre O'Brien, socialists, unionists, and land reformers to a new organization. Fatefully, preparing for the convention, Hyndman published a movement primer that plagiarized Marx's *Capital* without credit. Marx was infuriated, refusing any further dealings with Hyndman; Engels spurned him too, as a rank opportunist. But Hyndman went on to build England's only (ostensibly) Marxist organization. The founders included poetic luminary William Morris, Christian pacifist George Lansbury, Darwinian apologist Edward Aveling, and Aveling's partner Eleanor Marx, Karl's youngest daughter. In the early going the Democratic Federation debated its ideology and espoused one socialist proposal—nationalization of land. In 1884 it changed its name to the Social Democratic Federation (SDF), announcing that full-bore Social Democracy had come to England.[79]

The SDF had a central objective, an eight-point program, and nine remedies for social evils. The objective was to socialize the means of production, distribution, and exchange "to be controlled by a Democratic State in the interest of the entire community, and the complete emancipation of labor from the domination of capitalism and landlordism, with the establishment of social and economic equality between the sexes." Five ideological factions in the SDF debated every phrase of this objective, but Hyndman's quasi-Marxist faction got the upper hand, committing the organization to universal suffrage and publicly financed elections, abolition of child labor, free universal education, the replacement of the standing army with a national citizen force, a maximum forty-eight-hour workweek, the nationalization of land, and repudiation of the national debt. The SDF blasted the Liberal Party for pretending to champion the interests of workers, and it called for female suffrage mostly on solidarity grounds, a rare concession for Hyndman, who was dubious about feminism. There were constant complaints that Hyndman was domineering, sectarian, opportunistic, and obsessed with running for Parliament, which finally split the SDF in December 1884.[80]

Morris, Belford Bax, Eleanor Marx, and Edward Aveling charged that Hyndman was a bad Marxist for instituting a personal dictatorship and favoring electoral politics over union organizing. Most of the executive council walked out, launching a rival organization, the Socialist League. Engels was delighted, telling Eduard Bernstein he had seen through Hyndman from the beginning. Both societies claimed to be Marxian, more or less. Both were revolutionary, international, and anticlerical. But the federation was committed to electoral politics, and it took seriously the existence of nation-states. To the Socialist League, electoral politics was corrupting and nations were reactionary fictions; what mattered was to unite the workers of the world.

Morris wrote brilliant propaganda for the Socialist League's journal, *Commonweal.* He had grown up upper middle class in Essex, excelled in classics at Oxford, and won fame in the 1870s as a poet, decorative arts designer, and novelist. His epic poem *The Earthly Paradise* (1868–1870) retold Greek and Scandinavian myths. His novel *A Dream of John Ball* (1888) described the Great Revolt of 1381, featuring a rebel priest, John Ball. His utopian novel *News from Nowhere* (1890) featured a narrator who awoke to find himself in a future socialist society. All became landmarks of Victorian literature; the latter two were serialized in *Commonweal.* Morris imagined a society in which people flourished in cooperative communities and enjoyed being equal. He wanted socialism to be the next great world religion. But the tiny socialist sect in which Morris ended up quarreled endlessly over revolutionary purity. Anarchists gained control of it in 1892, Morris stopped writing for it, and the group died in 1895, a year before Morris died.[81]

Christian socialists watched all of this with a ready explanation: The socialist parties that sneered at Christianity were consumed by remorseless ideological battle. They had no grace and didn't know how to work together. Johnson lamented in the *Christian Socialist* that "there is a certain school of Socialists among us now who seem far more interested in attacking the great beliefs and institutions of mankind than in helping the victims of poverty all around us." Always there were debates about whether Christian socialists could work with fiercely ideological types who denounced religion. Many tried out the Labour Church on their way out of religion. Always there were more Christian socialists who stuck to church circles than those who consorted with Marxists or Anarchists or the Labour Church.[82]

The Fabian Society, however, offered a different kind of socialism. It was urbane, gradualist, not allergic to irony or introspection, and mildly welcoming to clerics. It had not come from the rough streets of Chartism, and it did not battle over ideological war-words. It was comfortable with its middle-class sensibility and did not speak of revolutionary smashing. It welcomed William Morris socialists and Christian socialists to a socialist organization that had no dogmas, although eventually it got one—Fabian Collectivism, the triumph of collectivism as defined by Sidney Webb. The *Christian Socialist* was sparing in its coverage of the SDF but lavished monthly attention on Fabian proceedings. George Bernard Shaw, speaking for the Fabian Society in 1889, said there were no "authoritative teachers of Socialism" at the present time. There were only "communicative learners" like himself and his fellow Fabians, trying to make sense. All Fabians were Social Democrats, Shaw explained. All believed in "the necessity of vesting the organization of industry and the material of production in a State identified with the whole people by complete Democracy." Fabian socialism was about achieving complete democracy, which could not be oppressive. To exalt "one particular cast of mind" above others in pursuit of complete democracy would not be democratic or Fabian. That seemed exactly right to many Christian socialists, notably Headlam, Howard, and Campbell. Shaw recruited Headlam to the Fabians, who recruited his friends to what was called the "ethical" wing of the society, which soon clashed with Fabian leaders about bureaucratic collectivism, imperialism, and eugenics.[83]

The Fabian Society sprouted from a pacifist vegetarian group in London influenced by the writings of Henry David Thoreau and Leo Tolstoy, the Fellowship of the New Life. Committed to simple living, its ringleader was Scottish intellectual Thomas Davidson; members included poets Edward Carpenter and John Davidson, sexologist Havelock Ellis, South African novelist and feminist Olive Schreiner, and future Fabian secretary Edward R. Pease. The Fellowship of New Life launched two study groups on the new stirrings for socialism in England, one focused on socialist spirituality and the other on socialist activism and economics. The Fabian Society morphed out of the latter group. It attracted prominent intellectuals and young activists, including Shaw, Pease, H. G. Wells, Annie Besant, Sydney Olivier, Ramsay MacDonald, Emmeline Pankhurst, and Frank Podmore. Most important, Sidney Webb joined the society and soon dominated it, eventually with his wife, Beatrice Webb. The group took its name from the Roman general Quintus Fabius Maximus—nicknamed "Cunctator," the Delayer—who shrewdly held back from attacking Hannibal's invading Carthaginian army until the right moment, refusing to be stampeded prematurely into action. That conveyed the identity of the new socialists. They were steeped in classical learning and committed to tracking the evidence. They were gradualists, not revolutionaries, proudly adopting the tortoise as their symbol. But they were serious socialists, committed to striking hard when the right moment came.[84]

The Fabians were tremendous pamphleteers and propagandists. They flooded every available discussion forum, making a case for gradual democratic socialism. They fashioned their club talks into pamphlets and articles, preserving the feeling of the spoken word, consciously creating a middle-class socialist reading public. Shaw was born in Dublin, Ireland, in 1856 and grew up on the edge of the middle class as the son of an Anglo-Irish civil servant lacking any real duties or pay and a frustrated mother who passed her love of literature to him. He had minimal formal education, a deep aversion to it, and a compulsion to write. Fabianism came along in Shaw's struggling novelist years. He became a riveting orator for the Fabians before he was famous and remained one afterward. Sidney Webb's path was more conventional, via academic achievement. Born in London in 1859, his mother was a hairdresser and his father collected rent and debt for merchants. Webb's parents hoped a good education would secure a career for him as a commercial clerk. He studied at the University of London and King's College London, became a barrister in 1885, and taught political economy at City of London College. He waxed idealistic about educational opportunity for the rest of his life. Webb and Shaw were both getting started when they joined the Fabian Society in 1884, three months after its founding. In 1890 Beatrice Potter met with Webb to ask him about trade unionism. He fell in love with her at their first meeting. She pleaded for friendship only, still recovering from Joseph Chamberlain. Webb was undeterred, wearing down her resistance, promising a mutually fulfilling partnership. They married in 1892, and three years later cofounded the London School of Economics with a bequest left to the Fabian Society.[85]

Their union was tremendously productive. Sidney and Beatrice Webb took pride in being sensible, balanced, industrious, middle class, and empirical, serving a colossal cause—a new civilization—through Sidney Webb's organizational achievement, the Fabian Society. It sponsored over seven hundred lectures in 1889 alone, when Shaw assembled a Fabian reader featuring chapters by himself, Sidney Webb, William Clarke, Sydney Olivier, Graham Wallas, Annie Besant, and Hubert Bland. Shaw described socialism as the secret desire of gamblers, liars, and cynics and the Social Democratic state as the means to achieve socialism: "For since in gambling the many must lose in order that the few may win; since dishonesty is mere shadow grasping where everyone is dishonest; and since inequality is better to all except the highest, and miserably lonely for him, men come greatly to desire that these capricious gifts of Nature might be intercepted by some agency having the power and the goodwill to distribute them justly according to the labor done by each in the collective search for them."[86]

Sidney Webb said in 1889 that socialism lacked any real basis in history because modern social consciousness had arisen only recently. All premodern precursors of socialism—from Plato and Thomas More to Babeuf and Owen—assumed a static society. Modern social consciousness was revolutionary because it swept away the idea of an ideal society as an unchanging state. Modern science, Webb explained, described a Darwinian world of becoming in which the constant growth and development of social organisms are axiomatic. Socialists understood this change better than apologists for laissez-faire political economics. Webb commended Hyndman for saying that a new form, socialism, had to grow through and beyond an old form, liberal reformism, letting pass that Hyndman said it against Marxists and Anarchists in his own group. Webb proceeded as though the smashers had already lost the argument; history had surpassed them. Socialism, Webb declared, was "a wave surging throughout all Europe," carrying the democratic revolution to its next stage of realization.[87]

Europe was awash in socialist movements because the past century of democratic movements and achievements had advanced this far. Webb understood the anguish of liberals, especially their opposition to mixing politics with social and economic issues. Liberals had not broken the power of the aristocracy to get this result. They were moved by hatred of the few, not love of the many. They were radicals in their time because they wanted to be lords. Now their time was past, even though they thought they were progressives. Utopians were equally quaint, being oblivious to blind social forces that wrecked every utopian dream of the past and remained uncontrollable. Webb described good socialism as a sophisticated synthesis of liberal democracy and utopian idealism. The lesson of democracy was that social reorganization occurs through the "slow and gradual turning of the popular mind to new principles." All organic changes in society are democratic, gradual, morally acceptable to the mass of people, and constitutional/peaceful. Democracy has its "freaks or aberrations," Webb allowed—the occasional brief monarchy or romantic dictatorship. But freakish episodes aside, democracies get more and more democratic and thus increasingly socialistic. England was like John Stuart Mill's *Principles of Political Economy*—every edition was more socialist than the one before, although England in 1889 had not caught up to Mill's seventh and last edition of 1871, which espoused Social Democracy.[88]

Webb piled up examples from English history and Mill. The social principle was gaining in every sphere of government, industry, and society. It started with Jeremy Bentham (1748–1832), who provided an ethical foundation for a new science, political economics. Utilitarian ethics changed the ethical standard to the happiness of humankind. Webb explained that if pleasure and pain are the sole masters of human beings, morality must be principally concerned with regulating pleasure and pain. The moral question is always whether a given act serves the greater good for the greater number. Bentham called for the abolition of slavery, the death penalty, and physical punishment on this basis. He taught utilitarian ethics to James Mill, who passed it to his son John Stuart Mill. Bentham's influence was so great that even theologians adopted utilitarianism; Webb cited Anglican apologist William Paley. Webb said utilitarian ethics challenged the usefulness of "every shred of social institution then existing." If England was "covered with rotten survivals from bygone circumstances," they had to be left behind. To be sure, Bentham-style utilitarianism was "a creed of

Murdstones and Gradgrinds," underwriting the interests of mill owners and merchant princes. It had to be warmed up by the Christian Romanticism of Coleridge, which led to Maurice and Kingsley, extending to the many. Though Bentham was a liberal of his time, his utilitarian liberalism led, logically and organically, to Social Democracy, exactly as John Stuart Mill maintained.[89]

In Webb's telling, modern history was a story of this logical, organic progression. The growth of government to serve more and more citizens was staggering. Liberal governments and Tory governments enacted a cascade of "Local Improvement Acts, Drainage Acts, Truck Acts, Mines Regulation Acts, Factory Acts, Public Health Acts, [and] Adulteration Acts," even as politicians of both parties mouthed conventional pieties about limited government. Politicians and academics railed against socialism as an affront to sturdy British individualism without acknowledging their sizable roles in socializing almost everything. Things that were previously left to private enterprise and treated as a legitimate source of individual investment were being taken over by the community through the state. Conduct of international relations headed this list, followed by the army, navy, police, and courts of justice. Further down the list, Webb cited "the post office, telegraphs, carriage of small commodities, coinage, surveys, the regulation of the currency and note issue, the provision of weights and measures, the making, sweeping, lighting, and repairing of streets, roads, and bridges, life insurance, the grant of annuities, shipbuilding, stockbroking, banking, farming, and money-lending." A longer list enumerated the new jobs that governance and public accountability created. Another list enumerated the growth of public institutions, beginning with parks, museums, libraries, lighthouses, and streets.[90]

Socialism, Webb said, was very far from being the foolish dream that politicians and the capitalist class condemned. It was already happening in every act of collective action that served the public good: "Such is the irresistible sweep of social tendencies, that in their every act they worked to bring about the very Socialism they despised; and to destroy the Individualist faith which they still professed. They builded better than they knew."[91]

This was the defining argument of Fabian Collectivism. Progress was happening constantly, and it happened best with a minimum of class war and killing. The Fabians were happy warriors committed to helping progress advance and to running things intelligently. The working class had a role to play in creating socialism, but intellectuals would decide how things should go. Webb and the Fabians advocated shifting the tax burden completely from workers to the recipients of rent and interest, with the goal of eliminating the renter and capitalist class. They called for a minimum wage and a maximum working day, a high-quality education for all children, generous welfare provisions for those unable to work, the elimination of private capitalists and middlemen, and full representation of all citizens in Parliament. Webb was not averse to an occasional exhortation: "We must abandon the self-conceit of imagining that we are independent units, and bend our jealous minds, absorbed in their own cultivation, to this subjection to the higher end, the Common Weal."[92] He welcomed Christian allies, lauding Maurice and Kingsley for founding Christian socialism and paving the way to new Christian socialist organizations. Webb cited the GSM and provided the name and address of Headlam's paper, the *Church Reformer*. He noted that ordinary Anglo-Catholics—not just the Headlam and Hancock intellectuals—were becoming socialists, a stunning confirmation of the Fabian argument. Even bishops were becoming socialists, Webb boasted, although most of them merely trembled that socialism was, in fact, happening.

"THE BANNER OF CHRIST IN THE HANDS OF THE SOCIALISTS"

Headlam was the Fabian Society's leading religious voice. Most of the Fabians were lapsed Evangelicals for whom socialism had replaced religion as a vehicle of redemption. They took pride in refusing to be distracted by old theological dogmas or new Marxist dogmas. Shaw explained that the Fabian Society had no party line on "peace or war, the Marriage Question, Religion, Art, abstract economics, Historic Evolution, Currency, or any other subject than its own special business of practical Democracy and Socialism." That relieved Headlam of defending his distinct theology in this group, or religion in general. He served on the Fabian Society's executive board and provided speaking venues for Shaw through the GSM. Headlam was simultaneously one of the most radical and conservative Fabians, embattled in the society on both counts. He was a fierce defender of the rights of the people, contending that landlords and capitalists should receive no compensation for anything the state nationalized. His rhetoric was hotter than that of most Fabians, and Webb counted on Headlam to uphold the organization's left flank. Headlam had a stump lecture, "The Sins That Cause Poverty," that pressed to the edge of what a Fabian or Anglican cleric could say because some audiences heard it as an incitement to class war. He lost a budding chapter of the GSM in Newcastle after getting that reaction. Many complained that Headlam was happy only when he battled for lost causes with angry rhetoric. To some, Headlam confirmed this impression by changing the motto of the *Church Reformer*. The original motto was clunky and clerical: "Readapting the ecclesiastical machinery to the wants of the age." The new one was sublimely searing, William Blake's poetic pledge:

I will not cease from Mental Fight,
Nor shall my Sword sleep in my hand,
Till we have built Jerusalem
In England's green and pleasant land.[93]

On the other hand, conservatism ran deeply in Headlam too. He was an Anglican priest who gloried in ritual practice and spoke to all manner of audiences with sermonic flourishes about God, morality, and the sacraments. His Fabian colleagues kept him out of their inner circle on this count; plus, Headlam stuck with the Single Tax long after most Fabians and Christian socialists left it behind as a half measure. Headlam reasoned that he upheld the radical mainstream of both Fabian wings. He boasted that GSM, under his leadership, moved far beyond the mild cooperative reformism of Maurice and Owen: "While showing all respect for cooperative shirtmakers and cooperative decorators, and for the many little communistic societies of monks and nuns, and for all other little private experiments, we at the same time call upon churchmen to take a wider view, and advocate and support such legislation as will help to remedy private evils."[94]

In the 1880s Headlam committed the GSM to political activism on three issues: public secular education, church reform, and the Single Tax. All conveyed some ironic aspect of his complex personality. Despite being High Church, Headlam roared for public secular education and was scathing about the corruption and privileges of the Church of England. He had to override Hancock's vigorous opposition to disestablishment, while downplaying that Hancock had Maurice on his side. For a moment, in 1885, Headlam hoped for ecclesiastical rehabilitation, as Jackson died and Exeter bishop Frederick Temple was called to London. Temple was a Broad Church sophisticate and a long-ago contributor to *Essays and Reviews*, but he blanched at music hall ballets, and he was an old school Liberal about political economy. Ballerinas were practically naked, he told Headlam; how could that not be an occasion of sin? Headlam published an account of their meeting that evoked ridicule for the new bishop of London, ending Headlam's hope of rehabilitation. Moreover, Headlam's insistence on sticking with the Single Tax puzzled many of his friends and allies. He countered that being radical should not preclude aiming for something achievable. In fact, going for achievable things was essential to being a good socialist, and socializing land was the core socialist necessity. Headlam supported the collective ownership of industry, but he never emphasized this aspect of the socialist platform because the Single Tax cut to something deeper for him—a vision of spiritual transformation.[95]

Headlam never lost the feeling of deliverance he got from *Progress and Poverty* and George's electrifying lecture tours. To George, as to Headlam, the Single Tax was spiritually liberating, not merely a regulative political scheme. George proclaimed that if rent were abolished, the sterile waste of centuries of parasitic landlords would be wiped away, and the barren places "would ere long be dappled with the shade of trees and musical with the song of birds." New creative powers of the human spirit would be unleashed: "Talents, now hidden, virtues unsuspected, would come forth and make human life richer, fuller, happier, nobler." George was an apostle of the Kingdom of Heaven, not merely an economist. He said so, passionately: "It is the culmination of Christianity—the city of God on earth, with its walls of jasper and its gates of pearl! It is the reign of the Prince of Peace!" Headlam retained that feeling about the Single Tax long after George was panned for leaving capitalism intact. George's breakthrough cut to something deeper than collective ownership. Thus to Headlam, George was the best of all socialists, despite disavowing the socialist name. Landlords were parasites who ruined everything. Headlam told his audiences that possession of the land preceded the problem of capital. If one owned a cow, one got the milk. If one owned the land, one got the capital. All unearned wealth and privilege flowed from landlordism. It followed that bypassing the land issue and fixating on the collective ownership of industry did not advance the socialist movement, no matter how many socialists disagreed.[96]

Headlam got a showcase venue for these arguments in 1892: Fabian Tract Number 42. His two-word title claimed to speak for a movement: *Christian Socialism*. He had learned the principles of Christian socialism, he said, from Maurice and Kingsley, long before there was a Fabian Society. Maurice had to correct people who thought Christianity was otherworldly and wrongly paired with socialism, and so did Headlam. Headlam believed, like Maurice, that nothing in life is secular because the Kingdom of Heaven sanctifies all life. Jesus said almost nothing about life after death, but he talked constantly about the Kingdom of Heaven, which Headlam described as "the righteous society to be established on earth." Though Headlam offended conservative Anglicans by addressing atheist organizations, he used the word "secular" only in table-turning mode, describing the miracles of Jesus as "secular, socialistic works: works for health against disease, works restoring beauty and harmony and pleasure where there had been ugliness and discord and misery; works taking care to see that the people were properly fed; works subduing nature to the human good, works shewing that mirth and joy have a true place in our life here, works also shewing that premature death has no right here." Clerics spoke comforting phrases about dying children going to a better place, but Jesus never talked that way. To Jesus, the death of a child was "a monstrous, a disorderly thing; not part of God's order for the world, but the result of wrong-doing somewhere or other." That got to the core of Christian socialism, Headlam said: "If you want a rough description of the object of Christian Socialism I should be bold to say that it was to get rid of premature death altogether." The gospel itself is about abolishing the conditions that kill children via poverty, disease, violence, and neglect.[97]

Headlam ran through the parables of the lily and the valley, the rich man in hell, and the sheep and the goats. He stressed that according to Jesus atheists who poured themselves out for the poor and afflicted went to heaven, while pious types who ignored the poor and afflicted went to hell. Headlam admonished that it took a lot of straining, spiritualizing, and special pleading not to see what mattered to Jesus: "So far as Christ's works and teachings are concerned, not only is there no contradiction between the adjective 'Christian' and the noun, 'Socialism,' but that, if you want to be a good Christian, you must be something very much like a good Socialist." He took a second run at the definitional issue: "If, again, you want a rough description of the object of Christian Socialism, I should say that it was to bring about the time when all shall work, and when, all working, work will be a joy instead of the 'grind' it is at present, and to bring about the time when the robbers shall be utterly abolished."[98]

Jesus, Headlam said, did not merely declaim against greed and unnatural suffering: "He deliberately founded a society to keep on doing, throughout the world on a large scale, what He began to do by way of example, in miniature, in Palestine." This was the primary business of the Christian Church, "doing on a large scale throughout the world those secular, socialistic works which Christ did on a small scale in Palestine." To be sure, the church had doctrines to teach and needed to care about "beautiful ritual and worship," but these were secondary matters if the church followed Jesus. Headlam stressed that sacraments teach and practice human equality, the Jesus ethic of loving enemies and all others as oneself. The very name Holy Communion "tells you that those who partake of it are bound to live in brotherhood, in fellowship, with one another." Headlam did not lack feeling for the church's sweet hymnody about being in communion with those whose work was done: "But it is even more important to have communion equally mystic and sweet with those whose work is going on. And that is what this great sacrament teaches us to have."[99]

Obviously, the Church of England was not known for teaching this understanding of its mission, let alone fighting for Social Democracy. Headlam told his Fabian audience that one cause of this tragedy trumped the others: "That you and your forefathers have allowed the Church to be gagged and fettered; instead of allowing the Church to elect her own bishops and clergy, you have forced them on her from outside." Instead of allowing the members of a parish to elect parish priests, the state church imposed upon parishes the whims of a landlord or a bishop or a college at Oxford or Cambridge or a builder with villas to rent or a peer "or a jockey at Newmarket." Establishment corrupted the church to the point of nullifying the gospel of Christ in it. Anglicans who cared about the gospel and Britons who cared about justice needed to disestablish the Church of England as the church of the state: "You cannot expect the Church to live up to the law of her being until you have disestablished and disendowed those whom you now allow to lord it over the Church, and left her free to manage her own affairs. A complete Christian Socialism cannot be brought about until the Church is free to use influence and discipline for the establishing of the Kingdom of Heaven upon earth."[100]

In the meantime some church leaders remembered that the state is a sacred organization no less than the church. A growing number of them united with the socialists "to seize the State and to use it for the well-being of the masses instead of the classes." Whenever he got rolling on this theme, Headlam downplayed that many Christian socialists did not agree with him about disestablishment. The *Church Reformer* got a lot of angry mail from Christian socialists saying Headlam should speak for himself and stop misrepresenting the movement on this issue. Headlam went on offending them. To him, using the state to create socialism and freeing the church from the state were both axiomatic. He had no concept of socialism without a state, he wanted the church to be free from the state, and he dismissed the many Christian socialists who said these two positions did not go together.[101]

He also dared to be boring. Public education was a boring issue compared to socializing the means of production, and the Single Tax was a mere reform. Headlam told Fabians not to denigrate such things. Education is a right, it allows the masses to get a better life, it helps them acquire discipline and the skills of interdependence, and it makes them discontented. Investing in universal education is the best way to lift the masses from apathy and ignorance: "We school them to a large degree with this in view, that they may know what is the evil they have to attack and how to attack it. We *do* want to educate them above their station." Headlam insisted that pressing for universal education and the Single Tax was not tinkering. He was a Christian socialist because he was not content with tinkering. To socialists who objected that a land tax would not benefit workers because workers did not pay land taxes, he replied that tax relief was not the important thing. The point was to get the primary means of production—the land—into the hands of the people, which would break the iron law of wages that impoverished workers. The Single Tax was the greatest of all reform measures. It was demanded by justice and consistent with morality. In fact, "morality is impossible without it." The land of every nation belongs by natural and inalienable right to the entire body of its people. Therefore, the people had no moral obligation to compensate landlords for what they wrongly claimed to own. The moral imperative was the other way around.[102]

Headlam said it another way since "Thou shall not steal" was endlessly cited against Christian socialists. In England, he observed, the rich robbed the poor every day, denigrated the poor, and passed laws justifying all of it: " 'Thou shall not steal' is just the commandment we want to get kept; we want to put a stop to the robbery of the poor by the rich, which has been going on for so long." For that matter, he even agreed that duty is a more sacred thing than rights—the other thing antisocialists were always saying. Did these people never consider what the Bible says about the duty that human beings owe to God and each other? "The earth is the Lord's, and therefore not the landlord's; the earth is the Lord's, and He hath given it unto the children of men." Headlam conceded nothing to those who prated about spirituality versus material concerns: "When once a man realizes the evils of our present social state, just because he is eager for the spiritual life of the people, he will be doing all he possibly can to put a stop to that robbery which is the main cause of poverty, and so by degrees to establish the Kingdom of Heaven upon earth."[103]

It was a good showing in a showcase forum, although not as representative as Headlam claimed. His own organization had many clerics and laity who opposed disestablishment, and by 1892 the Christian Social Union, Labour Church, and Christian Socialist Society outnumbered Headlam's group, while spurning the Single Tax. Headlam was ambivalent about celebrating their existence and their kinship to him. His capacious liberalism toward atheists and non-Christians did not extend to Nonconformist Christians. Headlam said it was better to be an atheist than a Calvinist because Calvinists maligned God with cruel doctrines. He had minimal sympathy for Christian socialist societies that admitted non-Anglicans because his Anglican chauvinism didn't allow him to like them. The *Church Reformer*, especially Hancock, routinely blasted Roman Catholicism and Evangelical Protestantism as distorted Christianities that should not exist.

For similar reasons, plus class snobbery, Headlam's paper opposed the idea of an independent labor party. In 1887 British Socialists debated whether to organize a labor party with a definite class program. Keir Hardie founded the Scottish Labour Party in 1888 and the Independent Labour Party (ILP) in 1893, the latter consisting of representatives from ninety-one ILP locals, eleven local Fabian Societies, four SDF branches, and miscellaneous others. The Fabian

Society in London raucously debated whether it should support the ILP. Many said that Fabianism was about permeating the Liberal Party with socialism, not putting workers into Parliament. Webb, Shaw, Headlam, and Pease opposed the new party on that basis. Fabians Hubert Bland and S. G. Hobson said it would be ridiculous for a socialist organization to oppose the ILP. How could Fabian leaders even imagine doing so? Webb and Shaw backtracked diplomatically, not really agreeing but trying to avoid bad appearances. Headlam did not backtrack, believing Hardie's group was too small, provincial, inchoate, and uneducated to be taken seriously. How did earning wages qualify anyone to deal with complex issues in Parliament? Headlam, though less elitist than most Fabians, believed that somebody had to stand up for what most Fabians said in private. He worried that a workers' party would scuttle the anti-imperialism of the Liberal Party, leaving England without a bulwark against Tory imperialism. Officially, the Fabian Society summoned workers to leave the Liberal Party, crying, "To Your Tents, O Israel!" It pretended to support the political aspirations of workers, not seeing how it could say otherwise. Headlam replied with disgust: "To advocate the introduction of workingmen, as such, into Parliament, as the Fabians now seem to be doing, is utterly absurd."[104]

Webb, Shaw, and Headlam preferred to run the social revolution from London, looking down on crude workers from the provinces that fudged on socialism. The Fabians were true Social Democrats dedicated to a classless society, but they blanched at accepting workers as comrades. Headlam grieved as they abandoned the Liberal Party, an anti-imperial bulwark. He was a socialist *and* a liberal, he said; the best strategy was to expand the socialist wing of Whig politics. To him, the Fabian Society was a liberal socialist alternative to SDF Marxism. If the Fabians could not fuse with Hyndman's group, how could they work with the overwhelmingly northern and provincial ILP? That question answered itself, to Headlam, as the ILP grew in the North. By 1895 the ILP had three hundred branches. One hundred were in Yorkshire, seventy in Lancashire and Cheshire, forty in Scotland, eighteen in the Northeast, and twenty-three in the Midlands. London had twenty-nine branches—an impressive achievement but not the main story. Hardie told reform pilgrims to visit the northern provinces if they wanted to see socialism getting somewhere because London sucked the life and hope out of people. The Fabians learned to be diplomatic about it, but not Headlam, who said the ILP represented crass, selfish, insular opportunism and nothing more. He loathed the idea of party discipline in voting, which seemed, to him, more antiliberal than prolabor. In 1895 he wrote scathingly, "To form a little party (and to give it a big name) pledged only to vote straightaway for the realization of your ideal, and to keep out all others who would help towards realizing it, is political suicide, immoral as all suicide is."[105]

That attitude, plus Headlam's ecclesiastical dogmatism, plus his fixation with divisive causes, caused his group to fall behind the gusher of Christian socialisms he helped to set off. In 1895 the GSM had almost four hundred members, of whom one-third were Anglican clergy. It made an impact far beyond its numerical base, as Headlam was good at publicity. His personal reach exceeded the GSM, and he trained some of the founding guild socialists. But Headlam and Hancock never shook their self-defeating belief that being devoted to Anglicanism made them more liberal, open, virtuous, and Christian than others. It was hard for Headlam to admit that liberal snobbery was illiberal or that he had a bad case of it.[106]

The GSM had many strong personalities, yet Headlam dominated it throughout its thirty-two-year run. He was an outstanding speaker and writer, yet no match for Hancock, who suffered the same shunned fate as Headlam as a cleric despite Hancock's devotion to the church. Hancock never attended college, having spurned his businessman father's attempts to force him into commerce. He apprenticed to a woodcarver and subsequently a sculptor, fell in with the poetic Rossetti siblings, Dante and Christina, in London, and found his way to Workingmen's College, where he found his role model, Maurice. Hancock idolized Maurice in the usual Mauricite fashion. He studied voraciously at the British Museum, won an essay prize, was ordained in 1863, and served several curacies in England and a chaplaincy in Germany. For ten years he barely survived in subsistence curacies. Finally in 1884 his friend Shuttleworth became rector of St. Nicholas Cole Abbey in London's business section and appointed Hancock as a lecturer—the only salaried job Hancock ever held. He later recalled of Shuttleworth, "He had given my youth back again to me and reopened the doors of the House of the Lord to one of His ejected priests."[107]

Hancock delivered lectures to tiny audiences at Cole Abbey that he fashioned into sparkling articles in the *Church Reformer*. There were over seventy in the *Church Reformer*, plus reviews in *Church Quarterly*. The state church was too corrupted by privilege and insularity to give him a job, but Hancock did not put it that way. He preached the pure Maurice gospel of aspiration for the church—it needed to become as catholic as the gospel itself, realizing and reflecting the divine order. All non-Anglican denominations and sects settled for a mutilated church not reflecting God's capacious moral order. The Church of England, in his telling, whatever its faults, was already more liberal, radical, and socialist than any denomination or sect had any chance of becoming.

Hancock said it fervently in issue after issue. The incarnation of Christ hallows all human life. All life must be treasured. The incarnation is the central teaching of Christianity, as Anglicanism teaches. Socialism is the best way to fulfill the Christian ideals of human dignity and equality. Therefore, Hancock taught, Anglican socialism combined the best church and politics. Calvinism was a horrible theology, the Methodist emphasis on saving souls for heaven made Methodism only slightly less illiberal than Calvinism, and the capitalist press was hopelessly capitalist—venal, predatory, and degrading. Hancock implored clerics to preach socialism unabashedly from the pulpit. Until more of them did so, those who did would be frozen out of pulpits, and England would continue to rot. Hancock had a dire warning on this theme. If the English people refused to be gathered together by the Son of Man, uniting the rich and poor as one family of equal brothers and sisters in Christ, an apocalyptic fate awaited them: "Unless England repents and rises out of her moral and social death, the Son of Man must appear and let loose 'the vultures' by whose dreadful ministry He will destroy the carcass of a corrupt and putrid civilization."[108]

This message spread Hancock's name and made him unemployable. He had a perch only because Shuttleworth was a socialist with a buoyant, backslapping, win-them-over personality. Only Shuttleworth had the standing and charisma to get away with challenging Headlam in the GSM. He was born in Cornwall, where his father was a cleric; later he studied only as much as necessary at Oxford. Shuttleworth was the model for Shaw's charming, popular, artistic, slightly vain and overconfident cleric, James Mavor Morell, in *Candida*, although Shaw added some of Headlam's intellectualism. Morell, according to Shaw, had the rare gift of being able to say "what he likes to whom he likes, to lecture people without setting himself up against them, to impose this authority on them without humiliating them, and, on occasion, to interfere in their business without impertinence." Shuttleworth was ecumenical, supporting the Christian Socialist Society. In 1894 he helped Baptist Fabian John Clifford found the Christian Socialist League; the following year he published a friendly, inclusive, optimistic book, *The English Church and the New Democracy*. Shuttleworth had atheist friends, notably Annie Besant, who later became a Theosophist, and Shaw respected him greatly for putting himself out for atheists and anarchists. Christian Social Union founder Henry Scott Holland, puckishly accenting that Headlam and Shuttleworth were tag team allies and intra-GSM rivals, called them "Headlong and Shuttlecock."[109]

The Queen's Jubilee, set for Thanksgiving 1887, set off testy exchanges in every Christian socialist organization. The *Christian Socialist* railed against

imperialism and queen-veneration, provoking a prominent Anglican contributor, E. D. Girdlestone, to object that despising the queen should not be compulsory for Christian socialists. To Girdlestone, the *Christian Socialist* waxed too
hot on this issue; he added that lockstep support for Irish Nationalists should
not be compulsory either. Then he added that Anglicans prayed for the queen
every Sunday, remember? Campbell replied that he strained to find anything
in British imperialism or the queen's character to commend. Headlam and
Shuttleworth, for a while, tried to finesse the queen issue. Both said jubilee
sentimentality was okay as long as it celebrated the monarchy and the people,
not just the monarchy. But Headlam was too republican to keep saying it, he
chafed at being outflanked by the *Christian Socialist*, and his rhetoric grew
angry. He blistered the monarchy as the quintessential symbol of England's worship of wealth, privilege, power, and itself. Reverencing the monarchy, he said,
kept the English from following Christ. Why should one lady have four palaces
when millions suffered in tenements? How dare the Church of England blas-
pheme about doing God's will?[110]

Meanwhile the SDF renewed an old Chartist tactic, interrupting church
services to demand sermons about poverty and justice. There were marches
featuring unemployed workers and strident banners. Then the SDF targeted
the great bastions of London Anglicanism—Westminster Abbey and Saint
Paul's Cathedral. A spectacular parade to Saint Paul's occurred on February 27,
1887. Protesters crowded into the cathedral and got a stern rebuke from the
canon in residence. Headlam and Hancock shook their heads. The protesters
were inviting the church to speak to them, and the church refused. The following Sunday Hancock pleaded with Anglicans to open their eyes. He sermonized
on the banners, delivering the mother lode sermon of Christian socialism, "The
Banner of Christ in the Hands of the Socialists":

> You see that they carry banners with mottoes upon them. Who is *the author*
> of those texts which express the social faith of this huge multitude? From
> what teachers have they borrowed the dogmas which they call upon all the
> city to read and respect, to observe and to obey? On whose authority are
> these innumerable crowds of the poor and rough doing this unwonted thing?
> They, or a great many of them, call themselves "Socialists." Let us read what
> is on their banners; let us discover *who* is the ultimate dogmatist of this
> multitudinous sect. . . .
>
> Oh, come all ye faithful! Look again and again at these inscriptions.
> Recognize while you have time, what they are: see, clergy and laity, out of
> whose mouth the cries of "the mob" have come. They are the words of
> *your* Master. They are the laws of the Eternal Father. They are the lessons

which he taught us by His son. They are the new commandments which you and I were pledged at our baptism to keep. "Feed *My* lambs." "*My* house is a house of prayer, but ye (capitalists and landlords) have made it a den of thieves!" "*I* was an hungered, and ye gave *Me* no meat, naked and ye clothed *Me* not." It is a small matter to what sect or party this great "multitude" fancies it belongs, or by what denomination it pleases to call itself. You can see to *whom* they have felt obliged to go in order to find the fullest expression of their faith. . . .

The undogmatic "socialism" of the desolate and oppressed, when it speaks freely out of its own heart and conscience, falls back upon the words with which the crucified and ascended Head of Humanity has provided His brothers and sisters. It reminds Christians that they are living in rebellion against Christ. It does not articulately name itself "Christian Socialism." No: but it declares inarticulately that the thing which economists, politicians, scholars—in hatred or in love—call "Socialism" is itself "Christian."[111]

This sermonic effusion had perfect pitch for its moment and movement audience. It was immortalized by citation for doing so. Shaw later recalled, "Religion was alive again, coming back upon men, even clergymen, with such power that not the Church of England itself could keep it out." The SDF, before marching on Saint Paul's, had asked if Archbishop of Canterbury Edward Benson or Bishop Temple might offer a service for the protesters. The canon and cathedral staff dismissed this request without bothering to float it upward. But the church hierarchy was not completely clueless about the social crisis. In October 1887 the Church Congress, meeting in Wolverhampton, put socialism on its agenda for the first time. SDF stalwart and *Christian Socialist* contributor H. H. Champion declared that socialism was gaining because it had a record of caring about oppressed workers. Had the Church practiced the Christian gospel, secular socialism would not have been necessary. Champion said socialists did not espouse violent revolution or abolishing the family, and there was still time for Christians and Socialists to work together. Many clerical leaders nodded approvingly while others fulminated at being compelled to listen to a Marxist, albeit a Christian Marxist from the aristocracy. Shuttleworth followed by urging the delegates to think about the sweated laborers who stitched their nice clothes. Headlam followed with a scathing speech expounding Ruskin's threefold division of humanity into beggars, robbers, and workers. The church taught that no one should live off the labor of others, but it blessed nobles who stole their wealth through rent. If the rich wanted to help the poor, Headlam said, they should start by earning their daily bread instead of stealing it.[112]

Headlam's speech set off an uproar against him, which he shrugged off, noting that at least church leaders now had to listen. The fading of the depression in 1888 stoked the socialist movement, as unskilled laborers waged strikes across the nation. Clerics who had hesitated to support union protests organized by Marxists did not hesitate when unskilled members of their congregations demanded decent wages. Benson, addressing the Diocese of Canterbury in 1889, provided quotable confirmation that Christian socialism had become respectable: "There is much in 'socialism,' as we now understand it, which honestly searches for some beneficial remedy—much of which is purely religious and Christian." Benson added that all clergy needed to learn about socialism and employ what they learned, advocating "the wisest social measures." That gave a green light to clerics, dons, and divinity students who wanted to join something without ruining their careers. Anglican socialism needed a better vehicle. Henry Scott Holland and Charles Gore founded the Christian Social Union to provide one.[113]

CHRISTIAN SOCIAL UNIONISM

The origins of the Christian Social Union (CSU) went back to Gore's and Holland's salad days at Oxford in the mid-1870s, which led to their landmark book of 1889, *Lux Mundi*. They had cut their teeth theologically on the hostile reaction to *Essays and Reviews*. By 1889 they were ready to try again, in print. It helped that Hegelian idealism was taking over British philosophy. More important was that late-Victorian intellectuals were publishing rueful poems and memoirs about losing their faith. Still more important was that English Anglicanism was overdue to legitimize biblical criticism and Darwinian evolution. More important yet was that the crisis of capitalist civilization had become unavoidable. Most important was that young Oxford theologians had conflicted feelings about their party, Anglo-Catholicism. The Broad Church party was too battered and defeated to spark a liberal renewal, and it lacked thinkers who burned for social justice. The spark had to come from an unlikely place, the Anglo-Catholic party.

E. B. Pusey's last protégés at Oxford exemplified the truism that generational experience cannot be replicated. In 1875 Gore was a new fellow at Trinity College and in need of supportive colleagues. Descended from long lines of Irish and English nobility, notably the second Earl of Arran, Gore was accustomed to leading and being followed. He started with three fellow Oxford dons, Holland (Christ Church), J. R. Illingworth (Jesus College), and Edward S. Talbot (Keble College). Later they added seven others—Francis Paget, Aubrey

Moore, R. L. Ottley, W. Lock, Arthur Lyttleton, R. C. Moberly, and W. J. H. Campion. All were Tractarians who worried that English Anglicanism was being suffocated by Tractarian rigidity and Evangelical anti-intellectualism. The group studied, socialized, and worshipped together, and Holland dubbed them "the Holy Party." By 1886 they had dispersed through career moves. Three years later they published a bombshell book: *Lux Mundi: A Series of Studies in the Religion of the Incarnation*.[114]

Lux Mundi had a tinge of nostalgia for college memories and a strong dose of modernizing admonition. The crisis of belief, to the authors, was undeniable; all had friends who had dropped Christianity. Gore's group judged that their teachers fixated on reactionary fantasies. Anglo-Catholicism had the right idea, but doctrinally it was rigid, ecclesiastically it was coercive, and politically it was reflexively right wing. It was nice that some Anglo-Catholic clerics ministered to the urban poor, but that would never break the identity of Tractarianism with religious and political reaction. If the church as a whole was to restore its credibility in a modernizing world, it had to stand for the right of free inquiry. John Henry Newman, grappling in the 1840s with the problem of historical consciousness, solved it by taking shelter in Roman Catholicism. Afterward, Tractarian leaders Pusey and Henry P. Liddon slammed the door on historical consciousness, clinging to an Anglo-Catholic orthodoxy that conceded nothing to biblical criticism. Gore and his friends struggled with this legacy during their years at Oxford. *Lux Mundi* was the fruit of their struggle.[115]

Gore was the first principal of Pusey House, a memorial to the Tractarian leader. He owed his appointment to Liddon, who viewed Gore as a likely successor. Talbot was the first warden of Keble College, named after Tractarian leader John Keble; Moberly was the son of a Tractarian bishop; Holland was a colleague of Liddon's at St. Paul's Cathedral, London. Holland and Headlam had been classmates at Eton before parting, respectively, to Oxford and Cambridge, and Holland renewed his friendship with Headlam after he became canon at St. Paul's in 1884. Holland regularly attended GSM meetings but never joined, nor did Gore, to Headlam's disappointment. Liddon judged, correctly, that Gore had the autocratic temperament to be a Tractarian leader; Gore spent much of his subsequent career as a bishop condemning the rise of a liberal modernist party. But in 1889 Gore opened the door to a liberal upsurge, declaring in the preface to *Lux Mundi*, "The epoch in which we live is one of profound transformation, intellectual and social, abounding in new needs, new points of view, new questions."[116]

The next generation of Anglican leaders, Gore said, had to be persuasive and relevant without falling back on coercion. He was against innovation in theology, which abandoned the church's founding truths. But theology needed to "take a new development" beyond intensifying an existing tendency. Gore offered a banner statement that shocked and sickened Tractarian leaders; soon it was famous in England. Instead of subordinating modern intellectual and moral problems to an assumed orthodoxy, the church was overdue to "put the Catholic faith in its right relation to modern intellectual and moral problems."[117]

In other words, the church had to stop treating modern thought as an enemy of Christian faith. Darwinian evolution and biblical criticism had to be accommodated, and British theology had much to gain from idealistic philosophy. All the *Lux Mundi* authors were influenced by the rising prestige of idealism in British philosophy, which traced to one person, Oxford neo-Hegelian T. H. Green. Green had studied under classicist Benjamin Jowett at Balliol College in the late 1850s, was elected a fellow of Queens College in 1860, and taught at Oxford until 1882, when he died of blood poisoning at the age of forty-five. Deeply involved in Liberal politics, he had a huge impact on English philosophy, swinging the field toward a spiritual interpretation of the world. Against David Hume's skeptical empiricism and John Stuart Mill's utilitarianism, Green argued that the existence of art, morality, religion, and science showed that reality does not reduce to the things of sense. Empirical psychologies wrongly reduced self-consciousness to a series of events, failing to explain its unity. Green taught his students to look for God in the self-generating spiritual consciousness of human beings, not in some ostensible beginning or end of nature. God, to exist as anything except an unrealized potential, must be actualized in the world.[118]

That was too pantheistic for Gore, who stuck with biblical and Nicene supernaturalism; Gore spurned Green's low Christology too. But Gore absorbed the ethical aspect of Green's idealism, and most of the *Lux Mundi* authors prized Green's spiritualizing impact on British philosophy. Holland and Illingworth were deeply influenced by Green, appreciating that neo-Hegelian philosophy refashioned the Logos theology of the Greek Fathers: the Incarnation is the incarnation of Universal Reason in humanity as a whole. This conviction put Holland and Illingworth in conversation with the metaphysical idealists who took over British philosophy in the 1880s and 1890s: Edward Caird, John Caird, Bernard Bosanquet, F. H. Bradley, R. B. Haldane, James Ward, Andrew Seth Pringle-Pattison, and Hastings Rashdall. Holland, for the rest of his career, lauded Green for rescuing Oxford students and British philosophy "from the sway of individualistic sensationalism."[119]

Lux Mundi, unlike *Essays and Reviews*, was a real book, carefully fashioned into a coherent statement about the Incarnation, evolutionary theory, and biblical criticism. It said that to take the Logos doctrine seriously is to see the Word at work in nature, humanity, art, science, culture, and everything else. Illingworth, rector of Longworth Church and sometime Fellow of Jesus College, exemplified the idealistic turn in British theology. *Lux Mundi* was Illingworth's breakout work as a theologian; afterward he wrote influential books on the sacredness of personality human and divine, blending Anglo-Catholic Platonism and post-Kantian idealism until his death in 1915. In *Lux Mundi's* signature chapter on evolution and the Incarnation, Illingworth said evolutionary theory helped the church recover its magnificent, neglected, cosmic vision of the reconsecration of the universe to God: "Evolution is in the air. It is the category of the age. . . . We cannot place ourselves outside it, or limit the scope of its operation."[120]

According to Illingworth, the Reformation fixed on justification, which reduced atonement to a selfish concern and widened the gap between things sacred and profane. It was "far otherwise," he argued, with the Church Fathers and Scholastics. The Greek Fathers, Augustine, Aquinas, and Bonaventure were "substantially unanimous" in upholding the Pauline and Johannine concept of Christ as the eternally preexistent reason and Word of God. To them, creation embodied divine ideas and thus revealed the divine character. Every creature is a theophany, a divine word telling something of God. The whole world is a kind of gospel of the Word by which the world was created. On Thomism versus Scotism, Illingworth was a Scotist, conceiving the Incarnation as the climax of creation, not contingent on the existence of sin, but he said that Thomas never lost the grand cosmic vision that the Church Fathers built out of Platonism and the Bible. The Protestant Reformers, on the other hand, did lose it: "In the countries most influenced by the Reformation it has dropped too much out of sight."[121]

Illingworth enthused that Darwinian evolution helped the church remember its true subject, the meaning and redemption of everything. Resisting Darwinian theory, some theologians held out for the essential difference between organized and inorganic matter; others drew a sharp line between human rationality and animal instinct. Illingworth cautioned against bottom-line dualisms. Science had already broken down seemingly impassable barriers between different kinds of things; moreover, science was sure to break down more of them. It was not good strategy to invest doctrinal significance in a scientific gap. God works behind and within every phase of matter. What matters is to be open to learning however God does it.[122]

Illingworth brushed off the Ritschlian School claim that the early church grafted too much Neoplatonism onto Christianity. This critique held "no force whatever" if the divine Logos works universally in the world in cooperation with human reason. Christianity was not contaminated by its contact with a declining Platonism. Rather, the decay of Greek philosophy allowed it to be incorporated into a larger, spiritually vital life. The true successors of Plato and Aristotle were the Church Fathers and Scholastics, not Celsus, Lucian, and Porphyry. Illingworth wanted modern theologians to approach other religions in the same way that Justin Martyr and other Fathers approached Greek wisdom, looking for signs of Eternal Reason while contending that only Christianity is truly universal: "The Incarnation opened heaven, for it was the revelation of the Word; but it also re-consecrated earth, for the Word was made flesh and dwelt among us."[123]

This was Anglo-Catholic music in a decidedly modernist mode. Critics and admirers of *Lux Mundi* devoted more attention to Illingworth than to any contributor except, predictably, Gore, an outsized personality who assigned himself the most explosive topic, biblical inspiration. Gore expressed great force of conviction and certainty in everything he did. A powerful thinker, always pressing to persuade, he brushed aside rival views before, during, and after his career as a bishop. His overflowing self-confidence flowed from being born to wealth and the Whig aristocracy in 1853, growing up in a Victorian mansion in Wimbledon, and winning highest academic honors at Harrow and Oxford. At the age of eight or nine Gore turned against his parents' Low Church religion, deciding he belonged in the High Church party. As an adolescent he attended Anglo-Catholic churches in London and identified with the Tractarian Movement, while retaining his parents' liberal Whig politics. At Harrow, Gore was influenced by B. F. Westcott, who taught him to prize rigorous scholarship and care about the needs of the poor. At Oxford he moved straight from Balliol scholarship student to Trinity Fellow, creating the "Holy Party" with his customary blend of conviction and industry.[124]

"I am profoundly convinced" was a favorite Gore phrase. At the age of twenty-five, in his first publication, Gore announced he was profoundly convinced that faith and reason go together, faith has a primarily moral basis, and faith is "natural and rational to a man" because it points to the divine ground of rationality and truth. Gore stuck to these core convictions for the rest of his life. In his late career, after years of bitter wrangling as a bishop, he wrote large books defending his theological position, offering a rare word of personal reflection: "I have, ever since I was an undergraduate, been certain that I must be in the true sense a free thinker, and that either not to think freely about a disturbing subject, or to accept ecclesiastical authority in place of the best judgment of my own reason, would be for me an impossible treason against the light. I must go remorselessly where the argument leads me."[125]

This freethinking aspect of Gore's personality came through in *Lux Mundi*, plus his remorseless tendency. Gore told British readers to stop pillorying German scholars for deconstructing the history of Hebrew scripture, because Julius Wellhausen's documentary hypothesis and Heinrich G. A. Ewald's seven-volume *Geschichte des Volkes Israel* were basically sound. It helped that Samuel R. Driver, Pusey's successor at Oxford, pioneered a British tradition of higher critical scholarship. Gore said the "Old Testament" abounded in "worldliness" and a "low standard of morals," evincing a low spiritual consciousness. Moreover, historical criticism showed that Chronicles is exaggerated compared to parallel accounts in Samuel and Kings. Priestly Code history is more idealizing than Deuteronomic history, and the doctrine of inspiration should not preclude recognizing the priestly tendency to idealize and exaggerate.[126]

On the other hand, Gore claimed, the New Testament has many fewer such problems: "It is of the essence of the New Testament, as the religion of the Incarnation, to be final and catholic: on the other hand, it is of the essence of the Old Testament to be imperfect, because it represents a gradual process of education by which man was lifted out of depths of sin and ignorance." Authority, he explained, is the process of education described by Plato in *The Republic*. Authority implants right instincts and antipathies in the growing mind of a child, enabling the child to grow into a "certain inner kinship" with the right reasons of things, making truth a friend. God's Spirit operated similarly in the Bible, gradually lifting believers from lower to higher ground.[127]

To reach the high ground of the New Testament, one first internalizes "a whole set of presuppositions about God, about the slavery of sin, about the reasonableness of redemption." Otherwise we could not understand the New Testament, something requiring the guiding hand of the church. Since the Bible does not tell us how to understand the Bible or what books belong in the Bible, we need the guiding hand of the church. Since we live in the fragmenting and corrosive age of modernity, we need the guiding hand more than ever. Gore said no mere Bible reader makes sense of Christ's divinity and humanity—such as, what Christians should believe about the self-emptying aspect of Christ's Incarnation.[128]

Philippians 2: 5–7 was his keystone Christological text: Christ "did not regard equality with God as something to be exploited, but emptied himself (*kenosis*), taking the form of a slave" (NRSV). The Incarnation, Gore said, was "a self-emptying of God to reveal Himself under conditions of human nature and from the human point of view." To construe how Christ could be divine and yet self-limited in some way, the Church needed to distinguish between what Christ revealed and what he used. Christ revealed God, God's mind and character, and within certain limits, God's threefold being. Christ also revealed "man's" sinfulness and spiritual capacities, God's purpose of redemption, and God's purpose in founding the Church. But Christ revealed these things under the conditions of a true human nature. Christ used human nature to feel and see as human beings ought to feel and see. These two things—revelation and use— are distinct; Christ revealed divine truth by using human nature. Thus his divinity is not at risk if Christ made statements about science, history, or the future that turned out to be inaccurate, for Christ restrained "the beams of Deity as to observe the limits of the science of His age, and He puts Himself in the same relation to its historical knowledge."[129]

As for biblical inspiration, Gore said it was an indispensable article of faith and the church never defined what it is. He was grateful for the latter fact. The Creeds said very particular things about the Virgin Birth, the two natures and resurrection of Christ, and the Trinity, so Christians were required to believe very particular things about these matters. But this was not true of biblical inspiration: "We cannot make any exact claim upon any one's belief in regard to inspiration, simply because we have no authoritative definition to bring to bear upon him."[130]

Only with the rise of modern critical knowledge did the Church sufficiently understand the development of the scriptural text to make sound judgments about the nature of its inspiration. Gore said historical criticism could be taken too far, as when German scholars favored novelty for its own sake, lacking a proper reverence for scripture. The right approach was to allow free inquiry within the walls of a faithful, confident Church that balanced criticism and reverence.[131]

Lux Mundi shocked, convulsed, and elated British Christians, running through ten printings in its first year and evoking strong reactions from every quarter. Opponents of biblical criticism, evolution, Hegel, modernity, and everything else the book accommodated condemned it ferociously. Evangelicals said *Lux Mundi* perpetuated the usual Anglo-Catholic slurs against the Reformation and betrayed the Anglo-Catholic reverence for scripture. Liberals said it was surprising but welcome that *Lux Mundi* took up issues raised by *Essays and Reviews* in 1860. High Church conservatives were mortified the book came from their party; Liddon was deeply distraught and enraged by it, especially Gore's contribution. According to Liddon, *Lux Mundi* was rationalistic and Pelagian, it demeaned the divine infallibility of the Bible, and, most grievously, Gore caused immense harm by claiming that Jesus held mistaken ideas. Reviewers debated Gore versus Liddon on the latter point long after *Lux Mundi* changed Anglican theology. Gore said the furor over the book surprised him because the authors settled on these positions in their school days. Holland, as usual, said the same thing more puckishly, claiming the authors expected only their aunts and mothers to read such a dull book.[132]

Headlam, never one to miss a good fight, stoutly defended *Lux Mundi* from its many conservative detractors, contending that scripture and Catholic tradition supported every statement in the book. Gore and his group got into trouble by defending intellectual freedom, but intellectual freedom is a bedrock principle of the Catholic faith. Authentic Catholic thought is a type of rational orthodoxy. Always inclined to accuse wrong-thinking people of being Protestants, Headlam claimed that most critics of the book were "Protestants daubed over with a little Catholic veneer." His only criticism was the book proceeded too gingerly. Gore's theologians stopped short of applying historical criticism to the New Testament, said nothing about the sanctity of politics and popular entertainment, and offered no call to action, unlike Maurice. Thus the authors missed a crucial opportunity. *Lux Mundi*, Headlam lamented, should have called for a social revolution in England. But that did not happen, a grievous loss for the Catholic theology of Incarnation.[133]

The meaning of *Lux Mundi* is indicated by what happened to its contributors. Moberly won a Regius chair at Oxford; Ottley succeeded Moberly in 1903; Paget became bishop of Oxford; Talbot became bishop, successively, of Rochester, Southwark, and Winchester. Holland became a major social reform leader while teaching for a total of thirty-two years at Christ Church, Oxford, interrupted near the middle by twenty-six years at St. Paul's Cathedral, London. Gore moved on to Westminster Abbey, served bishoprics at Worcester, Birmingham, and Oxford from 1902 to 1919, wrote prolifically on theological and social problems, and became the dominant church leader of his time, although he bruised too many feelings to make archbishop of Canterbury. Far from damaging their careers by producing a notorious book, the *Lux Mundi* authors swept to leadership positions in a modernizing church. Gore, tellingly, said the best name for his position and Anglicanism as a whole was "liberal Catholicism." Rightly understood, the Church of England blended Catholic substance and a liberal spirit.[134]

Lux Mundi was a sign of theological ferment in the heyday year of Christian socialism, 1889. It was the year when Britain's imperial trade pulled the nation out of a devastating trade depression, and when a Roman Catholic hierarch (Henry Cardinal Manning) mediated the Great London Dock Strike, while Anglican bishop Temple evoked embarrassment by dodging it. The success of the dock strike laid the foundation for a generation of union gains in England. The same year, Social Democrats from twenty nations founded the Second International, in Paris, determinately excluding Anarchists, and the Fabian

Society published *Fabian Essays in Socialism*. The same year, Holland and Gore founded the CSU. Holland later recalled that windows flung open from every side, barriers fell, "we were ready for a call, and it came." Holland's "we" were the donnish clerics who wrote *Lux Mundi* and founded the CSU. The Hegel vogue in British philosophy played a role, as did bits of Marxism, but Holland said these things "floated across to us, in dreams and visions, using our own Christian language, and involving the unity of the Social Body and the law of love, and the solidarity of Humanity." It no longer felt odd or embarrassing that Maurice and Kingsley called themselves Christian Socialists: "We woke up to Maurice. His influence, which had lain, as it were, alongside the Oxford Movement, now passed within it. . . . Christian doctrine showed itself as the very heart of a Social Gospel!"[135]

Holland had grown up as an aristocratic chum of Gore's at Wimbledon. His father had no discernible work besides hunting and travel, his parents met at a hunt ball, and Holland went to Eton and Balliol as a matter of course. Green and Arnold Toynbee were the chief influences on Holland at Oxford, in that order. Later Holland befriended B. F. Westcott, a prolific biblical scholar, Cambridge Regius Professor, and Broad Church theologian. In 1879 Holland cofounded a precursor of the CSU at Oxford called PESEK, a study group on politics, economics, socialism, and Christian ethics. Three bellwether books shaped the group's self-understanding and paved the way to the CSU. Foremost was *Progress and Poverty*. A second book, *The World as the Subject of Redemption* (1883), by Balliol Fellow W. H. Fremantle, made its signature claim in the title. A third book, *Christian Economics* (1888), by former Keble tutor Wilfrid Richmond, said political economy is rightly a branch of moral philosophy, not a self-standing science. Competition and cooperation, Richmond argued, are both important to economic life, contrary to economists who made no room for love, morality, cooperation, or justice. *Christian Economics* had a socialist bent without explicitly calling for the nationalization of the means of production, distribution, and exchange. To Holland, that was the right approach, which came to be called Christian social unionism. He founded the CSU on Richmond's call for a Christian political economy, adopting three aims: (1) recognize the Christian Law as the ultimate authority in social practice; (2) study the application of Christian principles to society; (3) follow the way of Christ in opposing wrong and standing for righteousness and love.[136]

That was purposively vague—Christian socialism in the broad sense of Maurician Christian idealism, not a political program. CSU implored Frederick Temple to intervene in the dock strike, but he fled to Wales to get away from it. A CSU pamphlet by Holland declared that political problems had given way to the industrial problem. The "ultimate answer" to the social question was the Person and life of Jesus Christ, but applying the "redemptive force of Christ to actual society" was highly complex and difficult. Introducing Richmond's next book, *Economic Morals* (1890), Holland said textbook economics offered little help because it trafficked in isolated laws detached from actuality: "We live as shuttle-cocks, bandied about between our political economy and our Christian morality. We go a certain distance with the science, and then, when things get ugly and squeeze, we suddenly introduce moral considerations, and human kindness, and charity. And then, again, this seems weak, and we pull up short and go back to tough economic principle. So we live in miserable double-mindedness. Each counter-motive intervenes at purely arbitrary points. When our economy is caught in a tangle, we fly off to our morality. When our morality lands us in a social problem, we take refuge in some naked economic law. There is thus no consistency in our treatment of facts; no harmony in our inward convictions."[137]

The CSU was an antidote to miserable double-mindedness and disharmony. From the beginning its Oxford branch was very academic and its London branch was activist. In 1889 the Oxford branch launched England's first economics journal, *Economic Review*; every issue challenged economic orthodoxy. The London branch was long on veteran GSM activists dedicated to influencing the general public and churches. Holland was the unquestioned ringleader of CSU, sharing leadership status with Gore and Westcott; Westcott provided older-generation respectability. In 1894 Holland and James Adderly founded a parish magazine expounding Anglo-Catholic personal and social religion, *Goodwill*, which Adderly edited for sixteen years, and in 1896 Holland founded the CSU's official national magazine, the *Commonwealth*, which he produced on a monthly basis until his death in 1918. *Commonwealth* was witty, interesting, very Anglican, and broad ranging, like Holland. Holland and Gore, though Anglo-Catholic like Headlam, did not share his ritualism, separatism, or contempt for ecclesiastical authority. They were fond of saying that Headlam's heart was better than his head. Holland kept the CSU Anglican because only Anglicans cared about redeeming Anglicanism, but he welcomed the High, the Low, the in-between, and the Liberal.

To Headlam, Christian socialism had to be Catholic; saying so could not be wrong. Roman Catholicism was beyond the pale, being papist and authoritarian, but Protestantism was the negation of Catholic soul. Protestantism meant three things to Headlam, all of them terrible — individualism, sectarianism, and otherworldliness. It amazed him that American Protestants embraced the social gospel, since they had to overcome Protestantism to get there. But even Protestants who clawed their way to the social gospel did so on deracinated terms, lacking a sense of the wholeness of things. Headlam warned repeatedly that if the GSM stopped being a devotional society, it would lose its revolutionary spirit. That would be tragic, but something even worse would occur: The GSM would lose its soul, the Catholic sense of the sanctity of life. The Christian Socialist Society, to Headlam, was Example A. It claimed that Christian socialism did not rest on any single theology or require any particular rituals. Headlam half-heartedly welcomed it, believing it would fail.[138]

It failed after only three years, vindicating Headlam's belief that sustaining an ecumenical socialist magazine—the *Christian Socialist*—was easier than building an ecumenical movement, and both were dubious projects. The CSU, by contrast, was a tremendous success. By 1895 it had twenty-seven branches and twenty-seven hundred members; the London branch alone had one thousand members by 1895 and fourteen hundred by 1900. The national group reached six thousand members; Westcott's call to the episcopacy in 1890 heightened the CSU's ecclesiastical prestige; and between 1889 and 1913, sixteen of the Church of England's fifty-three new bishops were CSU members. The London branch was a stronghold of GSM veterans—Adderly, Shuttleworth, W. E. Moll, Percy Dearmer, Lewis Donaldson, J. Cartmel-Robinson, and A. W. Jephson. Headlam tried to be gracious when his members joined the CSU. Holland and Gore used the GSM as a launching pad, and some GSM partisans had a snarky epigram about how CSU operated: "Here's a glaring social evil; let's read a paper about it." Certainly, there was a great deal of paper reading. But Holland and Gore built something that made an impact on the general public, the academy, and the Church of England, much like the Fabian Society.[139]

Meanwhile the GSM declined in the mid-1890s over Headlam's trademark fixations, anti-ILP liberalism, and refusal to emphasize public ownership of industries, plus, fatefully, the fallout over playwright Oscar Wilde. In 1895 Wilde was arrested for his sexual relationship with Lord Alfred Douglas, just after Wilde achieved a smashing success with *The Importance of Being Earnest*. Headlam barely knew him, but Headlam threw parties at his elegant Bloomsbury home—the origin of the legendary Bloomsbury Group—through which he knew many artists in Wilde's circle. Headlam disliked Wilde's aesthetic cynicism, which seemed narcissistic to him, a consequence of refusing to struggle for the kingdom of God. He also realized that helping Wilde would hurt the GSM. But Headlam posted bail and put himself out for many unpopular figures. When Wilde was arrested and punished with a very high bail of five thousand pounds, Headlam bailed him out, accompanied him to trial every morning, and steered him through jeering mobs every night. Wilde was convicted and sentenced to two years of hard labor, which destroyed his health.

Headlam got a torrent of hate mail and resignations, both of which he shrugged off. This was like getting fired from curacies. He was impulsive, he had a conscience, he stayed true to his character, and he accepted the consequences. Headlam disliked Wilde's sexuality in the same way he disliked the alcoholism of people he bailed out repeatedly. He was faithful to Late Victorian Christian morality even as he consorted regularly with dancers, poets, gays, atheists, and hard drinkers. But his radical style was high on the list of things that kept the GSM from CSU-like success.[140]

Two kinds of people flocked to the CSU, in Holland's telling: the "partly cracky, partly fervid set" and the mute "Respectables." Both tested his legendary good-spiritedness; Holland told Talbot they made him "oppressively anxious." The cracky talkers never stopped talking and nearly always lost their heads, while the others just sat there, never joining a committee or saying anything. Holland pulled at both ends and overworked, gifted with likability. Gore helped with exhortation, but this was Holland's group. Westcott symbolized the quiet, conservative, go-slow wing of the CSU, although he commended socialism at the 1890 Church Congress, explaining why it mattered: "Wage labour, though it appears to be an inevitable step in the evolution of society, is as little fitted to represent finally or adequately the connection of man with man in the production of wealth as in earlier times slavery or serfdom." Moving toward socialism was like getting rid of slavery because socialism advocated the abolition of the wage system, another form of slavery. Many clerics joined the CSU upon learning that even Westcott now talked like that.[141]

In 1893 the CSU committed itself to a consumer boycott of sweated industry. Oxford CSU compiled lists of sweatshops and firms paying trade union wage rates, and CSU branches launched boycott campaigns that manufacturers bitterly opposed. CSU used the same technique in the pottery industry, where lead poisoning was commonplace among pottery workers. In 1898 a London CSU deputation to the House of Commons demanded a revision of the factory acts. The group was studded with bishops, college heads, and other dignitaries not ignorable by Parliament. The House of Commons proposed a weak bill, CSU denounced it, the bill was withdrawn, and CSU helped to draft what became the Factory and Workshops Act of 1901. All of this was new in England—a Church of England group battling for legislation that benefited the working class. CSU London branch leader Percy Dearmer issued a Fabian-like call for more experts on social ills. If the church was to involve itself in solving social problems, it needed a brain trust of experts on Christian economics and Christian sociology, ensuring that CSU publication venues would have a long run.[142]

In this respect CSU resembled the Fabian Society, while Headlam protested that England needed fiery socialist clerics, not an economics journal. Headlam prized his leadership role in the Fabian Society and his annual election to the executive committee; for a dozen years he was among the top vote getters. But he realized from close acquaintance with Sidney Webb that Webb had the soul of a technocrat, and he was wobbly on imperialism. As long as Liberals ran the government, Webb and Shaw gave lip service to permeating the Liberal Party with Fabian socialism. In 1895, however, after the ILP split the progressive vote and Tories won the general election, Webb decided there was no reason why Fabians should not permeate the Conservative Party too.

Webb started by pulling back on the Fabian demand for secular education, contending that Fabians should be able to live with public funding of voluntary schools, most of which were Anglican. Then the Boer War of 1899–1902 provided a dramatic opportunity for Fabians to wave the Union Jack. Webb, Shaw, and Beatrice Webb said there was no reason to oppose Britain's war against the South African Republic and the Orange Free State. This was a flag-waving opportunity to prove that Fabians were patriots. The Boers deserved to be put down, the war was popular, and Fabians had a golden opportunity to expand their political reach. Fabian socialism had nothing to do with foreign policy, so why make trouble? Fabians hotly debated that position. Headlam headed the anti-imperial pushback, joined by S. G. Hobson, Ramsay MacDonald, Emmeline Pankhurst, and other left-Fabians; meanwhile Christian socialists across denominational and partisan lines condemned the Boer War. Shaw offended the left-Fabians by repudiating "the fixed-frontier ideals of individualist republicanism, non-interference, and nationalism." For a great power like Great Britain, he said, imperialism was unavoidable and not to be denigrated.[143]

The Fabians could not agree about the war, so they took no formal position. That was galling enough to anti-imperialists, but Shaw's much-quoted opinion was too much to stomach, setting off a flurry of resignations. Now Headlam was lonelier than ever in the Fabian Society. He feared that Webb was turning the society into a band of regulators lacking any radical spirit. Webb was smitten with authority, not the spirit of freedom. In 1901 Webb confirmed that he had opted wholly for bureaucratic collectivism, the rule of society by technocratic experts. The subtitle of his book, *Twentieth Century Politics: A Policy of National Efficiency*, offered his preferred name for it. Webb still preferred Liberals over the Tories and fledgling ILP, but not by much. He criticized Liberals for making a fetish of individual freedom, and he rejected the Liberal call for Irish Home Rule—the Irish needed good government, not racial autonomy. He implored Liberals and Conservatives to work together as "co-efficients." Efficiency, in this telling, was a middle-class white suprema-cist project.[144]

Fabian leaders were too enamored of bureaucracy, science, and themselves to resist imperial self-flattery, which made them ripe for the modern eugenics movement, a British invention. Eugenic weeding out went back to ancient Greece and Rome. Plato taught that human reproduction should be controlled by the state. Ancient Rome, Athens, and Sparta practiced infanticide as a form of phenotypic selection, and the fourth table of Roman law commanded the execution of deformed children. The Roman Empire practiced infanticide until Christianity abolished it. In 1865 Charles Darwin's cousin Sir Francis Galton called for new forms of eugenic weeding out, contending that social policies aiding the disadvantaged impeded the mechanisms of natural selection described by Darwin. Galton taught that intelligence and talent are hereditary traits in human beings. Social policies helping the mentally deficient are bad for society, dragging it downward. The less intelligent groups in British society were outbreeding the intelligent groups. British society needed eugenics—a term coined by Galton in 1883—the science of improving Britain's hereditary stock. Galton relied on social statistics to make his case, allowing room for socialization and environment as contributory factors. His protégé Karl Pearson developed a biometrical approach to eugenics, pioneering the field of biomet-rics; Pearson also claimed Galton was greater than Darwin. Eventually a school of biological reductionists arose, dividing the eugenics movement into rival camps. Galton and Pearson said their approach to eugenics perfectly fit progres-sive politics. In 1904 Galton expounded his prosocialization view in a speech at the London School of Economics, where Pearson was highly esteemed as a major statistician and Fabian stalwart.[145]

Pearson provided ample ballast for the bigoted Fabian mainstream. Webb, Shaw, Beatrice Webb, H. G. Wells, and Pearson wrote dire warnings that Britain was degenerating racially. The best white English, they warned, were not repro-ducing themselves, while Irish, Jews, and low-functioning whites were over-breeding. The poor were becoming dumber and more slothful as a consequence of reading smutty literature, breeding too many children, and being indulged. Pearson and Wells were strident on this theme, demanding that a serious eugenic policy had to begin with sterilizing the genetically deficient. Pearson declared in 1901: "My view—and I think it may be called the scientific view of a nation—is that of an organized whole, kept up to a high pitch of internal efficiency by insuring that its numbers are substantially recruited from the bet-ter stocks, and kept up to a high pitch of external efficiency by contest, chiefly by way of war with inferior races." In other words, there was only one way to attain a high level of civilization, "namely, the struggle of race with race, and the survival of the physically and mentally fitter race." Webb concurred that if England failed to curb the overbreeding of undesirable groups and to promote genetically sound marriages, there would be hell to pay. Either the nation would fall into irreversible racial degeneration or it would fall "to the Irish and the Jews." Shaw's Irish heritage did not stop him from agreeing that eugenics was an essential aspect of good governance. He and Pearson, plus Wells and both Webbs, plus coming liberal icons William Beveridge, John Maynard Keynes, and Margaret Sanger, unabashedly conferred moral and scientific respectability on eugenic bigotry, pitching it as progressive. Pearson won the first professorial chair of eugenics in 1911, funded by Galton's estate at the University of London, where he stumped for letting women vote and keeping Jews and other "inferior races" out of Britain.[46]

Margaret Cole, whitewashing this story decades later in her classic history of Fabian socialism, said nothing whatsoever about eugenics and confined Pearson to a single mention. Pearson, she noted, spoke for the trickle of Fabians who believed that small nations were not nations at all and thus should be policed for the sake of world prosperity. Cole was devoted to Beatrice Webb, fixed on Britain, and inclined to regard eugenics and racism as sideshow issues, plus belatedly embarrassing. Since she did not mention that the Fabian Society was deeply involved in eugenics bigotry, she did not mention that its Christian and ethical socialist members vehemently opposed it. Christian socialists stood against the Fabian majority by opposing imperialism and eugenics as morally repugnant. Headlam despaired that Fabian leaders paraded their racism as enlightened and defended the British Empire. The Webbs and their allies, he charged, were "grim ministers of technical education" out to create "a race of one-eyed specialists." It appalled him that Fabian leaders called their conceits socialist. Imperialism and eugenics, he said, were immoral for the same reasons. It was a disaster for Fabian socialists to be aligned with either, much less both.[47]

But Headlam stayed in the Fabian Society because his world oddly got smaller as socialism advanced. The GSM lost half its members in the late 1890s. Headlam could have found anti-imperial company in the CSU or Church Socialist League, but he was too proud for that. He clung to his diminishing role in the Fabian Society, finding Webb increasingly incomprehensible, the same thing Webb said about him. Meanwhile trade union socialism soared in England, which was also problematic for Headlam. S. G. Hobson, young Fabians G. D. H. Cole and William Mellor, and Christian socialists Conrad Noel, R. H. Tawney, and Maurice Reckitt opted for guild socialism, contending that trade guilds should replace the state bureaucracy. Headlam had a growing respect for unionism on its own terms, but he could not be a guild socialist because he believed that unions were too selfish to be trusted with the common good. The year 1906 was a turning point for socialism and Christian socialism, as the Labour Party was founded in England, the ILP played a ginger group role within it, and the northern-based Church Socialist League was founded. The Church Socialist League grew with the labor movement. It was Anglican, socially heterogeneous, and more radically socialist than the GSM or CSU. It had a dynamic leader, Noel, and it soared past other Christian socialist organizations, climbing with guild socialism.

Surpassed and isolated, Headlam gave a lecture in 1908 on how the Fabian Society had gone wrong. Good socialism had a Christian spirit, and it fixed on the land issue, he said. Since the Fabian Society claimed to be socialist, it was supposed to believe in the emancipation of land and industrial capital "from individual and class ownership, and the vesting of them in the community." But the Fabian Society no longer talked like that. Instead "the Fabian Society consists of Bureaucratic Collectivists and admirers of Mr. Bernard Shaw, and concerns itself with almost every social activity except the tackling of the land question." Headlam said he was not against parliamentary gradualism and did not cheer for anyone who shouted about overthrowing the capitalist state. The Fabians kept the faith on these two matters. But, incredibly, the Fabians made socialism boring and bureaucratic. They did not struggle to liberate the poor from the monopolists of land and capital. They took the path of technocratic opportunism, imagining that socialism was really about the rule of a superior bureaucratic class—themselves.[148]

The following year a declining Headlam shut down the GSM, unwilling to let others keep it going—a dismal end to the remarkable run that made other Christian socialisms possible. Headlam's biographer John Richard Orens rightly notes that Headlam lacked the intellectual heft of Gore and William Temple, and he was too impulsive and inflexible to be an ideal movement leader. But he was deeply anchored in two enabling convictions: "Headlam never lost faith in God or the people."[149]

IMPERIALISM OLD AND NEW

Gore and Holland were different kinds of church leaders. Gore was intense, voluble, and consumed with guilt feelings over the church's objective guilt. Everything he wrote radiated his moral passion, and much that he wrote registered his lacerating sorrow over the sins of the church. Repeatedly he thundered that the Church was not what Christ called it to be. Jesus provided the moral law of God's kingdom in the Sermon on the Mount, which the Church either ignored or trivialized. In 1891 Gore said the Church had become so corrupted by its immersion in commercial society that it didn't notice "its profound antagonism to the spirit of Christ. . . . There is not amongst us anything that can be called an adequate conception of what Christian morality means." Often he asked despairing questions that left his audience hanging, except to say they must not give up on the Church: "Why has it not spoken up for justice? Why does it cringe to wealth? Why has it not protested with a unanimous voice against this or that plain outrage upon brotherhood?" Gore did not aspire to march with Fabians or Marxists for a socialist society. He was too deeply a churchman for that, imbued with Maurice's dream of what the Church of England should be. Yet he was also prone to say that he hated—truly hated—the Church of England. Gore's revulsion at his church's corruption dissuaded him from believing that secular movements might be less corrupt or that he should link his beloved and loathed Church to them.[150]

Holland was famously otherwise—ebullient, teasing, hopeful, and wise-cracking—although he also raged when something made him angry. He emphasized folly rather than guilt. On a trip to Egypt in 1889 Holland kept a journal that his travel group read aloud; it was filled with humorous zingers, betraying no hint that he disliked Egypt and struggled with depression. He was fond of tweaking audiences at question time, "Every man his own grandmother!" When hecklers said the church should stay out of politics, Holland said they didn't mean it. They only wanted clerics like him to keep their liberal or radical politics out of the church. Conservatism, he said, never counted as politics in this indictment: "It was part of the immemorial system of nature. The parson was born a Knight of the Primrose League." Unlike Gore, Holland did not emphasize his qualms about Social Democratic overreaching. He said Christian socialists wanted very much to Christianize the state, getting as much as possible out of the state. Theologically and ideologically Holland blended High Church orthodoxy, Maurice-like modernity, Ruskin-like Romanticism, Gladstone liberalism, and ambivalently prounion Christian socialism. His core conviction was that God radically identifies with human beings at the lowest point of their need, in suffering. Theologian Donald MacKinnon explained: "He took with a simple penetrating seriousness God's self-revelation as love, as love active, concrete, working. He saw that the coming of Christ broke up indeed the foundation of our little world, our cosmos made to measure presided over by an idol fashioned after the image of our passing idealism."[151]

CSU was definitely anticapitalist and indefinitely socialist, in the manner of Holland and Gore. It campaigned for decent sanitary facilities, fair taxes, fair wages, protection of child laborers, and female county councilors, playing down its socialist aspirations. The group's left flank was eager to align with the ILP and the Labour Church, but Gore and Holland shared Headlam's qualms about that. In electoral politics CSU operated mostly in the left wing of the Liberal Party. Then the ILP split the Left vote in 1895, handing the government to the Tories, and Holland grieved that labor parties were self-defeating. He was inconsolable, writing to Adderly, "Down goes the middle-class Radicalism; and the Nonconformist conscience. They lie smashed in ruins. How shall we do without them? I sit in dread." The ILP had wreaked disaster on the nation: "They have handed England over to the strongest Government of property and capital and individualism which has been seen for a century. They have anni- hilated all the sympathetic Radicalism that could mitigate the roaring individu- alism of property. They have recklessly and thanklessly and barbarously ignored the forward action of the late Ministry, and have shut their eyes tight and fast to the enormous resistance which any forward attempt is bound to meet from the immense Conservatism of the English people."[152]

It was easy to sneer at Whigs and church radicals from an ILP perspective, but now the nation would pay the price of doing so, unleashing the political restraints on imperialism and whatever the capitalist class wanted. The Tory victory put Joseph Chamberlain in charge of the Colonial Office, yielding an upsurge of imperial aggression in India and Africa, plus jingoism about it. Here, CSU was not shy or vague. Except for Westcott, who accepted the British Empire as a too-late-to-stop fact of life, CSU leaders condemned British impe- rialism as morally repugnant and oppressive.

Westcott belonged to the last generation of the first British Empire, which ended with Tory prime minister Benjamin Disraeli's imperial adventures in Egypt, India, Afghanistan, and South Africa. The first empire was a school-days tale of mercantile colonization under the Stuarts and Cromwell; war victories against the Dutch, French, and Spanish in the seventeenth century; the acqui- sition of eastern North America, the St. Lawrence basin in Canada, numerous territories in the Caribbean, slave-trading outposts in Africa, and commercial interests in India; the consolidation of Britain's dominant financial and naval power; the loss of the U.S. colonies and the discovery of Australia; the expansion of Britain's East India Company into Afghanistan and Burma; the abolition of slavery in England in 1807; the end of the Napoleonic Wars in 1815; the acquisi- tion of Dutch South Africa; the freeing of slaves held elsewhere in the empire in 1833; the attempt to salvage something in Africa from the scraps of the slave trade; the inauguration of direct British rule in India in 1858, dissolving the East India Company; and the ascendance of industrialization and free trade ideology. The latter development undercut the old monopolistic trading corporations. English politics at the national party level had no principled issues between 1846 and 1868, as free trade and the economic boom yielded small-bore politics. The Victorians inherited the old mercantile empire and the new eastern network of commercial interests. They debated whether they needed to maintain either one, since Adam Smith contended in *The Wealth of Nations* (1776) that maintaining the empire was economically draining and self-defeating. Liberals cited Smith against their Tory opponents. Rhetorically, Gladstone versus Disraeli dominated electoral politics for two decades, pitting Whig liberalism against Tory nationalism. Gladstone radiated preachy Whig ambivalence about the empire and did not get along with Queen Victoria, while Disraeli bristled with imperial ambition and fawned over the queen.[153]

But the empire grew throughout the Victorian era under Whigs and Tories alike. Strategic factors were usually invoked, until racial paternalism worked better. Politicians did not say that capitalism inevitably created a demand for imperial expansion, no matter which party ruled. Holland and Gore came of age during the 1870s upsurge of national chauvinism that Rudyard Kipling later called the White Man's Burden. Faraway civilizations were said to be too backward to be capable of self-government, so the British nation was called to civilize backward parts of the globe. Disraeli said it stridently, urging Britons of all classes to unite in loving their empire, which he called "Tory Democracy." Disraeli's Jewish lineage conferred a patina of liberal respectability on British nationalism. It helped that he and Gladstone despised each other. Disraeli's first run as prime minister was a caretaker episode in 1868, when he famously quipped that he had "climbed to the top of a greasy pole." In 1874 the Tories swept the Whigs out of office, and Disraeli served again as prime minister, for six years. Foreign policy dominated his entire reign. Disraeli fended off Russia's attempts to gain from the decay of the Ottoman Empire. In 1875 he bought the Suez Canal Company, in Ottoman-controlled Egypt. In 1877 he conferred on Queen Victoria a coveted title, "Empress of India," overriding an outraged Whig protest in Parliament. Disraeli might have spared himself the controversy except for his devotion to the monarchy. In his last years in office he plunged the nation into a disastrous war in Afghanistan and a disastrous military campaign in South Africa, which swept Gladstone and the Liberals back to power.[154]

Anti-imperialists, both Christian and secular, were prone to say that empire was a problem of power lust and military overreach, cured by ethically decent politics, until the imperial plunder of the 1880s demanded a deeper economic explanation. The plunder began when Welsh-born American journalist Henry Stanley took an epic journey down the length of the Congo River in the late 1870s. Britain was skittish about venturing into Central Africa, but King Leopold II of Belgium invested in Stanley's plan to tap the Congo's riches, and the colossal ravaging of Central Africa began. The Royal Niger Company, the Imperial British East Asia Company, the British South Africa Company, and other British chartered companies struck hard. The European powers, meeting at Berlin in November 1884, sorted out their claims in Africa with ineffable hubris, although it took several years to sort out the details. England, having pushed earliest and hardest, got four million square miles of African territory; France got approximately the same amount; Portugal got three quarters of a million square miles; and Spain and Italy got substantial chunks. Stanley's exploits paved the way to the creation of the Congo Free State, which Leopold owned privately. All produced thuggish regimes of thievery and repression. Germany, a late player in this enterprise, was granted an area half the size of the entire German Empire in Europe—a huge payoff for joining the pillage of Africans lacking any say in the matter.[155]

W. E. B. Du Bois, later reflecting on this calamity, said the crucial point of the story was the equation of color with inferiority. The European powers took an important lesson from the British and American slave trades. The pillage and rape of Africa could be called something else if black people were less than human. France was keen to build a northern African empire stretching from the Atlantic Ocean to the Red Sea. Germany, shut out from Central and South America by the Monroe Doctrine, sought colonies in Africa and Asia. Portugal renewed and expanded its historic claims to African territory. In 1875 the European powers controlled one-tenth of the African continent. By 1900 they controlled virtually the entire continent. Du Bois said this was what drove Europe to war in 1914—the scramble for economic riches by rival capitalist nations creating mutually exclusive economic bases of power.[156]

British Christian socialists held a very similar interpretation long before World War I was the issue. They applied it to the Boer War, working with the English polymath John A. Hobson, who later influenced Du Bois. In his early career Hobson was a radical democrat, pacifist, and rationalist who specialized in economic theory. His first book, *The Physiology of Industry* (1889), originated the underconsumption theory of cyclical unemployment, arguing that capitalism created imbalances between the production of capital goods and consumer goods, yielding cyclical employment crises. In the 1890s he developed this theory in two books, *The Problem of Poverty* (1891) and *The Problem of the Unemployed* (1896), contending that the upper class chronically oversaved and that underconsumption was systemic and cyclical, producing mass unemploy-ment. Hobson wrote with a George-like moral passion that spoke to Christian socialists. He was deeply influenced by Ruskin, lectured regularly for the Ethical Culture Society, and collaborated with activists in the Christian Socialist Society and Christian Socialist League. In 1898–1899 he toured South Africa to investigate what became the Boer War. Hobson poured out articles and a book contending that British horror stories about the corruption and vio-lence of the Boer regime were made up. England fought the Boers, he said, because British gold and diamond miners wanted what lay beneath the Dutch farms of the Transvaal, not because British leaders cared about persecuted victims of the Boer regime.[157]

In 1902 Hobson published a soon-famous book, *Imperialism*, arguing that modern capitalism drove the capitalist powers into "undeveloped" markets. This story began, he said, when England established "imperialism as a political policy" in the early 1870s. As long as England held a virtual monopoly of world markets for important manufactured goods, it did not need modern imperial-ism; the old kind worked just fine. In the early 1870s competition from Germany, the United States, and Belgium impaired England's capacity to sell its manufac-tured goods at a profit. England was compelled to find new markets: "These new markets had to lie in hitherto undeveloped countries, chiefly in the tropics, where vast populations lived capable of growing economic needs which our manufacturers and merchants could supply." England tried to stay ahead of the competition, but its rivals seized and annexed territories for the same purpose: "Every improvement of methods of production, every concentration of owner-ship and control, seems to accentuate the tendency. As one nation after another enters the machine economy and adopts advanced industrial methods, it becomes more difficult for its manufacturers, merchants, and financiers to dis-pose profitably of their economic resources, and they are tempted more and more to use their Governments in order to secure for their particular use some distant undeveloped country by annexation and protection."[158]

Hobson's analysis was convincing to many Christian socialists and ethical socialists long before it became a pillar of neo-Marxist theory. Capitalism had structural flaws that drove investors to seek foreign markets for idle funds, fresh territories for railway construction, and the like. It kept itself going by exploiting colonized markets and exacerbating inequality at home. Hobson did not say that predatory capitalism explained everything. He made moral arguments, stressed that politics mattered, and wrote a book on the baleful psychology of jingoism. His work powerfully augmented the anti-imperial left. The *Christian Socialist* blasted English imperialism very much in Hobson's vein before

Hobson became famous for it. Marson said only a perverted form of Christianity legitimized imperial aggression, and the same thing was true of socialism. Christianity by itself should have been a bulwark against racism and imperialism. As it was, British Christian socialists belonged to a nation that savaged colonized people of color, and the "stupid bullies" of the Tory party gloried in doing so. Marson cheered the temperance activists for imploring that England really should stop exporting rum and syphilis to its colonies and stealing their resources. Working up to anti-imperialism needed to start somewhere: "It is something to get these watery worthies to admit this much, but Christianity ought to demand about ten thousand times as much, and does. To supply blacks with soda water and blue pills is not the end of our duties toward them. Our efforts to cheat, rob, murder and enslave them require as much denunciation as the fact that we dram, drug, and syphilize them. These temperance people are too modest." Marson implored readers to picture the missionaries and gunboats they sent abroad to tyrannize others, rendering null and void the distinction between Christianity and imperial violence.[159]

Holland said it from his high perch at St. Paul's Cathedral, fixing on Lord Robert Cecil of Salisbury. Salisbury served as Disraeli's India secretary in the 1870s, clashed with Gladstone over Irish Home Rule in the 1880s, and served three times as Tory prime minister. The nadir, to Holland, was the Boer War, a moral disaster fueled by lust for gold and diamonds and covered with hypocrisy. Holland said Salisbury extinguished ethical feeling as a factor in English politics. It was the worst thing he could imagine saying of a politician. In 1899, just after England went to war in South Africa, Holland lashed out at the demagogic patriots of "the War-party" and the "savage swagger of the music halls." He struggled to fathom, he said, "that we could fall so far from the very memory of Jesus Christ." During the siege of Ladysmith in 1900, when prowar feeling surged in England, Holland gave a blistering antiwar sermon declaring that England sinned against the Boers. Gore was equally scathing, with the same theological frame: England went to war in South Africa because England was arrogant and didn't care about God. Gore described British imperialism as "the worship of our unregenerate British selves, without morality or fear of God." He excoriated Salisbury and the military commanders for their hellish concentration camps in South Africa, condemning Britain's contempt for morality. On the other hand, two weeks after Gore attacked Salisbury, Salisbury appointed him to his first bishopric, at Worcester. That was England, too.[160]

Opposing imperialism was straightforward and clear compared to anticapitalism. Anti-imperialism was fundamentally moral, it had a place in party politics, it was severable from questionable ideologies, and it was hard to deny that clerics had a right to pronounce about war and killing, although many denied it anyway. Socialist economics had none of that going for it. Capitalism was exceedingly complex, it had good features along with the bad ones, and socialist activism raised difficult questions about allying with trade unions and worker parties. The Christian socialists were well aware of an additional complicating factor. They faced it every week in the pulpit, preaching to the bourgeoisie. Headlam acquired some independence by blowing up his clerical career, but Headlam had a guaranteed income. The *Christian Socialist* was strong and clear, but it lasted only eight years. CSU made inroads in the House of Bishops, but that truncated how far it would get and how radical it would be. CSU never really tried to bond with workers. Only the Church Socialist League broke into the working class, and it did so by riding on the back of northern trade unionism and the guild socialist movement.

The version of Anglican socialism that had the longest run was the one that seeped into the episcopacy. CSU lost members to the Church Socialist League and eventually merged, in 1919, with the Navvy Mission Society to form the Industrial Christian Fellowship, thus losing its separate identity. It still exists as the Industrial Christian Fellowship. Meanwhile CSU transplanted to the United States shortly after it sprouted in England. John Carter, a Canadian cleric educated at Exeter College, Oxford, was closely allied to Gore as one of the first four priests to join the monastic order Gore created at Yorkshire, the Society of the Resurrection. He contacted two Episcopalian scholar-activists, political scientist Richard T. Ely and cleric W. D. P. Bliss, who founded a CSU organization in the United States. Ely and Bliss were astute thinkers, energetic organizers, and major figures in what became the American social gospel. The high-water mark for CSU came in 1908, when the Pan-Anglican Conference met at Lambeth. Two young clerics with illustrious futures, Percy Dearmer and William Temple, commended Christian socialism. Headlam scolded the assembly that Christian socialism was about justice, not about charity. The Church Socialist League, meeting at nearby Memorial Hall, gave CSU its due, calling the Lambeth conference "a triumph for Christian Social-Unionism." Ludlow took a bow at Lambeth as the grand old man of Christian socialism. According to Holland, Ludlow "made the rest of us look very cheap. . . . The fire gleamed still in his eyes."[161]

It was a buoyant moment, chastened by Gore. On the one hand, Gore said, Christian socialists deserved credit for proving that socialism at its best had nothing to do with abolishing marriage, the family, individual freedom, or a spiritual conception of reality. Socialism was fundamentally an ethical critique of injustice and thus a modern expression of Christian ideals: "The indictment of our present social organization is indeed overwhelming. And with the indictment

Christianity ought to have the profoundest sympathy. It is substantially the indictment of the prophets." On the other hand, the church was so deeply implicated in sin that celebrations were grotesque. The Victorian church failed its people, Gore admonished: "How vast has been our failure!" Now the church had to repent its role in the "crushing of weak lives" and its betrayal of the gospel. Redeeming the church would require nothing less than a "tremendous act of penitence for having failed so long" and a penitent willingness to repair the damage: "We must identify ourselves with the great impeachment of the present industrial system." He also said it positively: "We must identify ourselves, because we are Christians, with the positive ethical ideal of socialistic thought." Otherwise, Gore warned, God would judge the church very harshly.[162]

This was the keynote of CSU socialism to the doorstep of World War I. Holland pleaded against arming for war and hating Germany. He preached on the anti-Christian hellishness of war and did not stop until Germany invaded Belgium. His biographer Stephen Paget, otherwise admiring, found this part of Holland's witness unbearably "horrible," a terrible blot on Holland's legacy. After the war began Holland told a friend he had one consolation: "My one comfort now is to remember that I never insisted on War as inevitable, never shouted Armaments, never saw the Kaiser as the one unspeakable devil." One night, eating dinner with a student who had enlisted to fight, Holland asked if the student still wanted to love Germans. He said yes, and Holland scurried to his piano, where he joyfully crooned German folk songs.[163]

Holland and Gore wanted to believe that capitalism did not always overpower religious and secular movements for social justice. But the Western movements for democracy and "progress" helped to accelerate the flow of finance capital to far-off lands, thus ratcheting up the clash of empires. Democracy was supposed to be the answer to the terrible problems of inequality, exploitation, and oppression. The ship of state was supposedly launched on the great tide of democratic expansion. Yet as democracy spread, so did the rule of might, regardless of which party won office. Democracy and imperialism grew together, unless—what? In England the Labour Party became the vehicle of the socialist and Christian socialist answer, betting on Fabian ideology just as the Fabian Society and its ethos of Edwardian progressivism faded. In the United States the religion of democracy got a longer run by virtue of geographic advantage and the American faith that history did not apply to the United States. In Germany socialism and Christian socialism proved to be no match for nationalistic fearmongering, shredding the hopes that democracy, Marxism, Progress, or some conflation of these things might thwart the march of nations toward catastrophe.

3

GERMAN SOCIAL DEMOCRACY: MARXISM AS THEORY AND POLITICS

British socialism got along for nearly a century without a significant Marxist tradition. Marx and Engels dismissed Britain's tiny Marxist party as not worth mentioning, Marxism played almost no role in the Labour Party, and it lacked any notable British following until the 1930s. Even its book club following in the 1930s was a Popular Front episode steeped in British liberalism. British socialists, religious and not, saw little reason why they should immerse themselves in Marx's problematic legacy. Marx was highly theoretical, dogmatic, and abstract, he condemned religion and derided religious socialism, his followers were atheistic anti-Christians, his legacy was notoriously ideological and factional. Every one of Marx's defining claims was a subject of contentious dispute, and some were incompatible with any conceivable form of Christian or religious socialism. Why bother with any of that?

In Germany this dismissal was not possible, which later made it impossible elsewhere. Marxian theory is the most creative and sophisticated tradition of anticapitalist criticism ever devised. Marx argued powerfully that capitalism is not the most natural way to organize a society, he stressed that capitalism was founded on the dispossession of peasants and the poor from their land, facilitating "primitive accumulation," and he focused brilliantly on the question of who produces and who receives the surplus value. This critique so far surpassed all others that very different schools of socialist thought felt compelled to appropriate it. The founder of the General German Workers Association, Ferdinand Lassalle, considered himself a Marxist, although he was also a German nationalist and monarchist, a collaborator with Prussian minister president Otto von Bismarck, a self-styled democratic socialist, and a self-dramatizing eccentric who died early from a stupid duel. The founders of the Social Democratic

Workers Party, Wilhelm Liebknecht and August Bebel, similarly claimed to be Marxists, on terms shaped by their regional and political interests. Six years after Lassalle founded the General German Workers Association in 1863, Liebknecht and Bebel founded a rival party, contending that Lassalle and his eventual successor, Johann B. von Schweitzer, sold out the revolutionary vision of the *Communist Manifesto*. But in fact all four party leaders were radical democrats with select socialist and Marxist tendencies. The dubious Marxism of Germany's original socialist parties caused Marx himself to explain, scathingly, in 1875 what socialists should believe if they aspired to the real thing.[1]

The party of Lassalle came chiefly from Prussia, it was straightforwardly statist, and it set democratic socialism against liberalism. It proposed to achieve socialism, defined as state-funded producer cooperatives, through the three-class franchise quasi-democracy that Bismarck introduced in Prussia. In Germany the middle class was unable to bid for political power until capitalism entered the industrial phase. It finally happened under Bismarck, a conservative royalist who hated liberalism, but realized that co-opting the rising middle class was politically imperative. In 1863 Bismarck colluded secretly with Lassalle over their shared contempt for liberalism and their dream of a unified German empire. Lassalle wanted to forge an alliance with Bismarck against the bourgeoisie. Instead Lassalle got himself killed, von Schweitzer took over the party, Bismarck annexed Hannover and other pro-Austrian states after defeating Austria in the war of 1866, he tried to fuse Prussia's military aristocracy with the bourgeoisie, bargaining with the National Liberals, Liebknecht and Bebel founded a new party in 1869, and, in 1871, Bismarck unified Germany as chancellor of the German Reich. Liebknecht and Bebel said that celebrating the new German Empire had nothing to do with building socialism. They were called "Eisenachers" for founding their party in Eisenach, the birthplace of Johann Sebastian Bach, a town in the forested hills and farms of central Germany, in the state of Thuringia. The Eisenachers despised von Schweitzer as a dictatorial bully and a toady for Bismarck's wars. Liebknecht and Bebel, like Marx, opposed Prussia's war against France and cheered the Paris Commune of 1871. They said, like Marx, that religion was a narcotic for the weak and a consolation. But Liebknecht and Bebel were like Lassalle in fusing bourgeois radicalism to the parts of Marxism they accepted, and very few of their comrades knew what Marx taught anyway.

In 1874 both socialist parties did remarkably well in the Reichstag elections, compiling 352,000 votes, 6 percent of the total. They also did equally well, splitting the socialist vote. To move forward they had to unite, which was hard because each party accused the other of selling out, and neither was strong

enough to swallow the other. In 1875 the two parties merged at Gotha to form
the 25,000-member Socialist Workers Party of Germany, which changed its
name in 1890 to Sozialdemokratische Partei Deutschlands (SPD). The unity
platform in 1875 was Lassallean, not Marxist. At least that was how Marx characterized the Gotha Program, which advocated universal voting rights, civil
rights, a free state of the people, state-supported producer cooperatives, equal
distribution of the national product, and religious toleration.[2]

Marx raged against it, chastising the new party for capitulating to its reformist
flank. He was offended that the Gotha Program contained none of his analysis
of capitalism and nothing about revolution or the class character of the state.
He was furious at Liebknecht, his personal link to German Social Democracy,
who had to bear Marx's anger for months afterward, hoping to be vindicated.
Marx said it was pathetic for socialists to rattle on about a "free state" and their
support of democratic rights, direct legislation, and religious freedom. Marx
supported democratic rights and religious freedom, but these were secondary
issues for a revolutionary movement, and revolutionaries did *not* conceive the
state as an independent entity possessing its own freedom and ethical basis.
They did not give priority to bourgeois issues or dream of setting the state free
or cater to the anxieties of liberals or monarchists. Marx countered that true
freedom consists in converting the state from an organ superimposed upon
society into an organ completely subordinate to society. States are free exactly
to the extent they curtail the freedom of the state. The Gotha Program confirmed to Marx that the Lassalleans were "not even skin-deep" socialists. So-
called democratic socialism addressed its demands to something called "the
present-day state," a fiction existing nowhere. Marx said states were as numerous as the many "civilized" countries. What they held in common was that all
were based on modern bourgeois society.[3]

This reading was faulty as history and analysis. Nearly every specific demand
about rights and liberties in the Gotha Program came straight from the
Eisenacher platform written by Liebknecht. Moreover, the Gotha Program's
emphasis on a free people's state was a bedrock demand of the Eisenach party,
not a concession to a sellout Lassalle party. The Lassalle party, to be sure, based
its socialism on political democracy, emphasized reform issues, and reeked of
Lassalle's Hegelian cult of the state—the state as the guardian of order and high
culture. But the free state issue mattered more to the South German base of the
Eisenach party than to the Lassalleans. The South German labor organizations
in the Eisenach party had a strong case of *Preussenhass*—hatred of Prussia.
They were anti-Prussians first and socialists second. The Lassalleans sought
to achieve socialism by uniting the proletariat and the state against liberals.

The Eisenachers sought to achieve socialism by uniting the proletariat and the liberal bourgeoisie against the state. Many Eisenachers prized their region's independent farming ethos and believed that Marx and Engels were wrong about constantly worsening misery. They rejected the Marxist line on abolishing private ownership of land and resisted his fixation with factories and the industrial proletariat. Thus even Liebknecht's aspiring "Marxist" party had a non-Marxian base, and Liebknecht's Marxism was practical and selective, as Marx knew.[4]

Marx had to look past all of that to say that Lassallean reformism was the problem at Gotha. He said it forcefully because everything was at stake at Gotha. The uniting Gotha socialists failed to conceive the existing society as the basis of the many existing states, so they failed to say what genuine socialism was about: abolishing bourgeois society to make way for a communist society that abolishes classes, state domination, and alienation. Marx tried to push the new party further toward Marxism than either party had been previously. Nearly every subsequent debate about Marxism cut to an argument about what that meant and how one should think about it.

MARXIAN ECONOMICS AND REVOLUTION

The Gotha Program united the two German socialist parties eight years after Marx published the first volume of his masterwork, *Capital: A Critique of Political Economy*, and two years after he published its second edition. He never completed volumes 2 and 3, so, in everyday discourse, volume 1 became *Capital*. The Eisenachers had only one leader, Liebknecht, who came from Marx's generation and knew Marx personally. Liebknecht conveyed to his comrades what Marx believed about Lassalle and his legacy: Lassalle cribbed Marx's ideas, sometimes plagiarized Marx without acknowledgment, refashioned Marxism for existing German society, and sold out the proletarian revolution. Liebknecht and Bebel sympathized with Marx on these points, without believing that Marx was always right. They coped with messy historical realities that Marx dismissed, especially the worldview of South German unionists whom Bebel recruited to socialism. They also regretted Marx's obscurity. For most of his career Marx poured out articles and books that academics, middlebrow critics, and the general public ignored. Then in the early 1870s he began to win some attention, although he protested that reviewers almost never got him right.

The preface to the second edition of *Capital* put it vividly. Marx recalled that when his massive masterwork appeared in 1867, German intellectuals tried to kill it by ignoring it, just as "they had managed to do with my earlier writings."

In 1871 a political economist at the University of Kiev, A. Sieber, noted that Marx amplified the Smith–Ricardo theory of value and capital, and the following year a Russian edition of *Capital* was published. That exhausted Marx's list of hopeful portents, aside from his meager following in the dying First International. Marx owed his few reviews in nonsocialist publications to his socialist following, a point of pride and frustration to him. He lamented that political economics was a "foreign science" in Germany, where capitalism had a delayed beginning and the professors "remained schoolboys." Thus *Capital* got shallow reviews complaining that the book was dry, long, cumbersome, and boring. Most reviewers failed even to recognize that he had adopted the deductive method of the Smith–Ricardo English school.[5]

One reviewer, catching Marx's favorable reference to Hegel, admonished that the Hegel vogue was long past and Marx needed to get his clock fixed. Marx set the record straight. Yes, he was a protégé of Hegel, "that mighty thinker," because Hegelian dialecticism was powerfully important to him. Hegel recovered and refashioned an indispensable form of ancient Greek thought, he rightly put conflict and negation at the heart of all things, and Marx employed distinctly Hegelian tropes in his theory of value. But Marx contended that his dialectic was the opposite of Hegel's. To Hegel, ideas were ultimate reality, and real things were exemplifications of ideas. Marx said Hegel's idealism turned everything upside down. Hegel fashioned the life-process of the human brain—the process of thinking—into an independent subject, which Marx called "the demiurgos of the real world." To Marx, "the ideal is nothing else than the material world reflected by the human mind, and translated into forms of thought."[6]

Marx had judged in his early intellectual career that Hegel's celebrated philosophy enabled German academics to glorify their own culture and society. Thirty years later intellectual fashions had changed, and Marx told "peevish, arrogant, mediocre" intellectuals they had no reason to look down on Hegel, a colossal thinker who got crucial things right. Hegelian dialecticism was vastly superior to the simplistic worldview that German academics took from English economists. Hegel grasped that everything is in motion, everything has a transient nature and a momentary existence, and thus the ever-fluid process of life "is in its essence critical and revolutionary." On the other hand, it was terribly important to repudiate what came from Hegelians who ignored Hegelian negation and/or couldn't get religious idealism out of their heads. Marx boasted that he managed it fresh out of graduate school. Hegel stood the dialectic on its head; Marx turned it on its feet and thereby discovered "the rational kernel within the mystical shell." Both claimed to be scientific in the sense of German *Wissenschaft*—a systematic body of knowledge in which objectively necessary relationships are established—but the early Marx better earned the name by showing that Hegel's puffed-up talk about civil (*bügerlich*) society abstracted from its class character as *bourgeois* society.[7]

Capital came late in Marx's career, and it needed many years afterward to grow into its career as the basis of Marxism—a fundamental critique of capitalist political economy. It expounded a labor theory of value and capital that amplified Ricardo's labor theory of price, with a radically different upshot, and a theory of capital, surplus value, and exploitation that expounded what was at stake in the proletarian struggle. The book's first three chapters summarized the theory of value and money that Marx developed in *A Contribution to the Critique of Political Economy* (1859), which settled his previous uncertainty about whether alienation is primarily a by-product of commodity production per se or the appropriation of the product by capitalists. The early Marx seesawed on this question, but in *Contribution* he argued that capitalist appropriation is the crux of the matter.

His thought reversed the logic and history of classical economics. Marx began, like Smith and Ricardo, with the concepts of supply and demand, competition, and the market. But unlike classical theory Marx did not move into quantitative formulas about market relations and the flow of exchange value. He applied Hegelian dialecticism to economics, seeking to reveal the essential-whatever behind the phenomenal appearances of market relations. Marx's pursuit of this post-Kantian project led him to examine production and relations of production, first generally and then specifically under capitalism. *Contribution* was the overture to *Capital*. Marx scrapped his first introduction to *Contribution*, explained that it was pointless "to anticipate results which still have to be substantiated," and substituted the only summary of his philosophy he ever published: Human beings enter relations of production in the social production of their experience that correspond with a given stage of economic development and that are independent of their will. The totality of these relations of production constitutes the "real foundation" of society, "on which arises a legal and political superstructure with corresponding forms of social consciousness. The mode of production of material life conditions the general process of social, political, and intellectual life." Social existence determines consciousness; philosophies and ideologies rationalize economic interests; and no social order is ever destroyed "before all the productive forces for which it is sufficient have been developed."[8]

The tight summaries of the preface provided proof texts for vulgar Marxists for decades to come. Had Marx stuck with his ambivalence about preface summarizing he might have inspired much less vulgar Marxism. *Contribution* plunged immediately into its gritty, detailed, demystifying business, analyzing capital in general. It began with commodities and commodity production, distinguished between use value and exchange value, and developed an analysis of money as a universal measure of value and medium of exchange. It favored Ricardo over Smith because Ricardo emphasized the problem of production. Marx argued in *Contribution* that exchange relations—the appearances of the market—express the *social* relations of labor activity and the division of labor that fundamentally constitute society itself. Under feudalism, capital consisted mostly of tools and secondarily of money capital, retaining an agrarian character. Under capitalism, the reverse took place. Agriculture became largely a branch of industry, dominated by capital. The same thing happened to rent.

Put differently, in sociological concepts reaching back to Marx's earliest work, in precapitalist societies the relation of laborers to their work was transparent and often more natural and human than under capitalism, though Marx did not conceive slavery and serfdom as being either human or natural. The crucial difference was that human relations in precapitalist societies were undisguised throughout the process of production, exchange, and consumption. Under capitalism, the same relations were veiled through institutions shrewdly dubbed the "free market" and "private property." Relations between people were replaced by what appeared to be relations between things. Marx's unwieldy name for this process, *Verdinglichung*, had no English equivalent; translators usually opted for "reification." The problem of alienation is distinctive to capitalist society, he contended. To be sure, "natural relations" still exist in capitalist society wherever landed property remains the decisive factor. But wherever capital predominates, it changes everything: "Capital is the economic power that dominates everything in bourgeois society. It must form both the point of departure and the conclusion and it has to be expounded before landed property. After analyzing capital and landed property separately, their interconnection must be examined."[9]

Marx got that far in *Contribution*, which summarized parts of his sprawling unpublished notebooks of 1857–58, *Grundrisse der Kritik der Politischen Oekonomie*. He had worked out his method and the gist of his argument but needed a deeper base of evidence for his challenge to classical theory. That required nearly another decade of work. Engels announced that Germans finally had a great political economist, one who, on the basis of *Contribution* alone, already surpassed Smith and Ricardo. Moreover, *Contribution* was just "the first result" of ongoing work. Engels defied readers to compare Marx to Smith: "Anyone wishing to find a striking instance of the fact that the German dialectic method at its present stage of development is at least as superior to the old superficially glib metaphysical method as railways are to the medieval means of transport, should look up Adam Smith or any other authoritative economist of repute to see how much distress exchange value and use value caused these gentlemen, the difficulty they had in distinguishing the two properly and in expressing the determinate form peculiar to each, and then compare the clear, simple exposition given by Marx."[10]

Textbook economics treated the behavior of money as the essence of economic activity. Commodities are objects of human want and need, all societies turn commodities into money and back again in a circular flow of exchange value, and economics tracks the flow of money in satisfying human needs and wants. *Contribution* explored Marx's seemingly simple question about where the value of a commodity comes from in order to show, as Marx argued powerfully in *Capital*, that the capitalist system of production and exchange is contradictory and oppressive, rendering human labor literally inhuman by turning commodities into fetishes. Marx spurned commonsense presumptions that money originated in circulation or that capitalists buy commodities below their value or sell them above their value. Common sense was superficial—and wrong. Capitalists buy and sell commodities at their value, but somewhere they withdraw more value from circulation than they put into it. The answer to the riddle lay in the process of production itself, which makes it structural and objective, not a function of something subjective, like a desire.

He distinguished between the use value of a commodity (a property intrinsic to the commodity) and its exchange value (the value relative to other commodities in an exchange situation), asking how it could be that commodities with different use values were measured in the same units. Ricardo developed a cost of production theory of value, not a simple labor theory in which the cost of production and the value of a product were the same thing. But in *Principles of Economy and Taxation* (1817), Ricardo seemed to endorse the simple theory, declaring that the value of a commodity "depends on the relative quantity of labor which is necessary for its production, and not on the greater or less compensation which is paid for that labor." Economists interpreted Ricardo as a proponent of the simple labor theory, and Marx began with it: The price of a commodity represents the labor that goes into it. Or, formally: The universal measure for value, expressed as money, corresponds to the amount of labor time that goes into the making of a commodity. Commodities holding different use values have only one thing in common, the amount of labor time that goes into making them. Thus labor time is the only criterion by which commodities with different use values are comparable in exchange situations. The value of a commodity consists in the socially necessary labor that is expended upon it, measured by time.[11]

Marx cautioned against the appearance that commodities are readily understood. Use values, he allowed, such as making a table out of wood, are not mysterious, and neither are the determining factors of value, which are functions of
human organisms. The exchange process, however, turns a commodity into "a
very queer thing, abounding in metaphysical subtleties and theological niceties."
Marx's famous theory of commodity fetishism built on this insight. Commodities
are mysterious because they stamp the social character of human labor upon the
product of labor *as an objective character,* and they present the relation of the
producers to the sum total of their labor as a social relationship *between the products of their labor,* not between the producers. Capitalism renders the social
relations between who makes what, who works for whom, and the production
time required to make a commodity as economic relations between objects—
the value of a given commodity when compared to another commodity. The
market exchange of commodities thus obscures the actual human relations of
production, "social things whose qualities are at the same time perceptible and
imperceptible by the senses." Perception, Marx reasoned, requires a physical
relationship between physical things. An actual passage of light occurs between
an external object and the optic nerve of an eye. But there is absolutely "no connection" between the physical things that become commodities and their labor-
produced value, on the one hand, and the physical nature of the commodity and
material relations arising out of the exchange process, on the other.[12]

Marx called commodity fetishism "the fantastic form of a relation between
things." To find an analogy, one had to take flight into the misty world of religion, where productions of the human brain appeared as really existing individuals who interacted with human beings. Commodity fetishism was very
much like religion: "This I call the Fetishism which attaches itself to the
products of labor, so soon as they are produced as commodities, and which is
therefore inseparable from the production of commodities." Capital is more
expansive than commodities, Marx argued, because all manner of societies at
various stages of economic development created commodities. The barter system began with a social division of labor that separated use value from exchange
value. Capitalism, however, rests on historical conditions that were not given
with the mere circulation of money and commodities. Capitalism sprang into
life only when an owner of the means of production and subsistence engaged a
laborer in the market selling his or her labor power: "And this one historical
condition comprises a world's history. Capital therefore announces from its first
appearance a new epoch in the process of social production."[13]

Though *Capital* credited Ricardo with the labor theory of value, Marx
blasted Ricardo and his school for blithely assuming surplus value. Ricardo took

for granted that surplus value is inherent in the capitalist mode of production, and his successors reduced economic activity to the behavior of money. Marx countered that production and exchange are social institutions. Monetary values obscure the complex social aspects of commodities because the entire production of commodities is a social process that depends on an exploitative system of production and exchange.

Basically Marx accused economists of screening out most of their subject, capitalism—a social system of intense accumulation of commodities. Though Ricardo rightly identified labor productivity as the originating cause of surplus value—Marx's favored term for profit—Marx said the entire Ricardo school was conveniently incurious about how profits are generated. Surplus value, according to Marx, consists in the difference between the labor value of products and the payment for the labor *power* expended in production by workers. He found it amazing that John Stuart Mill, a half century after Ricardo, was no more curious than the Ricardo school about how surplus value works, even though Mill touted his superiority over the mercantile tradition. Marx put it sarcastically in Mill's case: "Strange optical illusion to see everywhere a state of things which as yet exist only exceptionally on our earth." The fact that Mill added Social Democratic elements to later editions of his work made it more pitiful to Marx because Mill still assumed the Smith–Ricardo model of economic activity. Marx countered that all precapitalist systems conceived money as a means of exchanging some commodities for others: commodity–money–commodity. Capitalism turns money into something else: capital, to be sought for its own sake. Capitalism is about money being used to obtain more money: money–commodity–money. Capitalists cared about accumulating capital, not about people or making things, and to accrue their capital they bought the labor power of vulnerable workers and exploited it.[14]

Smith, upon naming capitalism and launching classical economics, defined capital as the command over labor. Marx said that was half right, as capital is essentially and more importantly the command over unpaid labor. All surplus value, whether deriving from profit, interest, or rent, is in substance "the materialization of unpaid labor." The value of labor power is determined by the value of the necessities of life "habitually required by the average laborer," and the secret of the self-expansion of capital lay in quite specific social processes that classical economists ignored. When Smith and Ricardo discussed the value of labor, Marx said, they reversed and obliterated what was actually at issue. To invoke the value of labor as an abstract concept is no more meaningful than to invoke the value of the earth. The real value of labor arises from relations of production, which are categories for the "phenomenal forms of essential relations." Marx chided that every science except economics recognized that things in their appearances often represent themselves in inverted forms. Classical economists, by contrast, carried on the old physiocrat doctrine of a "necessary price," rephrased by Smith as the "natural price" of labor, a commodity value expressed in money. Marx countered that what economists called the value of labor is in fact the value of the labor power of a human personality—a value as different from its laboring function as a machine is different from the work it performs.[15]

In precapitalist economies the instruments of labor in artisan workshops, among individual peasants, and to some degree in early mercantile enterprises belonged to the producer. Marx said capitalism changed the world by turning scattered, individually owned means of production into powerful levers of production. This process had three phases, starting with simple cooperation, moving to manufacturing, and culminating in modern industry. But the crucial point was that the transformation of individual instruments of labor into mighty productive forces turned the means of production into *social* means of production. Products became social products, joint productions of laborers operating machinery workable only by collectivities. Capitalism socialized the producers, the means of production, and the products, yet bourgeois society treated all three as though nothing had changed; the means of production and products still belonged to individuals.

Capitalism abolished the conditions upon which individual owners owned their own products and brought them to market, but it allowed owners of the means of production to appropriate the products of labor to themselves, notwithstanding that others did the producing and created the value. This contradiction is unsustainable, Marx contended; it is the key to the crisis of capitalist civilization. The more the capitalist class attains mastery over the many fields of production through the new mode of production, the more it reduces individual production to marginal status. Capitalists socialize production without socializing appropriation. They get away with it by firing troublemakers, thwarting unions, holding down wages, rewarding compliant lawmakers, and maintaining an industrial reserve army of unemployed workers. The latter concept inspired one of Marx's most colorful passages in *Capital*: "This antagonism vents its rage in the creation of that monstrosity, an industrial reserve army, kept in misery in order to be always at the disposal of capital; in the incessant human sacrifices from among the working class, in the most reckless squandering of labor-power, and in the devastation caused by a social anarchy which turns every economical progress into a social calamity."[16]

Capital brimmed with bristling asides about famous apologists of England's capitalist ascendancy. Marx said economist F. M. Eden was the only eighteenth-century disciple of Smith worth reading. He said Ricardo's disciples were wretchedly evasive "vulgarizers" whose recycled nostrums perfectly fit the "imbecile flatness" of the bourgeoisie. Thomas Malthus, a mediocre parson scribbler, was wrongly famous for warning about population trends. Marx said Malthus plagiarized better writers such as economist James Steuart, he unfortunately lured many parsons to scribble about population doom, and they unfortunately did not apply this obsession to themselves, breeding large families of future parsons. Bernard de Mandeville had a shaky reputation for contending in *The Fable of the Bees* (1714) that a growing society needs a large multitude of people who remain mired in abject poverty despite working very hard. Marx, however, prized Mandeville as an "honest, clear-headed man" who understated his thesis, having witnessed capitalism in its early eighteenth-century germination. Mandeville did not grasp, Marx said, that the process of accumulation increases the laboring poor masses along with capital. Repeatedly Marx said the accumulation of capital at one pole corresponds with an accumulation of misery and brutality at the other pole. He said it so emphatically that orthodox Marxists were stuck with it, although Engels played it down after witnessing the capitalist boom of the 1880s and early 1890s.[17]

The capitalist mode of appropriation is a consequence of the capitalist mode of production, which produces capitalist private property. Marx said it in the language and method of Hegelian dialectics, describing the production of capitalist private property as the "first negation" of individual private property. Capitalist production always begets its own negation: "It is the negation of negation." Capitalism does not reestablish private property in a modernized form for the producer. It *gives* individual property to the capitalist from the social bounty of modern expropriation and accumulation. Marx seethed at the "effrontery" of capitalist apologists who employed the language of freedom to describe wage slavery and "the despotism of capital." He stressed that the transformation of individual private property into capitalist private property was a far more wrenching, violent, and protracted process than the current struggle to transform capitalistic private property into socialized property. Capitalism, after all, expropriated the mass of the people "by a few usurpers." The proletarian revolution expropriated a few usurpers for the sake of the many.[18]

But socialism needed real socialists, not reformers like the Lassalle democrats. Just before the Gotha Program united the two socialist parties, Marx wrote to Liebknecht, Bebel, Wilhelm Bracke, and other Eisenacher comrades. He recalled that Lassalle knew the *Communist Manifesto* by heart, and he knew what he was doing. Lassalle modified Marxian socialism to make it fit into existing German society. He attacked the capitalist class but not the landowners, and he introduced pet phrases about "the proceeds of labor" and "a fair distribution" that watered down the real thing. Then the Gotha Program featured these ideas. Marx said the former phrase was purposely evasive, since the proceeds of labor might be the product of labor or its value, and if the latter it might be the total value of the product or merely the part of the value that labor added to the value of something produced. As for fairness, every liberal crowed about being fair. The idea of "fair distribution" reeked of the self-serving bourgeois view that economic relations are regulated by legal conceptions, contrary to the Marxist view that all legal relations arise from economic arrangements.[19]

That was a deadly retrogression to bourgeois economics, Marx protested. He called it "vulgar socialism." It was a terrible mistake to feature the idea of fair distribution in a socialist program because doing so capitulated to the bourgeois assumption that the distribution issue is independent of the mode of production. Marx countered that any distribution of the means of consumption is never more or less than a consequence of the distribution of the conditions of production. Moreover, the distribution of the conditions of production is always a feature of the mode of production. In capitalist production the material conditions of production belong to nonworkers, the owners of capital and land, while the working masses own only their labor power. Grossly unequal distribution is a by-product of the system, not the issue that matters. Marx yearned for a movement that straightforwardly proclaimed what the revolution was about and that galvanized the working masses to abolish capitalist society. Instead Lassalle polluted the movement with "ideological nonsense about right and other trash so common among the democrats and French socialists."[20]

Once capitalist society was eliminated, Marx said, a transition period leading to a communist society would occur, just as the *Communist Manifesto* proclaimed. No one could say what functions the state would need to retain or adopt during the transition. He even suggested that no one could say what functions the state might need to perform in communist society. But politically, during the transition, "the state can be nothing but the revolutionary dictatorship of the proletariat." Marx recycled his most notorious concept to accentuate his opposition to reformist socialism. In his view it accomplished nothing whatsoever to combine the word "people" with the word "state." The Lassallean socialists blathered about voting rights because they didn't want to seem threatening to liberals and democrats, they opposed middle-class liberals while playing a liberal game, they prized their seven seats in the National Assembly, and they wanted very much not to get thrown into prison. Thus they carefully assured that they operated within the existing state, the Prussian–German Empire. Marx taunted them for lacking decency and a spine—demanding things that meant something only in a democratic republic. Their nation was a "police-guarded military despotism," so their boasts about being liberal and democratic were meaningless, aside from conveying that they were no threat to anybody.[21]

It galled Marx that his labors had yielded so little—a workers' party that bragged of its feckless liberal democracy. He protested that the Lassalle group employed the words "equality" and "democracy" as magic wands that somehow redeemed everything they touched. He charged that the Free Trade party had an "infinitely" higher internationalism than the Gotha Program, which reduced internationalism to the moralistic shibboleth of the bourgeois League of Peace and Freedom, "the international brotherhood of peoples." He accused the Lassalleans of reducing socialism to the plea that slavery should be abolished because the feeding of slaves under slavery should not exceed "a certain low maximum." He ridiculed the Lassalleans for adopting bourgeois newspaper twaddle about "the social question" and its "solution," a pathetic substitute for the revolutionary transformation of society. Thanks to "Lassalle's imagination," the Gotha Program proposed to build a new society with state loans for producer cooperatives, a sop borrowed from Buchez that Marx said was too ridiculous to merit a refutation. Lassalle's devotion to state-supported producer cooperatives reduced a class movement to sectarian reformism, and his group's pious advocacy of "equal elementary education" was equally ridiculous, a leveling concept that would not work in capitalist society.[22]

"Freedom of conscience" played a similar role in the Gotha Program. Marx paused for a rare one-sentence concession, mindful that Bismarck's *Kulturkampf* against the Catholic Church was ongoing. Bismarck distrusted the loyalty of Catholics to Prussia, and in 1870 the declaration of papal infallibility at Vatican Council I confirmed his distrust. The following year Bismarck abolished the Catholic bureau in the Prussian Ministry of Culture and forbade priests from voicing political opinions in the pulpit. Marx said if German socialists were determined to be liberals on religious freedom and nice to Catholics in particular, they might say that everyone "should be able to attend to his religious as well as his bodily needs without the police sticking their noses in." That was Marx's approach. Instead the Gotha Program framed the religion issue under a sacred cow principle, freedom of conscience. Marx countered that a workers' party needed to condemn the evils of religion, not emphasize the freedom to be a religious idiot. The party needed to express its "awareness of the fact that bourgeois 'freedom of conscience' is nothing but the toleration of all possible kinds of religious freedom of conscience, and that for its part it endeavors rather to liberate the conscience from the witchery of religion." All religions are backward, reactionary, and stupefying, stripping people of their human dignity and power. The party needed to say so, without transgressing the bourgeois toleration of religion. Overall, Marx said, the Gotha Program, "for all its democratic clang, is tainted through and through by the Lassallean sect's servile belief in the state, or, what is no better, by a democratic belief in miracles, or rather it is a compromise between these two kinds of belief in miracles, both equally remote from socialism."[23]

Marx's *Critique of the Gotha Program* is one of the major texts of the Marxist canon. The First International was on its deathbed in 1875, and Marx held a low view of every party in it. Building a revolutionary movement in Germany was crucial to him; thus he skewered the Gotha Program as a pathetic concession to the liberal opportunism of the Lassalle party, conveniently overlooking that the Eisenachers had just as many non-Marxist convictions. When Bismarck created the Reich, there were seven Lassalleans in the North German Reichstag (led by party leader Wilhelm Hasenclever) and two Eisenachers (Liebknecht and Bebel). Bismarck founded the Reich on his dream of an alliance between Prussia's military aristocracy and the German bourgeoisie. That was hard to pull off, especially because he despised liberals. Harder yet was to imagine how he would keep the working class productive, loyal, and obedient. Socialism was a response to the wretched condition of a denigrated working class in a rapidly industrializing society, but the two socialist parties operated very differently in the Reichstag. The Lassalleans worked for lesser evils in the government, touted their Prussian nationalism, and played down rumors that Lassalle colluded with Bismarck back at the founding. The Eisenachers treated the Reichstag as a platform for proletarian declamation and derided Lassallean patriotism. Thus the Lassalleans voted to support the Franco-Prussian War of 1870–1871 and the Eisenachers abstained, refusing to support the war, ostensibly regardless of who started it. Liebknecht and Bebel believed that King Wilhelm I of Prussia started the war to unite Germany as a nation-state and create a German Empire, which happened on May 10, 1871. Afterward the entire socialist bloc in the National Assembly called for peace and opposed the annexation of French territory, Alsace-Lorraine (Reichsland Elsaß-Lothringen). Bebel dramatically declared in the Reichstag that real German socialists sympathized with the Paris Commune and the entire European proletariat.[24]

That was an electrifying moment for German socialism. It set off a surge into the Eisenacher party and got Bebel and Liebknecht thrown into prison for two years for treason. Liebknecht, on his way to prison, declared, with customary dramatic flair, "I am not the degraded adventurer that my calumniator would make of me. . . . I have never sought my own personal advantage. . . . I am not a professional conspirator; I am not a knight-errant of subversion. But I should have no objection to your terming me a soldier of the revolution." In 1874, upon leaving prison, Liebknecht and Bebel were promptly reelected to the Reichstag. To a surging socialist base, they were heroes for defying the ruling class and suffering for it. Now the socialists had to unite; it was absurd to keep splitting the socialist vote. At least, Liebknecht thought it was absurd. Bebel chafed at the prospect of uniting with Lassalleans, and so did Engels. Engels told Bebel it was better to uphold Marxist principles than to unite with a non-Marxist party that sold out the revolution. The founding of a united German Social Democracy and what became the SPD was remarkably astute, brave, and strategic in that context. It was a counterword to the militaristic gore of a triumphant new empire *and* a resolute calculation, principally by Liebknecht, that uniting the socialist movement was more important than satisfying Marx and Engels. Once they stopped splitting the vote, they could argue about ideology as comrades and perhaps agree about how to be revolutionary and reformist at the same time.[25]

Liebknecht was born to a Hessian public official, studied theology and philosophy at Berlin and Marburg, got in trouble during the revolution of 1848, and spent the 1850s in exile in London, where he forged a close alliance with Marx. In 1862 he took the amnesty for 1848 revolutionaries and joined Lassalle's party in Berlin, coediting its journal, published by von Schweitzer. He clashed with von Schweitzer and Lassalle, however, over the party's friendly relationship with the new minister-president, Bismarck. Liebknecht refused to publish a letter from Bismarck, resigned from the journal, and eventually resigned from the party in 1865. He spoke against Bismarck at public labor meetings and got expelled from Berlin. He moved to Hannover and then Leipzig, making a spare living off lectures and writing. He met Bebel, a fiery wood turner by trade who was fourteen years younger than Liebknecht.

Bebel was born in a Prussian military barracks in Cologne and hardened by many years of abject poverty, traveling in search of work. He converted to socialism by reading Lassalle but quit the Lassalle party in 1867 after meeting Liebknecht. Liebknecht was a radical intellectual, a nature lover, a commanding speaker and writer with a racy, avuncular, dramatic style of expression, and a forceful personality, but he was not good at anything practical. Bebel became his lieutenant; later he recalled that Liebknecht liked to force matters and stir things up, so Bebel spent years eating the soup that Liebknecht stirred. Bebel bristled, however, when comrades said that Liebknecht converted him to Marxism because Bebel read *Capital* as soon as it came out, whereas Liebknecht never bothered. Still, Bebel allowed that absorbing Liebknecht's stump speeches made Marx comprehensible to him. In 1859 he had tried to read

Marx's *Contribution* and completely failed. Eight years later he and Liebknecht founded a people's party in Saxony. In 1869, when Liebknecht and Bebel founded the Eisenacher party, it was a very modest beginning. Six years later they led a union of two surging socialist parties.[26]

In 1877 the united Social Democrats polled 494,000 votes, more than 9 percent of the total, electing a dozen members to the Reichstag. There should have been more seats but Bismarck gerrymandered the electoral districts, favoring agrarian areas. Still, the election made the Social Democrats the fourth biggest party in the nation, and Bismarck struggled to contain the socialist contagion. He proposed an antisocialist bill in 1878, which was defeated by a coalition of Progressives and left-flank National Liberals. Two failed attempts by deranged attackers to assassinate Emperor Wilhelm I gave Bismarck a pretext to try again. He dissolved the Reichstag, called for new elections, played the fear card, and got a more compliant National Assembly. The Progressive Party, (Catholic) Center Party, and Social Democrats voted against the new antisocialist bill, and Germany's two conservative parties supported it. Fatefully, the National Liberal Party supported it, after a bitter fight that decimated the party's left flank. Socialists were banned from holding meetings, distributing literature, and organizing unions and cooperatives. Even socialist glee clubs were outlawed.[27]

Bismarck said these new socialists were a menace, unlike Lassalle. For fifteen years Bismarck had sought to create a parliament of propertied stakeholders who depended on the state and him. He wanted to impose protective tariffs and create state monopolies, but liberals stood in his way, preaching limited government, self-help, free trade, and political freedom. Eduard Lasker, leader of the National Liberal Party's left wing, tormented Bismarck in the National Assembly. Then the founding of the German Reich and the rise of right-wing liberalism changed the political calculus. The liberal right was nationalistic and imperialist, it grew anxious about the seeming plague of Social Democrats and politicized Catholics, it boasted prominent intellectuals such as political historian Heinrich von Treitschke and philosopher Rudolph Haym, and some right-liberals pulled back from universal suffrage in the National Assembly. Treitschke bailed out on universal suffrage in 1874, declaring that it empowered irrationality over intelligence, soldiers over officers, and workers over employers. Three years later Haym said the same thing, describing Germany as a besieged fortress. This was the siege mentality that backed Bismarck's attacks on socialists and Catholics. Republican government was an instrument of Bismarck's rule. In the early going socialist leaders hoped that liberals would regroup and reassert their liberalism, defying Bismarck. Most liberals held fast to universal suffrage for the Reichstag, and many still favored its extension to the state and local levels. But standing up for the rights of socialists was otherwise not in play for the new mainstream of the National Liberal Party, and its left flank bolted the party in 1881.[28]

For twelve years the socialists were hounded, persecuted, and repressed by the government, unsuccessfully. They forged a unified party that thrived on persecution and crisis, and they became stronger Marxists. Liebknecht and Bebel bravely defied Bismarck in the Reichstag but carefully refrained from breaking any laws. Both were immensely able—gifted at speaking extemporaneously, firing off articles at a moment's notice, and inspiring socialists to hang together. Both said there was no real socialism without democracy and no real democracy without socialism. Marx and Engels cheered for them admiringly, while fretting constantly that German socialists were prone to reformism, enjoying their perches in the Reichstag too much. Prussia's three-class franchise consigned almost the entire working class to the third class, outnumbered in voting power by the two higher classes, even though class three vastly outnumbered the other two combined. The right and left flanks of German Social Democracy had perennial internal battles over how much time and energy they should devote to electoral politics. During the years of persecution, however, the party could not meet to debate the issue, and Bebel became its dominant leader, defining the party with his fiery militancy.[29]

The years of persecution heightened the party's antireligious image. Many Social Democrats had retained at least nominal ties to religious communities, and the party did not pressure them to leave. That changed under the antisocialist repression. Social Democrats renounced their ties to Christian and Jewish religious institutions, making antireligious pronouncements at secret congresses in Switzerland, Denmark, and St. Gall. In public they stuck to a scripted two-track approach to religion, in Marx's fashion. Always they said that religion was a private matter and that Social Democracy would not abolish anyone's right to be religious. Liebknecht wrote the script: "The Social Democracy as such has absolutely nothing to do with religion. Every man has the right to think and believe what he will and no one has the right to molest or limit another in his thoughts or beliefs." This assurance jostled uneasily, however, with Liebknecht's other belief about religion: "It is our duty as socialists to root out the faith in God with all our zeal, nor is anyone worthy of the name who does not concentrate himself to the spread of atheism. . . . Socialism must conquer the stupidity of the masses in so far as this stupidity reveals itself in religious forms and dogmas." Bebel was equally quotable on the latter theme: "Christianity is the enemy of liberty and civilization. It has kept mankind in slavery and oppression. The Church and State have always fraternally united to exploit the people. Christianity and socialism are like fire and water." On this basis Social Democrats disavowed any interest in making alliances with religious socialists or religious anything, and church leaders gave it right back, condemning Social Democracy as an anti-God, anti-German, anticivilization menace. In 1881 Bebel declared in the Reichstag that Social Democracy was republican in politics, socialist in economics, and atheist in religion.[30]

Young party stalwart Eduard Bernstein reflected the drama of this period and contributed mightily to it. He was born in January 1850 in Berlin, just as the mighty postrevolutionary backlash in Germany unfolded. Bernstein's family tree had numerous rabbis, physicians, mathematicians, and other high achievers, his father was a locomotive driver, and his parents attended the Reform Temple on the Johannistrasse, where services were held on Sunday. One of his uncles, Aaron Bernstein, was a prominent liberal journalist and religious reformer. Bernstein was schooled at a gymnasium until the age of sixteen and took a job as a bank clerk. He renounced Judaism on the day after his mother died, and in 1871 he cheered for Liebknecht and Bebel during the Franco-Prussian War. Then he was repulsed when Liebknecht and Bebel were convicted of treason. Bernstein studied up on the Eisenachers and Lassalleans, converting to socialism by reading Lassalle and popular intellectual crank Eugen Dühring. He joined the Eisenacher party in 1872, mostly out of hero worship, still knowing hardly anything about Marxism.

Bernstein learned his socialist theory in the movement, lecture touring for the Eisenach party. His winsome sincerity helped him play a unifying role at the Gotha conference. In August 1878, while Bismarck campaigned to outlaw socialism, Social Democratic patron and *Die Zukunft* publisher Karl Höchberg asked Bernstein to accompany him as his secretary on his foreign travels for the paper. Bernstein's activism had attracted attention from the police, and he had never seen a foreign country, aside from a vacation in Vienna as a teenager. So he eagerly accepted, clueless that this trip would exile him from Germany for twenty years. In Switzerland he befriended young Karl Kautsky and steeped himself in Marxist theory. He won over Engels, took over the Swiss version of the *Social Democrat*, and flooded Germany with twelve thousand weekly copies of the smuggled paper. Socialism surged in Germany. The Social Democrats made spectacular gains in nearly every industrial city and substantial gains in rural areas, winning 312,000 Reichstag votes in 1881, 550,000 in 1884, 763,000 in 1887, and 1,427,000 in 1890. By 1890 the renamed SPD held 20 percent of the National Assembly, making it the largest single party in Germany.[31]

Meanwhile the booms and busts of Germany's growing economy heightened its volatile political climate. A speculative bubble burst in 1873, throwing many out of work and their homes. Then came the great expansion of the 1880s, a boom exceeding England's because it came late and benefited from technology developed in England. Nearly all German socialists, except for a few leaders, were movement proletarians, a much smaller group than the following who voted socialist. However, the social dislocations wrought by Germany's capitalist boom created anticapitalists far beyond Germany's movement proletarian class. Antibourgeois conservatives wanted the state to wrest control over capitalist anarchy, Catholics remained loyal to unions affiliated with Social Democracy, and National Liberal leaders relied increasingly on the state to hold the nation together. Wilhelm Emmanuel von Ketteler's embattled successors in the Center Party got dramatic vindication in 1891, when *Rerum Novarum* condemned laissez-faire capitalism and atheistic socialism, defended trade unions, and asserted the right of the Catholic Church to act on its teaching about such things.[32]

Bismarck never broke the loyalty of Germany's large Catholic working class to struggling trade unions, most of which belonged to the SPD, and to Catholic political institutions, especially in the Rhineland. But he shrewdly co-opted some of the surging anticapitalist sentiment in Germany by creating a first-of-its-kind welfare state of state monopolies and social insurance, publicly embracing the state's responsibility to care for the poor and vulnerable. Health insurance came first, in 1883; accident insurance became law in 1884 and 1885; old age insurance was enacted in 1889. To Bismarck, social insurance adroitly made the working class dependent on the state, at a manageable financial cost, while thwarting full political rights and radical socialism. He lauded the historical economists, now called "State socialists," who contended that increasing the power and prosperity of the state was the best way to head off the bad kind of socialism. Historical economist Gustav von Schmoller was prominent in this cause, producing many disciples. They advocated government programs to ensure high employment, improve labor conditions, regulate the employment of women and children, equalize the distribution of wealth through taxation, nationalize the railways, and maintain a strong military. Schmoller and his protégés prized their respectability in German society, forging alliances with like-minded religious leaders.[33]

The leading figures in the latter group were eminent historical theologian Adolf von Harnack, pastor and court chaplain Adolf Stöcker, and church activist Friedrich Naumann. Young theologian Ernst Troeltsch, not yet renowned or involved in social issues, got his social Christian bearings by watching Harnack and Naumann. In 1890 the dramatic gains by socialists abruptly ended Bismarck's reign. He proposed to double down on repression, but the new emperor, Wilhelm II, judged that repression had already failed. Bismarck was forced to resign, and the emperor issued several decrees on social questions. He encouraged church leaders to defend the Reich's conservative welfare state. Harnack, Stöcker, and Naumann obliged him by founding the Evangelical Social Congress as a forum for German social Christianity.

GERMAN SOCIAL CHRISTIANITY

Harnack could see radical Christian socialism coming on the wing of the proletarian movement, which would not be good for Germany or modern Christianity. Already a prominent figure in theology for his prolific scholarship on Christian history, he became more so through the 1890s and early twentieth century as the epitome of Culture Protestant respectability. Harnack came to the church, academy, and German establishment by family tradition, although he had to struggle for the German part, in Russian territory. Born in 1851 in Dorpat (today Tartu), a Russian-majority town in Livonia (then a province in Russia, today in Estonia), Harnack belonged to the German-speaking Russian nationalist elite that ruled his hometown. He also belonged to the generation that witnessed the transformation of the North German Federation into the German Empire in 1871, which turned the Prussian king Wilhelm I into the German emperor, which was not quite the same thing (to the relief of Austrians, federated monarchs, and Swiss) as being emperor of Germany. Both of these identity markers cast a long shadow over Harnack's life and thought.[34]

The son of a church historian in Dorpat, Harnack belonged to a German aristocracy that fought off all encroachments on the superiority of German culture, politics, and religion. His brilliance whisked him from a teaching position at Marburg to a chair at Berlin, although he had to withstand an appointment controversy over his theology in 1888, the "year of three Emperors." The Supreme Council of the Evangelical Church vetoed Harnack's appointment to Berlin, declaring that he was too liberal to deserve a prestigious chair supported by the state. Emperor Friedrich died, leaving Emperor Wilhelm II and Chancellor Bismarck to decide whether church conservatives should prevail over the authority and prestige of the academy. Wilhelm II overruled the church office, tartly declaring that he wanted no bigots in his university. Harnack quickly became Kaiser Wilhelm's favorite academic. He spoke for the mainstream of the Evangelical Social Congress, which was academic in its ethos, evangelical-liberal in its theology, and more genteel than the group's factional wings.

Stöcker and Naumann led the two wings. Stöcker sought, at first, to lure the working class away from Social Democracy. He founded the Christian Social

Labor Party in 1878, served in the Reichstag for thirty years, revamped the Christian Social Party as a bourgeois outfit, and enthralled his conservative churchly following with emotional rhetoric. In his telling, Germany's precious Protestant heritage was under attack by Social Democrats, all of whom were Marxist wreckers: "Their god is the party, their sin is private ownership, their savior is revolution, their Kingdom is the *Volksstaat*." A court chaplain to the kaiser from 1874 to 1890, Stöcker sprinkled anti-Semitic asides into his speeches. Jew-bashing revved up his crowds like nothing else, so Stöcker relied on it increasingly in the 1890s, ramping up his following. In 1896 he quit the congress to form a conservative rival, the Church Social Conference. Naumann began as a Stöcker protégé but clashed with him when Stöcker gave up on the working class. Naumann's close friendship with Max Weber also played a role, for a while, in dissuading him from Stöcker's kaiser-veneration.[35]

In the early 1890s Naumann was the great hope that progressive social Christianity might amount to something in Germany. He published a weekly magazine that addressed labor issues, *Die Hilfe*. But in 1895 Naumann began to say that Germany needed a powerful national state more than anything else. To repel the Russians and hold off the Social Democrats, good socialism had to be nationalistic. Naumann scoffed at the fate of Christoph Friedrich Blumhardt, the first Lutheran pastor to join the SPD, who lost his career in the state church in 1899 for joining the SPD. Increasingly, church people annoyed Naumann, being too squishy and moralistic for him. He cheered for Germany's military build-up that began in 1905, winning election to the Reichstag two years later. Naumann was an early exponent of national existentialism, a trope with a toxic future in Germany. By August 1914 he was a full-fledged monarchist and imperialist, with a liberal veneer. During the war he gave forceful proannexation speeches, and in 1919 he cofounded the German Democratic Party, serving briefly as its president before his death the same year.

Holding together a congress flanked by Stöcker and Naumann was politically taxing from the beginning. Harnack pulled it off by stressing, with characteristic self-confidence, that his mannered, civil, academic, mildly churchy, liberally evangelical approach was the best one for the congress. Harnack respected the moral power in Social Democracy and the fact that it resonated with many clerics. He said that Christian socialists were mostly right about capitalist ideology, which he called "Manchesterism." Any gospel-centered civilization had to curb the worst abuses of its economic order. The abuses of modern industrial society were no exception. But Harnack added that the gospel of Jesus was above politics, focusing on the moral and spiritual character of individuals. Moreover, there had to be a third way between radical socialism and its opposite, British and American capitalism. In his telling, these were the twin concerns of German social Christianity. It had a social conscience but focused on individual morality. It left policy questions to experts and denied that the church had any business trying to transform the social order.

Harnack's address to the 1894 Evangelical Social Congress was a milestone in the group's history and collective identity. The SPD had emerged from its twelve years of persecution as a hardened, militant, surging party, and it scared Harnack's church crowd. He argued that the social mission of the church had changed in modern times, but the gospel had not changed, including the limits it placed on social action. Some congress conservatives disputed that anything had changed or should have changed; Harnack tried to assure them he was mostly on their side. The church's first and primary obligation, he declared, was still to preach the gospel of personal faith. Its second obligation was to strengthen and renew Christian congregations as formative spiritual communities. Harnack lamented that the SPD was better than the churches at communal fellowship: "It has succeeded in creating and maintaining, among a migratory population, and in face of obstacles of every kind, an organization closely knit, operative alike in the cities and the provinces, both national and international. Why could we not do the like?"[36]

He warned that if the churches did not renew themselves as mission-oriented spiritual communities, it was pointless even to speak of the church's social mission; the preconditions for carrying out a social gospel would not exist. Harnack's favorite theologian, bourgeois liberal Albrecht Ritschl, got this right before the social gospel emerged: the church had a mission to do something about the social order. This was especially true in Germany, Harnack said, where "our Church still holds a great and influential place in the State, and in the life of the nation." He warned that if the church neglected the social ideals of the gospel, it would be condemned as "an accommodating tool in the hands of an 'Aristocratic Government.'" Admittedly, this was the situation already; the church had to change it by advancing "evangelical social ideals."[37]

What did that mean? Harnack said it did not mean the church should advocate economic justice, for the gospel has nothing to do with economic policy issues: "It has nothing to do with such practical questions of social-economics as the nationalization of private property and enterprise, land-tenure reforms, restriction of the legal hours of work, price-regulations, taxation, and insurance." The church was not competent to make pronouncements on economic policy, and even if it acquired the competence, it had no business doing so, since meddling in such matters led straight to secularization. Harnack did not want Christian thinkers to compromise the church's spiritual standing or integrity by taking a position on tax fairness. The gospel was above anything having to do with economic justice or policy.[38]

But "serious moral evils" belonged to a different category, he judged. The church had to oppose prostitution, even if that required meddling in politics. It had to oppose dueling and anything that undermined the sanctity of marriage and family life. It had to support welfare provisions that lent a helping hand to people in distress. It had to speak against class prejudice of every kind. It had to speak *as* the church, something Harnack managed better than Naumann, although both had problems in this area. And it had to be an advocate of peace. Harnack was a "peace through strength" type who squared the gospel command to peacemaking with German militarism by claiming that a strong German nation was indispensable to the peace and unity of Europe. He believed that the greatness of Germany rested on two pillars: the German armed forces and German scholarship. From 1908 to the summer of 1914 Harnack spoke for peace through strength, urging his audiences to step away from the path to war. In 1909 he told a group of British clergy, "On the soil of science and Christianity the cry 'war' is as madness, a cry out of an abyss from which we have long ago emerged."[39]

In Harnack's case one act of loyalty to Fatherland, Emperor, and Culture Protestantism led to another. In 1903 he assumed the presidency of the Evangelical Social Congress. Two years later he became director general of the Royal Library, renamed the Prussian State Library after World War I. Harnack held these two positions concurrently for six years, greatly expanding the library on Berlin's main avenue, Unter den Linden. In 1911 he gave up the congress presidency because the emperor asked him to run the Kaiser Wilhelm Gesellschaft, founding scientific research institutes. For ten years his twin directorships for the emperor overlapped. On August 1, 1914, the emperor asked him to compose a call to war. The enemy nations, when Harnack started to write it, were Russia and France. Before he had finished he was told to add Great Britain, which staggered him; Harnack prized his British friends. Within a month he had lost most of them. Harnack spent the war years sharply rebuffing critics of Prussian militarism. All Germans were obligated to sustain the glorious legacy of German civilization, he said. He signed numerous declarations that said it defiantly. He taught until 1921, when he left the Royal Library, but Harnack presided over the research foundation through years of postwar political crisis, monetary deflation, economic depression, and demands to change the foundation's name, which he resisted until his death in 1930; afterward it was renamed the Max Planck Gesellschaft.

Harnack never doubted that his social prominence and devotion to high-brow German culture were good for Christian theology, although he lived to see both ridiculed by a postwar generation. Once the crashing commenced, he perfectly symbolized everything that the postwar generation of theologians needed to repudiate. He played exactly that role for young Karl Barth, one of Harnack's former students. Barth grew up religiously conservative, turned theologically liberal under Harnack at Berlin and Wilhelm Herrmann at Marburg, and got his first taste of antibourgeois radicalism by joining the religious socialist movement in Switzerland. There he learned that Christian socialism was not always the nationalistic culture religion he had encountered in graduate school. There he belatedly learned what German Social Democrats had been fighting over for the past twenty years, and why it mattered.

MARXIAN REVOLUTION, FRIEDRICH ENGELS, AND GERMAN SOCIAL DEMOCRACY

The great blowout over Marxian orthodoxy went back to the years of persecution that hardened Social Democratic leaders. Always there were disputes about who was sufficiently militant, what Marx taught, and who had sold out. Bebel and Liebknecht led the party through the plague of antisocialist repression, holding fast to proletarian radicalism. With steely discipline they censured the party's anarchist flank and its flank of reformists who wanted to accommodate Bismarck. Anarchists condemned the Social Democrats for running for office, so leading anarchists had to be expelled, notably Johann Most and Wilhelm Hasselmann, painfully in both cases. Reformers believed that reforms were important ends in themselves. A true Marxist never believed that. The years of persecution radicalized and unified the Social Democrats, at least in public. Meanwhile, after Marx died in 1883, the prestige of Marxist doctrine grew in France and Germany, which propelled French and German socialists to create the Second International, never mind that Marx had opposed doing so.

The appeal of Marxism grew with industrialism itself. Most of the working class was not industrialized, and the majority of factory workers were unskilled and not unionized. Marx's focus on the industrial proletariat was both appealing and troubling to unskilled workers. Every socialist party had to cope with the fact that Marxism addressed some oppressed communities directly, others ambivalently, and still others not at all. Peasants and petit bourgeois shopkeepers would never overthrow capitalism. Marx's critique of capitalism grew by speaking to a growing mass of industrial workers. Socialist leaders recruited streams of industrial workers into class-conscious parties, using a pamphlet written by Engels. *Capital* was too long and demanding to be widely read, and Marx never finished volumes 2 and 3, which Engels completed. *The German*

Ideology never secured a publisher, and Marx never whipped the *Grundrisse* into a publishable book. Marx's *Civil War in France* (1871) was well known, but it was a journalistic defense of the Paris Commune.

The movement needed an accessible summary of Marxist doctrine, which Marx never wrote. However, in 1878 Marx contributed a chapter on political economy to Engels's takedown of Eugen Dühring, *Anti-Dühring*. Dühring wrote popular books combining positivist philosophy, ethical socialism, racism, anti-Semitism, atheism, American economist Henry C. Carey's protectionism, and anti-Hellenism. Real socialism was German, Dühring said, an antidote to Jewish Social Democracy. Marx and Engels were appalled that some Social Democrats embraced Dühring's stew of bigotries, quackery, ethical claims, and positivism. Engels said Dühring was the worst kind of socialist, a pathetic alternative to Marxian scientific socialism. In 1880 Engels refashioned three chapters of *Anti-Dühring* as a pamphlet titled *Socialism: Utopian and Scientific*, and the movement acquired a classic summary of Marxism.[40]

Engels told a triumphal story about the Enlightenment leading to Marxist criticism and revolution. The Enlightenment commendably attacked "superstition, injustice, privilege, and oppression" by appealing to eternal reason, but that proved to be "nothing more than the idealized kingdom of the bourgeoisie." Eternal rights were realized in bourgeois justice, the equality principle reduced to bourgeois equality before the law, bourgeois property was elevated to an essential right of humankind, and the social contract of Rousseau became a democratic bourgeois republic. Engels stressed that bourgeois reformers unabashedly claimed to speak for all suffering humanity, not merely their own little class. The best reformers—Owen, Saint-Simon, and Fourier—were utopian socialists who took a major step forward. Engels praised them heartily for condemning the emerging industrial system and proposing communal socialist alternatives to it. But the utopian socialists were true believers in Enlightenment rationality who failed to grasp that the new order of things was rational only to a point. They believed that all social problems could be solved by reason, which cut off any impulse they may have felt to view society from the standpoint of the working classes for which they spoke.[41]

Meanwhile two related breakthroughs led to Marx. Engels noted that both recovered something precious from ancient Greek thought. The first was the renewal of natural science in the late fifteenth century, which was rooted in the mathematics of Euclid and Archimedes during the Alexandrian period. Modern science broke nature into its individual parts, grouped the different processes and objects into appropriate categories, and studied the anatomy of organic bodies in their many forms. Engels said science alone was not enough to set philosophy on the right path; instead it yielded the narrow rationalistic metaphysics of the John Locke tradition and its early Enlightenment variations. Locke sorted out things from ideas, assigning both to fixed places that left nothing out of place and nothing in irresolvable tension with itself or something else. The second breakthrough was the rediscovery of dialectical reasoning by Descartes, Spinoza, Kant, and various post-Kantian idealists, supremely, Hegel, who synthesized the riches of philosophical idealism. Modern idealists rightly went back to the Socratic method of interrogating claims and premises to draw out contradictions and inconsistencies. Kant described ancient Greek dialecticism as the logical method of identifying false appearances. Hegel said that every organic being is the same and yet not the same in every moment. Every being assimilates matter from without and dispenses other matter, constantly. Nature itself proves the superiority of dialectical logic. Hegel was the greatest in this line because he synthesized the natural, historical, and intellectual development of the world as a dynamic, interrelated process of constant motion and transformation.[42]

Engels said Hegel got farther than everyone else because he had the most encyclopedic mind of his time. But there were three problems with Hegel. His knowledge was limited by human limitation, which made it impossible to solve the ambitious problem he addressed. His knowledge was limited by the limitations of his era, also unavoidably. And he was an idealist, regrettably. Engels explained that Hegel did not conceive the thoughts in his brain as abstract pictures of actual things and processes. He conceived the things and their evolution as realized pictures of eternal ideas. Hegel got many things brilliantly right, Engels allowed, but his idealistic system was "a colossal miscarriage" that distorted real particulars at every turn, foundering on a fundamental contradiction. It rightly conceived human history as a process of evolution that inherently confounds every human attempt to discover absolute truth, but Hegel claimed to understand the essence of absolute truth. He freed history from metaphysics by making history dialectical, but his concept of history was still essentially idealistic, a throwback to Platonism and Christian theology. Engels confirmed Marx's boast about bringing the dialectic to earth. Marx made an epochal breakthrough by driving idealistic philosophy from its last refuge, the philosophy of history. His materialistic philosophy of history explained human knowing by human being—interpreting history as the struggle between dominant and oppressed classes. Engels generously did not mention that he pushed Marx in this direction back when Marx was struggling with Hegel's political philosophy.[43]

In the modern period, Engels observed, the struggle that mattered pitted the oppressed proletarian masses against a bourgeois class of oppressors. The early socialists grasped that capitalism was predatory and oppressive, but they did not understand what made the capitalist mode of production so destructive, so they had no solution for it. All they could say was that capitalism was bad. Engels said Marx laid bare the essential character of capitalism. The key to Marxism was the discovery of surplus value, the secret of capitalist productivity and destruction. The capitalist mode of production is based on the appropriation of unpaid labor, which exploits every worker under capitalism. Even when capitalists buy the labor power of workers at its full value as a commodity on the market, they extract more value from the labor than they remunerate. The resulting surplus of value is heaped upon other masses of capital that the possessing classes control.

According to Engels, Marx's relentless explanation of the genesis of capitalist production and the production of capital transformed socialism into a science. The twofold key to scientific socialism was Marx's materialistic conception of history and his discovery that capitalist production depends upon the extraction of surplus value from alienated labor. Marxian materialism explained how the production of the means to support human life and the exchange of things produced undergird everything else in society. All questions about social rank, individual rights, love and marriage, aesthetic fulfillment, distributive justice, and the like are secondary to the questions of what is produced, how something is produced, and how the products are exchanged.

Engels put it aggressively, disputing commonsense conventions. All significant social changes come about through changes in the modes of production and exchange, not by advancing noble thoughts about truth or justice. Economics always matters more than philosophy. Feudalism could not compete with the capitalist mode of production, so the privileges and ethos of the feudal system were obliterated. The bourgeoisie replaced feudalism with a kingdom of free competition, plus personal liberty and equality for commodity owners, because the capitalist mode of production yielded staggering gains for capitalists. But Engels cautioned that capitalism did not extinguish the fatal contradiction of feudal society; it exacerbated the contradiction. Under feudalism, manufacturing and handicraft increasingly collided with the guilds. Under capitalism, the same thing happened and kept happening at ever-higher levels of expropriation as new forms of capitalistic production collided with the early industrial system and outstripped it. Summarizing Marx's analysis of the production of relative surplus value, Engels explained that the productive forces of modern capitalism were far more powerful than the capitalist mode of production. Scientific socialism was nothing more or less than the reflex, in thought, of the factual materialistic conflict between capitalist productivity and the capitalist mode of production.[44]

He repeated and accentuated Marx's claims about the industrial reserve army and the accumulation of misery. Expecting a different distributive result from capitalism, Engels said, was like expecting the electrodes of a battery not to decompose acidulated water. All economic crises under capitalism go through the same drama of overproduction and financial collapse. There were six crashes between 1825 and 1877, and all exposed the contradiction between socialized production and capitalist appropriation—the rebellion of the mode of production against the mode of exchange. Engels took for granted that more trusts and monopolies were coming, plus more ventures in state socialism, which he called "flunkeyism." Corporations were naturally driven to form mergers to monopolize their markets, and no nation was likely to put up with the exploitation of communities "by a small band of dividend-mongers." Sooner or later every industrialized nation would take the path of Bismarck, just as the Fabians said. Wherever the means of production and distribution outgrew the joint-stock company model, state takeovers were inevitable. Engels cautioned against cheering for flunkeyism, the last refuge of the capitalist state. Every form of the modern state is "a capitalist machine." Wherever states got bigger, taking over national economies, greater numbers of citizens were exploited. Engels believed in collectivist inevitability, but he also believed in political will. Social forces were like natural forces. They could be controlled only if they were understood, mastered, and subjected to human will. The difference between capitalism and socialism was like the difference between lightning in a storm and electricity charging a telegraph. The "social anarchy of production" drove every industrial society inevitably toward collective control, but only the kind that created a communist society was worth having.[45]

It mattered that states were already showing how to transform this vast industrial machine into state property; Engels said that history was moving very fast. Soon the proletariat in many places would seize political power and turn the means of production into state property. But in so doing the proletariat would abolish itself as a proletariat, abolishing "all class distinctions and class antagonisms," which would leave the state with nothing to do except expire. Every state represented society as a whole, but only insofar as it represented the class that represented society as a whole. In ancient times the state represented the class of slave-owning citizens; in medieval times it represented the feudal lords; in modernity it represented the bourgeoisie. As soon as the proletarian revolution succeeded, the state would become the true representative of the whole of society and thus become unnecessary. No one would be held in subjection, so society would not need a state. Engels said it plainly and repeated the point, driving home the utopian expectation of Marxian theory. He and Marx did not believe in abolishing the state. They believed the state would swiftly die out amid an explosion of universal emancipation.[46]

Engels's authority lifted his pamphlet and its book version to an exalted place in the canon of Marxist works that vast audiences actually read, exceeded only by the *Communist Manifesto*. *Socialism: Utopian and Scientific* was more didactic and accessible than Marx's writings, which helped it find a huge popular audience. The book version, *Anti-Dühring*, had a parallel career for intellectuals and book readers, notably Kautsky and Bernstein, who cut their Marxist teeth reading it. *Anti-Dühring* played a similar role for many French Marxists, notably Jules Guesde and Marx's son-in-law Paul Lafargue, although Marx said they were prone to "revolutionary phrase-mongering" that needlessly spurned achievable reforms. Upon reading Guesde and Lafargue hold forth on Marxist principles, Marx famously declared to Engels, "What is certain is that I myself am not a Marxist!"[47]

France was always a special case, culturally and historically. French radicalism had deep strains of anarchism, communalism, and utopianism, plus, more recently, anarcho-syndicalism. The Blanquist, Proudhonist, and Bakuninist traditions retained popular followings in France, and many French radicals assumed that true radicalism was Jacobin, not Marxist. Many resented that Marx ridiculed Proudhon in *The Poverty of Philosophy* for opposing strikes, misusing Hegelian dialectics, accusing Marx of dogmatism, and rationalizing his own incoherence as Hegelian. France's great radical, they believed, deserved far greater from Marx. Marx relied on Proudhon's critique of private property even as he spurned it, while claiming that Engels vastly surpassed Proudhon. Then Marx tarred Proudhon forever with a quotable zinger: "He wants to be the synthesis—he is a composite error."[48]

In addition, France's two leading Marxists, Guesde and Paul Brousse, were bitter factional rivals. Guesde was an orthodox Marxist, adhering closer to the Marx/Engels line than Liebknecht or Bebel. He was born Jules Bazile in Paris, wrote for Republican newspapers in the 1860s under the Second Empire, and took his mother's maiden name as his pen name. In 1871 he fled to Geneva after defending the Paris Commune. There he read Marx and converted to Marxism, returning to France in 1876 and enduring a six-month prison term in 1878. In 1880 Guesde founded the Parti Ouvrier (PO), consulting with Marx on its program; Marx wrote the preamble. Guesde disdained parliamentary reformism except for propaganda purposes, he sought to build a centralized mass party that overthrew the capitalist state, and he held fast to revolutionary Marxism—at least until August 1914, when he rallied to France's defense against Germany. Brousse was France's leading reform socialist, working through parliament to achieve socialist objectives. Guesde attacked him scathingly as a sellout "Possibilist." Marx and Engels favored Guesde but wished he would tone it down, which yielded the "revolutionary phrase-mongering" complaint. French socialism never pulled together in the nineteenth century because it had venomous rivalries and too much history to overcome. Socialist unity had to wait until 1905, when a charismatic democratic socialist, Jean Jaurès, surpassed Guesde as France's leading socialist and surpassed all other European socialist leaders.[49]

Throughout the 1880s there were calls to build a new International Workingmen's Association. Marx and Engels were dubious, preferring to build strong national parties first, but that argument was unpersuasive to many, especially in France and Germany. Guesdists and Broussists agreed that a Second International should be founded, and it should happen in Paris on the one hundredth anniversary of the French Revolution, July 14, 1889. But the two French parties could not work together, so each organized a founding congress. Delegates from other nations had to shuttle between the two conventions. Engels supported the Guesdist congress but did not attend. English Socialist League delegate Frank Kitz reported that Belgian and Italian delegates wasted two days "in a useless discussion" over how the two conventions might be fused. Kitz's poet-comrade William Morris reported that many of the fusion enthusiasts "were very hot about it." Afterward the Broussist party faded, and the Guesdist congress was recognized as the founding of the Second International. It elected Liebknecht and Édouard Vaillant, a former Paris Communard, as copresidents. Their cooperation was heralded as a sign of socialist solidarity, contrasting with the toxic nationalism of the German and French governments.[50]

From the beginning the Second International bore the same ideological tensions as the SPD. It vowed to be revolutionary, not reformist, but its resolutions were reformist, presuming that years of peaceful evolution lay ahead. It gave an exalted place to Engels, naming him its honorary president in 1893, but Engels died two years later. Every congress of the International debated its ideological identity.

In 1891 two French delegates at the Brussels congress demanded a condemnation of Jewish bankers. A tense discussion followed. The International had a smattering of anti-Semites who chose a bad way of denying that Social Democracy was Jewish. Sometimes they cited Marx's ugly sneer that Jewish selfishness, haggling, and worship of money, not Judaism, disclosed "the secret of the Jew." But the International usually censored anti-Semitism when it surfaced. At the 1893 congress in Zurich Bebel pushed through a resolution requiring that all groups belonging to the organization accept political action. That confirmed that

German Marxists were in control of the International. Two governing principles won out: Every nation needed to create an independent working-class party, free of bourgeois domination or affiliation. And every group in the International had to favor parliamentary political activism over revolutionary direct action. There were fierce debates about the second principle at the London congress in 1896 because anarchists flooded the meeting. The cracks in Social Democracy widened at London. More than half the 782 delegates were British, many were Fabians, and radicals protested vehemently that reformists were taking over. The 1900 congress in Paris featured more of the same, with a fateful twist, as the Russian Social Democratic Labor Party splintered into numerous factions, one of which became the Bolsheviks in 1903.[51]

The SPD was by far the strongest player in the International and the prime shaper of its ideological identity, as expressed in the Erfurt Program. In 1890 the renamed SPD conducted fierce debates over its identity and mission as soon as it convened again in legalized gatherings. Anarchists and extreme Marxists wanted to renounce parliamentary politics; reformers wanted to strengthen alliances with liberals and retain the party's demand for state-supported cooperatives; Bebel and Liebknecht were stung by young radicals from Berlin who looked down on speech making in the Reichstag. The party's bruising debates, however, vindicated Bebel and Liebknecht, who were lauded for steering German socialism through its years of persecution. The upshot was the Erfurt Program, adopted at the SPD Congress of 1891 in Erfurt.

The Erfurt Program committed the SPD to a Marxian agenda compatible with democratic socialism. It had two parts. Part 1 was pure *Communist Manifesto*, declaring that capitalism cheated workers of the fruits of their labor, creating ever-mounting misery, debasement, and exploitation that led inevitably to a proletarian industrial explosion against the capitalist state. The revolutionary struggle against capitalism was the work of the working class alone, for all other classes were bound to private property and its defense. Part 2 was pure Gotha Program reformism with a revolutionary spin, detailing the reformist agenda of a revolutionary party in a nonrevolutionary period. It eliminated the party's demand for state-supported cooperatives and added references to race and gender. It said that equal rights, universal suffrage, freedom of speech, sexual equality, public education, and progressive income taxes were socialist causes. It called for a revolutionary new order via ordinary, legal, political action: "The German Social Democratic Party therefore does not fight for new class privileges and class rights, but for the abolition of class rule and of classes themselves, for equal rights and equal obligations for all, without distinction of sex or birth. Starting from these views, it fights not only the exploitation and oppression of wage earners in society today but also every manner of exploitation and oppression, whether directed against a class, party, sex, or race."[52]

Kautsky wrote the Erfurt Program, with help from Bebel and Bernstein. Kautsky was perfectly suited for this task for reasons that marked his entire career. He founded the party's theoretical organ, *Neue Zeit*, in 1883, as a monthly in Stuttgart. He lived in London from 1885 to 1890, collaborated closely with Engels, broke through in 1888 when Engels asked him to edit Marx's *Theories of Surplus Value*, and turned the magazine into a weekly in 1890. *Neue Zeit* was already the world's most important Marxist publication when it became a weekly. Many socialists learned German to be able to read it. Erfurt crowned Kautsky's importance to the movement, confirming his belief that theoretical concepts unified the various ideological and political tendencies in Social Democracy. Theory was not just for people who liked to theorize. It was indispensable to the clarifying and unifying work of Social Democratic leadership. This conviction, though disputed by many Social Democrats, lifted Kautsky to an eminent stature in the SPD exceeded only by Bebel and Liebknecht, whom he eventually succeeded.

The Erfurt Program established how a revolutionary Marxian party should describe itself in a nonrevolutionary context. It identified with the industrial proletariat while assuring that a "stampede" of farmers and small capitalists would pour into the SPD and had already begun to do so. It said that the economic development of bourgeois society led necessarily to the overthrow of this system, exactly as Marx said, because capitalism separated workers from their tools, turning workers into propertyless proletarians. The means of production belonged increasingly to a monopoly of capitalists and landholders. Productivity increased but so did monopolies. For the disappearing middle class the result was constantly greater misery and degradation. Kautsky wrote the party's official commentary on the platform, *Der Erfurter Programm* (1892), a book written with commanding certainty that found the sweet spot between pamphleteering and technical theorizing. Kautsky said the SPD understood where history was going because the SPD was Marxist: "The more unbearable the existing system of production, the more evidently it is discredited, and the more unable the ruling parties show themselves to remedy our disgraceful social ills, the more illogical and unprincipled these parties become and the more they resolve themselves into cliques of self-seeking politicians, the greater will be the numbers of those who stream from the non-proletarian classes into the Socialist Party and, hand in hand with the irresistibly advancing proletariat, follow its banner to victory and triumph."[53]

This vision put the catastrophe doctrine of the *Communist Manifesto* at the center of Social Democratic conviction, defying certain appearances of the moment—the millions lifted out of poverty in the 1880s and the growth of big business. It also rationalized the mismatch between the SPD's everyday politicking and its revolutionary rhetoric. SPD leaders rightly took pride in having braved the years of persecution, which sealed the party's heroic self-image. But their insistence that capitalism would soon implode was not plausible to many or even intelligible. Thus there was no stampede from other sectors of German society. Historian Dieter Groh, in 1973, coined the two phrases by which Erfurt's strange combination of revolutionary rhetoric and practical inertia came to be marked, both in the title: *Negative Integration und revolutionärer Attentismus.* Erfurt Marxism, Groh argued, negatively integrated the SPD into German society, instituting a tradition of verbal radicalism that did not further the revolution. Thus it weirdly identified orthodox Marxism with a wait-and-see posture, "revolutionary attentism."[54]

Meanwhile Social Democracy grew with the growth of industrialism, on the back of a growing union movement that was practical and reformist, not radically ideological. This reality alone made Marxian revisionism inevitable. The revisionist challenge had Prussian roots in the Lassalle movement and South German roots in the Eisenach party. Capitalism did not develop as rapidly in Saxony and Bavaria as in Prussia, although Saxony eventually became Germany's most industrialized state. South Germany had a rural democratic ethos that yielded a reformist brand of socialism. It had weak but growing unions that fixed on practical economic gains. Georg von Vollmar, the SPD's leader in Bavaria, never accepted Marx's revolutionary antistatism or his claim that capital and land (especially land) concentrated in fewer and fewer hands. Rejecting basic Marxian doctrines did not stop Vollmar from achieving a prominent role in the SPD. Thus Bernstein's historic challenge to Marxian orthodoxy did not come from nowhere, except in a personal sense, as he had played a large role in establishing orthodox Marxism.

REVISING MARXIAN SOCIAL DEMOCRACY: EDUARD BERNSTEIN

The patron who whisked Bernstein to Switzerland, Karl Höchberg, sorely tested the party's tolerance for non-Marxism. He was wealthy, connected, intellectual, generous to the party, and, by his lights, eager to advance it. He was also naïve and presumptuous in the manner of well-to-do socialists, eager to give privileged advice. Höchberg founded a semimonthly journal for the SPD, *Die Zukunft,* and wrote idealistic articles for it, not fathoming Marxism. He liked Bernstein, who still lacked a grasp of Marxism or a view of it, so he asked

Bernstein to be his secretary. On October 12, 1878—the day the Reichstag passed the antisocialist law—Höchberg and Bernstein journeyed from Berlin to Frankfurt, on their way to Switzerland. Two days later they entered Basel, spending the winter in Lugano. The following April, Höchberg moved his headquarters to Zurich, anxious to help the outlawed Social Democrats survive.

For Bernstein, the experience was culturally and ideologically challenging. He tried not to look down on Schweizerdeutsch, especially its guttural flattening of German vowels that made all Swiss German speakers sound lower class to him. He struggled with his feelings about it for months, realizing that snobbery was not very socialist. He admired Höchberg's literary sophistication and devotion to Immanuel Kant, resisting suggestions by comrades that these were not things to admire. One day a distinguished Swiss intellectual confessed to Bernstein that he was never comfortable with Germans because he always feared being corrected for a linguistic blunder. Bernstein had a flash of recognition. If this highly literate Swiss gentleman feared German snobbery, how could Bernstein do better with Switzerland's swirl of working-class nationalities? On another occasion he got a dinner invitation in a mountain village from a comrade whose brother was a Catholic priest. It turned out that the brother would be attending, along with five other priests. Bernstein was mortified. How could this possibly go well? He loathed religion as the enemy of enlightenment. He feared a disastrous dinner in which he would have to make an ugly scene. But the priests were friendly, they bantered charmingly with no prayers or mention of religion, and Bernstein had another startling insight: Perhaps in a mountain village, where people lived in scattered houses with no access to libraries, museums, universities, and city sophistication, the church seemed "less repugnant" to reasonably intelligent and well-adjusted people.[55]

Zurich proved to be more surprising to Bernstein, as its hardy Social Democratic tradition had a Christian socialist core, a strain of radical Reformed theology centered at the University of Zurich. Friedrich Salomon Vögelin, a distinguished historical theologian and brilliant speaker, was the catalyzing figure in labor and democratic movements that led to Social Democracy in Switzerland. Vögelin was an intellectual fighter for democracy, rallying audiences with ethical passion and sarcastic asides. He spoke at Labor conferences on factory legislation, played a leading role in the Democratic Party of Zurich, and inspired a like-minded following of Reformed pastors, ex-pastors, and academics. Three of his ex-pastor disciples edited the house organ of the Democratic Party, and Bernstein admired Vögelin enormously, amazed that radical Reformed theologians existed. Reformed clerics and ex-clerics were prominent in the founding of the Swiss Workers League in 1874, which still existed when

Bernstein arrived in Switzerland. In 1879 Vollmar founded a Zurich edition of the banned German Social Democratic paper, *Die Sozialdemokrat*, and the following year Bernstein and his comrades held a farewell ceremony for the league, having launched a thriving Social Democratic outpost in exile. Bernstein worked on the paper and helped Julius Motteler smuggle it into Germany. In the early going he was awed when Bebel and Liebknecht came to town, and he formed a close friendship with Kautsky. For amusement Bernstein and Kautsky sang silly ditties mocking Christianity. They tried to stay out of trouble while attending three secret congresses, which proved not to be possible. Bernstein's early work on the paper and his friendship with Kautsky compelled him to make a decision about Marxism. He began to regard himself as a Marxist just before he had to prove it to Marx and Engels in person.[56]

Höchberg was happy to let go of *Die Zukunft* because he had bigger projects. One was a German edition of a Fabian-like book by A. E. Schäffle, *Quintessence of Socialism*. Marx said Schäffle wrote vulgar twaddle; Höchberg had no idea. His clueless dream was to convert the European intelligentsia to socialism. Meanwhile Engels published *Anti-Dühring*, and Bernstein was enthralled by it though also embarrassed, as he had thought Dühring was a great socialist. Engels's book was a revelation to Bernstein: "It converted me to Marxism." Shortly afterward Höchberg and Bernstein published a social science yearbook, proudly sending it to Marx and Engels, who were appalled. One article was especially offensive. Anonymously written by Karl Flesch (later a prominent Frankfurt reformist), it said that German socialists bore much of the blame for getting outlawed because they relied too much on proletarians, disdaining the liberals and progressives who wanted to help. Marx and Engels said something had to be done about Höchberg and this Bernstein person, who embarrassed German socialism with bourgeois trash. If the party had to forgo Höchberg's money, so be it. If Höchberg and Bernstein didn't understand that only the industrial proletariat would emancipate the proletariat, they had to be expelled. Bernstein pleaded to Bebel that the article wasn't his fault, and he didn't agree with it. That persuaded Bebel to take his first trip to London, with Bernstein in tow. It was the first sea voyage for both and as stormy as they feared. Shaken from the trip, Bernstein and Bebel made their way to Engels's home on Regent's Park Road in London.[57]

Engels greeted Bebel warmly and Bernstein politely before grilling Bebel about the paper. Engels was rough and volcanic, plus hard drinking. Bebel held his ground for an hour, and Engels declared it was time to visit "the Moor," who lived nearby on Maitland Park Road. Catching Bernstein's puzzlement, Engels said he always called Marx "the Moor," a reference to his sallow complexion and no-longer-black hair. Marx surprised Bernstein by being much nicer than

Engels—friendly, charitable, and welcoming. Finally Bernstein was asked to account for the yearbook. He won over Marx and Engels by assuring that he understood Marx's scientific doctrines, he was a believing Marxist, and he was not an arrogant academic type. Far from the latter, he was totally a movement activist and steeped in Marxian science. Marx and Engels were delighted with this information, especially Engels. Engels warmed to Bernstein, showing him the usual tourist hotspots, plus Marx's desk at the British Museum. Bernstein met Jenny Marx and her four daughters, warming especially to young Eleanor Marx, and learned that the Marx women intensely disdained Lassalle from his visit in 1862. Lassalle struck them as a conceited dandy who helped himself to Marx's ideas. Marx said they were too hard on Lassalle, who had some good points. Bernstein's standing in the party soared after he returned from London. He became more involved in the paper, and in 1881 he took over as editor.[58]

Bernstein ran the paper through its glory run, until it was no longer needed in 1891, writing winsome articles that brought thousands of German readers into the party. He explicated Marxian orthodoxy impeccably, as expounded by Engels and Kautsky: Parliamentary politics would never create a socialist society; German socialists needed to prepare for the inevitable revolution that delivered Germany from capitalism; but first they had to survive Bismarck, so they had to be vigilant, intransigent, unified, and careful, breaking no laws. If the party stayed defiant but legal in the Reichstag and the exiles in Zurich kept it alive, the downtrodden masses would flock to Social Democracy. Policy vigilance was crucial. Engels, Bebel, Liebknecht, and Kautsky said Bismarck's social legislation was obviously a crude form of blackmail that kept the monarchy and propertied classes in charge. Bernstein endeared himself to them by saying it persistently. Engels did not oppose reform legislation that helped working people as long as it did not strengthen the government against the people. Bismarck's entire welfare program, however, failed this test, as did state subventions for the steamship industry that enabled imperial expansion. It didn't matter that working people liked health insurance and subventions financed dockyard jobs. This was a difficult argument to make; the party's right flank, especially in the unions, howled against it through the 1880s. Bernstein survived the loudest challenge to his editorship by opposing all steamship subsidies. He became a hero to SPD leaders by sticking to a hard line and winning hearts and minds.[59]

In 1884 Bernstein made a second trip to England, representing the Swiss Labor Movement and Swiss Social Democracy at a conference. He looked up Engels and got a taste of Engels's later life, poring over Marx's literary remains through several long days and nights of labor. He heard Guesde give a strong speech that made him hopeful for French Marxism and liked that Guesde won the crowd without drawing attention to himself. He met socialists who pined for state-supported producer cooperatives; Bernstein replied that capitalism and socialism had developed far past the point at which Lassalle's pet idea made any sense from a socialist standpoint: "A resolute workers' party is now in open combat with the whole of the old world of exploitation, which knows full well how significant this struggle is and whose one desire is therefore to conceal it as far as possible, to blunt its impact, to *emasculate* its fighters, or some of them at least." Begging the state to support cooperatives "would *emasculate* the workers," he warned, punching the key word again; it would also corrupt socialism. Three years later Bernstein returned to England for another conference, unaware that his life was about to turn a corner.[60]

In 1888 Bernstein lost his refuge in Switzerland, as Bismarck persuaded Swiss authorities to shut down *Der Sozialdemokrat*. Bernstein moved the paper to London, in Kentish Town, where his comradely relationship with Engels grew into a close friendship. Engels had a few friends who were not movement Marxists, notably German democratic republican Eugen Oswald and German publisher Rudolph Meyer. The leading English Marxist, H. M. Hyndman, never won Engels's favor, as Engels found him arrogant, sectarian, and dishonest. Engels grieved that England's only Marxist party had no allies because Hyndman liked it that way. Bernstein later wished Engels had similarly marginalized the narcissistic Edward Aveling, who attached himself to Eleanor Marx and betrayed her, driving her to suicide. As it was, Aveling and Eleanor Marx were the only English socialists in Engels's inner circle, except for contrarian gadfly Ernest Belfort Bax.[61]

Bernstein surprised himself by reaching beyond this group, befriending numerous socialists and Christian socialists who were nothing like Engels. He greatly admired William Morris, whom Engels respected and occasionally hosted. Morris showed that one could espouse socialism from a Romantic poetic standpoint without being an aesthete. But Morris was a star with his own following, approaching socialism through his artistic imagination, very unlike Engels. For a while Bernstein spurned George Bernard Shaw, Sidney and Beatrice Webb, and all other Fabians because he was prejudiced against Fabianism. That changed after Bernstein heard Shaw give a sparkling Fabian lecture studded with insight, paradoxes, and conviction. Gradually Bernstein relinquished his prejudice that Fabians were not serious socialists. He marveled at their industry, the high quality of their publications, and their impact on British society. He befriended the Webbs and eventually formed a judgment about them: Both were brilliant, but Beatrice Webb seemed more brilliant than her husband only because she grew up privileged and classically trained. Bernstein identified with

Sidney Webb, another self-made intellectual from the lower middle class who lacked polish but was actually smarter than everyone else.[62]

Consorting with this crowd brought Bernstein into contact with Christian socialists, who surprised him even more. One was an Oxford-educated Anglican priest in South London named William Morris, who lived among the poor, ardently supported the labor movement, and was dubbed "Brother Bob" by socialist comrades. Eleanor Marx took Bernstein to a cooperative society event in East London at which Brother Bob regaled the crowd with comical songs. Brother Bob had nothing in common with Bernstein's stereotype of the Anglican cleric. Bernstein was still thinking about it when he met Stewart Headlam, who exploded the stereotype. Bernstein delighted in Headlam's forceful defense of freethinkers, enthusiastic defense of theater and ballet, and robust advocacy of Anglican socialism, a cause pioneered by "the admirable Frederick Denison Maurice." Bernstein also treasured Percy Dearmer for espousing radical Anglican socialism with no hint of churchy affectation, but his favorite Christian socialist was Thomas Hancock. Headlam introduced him to Hancock, whose kindness, humility, and "peculiar selflessness" moved Bernstein deeply. He learned that Hancock spent his entire career helping others find their way with no thought of reward. Hancock's expertise on the English Revolution helped Bernstein write a notable book about the roles of the Leveller movement and the Communist Diggers, especially Gerrard Winstanley. Hancock was quietly generous throughout Bernstein's research and writing phases, a new experience for Bernstein. Many years later Bernstein wryly reflected that Germans often boasted of being the only people ever to do anything for its own sake with no thought of reward. He winced whenever he read it, wishing his compatriots had known Hancock.[63]

All of this was cited against Bernstein after he rocked the SPD and Socialist International by contending that some aspects of Marxism were wrong. British progressives had seduced him! Always he denied it, contending that his mind was changed by factual evidence, not personalities. *Die Sozialdemokrat* shut down in 1891, but that liberated Bernstein from the weekly grind, plus the constraints of producing party propaganda. He was in great demand as a writer and speaker, although he couldn't go home, being still under indictment for sedition. He wrote think pieces for *Neue Zeit*, enjoying the charms of theory, and produced a three-volume edition of Lassalle's works. Bernstein did not say he spoke for himself because he identified completely with the SPD and Marxian solidarity. But it began to happen in the mid-1890s, before anyone noticed, including Bernstein. Engels did not detect that his friend was changing, nor did Kautsky. When Engels died Bernstein and Kautsky inherited his literary estate, and Bernstein scattered his ashes off Beachy Head near Eastbourne. Engels trusted Bernstein and Kautsky above all others.[64]

There were a few signs of wobbling. In 1893 Bernstein said the SPD should enter an electoral alliance with liberals because the political situation had changed and elections were just a means to an end. The socialist end had not changed, he reasoned, but there was nothing sacred about any means to an end. The same year he wrote a review article that skirted around Julius Wolf's detailed refutation of the labor reserve doctrine; Bernstein settled for derision, calling Wolf "the latest destroyer of Socialism." The following year, after Engels published the third volume of *Capital*, Bernstein gave it a lukewarm review, without saying why. He did not want a ruckus over his disappointment that Marx/Engels did not persuasively refute marginalist critiques of Marxism. Bernstein grappled with this issue for years before deciding that Marxism and marginal analysis were about different things and thus compatible. In 1896 the SPD tensely debated whether it should support nationalist movements in Poland and Turkey. Bernstein said socialists should support whatever advanced the cause of civilization. Armenians were more civilized than Turks, so socialists should support the Armenians. Bax replied incredulously in *Justice* that this was not a Marxist argument. According to Bax, Bernstein had become a Fabian without knowing it. Bernstein countered that Marx and Engels cared about civilization, unlike sectarian Marxists like Bax. He denied being a Fabian but commended the Fabians for realizing that industrial oppression was not the only or worst form of oppression. Having to deny he was a Fabian was telling, as Bernstein soon realized. He was known for complimenting England's free atmosphere and for believing that England was more civilized than any nation; Engels bristled when Bernstein said it at dinner parties. In 1896 Bernstein wrote a series of articles, "Problems of Socialism," defending Marxian orthodoxy with a bit of straining. He had one article remaining in the series when he had a light-goes-on moment with the Fabians.[65]

On January 29, 1897, Bernstein gave a lecture to the Fabian Society titled "What Marx Really Thought." He did not set out to improve upon Marxism to make it persuasive to Fabians. He was committed to his title. As he delivered the lecture, however, Bernstein realized he was not persuading himself. He later explained to Bebel, "As I was reading the lecture, the thought shot through my head that I was doing Marx an injustice, that it was not Marx I was presenting." Fabian stalwart Hubert Bland asked "a few innocuous questions" on this point. In years past Bernstein would have handled Bland readily; now he felt overwhelmed: "I told myself secretly that this could not go on. It is idle to attempt to reconcile the irreconcilable. The vital thing is to be clear as to where Marx is still right and where he is not."[66]

The next article was plainly different; Bernstein's foremost virtue, among many others, was integrity. Writing about the relationship between the individual and the state, Bernstein said states were historical and various, like everything else. Engels wrote about the withering away of the state because every existing state was an instrument of class rule, plus Engels had to negate Lassalle's cult of the state. But Marxism was not an ahistorical doctrine about a perfect society, Bernstein argued. Too many Marxists were like medieval scholastics, wielding a doctrine about a necessary perfect ideal. Meanwhile democracy was advancing, and a fully realized democracy was not hard to imagine. Democracy changed the equation because it compelled states to meet the needs of common people, no longer serving merely a class interest. In Europe and the United States democracy was already the best road to socialism. Moreover, huge industrial firms were growing in size and number. Advanced economies needed the rule of law and considerable planning, with or without capitalism: "However decentralized an administration we envisage, there will always be a large number of social tasks which are incompatible with the notion of the autonomous activity of society." Bernstein said Social Democracy should be synonymous with social responsibility and civilization. Rightly understood, Social Democracy was not a fantasy about "society" somehow transforming the transport system into something requiring no governmental administration. Moreover, Marx did not say that great nations should be torn apart; he said the proletarian revolution sought to find a new basis of unity. Bernstein concluded, "Whether this can be achieved in every case in the way which Marx describes in this work need not concern us here."[67]

But Marxists cared very much about Marxism. For a few months the pushback was mostly local. Hyndman and others in his party took up Bax's charge that Bernstein had become a Fabian, which was never quite right. Democracy was more important to Bernstein than to the Webbs, and he was a neo-Kantian in the mold of Marburg philosopher F. A. Lange, not a British utilitarian. In the early going Kautsky puzzled that SPD leaders held back from the contention over Bernstein. Was it possible they didn't actually read *Neue Zeit*? Then a second exchange between Bax and Bernstein, now in *Neue Zeit*, ignited a firestorm. Bax was quotably opinionated, contending that males were the oppressed gender, Bernstein was a philistine for prizing modern civilization as a fruit of capitalism, and "too much Jewry is no blessing for mankind," although Bax denied being an anti-Semite. Bernstein replied that Bax had eccentricity issues; moreover, the *Communist Manifesto* lauded the progress of Western civilization under capitalism, comparing it to the pyramids. Bernstein put it in Kantian fashion: "One of the main achievements of this civilization is to value

the rights of *personality*, of *human life*, which, in the general and broad interpretation they enjoy today, were unknown to any earlier civilization." The following month, in January 1898, Bernstein cut to the core of his debate with Bax.
Capitalism was not destroying itself, contrary to Marx, and it was not very scientific to ignore the facts about capitalist expansion. Even Marx, at the end,
backed off his idea of a ten-year production cycle. Bernstein implored socialists
not to deny that Marx and Engels got various things wrong. What mattered was
the movement, not a belief about where socialism was going: "I frankly admit
that I have extraordinarily little feeling for, or interest in, what is usually termed
'the final goal of socialism.' This goal, whatever it may be, is nothing to me, the
movement is everything." That is, society's general movement toward socialism
was what mattered, not only the advances of the organized socialist movement.[68]

The German radical press exploded with anger and accusation. The
Volkszeitung doubted that Bernstein had ever been a genuine radical. The
Sächsische Arbeiter-Zeitung declared that Bernstein was trying to sabotage
the revolution in Germany by denying it was achievable; editor Alexander
Helphand ("Parvus") wrote seventeen articles in two months on this theme.
SPD journalist and historian Franz Mehring, soon a major figure in the party's
left wing, said Bernstein had regressed to utopian socialism. Bebel raged against
Bernstein bitterly. Bernstein took it hard, falling into depression. Eleanor Marx
lamented that her friend became miserably irritable, uncharacteristically snap-
ping at people. Then she committed suicide over Aveling's secret marriage to
another woman, wounding Bernstein deeply. Bernstein fought back against the
barrage of criticism, contending that Marxian dogmatism did not exempt
Marxists from the problems of idealism and fallible knowledge. Materialism is
an idea, he stressed. All knowledge of physical reality is unavoidably hypothetical and thus ideal. Science is open-ended and revisionist, rooting out errors;
thus scientific socialism must be sufficiently open-ended and revisionist to correct its errors.[69]

Kautsky held back from joining the barrage against his friend. Friendship
mattered to him, plus Bernstein never said the SPD should change the course
of direction that Engels charted and Bernstein previously defended. Everything
that Bernstein revised was at the level of principle, not policy. In addition
Kautsky was somewhat unnerved that perhaps SPD leaders did not read *Neue
Zeit.* Then Bernstein's later replies to Bax confirmed he had opted for reform
socialism, and Kautsky realized the Bernstein problem would not fade away, at
least not without moving away. Kautsky urged Bernstein to move to Zurich or
Vienna; Bebel countered that moving would solve nothing because Bernstein
was lost to the movement.

Young Rosa Luxemburg weighed in, dramatically introducing herself to German socialists. She was born in 1871 to a Jewish merchant family in Zamosc, a town near Lublin in the Russian-occupied section of Poland. Her family was rich in nurture, culture, and support of her stunning brilliance but poor financially. Luxemburg had a tiny frame and a congenital hip ailment, probably dysplasia. She read voraciously in Polish, Russian, Hebrew, and German, achieving fluency by the age of ten. She consumed *Capital* as a youth and joined the Polish Marxist party Proletariat as a fifteen-year-old. The tsarist authorities ran a viciously repressive state in Poland, hunting down revolutionaries and confining Jews to ghettos and shtetls. Being tiny, Jewish, female, and a teenager endangered Luxemburg and drew dangerous attention to her comrades, who changed their identities frequently to avoid detection. In 1889 government forces smashed Proletariat, and Luxemburg was smuggled out of Poland to Zurich, telling her parents she had to get there because the University of Zurich admitted women.

She studied botany and zoology at first, her first passions, but switched to philosophy, political theory, and economics. Russia's best socialists were in exile in Zurich, so Luxemburg befriended them, plus an extraordinary Lithuanian revolutionary, Leo Jogiches (1867–1919). He was dedicated, learned, connected, and winsome, albeit a bad writer. He persuaded her the *Communist Manifesto* was wrong about Polish national emancipation because Prussia and Russia would crush any revolutionary uprising in Poland. Socialist revolutions had to occur in Germany, Austria, and Russia before Poland achieved independence. From 1890 to 1905 Jogiches was Luxemburg's lover and mentor, remaining her friend and comrade afterward. She was active in Polish revolutionary émigré groups in Switzerland and France and attended the Second International's 1893 congress in Zurich, where she met Engels and the founder of Russian Marxism, Georg Plekhanov. In 1897 Luxemburg completed her doctoral dissertation on Poland's industrial development. She had just moved to Germany and joined the SPD, in 1898, when the controversy over Bernstein revisionism broke out. Her fiery Marxist attacks on Bernstein stoked the controversy distinctly. She told Jogiches, "I want to affect people like a clap of thunder, to inflame their minds not by speechifying but with the breadth of my vision, the strength of my convictions, and the power of my expression." For SPD leaders she was hard to take in every way: female, Polish, Jewish, young, brilliant, eloquent, pushy, and critical, with a colorful personality. Richard Fischer, editor of the SPD's chief organ, *Vorwärts*, described Luxemburg as a "guest who comes to us and spits in our parlor." Luxemburg powerfully contended that Social Democracy needed to stand for proletarian revolution, brushing past party leaders who resisted hearing it from her.[70]

The controversy over revisionism spilled into the SPD Congress at Stuttgart in October 1898. Bernstein was still barred from Germany. Was he right that Social Democracy did not have to agree about its final goal? Bernstein wrote to the congress defending his view, and the delegates tried to address the question without discussing Bernstein. Wolfgang Heine said yes; the very idea of a final goal was repugnant, as though history stopped at the achievement of a socialist victory. Vollmar also said yes; he wearied of comrades who yearned for sectarian irrelevance or violent insurrections. Bebel vehemently disagreed—a fighting party had to have a final goal. Otherwise it would not fight and would not be socialist. Luxemburg agreed with Bebel. She told the congress that socialists had no short-term practical objectives of their own. What made socialist parties different from other progressives was their commitment to the conquest of political power that produced a communist society. Lacking that, there was no reason to be a Social Democrat. Vollmar countered that Luxemburg perfectly described Blanquism, not Social Democracy. There was nothing intrinsic to socialism about violently seizing power and much to dread in it. Luxemburg advised Vollmar to check his patronizing tone. As for "the bogey of Blanquism," how could Vollmar not see the difference? Blanquism was a handful of vanguard revolutionaries seizing power in the name of the working class; Social Democracy was the working class itself seizing power: "I know quite well that I still have to win my spurs in the German movement, but I intend to do so on the left wing of the party where they fight the enemy, and not on the right where they compromise with him."[71]

It was unclear where this debate was going, but Bebel forced the congress to talk about Bernstein. Kautsky dramatically broke his silence about Bernstein, declaring it pained him to speak against his long-treasured friend. Moreover, there were caveats to make. England was unique in many ways. It had no standing army, bureaucracy, or peasantry, and its agricultural sector was small. In addition, even Marx conceded that England might be able to make a peaceful transition from capitalism to socialism. But Kautsky warned that none of this justified Bernstein's reformism. Bernstein had lost touch with the movement in Germany; everything he wrote generalized from his experience of England. Bernstein claimed that capitalism was advancing. If this were true, Kautsky said, it would mean that socialists had no hope of reaching their goal! That had to be wrong. Bernstein had gone over to the ethical socialists, who believed that achieving democracy came first, followed by leading the proletariat to victory. Kautsky countered that true socialists believed the reverse. The victory of the proletariat was the precondition of the victory of democracy. Though Kautsky yearned for a victory without catastrophe, he did not believe it was possible. The German socialists roared with approval—loud, sustained, and fervent. Liebknecht declared that Bernstein had been "exceedingly foolish" to say the movement was everything and the goal was nothing; on the other hand, Luxemburg was wrong to say the opposite. The movement and goal were both indispensable, and the goal was "the overthrow of capitalist society." The congress roared again with approval and ended.[72]

The conquest of power yielding a classless society was the only thing that fused the revolutionary rhetoric of Social Democracy to its everyday practices. As long as the party had a constant final goal it could rationalize all manner of electoral and parliamentary maneuvers. Running for office was a revolutionary tactic as long as it was only a tactic, an expedient implying no commitment to parliamentary democracy. No tactic was right or wrong in itself. The right means had to be found to achieve the given end. Plus, the party shrewdly made a fetish of its supposed revolutionary purity by refusing to vote for a national budget. What made *anything* revolutionary, as Kautsky said repeatedly, was its end, never its means. As long as the party had a defining final goal, everything else in the Erfurt Program and the party's day-to-day politicking made sense. So the party's center radical leaders believed. They perceived that Bernstein's argument undermined the SPD's ability to make sense to itself. This was more threatening than anything else in the back-and-forth over revisionism.

Bernstein tried to rephrase his offending statement about the final goal, declaring that the movement meant everything to him because it bore its goal within itself. Better phrasing, however, did not mollify party leaders because the rift in the party cut to its core identity. Bebel and Mehring demanded Bernstein's expulsion, Luxemburg stopped short of demanding it, and Kautsky was coy about it, telling Bernstein he should resign without putting the party through an expulsion drama. He added that Bernstein was no longer a German anyway, so he should embrace his new life: "You have decided to be an Englishman—take the consequences and become an Englishman. You have a completely different position with the English press than with the German." According to Kautsky, Bernstein had "completely lost touch with Germany" and should stop deceiving himself. He had already abandoned German Social Democracy, so make the best of it: "Try to achieve a place in the English movement and to become a representative of English Socialism." Bebel said Bernstein had a history of changing his skin. He began as an Eisenacher, converted to Dühring's crackpot stew, morphed into Höchberg's bourgeois idealism, adopted Marxism barely in time to qualify for "the high point of your life," and was ruined by English liberals and liberalism: "I think that you are floundering in glaring contradictions and that you are drawing many false conclusions." To Bebel, it seemed that "you see only what you want to see and that, when you see nothing at all, you make things up."[73]

Bebel insinuated that Bernstein waited until Engels died before he sprung his Fabian reformism on the party. To Bernstein, that was insulting in every way. He still agreed with SPD policies but argued that the party lacked a theory fitting its policies because Bebel and other leaders dogmatized the catastrophe rhetoric of the *Communist Manifesto*. He refused to resign, waiting to see if Bebel would follow through on expelling him, which didn't happen, chiefly because Austrian Social Democratic leader Victor Adler persuaded Bebel to back down. Adler founded the Social Democratic Workers Party of Austria in 1888, his political skills were extraordinary, and he strongly disagreed with Bernstein. Thus he had unusual pull with Bebel. Adler said being wrong did not disqualify Bernstein from party membership. Revolutionary Marxism versus nonrevolutionary socialism was a legitimate debate *within* Social Democracy, and Bernstein was an able champion of the latter option. If the party expelled Bernstein it would have to expel many others. On that basis Bernstein kept his place in the party and won others to it with a famous book, *The Preconditions of Socialism* (*Die Voraussetzungen des Sozialismus*, 1899). Kautsky called it "the first sensational book in the literature of German Social Democracy." That was rueful, as Kautsky regretted having challenged Bernstein to write a book version. On the other hand, the controversy over revisionism enhanced Kautsky's eminence in Social Democracy as the intellectual defender of what mattered. The English edition of Bernstein's book aptly conveyed its argument by changing the title to *Evolutionary Socialism*.[74]

EVOLUTIONARY SOCIALISM

Bernstein had a choice between playing down his differences with Marx and Engels, as he had done previously, and making a maximal version of his argument. He created a sensation by going maximal but began in the former mode, contending that his position should not have elicited such an outcry since it rested on something obvious: Bourgeois society was not on the verge of collapse. Thus Social Democracy needed to stop fusing its rhetoric and tactics to an imminent catastrophe. According to Bernstein, Marx and Engels did not treat the catastrophe assumption of the *Communist Manifesto* as an immutable given of scientific socialism. He pointed to their preface in the 1872 edition of the manifesto, which denied that the working class could readily seize state machinery for its own purpose; the Paris Commune proved the point. Moreover, in 1895 Engels wrote that socialists had to pursue "slow propaganda work and parliamentary activity." Bernstein, in his telling, was condemned for saying the same thing. He did not believe that seizing power for a utopian end defined Social Democracy. Struggling for power and expropriating capitalists were means to achieve a socialist order. As such, they were demands in the program of Social Democracy. All Social Democrats accepted these demands, but nobody knew the circumstances under which they would be fulfilled. Struggling for the realization of these demands entailed fighting for the political and industrial rights of German workers. Saying so was merely sensible, but he was condemned for saying it.[75]

That was a shaky beginning and misleading, a rerun of Bernstein's letter to the Stuttgart congress. Bernstein knew very well that Marx and Engels never stopped believing that a violent revolution was inevitable. The later Engels said a climactic political crisis would occur, and capitalism would implode, but the era of barricades and street fighting was over because modern governments possessed overwhelming military technology. Thus to Engels it was crucial for socialists to stay out of trouble before the crisis and implosion, avoid confrontations with the state, and build up popular support through electoral politicking. Bernstein strained to make Engels sound like Bernstein, which persuaded no SPD insider.

Then he made two deft moves. First, he announced he would no longer play down his differences with Marx and Engels because the crisis in Social Democracy demanded candor. Second, he distinguished between pure theory and applied theory. Pure theory consisted of principles derived from the pertinent data that were universally valid, "the constant element in the theory." Applied theory applied the principles to specific phenomena and practices, "the variable element in the system." Both were conditional, Bernstein allowed, because the principles of pure science were subject to correction and modification, and some applications were valid across variable contexts. He seemed to be building an argument for affirming Marx's pure theory while rejecting certain applications of it, much like Harnack separated the kernel of the gospel from its dispensable husk. Surplus value and historical materialism might have qualified as pure Marxian theory, as distinguished from Marx's account of capitalist development. But Bernstein no longer cared whether SPD radicals considered him an orthodox Marxist. He was done with passing whatever minimal requirements Engels and Kautsky established for it. So he said that Marx's theory of capitalist development was a staple of Marx's pure theory.[76]

Specifically, Bernstein said the pure science of Marxism had six planks: historical materialism, the general theory of class conflict, the specific theory of the conflict between the bourgeoisie and the proletariat, surplus value, the theory of the mode of production of bourgeois society, and the theory of capitalist development. Historical materialism was the foundation of Marxian theory, a fact disputed by no one, including Bernstein. He took for granted that Marxism stood or fell with Marx's theory of history. All events are necessary in the sense that matter moves of necessity in accordance with certain laws. There is no cause without its necessary effect and no event without a material cause. The movement of matter determines the formation of ideas and the directions of human will, so everything falling under these categories is also necessitated, like all other human events.

If all events are necessary, Bernstein said, the problem for materialists is to discern how various factors of force relate to each other and how nature, the economy, legal institutions, and ideas should be understood. Marx's theory of the material forces and relations of production was his answer to this problem: Productive forces and relations are the determining factors. Marx taught that the bourgeois mode of production was the last antagonistic form of the social process of production, and the forces developing within it created the material conditions needed to end the antagonism. Human society would end its prehistorical phase when the contradictions of capitalism yielded a communist society. Bernstein said the part about communism was hypothetical, belonging to the future, so he passed over it. He did not like Marx's reductionism about human ideas and will, which rendered human beings as "nothing but the living agents of historical forces whose work they carry out against their knowledge and will." Marx had a place for ideological consciousness, since Marx distinguished between the material conditions of production that caused social revolutions and the ideological forms that revolutions engendered. But Marxism was undeniably a strongly deterministic theory in which human subjectivity was far subordinate to material movement.[77]

On occasion Engels wrote passages that softened Marx's determinism, and Bernstein acknowledged that Marx and Engels were too deeply enmeshed in revolutionary politics to ignore that willing and reasoning human beings wage revolutions. Still, they ridiculed all who appealed to human feeling or idealism and even human willing and rationality. Bernstein angled for a humanistic revision of historical materialism. The English edition of his book omitted his chapter on Marxism and Hegelian dialectic, apparently on the premise that Britons and North Americans didn't want to read about Hegel. To Bernstein, the Hegel chapter was crucial because he thought Kant's critical idealism better suited Marx's attempt to track the empirical facts of history.

Putting the dialectic on its feet still trapped Marx in the Hegelian puzzles of the self-development of the concept. Bernstein said this problem increases as the object gets more complex. The greater the number of elements involved, with variations in nature and force relations, the more danger there is of distorting empirical reality. The negation of the negation yields questionable deductions about inevitable transformations, producing arbitrary constructions about where history is going. Bernstein granted that Hegel's idea of development through antagonisms was brilliantly illuminating; he shared neo-Kantian F. A. Lange's high estimate of Hegel's achievement. But he also concurred with Lange that Hegel and Marx overbelieved in it, as evidenced by the *Communist Manifesto*, where Marx and Engels declared that the bourgeois revolution was the prelude to an immediately succeeding proletarian revolution. Bernstein doubted that Marx would have been so self-deceived had he not overbelieved in contradiction dialectics. As it was, Marx "never completely got rid of it," and neither did Engels.[78]

For the same reason, Bernstein argued, the Marxist tradition never quite threw off Blanquism. The program of revolutionary action in the *Manifesto* was thoroughly Blanquist. On various occasions afterward Marx and Engels described Blanquists as the best exemplars of proletarian struggle, notably in the circular to the Communist League of March 1850. Marx and Engels extolled proletarian terrorism as a near-miraculous force that propelled the revolution forward. To be sure, Bernstein acknowledged, they stopped talking like that in the 1850s, but their Blanquist phase revealed a dualistic defect in Marxian theory, not merely a "passing mood." This defect preceded Marxism and runs through the entire socialist movement, pitting two streams of thought into constant tension. One is constructive in variously utopian, sectarian, or peacefully evolutionary forms. The other is destructive in variously conspiratorial, demagogic, or terroristic forms. Constructive currents conceive emancipation as occurring primarily through economic organization. Destructive currents conceive emancipation as occurring primarily through political conquest and expropriation. Bernstein argued that Marx combined the essential elements of both streams, synthesizing the constructive investigation of the economic and social preconditions for liberation with the revolutionary conception of liberation as a political class struggle, and Marxism still featured this twofold character.[79]

Marxism superseded Blanquism in only one respect—method. Bernstein recalled that Marx and Proudhon depicted the revolution of 1848 very similarly, describing it as a historical process in which every major episode marked a defeat for the revolution. But unlike Proudhon, Marx believed the counterrevolution was good for the proletarian revolution, which needed a hardened, fighting revolutionary party. The proletarian revolution could move forward only if the revolutionary party became truly revolutionary, clashing with the state.

According to Bernstein, Marx still burned with Blanquist zeal when he wrote *The Class Struggles in France* in early 1850, although Marx said that an economic crisis was the necessary precondition of any proletarian revolution. Bernstein pressed hard on an uncomfortable point. Marx did not merely miscalculate what happened in 1848–1849. He never fully acknowledged his error on the level of principle, so Marxism was never purged of Blanquism. Marx and Engels continued to say the proletarian revolution would follow the pattern of the revolutions of the seventeenth and eighteenth centuries. First, a progressive bourgeois party would take power, aided by revolutionary workers as a propelling force. It would rule for a while, run its course, and give way to a radical bourgeois party, which would soon be overthrown by the revolutionary party of the proletariat. In his preface to *Revelations on the Communist Trial* (1887) Engels was still saying that petit bourgeois democrats "must certainly be the first to come to power." This "certainty" was not based on historical evidence. It was something on the level of principle for Engels, something *necessary* for a successful socialist revolution to occur.[80]

Bernstein no longer believed it because modern revolutions tended to immediately thrust forward the most radical party. It happened in France in 1848 and 1871, and since then the socialist movement had grown strong. There was no reason to believe that next time socialists and revolutionaries would take a back seat to bourgeois radicals or liberals. It was far more likely that bourgeois types would withdraw, leaving political responsibility to the proletarians. Bernstein doubted that a radical bourgeois government would last a single day in Germany. In that case, socialists needed to be ready to govern Germany, something he shuddered to imagine for the SPD as he knew it. SPD bigwigs trivialized what Blanquism was about, routinely reducing it to a stereotype about a handful of vanguard conspirators waging terrorism which had nothing to do with them. Bernstein said this was convenient for them but wrong. Blanquism is the theory that the overthrowing power of revolutionary force is immeasurably creative and indispensable. This cult of force, a legacy of the French Revolution and contradiction dialectics, is toxic and hard to uproot, it condemned Bernstein at the Stuttgart congress, and the SPD was overdue to be purged of it.

There were similar problems with other Marxian concepts. Bernstein cautioned socialists against assuming that Marx's theories of value and surplus value are the last word on both subjects because Marx's measure of commodity value involves too many abstractions and reductions to be intelligible. It starts with pure exchange value being abstracted from the particular use value of individual commodities. To get a concept of general human labor, one must set aside the peculiarities of numerous particular kinds of labor. To get the socially necessary labor time that measures the value of labor, one must set aside differences in the work habits, ability, and equipment of workers. To convert value into market value, one must set aside the labor time required for commodities taken separately. The labor value thus derived requires another abstraction because under capitalism commodities are sold at the cost of production, plus a given profit rate, not at the cost of their individual values. On Marx's account, Bernstein argued, value is an abstracted construct stripped of concrete content, and surplus value is the difference between this mental construct and the labor power expended in the production of products. Surplus value, however crucial it may be in fact, is a formula resting on a hypothetical construct.[81]

Bernstein commended Engels for struggling mightily with this problem in volume 3 of *Capital*. He judged that Engels ably substantiated much of Marx's analysis about the development of the profit rate in economic history. But economic historians were already shooting down things that Engels got wrong about feudal relationships, guilds, and other monopolies. More important, Engels did not improve upon Marx's abstract quandaries about value. Bernstein judged that Marx and Engels would have done better to let go of gauging the value of individual commodities, since commodities are sold at the price of their production, plus profit. What matters is the value of the total production of society, plus the surplus of this value over the sum total of wages paid to the working class.

That is, the social surplus value, measuring production as a whole, matters more than dubious calculations about individual value. Surplus value is real only for the economy as a whole. Of course, this is problematic too, since there is no reliable measure for the total demand at any given time for given commodities. Bernstein wished that Marx had not wagered so much on this enterprise; labor value is merely a key, at best. Engels, in volume 3, responded to the neoclassical turn in economic theory, the marginal utility school of Austrian economist Carl Menger and English economist William S. Jevons. Marginal theorists denied that value could be calculated from the cost of production or labor embodied in the product. They held that value is a function of utility derived from the cumulative desires of consumers. Value is determined at the margin, depending on the relationship between desires and supply. The leading Fabians—Shaw and Sidney Webb—embraced marginal theory, as did much of the academy. Bernstein watched this trend with a sinking feeling, fretting that his Marxian comrades were willing to go down with a discredited doctrine about the objectivity of value. In *Neue Zeit* he toyed with a synthesis of marginal analysis and Marxian theory, reasoning that Marx's theory of value is merely a means of analysis, not a demonstrative proof of anything, and the social surplus is real whether or not the theory of value is valid.[82]

Socialists had bigger things to worry about than Marx's reputation in the academy; Bernstein was not talking only about that. The bigger problem was that socialists invoked Marx's authority in claiming that the labor theory of value measures the exploitation of workers. Often they described the rate of surplus value as the rate of exploitation. Bernstein countered that value and distributive justice are both more complicated. The highest paid workers usually toiled in trades with the highest rates of surplus value, while the most brutally exploited workers toiled in places with low rates. The labor theory of value did not provide a sufficient basis for socialism, so Engels said in his preface to the first German edition (1884) of *Poverty of Philosophy* that Marx based his socialist demands on something else—the inevitable collapse of capitalism. Actually, Bernstein was cheating again to make Engels sound like Bernstein, but Engels did believe that the inevitable collapse of capitalism trumped everything else.[83]

This was the crucial matter, and to Bernstein the truth was a mixture of yes, no, and not-yet-known. In Marxian theory, capitalism produces surplus value to make a profit but draws surplus value only from living labor. Capitalists angle for market advantage by reducing the costs of production, either by lowering wages or raising the productivity of labor via machinery. To save human labor power, however, is to put value-producing labor out of commission, reducing profits. Marx also said that overproduction of commodities is endemic to capitalism, creating booms and busts of depreciation, capital destruction, and stagnation followed by periods of equilibrium in which the dance of profitable capital investment begins again, now with greater centralization of capital, greater concentration of enterprises, and worse exploitation than before the last round of booming and crashing.

All of this is true, Bernstein said—as a tendency. The structural forces that Marx described are real, as are the fall in the rate of profit, the periodic destruction of capital, the concentration and centralization of industrial capital, and the increase in surplus value. In principle, every plank of Marx's critique of capitalism holds up, even though Marx misconstrued the situation under capitalism. Bernstein pressed hard on the latter point. Capitalism took longer to develop than Marx expected, he mistook an early phase of its development for its fall, the number of property owners grew throughout the 1870s, 1880s, and 1890s, and the enormous increase in social wealth went along with a similar increase in the number of capitalists of all levels. Marx's picture did not describe much of what happened. He completely ignored key factors that blunted the structural antagonisms he described, and he gave misleadingly short shrift to others. He stuck relentlessly with his critique, which got many things right but not the social reality confronting socialists at the end of the century.

Marx treated the rise of the joint-stock company only as an example of the concentration and centralization of capital, failing to recognize that joint-stock companies create a significant counterweight to the centralization of wealth by centralizing business enterprises. Joint-stock companies permit already concentrated capital to be extensively divided, making it unnecessary for capitalist titans to appropriate capital to concentrate their enterprises. Bernstein said socialists were slow to grasp what made corporate capitalism different because Marxian theory steered them away from doing so. Plus, Marx said the concentration of industrial entrepreneurs runs parallel with the concentration of wealth, which is not true. Bernstein brandished a slew of graphs dramatizing the ongoing capitalist blowout in Germany, England, Holland, and France. He implored that socialism had a viable future because social wealth was increasing, not decreasing. The movement had to give up its dire dogma that its future depended on an imminent catastrophe—a diminishing capitalist class that sucked up all surplus value. Modern production greatly increased the productivity of labor, which greatly increased the mass production of goods for use, generating enormous new wealth. If capitalist magnates ate ten times as much and employed ten times as many servants, their consumption would be "a feather in the scales." To be sure, they exported much of the surplus, but foreign customers paid in commodities that fueled larger middle-class sectors on both sides.[84]

Socialists had to stop pining for a capital crisis that wiped out the growing middle classes of the world. Bernstein pointed to Kautsky's plaintive protest at Stuttgart that socialists would never reach their goal if capitalists were increasing, not the proletariat. Bernstein had never said the industrial proletariat was not increasing. He still believed, with Marx, that the proletariat grew as capital grew. Kautsky's fixation on orthodox Marxism prevented him from imagining that capitalists and the proletariat might increase simultaneously. Kautsky had a zero-sum understanding of capitalism that identified capital with capitalists, but Bernstein knew volume 3 of *Capital*, where Marx developed the idea of the organic development of capital. Marx taught that constant capital increases and variable capital decreases in modern capitalist development, such that the absolute increase of capital causes a relative decrease in the enterprises concerned. Thus the absolute increase of capital causes a relative decrease in the proletariat in the economy as a whole. However, the workers who become redundant through the growth of capital and technology find new jobs only to the extent that *new* capital is infused into the market. Marx perceived that the number of industrial workers could and did increase as long as capital increases proportionally even faster. Bernstein boasted that he, not Kautsky, had Marx on his side. The contradiction of capitalist development looms large in the qualifier precondition—"as long as"—but there is a basis in Marxian theory for granting that big capitalism, the middle class, and the proletariat might grow simultaneously for prolonged periods of time.[85]

That was not what Marxists said, however. Moreover, Bernstein knew very well that Kautsky and Luxemburg would win a proof-texting contest. He said Marxian theory was more capacious than the catastrophe version propounded by Kautsky and Luxemburg, but he also said that making sense of reality was more important than getting Marx right. Luxemburg treated credit as an entirely destructive phenomenon, contrary to Marx's view that credit is half fraudulent and half creative. On stronger ground, Luxemburg stressed Marx's generally correct belief that overproduction is unavoidable in capitalism. Even here, Bernstein cautioned that overproduction in individual industries does not necessarily lead to a general crisis. Overproducing industries must be systemically significant to produce a general crisis, bringing down industries in other areas. Bernstein believed that wealthy nations with advanced credit systems faced little danger of collapse because their wealth multiplied their capacity to make adjustments. Even Marx said contractions at the center of the money market are more readily overcome than at the periphery, although he also warned in volume 3 that expanding markets lead to extended credit, which leads to speculation becoming the dominant feature of business. Bernstein agreed but noted that communication technology grew spectacularly after Marx's death, erasing the perils of distance.[86]

Social Democracy, Bernstein urged, could easily be more compelling and up-to-date than the dire apocalyptic face it presented to the world. The key to socialism is the idea of cooperation, but much of the socialist movement had forgotten how to say it, losing the etymology of the word: *socius* = associate. Marxian Social Democracy rested everything on a theory about the structural contradictions of capitalist production and an argument about the exercise of political power by a class party of workers, described in the transition period as a dictatorship of the proletariat. All three parts of this platform were problematic, and the third part was repellant. Social Democracy needed to acknowledge that wage earners were not the homogeneous mass devoid of property that the *Communist Manifesto* depicted. Moreover, the most advanced industries produced highly differentiated labor hierarchies in which feelings of solidarity were tenuous at best. Bernstein grieved that barricade rhetoric prevailed at Stuttgart. It may have felt exciting to proclaim, but it repelled toolmakers who made decent wages and farmers who wanted to own their land.

Social Democracy fixed so intently on the seizure of political power that it no longer talked about cooperatives, where socialism began. Marx's baleful comments on cooperatives in the *Manifesto*, *The Eighteenth Brumaire of Louis Bonaparte* (1851), and the *Critique of the Gotha Program* settled the matter for many Social Democrats. Marx said cooperatives were small bore and a distraction, although in volume 3 he allowed that they played a role in the transition to socialist production. Here and there in the 1860s and 1870s, Bernstein recalled, some socialists created producer cooperatives, accepting consumer cooperatives only as part of the bargain. Socialists didn't like consumer societies because they held down wages and morphed into retail outlets. But the producer experiments usually failed outside the handicraft trades, while consumer societies flourished. Producer cooperatives never became an economic force, exactly as Marx said. They had trouble getting capital and credit, and they did not scale up, mainly because equality breaks down as soon as a cooperative firm gets big enough to require differentiation of labor. Very few producer cooperatives were both sizable and successful, and the few exceptions succeeded by compromising the equality principle. Bernstein said Beatrice Webb was right about cooperatives: Producer cooperatives are still a form of private ownership and thus individualistic, while consumer societies are more broadly democratic. Bernstein still liked producer cooperatives, but, more important, he wanted Social Democracy to learn from the success of consumer societies because they dwarfed producer cooperatives as an economic force. Producer cooperatives required technical skills and habits of cooperation that took many years to develop. Socialists were too quick to say the price wasn't worth paying. Routinely they disparaged cooperatives for being bourgeois, paying salaries to officials, paying workers with wages, and paying interest and dividends. But these very features of cooperatives made them broadly accessible to working-class people. Not being snotty about that, Bernstein believed, should have been a socialist trademark.[87]

Consumer cooperatives seek to enhance the rate of profit in trade, while trade unions seek to enhance the rate of profit in production for the benefit of workers. Marxian Social Democrats were conflicted about unions in the same way they were conflicted about democracy: They were for unions as long as unions did not thwart the revolution. But many unionists did not dream of Social Democracy, so the SPD had constant debates about restraining the agency and standing of unions. Bernstein was emphatically on the side that supported unions as bulwarks of democracy and democracy as the essence of socialism.

Marxian theory came from an era in which democracy was merely a form of government and thus not really the point for a Marxist. To be sure, the root of democracy—government by the people—was very much the point, but not as interpreted by liberals. Bernstein said democracy changed into something else in the late nineteenth century. Socialists, radical democrats, and progressive liberals brought out the negative meaning of democracy as the absence of class government. No class should have a political privilege against the community as a whole. Progressives got clear about this in fighting against the antidemocratic privilege of the monopolistic corporation. Moreover, Bernstein argued, the negative definition brought out the idea that a majority's oppression of the individual is repellant. Generalizing his own feeling, Bernstein said that repressing individuals and minority communities was "absolutely repugnant to the modern mind." Modern people recognized that abusing minorities is profoundly antidemocratic: "As we understand it today, the concept of democracy includes an idea of justice, that is, equality of rights for all members of the community, and this sets limits to the rule of the majority." Socialists played a key role in establishing that democracy is democratic only if it protects the equal rights of all people of the community. Bernstein wanted socialists to name and own their contribution to full-orbed democracy: "The more democracy prevails and determines public opinion, the more it will come to mean the greatest possible degree of freedom for all."[88]

Bernstein was out of touch, and not. He claimed that European democracies already upheld the rights of minorities and believed that democracy was not merely the rule of a majority. That was wildly off the mark. He also knew that his emphasis on democracy smacked of sellout liberalism to his chief audience, so he said it aggressively. Both things registered as "out of touch," but his book was a movement polemic, not academic sociology. Bernstein's insistence that democracy was not another name for lawlessness showed that he understood how the prodemocracy argument usually played out. He implored audiences to stop denigrating democracy because it abolished laws granting privileges to property, birth, and religious confession, laws infringing individual rights, and laws denying to any citizen the equal right of all to the liberties and goods of society. It was vulgar and dishonest, he said, for anyone to describe democracy as the tyranny of the majority or the rule of lawlessness. He flattered his audience to win the point: "In our times, there is an almost unconditional guarantee that the majority in a democratic community will make no law that does lasting injury to personal freedom, for today's majority can easily become tomorrow's minority and every law oppressing a minority is thus a threat to members of the current majority." That did not describe terribly well Bernstein's experience as a socialist from a Jewish family in Germany or his still exiled status. But it described very well why he wanted full-orbed democracy to prevail.[89]

To Bernstein, democracy was the means and the end of socialist struggle: "It is a weapon in the struggle for socialism, and it is the form in which socialism will be realized." He acknowledged that it did not perform miracles. In Switzerland the industrial proletariat was a minority of the population, so democracy had no chance of bringing the proletariat to political power. In England the industrial proletariat lacked the will and organization to try. But Switzerland, England, France, the United States, and the Scandinavian nations had socialist and radical democratic movements that were powerful levers of social progress. Where such movements existed, democracy already stood for the abolition of class government, despite lacking the actual abolition of classes. Bernstein allowed that the customary Social Democratic response—democracy is conservative—had a kernel of truth. Democracy compelled all parties to recognize the limits of their power and reach. Working democratically was messy and prosaic, requiring constant bargaining. It was nowhere near as emotionally cathartic as revolutionary socialism, which abounded with absolutist rhetoric. The entire Blanquist tradition conceived democracy as a repressive force. Social Democracy had to stop drawing from that well. In practice, he acknowledged, Social Democracy always supported the democratic doctrine of universal suffrage. But everyone knew that socialists "have often offended against this doctrine in their pronouncements, and such offenses still continue."[90]

For example, how could it be that SPD literature still called for the dictatorship of the proletariat? This phrase, in its time, may have marshaled opposition to the absolute reign of property in Europe, but all attempts to salvage it were stupendously wrong. Bernstein put it sharply: "Class dictatorship belongs to a lower civilization." Democrats had the German language against them on this point, so Bernstein said it as plainly as possible. German had no word that distinguished a citizen with equal rights in a community from the concept of a privileged citizen. Since no special word marking the former existed, Bernstein proposed to reserve the loanword "bourgeois" for the privileged citizen, not Bürger (citizen), because otherwise it sounded like German socialists wanted to wipe out civil (bürgerlich) society. Social Democrats needed to speak of opposing the bourgeoisie and abolishing bourgeois society without being grossly misunderstood. Bernstein could have said that Marx tried to disentangle the linguistic ambiguity of bürgerlich—which sometimes means "civil" and sometimes means "bourgeois"—by coining the neologism "bourgeois." But what mattered was that Marxists gave the impression they wanted to abolish civil society. Bernstein said they had to take responsibility for the upshot of their rhetoric. Social Democracy, rightly understood, did not aspire to destroy Germany's civilized community—civil society—in favor of turning everyone into a proletarian. To the contrary, the goal was "to raise the worker from the social position of a proletarian to that of a citizen [Bürger]." Social Democracy was about making citizenship universal: "It does not want to replace a civil society with a proletarian society but a capitalist order of society with a socialist one."[91]

Social Democratic literature made it too easy for reactionaries to claim that Social Democrats were tyrannical smashers. Bernstein said Lassalle was better "than we are today" in this area. Lassalle, in his *Workers' Program*, denied that his opposition to the bourgeoisie entailed any animus against *bügerlich* society: "It does not have this meaning for me. We are *all citizens*: the worker, the petit bourgeois, the big bourgeois, etc. In the course of history, the word bourgeoisie has rather acquired a meaning which denotes a well-defined political tendency." For similar reasons, Bernstein added, Social Democrats had to stop bashing liberalism indiscriminately. This was another hangover from decades past. Before liberalism bonded with democracy, liberals were procapitalist enemies and old-fashioned liberals still were. It mattered greatly that most liberals now supported democracy. Bernstein did not stop there. He made a stronger claim about liberalism and its affinity with Social Democracy, one guaranteed to offend. Social Democracy, he contended, prized civil liberties above everything else. Liberals did not own this issue because whenever Social Democrats had to choose between defending civil liberties and promoting economic justice, they always chose liberty. Here again, the practice was better than the official rhetoric. Social Democracy throughout its history had a freedom-loving, ethical, democratic, humanistic core: "The aim of all socialist measures, even of those that outwardly appear to be coercive measures, is the development and protection of the free personality. A closer examination of such measures always shows that the coercion in question will *increase* the sum total of liberty in society, and will give *more* freedom over a *more extended* area than it takes away."[92]

Limits on the workday belonged in this category, as did prohibiting slavery. Bernstein insisted that everything Social Democracy struggled to achieve was for the sake of human freedom: "Socialism will create no new bondage of any kind whatever." Anarchists demanded to be free of all duties to the community; socialism was about creating a good society that abolishes economic compulsion. It was not achievable without freedom-loving organizations: "In this sense, one might call socialism 'organized liberalism.'" Socialism, in this telling, was a fusion of feudalism and liberalism, bonding feudal institutions and the principle of the common good to liberal freedom and democratic constitutionalism.[93]

Bernstein felt the limitations of the Marxism story that Social Democrats told, and he realized his emphasis on the French Revolution had similar problems. At meetings, newcomers said his message reminded them of what they learned in the Bible. Sometimes they pulled out a Bible to show him. Bernstein didn't know what to say to that. He knew enough religious socialists not to smirk, his personal atheism was not in question, and he realized that religion was a problem for Social Democracy. Meanwhile he said that Social Democrats had to rethink the national question, no matter how much it disturbed them. In Germany the national question had become unavoidable because Social Democrats were close to attaining power. Bernstein declared that he had no chauvinistic inclinations and no cause to have them: "My esteem for internationalism is as high today as it ever was." He did not compromise socialist internationalism. It was important to say, however, that internationalism "is no reason for yielding weakly to the pretensions of foreign interested parties," a point made by Marx, Engels, and Lassalle. Germany had legitimate national interests, like all other nations, and German Social Democrats were compelled to defend Germany if they attained power. Bebel, holding forth in the Reichstag, said that if Russia attacked Germany he would call Social Democrats to defend Germany. Bernstein agreed that Social Democrats should not be purists about nationality and war, hard as it was to give up the purity pose.[94]

He inched into perilous territory. Bernstein opposed Germany's recent occupation of Kiaochow Bay, but not as a matter of principle. Germany had a legitimate interest in ensuring free trade with China, there were hard choices to make, the SPD rightly opposed the occupation, and knee-jerk anticolonialism was stupid. Bernstein believed that imperialisms ranged from the defensibly not so bad (when they promoted "civilization") to the indefensibly horrid. British imperialism was mostly of the former sort, like Periclean Athens and Republican Rome, while Genghis Khan and tsarist Russia practiced horrid imperialism. In 1899 Bernstein still hoped that Germany would aspire to the British standard of colonizing. He said it was out of the question for Social Democrats to support Germany's recent binge of colonizing, but socialism was not absolutely anticolonialist. The old chestnut that acquiring colonies delayed the march of socialism was a hangover from the ever-worsening-misery theory. Colonialism, he declared, was not an impediment to socialism, so socialists could be trusted to be reasonable in this area. Bernstein put it negatively: "German Social Democracy would have nothing whatsoever to fear from the colonial policy of the German Reich." Implicitly, it also worked the other way around, if Social Democrats attained power and the German people still wanted colonies. Bernstein anticipated a socialist Germany of the near future that acquired new colonies. After all, Germany already imported colonial produce. Why not get it from Germany's own colonies? To be sure, he allowed, this was a far cry from international socialism, but it would be a long time before many countries went socialist. Then he said it with howling Enlightenment bigotry: "It is not inevitable that the occupation of tropical countries by Europeans should harm the natives in their enjoyment of life, nor has it usually been the case up till now. Moreover, we can recognize only a conditional right of savages to the land they occupy. Higher civilization has ultimately a higher right. It is not conquest but the cultivation of the land that confers an historical right to its use."[95]

Native peoples had rights that civilized people were bound to respect, but they had no right to their lack of "civilization." Bernstein heard plenty of that at Fabian meetings, plus protests against jingoism and imperialism. He said he kept his balance between the extremes of his friends. Superpatriotism repelled him, but so did antipatriotism. British Christian socialists railed against imperialism, but they were moralists at heart; mainstream Fabians kept their balance, like him. Orthodox Marxists took unwarranted pride in spurning morality, yet they clutched proletarian internationalism as a moral dogma. Bernstein pitched his case to the quiet majority of Social Democrats he believed was out there. They knew Marx was wrong about many things but were expected to pretend that Marx was always right. Bernstein believed his arguments for democratic socialism fit his case for colonial progress. If he got to return to imperial Germany he would not stand in the way of its interests and colonial ambitions and saying so might help him return. More important, the SPD had to become trustworthy in this area, without going overboard. In foreign policy, he said, healthy debates between democracies are healthy. In fact, "an exchange of ideas between the democracies of the civilized countries" is the only way to work for peace.[96]

When Bernstein made his fateful declaration about the final goal, he had in mind a sentence from Marx's *Civil War in France*: "They have no ideals to realize, but to set free the elements of the new society with which old collapsing bourgeois society itself is pregnant." Bernstein believed his statement about the movement being everything was an apt restatement of Marx. The movement mattered, not any preconceived idea about the outcome of the movement. Sometimes he said he was a better Marxist than his left-flank accusers; then he added that this was not the right issue. Georg Plekhanov angrily declared that Bernstein's sellout of Marxism reduced to one thing—his claim that the condition of the worker in bourgeois society was not hopeless. All his errors sprang from this one, which made Bernstein an enemy of scientific socialism. Bernstein replied that Plekhanov degraded the word "science" "to pure cant." Real science was open-ended, tracked the evidence, and corrected its errors. The dogma about the hopeless condition of the worker had become a form of bad faith in Marxism. It was the basis of an entire belief system or at least "an indisputable axiom of 'scientific socialism.'" To cite a study by a bourgeois economist had become an unforgivable offense in Marxism, if the study contradicted something Marx said in the 1840s. Bernstein put it blandly, knowing he would offend anyway: "The fact that Marx and Engels once subscribed to an error does not justify continuing to maintain it; and a truth does not lose its force because it was first discovered or expounded by an anti-socialist or not completely socialist economist. In the field of science, bias has no claim to privilege or powers of expulsion."[97]

Bernstein acknowledged that Luxemburg was right about the upshot of his revisionism. On his interpretation, socialism had no objective historical necessity, and it needed an idealistic basis. The middle class was not vanishing, the number of capitalist magnates was not declining, and socialists had to stop embarrassing themselves on these points. To learn that property owners were increasing in number, one had only to consult the records of tax authorities: "Why should the achievement of socialism depend on its denial?" The SPD, Bernstein said, knew better than its rhetoric, as proved by its everyday practices. If the SPD really believed that socialism was impossible if the number of capitalist magnates grew, it should have supported policies that heaped capital in fewer and fewer hands. But only a few wingnuts held out for that. In its politics the SPD was a reformist party, not an agent of apocalyptic sectarianism. Bernstein never said how much of the national economy should be socialized, as this was a pragmatic economic matter. Socializing everything would be insane, and some private industries were better left under private management. As for idealism, Bernstein owned up to it, confessing he was a Kantian ethical idealist, as interpreted politically by Lange. Kant's imperative about treating all people as ends in themselves, never as a means to an end, could be fulfilled only under democratic socialism, as Lange contended. Marx's denigration of moral reason had long grated on Bernstein, and he was happy to shuck it off.[98]

The Preconditions of Socialism was an earthquake in Social Democracy. Bernstein was pilloried for betraying Marxism, capitulating to English liberalism, and demoralizing Social Democrats, but he had heard all that before. More important, the book was a supercharger for his revisionist faction of the party, the broader reform wing to which it belonged, and the party's growing union faction. Bernstein shot to the top of the quiet party majority he believed was there. He compelled orthodox Marxists to clarify what orthodox Marxism was and was not, which Kautsky graciously said was a real service to the party. Liebknecht, shortly before he died in 1900, said Bernstein's "sentimental philanthropic striving after human equality" was ethical socialism, not class struggle socialism, two entirely different things. He hated that a wholly nonrevolutionary ideology had arisen in Social Democracy, something Liebknecht insisted had not happened at Gotha. Now the true socialists had to reassert that Social Democracy stood for proletarian revolution and "no political trading."

Liebknecht wagered that fewer than ten thousand SPD comrades actually read Bernstein's book, so the sky was not falling. Center leftists and radical leftists still defined Social Democracy. Bernstein's renown, however, swept him home in 1901, as Chancellor Bernhard von Bülow figured that Bernstein's return might split the SPD. Bernstein defended his position in person for the first time at the Lübeck congress of 1901. Vehemently condemnatory resolutions against him were introduced and defeated. Bebel took it hard, offering a milder resolution that censured Bernstein for one-sided criticisms of Marxism and Social Democracy. Bebel's resolution passed, but the Lübeck congress was a victory for Bernstein, and a vindication.[99]

The reformist side of the party had never had a theorist, much less a star with a storied history in the SPD. Bernstein plunged into party activism and was promptly nominated for the Breslau-West seat in the Reichstag. He beat Breslau radical Oscar Schütz and young radical lawyer Karl Liebknecht in a party runoff before crushing his opposition in the March 1902 election. Everywhere he spoke he drew crowds of supporters who called themselves "Bernsteinians" or "Revisionists." They launched a journal, *Sozialistische Monatschefte*, and Bebel grudgingly accepted that the gradualist side of the party had a theory and a journal, not just a grab bag of compromises. Bernstein savored that he had proven Bebel and Kautsky to be wrong about his place in Germany. Luxemburg demanded the expulsion of the revisionists from the SPD, which did not happen at the party's climactic debate at Dresden in 1903. Bebel and Kautsky remained in control of the party, the radical wing was rebuked for divisiveness, and the revisionists were censured for selling out socialism but formally indulged.[100]

At the intellectual level the controversy over revisionism never ceased. But the revisionist heresy made its greatest impact on large sectors of the party that were averse to intellectualism. Most reformers did not read *Neue Zeit* or go in for theory, so Bernstein got little help from them, even as he legitimized their role in Social Democracy. His challenge to Marxian orthodoxy also helped trade unionists assert themselves, also with little thanks. The Bernstein controversy and the rise of the unions hit the party at the same time. Until the late 1890s unions had a secondary status in the SPD. They were too weak and dependent to create party leaders, they took no interest in intellectual debates, and they acquiesced to the party's patronizing slogan from Marx that unions were schools of socialism, not central to socialism.

That began to change at the 1893 party congress in Cologne when Carl Legien, leader of the Free Trade Unions, said SPD unions should concentrate on labor organizing and not require their members to support the SPD politically. Politically, he was for don't-bother-us neutrality because many union members did not want to be saddled with Social Democracy. This position caused heartburn at SPD conferences, where radical leftists insisted on union subordination to the party, as did the party's center leftist leaders, Bebel and Kautsky. In 1893 Social Democratic votes outnumbered the unionists by eight to one. Then the ratio changed dramatically, falling to four to one in 1898 and three to one in 1903. Union leaders felt their surging power and used it, demanding to be treated as partners, not pupils. By 1906, when the SPD took its first census, it turned out that the party had 385,000 members and the unions had 1,700,000 members. Bebel and Kautsky infuriated the radical wing by giving in to numerical reality, granting equal status to the unions in the Mannheim Agreement of 1906.[101]

Bernstein's gradualist agenda and support of unionism were highly congenial to the worldview and interests of a surging union movement. He opposed the syndical dream that all-powerful unions should run the country, but so did most unionists. The coming of Bernstein revisionism helped unions gain power in the party and achieve their goals. Union leaders, however, did not take a stand on revisionist versus orthodox Marxism. They said that intellectual debates about Marxism were boring and irrelevant to them. Neither did Bernstein's followers break into the unions. The revisionist school attracted intellectuals—Vollmar, agrarian theorist Eduard David, ethical idealist Ludwig Frank, economist Conrad Schmidt, political historian Paul Kampffmeyer, and future Bavarian prime minister Kurt Eisner. Most were from South German states, where the three-class electoral system did not exist (although Saxony adopted it in 1896) and Social Democrats had a history of collaborating with liberals. The Bernstein revisionists defended their role in the party and their right to the Marxist name with spirited unity, hanging together until August 1914. They stood for something much bigger than their little group of intellectuals, but no faction of the SPD held true to socialism when catastrophe struck in August 1914.[102]

DEFENDING REVOLUTIONARY MARXISM: KARL KAUTSKY AND ROSA LUXEMBURG

The task of defending Marxian theory and strategy fell to Europe's leading Marxian theorist, Kautsky, who earned an ironic title, "the Pope of Marxism," by defending Marxian orthodoxy against his former friend, and to the scintillating Luxemburg, who despaired that she failed to pull Kautsky to the left. For years they had been allies in defending the revolutionary character of Marxism and Social Democracy from reformist forces in the SPD. But the center did not hold in German Social Democracy. Kautsky found himself fighting the radicals more than the right flank, and then catastrophe struck. Two world-historical movements came out of German Social Democracy, but neither expounded the conception of Marxian revolution that Kautsky and Luxemburg very differently espoused.

Kautsky established for many what respectable Marxian radicalism looked like. Born in Prague in 1854 to a Czech nationalist father and German mother, both artistic and middle class, Kautsky grew up in Vienna, where Czechs were denigrated. He told audiences that being Czech in Vienna was very much like being a Jew in Germany and Austria. He studied philosophy and economics at the University of Vienna, joined the Austrian Social Democratic Party as a student in 1874, and joined Höchberg's group in Zurich six years later. Kautsky's belief in the supremely important role of correct theory lifted him to a leadership role. He was slow to realize that Bernstein fell away, in Kautsky's magazine, unlike Luxemburg, who noticed immediately. Luxemburg said it was terribly important not to speak of revisionist Marxism because Bernstein was an opportunist with no arguments of his own, only objections to something incomparably great, Marxism. She befriended Kautsky, clashed with German socialist leaders, sustained a tense and conflicted friendship with Kautsky, and failed to move the SPD center to the left, which yielded a painful break with Kautsky. She also clashed with Bebel, who wrote a book about recruiting women to socialism but made sexist remarks about Luxemburg. Later she symbolized for many the martyred tragedy of a road not taken.[103]

Luxemburg said Bernstein began by abandoning the cornerstone of scientific socialism, the theory of capitalist breakdown, so in logical fashion he dumped all other Marxist doctrines one by one. If capitalism did not break down, it was impossible to expropriate the capitalist class, so Bernstein renounced expropriation, substituting "a progressive realization of the 'cooperative principle.'" But cooperation was impossible within capitalist production, so Bernstein renounced the socialization of production, falling back on consumer cooperatives. But the dream of a cooperative commonwealth was incompatible with "the real material development of capitalist society," so Bernstein dropped historical materialism. Since Marx was evidently wrong about capitalist development, Bernstein dumped the theory of value and surplus value, leaving nothing of Marx's economic theory. The class struggle came next, which Bernstein happily dropped, since he wanted very much to be reconciled with liberals. That led him to discard even the idea that classes exist in society, for Bernstein said the working class is a mass of individuals with various conflicting economic interests. Thus in "rigorously logical" fashion Bernstein passed from the materialist conception of history to the commonsense prattle of bourgeois editorialists.[104]

To Luxemburg, Marxism was magnificent precisely because it grasped capitalism as a totality. Bernstein viewed society from the standpoint of individual capitalists and individual units of capital, so he missed the crucial point of Marxian analysis, while believing his myopic empiricism constituted a devastating critique. Perhaps it was true that the credit system enabled individual firms to overcome some of the anarchic features of capitalist competition, but expanding productivity in this fashion exacerbated the mal-distribution of power between those who owned capital and those who were employed by it. Socializing production within capitalism pushed the structural contradictions of capital to a higher level. Monopoly capitalism was not sustainable, but Bernstein, absurdly infatuated with England, shucked off everything he once knew about why Marxism mattered. Having dropped the entire socialist critique of capitalist society, Bernstein had one last step to take, which he took in vulgar empiricist style. He told socialists to recognize that capitalist society was in pretty good shape. Workers were doing better and the bourgeoisie was politically progressive; even bourgeois morality was healthy, more or less.

By the end, Luxemburg said, there was nothing left of socialist criticism to throw away: "He began by abandoning the *final aim* and supposedly keeping the movement. But as there can be no socialist movement without the socialist aim, he ends by renouncing the *movement*." She cackled at Bernstein's bits of Marx, Kant, Lassalle, and Lange sprinkled through his book. In his Marxist days Bernstein had a profound intellectual axis and a political compass, but now he had neither. He thought this freed him of a mere class morality, prizing his newfound intellectual freedom. Somehow he forgot that society consists of classes holding diametrically opposed interests and desires. Since the class struggle was terribly real, Luxemburg said, "a general human science in social questions, an abstract Liberalism, an abstract morality, are at present illusions, pure utopia." Incredibly, Bernstein believed that "bourgeois" was a universal idea, not a class expression. His book was the first attempt to provide a theoretical basis for steamship subsidies, South German agrarian socialism, Vollmar's state socialism, and other opportunist nostrums plaguing Social Democracy. Until now, Luxemburg wrote, opportunism had no theory because the whole point of opportunism was to have no principles, unlike Marxism, which disciplined the aims, means, and method of struggle. Bernstein deserved credit for showing that opportunism was incapable of being seriously theorized. But Bernstein opportunism was very good at smoothing the way for unions to sell out the socialist basis of the labor movement. It did so by making moral appeals to justice, criticizing the mode of distribution, and enacting the cooperative principle, "all the nice notions found in Bernstein's doctrine."[105]

These notions, Luxemburg said, had a legitimate place in the socialist movement before Marx formulated the principles of scientific socialism. To return to them afterward was ridiculous. She put it stronger than she believed because Luxemburg radiated ethical idealism and believed in it, telling Jogiches she was a moral idealist just like Bebel and many others who felt obligated to claim otherwise: "I am and will remain an idealist in the German as well as in the Polish movement." Her takedown of Bernstein was a public performance driven by a movement imperative flowing from her passionate belief in Marxian theory. All that came from Bernstein had to be shredded. To Luxemburg, the surprising thing about Bernstein's book was "its feebleness." As long as opportunism fixed on steamship subsidies or workplace issues, it seemed to have a serious basis in something: "But now that it has shown its face in Bernstein's book, one cannot help exclaim with astonishment: 'What? Is that all you have to say?' Not the shadow of an original thought! Not a single idea that was not refuted, crushed, reduced to dust, by Marxism several decades ago." It was good to learn that opportunists had nothing to say. On second thought, she said, the Bernstein episode represented something bigger: "For only dialectics and the materialist conception of history, magnanimous as they are, could make Bernstein appear as an unconscious predestined instrument, by means of which the rising working class expresses its momentary weakness but which, upon closer inspection, it throws aside contemptuously and with pride."[106]

Kautsky could not compete with that. He specialized in casuistry, lacking Luxemburg's talent for sarcasm and turning a phrase, and he had to think about his role as a party leader. Kautsky treated Bernstein more respectfully, acknowledging that he buoyed many Social Democrats, and he made sense on his own terms. But Bernstein's perspective wasn't Marxism, so Luxemburg was right about revisionist Marxism. Like Luxemburg, Kautsky stressed that capitalism was self-destructive, and Bernstein fell into the vulgar empiricist trap of misconstruing temporary adjustments in capitalism. Like Luxemburg, Kautsky reaffirmed the theory of "immiseration" (*Verelendung*)—a concept so central to orthodox Marxism that English translators had to establish the term by usage. Bernstein was overly impressed by the temporary prosperity of capitalism during its monopoly phase, a mentality Kautsky knew well from battling SPD unionists over steamship subsidies.

Kautsky said the proletariat received a smaller share of the gross product under monopoly capitalism than under earlier phases of industrialization. The structural contradictions in capitalism were intensifying, not receding. Capitalism grew in the 1890s by breeding cartels that eliminated competition from production and monopolized entire industries. The struggle against big cartels generated super cartels that merged various kinds of businesses into a single gigantic enterprise. This process had barely begun when Marx died, but Kautsky contended that Marx's theory of the concentration of capital uniquely explained its structural dynamics, growth, and inevitable failure. Bernstein misconstrued a desperate monopoly phase of capitalism as a refutation of Marx, treating select evidence of a few years' time as a refutation. Marx's predictions about when and how fast capitalism would fall were not essential to Marxism. What mattered was that Marx grasped the big picture and the coming implosion of capitalism.[107]

That put the fluctuations of industry and politics at the center of Kautsky's defense. The revolution of 1848 broke out during an economic crisis. The industrial expansion of the early 1850s thwarted proletarian efforts to try again. The crisis of 1871 came from dynastic wars and political unrest in a time of tremendous economic growth. Kautsky said the industrial and political spheres experienced periods of prosperity, crisis, and stagnation yielding social struggles and reform phases. The ups and downs in each sphere had an impact on the other sphere, and the current phase of bourgeois civilization ran longer than Marx and Engels expected. One sweeping admission cleared the ground for Kautsky: "For some years now we have been witnessing a period of economic prosperity, although this particular period is lasting longer than 1871." He acknowledged that a highly developed economic base extended the current growth run, yielding a period of dismally stagnant politics. Bernstein's book was perfectly geared to this situation: "His emphasis on small-scale practical economic work does correspond to actual existing needs; his skepticism regarding the probability of significant and rapid political transformations—catastrophes—is entirely in keeping with the experience of the last years."[108]

The practical types who cheered for Bernstein, Kautsky said, did not care about his theories or even know what they were. All they cared about was making things better in the present situation. Kautsky understood why ordinary people spurned theory, focused on short-term practicality, and shuddered at militant rhetoric. Bernstein gave them what they wanted. They wanted to believe that bargaining for gains under monopoly capitalism would keep paying off. But that was naïve and shortsighted, for quintessential Marxian reasons. Bernstein's reformist prescription for Social Democracy reflected a passing moment in time. He took far too seriously the achievements of bourgeois society and the qualms of middle-class lecture audiences.

Kautsky reminded lecture audiences that the old petit bourgeois liberals had a fighting spirit. They fought for their rights to make money and vote, and they fought to prevent capital from devouring them. The new liberals, however, especially the intellectuals, were averse to fighting: "They detest the class struggle, and according to them it should be eliminated or at least weakened. Class struggle means insurrection, rebellion, revolution; and these forces are to be rendered superfluous by social reforms." Kautsky detested café socialism, a revival of the twaddle that Marx and Engels blasted in the *Manifesto*. Repeatedly he invoked the *Manifesto* for getting the main thing right, proletarian revolution, albeit with some faulty calculations. Kautsky wearied of progressives who said that "proletarian brutality" was the only thing preventing them from joining the Social Democrats: "What actually keeps them from becoming involved are not externals, but their own lack of character and insight." Progressives did not understand "that it is neither possible to save the given social order nor to prevent the final victory of the proletariat. They are either unaware of their impotence to alter the course of the development of society, or they simply lack the strength and courage to admit that and to break with bourgeois society." In either case, now they had a prominent Social Democrat who told them they were right, a very troubling development for Social Democracy.[109]

Kautsky watched the problem grow at party meetings. He tried to correct the revisionist theorists and theory-less reformers: "It is an attractive picture they have painted, and again it cannot be truthfully said that it is wholly built in the air. The facts upon which it is founded actually exist. But the truth that they tell is only a half-truth." Legislative reforms stopped at the capitalist doorway. Trade unions cared only about unions. Consumer cooperatives were nice, so nobody criticized them except small merchants, but that was a clue to the feebleness of cooperatives. Kautsky said the capitalist class indulged cooperatives because they pleased squishy progressives without threatening the power of capital. Union leaders compounded Kautsky's distress by imploring him to stop quarreling with revisionists over mere words. Kautsky feared that attitude more than Bernstein revisionism. It was true, he allowed, that "both currents" in the SPD worked for the same sociopolitical and democratic reforms. But the question of the party's final aim was not a negligible wrangle over words. It concerned whether or not the SPD was a proletarian revolutionary party. If the SPD opted for revisionist socialism, which Kautsky called "the consummation of liberalism," it would morph into a people's party (*Volkspartei*) embracing all the bourgeois democrats and café socialists. To Kautsky, that was a nightmare of capitulation.[110]

His blend of revolutionary Marxism, stodgy intellectualism, and party leader practicality made him hard to pin down. Vladimir Ilyich Ulyanov, already going by "V. Lenin" in 1901, profusely lauded Kautsky's work of this period. Lenin launched the Bolsheviks in 1903 from a schism in the Russian Social Democratic Labor Party, a year after he wrote his manifesto for vanguard revolution and proletarian dictatorship, *What Is to Be Done?* There he praised Kautsky's "profoundly true and important utterances" on the either/or of class struggle. Marx and Engels, defining Marxism as radical ideology-critique, denied that Marxism is an ideology. Lenin followed Kautsky in treating this denial as self-flattery. Obviously Marxism was an ideology; the crucial thing was to police the choice between bourgeois ideology and socialist ideology. Lenin said Kautsky did it in exemplary fashion. There is no third option, Lenin contended, "for humanity has not created a 'third' ideology, and, moreover, in a society torn by class antagonisms there can never be a non-class or above-class ideology." According to Lenin, Kautsky profoundly understood what was at stake in Bernstein's opportunism: "To belittle socialist ideology *in any way*, to *deviate from it in the slightest degree* means strengthening bourgeois ideology."[111]

Lenin wanted to believe that Kautsky was a Leninist at heart. He appreciated Kautsky's revolutionary elitism, rejection of parliamentary reformism, and denigration of the liberal bourgeoisie, although Lenin later claimed to have detected from 1900 onward that Kautsky was a rank opportunist. *What Is to Be Done?* famously declared that class consciousness must be brought to workers from without. This slogan came straight from Kautsky, grievously to Luxemburg, who tried to dissuade Kautsky and Lenin from revolutionary elitism. Neo-Marxian social theorist Jan Rehmann, in his finely reasoned *Theories of Ideology* (2013), elaborates on the subterranean connections between Kautsky and Lenin, in his case from the viewpoint that Kautsky, Bernstein, and Lenin wrongly encouraged two generations of Marxists to relinquish the fundamental concept of Marxism as radical ideology-critique. Luxemburg, in this persuasive telling, was the true Marxist.[112]

Kautsky and his wife, Luise Kautsky, were Berlin–Friedenau neighbors of Luxemburg. They bonded over proletarian revolution, their shared revulsion of revisionism and imperialism, and Kautsky's friendships with Russian émigré Marxists, especially Plekhanov. Kautsky did not convey the usual SPD snobbery toward Russians, and he defended Luxemburg when she offended party leaders. Thus he and Luxemburg formed a comradely friendship. But the Russian Revolution of 1905 shook the SPD, enthralling its left wing, traumatizing its right wing, and squeezing party leaders. Kautsky zigged and zagged on what to say about mass strikes and how to deal with German unions, which strained his relationship with Luxemburg for years before it broke.

Kautsky stressed that the fall of capitalism did not depend on the will or zeal of any group. Even more, it did not depend on the conspiratorial cunning of a vanguard. Violence, he implored, is a weaker weapon than propaganda, conventional strikes, and organizing; the entire history of the labor movement

proved it. During placid periods good revolutionary work is prosaic, even boring. Kautsky did not have to be the most radical person in the room. He got
along with SPD officials who said that Luxemburg was rude and her ideas were
too Russian. They did not burn for revolutionary action like she did. Kautsky
fixed with steely scientific concentration on building up the SPD and restraining the masses from intemperate action. Ethics had a role in the struggle, subordinate to science. In a book on materialistic ethics Kautsky argued that
morality is like the rest of the ideological superstructure standing above the
mode of production. For given periods of time morality is sufficiently real to
break away from its base and carry on a life of its own. Thus Marxists had to be
vigilant about keeping morality in its place. Immorality, though terribly real,
exists only as a deviation from one's own morality. Kautsky reasoned that some
timeless and universal moral truth undoubtedly exists, but every idea about it is
determined by class interests and changing conditions. All moral precepts are
subject to continual change, a shaky foundation for what matters. To be sure,
Kautsky granted, Marx's moral passion occasionally broke through in his writings: "But he is continually aiming, and rightly, to banish it wherever possible.
For in science a moral ideal becomes a source of error if it gets to the stage of
attempting to dictate goals."[113]

Kautsky stuck determinately to that mode and mood, chiding that he was
not a r-r-radical like some others. Luxemburg epitomized r-r-radicalism, once
writing to herself: "Determined revolutionary activity coupled with a deep
feeling for humanity, that alone is the essence of socialism. A world must be
overturned, but every tear that flows and might have been stanched is an
accusation." Luxemburg hated the casual slurs against Russians and colonized
peoples she heard at political meetings. She was deeply involved in the Polish
and Russian revolutionary movements, heading (with Jogiches) both of Poland's
successive Social Democratic parties, which she tried to affiliate with the
Russian Social Democratic Party (RSDRP). She knew Lenin personally,
respected him greatly, worked with him, and was decidedly pro-Bolshevik in
the factional rivalry between Bolsheviks and Mensheviks, all despite vehemently opposing Lenin's dictatorial animus. Luxemburg described Lenin's dictatorial centralism as a mirror image of what she disliked in German Social
Democracy. In 1904 she observed that Russia was a special problem for socialists because the sheer force of Russia's absolutist state veiled the domination of
the bourgeoisie. Socialist criticism seemed abstract by comparison with ongoing revolutionary action. In her telling, Lenin's "pitiless" ultracentralism was
Social Democratic centralism vengefully exaggerated, resting on two principles: "1. The blind subordination, in the smallest detail, of all party organs, to

the party center, which alone thinks, guides, and decides for all. 2. The rigorous separation of the organized nucleus of revolutionaries from its social-revolutionary surroundings."[114]

This strategy, Luxemburg said, was a mechanical transposition of Blanquist organizing principles into the Russian working class and a looming disaster for Russian socialism. Lenin said that a revolutionary Social Democrat was a Jacobin joined to the organization of a class-conscious proletariat. Luxemburg countered that Social Democracy *was* the proletariat, not joined to it. True Social Democracy got rid of Blanquist centralism. Two things defined Social Democracy: a large contingent of workers who grasped its class interests, and a "regime of political liberty" that allowed the proletarian vanguard to affirm and realize its capacity for self-direction. The first condition, she argued, was emerging in Russia, but Leninism snuffed out the spirit of freedom in the name of proletarian dictatorship: "The ultra-centralism asked by Lenin is full of the sterile spirit of the overseer. It is not a positive and creative spirit. *Lenin's concern is not so much to make the activity of the party more fruitful as to control the party— to narrow the movement rather than to develop it, to bind rather than to unify it.*" The last phrase is better translated as "tying the movement up and not drawing it together." In either case Luxemburg recoiled at Lenin's vengeful arrogance, which denounced the slightest demurral from "military ultra-centralism" as opportunism. Lenin claimed that only opportunistic intellectuals chafed at the absolute authority of a revolutionary elite. Luxemburg was repulsed by Lenin's conceit that the true proletarian felt "a kind of voluptuous pleasure in abandoning himself to the clutch of firm leadership and pitiless discipline."[115]

To be sure, she allowed, socialist intellectuals were naturally prone to opportunism. They prized their individual egos and usually came to socialism against their class inclinations, so they had to be watched. Still, Leninism was the crowning evidence that intellectuals had important work to do in revolutionary movements. Intellectual criticism was an antidote to mechanical application and the tyranny of dictatorship. Lenin described every variation of the preference for decentralization as opportunism, the hallmark of intellectuals. Revolutionary organizations had to ruthlessly expunge their ranks of intellectual opportunists who paralyzed the movement to boost themselves. Luxemburg said Lenin misconstrued and exemplified the very thing that obsessed him, opportunism. Opportunism had only one principle, the absence of principle. Leninism was the epitome of opportunism, the exaltation of a revolutionary elite over all others, bound by no principle: "It is by extreme centralization that a young, uneducated proletarian movement can be most completely handed over to the intellectual leaders staffing a Central Committee."[116]

In her telling the Eisenach party was vastly better than the Lassalle party on this point, since Lassalle and von Schweitzer were unabashed centralizers. Now it was happening in Russia, the site of a magnificent proletarian struggle for liberation. Opportunistic intellectuals predictably favored "despotic centralism" wherever they led struggling movements groping for an answer, "as is the case now in Russia." Equally predictably, they favored decentralization wherever they operated under parliamentary regimes and were allied with strong labor parties. Luxemburg implored that Leninism was the worst possible organizational model for the proletariat in the revolution "soon to break out in Russia," which would be a bourgeois revolution. Bourgeois intellectuals were about to have their day in Russia. An unleashed proletariat was the best guarantee against opportunism. Social Democracy had to get its head straight, standing for the real liberation of the entire proletariat: *"Nothing will more surely enslave a young Labor movement to an intellectual elite hungry for power than this bureaucratic straight jacket, which will immobilize the movement and turn it into an automaton manipulated by a Central Committee."*[117]

Marxist theory, she believed, was an indispensable guide to recognizing and combating opportunism, but socialism was a mass movement. The perils of socialism arose out of unavoidable social conditions, not the machinations of individuals or groups. Lenin's obsession with opportunism was self-defeating and self-fulfilling. Luxemburg implored SPD comrades that the perils of Leninism were no reason to hold back from proletarian solidarity in Russia. To the contrary, the proletarian faction of the revolutionary movement desperately needed help.

Bloody Sunday in St. Petersburg—January 22, 1905—and a stunning coal strike in Germany's Ruhr basin convinced Luxemburg that the proletarian masses were moving in Russia and Germany, outracing their ostensible leaders. In Russia an explosion of worker strikes, peasant rebellions, and military mutinies swept through vast areas of the empire after troops fired on a defenseless crowd of workers in St. Petersburg. In Germany the coal strike was wholly spontaneous and historically unprecedented in scale. Luxemburg enthused that the RSDRP, barely seven years old, already surpassed its European counterparts. Socialism was changing, no longer constrained by the debates of the 1890s over revolutionary mass action. Until now, she said, anarchists owned the general strike as a spark for social revolution, while socialists focused on the daily political struggle of the working class. Socialists regarded mass strikes as either premature or unnecessary. If a mass strike lacked the requisite organizational strength and financial resources to succeed, it was wrong to strike. If the means existed, a mass strike was unnecessary. German Social Democracy deeply absorbed this Marx versus Bakunin lesson, but the Russian Revolution achieved "a grandiose realization of the idea of the mass strike," changing everything. The masses did not have to be trained and herded by organizations. Spontaneity no longer took a back seat to organization, for spontaneous strikes were the engines of revolutionary struggle. Luxemburg noted that anarchists had a negligible role in the Russian Revolution despite decades of Russian anarchism. Socialists had suddenly acquired "the most powerful weapon of the struggle for political rights," which German socialists needed to use in Germany. With this argument, Luxemburg broke free on her own, no longer hewing to Jogisches or romantically involved with him.[118]

Kautsky swung behind her, deeply moved by the Ruhr strike. In September 1905 Luxemburg's left radicals took their case to the SPD Congress at Jena, where Bebel gave a dramatic three-hour address that strained to say yes in a nonthreatening fashion. Bebel claimed that nothing in Russia applied to Germany because Russia was too backward to be an example for Germany. In Germany the mass strike had a legitimate role as a defensive weapon in the arsenal of the SPD and its unions. Germany, Bebel said, had two great organizations, both reflecting the Prussian–German genius for organization: the SPD and the army. Any use of the mass strike in Germany would be waged carefully and intelligently. That watered down Luxemburg's argument, pretending that spontaneity and unruly rebellion were not in play in the German context. To her, the mass strike was sharply distinct from conventional strikes because it was revolutionary. A planned strike of limited duration, such as the annual May Day strike, was a small thing. The revolutionary strike was something else entirely. Party leaders could not manage it, and when the revolutionary period came workers would not be taking orders anyway. They would launch mass strikes on their own. Luxemburg realized that SPD delegates would not vote for that, so she supported Bebel's resolution. For the first time the party declared itself ready to support a general strike in pursuit of its aim. Briefly Luxemburg hoped the party was moving in her direction. The following year the unions struck back at the Mannheim congress, winning independent parity with the party, and Luxemburg despaired that Kautsky and Bebel sold out. Caving to the unions meant the SPD was not a revolutionary party. When forced to decide whether the SPD was a revolutionary party with a parliamentary strategy or a reform party with revolutionary rhetoric, Kautsky and Bebel chose the latter.[119]

Always there were tensions and skirmishes about that. Kautsky and Bebel papered over the dichotomy between mass party revolution and parliamentary reform by exalting the organization. Anything that grew the party was revolutionary, since the SPD *was* the proletarian revolution in Germany. To Kautsky and Bebel, the purpose of the party was to grow. Orthodox Marxism, on this telling, was a form of organizational fetishism. To Luxemburg, that was pathetically self-deceiving. Kautsky told comrades that Luxemburg was extremely talented "but tact and a feeling of comradeship were completely foreign to her." She said he was "dull, unimaginative, and ponderous," and his ideas were "cold, pedantic, doctrinaire." In 1907 Luxemburg attended the RSDRP Congress in London, where she lauded the Russians for surpassing their German comrades. Russian Social Democrats were the first to apply Marx's teaching "in a stormy revolutionary period," something very different from Germany's parliamentary situation. Marx himself was the only one to try it previously, and only briefly in his case, during the 1848 revolution. Pointedly she reminded the delegates, "Without the slightest vacillation he supported and defended every action of the proletarian masses." Marx worked with bourgeois radicals but always with a revolutionary purpose and aim. Luxemburg boasted that proletarians were the only true fighters for democratic rights even on bourgeois terms, whereas liberals, in every case without exception, were "treacherous" allies. She loved her Russian comrades and cheered them on: "The Russian Revolution is not just the last act in a series of bourgeois revolutions of the nineteenth century, but rather the forerunner of a new series of future proletarian revolutions in which the conscious proletariat and its vanguard, the Social-Democracy, are destined for the historic role of leader."[120]

Upon returning to Germany she regaled lecture audiences on the necessity of mass action, imploring that too much of it was not possible in Germany. Only mass action would catalyze the broad masses and purge German Social Democracy of small-minded opportunism. SPD leaders chafed at hearing it. Luxemburg told her friend Clara Zetkin she felt increasingly marginalized: "I feel the pettiness and indecisiveness which reigns in our party more brutally and painfully than ever before." Bebel and Kautsky, she said, accepted her help against Bernstein "because they were shaking in their shoes," but now they shunned her. That year, 1907, the SPD lost nearly half its seats in the Reichstag. Alarmed party leaders vowed to double down on electoral work, depressing Luxemburg. The party's unbroken string of electoral victories had fueled a progress narrative about marching relentlessly to socialism. Now the record was broken, and the progress story was in doubt, which strengthened the reformers who had never felt conflicted about electoral pragmatism. Luxemburg likened it to a bad dream. She complained about Kautsky to her friend Luise Kautsky, but that was awkward, especially after Kautsky heard, so Luxemburg had to dissemble. She told her lover Kostya Zetkin, Clara's son, that Luise "complains to various people about my imaginary sorrows." The following year Luxemburg told Kostya more candidly, "Soon I shall be unable to read anything written by Kautsky."[121]

Kautsky felt her scorn and rankled at it. In 1908 Karl Liebknecht won election to the Prussian parliament from his prison cell in Glatz, Prussian Silesia. Liebknecht was much like his father, the party's founder, and deeply antimilitarist. Kautsky wanted the respect of radicals like Luxemburg, Liebknecht, and Mehring. In 1909 Kautsky conducted a debate with revisionist Max Maurenbrecher that pulled him closer, for a moment, to the left wing, yielding his most radical book, *The Road to Power*. Kautsky declared that a period of climactic fighting had almost arrived: "The power of the state is everywhere an organ of class rule. . . . I can say definitely that a revolution brought about by a war will happen but once. . . . We are revolutionists, and this not simply in the sense that the steam engine is a revolutionist." Revisionists were deluded because there was no third way. Bernstein's so-called peaceable growth into socialism was "the growth in power of two antagonistic classes, standing in irreconcilable enmity to each other." These forces hurtled toward an explosion that would shatter the state and overthrow the capitalist class. Kautsky clarified what that did not mean. His centrist leftism had not changed. He was revolutionary *and* rational, organizational and controlled. The SPD, he said, was a revolutionary party, not a revolution-making party. No party caused a revolution: "It is no part of our work to instigate a revolution or to prepare the way for it."[122]

He knew nothing about how or when the revolution would occur or whether it would be bloody. Kautsky stressed that Social Democrats did not agitate for violence. On the other hand, he allowed that a strain of violent mass rebellion was growing. Anarchists provoked police as their second favorite activity— antagonizing socialists was number one—and some socialists were starting to sound like anarchists. Kautsky implored that people who lusted for violence harmed the movement and delayed the revolution. The rulers wanted to be attacked, and anarchists stupidly obliged them. This was starting to sound like a polemic against Luxemburg, which it was, although Kautsky preserved deniability by targeting anarchists. Then he swung back to something he and Luxemburg shared, their antipathy to racism. The socialist movement had to stand against colonial racism, he said, something that should not exist at Social Democratic congresses. Kautsky implied it was increasing because revisionists spewed it openly, "to be sure, in an ethical manner." He blasted the conceit that peoples not belonging to European civilization were incapable of civilized development: "The people of other races are looked upon as children, idiots, or beasts of burden who may be handled with more or less gentleness, and in any case are beings of a lower stage, which can be controlled according to our desires." Human equality, Kautsky argued, is not a mere phase or moral ideal. It is a real power in history and society. To be sure, colonized peoples lacked the power of resistance, but that was not due to "any natural inferiority, as the conceited ignorance of European bourgeois scholars would have us believe." Imperialists crushed and exploited colonized peoples, then said they were better off for being conquered.[123]

Lenin greatly admired *The Road to Power* or at least said so. Then another mass strike in Russia, in 1910, set off another frenzy of debate in the SPD over mass action. Luxemburg wrote an article on the mass strike that *Vorwärts* refused to publish. Kautsky refused to publish it too, ostensibly because Luxemburg called for a republic in Germany, something the SPD had carefully avoided. A bitter exchange of letters ensued. Kautsky contended that he did not muzzle Luxemburg and that the offending issue was the republic, not mass strikes. She demanded an honest reply, and he clarified his position, borrowing the concepts of overthrow (*Niederwerfungsstrategie*) and attrition (*Ermattungsstrategie*) from military historian Hans Delbrück. Kautsky charged that Luxemburg's agitation for mass strikes and overthrow took leave of scientific rationality, ignoring the likely consequences. He espoused the attrition strategy of wearing out the enemy on multiple fronts and avoiding big, decisive battles. His approach did "not go forward directly to the decisive struggle, but prepares it for a long time, and only begins it when it knows that its opponent is sufficiently weakened." Kautsky did not mention that this very argument named the Fabians. Pointedly he said that Luxemburg overgeneralized her fixation with Russia: "The conception put forward here by Comrade Luxemburg was very well suited to the conditions of the Russian Revolution, conditions in which the overthrow tactic was appropriate. But it completely contradicts the experiences upon which the strategy of attrition of our party rests." He and Bebel prized party unity and their proud German civilization over Luxemburg's overgeneralized solidarity with Russian street rebels.[124]

Now their feud was public. Luxemburg's blistering reply bristled with ripostes and score-settling facts. She would have let Kautsky cut her section on the republic, but that called his bluff, and he returned the offending article anyway. Kautsky exaggerated the novelty of demanding a republic in Germany; as it was, he was responsible for making it seem out of bounds in the SPD: "Comrade Kautsky has handled himself badly." On Germany and Russia she wearied of Kautsky's obnoxious refrain that Germany was great, mighty, enlightened, free, and very advanced while Russia was weak and four kinds of backward. He described Russia's mass strikes as chaotic, primitive, unplanned, and lacking any specific demands or successes, which she said was wrong on every count: "These Russian strikes and mass strikes were so far from being 'amorphous and primitive' that in boldness, strength, class solidarity, tenacity, material gains, progressive aims and organizational results, they could safely be set alongside any 'West European' government." Luxemburg granted that most of Russia's political and economic gains were lost after the revolution was defeated, but that was another matter. Similarly, she ripped Kautsky's howler that Russia's mass strikes were products of economic and proletarian backwardness, which overlooked Russia's industrialized economy and its superior proletarian movement. Kautsky said Russian proletarians raged and stormed in fruitless strikes while German socialists attended meetings, won elections, and built up the SPD. Luxemburg countered that strikes advanced socialism better than anything, and everyone knew it. Only German socialist leaders didn't know it.[125]

This verdict was rendered just before the SPD took a deeper plunge into accommodation that sealed the rift between SPD leaders and Luxemburg's radicals. The break between Luxemburg and Kautsky stunned most of the SPD but not with discussion that registered its historic significance. It seemed mostly personal at the time. Lenin stayed out of it, still believing that Kautsky was the greater figure, a view he maintained until August 1914. Meanwhile Kautsky and other party leaders changed their view of the chief struggle within the SPD. Fighting off revisionism was no longer the party's chief internal problem because the party needed to overcome its electoral setback of 1907. Putting down revisionists became far less important than electing Social Democrats of whatever kind to the Reichstag—a revisionist agenda. In 1910 German progressives facilitated the SPD's deeper plunge into accommodation by uniting several groups to form the Progressive People's Party, which renewed an old SPD debate about cooperating with progressives. Two years later the party dropped its policy against formal electoral alliances, cooperating with Progressive candidates. Both parties ran candidates in the first round and agreed to throw in with the winners in the second round. The aim was to win a left/liberal majority of SPD, Progressive, and National Liberal representatives in the Reichstag, breaking the rule of a center/right coalition, the Blue-Black Bloc.

Bebel and Kautsky went full bore for electoral campaigning. At the Jena Congress in 1911 Bebel barely mentioned the threat of war, committing the SPD to a campaign emphasizing tax fairness, tariff issues, and military spending. The deal with the Progressive People's Party paid off tremendously for both parties, at least in electoral terms. The SPD won 110 seats in the Reichstag and a million new votes (from 3.25 million to 4.25 million)—totaling twice as many votes as the second-place Centre Party. Kautsky hailed the outcome as a historic victory made possible by the rise of a new class of progressive-leaning salaried workers, which he called a "new middle class." He quantified the phenomenon, explaining that the new middle class grew from 2.4 percent of the earning population in 1882 to 6.6 percent in 1907. This group was increasingly important, Kautsky said. It changed what was possible politically, not mentioning that Bernstein revisionists had been saying so for the past decade.[126]

The moment was very short lived. The SPD was trying to gain leverage by addition, much like the French Socialist Party (Section Française de l'Internationale Ouvrière, SFIO) had done by uniting socialist and progressive groups in 1905. Suffrage in Germany, however, had been granted from above, and Chancellor Theobald von Bethmann-Holweg did not need a parliamentary majority. To break the Blue-Black Bloc and force concessions from Bethmann-Holweg the SPD had to work with Progressives and National Liberals. Instead the Social Democrats proved far more willing than Progressives to keep party discipline, hold their noses, and support the coalition candidate. Then the National Liberals cut a deal with the Blue-Black Bloc. Social Democrats felt denigrated by Progressives and betrayed by National Liberals. Victory turned very bitter and demoralizing. The Luxemburg wing excoriated party leaders for abandoning the party's independence and demoralizing the party. Luxemburg said the SPD had one chance to redeem itself—by lifting its struggle against imperialism above everything else. Ministerial governance and parliamentary maneuvers paled by comparison because imperialism was the last gasp of the capitalist system.[127]

Luxemburg put it plainly in her book *The Accumulation of Capital* (1913): "Capitalism needs non-capitalist social strata as a market for its surplus value, as a source of supply for the means of production and as a reservoir of labor power for its wage system." The struggle of the great powers for colonial markets for surplus capital, she believed, had reached its final phase. It was not the creation of any nation or group of nations but the product of capitalism as a global system. Capitalism was driving the world to war, which would open the way to a socialist revolution. This conviction had burned in Luxemburg since the Socialist International Congress in 1907 at Stuttgart, where the International debated what it should say about imperialism and militarism. One proposal carefully rejected colonialism in principle but added that a certain amount of colonial exploitation was inevitable in practice. Kautsky and British delegate Harry Quelch objected that a socialist colonial policy was a contradiction in terms. A protracted debate yielded a compromise declaring that only a socialist victory would make it possible to abolish colonialism. The debate over militarism was similarly taxing. Jean Jaurès and Édouard Vaillant offered a resolution calling the working class to oppose war through public agitation, parliamentary intervention, mass strikes, and all other available means. Bebel countered that the SPD could not endorse such a position in Germany, so Jaurès substituted "historical struggles" for "methods of struggle," revising Bebel's resolution. Luxemburg and Lenin raised the ante on militarism, urging the International to say that militarism was "the chief weapon of class oppression" and that opposing war was not the end-all of antimilitarism. Any future war had to be treated as an opportunity to overthrow the bourgeoisie. Luxemburg and Lenin got the International to say it. That was foremost in her mind in 1913 and 1914. The antithesis that mattered, she said, was imperialism versus socialism.[128]

This position drove Luxemburg and her radical left comrades—especially Mehring, Clara Zetkin, and Julian Karski—to criticize the antiwar activism of their party as a half measure. Imperialism, they argued, was inevitable in the present stage of capitalism, and militarism went along with imperialism. Thus it was counterrevolutionary to call for limitations on armaments and military spending, notwithstanding that the SPD had been doing so in the Reichstag since 1909. Antimilitarism was okay as far as it went but no substitute for the fantasy of an unorganized proletariat overthrowing the bourgeoisie. Luxemburg's apocalyptic turn alarmed Kautsky and most of the SPD. Bebel died in 1913, leaving Kautsky alone at the top. Kautsky renounced his long-held position that the arms race was an inevitable by-product of imperialism. Certainly, he allowed, the arms race had economic causes, but it was not an economic necessity like the drive for new markets. Imperialism was like the growth of monopoly capitalism, which began with rivalries between national monopolies that led to international treaties regulating cartels. Kautsky argued that Britain and Germany were fully capable of curtailing their armaments to serve their imperial interests. Not pressing them to do so was unthinkable for a socialist movement. He said it for two years during the run-up to Austria's ultimatum to Serbia in 1914, then said it frantically: Imperialism was digging its own grave, it could not go on for much longer in its present mode, but war was not inevitable. From a purely economic standpoint, he contended, "it is not excluded that capitalism may live through another new phase, the transference of the policy of cartels to foreign policy, a phase of ultra-imperialism." If so, socialists would make adjustments and fight against ultra-imperialism. Shortly after Europe descended into war Kautsky stressed that nationalism was still a powerful motivating force in Austria and Serbia, perhaps equal to imperialism.[129]

SPD leaders had inveighed against militarism and imperialism for years, opposing the blustering pronouncements of Kaiser Wilhelm II. To the extent that the party had an official foreign policy, it rested on two principles: Foreign affairs are functions of domestic politics, and socialists are internationalists.

Basically there were three party factions heading into 1914. The radicals said that imperialism inevitably led to war and could be combated only by revolutionary action. The right-wing "social imperialist" bloc supported the Reich in its military policies. The center leftists strove to be antiwar and pro-German simultaneously. Kautsky and Hugo Haase led the center leftists, upholding the party's traditional distinction between aggressive and defensive wars, although the right wing invariably claimed that Russia and Serbia were the true aggressors. The closer Germany drew to war, the more Bernstein drifted to the center left faction. He loathed the imperialism of Wilhelmine Germany, ranking it far below the colonizing, not-so-bad kind. He condemned the policies of Chancellors Bülow and Bethmann-Hollweg during the run-up to the war, protesting that Wilhelmine *Weltpolitik* was reckless, militaristic, beholden to Junker interests, and vaingloriously nationalistic. The deep divides in the SPD showed when the Reichstag voted on military taxes, yielding slightly more yes votes than no votes and abstentions.

Officially the SPD was always for pan-Europeanism, refusing to take sides in rivalries. In reality anti-British and anti-Russian feeling pervaded most of the party, and much of the right wing that supported Bernstein despised England nearly as much as it feared and hated Russia, awkwardly for Bernstein. He wanted Germany to forge an entente with liberal Britain and republican France. If Germany formed a naval détente with Britain, mutual enmities would dissipate. If home rule were granted to Alsace-Lorraine within the German Empire, France might be mollified. If Germany liberalized politically, new alliances would become possible. In 1911 Bernstein wrote a book titled *Die englische Gefahr und das deutsche Volk* (The English peril and the German people). He implored that the English peril was almost completely made up. German officials and journalists were scaring the German people with a smear campaign against Britain lacking almost any evidentiary basis. The popular fear of "encirclement" was ridiculous, as France was not hell-bent on helping Russia strangle Germany. Germany's concerns about colonial rivalry were negotiable because German colonialism was mostly a sop to the Junker class, Prussia's landed nobility. Bernstein warned that fearmongering led to war, which would be catastrophic.[130]

Being right about that did not help Bernstein in August 1914. A Serbian nationalist assassinated Archduke Franz Ferdinand in Sarajevo on June 28, 1914. Europe's tangle of alliances triggered a chain reaction of preparations for war, while Social Democrats held frantic antiwar rallies across Germany. Then a French nationalist murdered Jaurès on July 31. Bernstein loved and admired Jaurès above all socialist leaders. He believed that Russian agents killed him, and Bernstein held the usual German dread of Russians. Kaiser Wilhelm had eviscerated Bismarck's policy of allying with Russia, and for over a decade Bernstein had dreamed of unlikely alliances with France and Britain to stifle the Russian peril. All of Bernstein's compatriots feared a Russian invasion. Going to war against Russia seemed inevitable to him, and not wrong, because Bernstein believed that Russia and Serbia wanted war. Still, Bernstein was an individuated case, and the party leadership was vehemently antiwar in its public pronouncements. On July 25 the party issued a blistering call for mass demonstrations against the war: "The class-conscious proletariat of Germany, in the name of humanity and civilization, raises a flaming protest against this criminal activity of the warmongers. It insistently demands that the German Government exercise its influence on the Austrian Government to maintain peace; and, in the event that the shameful war cannot be prevented, that it refrain from belligerent intervention. No drop of blood of a German soldier may be sacrificed to the power lust of the Austrian ruling group [or] to the imperialistic profit-interests."[131]

Five days later the stampede to war was obvious, and the party issued a despairing, anxious second statement, declaring that Social Democrats had done everything they could to halt the dreadful march to war. On August 1 the entire right wing of the SPD parliamentary delegation announced it would vote for war credits whether or not the party approved, an unprecedented breach of party discipline. This group included the trade union bloc, which constituted one-fourth of the entire delegation. On August 3 the Reichstag deputation caucused to discuss the next day's vote on war credits. The right wing reiterated its position, now demanding no abstentions or negative votes from SPD deputies. The radicals were conflicted about what to do, and only fourteen SPD deputies, led by Hugo Haase, opposed voting for the war credits, out of ninety-two deputies. The fourteen dissenters agreed to line up with the others, accepting the norms of party discipline. Some dissenters believed the party would soon regain its courage and renounce its position, so it was best to hang together. That was sadly not to be. That night Britain declared war on Germany.

German Social Democrats, it turned out, were terrified of being pariahs under the coming state of siege. The social imperialist bloc was straightforwardly militaristic, the center leftists turned out to be nationalists when it mattered, and fear of Russia trumped everything for many. Then war psychology kicked in, as prowar jubilation swept German society. There were individual exceptions in all factions. Paul Lensch flipped from the Luxemburg camp to outright imperialism, and Kurt Eisner flipped from prowar to antiwar. But that is what usually happens when nations march to war. The Social Democrats were supposed to be different, having claimed that proletarian solidarity made them immune to the sirens of war and patriotic gore. Thirty-nine years of claiming it were obliterated in a few minutes on August 4, 1914. Every deputy who voted no on August 3 had to do so with the expectation that the punishment for opposing the war credits would be harsh and humiliating, leading to a prison cell. The state of siege law turned military commanders into dictators accountable to no civilian authority except the king–emperor. Very few Social Democrats were ready to pay the price, and party discipline saved all from paying it until Karl Liebknecht broke ranks in December. Soon the same capitulation to war happened in France, with barely a word about the Second International, with the significant difference that France did not pine for war in July 1914. In Germany and France socialists said they voted for war to avoid being trampled by their own followers.[132]

Kautsky disbelieved until August 1 that his party would vote for war. Then he drafted a preemptive condemnation of annexations and violations of neutrality, which the German foreign office blocked, ominously. Then he justified his support for the war by saying the usual shabby things about defending the fatherland. For most German Social Democrats the logic of repelling Russia negated Second International fantasies about responding to war with a mass strike. A strike would have made Germany vulnerable to a Russian invasion, a horrifying prospect to Germans steeped in fear of "barbaric Cossack hordes." European balance-of-power politics drove France to ally with Russia, so French socialists became enemies too. The lightning speed of the German attack blew away normal Reichstag dickering. The Reich's strategy was based on Germany's presumed ability to quickly smash France before Russia invaded Germany. France was fortified on its German border, so the Reich invaded neutral Belgium to get to France, disastrously. Tiny Belgium fought off the German army, slowing it down, yielding carnage that sullied Germany's global reputation for decades. German Social Democrats were no different from other Germans in believing that Germany's mighty army would crush all its enemies. Losing that expectation proved hard to swallow.

In the early going the right-flank socialists welcomed their novel respectability, enjoying their prowar solidarity with government officials. For the small group of center leftists and radical leftists who could not cheer for the war, the war was sickening, a calamity. Every week there were debates and votes in the Reichstag pitting loyalty to socialist principle against loyalty to nation and party unity. The party had been everything to SPD leftists. Social Democracy was their religion, and the SPD was their church, providing a source of family belonging, emotional security, ethical aspiration, and social conviction. Activists who were nobody in German society knew Kautsky and Mehring as comrades. Now the real thing was shattered, leaving only pretenders and guilty choices. Bernstein reached out to Kautsky after years of no words between them, and to Haase, one of the few center leftists who had always remained friends with him. In late September Bernstein wrote an article denying the popular shibboleth that Britain and France wanted the war. *Sozialistische Monatschefte* refused to publish it, and Bernstein announced in December that he no longer belonged to his group. He had voted for war on the basis that Russia was at least as guilty as Germany of causing it and that Germany's war aim was defensive. By September he already believed that Germany was the chief culprit and the SPD should have voted no.

Liebknecht, the strongest antimilitarist among SPD officials, challenged the party's war policy on December 3, 1914, by voting against the second war credits bill. He tried to recruit additional no votes and failed, which split the war dissenters into two hardened camps. The radicals cheered for Liebknecht as he cast lonely votes against the war in March and August 1915; meanwhile Kautsky, Haase, and Georg Ledebour held together the center left group, which censured Liebknecht for breaking ranks. This resumed the argument of 1912, by the same people, with greater intensity. The center leftists tried until the summer of 1915 to stay out of trouble without selling out. They defended the right of Germany to defend itself, contended that imperial rivalries caused the war, and opposed any expansion of Germany's territory. They were for peace based on the status quo, not victory or defeat. To them, this was a Marxist position. They did not support the war on the basis of a noxious patriotic principle, like the right wing, or oppose the war on a radical principle, like the left wing. But the war dragged on, and the center leftists bridled at the censorship, state of siege, and treatment of national minorities, broaching these issues in the Reichstag. Then the annexation issue drove them into opposition. In June 1915 Bernstein coauthored a pamphlet with Kautsky and Hasse, *The Demand of the Hour*, opposing annexation. They argued that the war had become an imperialist venture on the part of the German government, which made it intolerable for Social Democrats to keep voting for war credits. A party conference in August 1915 vehemently debated this contention. Bernstein spoke for the center leftists, Eduard David led the opposition, and nearly two-thirds of the SPD officials and Reichstag caucus members voted against Bernstein.[133]

That month Bernstein abstained on a war credit vote along with thirty center leftists. In December Bernstein and eighteen other center leftists voted no, plus Liebknecht. SPD Reichstag leaders Lensch, Legien, and Philipp Scheidemann were brutally accusatory in response, condemning the dissenters. To radicals, however, the conversion of the center leftists was pitifully late and still about the wrong thing, a negotiated peace. Luxemburg cited Revelation 3:16; Jesus hated lukewarm followers and so did she. If the center leftists needed the annexation issue to get on the right side, they were untrustworthy allies. In January 1916 party leaders expelled Liebknecht from the Reichstag delegation, mostly as a warning to center leftists, while the radicals began calling themselves the Spartacus League. This was a moment for revolutionary clarity, they said, not unity. Haase was expelled from the SPD in March for condemning the war in the Reichstag. Bernstein and sixteen other center leftists were expelled from the Reichstag, and the government cracked down on the growing opposition, throwing Liebknecht into prison for treasonous statements in a May Day speech. That sparked demonstrations, so the government imprisoned Luxemburg for a second time, with other radicals. On Easter Sunday 1917 Haase gathered the center leftists and Spartacus League to found a new party, the Independent Social Democratic Party of Germany (USPD).[134]

The new party had its founding conference at Gotha. It had a right flank led by Kautsky espousing a stop-the-war platform, a Spartacus flank operating as an independent caucus, and a middle group mediating between the two flanks. Haase, by then, had converted to radical leftism, although he urged the factions to work together. Bernstein felt uncomfortable among so many radicals. He and Kautsky voted against a new party, preferring to unite the antiwar opposition, but they went along with the party that emerged. The USPD reaffirmed its commitment to the Erfurt Program, overriding Spartacus objections that Erfurt was a dead letter from a bygone time. Most of the comrades who gathered sorrowfully at Gotha did not fathom how Erfurt could be a dead letter or how Luxemburg viewed the world. The Spartacus radicals were closer to Lenin's worldview than to Kautsky's, except they also vehemently rejected all forms of hierarchy and centralism. Luxemburg's group shared Lenin's conception of imperialism and his bitter critique of Kautsky opportunism but hated authoritarianism.

Lenin was horrified that Kautsky supported the war: "How dangerous and scoundrelly his sophistry is, covering up the dirty tricks of the opportunists with the most smooth and facile phrases." Kautsky, to Lenin, instantly became "more harmful than anyone else." Kautsky's evil outstripped all others because it was "diplomatically colored over, contaminating the mind and the conscience of the workers, and more dangerous than anything else." Lenin's bad list, now headed by Kautsky, included all European socialist leaders. In September 1915 Italian socialists convened an emergency meeting of neutral nation socialists at Zimmerwald, Switzerland, to save the soul of the Second International. It helped that Italy had not been invaded in August 1914. The delegates saw themselves as brave guardians of European socialism. Lenin was a delegate, having helped to organize the conference from his exile in Zurich, but he ripped the socialists scathingly. Their parties were anemic because *they* were corrupted by imperialism and "social pacifism." He was interested only in hard revolutionaries who accepted the discipline of democratic centralism and harbored no fear of violence. Lenin's commanding self-confidence contrasted with the gloom and anxiety of the Social Democrats. He waged fiery duels with them, deriding them as pseudorevolutionaries. G. M. Serrati, leader of the radical wing of the Italian Socialist Party, was so offended he had to be physically restrained.[135]

The following year Lenin wrote *Imperialism, the Highest Stage of Capitalism*, contending that late-capitalist imperialism was based on the dominance of finance capital, not old-fashioned colonial empires. Capitalism in its highest stage dominated poor nations simply by the export of capital. It was no longer necessary to colonize foreign lands and steal raw materials for European industries; now the capitalist class simply collected ongoing income from its capital. The book heaped scorn on Kautsky's betrayal and mendacity. Kautsky described imperialism as a product of advanced industrial capitalism that drove capitalist nations to annex large agrarian regions without regard to national sovereignties in question. Lenin said this analysis, besides being "utterly worthless," obscured what mattered.[136]

Kautsky focused on industrial capital instead of finance capital, and political imperialism instead of economic imperialism. Lenin was influenced by SPD economist Rudolf Hilferding's contention that monopolistic finance capital created a different kind of capitalist system, one in which the capitalist class dominated the state. Hilferding was Austrian, a Kautsky protégé, and close to Kautsky. His major work, *Finance Capital*, was published in 1910, so Lenin was incredulous that Kautsky wrote outdated prattle emphasizing the nexus of political and industrial imperialism. Lenin said Kautsky played down monopolistic finance, overlooked the violence of political imperialism, and identified industrial imperialism with agrarian usurpation—as though Germany had not devoured industrialized Belgium and France not devoured Lorraine. Kautsky had regressed to the point of being inferior to John Hobson, a mere liberal. To claim, as Kautsky did, that imperialism was only one form of capitalism, so destroying imperialism was not the essential thing in struggling for socialism, was incredible. Lenin was done with Kautsky. He said it repeatedly. Kautsky's theory was "a most reactionary method of consoling the masses with hopes of permanent peace being possible under capitalism." Instead of attacking imperialism, "we have nothing but a reformist 'pious wish' to wave it aside, to evade it." Kautsky's position "has nothing in common with Marxism and serves no other purpose than as a preamble to propaganda for peace and unity with the opportunists and social-chauvinists." Most important in 1916, "Kautsky obscures the question, which has become very serious, of the impossibility of unity with the opportunists in the epoch of imperialism."[137]

This verdict, to Luxemburg, was exactly right. Her spectacular "Junius" pamphlet of 1915, published under the pseudonym Junius while Luxemburg languished in prison, became the manifesto of the Spartacus League. "The show is over," she declared, although the war still had three years to go. "Shamed, dishonored, wading in blood and dripping with filth, thus capitalist society stands. Not as we usually see it, playing the roles of peace and righteousness, of order, of philosophy, of ethics—but as a roaring beast, as an orgy of anarchy, as a pestilential breath, devastating culture and humanity—so it appears in all its hideous nakedness." Luxemburg interrogated the stunning capitulation of German Social Democracy. She recalled nostalgically that the SPD was long the "jewel" of European socialism—an exemplar for Italians, French, and Belgians and an object of "almost unquestioning admiration" for Russians and Slavs. Every socialist everywhere took pride in the SPD. Then German Social Democracy crashed in "the mightiest cataclysm."[138]

Did it have to crash? Luxemburg acknowledged that a Marxist could not just blame the leaders, so she blamed the movement as a whole: "Our readiness to fight has flagged, our courage and convictions have forsaken us." She blistered SPD leaders and workers for fearing a Russian invasion more than they hated capitalism and world war. The SPD did not capitulate because it adopted the wrong policy, she said. It capitulated because it had no policy. The party delivered the nation "to the fate of imperialist war without to the dictatorship of the sword within," all without a word of protest. The government did not need Social Democratic votes, but it got them anyway, which shamefully conferred the moral authority of Social Democracy on killing for fatherland and empire. Shame was very much the issue, she said. Bebel and the elder Liebknecht, in the 1880s, never gave a moment's consideration to retreating or capitulating: "They stuck to their posts, and for forty years the Social Democracy lived upon the moral strength with which it had opposed a world of enemies. The same thing would have happened now."[139]

She lingered there, imagining a German socialist party that "stood in the midst of this mad whirlpool of collapse and decay like a rock in a stormy sea." She grieved at losing German Social Democracy but cautioned that French socialists would not abolish imperialism or even militarism by overthrowing Germany: "Imperialism, and its servant militarism, will reappear after every victory and after every defeat in this war." A victory by either of the warring sides would be a disaster for the proletariat. The only way to abolish imperialism was for the international proletariat to abolish capitalist states everywhere. One thing only, Luxemburg said, could be said for the war: It created the preconditions for the final overthrow of capitalism. Her last word was an echo of the *Communist Manifesto:* "This madness will not stop, and this bloody nightmare of hell will not cease until the workers of Germany, of France, of Russia and of England will wake up out of their drunken sleep; will clasp each other's hands in brotherhood and will drown the bestial chorus of war agitators and the hoarse cry of capitalist hyenas with the mighty cry of labor, 'Proletarians of all countries, unite!' "[140]

The collapse of the tsarist state in Russia in March 1917 commenced, from a Marxist standpoint, Russia's bourgeois revolution. Like Kautsky and most Russian Marxists, Lenin had long believed that Russia's bourgeoisie was too soft and dependent on foreign capital to fight like the nineteenth-century English and French liberals. He brushed aside the contention of Kautsky and most European socialists that Russia's working class was too small and its capitalism too undeveloped to produce a successful Marxist revolution. Then the March revolution took Lenin by surprise in exile, and he had to persuade reluctant Bolsheviks to strike for power immediately. The cunning and discipline of Lenin and Leon Trotsky, plus a surge of mass protests in the fall of 1917, lifted the Bolsheviks to power in November. Lenin protected the revolution from a German invasion by signing the Brest-Litovsk Treaty, followed by civil war against the anti-Bolshevik White Army.

One year after the Bolsheviks took power the German front collapsed, and German sailors mutinied in Kiel. A wave of protests swept aside the German monarchy in a few days. Workers and soldiers' councils were organized, SPD militarist Gustav Noske was commissioned in October 1918 to restore order, and Liebknecht, Luxemburg, and other political prisoners were freed. The last wartime chancellor, Max von Baden, announced on November 9 that Wilhelm II had abdicated as emperor. Von Baden, with no legal warrant, selected as chancellor SPD leader Friedrich Ebert, who retained the recently appointed Philipp Scheidemann as a cabinet secretary, who dramatically declared from the balcony of the Reichstag, also with no legal warrant, that Germany was a republic. The emperor had, in fact, not yet abdicated. Ebert and von Baden had hoped to found a constitutional monarchy, and Ebert furiously told Scheidemann he had no right to declare a republic. Now the republic pledge seemed irreversible, while Liebknecht proclaimed at the Berliner Stadtschloss that Germany was a Free Socialist Republic.

All of this was on November 9. From November 1918 to February 1919 Ebert headed a six-member ruling council that got Germany to the founding of the Weimar National Assembly in February. It consisted originally of three SPD officials, including Scheidemann, and three USPD officials led by Haase. This provisional cabinet of Social Democratic ministers instituted historic reforms, including an eight-hour workday, worker councils, collective bargaining rights, abolition of press censorship, national health insurance, and universal suffrage in local and national elections. It also contained the German Revolution within bourgeois boundaries, cutting deals with the capitalist class and royalist-reactionary military officers, and suppressing communist uprisings, which sundered the SPD/USPD coalition.[141]

The two socialist parties disagreed fundamentally about the aims of the German Revolution and had four years of wartime enmity to overcome. Kautsky served briefly as undersecretary of state in the Foreign Office. Bernstein, serving as assistant secretary to the treasury secretary of state, made a stirring speech in mid-December pleading for reconciliation. His contribution to the November Revolution was to mediate between the USPD and SPD, trying to hold them together. But Ebert and Scheidemann cut deals with the army and big business that drove out the USPD officials, agreeing with army general Wilhelm Groener not to reform the army as long as it vowed to protect the state. The USPD refused to be associated with a government that tried to buy off every power bloc except the revolutionaries demanding a socialist republic. Bernstein alone did not walk out. He rejoined the SPD, kept his membership in the USPD, and pleaded for Social Democratic unity. Meanwhile the German Communist Party (KPD) was founded on the last day of 1918, replete with a speech from Luxemburg repudiating the Second International as a fatally mistaken enterprise from the beginning.[142]

Her friends were stunned to see her emaciated condition upon leaving prison because Luxemburg wrote buoyant letters from prison about staying cheerful, being a *Mensch*, and enjoying life. She admonished her devoted friends Mathilde and Emanuel Wurm to stop moaning and feeling sorrowful: "*You* people are a different zoological species than I, and your grousing, peevish, cowardly and half-hearted nature has never been as alien, as hateful to me, as it is now." Buck up! That was in December 1916, after receiving a kindly Christmas letter from Mathilde. When Luxemburg thought of "the adorable Haase [and] the uncertain pastor Kautsky" the Wurms admired, "a creepy feeling comes over me." These were the creepy leaders who destroyed Social Democracy. She told the Wurms what to expect when she got out of prison: "As for me, although I have never been soft, lately I have grown hard as polished steel, and I will no longer make the smallest concession either in political or personal intercourse." She implored them to stop whining: "Being a *Mensch* is the main thing! And that means to be firm, lucid and cheerful. . . . The world is so beautiful even with all its horrors, and it would be more beautiful if there were no weaklings or cowards." Later she told Mathilde, who looked up to her, that she differed from other SPD leaders because she did not get distracted by anxiety, routine, or "parliamentary cretinism."[143]

In December 1917 she was still in prison in Wronke and mindful that Liebknecht had been imprisoned for the past year, so she wrote to his wife, Sophie Liebknecht, who had brought her a Christmas tree the previous year. There was not a word of sorrow in Luxemburg's long letter. "I am as tranquil and cheerful as ever," she reported. She could not say why, exactly, she was so joyful: "I believe that the key to the riddle is simply life itself. This deep darkness of night is soft and beautiful as velvet, if only one looks at it in the right way." She went on about blackberries, poetry, and Lange's book *History of Materialism*, which she liked very much. Finally there was a parting postscript: "Never mind, my Sonyusha; you must be calm and happy all the same. Such is life, and we have to take it as it is, valiantly, heads erect, smiling ever—despite all."[144]

She celebrated and criticized the Russian Revolution, writing a detailed assessment in September 1918 from prison. Luxemburg hailed it as the greatest event of the war and an overwhelming refutation of the standard Social Democratic line championed by Kautsky. The Bolsheviks, she enthused, knew better than Kautsky, the Mensheviks, the opportunist wing of Russian union-ism, and everyone else who said that only a bourgeois revolution was feasible in Russia. The Bolsheviks rightly based their actions on the global proletarian revolution proclaimed in the *Communist Manifesto*. They cast aside the "par-liamentary cretinism" of "the parliamentary nursery" about first winning a majority of the people, revealing the true dialectic of revolutions: first the revo-lution, then democracy: "That is the way the road runs. Only a party which knows how to lead, that is, to advance things, wins support in stormy times." Luxemburg agreed with the Bolsheviks that bourgeois democracy was not the road to socialist democracy, but its enemy. She lauded the Bolshevik uprising for saving the Russian Revolution and the honor of international socialism by audaciously imposing "a dictatorship of the proletariat for the purpose of real-izing socialism." Now the challenge was to create a revolutionary democracy after the seizure of power.[145]

Here there were serious problems because Lenin and Trotsky still thought like Kautsky about the dictatorship of the proletariat. Luxemburg said socialism did not work without a flourishing, educated, liberated mass of the people.

Bourgeois class rule worked without it, which Lenin overlooked, but not socialism, which Lenin denied. Luxemburg lamented that Lenin and Trotsky conceived the dictatorship of the proletariat as a ready-made formula owned by the revolutionary party that officials carried out. Like Kautsky, they conceived dictatorship as the opposite of democracy, except that Kautsky advocated bourgeois democracy. Luxemburg feared that Lenin and Trotsky used the dictatorship of the proletariat as a club to silence and smash the democratic aspirations of the masses. Trotsky famously sneered that Marxists did not worship formal democracy; Luxemburg replied that true Marxists did not worship socialism or Marxism either.

She believed in the dictatorship of the proletariat, "but this dictatorship consists in the *manner of applying democracy*, not in its *elimination*, in energetic, resolute attacks upon the well-entrenched rights and economic relationships of bourgeois society, without which a socialist transformation cannot be accomplished." Dictatorship, in the Marxist sense, had to be the work of the entire proletarian class. It was emphatically not something owned by a revolutionary elite. It had to flow out of the active participation and direct influence of the masses; otherwise it was another form of tyranny. Luxemburg granted that Lenin and Trotsky had to use brutal tactics to gain power and defend the revolution. She feared that they made a virtue of necessity, building a suffocating system out of the tactics forced upon them and calling it Marxism. Still, she said, the Bolsheviks were the only ones thus far who had earned the right to say, "I have dared!"[146]

Luxemburg wrote this piece for the Spartacus League but had not finished it when she was released from prison in November 1918, when she had two months to live. It was not published until 1922, when her lawyer, Paul Levi, published it as a marker of his expulsion from the KPD. She plunged into the revolutionary ferment of the moment, producing a daily paper for the Spartacus League, conferring with the Berlin USPD and Revolutionary Shop Stewards, and giving speeches. She came out of prison declaring that the monarchy had never been the real enemy but merely the façade of the ruling imperialist capitalist class—"This is the criminal who must be held accountable for the genocide." The real German Revolution put all power in the hands of the working masses through the new workers' and soldiers' councils and a not-yet-organized national council of workers and soldiers. It had begun, she said, and it would not stand still because the vital law of a revolution is to outgrow itself. It would sweep away the Junker landowning aristocracy that still owned everything in East Germany and the private capitalists who owned everything else. Luxemburg implored audiences that they could not build socialism "with lazy, frivolous, egoistic, thoughtless and indifferent human beings." Socialism was about the many coming alive, overthrowing barbarism.[147]

Moral idealism was very much in play. Luxemburg urged audiences to "acquire the feeling of responsibility proper to active members of the collectivity which alone possesses ownership of all social wealth." She put it negatively—a government bureaucrat nationalizing a few factories was not socialism. That was a dead word, an empty phrase. She soared beyond moral idealism to John 1:4, declaring that only the organized and active working class "can make the word flesh." To achieve control over production and thus acquire real power workers had to struggle with capital on a shop-by-shop basis, hand-to-hand, with strikes and direct mass pressure. They had to disarm the police, confiscate all weapons, create a people's militia, expel all officers from the soldiers' councils, prosecute the war criminals, replace all parliaments and municipal councils with workers' and soldiers' councils, abolish all differences of rank and sexual discrimination, confiscate all dynastic wealth and income, repudiate war debts, and support socialist revolutionaries across the world. She invoked the gospel passion narrative, with the socialist movement in the role of Jesus. Capitalists, the petit bourgeois, military officers, the anti-Semites, the press lackeys, and the SPD social imperialists called out for crucifixion. Socialists had taken over the Jesus role of struggling "for the highest aims of humanity."[148]

Cofounding the KPD with Liebknecht, Luxemburg repudiated the Second International. She had not begun as an organization person, but Jogiches persuaded her that a socialist had to have an organization, so she held her nose in the SPD. She had long felt that Social Democracy was not about the right things. Finally she was free to say why. Marx and Engels, she believed, got it right in the *Manifesto*—all that is necessary is to spark a political revolution, seize the power of the state, and fulfill the socialist idea. But Marx and Engels abandoned this belief after the Paris Commune, for what seemed like good reasons at the time. Social Democracy replaced the original Marxian scheme with a compound of reform and revolution that Marx endorsed, more or less. A decade after Marx was gone, Engels wrote the famously dispiriting preface to Marx's *Class Struggles in France* acknowledging how wrong he and Marx had been about the near future of capitalism. Engels went on to say that parliamentary socialism worked better than street fighting. Luxemburg still believed that Engels would have been repulsed to see what came of Social Democracy long before August 4, 1914, but she stressed that he paved the way to it: "The Preface was the proclamation of the parliamentarism only tactic."[149]

Engels gave way to the Kautsky era of sterility and degradation. To Luxemburg and other left radicals these were years of bitterness at every party congress, where everything that was not parliament-only was stigmatized as "anarchism, anarcho-socialism, or at least anti-Marxism." Then came the debasement of August 4 and the war, to the last day of 1918, when Luxemburg declared that true Marxism was reborn in Germany. False Marxism led to "the henchmen of Ebert." True Marxism repudiated the debilitating dualism of the Erfurt Program, which separated the minimal demands of the political and economic struggle from the maximal demands of the struggle for socialism. Founding the KPD was a repudiation of Erfurt: "For us there is no minimal and no maximal program; socialism is one and the same thing; this is the minimum we have to realize today." The movement began on November 9, it was not about the monarchy, and the external form of the ongoing struggle for socialism was the strike. Luxemburg only half expected that a National Assembly would be created, and she did not say the KPD would have nothing to do with it. Neither point really mattered because both looked in the wrong place. What mattered was to build a revolutionary movement at the base. The masses would learn how to use power by using power. In the beginning is the act.[150]

But Luxemburg did not know if the workers' and soldiers' councils would support the KPD, and in Berlin all radical groups counted on sympathetic treatment from the chief of police, Emil Eichhorn, a USPD stalwart. On January 4, 1919, the provincial government fired Eichhorn. The following day over one hundred thousand workers responded to a call from the Berlin USPD, the Revolutionary Shop Stewards, and the KPD protesting the firing. Liebknecht and other leaders of the three groups, impressed by the turnout, formed an emergency committee that voted the same night to overthrow the Ebert government. On January 6 over half a million workers marched in Berlin demanding a new government, but failed to win soldiers to their cause. The following day three hundred Spartacists tried to overthrow the government and were crushed by government forces. Luxemburg apparently believed the insurrection was premature, especially lacking soldiers from the Berlin barracks. But she did not oppose it, after which she and Liebknecht were forced into hiding. Ebert enlisted the Freikorps—paramilitary thugs armed by the government—to hunt down Luxemburg and Liebknecht. Meanwhile she taunted Noske that he was much better at killing German workers than he had managed against the French, British, and Americans. She had not expected to win, given the "political immaturity of the masses of soldiers," and she allowed that Spartacus Week ended badly. Nonetheless, this defeat would be the seed of a great victory. Luxemburg blistered Ebert and Noske for proclaiming that order reigned in Berlin: "You stupid lackeys! Your 'order' is built on sand. The revolution will 'raise itself up again clashing,' and to your horror it will proclaim to the sound of trumpets: *I was, I am, I shall be.*"[151]

The Freikorps captured Luxemburg and Liebknecht on January 15, interrogated and tortured them and murdered them. His body was dumped at the city morgue. Her disfigured body was discovered months afterward in the Landwehr canal. The tacit consent of Ebert and Noske conferred a special odium on the SPD in the orbits of the USPD and KPD. Socialists had not merely slaughtered socialists to preserve the bourgeois order. They commissioned the forerunners of the Nazi Brown Shirts to do their dirty work. The social imperialists who ran the provincial government were terrified of Bolshevism, contemptuous of left-wing socialists, unprepared to govern, obsessed with law and order, and timid before the old bureaucracy. In February and March 1919, after the republic was founded at Weimar, Ebert went on to suppress communist uprisings in Berlin and Munich, with over one thousand casualties. In April the Communists briefly set up a republic in Bavaria, the heart of Catholic Germany, which was liquidated the following month, yielding a Red scare in Munich that persisted for decades and gave Adolf Hitler his start.

WEIMAR HUMILIATION

Bernstein furiously condemned the murder of Luxemburg and Liebknecht. He had long regarded Luxemburg as his best critic and admired Liebknecht as an exemplar of socialist courage. He also believed that Luxemburg and Liebknecht had overplayed their hand, beginning with Liebknecht's November 9 call for "all power to the councils," which invited the counterrevolutionary backlash. In 1917 Bernstein lauded Liebknecht just after he was arrested, calling him the "true son of his father," gifted with "unbounded optimism," curiously indifferent as to "what might befall him personally," and equally indifferent to formal rules. Father and son, Bernstein said, caused stormy scenes in the Reichstag and never for a selfish or calculating reason. Both were intoxicated with "the interest of humanity." Bernstein's role in the revolution of November 1918–February 1919 consisted entirely of imploring the two Social Democratic parties to work together. His failure in this impossible effort was a colossal tragedy. The bitterest symbol of this failure was that Social Democratic officials consented to the murder of Luxemburg and Liebknecht. Haase was next, murdered in November 1919 by an unhinged right-wing assassin. To the end of his days Bernstein regretted that Haase, Kautsky, Wilhelm Dittman, and Emil Barth had resigned from the provincial government, leaving no counterweight besides Bernstein within the government. His only success was with himself.[152]

The National Assembly elections of January 19, 1919, secured for the SPD the very thing it had sought since 1875—control of the government through electoral victory. The SPD won almost 38 percent of the vote in the nation's first free and fair election and the first one with women's suffrage. The three pro-Weimar parties—the SPD, Centre Party, and German Democratic Party (DDP)—formed a majority governing coalition, with Ebert as president of the German Reich. Scheidemann became minister president, an office later renamed chancellor after the Weimar Constitution came into force in August 1919, without Scheidemann. The SPD retained its wartime practice of calling itself the Majority Social Democratic Party, a reminder that most Social Democrats supported the war and the USPD was a fringe group. "One man, one vote," now including women, was deeply ingrained in the SPD. Dictatorship of the proletariat, whatever its force as a rhetorical totem, had nothing to do with depriving the bourgeoisie of the vote. SPD officials did not regard the worker and soldier councils of the November Revolution as viable state organs, unlike the USPD, which pushed for a council system (*Räterepublik*). To the radical majority of the USPD, council Marxism was better than parliamentary democracy. To the newly empowered SPD, the worker councils were not foundations of an alternative government or society. Syndicalism was imaginable only on the basis of an actual dictatorship of the proletariat, a nonstarter.

Thus the SPD fought off the radical socialists and Communists, which did not stop right-wing nationalists from vilifying the SPD as a traitorous enemy. The SPD became a perfect scapegoat for losing the war and accepting the punishing terms of the Versailles Treaty. Article 231 decreed that Germany was solely responsible for the war and its carnage. Most SPD officials in the Reichstag voted to swallow it on June 23, 1919, although Scheidemann dramatically resigned as minister president in protest, warning that Versailles put Germans in chains. Scheidemann went on to stoutly defend all the Weimar governments, making himself a symbol of Weimar treachery to the right wing, along with Ebert. He and Bernstein differently symbolized the fate of the SPD. Scheidemann was popular in the SPD and Bernstein was not; Scheidemann roared against Versailles vengeance and Bernstein did not; and Scheidemann was far to the right of Bernstein politically. But both spent the early Weimar years pleading that only a strong SPD could make the Republic work in the face of recrimination, conspiracy politics, postwar trauma, Communism, and hypernationalism.[153]

Instead right-wing movements sprouted noisily, the split between the SPD and USPD weakened the SPD, and SPD leaders derided Bernstein as a has-been and wailing Cassandra. Bernstein remained in the USPD until March 1919, when it prohibited dual memberships. Then he found himself hopelessly isolated in the SPD and Reichstag. The self-pitying chauvinism of the National

Assembly appalled him. Somehow Germany's enemies were responsible for all of Germany's problems, even to SPD delegates who voted bitterly to swallow Versailles. Bernstein rejoined the SPD too late to be a delegate at the founding National Assembly, but he gave a speech at the Weimar Party Congress of the SPD in June 1919 that bravely tried to dissuade the SPD from its cherished nationalistic self-pity.

He began with August 3 and 4, 1914: "Our vote was a disaster for our people as well as for the civilized world." Had the SPD voted no, Bernstein said, things could not have gone worse for Germany, and millions of lives might have been spared. He shredded the usual fiction about France and Britain, declaring that the French and British governments wanted peace in 1914. He turned to the requirements of the Versailles Treaty to disarm, make territorial concessions, and pay huge reparations, allowing that all were hard and some were impossible, but 90 percent were necessary. The jeering turned uproarious. A stormy, angry chorus of "No!" and "Scandal!" made it hard for Bernstein to be heard. He said it again, adding that France suffered worse than Germany in the war. The roaring got louder and angrier. Bernstein told the delegates to think about what Germany did in Belgium. They cried back that he should think of East Prussia. He replied that Germany was responsible for the sacrifice of East Prussia. Germany, claiming it had to repel Russia, spent most of its firepower smashing Belgium and France—two nations that didn't want war. A succession of offended speakers came forward to denounce Bernstein for hurting and maligning Germany, sacrificing German territory, and lionizing Germany's enemies. Every speaker and nearly every delegate poured out wounded outrage and repudiation. Blaming Germany's wartime leaders for a disastrous war was anathema.[154]

This contention carried on through the 1920s, as Bernstein refused to back off, featuring two arguments: (1) The German government bore a grave guilt for being chiefly responsible for the war. (2) The same government and its army proceeded to lose the war on the battlefield. Both arguments made Bernstein an object of ridicule and shunning to Reichstag opponents and his party. He caused a ruckus at the Reichstag budget debate of 1921 by compelling the assembly to discuss his contention that Imperial Germany bore the guilt for starting the war. To him, it was bad enough that conservatives and tabloid editorialists wailed about affronts to the honor and dignity of Germany. It sickened him to read similar vengeful fare in *Vorwärts*.

In 1920 the SPD suffered a crushing defeat in the federal election, sliding from 37.9 percent of the vote in January 1919 to 21.7 percent in June 1920. The SPD finished well ahead of all other parties, but lost sixty-three seats, nearly all to the USPD, which won 17.9 percent of the vote. Unsuccessfully, Bernstein implored SPD leaders to join a governing coalition led by the German People's Party (DVP), the party of big business, finance, liberal intellectuals, and the business establishment. Warily he noted that the far-right German National People's Party polled third with 15 percent. On the left, the election story was that left-wing socialists swung to the USPD out of support for the revolutionary councils and grief over Luxemburg, Liebknecht, and other Communist martyrs. Nearly half of the USPD wanted to preserve some form of worker control in democratic socialist fashion that reestablished parliamentary democracy. But the party imploded over Communism, voting in October 1920 to join the Communist International. In December the majority half of the USPD—four hundred thousand members—joined the KPD, merging as the United Communist Party of Germany. The smaller half, including three-fourths of the party's Reichstag members, stayed with Arthur Crispien and Georg Ledebour in the USPD, sticking with radical democratic socialism. There were not enough of them to make a difference, and it took two years for the rump-USPD group to reunite with the SPD. Losing the USPD to Communism shattered the dream of a democratic socialist government at the outset of the Weimar experiment. Amid this drama the Reichstag made slight amends for dissolving the revolutionary councils by enacting a mild reform bill, the Works Council Act, which established consultative worker councils at the firm level, the foundation of German codetermination after World War II.[155]

Reinventing the nation amid the ravages of war defeat and soaring inflation was torturously difficult. The Weimar Republic inherited a massive war debt and punitive reparations that it could not pay. In 1923 Germany defaulted on its war reparations, French and Belgian troops occupied the Ruhr valley coal and steel industries, and center-right politician Gustav Stresemann put together a "great coalition" of the SPD, DDP, Centre Party, and Stresemann's DVP. Stresemann went on to serve eight successive Weimar governments as foreign minister, holding many of them together, more or less. He tamed Germany's hyperinflation by creating a new currency, the *Rentenmark*, got the French and Belgian occupiers out of the Ruhr, and drove himself to an early death by a stroke in October 1929 at the age of fifty-one. In Stresemann's first government of 1923, the fabled "year of crises," he served as chancellor and foreign minister, appointing Hilferding as finance minister. Hilferding rejoined the SPD through its merger in 1922 with the rump-USPD socialists. Then he succeeded his mentor, Kautsky, as chief theorist of the SPD. In two tenures as finance minister Hilferding got a close-up experience of the reality he had theorized—the domination of the capitalist state by monopoly interests. He laid much of the groundwork that stabilized Germany's new currency, and he played a crucial role in persuading the SPD to accommodate the moderate bourgeois parties on foreign policy. In 1924 two Reichstag elections boosted all the right-wing parties and the KPD, compelling the SPD to grimly cooperate with Stresemann's DVP or at least try to do so, unsuccessfully, in the face of vitriolic campaign rhetoric.[156]

Hitler surpassed his ample right-wing competition by winning the youth. He joined the German Workers' Party in 1919, discovered a gift for demagoguery, and regaled vast crowds in Bavarian beer halls. In 1921 he took over the renamed National Socialist German Workers' Party. Two years later he tried to overthrow the Bavarian state government in Munich, which yielded a five-year prison sentence for treason, less than a year served, and Hitler's autobiographical screed, *Mein Kampf*. Bernstein denounced the vengeful mania that Hitler mobilized *and* the fact that Communists had too much in common with it. Always he said that Bolshevism was terrible Marxism, a willful perversion resting on a few sentences from the *Manifesto* and Marx's Blanquist utterances of the succeeding few years. Bernstein warned that Communism had already proved disastrous for the Russian people, and German Communism would be no different. In his last years he said it to a stream of youthful visitors. He knew and loved Engels, who was nothing like a Leninist. The Bolshevik lust for power distorted Marx's teaching and erased Marx's democratic radicalism, rendering a vulgarized concept of the dictatorship of the proletariat as the essence of Marxian revolution. Bernstein did not have to take back his criticism of Marx and Engels along this line to say they deserved better than a Leninist legacy. He said it constantly, decrying that Lenin and Trotsky brushed aside Marxian reasons for eschewing revolutionary violence in Russia.[157]

The SPD was a party of grizzled warhorses in the 1920s, lacking almost any youth, and the Weimar Republic was a semipresidential democracy still named the Deutsches Reich; it was not called the Weimar Republic until 1933, when Hitler's name for it caught on. *Vorwärts* refused to publish Bernstein's articles because criticizing Germany was repugnant. In 1921 the party retreated from Erfurt Marxism, discarding it in the Görlitz Program, which gave Bernstein his last hurrah at party conferences. The following year the merger of the rump-USPD with the mother party set off a chain reaction of coalition rearrangements. The Centre Party and DDP, fearing a strengthened SPD, linked arms with Stresemann's DVP, hitherto regarded as too right wing to be a pro-Weimar party. Hilferding was willing to deal with Stresemann and the DVP, but most of his former USPD comrades were not. Two SPD coalitions with Stresemann governments collapsed for that reason; meanwhile the SPD went back to Erfurt Marxism, in the Heidelberg Program of 1925. Erfurt Marxism, at least as rhetoric, suited the SPD during its wilderness years from 1925 to 1928. Ebert served as president until his death in 1925, right-wing war hero Paul von Hindenburg was elected president to succeed Ebert, and the SPD achieved more social legislation as an outside pressure group than it managed during its own governments. Briefly, the economy grew and the unions surged, strengthening the SPD. Right-wing nationalists stoked a myth of betrayal and vengeance in which everything wrong in Germany traced to Jewish bankers, Jewish intellectuals, Jewish Social Democrats, other kinds of Social Democrats, intellectuals, and liberals and their collaborators. In 1927 Hindenburg wailed at Tannenberg that the Versailles reparation crippled Germany, not mentioning that Germany paid only a small portion of it. Bernstein replied that German leaders had to stop pedaling a demagogic victim story that harmed a struggling republic.[158]

The following year Bernstein retired from the Reichstag, acknowledging he had no influence in the SPD or the Reichstag. He told friends gloomily he was politically dead in Germany. Party leaders spurned Bernstein as out of touch, idealistic, and politically naïve, consumed with an ethical socialism that did not fit the new Germany. At the time they had reason to feel good about themselves. In 1928 the SPD, already the largest party in the Reichstag, won a huge electoral victory that more than doubled the vote total of the second place, right-wing German National People's Party (DNVP). SPD leader Hermann Müller, a former chancellor in 1920, assembled a Great Coalition of the SPD, DDP, Centre Party, and DVP. This was a throwback to the coalition preceding the rise of Stresemann and the leftward swing of the SPD. As late as 1928 the SPD won 29.8 percent of the vote, no other party won more than 14 percent, and the Nazis won 2.8 percent.

But the Müller government never gelled as a governing coalition. Internal rivalries consumed it from the beginning, conservative factions angled for a presidential system with strongman rule, and the SPD was no better than others at getting along, having never entered a coalition government with a constructive attitude. The SPD joined coalition governments only when it felt compelled to thwart the reactionary parties, especially in foreign policy. It viewed coalition politics purely in tactical terms, fatefully in March 1930, as the party terminated the last Weimar cabinet able to rely on a parliamentary majority. Müller asked Hindenburg for emergency powers, he refused, and Müller resigned, ending the Weimar Republic's last genuinely democratic government. Hilferding's second tenure as finance minister—1928–1929—turned out badly, just before the Depression and Keynesian theory. Hilferding battled inflation in standard textbook fashion, believing that deficit-financed government spending would be ruinous. Instead Germany reaped a colossal ruin for starving its own people.[159]

Bernstein had two slight strokes in 1925 but hung on for three more years of Reichstag debates, mostly in Cassandra mode. It sickened him that his party bailed out on parliamentary governance whenever governing got really hard because that made the SPD a hindrance to democracy. Supporting democracy, to Bernstein, was a categorical imperative. By the end he was a dinosaur in Germany and deeply aware of it. He had never shown how bourgeois society could grow gradually into socialism. All he could say was that democratic politics needed to achieve this result. The chasm between this dream and reality made him sadly irrelevant. Bernstein did far better among foreigners, welcoming streams of foreign students to his campus lectures and home. He helped many obtain residence permits and conduct research projects. American historian Peter Gay described the later Bernstein as "helpful to others, beloved by his friends and relatives, ignored by his own party, [and] fearful of the future."[160]

Bernstein and Kautsky wrote friendly letters to each other until the end. During the war they went back to their youthful nicknames for each other—Ede and Baron. Afterward they remained friends while competing for Bernstein versus Kautsky influence in the SPD. Kautsky returned to Vienna in 1924, and Bernstein praised him for being a real theorist, moving from a theoretical starting point to a theoretical conclusion, whereas Bernstein started with praxis and moved up to theory as a guest performance. His last letter to Kautsky was written in January 1932, just before Bernstein died. Bernstein said he felt immense dread about Germany and the world but willful optimism about the SPD. He feared the Nazis and Communists would unite against democracy and Social Democracy. He exhorted Kautsky to keep believing that Social Democracy would prevail.[161]

American Social Democrat Sidney Hook, visiting Bernstein in 1929, found him to be as generous and friendly as everyone said. Hook admired Bernstein's intellectual integrity and his willingness to admit that Marx had a Bolshevik streak in his personality, which came through in his vituperative treatment of others. To Hook, Bernstein exemplified the possibility of Marxian revisionism, which Marx and Engels pioneered by revising their analysis and agenda, exactly as Bernstein said. British political historian Henry Tudor later countered that Bernstein never grasped why true Marxists opposed him. Bernstein believed he was like Engels, addressing awkward facts in a scientific spirit. In truth, Tudor said, Bernstein discarded every assumption that defines Marxism. Kautsky versus Bernstein was a confrontation between "two incommensurate ideologies," not an argument about whether Social Democracy should be very Marxist or much less Marxist. Marxism had no meaning if Bernstein counted as some kind of Marxist.[162]

But this argument has a long history of failure that dismisses the self-understanding of a great many Marxists. Hook became a good example, twice over. In his early career Hook was a Bernstein Social Democrat whose astute exposition of Marx helped a large readership grasp the basic concepts of Marx's thought. Later he turned neoconservative and policed an orthodox understanding of Marx that Hook's early work undermined. The later Hook ridiculed Michael Harrington's interpretation of Marxism and his claim to be a Marxist, notwithstanding that Harrington recycled arguments from Bernstein and the early Hook. Orthodox policing is always a dubious enterprise of that sort. According to Tudor, Bernstein's opposition to World War I was artificial because his socialism was about accommodating the bourgeoisie. Had Bernstein stayed true to revisionist Social Democracy he would have supported the war and kept his place in the mainstream of the SPD, which Tudor claims he reacquired after the war ended. Tudor was wrong on both counts, not fathoming what Bernstein's moral convictions meant to him and what they cost him in the party. There was nothing strange or artificial about Bernstein's opposition to the war, and he never believed the war question reduces to whether a war serves the proletarian revolution. He loathed World War I and the nationalistic chauvinism of his party for the same reasons he loathed the carnage in Stalinist Russia and would have loathed the horror he barely missed.[163]

As it was, German Social Democracy bore too much guilt for the hated Weimar Republic to impress the generation of intellectuals who cut their teeth on Bernstein versus Kautsky versus Luxemburg. Moreover, Bernstein spoke the same language of progress and rational optimism that befell the remnants of progressive German Christian socialism after World War I, and he had no heirs in the SPD that amplified his work. Progressive Christian socialists in Germany tried to regroup after World War I, renewing religious socialism as an option in the USPD, the SPD, and the churches. For a while the two greatest theologians of the twentieth century, Karl Barth and Paul Tillich, were luminaries in the project of rethinking Christian socialism, but very differently. Barth pulled back from the socialist movement just before Tillich joined it. Barth blasted the attempt to renew Christian socialism, while remaining a Christian *and* a socialist, with no contradiction by his lights. Tillich took up the very enterprise Barth criticized, now with stronger interreligious and Marxist elements. In both cases it mattered greatly that Christian socialism in Germany had very little history that was not nationalistic or fatally identified with Culture Protestantism. Barth and Tillich had contrasting theologies but similar feelings about the SPD of 1919: The party had lost its way and had to be overcome.

In many renderings the failure of the November Revolution led inevitably to the SPD failures of the late 1920s and early 1930s. The November Revolution halted at the gates of the factories and barracks, preventing a formal democratic

revolution from converting to a socialist revolution. Afterward the SPD qualified for a place at the governing table by accepting capitalism, the capitalist
state, and capitalist foreign policy. Tillich said it repeatedly, never quite assimilating that his politics put him in the mainstream of the SPD. In the 1960s and
1970s three bellwether historians of German Social Democracy—Eberhard
Kolb, Susanne Miller, and Heinrich Potthoff—reiterated this critique. Rightly
they stressed that the fallout between the SPD and USPD made the SPD pitiable in power, and the SPD was co-opted by its willingness to play a governing
role. But the SPD did not indulge nationalist victim-mongering or practice fiscal conservatism because Germany failed to build a council system. Even its
marginalization of left-wing socialists was not inevitable but chosen. The either/
or of Marxist historiography is too determinist about the supposed significance
of one thing—a pure council alternative that disenfranchises the bourgeoisie
and has never succeeded anywhere. On the other hand, the SPD never recovered from the steep losses it suffered in the 1920 election for killing Communists
and radical socialists. Bernstein perceived correctly that nothing was more
important than holding the SPD and USPD together. Swiftly he became the
symbol of that failed dream.[164]

Then the SPD suffered a punishment for Versailles and an enemy-imposed
Republic. When Bernstein died in 1932 he seemed an utter failure in Germany
and was treated as such. His death passed without notice. Whatever he represented was obsolete. There were no books about him until a trickle began in the
1950s, all by non-Germans, notably Gay in 1952, Pierre Angel in 1961, and Bo
Gustafsson in 1972. It was not until the 1970s that Bernstein began to get his due
in West Germany, just after the resurrected SPD climbed into power. SPD
political theorist Thomas Meyer, writing in 1977, lauded Bernstein for grasping
the internal complexity of capitalist economies and paving the way to modern
Social Democracy. Meyer said Bernstein had sagelike wisdom, and his praxis
orientation was not a deficiency. By then many Social Democrats said Bernstein
was the greatest of the Social Democratic founders. SPD political historian
Roger Fletcher, writing in 1987, felt that Bernstein's resurrection had already
carried too far because Bernstein was pragmatic, an empiricist, and a moral
idealist, three deficiencies in his telling. But Fletcher acknowledged that
Bernstein was "a man of impeccable intellectual honesty and moral probity"
who deserved to be remembered with appreciation, though well below Marx,
Engels, and Lassalle.[165]

The same qualities that discredited Bernstein for decades made him
somewhat admirable or very admirable after Social Democracy survived the
Nazi catastrophe, reestablished the SPD, and eventually embraced Bernstein

revisionism. In his time all he could do was protest that a better world was possible. He stuck with the USPD as long as it allowed, trying to prevent the disaster of losing most of it to Communism. He could imagine a Social Democratic movement that acknowledged what went wrong in 1914, which did not happen. The upshot was baleful for religious socialism. The SPD proudly repelled religious people during its heyday and was too discredited afterward to attract the next generation of radical religious thinkers. Bernstein saw the problem, pleaded for another possibility, and became a lonely figure by doing so. The idea of a democratic socialism that socialized as much industry as necessary, supported codetermination and economic democracy, doggedly supported political democracy, and was genuinely open to religious socialists remained to be achieved. Bernstein was not willing to kill people to achieve socialism, and calling it class war did not dissuade him. He had no interest in imposing socialism on people who didn't want it, and he prized his own intellectual freedom as something not negotiable. That made democracy the road to socialism, however long the road turned out to be.

German Social Democrats thought they were covered on the religion issue if they said they did not prohibit religion. Those who knew their Marx added that Marx agreed with them. Religious socialists who winced at being tagged as drug addicts were supposed to be assuaged that Marx said it sympathetically. Their sad condition compelled them to hold desperately to religious illusions.

Social Democracy, however, had another thread of reflection on this subject. A few socialists took interest in the Christian background to socialism, knowing it mattered. Engels, Kautsky, and Luxemburg propounded versions of the argument that socialism resumed the revolutionary spirit of the Jesus movement. Engels drew on his youthful studies of left Hegelians to stress the "notable points of resemblance" between early Christianity and modern socialism. The early Christians, he said, were fired by their opposition to Roman domination and the hope of equality in heaven: "Christianity was originally a movement of oppressed people; it first appeared as the religion of slaves and emancipated slaves, of poor people deprived of all rights, of peoples subjugated or dispersed by Rome." Kautsky, updating this argument, said Engels was basically right, but early Christianity was not entirely plebeian, and its preaching of the kingdom of God was more worldly than Engels grasped. Kautsky observed that the free proletariat in the urban centers of the ancient world flocked to Christianity, hearing the message of rebellion in the gospel. He played up the political dilemma faced by the gospel writers in dealing with the Roman oppressor and a daunting Jewish background: "The crucifixion of the Messiah was an idea so alien to Jewish thought, which could only imagine the Messiah in all the glory of a conquering hero, that it would require an actual occurrence, the martyrdom of a champion of the good cause, who had made an indelible impression on his supporters, to make the idea of the crucified Messiah at all acceptable."[166]

Kautsky appreciated that the Jesus story was inherently threatening to power; thus it had to be domesticated to survive persecution. He argued that Christianity survived and then flourished, albeit in mutilated form, for two reasons: It created a scrappy organization that kept alive the memory of its martyr founder. And its savior figure was a social Messiah who appealed to the poor of all nations, not a national Messiah who died with the destruction of the temple in Jerusalem. Jesus was a proletarian communist martyr whose essential character had to be obscured by the church but which came through anyway. Kautsky said he sought to be objective; this was scholarship, not propaganda.

Still, it was hard not to project. If Christianity defeated Rome and conquered the world by distorting its founder, and if modern socialism took up the Jesus cause of abolishing domination and oppression, was there a danger that Social Democracy would become a bastardized state religion just like Christianity? At least Kautsky asked the question. He answered, in 1908, that such a tragedy had no chance of occurring. Christianity, he explained, emerged during a period of spiritual decline, which sabotaged true Christianity from the beginning. Socialism, however, rode on the back of the tremendous economic, cultural, and scientific progress of the entire nineteenth century. Socialism fused and was fired by everything that made the nineteenth century a spectacular era of progress. Kautsky declined to revise *Foundations of Christianity* after World War I shredded his assurances. Returning to Vienna in 1924, he stayed until the Nazis annexed Austria in 1938, barely made it to Amsterdam, and died the same year. His second wife, Luise Ronsperger, did not escape the Nazis, perishing in Auschwitz. German Social Democracy seemed to be eviscerated by the Nazi nightmare; even unions were abolished under Hitler. Afterward it arose from the dead with remarkable resiliency and outdated dogmas.

4

GERMANIC POLITICAL THEOLOGY: SOCIAL DEMOCRACY AS THEOLOGY

The ravages of the Great War and the peculiarities of German politics reverberated across theology for decades, producing a generation of theological giants. England resembled a defeated nation in the 1920s, with little sense of having caused any of it, which left English theology largely unchanged. In Germany the war was an occasion of convulsion and revenge, yielding dialectical theologies that repudiated the bourgeois myth of progress and nationalistic theologies that blamed Germany's enemies within and without for the woes of the nation. In the United States the war was a foreign venture, belatedly entered and successfully prosecuted, which confirmed the national myth that history did not apply to the United States. Social Democracy surged ahead in familiar channels in England and Switzerland as Anglican socialism developed in Fabian, guild socialist, cooperative, and Labour Party forms, and religious socialism played a similar role in Swiss Social Democracy. But an offshoot of Swiss religious socialism, Barthian dialectical theology, soared to the top of the theological field in much of the Continent, notably Germany, where Social Democracy was fatefully synonymous with the Weimar Republic, religious socialism was a handful of intellectuals, fascism gained power, and dialectical theology splintered into factions.

The peculiarities of the German situation overdetermined much of European and North American theology. Heading into the Great War, Germany had forty million Protestants, twenty-four million Catholics, and five hundred thousand Jews. The Protestant *Land* (regional state) churches were Lutheran, Reformed, or Union—an alliance of Lutheran and Reformed—although the majority were Lutheran. Lutheran theology began as a critique of indulgences, teaching Lutherans to respect the authority of the state and the divine orders of creation. Calvinist theology began as a critique of idolatry, emphasizing the transcendent glory and unknown decrees of God. Meanwhile many Union leaders were Cultural Protestants who touted the socially cohesive role of religion.[1]

Liberals dominated German academic theology, a legacy of the German Enlightenment. Germany's leading theologians—Adolf von Harnack, Wilhelm Herrmann, Ernst Troeltsch, Friedrich Naumann, and Julius Kaftan—were liberal theologically and moderately conservative politically. They were patriotic, boastful about Germany's superior military and universities, usually monarchist, and usually Lutheran. They espoused the bourgeois myth of progress, Prussian civil religion, and a theory of enlightened Christendom—Cultural Protestantism. They had a place for democracy and political liberalism, usually subordinate to nationalism and political conservatism. Moreover, they were the intellectual elite, addressing church audiences that were usually more conservative. "Liberal theology" meant all these things to the Barthian dialectical theologians who overthrew it in the 1920s.

Twentieth-century theology began in August 1914. Karl Barth, a pastor in Safenwil, Switzerland, was stunned and repulsed that German Social Democrats rolled over for the war and that his German theological teachers cheered for it. He later described the spectacle as the twilight of the gods. Social Democracy provided no brake whatsoever on the rush to war, which negated much of Barth's rationale for being a Social Democrat, at least an active one. More important to him, if German theology was so easily turned into an instrument of militaristic gore, what good was it? If German theologians shucked off the gospel as soon as the kaiser called the nation to war, how could Barth trust anything they had taught him?

Twentieth-century theology began with these questions. The "crisis theology" movement that overtook Continental theology in the early 1920s displaced the liberal tradition with a neo-Reformation perspective emphasizing divine transcendence and shattered illusions. In Barth's case it combined dialectical brilliance, prophetic spiritual power, a return to *sola Scriptura* biblicism in a modernized form, devotion to the Reformed tradition, and a great and strange narrowness. Barth turned away from the Christian socialisms of Hermann Kutter and Leonhard Ragaz, even though both had a theological basis, and even as Barth remained a democratic socialist. In Paul Tillich's case, crisis theology combined dialectical brilliance, post-Kantian German idealism, Lutheran roots, cultural theory, and religious socialism, repudiating narrowness.

Barth adopted Swiss religious socialism as an antidote to bourgeois captivity before deciding that all things political should be secondary issues for Christian theology. Tillich renewed the very tradition of religious socialism that Barth pushed aside, having come late to it as a typical middle-class nationalist in a nation lacking a tradition of progressive religious socialism. Tillich always thought of himself as living on the boundary between two options; for many years he worried that he over-identified with Shakespeare's Hamlet. On political theology he straddled the boundary between Lutheranism and proletarian socialism, in a German context in which Lutheranism had lost its power to stir the masses. After 1848 the world of the working class became a foreign country to Lutheran leaders, who hung on by allying with Prussian conservatism. Tillich became a socialist through his traumatic introduction to the world of the working class during World War I. Then he bonded with Jewish socialist intellectuals for whom religion and ethnicity no longer mattered and opposed Germany's plunge into fanatical racist nationalism and militarism.

Karl Barth was born in Basel, Switzerland, in 1886, where he spent most of his life, although not as a youth. His mother, Anna Barth, was a hard-edged personality who made Barth allergic to strong-willed women for the rest of his life. His father, Fritz Barth, a former pastor, taught at the College of Preachers in Basel, a new institution dedicated to opposing liberal theology and training preachers in biblical theology. In 1888 a group of theological "positives" (conservatives) at the University of Berne called Fritz Barth to succeed Adolf Schlatter as a biblical theologian; thus Karl Barth grew up in a conservative Reformed household near the university, in the Swiss capital.

Fritz Barth was reliably orthodox, with an independent streak. He prized scholarship, had friendly relations with Harnack, and tried to mediate between his orthodox base and an ascending liberal opposition. In 1904 Karl Barth began his studies in theology, at Berne, where he embraced biblical criticism, dismaying his father. Aching for the real thing, Barth moved to Berlin for a semester in 1906 and hung on Harnack's every word, admiring his lectures on Christian doctrine, although Barth did not join the cheering in Harnack's classroom when nationalist parties drubbed the SPD in the February 1907 election. At Fritz Barth's behest, Barth moved to Tübingen to study under Schlatter, where he sneered at Schlatter's conservatism. After that he studied under Wilhelm Herrmann at Marburg, where he adopted Herrmann's existential Pietist conflation of Friedrich Schleiermacher and Albrecht Ritschl—two kinds of liberal theology. In 1908 Barth was ordained in a service conducted by his father at the Berne cathedral. Years later he recalled that he entered the ministry as a pure Marburg liberal who had "absorbed Herrmann through every pore."[2]

Herrmann's warmhearted devotion to Christ assured Barth that liberal theology retained the essential gospel faith. Rationalistic forms of liberalism did not appeal to Barth, and Ernst Troeltsch's historicism left him cold, but Herrmann had the gospel spirit. Barth later reflected: "One of the best remedies against liberal theology and other kinds of bad theology is to take them in bucketsful. On the other hand, all attempts to withhold them by stratagem or force only causes people to fall for them even more strongly, with a kind of persecution complex." The moral of the story: Fritz Barth saved his son from a lifelong fascination with liberal theology by allowing him to study bad theology at prestigious schools. But when Barth turned away from his acquired liberalism, his father's conservative orthodoxy was not an option.[3]

For two years Barth preached liberal sermons at a German-speaking Reformed church in Geneva where Calvin had preached and where his tiny audience found him strange. Afterward, moving to Safenwil, he preached to a tiny congregation of farmers, shopkeepers, and workers who shook their heads in perplexity. In both places only women attended church. Barth urged them to cultivate their feeling for the spirit of Jesus and to strive for the highest ideals. After services he puzzled that no one found his ideas as inspiring or edifying as he had when he heard them from Herrmann. Some parishioners worked in a knitting mill or in one of the area's mill and dye works factories. Wages were low, working conditions were dangerous and grueling, and workers had no trade union to help them. The fact that only Social Democrats seemed to care about the misery of working people made a deep impression on Barth—enough to make him rethink the sneering things that Harnack, Herrmann, and Friedrich Naumann said about Social Democracy.[4]

Ministry proved unsettling at best, but Barth found inspiration in the religious socialist movement, which arose in Switzerland during Barth's early ministry. Zurich pastor Hermann Kutter and University of Zurich theologian Leonhard Ragaz were its cofounders and leaders. Religious socialism had a Swiss backstory in the activism of University of Zurich theologian Friedrich Salomon Vögelin and his followers in the Democratic Party of Zurich, plus the Swiss Workers League, all of which led to the founding of Swiss Social Democracy in 1880. Kutter and Ragaz shared the role in Switzerland that Walter Rauschenbusch played for social gospel socialism in the United States, boosting an ascending movement. Both admired German pastor Christoph Friedrich Blumhardt (1842–1919), a charismatic spellbinder who broke the taboo in 1899 against joining the SPD and thereby lost his clerical career in the state church. Kutter and Ragaz wagered that Switzerland should be more hospitable to Christian Social Democracy. They broke through in 1903, both separately and together, to build a movement.

KUTTER, RAGAZ, AND SWISS RELIGIOUS SOCIALISM

From the beginning there were differences between Kutter and Ragaz that yielded different kinds of religious socialism. Kutter was emphatically a church minister, despite being sharply critical of churches, while Ragaz struggled with his alienation from the church. Kutter confined his socialist activism to the sphere of the church, which never made sense to Ragaz. Kutter was more deeply grounded in Reformed theology and more radically socialist than Ragaz, two things that went together in Kutter's case, except when they did not.

Kutter was born in 1863 to an engineer's family in Bern; he studied theology in Basel, Bern, and Berlin; and he fervently espoused Reformed teaching on the sovereign glory of God. In his early career, from 1887 to 1898, he ministered in a village church, Vinelzam-Bielersee. Then he was called to the charge of Zurich New Minster, where he preached until his retirement in 1926. Ragaz was born in 1868 to a German-speaking farm family in Canton Graubuenden, a small mountain village. He studied theology in Basel, Jena, and Berlin and began his ministerial career as a neo-Hegelian liberal in the mold of Swiss Hegelian theologian A. E. Biedermann.

The two ministers took different things from their theological training in Germany. The early Ragaz embraced Germany's literary, philosophical, and theological traditions while disliking German militarism. Kutter was too orthodox to admire bourgeois German theology, but he identified more than Ragaz with Germany. Ragaz preached liberal theology for three years at mountain village churches in Canton Graubuenden. He washed out in 1893, taught at a school in Chur for two years, and retooled intellectually, reading Hegel, Naumann, Ritschl, Søren Kierkegaard, and Charles Kingsley. In 1895 he returned to the Reformed ministry, in Chur, as a social gospel progressive. Ragaz interpreted the social Christianity of Ritschl, Naumann, and Kingsley as a corrective to bourgeois individualism, and Kierkegaard as a corrective to domesticated church religion. He flourished in Chur, developing a social justice ministry, and accepted a call in 1902 to Basel Minster in Basel, a Reformed landmark and former Catholic cathedral.[5]

Kutter and Ragaz had the same exemplar, Christoph Blumhardt. Both absorbed Blumhardt's emphasis on the kingdom of God and his idea that Social Democracy was an unwitting instrument of God's action in the world. Both loved the story of the Blumhardt family legacy in Germany, which started with Johann Christoph Blumhardt's ministry in Möttlingen, a village in Württemberg at the edge of the Black Forest in Southern Germany. The elder Blumhardt became a famous faith healer despite his sincere efforts to discourage sensationalism and his growing legend. He moved his ministry to a resort hotel in Bad

Boll to relieve Möttlingen of the hordes flocking to him. His son Christoph succeeded him as an evangelist and faith healer, conducting mass crusades and building a national ministry.

Both Blumhardts succeeded spectacularly by contradicting the stereotype of the faith-healing evangelist, but the younger Blumhardt tired of the fixation on personal health and illness. He implored that the kingdom was about more than healing, to no avail. A mass crusade in Berlin in 1888 pushed him over the edge. To fix on the "more," Blumhardt had to pull back on crusading. He went home to Bad Boll and set off a furor in German churches by joining the enemy, the SPD, which welcomed him with surprised fascination. Blumhardt served a six-year term as an SPD delegate in the Württemberg legislature, although he wearied of politics too. Through all of it he preached that the kingdom of God is about the coming of a new world: "God is now creating a new reality on earth, a reality to come first among men but finally over all creation, so that the earth and the heavens are renewed." The god of philosophers, he said, did not interest him, but the living God of the kingdom was the most real, interesting, and difference-making reality in the world: "The kingdom of God comes not through logical concepts but through surprises."[6]

In 1903 Ragaz heralded a construction workers' strike, declaring that if the church did not support the striking workers, it could only mean that the salt of the earth had gone putrid. Jesus was on the side of oppressed workers, and the labor movement was a sign of the kingdom of God, which humanized human beings and fulfilled God's will. This sermon was widely lauded and condemned, changing Ragaz's life. He spoke on labor issues as the preacher of the "Bricklayers' Strike Sermon" and met Kutter. The same year Kutter published a manifesto, *They Must; or, God and the Social Democracy*. Kutter wrote in a flaming style that summoned readers to action. He likened Social Democrats to the early Christians who opposed their time and inaugurated a new era: "They all have a force in them which will not abide question, an imperative which hardly realizes itself, but which will and must create that to which it impels. *They must!*"[7]

Kutter grieved that Christian socialism was almost impossible in the Germanic nations, owing to implacable hostility on both sides. He put it bluntly in his preface to the American edition of *They Must* (1908), declaring that Christian socialism in the United States was "an entirely different thing from what is called the Christian Social movement in the Germanic countries." Americans, he said, could scarcely imagine the obstacles he faced. In his telling, the socialist and social gospel movements in the United States were compatible, sounding much alike. American society was sufficiently free and open-ended that ministers could become socialists and socialists could become ministers. Kutter said social Christianity in the Germanic nations was nothing like that. The Germanic nations had no concept of an energetic Christianity that acted on its own impulses and was not controlled "either by state or by society." He marveled at the audiences that American social gospel leaders Washington Gladden, George Herron, and W. D. P. Bliss routinely attracted. Liberated from a state church, American social gospel ministers preached the gospel as they understood it. At the same time, according to Kutter, American social Christians faced nowhere near the hostility from organized socialism that Germanic social Christians confronted. He asked American readers to keep all that in mind as they read him.[8]

The Germanic state churches, he said, were so "fettered and bound" that it was almost impossible to preach about the original revolutionary spirit of Christianity. Reformed versus Lutheran differences made little difference in this area. Socialism versus Christianity was the upshot: "Thus we had a weak capitalism and a weak Christianity; but over against them, a strong Social Democracy, holding fast to a philosophic doctrinairism which the giant mind of Marx had carried to an extreme height." Marxist theory gave the socialist movement an impulse toward theory, abounding in the formulation of theses and negations. Kutter shared this dialectical style of reasoning but claimed to resist it because dialectical reasoning gave too much weight to abstractions. More important, in Germany it set social Christianity against Social Democracy. Kutter pressed hard on the fateful upshot. German social Christianity, having originated as a form of opposition to Social Democracy, was wholly identified by this antagonism. Harnack, Stöcker, and Naumann based their positions on their different ways of warning that Social Democracy was destructive, overreaching, anti-Christian, and unpatriotic. Kutter countered that social Christianity needed to affirm the Christian core of the socialist movement. Socialism was a secular parable of the kingdom, a recovery of the kingdom of God with God left out. It desperately needed a spiritual infusion—Christian socialism—something "unthinkable" to the founders of German social Christianity.[9]

Stöcker and Naumann loomed large in Kutter's book, both as mirror images of the "sad and fatal error" of anti-Christian Social Democracy. Stöcker, Kutter recalled, founded a Christian Social Labor Party in Berlin, but it flopped and was soon absorbed by the Conservative Party. Stöcker did better with middle-class audiences, so he revamped his Christian Social Party into a bourgeois enterprise emphasizing social issues, not economics, which made it suitable for absorption by the Evangelical Social Congress in 1890. Kutter acknowledged that the congress published some worthy papers. Nonetheless, it did nothing for the suffering masses, exactly as Harnack intended, while posing as an antidote to Social Democracy. In Kutter's telling, Naumann gave the congress its only chance to become what it should have been because Naumann was brilliant, and for a while he cared about working people. But power, prestige, his friends, and his own conceits seduced Naumann. By 1907 Naumann was a shill for Chancellor von Bülow's craven militarism, imperialism, anti-Catholicism, and antisocialism. Kutter grieved that the congress made everything worse, heightening the impression that "Evangelical" meant "anti-Socialist."[10]

This was what came of setting Christianity and Social Democracy against each other: "The Evangelical Socials never perceived that the oneness of the social needs and tasks of the working class is fatal to any cleavage on religious or national lines. Wrapped up in their religious prejudices, and alarmed by the radicalism of the leaders of the Social Democracy, they did not recognize the providential importance of that rising movement; and they never saw deep enough to discover the elementary truth that the Social Democracy, in spite of all its one-sidedness, is, in its essentials, simply right." The great biblical idea of justice as a ray emanating "from the very life of God" and scornful of religious dogmas, they never fathomed.[11]

Kutter pleaded not to be misunderstood. He did not write as a partisan of any Social Democratic party and did not belong to one. He voted for Social Democrats without wanting a red card. He cared only about the great idea of social justice that God cared about. When Kutter compared Social Democracy to the churches, he was embarrassed for Christianity. Since the monikers "Christian Social" and "Evangelical Social" had tainted legacies, he and Ragaz had to call their group something else. They started gingerly with "Religious Social" before owning up to the S-word. Kutter said he and Ragaz sought to unite "the radicalism of the Social Democratic belief with a warm and enthusiastic religious devotion." The old watchwords—conservative, radical, orthodox, and liberal—had become meaningless. Religious socialism breathed a fresh new spirit of radical expectation, dialectically absorbing Social Democracy while being transformed by it: "The Spirit of God, whose express purpose is to bring creation, corrupted by sin, back under the sway of justice and love, makes us glad and strong, so that we, for the sake of the great common goal, are able without hesitation to walk hand in hand with the Social Democracy."[12]

Kutter believed passionately that it should make all the difference in the world whether one believed in God. He featured this belief and put it bluntly, very much like Blumhardt. Unlike every theological system and creed, Kutter said, the Bible has no doctrine of God. The Bible exalts God's glory, longs for God's presence, and expresses every way of relating to God but contains no proofs of God's existence or attributes. Scripture simply attests that God lives, exuding the immense spiritual power that comes from believing it. Theologians and preachers rendered faith in God as the end of an argument; Kutter countered that the Bible unfolds its ideas from the premise that God lives. He put it sharply, contrasting normal everyday existence to the worldview of the Bible. In normal life many things were realities, and God was one of them. In the Bible only one reality really matters, God. Kutter was a thoroughly Calvinist idealist concerning God's reality. Churchgoers, he said, vacillated between trust and doubt, as did their ministers. In the Bible only God is truly interesting and real, so doubt is not an issue: "The Bible is diametrically opposed to our Christianity." Kutter insisted that religion is one of the greatest hindrances to recognizing the living God. Thus it was not surprising that it took an anti-Christian movement to recover the ethical meaning of the Christian worldview. Jesus dwelt fully in the presence and power of the living God, but Christianity lived by ideas about Jesus and God.[13]

Kutter despaired that modern Christians did not fathom what it means to hunger and thirst after righteousness. The Sermon on the Mount washed over them without comprehension, especially the saying about being reviled for the sake of Jesus, which was *totally* incomprehensible. Modern churchgoers were accustomed to being the revilers, looking down on Social Democrats and the poor: "The despised of all people today are the Social Democrats. I am tempted to believe that *there* is today's revelation of God." Kutter piled up antitheses in that vein. Socialists were atheists, yet they waged the fight against false gods and injustice that God cared about. Anyone who truly believed in the living God had no reason to fear socialist atheism. Socialists were materialists in theory, yet they tried to change material conditions, evincing a powerful spiritual vision that put Christians to shame. In theory socialists derided the language of sin, yet they battled the social ravages of sin, unlike the churches. At every turn, Kutter said, Christian churches reduced the religion of Jesus to something innocuous and private, while socialists called for repentance and social salvation: "Christianity has lived its self-satisfied life from century to century, without bothering itself about the poor, otherwise than to throw them the hard bread of alms. It hardly thinks of the commands of the Gospel on its every page to dispel the power of evil and sin."[14]

Piling up antitheses in this fashion was a form of repentance for Kutter because it contrasted with the repugnant fare that churches spewed against Social Democracy. Stöcker was his stock example. Stöcker railed that Social Democrats hated their country and hated God, so they had to be fought before they turned Germany red with blood. He claimed that he took the social problem seriously but in a way that loved Germany, order, Christianity, and God. Kutter shuddered that Stöcker won a popular following with this tripe. Whatever might be wrong with Social Democracy, Social Democrats poured themselves out for the poor and oppressed, exactly as the Bible commends. Stöcker's brand of social Christianity, by contrast, "has too much of the trader spirit." There was nothing in it for God to use. Kutter blasted theologians for objecting that Social Democracy was revolutionary. If they didn't get that Christianity is supposed to be revolutionary, they had no idea what it meant to believe in the living God. As for violence, Kutter affirmed Marx's maxim in *Capital* that violence is the midwife of "every old society which is pregnant with a new one." He noted that Bernstein revisionism steered much of Social Democracy away from revolutionary violence, but Kutter did not say it to commend Bernstein to churchgoers. The violent end of the old world, Kutter said — revolution — is on every page of the New Testament. Christianity is not a sentimental substitute for it: "The living God laughs at this bastard, fearful Christianity." God *uses* violence to make a new world and lay waste to human vanity. God is "the greatest of all revolutionists" and the "most ruthless of destroyers!"[15]

In modern society, Kutter said, only one thing is great — Mammon. Mammon produces, governs, determines, and destroys, making everything small and mercenary. Only the Social Democrats dared to oppose the idolatry of money, so God worked through the Social Democrats, building the kingdom of righteousness and community. Guardians of Reformation theology objected that the Word alone must accomplish God's purpose; Christians have no business helping God build the kingdom. Kutter did not counter in stock social gospel fashion with Matthew 25 or the like. He had an answer but was slow to give it. Kutter was assiduously church-centered and Calvinist in the way he thought about socialism and the divine kingdom. He eschewed ethical language about building the kingdom and did not urge Christians to join Social Democratic parties. To him, the kingdom was God's business, which God was bringing about through the socialists. Kutter wanted Christians to learn from the socialists how to transform the churches. The churches had to become Christian before they could be useful to God. Kutter did not say it this clearly in 1903, so his response to his own rhetorical question about Reformation theology gave the appearance of changing the subject in mid-paragraph. He said that Social Democrats went overboard in assuring they wanted a revolution without violence.

He was still talking about God using violence to make a new world, despite the appearance that he had moved to another topic. Kutter pointedly refrained from saying that he prayed for a revolution without violence. The Social

Democrats cultivated a noble idealism in this area, he said. Kutter was more radical, like God, wishing that Social Democrats were less squeamish and idealistic. The rule of Mammon would not be swept aside by a word or any form of moral idealism because it pervaded every institution in modern society. Kutter admonished that the "slightest sign of Social Democratic disturbance" brought out hordes of police to preserve the rule of Mammon. Social Democrats and everyday unionists had to be much tougher than churchgoers to withstand how capitalism defended its arrangements. However, Kutter compensated with the usual Social Democratic assurance about strikes. In the long run, he said, strikes were good for peace and stability because they turned desperate, hungry, and oppressed bands of workers into stable communities.[16]

Kutter knew many well-meaning churchgoers who prayed sincerely for the poor and thought it was nice to be nice. They used the word "ought" a great deal, showing their moral sensitivity. The church ought to do this and society ought to do that. Kutter said they talked so earnestly and so much because they were powerless to do anything: "We cover our moral nakedness with these imperatives." What good was any ought that did not get to must? The good is not merely an ought, he urged. The good must be, for it alone is real, the life of the living God in the world. Mammon is a false god that must be overthrown: "This *must* glows in the souls of the Social Democrats. Hence society accuses them of overthrowing morality." Social Democrats were the enemies of pathetic do-nothing morality. Kutter held one objection to the end, knowing his church audience. Socialists were said to be enemies of the family, advocating free love. This line of attack, Kutter said, rested on one person, August Bebel, who wrote a book deriding marriage as a form of slavery. Kutter greatly admired Bebel but not on this subject, on which Bebel misled many into believing that Social Democrats wanted to abolish marriage. Kutter said socialism would be tremendously good for families, relieving women of the struggle not to starve. Social Democrats were the most deeply moral and self-sacrificing people he knew, "leading lives irreproachable, according to the moral standards of our day."[17]

He had to finish with patriotism because nationalism had grown virulent in Europe, and socialists were accused of trampling "the holiest of all things, the love of fatherland." Kutter said Social Democrats were trustworthy patriots who wanted world peace as much as anyone else. There were two kinds of patriotism, he reasoned. Chauvinistic patriotism was insular and mean, always looking down on foreigners. Good patriotism, however, respected the aspirations of other peoples and desired world peace. Socialists were the best kind of good patriots because their love of country extended to all nations and people. They were emphatically not antipatriots spoiling for a global class war. In France,

Russia, and everywhere else the poor were much the same, for hunger "knows no Fatherland." Social Democrats were internationalists because they cared about the oppressed everywhere. According to Kutter, they established a new standard about how to be a good patriot. Social Democrats taught the world that "no people is free until all are redeemed from oppression." He said the same thing differently, describing true patriotism as cosmopolitan love of all human beings regardless of nation or ethnicity. Kutter was repulsed that Stöcker accused Social Democrats of hating their country and Naumann shamelessly named his group the National Social Party. Both betrayed Christianity by stooping to the bad kind of patriotism. True patriotism, a robustly cosmopolitan faith, could not be achieved under capitalism: "Without the destruction of capitalism, true patriotism cannot exist."[18]

They Must electrified Kutter's Swiss audience and stunned German theologians, sparking a movement on the initiative of Ragaz, who moved from sermonizing "ought" to organizing "must" by reading Kutter. The only comparable Christian socialist work of its time for making an impact was Rauschenbusch's *Christianity and the Social Crisis*, published in 1907, which oddly never cited Kutter. Kutter and Ragaz bonded over Ragaz's enthusiasm for the book. They founded a movement organization in the home of a Degersheim pastor, Hans Bader, in which Ragaz played an active role and Kutter played the role of distant seer. Both traded on Switzerland's distinct political and ecclesiastical history but without rattling on about Calvin and Zwingli because religious socialism was not just for Swiss.

The group launched a journal edited by Ragaz, *Neue Wege,* and a journal representing the Kutter camp edited by Georg Benz and Otto Lautenburg, *Freie Schweizer Arbeiter.* Just as this two-track movement got rolling in 1906 Ragaz urged a large ministerial gathering in Basel to focus on the big picture. The church was too middle class to be a real community, he said. Socialism reminded the churches of what they were supposed to care about, and it would not nationalize small firms, only the big ones. When parishioners mouthed "the domineering point of view," ministers needed to set them straight. Democracy and equality were coming, and capitalism was compatible with neither. It was "false in every respect" to proclaim that one was the master of one's house or business. The old master, Ragaz said, got away with talking like that because he cared for his servants in sickness and old age, and there was no democracy. Now husbands and employers had to be told that patriarchy and feudalism were gone and discredited: "Now an order is emerging which people work together for a common goal, no longer against each other but for each other."[19]

Ragaz preached a theology of hope a half century before Jürgen Moltmann launched a school bearing this name. He told his Basel congregation in his farewell sermon that God was ever before them, luring them to liberation from guilt, hate, and oppression: "Hope and future I have proclaimed to you." Since they were Reformed children of Calvin and Zwingli they were supposed to believe that the will of a holy God should be embodied in the world. Ragaz said three things kept them from believing it. They thought of God too theoretically, associated God with a past age, and felt defeated by the evil in the world. He said he spent his early ministry committing all three mistakes. But God kept working on him—the God of becoming who has always just begun to save the world. The God of the future, Ragaz taught, cannot be captured in a system and does not belong only to the past. The living God is the ground of hope that wills the redemption of all people and the earth: "We are to breathe freely in the freedom of God and become united in a Kingdom of freedom, purity, justice, and love." On this basis social Christianity was critical of the church and society, daring to embrace God's hope for the world. The more he believed it, Ragaz said, the more he found himself loving other people. It wasn't his doing because God gave this love to him. But woe to him had he not obeyed: "Something compels, forces me to show the worker that I understand him, that I would like to do justice by him."[20]

In 1908 the University of Zurich called Ragaz to its chair in systematic and practical theology. He had not expected to become an academic but appreciated what it meant for modern theology that his activism lifted him to this position. Ragaz judged that Blumhardt and Rauschenbusch were the two theologians closest to his way of thinking, so he reached out to them, forging friendships. Blumhardt and Rauschenbusch had the eschatological emphasis that marked Ragaz, and both were prophetic exemplars to him. On Ragaz's initiative, Rauschenbusch's *Christianity and the Social Crisis* was published in a German edition translated by Ragaz's spouse, feminist peace activist Clara Ragaz-Nadig. Barthian theologian Emil Brunner later recalled that Ragaz had a powerful impact on him and others during his student days at the university: "That was a great time, when Ragaz came to Zurich. Then theology was interesting, not as a science, but as a proclamation in our time, as encounter with historical reality, with the labor question, with the war issue." Barth similarly recalled that when he returned to Switzerland to begin his ministerial career religious socialism was sweeping the churches: "Every young Swiss pastor who was not asleep or living somehow behind the moon or for whatever reason errant, was at that time in the narrower or the wider sense a 'Religious Socialist.' We became—in negative things more certain to be sure than in the positive—powerfully *antibürgerlich*."[21]

Barth's closest friend and fellow minister in the Aargau, Eduard Thurneysen, knew Kutter and Blumhardt personally and Ragaz less so. He encouraged Barth to see that religious socialists were different from the German liberals and social Christians he knew in graduate school. The religious socialists were religiously serious in a way that was new to Barth. They spoke and behaved as though it mattered immeasurably whether one believed in God. Kutter impressed Barth by saying it emphatically. Barth later recalled, "From Kutter I simply learnt to speak the great word 'God' seriously, responsibly, and with a sense of its importance. From Blumhardt I learned just as simply (at least at the beginning) what it meant to speak of Christian hope." Barth's exposure to religious socialism shook loose some of his acquired culture religion. He told his congregation that without a commitment to a kingdom-bringing social justice their religion was a pack of lies. Having been touched, as he later recounted, "for the first time by the real problems of real life," he immersed himself in trade union issues and socialist theory, blending liberal theology with socialist politics. He read Werner Sombart on socialism and found himself poring over factory legislation: "I had to read the Swiss trade-union newspaper and the *Textilarbeiter.*"[22]

Barth still assumed, with Schleiermacher and Herrmann, that religious experience must be the generative ground of theology. At the same time he resisted the disturbing suspicion that he had been corrupted by the cultural chauvinism and nationalism of his German teachers. This suspicion helped to motivate Barth's railing against militarism, which he kept up nearly every week from the pulpit for a year before Europe descended into war. He urged his congregation to accept that the teaching of Jesus was irreconcilable with the murderous violence of war, and Christians had to be antiwar. For a while Barth imagined that at least some of his teachers must have agreed. Then the kaiser called Germany to war in an address written by Harnack. Two months later, ninety-three prominent German intellectuals issued a ringing manifesto of support for the war. Barth read it with revulsion, finding the names, as he told the story, of nearly all his German theological teachers. He recalled that reading this "horrible manifesto" was "almost even worse" for him than Germany's invasion of Belgium. He put the personal upshot dramatically: "An entire world of theological exegesis, ethics, dogmatics, and preaching, which up to that point I had accepted as basically credible, was thereby shaken to the foundations, and with it everything which flowed at that time from the pens of the German theologians." Bourgeois theology was obviously bankrupt, and he had to find an alternative to it.[23]

Actually it was not that simple. The story of how Barth rebelled against his liberal teachers and changed the direction of modern theology is the founding narrative of twentieth-century theology, notwithstanding that a good deal of it is wrong or exaggerated. Contrary to the story Barth told, only two of his teachers signed the manifesto, his career did not consist of a series of dramatic conversions, it took him six years to break from liberal theology, his development of an analogical method was an elongated affair too, he never stopped being a dialectical theologian, his theology retained and refashioned numerous elements from Herrmann, Kant, Hegel, Schleiermacher, and Ragaz, and Barth remained a socialist for the rest of his life, although not a religious socialist. His path to Barthian theology was more winding and complex than the usual rendering of it, partly because Barth told the story from the perspective of his later theology and because conversion stories are dramatically compelling. I dissected this extremely tangled story in *The Barthian Revolt in Modern Theology*. Here it is enough to summarize, emphasizing his involvement in religious socialism.[24]

The differences between Kutter and Ragaz yielded factions in Swiss religious socialism from its early days onward. Kutter said that plunging into Social Democratic politics would corrupt and politicize the churches. Ragaz said that being a Christian socialist should lead to being involved in Social Democratic politics. Kutter kept his direct involvement in the organization to a minimum, while Ragaz spoke and wrote for it constantly. On militarism and the war and on politics more generally the two founders divided sharply. Kutter sympathized with Germany and kept quiet about the war, quietly cheering for a German victory. Ragaz blasted German militarism, condemned the war unequivocally, and called the churches to Christianize the Social Democratic drive for social justice. Ragaz and his followers were antiwar radicals on militarism and war, holding fast to Christian socialist antimilitarism. But ideologically Kutter was more radical, prizing Social Democracy as the hammer by which God would smash capitalism. He stuck to his positions and did not referee the swirl of debates within his camp or religious socialism as a whole. Kutter was a Marxist in the Kautsky mode, while Ragaz agreed with Bernstein's critique of Marxism. Ragaz's Christian ethical idealism fit the Bernstein agenda for Social Democracy, in a Swiss context. Kutter's radical Calvinism put him on the side of Marxian revolutionaries, albeit within the confines of the church.[25]

Barth was torn between them. Politically he tended to side with the Ragaz idealists. What was the point of advocating socialism if you refused to work with unions and socialist parties? Barth admired Ragaz's nervy support for the general strike of 1912 in Zurich, which evoked protests to fire Ragaz from the university. Government troops crushed the strike, deepening Ragaz's commitment to antimilitarism. He played a leading role in the Peace Congress of the Socialist International, which met in Münster in 1912 to plan a world conference on social Christianity, slated for 1914 in Basel. Instead Europe went to war. To Barth, the moral difference between Ragaz and Kutter seemed overwhelming.

Barth had a son-like relationship with one of his German teachers, Marburg theologian Martin Rade, who founded *Die christliche Welt* (The Christian world) in 1888 and joined the Marburg faculty in 1904. Rade and his paper played leading roles in the Evangelical Social Congress and German Protestantism. Barth had worked on the paper during his student days, and he trusted Rade to an unusual degree, partly because Rade was as politically progressive as a Harnack protégé and establishment insider could be. Rade played this role throughout his long career. In 1914, however, Rade supported the war for the same reasons as Harnack and Herrmann. Barth trembled with revulsion at the paper's early wartime issues. He told Rade on September 8 that *Die christliche Welt* had ceased to be Christian, lining up "simply with *this* world." Barth said he was willing to leave the political judgments aside. Christian integrity was the issue. What had happened to the Christian part of German theology? On October 1, two days before the manifesto, Barth told Rade his long-held respect for the "German character" was being destroyed. The Christian part of German theology, as far as he was concerned, had broken into pieces under the pressure of a war psychosis.[26]

Then the manifesto came out, Barth wrote an incredulous open letter to Herrmann, and Rade tried to talk him down. Rade told Barth his Swiss citizenship made him incapable of understanding the German situation. He lacked the German war experience, a commanding reality that united all Germans. Barth was appalled that any theologian considered this a serious reply, much less the German theologian he trusted most. Germany's war psychosis compelled him to silence, even reverence? Barth despaired that the entire tradition of German theology was dead to him, except Schleiermacher, who surely would not have signed the horrible manifesto. In January 1915 he belatedly joined the Social Democratic Party of Switzerland, which was officially neutral in the war. It mattered to Barth that Ragaz had joined the party in October 1913, mainly to stand against militarism and war. Now Barth was clinging to the anti-militarism of Ragaz's wing of the party. Kutter, meanwhile, apologized to Germans for the Swiss socialists who blamed Germany for the war, and his *Freie Schweizer Arbeiter* editor Gustav Benz declared that the moment called for silence, not righteous antiwar sermons.[27]

All of that militated against taking Kutter seriously, and it got worse in 1916, when Kutter published a book titled *Reden an die deutsche Nation* (Speeches to the German nation) in which he repeated the apology and invoked the living God of mysterious ways, still cheering for a German victory. Thurneysen,

however, cautioned Barth against dismissing Kutter. Kutter's emphasis on waiting for God, Thurneysen said, contained a deeper spiritual wisdom than Ragaz's
eagerness to see signs of the kingdom in the antiwar opposition and the socialist
movement. Kutter understood that every hearing of the Word of God is problematic. Ragaz conflated too readily the gospel faith with the politics of Social
Democracy, but Kutter and Blumhardt preached that people are enslaved without God. The preaching reference mattered because Barth and Thurneysen
faced the problem of the sermon every Sunday.

What did they believe that had to be preached? In April 1915 Barth and
Thurneysen attended the wedding of Barth's brother Peter to Rade's daughter
Helene. On the way home they visited Blumhardt for five days in Bad Boll.
Blumhardt made a riveting impression on Barth. He did not fumble over his
Christian identity or the problem of the sermon. God was real to Blumhardt as
the presence of the kingdom. As Barth put it, "God is the end, and because we
already know Him as the beginning, we may await His consummating acts."
That summer Barth studied the sermons of both Blumhardts. By the fall of 1915
Barth agreed with Thurneysen that Ragaz identified the kingdom too readily
with the activism of religious socialists and their kin. Christian socialists needed
to wait upon a God that does not submit to human plans. The kingdom of
Christ, Barth reasoned, is a new world breaking into the existing world that calls
into question everything human. He thanked Thurneysen for helping him to
see that Kutter understood the kingdom better than Ragaz: "You really made
him accessible to me. That was an act!"[28]

This was the crucial turn in Barth's twisting and turning path to a neo-
Reformation theology. To Barth, Ragaz showed what Christian socialism looked
like on Herrmann's terms, still expounding a liberal theology of religious experience. Barth judged that if Kutter was better than Ragaz, he had to start over,
waiting upon a Wholly Other God of grace and glory. It took Barth ten years
and two very different versions of the same book even to get to the point of
becoming a dogmatic theologian, all the while characterizing Ragaz in ways
that favored Barth and were unfair to Ragaz. Then Barth went through another
prolonged process of sifting and rethinking, still focused on the problem of how
one knows anything about God.

I agree with Barth scholars Ingrid Spieckermann and Bruce McCormack
that Barth's turn in 1915 over Kutter versus Ragaz is the key one in his thought.
But I do not accept Barth's polemical rendering of Ragaz's theology, which
owed some of its polemical animus to competitive rivalry and some to the
fact that Ragaz propounded key Barthian tropes before Barth. Moreover,
Ragaz developed these concepts with greater theological sophistication than

Blumhardt or Kutter. Barth became famous during his crisis theology period for expounding themes he got from Blumhardt, Kutter, and Ragaz, but he fashioned these tropes as reasons not to support religious socialism. He contrasted the kingdom of God with religion, identified the gospel with the promise of a divine new order, and described the kingdom of God as the abolition of religion, in every case taking over a signature trope of Ragaz.

During the war Ragaz accentuated that the kingdom of God comes from God as the negation and abolition of religion. He put it with customary candor in 1917: "This new world, the Kingdom of God, is different from the other kingdom that has usurped its place under the pretense of being the Kingdom of God itself. The other kingdom is so strong that it obscures the view into the nature of the genuine Kingdom of God. It even persists in concealing Jesus. We must try to free Jesus and his cause from the obscurities and distortions that have surrounded him so that the free and deep spirits who are now on the way to God might know what we are talking about." He also said it sharply: "First of all, it needs to be said once again that the Kingdom of God is not a religion, but rather its opposite. . . . The Kingdom of God is no religion but rather the abolishment of all religion. . . . Moses wanted no religion, and the battle of the prophets was a battle *against* religion. . . . Jesus also stands in this line; he follows it to the end. . . . He does not want a religion, but rather a Kingdom, a new creation, a new world."[29]

Religion, Ragaz said, is a human creation, a product of the human struggle and desire for spiritual meaning: "It is a whole world of dispositions, an unending symphony of sentiments. The scale of religious feeling reaches from the deepest hell to the highest heaven. All jubilation and all agony, all light and all darkness that inhabit the infinite reaches of the human soul find their strongest and fullest expression in religion." Jesus didn't want any of that. Jesus fixed on the kingdom with no hint of any interest in worship etiquette or cultivating personal piety. He cared only about the coming of a new order. Ragaz urged, "We cannot think realistically enough about the cause of Jesus." Protestants liked to say the true church is invisible, but Jesus spurned invisible spirituality: "What Jesus wants is a world order based on God, not a religion." Ragaz implored Christians not to claim that religion does more good than evil. It was hard to say whether this claim is true, and beside the point anyway. What matters is to care about what God cares about: "He is the God of justice and love, from whom comes the Kingdom. It is there he rules, and there only."[30]

These arguments had an explosive impact on theology only a few years later, when Barth gave them an otherworldly spin that credited Blumhardt, who was easier to bend to Barth's purpose. Ragaz carried on the activist and ideological work that Barth cast off on his way to becoming a dogmatic theologian, and Ragaz stressed that God and the divine kingdom, not religion, make religious experience sacred. To Ragaz it made no sense to advocate democratic socialism without joining others in the political struggle for it, just as it made no sense to advocate peace without joining actual peace movements. The war drove him to emphasize antimilitarism more than prosocialism, but the two things fused together for him anyway. Similarly, after the Bolsheviks took power in Russia Ragaz said it was imperative for Social Democrats to repudiate Bolshevism. Democracy is not an optional matter for socialists, he insisted. Socialism *is* democracy applied to the society and economy. Thus Bolshevism was an enemy of socialism, every bit as anathema to socialism as militaristic capitalism.

He said it as an intellectual leader in the Swiss Social Democratic Party. Ragaz shuddered at Social Democrats who said that Bolshevism was socialism in a hurry or the best that Russians could manage. He warned that the Bolsheviks would not allow democratic institutions to develop because Leninism was a justification of tyranny by a revolutionary elite. Leninism was "a perversion of socialism," a cynical creed and strategy that valued power more than truth. It had to be fought with the same principled, ethical, freedom-loving militancy that democratic socialists mustered against capitalist tyranny: "On the one side stands the new democracy which wants to transform the world politically and socially on the basis of justice and freedom and in the light of a moral ideal. Against it stands Leninism with its proletarian imperialism." Ragaz pleaded with Social Democrats to stand against what they hated: imperialism, dictatorship, and militarism. Leninism was all three, in a left-wing form that implicated Social Democracy if Social Democrats did not forcefully oppose it: "Everywhere Bolshevism entails a belief in violence rather than justice, in dictatorship rather than democracy, in absolutism rather than freedom, in matter rather than spirit."[31]

Ragaz led Swiss Social Democracy's cheering section for Woodrow Wilson's Fourteen Points and was crushed when Versailles went badly in 1919. The same year he was a major player in the Swiss Social Democratic debate over whether the party should join the Communist International founded by Lenin in March. Ragaz went straight for an argument about having a soul. The soul of socialism is its "deep reverence for persons," he urged. Nothing cuts deeper in socialism than its soulful regard for the freedom and dignity of every human life. Socialism is a moral ideal and a form of community based on the principle of solidarity. To him it was unthinkable that Swiss Social Democrats would join the Communist International, unless Swiss Social Democracy had lost its soul. Never an absolute pacifist, Ragaz took wars one at a time, accepted the principle of self-defense, and based his argument for antimilitarism on an ethical critique of the demonic character of human power. To begin with violence, he argued, is to guarantee that one will never be rid of violence. Using violence to obtain power is the sure way to build a despotic kingdom. The only way to build a democratic socialist society is to begin with a deep respect for the intrinsic value and inner freedom of others, seeking to persuade, not to rule: "Truth has its origin in freedom. All freedom originates in belief, and all denial of freedom is disbelief." The socialist movement, he said, stood at a fateful crossroads, an either/or about the kind of movement it was to be. Obviously the Communist parties would join the Third International. If any Social Democratic party joined, it would be a calamity, a betrayal of socialism.[32]

Ragaz did not know exactly where to draw the line between politics and good religion—defined as the spirit of Christ—but he felt compelled to try. It was a divisive issue for many socialists and for what became the Barthian reaction. To give his usual spiel against religion would have been incomprehensible to non-Christian socialists, and Ragaz had much at stake in being persuasive. He reasoned that politics necessarily involves a struggle for worldly power, contrary to the religion of Jesus. To follow the way of Jesus is to reject all power in the service of God and humanity. Politics is about ruling, and the religion of Jesus is about serving. Many socialists and Christians preferred to keep this dichotomy in place, identifying socialism completely with politics, for better or worse, and debating the relative badness of religion. None of that was the point this time because Ragaz needed to explain himself and others like him. The socialist movement, as he experienced it, was not wholly political. It was partly political and partly religious in the sense of good religion because on both sides it sought to replace the old order of domination with a new order of justice and solidarity. Ragaz said the socialist movement, as he experienced it, was a low-medium form of good religion. Being political, it had no chance of reaching the kingdom level, but it was about the same things the kingdom was about: "The wish of each Christian remains that socialism would some day dissolve in the Kingdom of God, allowing politics and religion to converge, but today we are only on the way."[33]

That was not where Barth wanted to land. Ragaz despaired of church conservatism and the academy, both of which compared poorly to trade unions, Social Democracy, and community church groups. In 1921 he gave up his faculty chair and moved to a working-class section of Zurich, where he edited *Neue Wege* and ran an educational center for the rest of his career. He had to be with the people who struggled for what mattered, even if that meant losing his place in the academy and institutional church. Ragaz fought against fascism as soon as it arose, he was a North Star of progressive religious Social Democracy, and he struck

Barth for many years, wrongly, as the epitome of a politicized religious socialist who tossed theology overboard. Ragaz criticized church and society on the basis of his understanding of the divine will, not the postulates of social theory. He did not identify the kingdom with social movements, although Barthians described him that way until 1945, when he died. To Ragaz, the movements for peace, worker rights, feminism, and Social Democracy were *signs* of the divine commonwealth. He sought repeatedly to formulate the optimal relationships among theology, social theory, politics, and ethical idealism, notably in his book *Von Christus zu Marx, von Marx zu Christus* (1929), which argued that Marxian materialism was "the true child of idealism," the transformation of ideals into reality. Ragaz went only so far with Marx because Ragaz believed in the creative power of Spirit divine. But he accepted Marx's critique of humanistic idealism, and he lauded Marx for subduing the world to the spirit of Marxian criticism.[34]

Ragaz was a restless seeker of the divine will, committed to grappling with an unsolvable problem. After he was gone, many said he deserved better than to be reduced to a stereotype about politicized religion; Barth was one of them.

CRISIS THEOLOGY

The Barthian revolt, shortly after it won a following, was called "crisis theology." Barth wrote that before the kingdom of God can become real to modern Christians "there must come a crisis that denies all human thought." Crisis theology was a reaction to the slaughter and destruction of World War I and the complicity of Barth's teachers in lionizing Germany's invasion of Belgium and France. More broadly, it was a response to the ferocious judgment of the war on European cultural pretension. Liberal theologians gave the impression of being comfortable with God and proud of their sophistication. Crisis theology was about shattered illusions, the experience of emptiness before a hidden God, and what Barth called the unexpected surge of spiritual meaning he found in "the strange new world within the Bible."[35]

In January 1916 Barth told Thurneysen he was becoming "frighteningly indifferent" to historical questions. To be sure, he allowed, he was prone to antihistoricism, which showed in his attraction to Herrmann. For years Barth debated Paul Wernle, a Troeltschian theologian at Basel, on this point. Wernle contended that historical consciousness is enriching and the future of theology belonged to the history of religions school, which studied religions from an objective academic standpoint not giving privilege to any particular religion. To Barth, this was a very dismal prospect. Historicism made theology weak and shallow, and he doubted that any theologian would embrace Troeltsch's historicism without being devoured by it. In a lecture in November 1915 titled "Wartime and the Kingdom of God," Barth said God was absent from modern life, and Wernle cautioned that Barth was falling into an apocalyptic mentality. Two months later Barth told Thurneysen that soon they would have to "strike a great blow against the theologians."[36]

The following July he mentioned to Thurneysen that he was assembling a "copy-book" of comments on Paul's letter to the Romans that summarized Paul's message in modern language. Barth said he had discovered a "gold mine" for this project, a collection of biblical commentaries written by his father's favorite teacher, Württemberg biblical scholar Johann Tobias Beck. "As a biblical expositor he simply towers far above the rest of the company, also above Schlatter." Beck had taught biblical interpretation to Barth's father and grandfather. His respect for the divine inspiration and canonical integrity of scripture gave his scholarship a spiritual depth that Barth missed in liberal criticism. It also brought Barth closer in feeling to the memory of his recently deceased father. He told Thurneysen that Beck's old-fashioned approach was "in part directly accessible and exemplary for us." It disclosed the spiritual world of the Bible that liberal scholarship never managed to find. Barth remarked, "The older generation may once more have some pleasure in us, but a bit differently from what it intended."[37]

Barth didn't know where he was going, but he knew he needed something stronger than his acquired liberalism. He fastened on the problem of the sermon, partly from practical necessity. He gave talks to pastors, protesting that theologians reduced the gospel to their own "pitiably weak tones." Biblical criticism deconstructed the literary and religious history of the Bible to get its meaning, which obscured the spiritual truth of scripture, negating the driving spiritual force that makes the Bible holy scripture. Barth declared, "If we wish to come to grips with the contents of the Bible, we must dare to reach far beyond ourselves. The Book admits of nothing less." The answer that scripture gives is its own strange new world, "the world of God." There is a rushing stream in the Bible that carries us away if we allow ourselves to be taken by it: "We need only dare to follow this drive, this spirit, this river, to grow out beyond ourselves toward the highest answer."[38]

Faith opens the strange new world of the Bible to us, Barth said. We cannot enter the world of scriptural truth by reading the Bible with false modesty or academic restraint, for these are passive qualities. Faith is a form of spiritual daring. More important, scripture offers an invitation to dare, an expression of divine grace. A new world enters and suffuses our ordinary world by the grace of God's Spirit, through faithful openness to the Word that scripture contains: "We may not deny nor prevent our being led by Bible 'history' far out beyond what is elsewhere called history—into a new world, into the world of God."[39]

Barth reasoned that the kingdom of God is not a second world standing apart from the existing "real" world. It is this existing world made new through the in-breaking power of the Spirit. At the same time, the Bible is not about how to find one's way to God, and it is not terribly helpful with moral and practical questions. The Bible is about God's glory and sovereignty and how God found the way to estranged human beings. Barth praised the old conservatives for holding to this truism against Schleiermacher and biblical criticism; rightly, they took revelation seriously: "Our fathers were right when they guarded warily against being drawn out upon the shaky scaffolding of religious self-expression."[40]

That raised the slippery issue of Pietism, since the "fathers" were conservative-leaning Pietists: Beck, Friedrich August G. Tholuck, and C. H. Rieger. These were Barth's guides as he worked through Romans, in addition to commentaries by Calvin and Johannes Bengel. He also drew on his father's lecture notes and Kutter's articles on Romans. Barth was wary of Pietist enthusiasm. At its worst it yielded gruesome revival preaching and fearmongering threats of hellfire that Barth found repugnant. Even at its best it turned into a stopgap for the evangelical liberalism that Barth was trying to overcome. He told Thurneysen that when the moment came to strike the blow against the theologians, they would have to untangle the web of Pietist and historicist influences they imbibed from their teachers.

Barth fretted that his conversion to biblical revelation came too late, telling Thurneysen, "If only we had been converted to the Bible *earlier* so that we would now have solid ground under our feet!" In fact, his turn against his teachers was perfectly timed. The colossal carnage of the war refuted, in Germany, the prowar sermons of the early war. In Switzerland Barth preached to congregants who feared the war would never end or would spill into their country. After February 1917 many feared the Bolshevik revolution would spill into their country. By then all were pressed hard by commodity shortages and inflated living costs. Barth was never one to flatter his congregation with easy religion; even during wartime he gave a blistering sermon against the kind of congregation that yearned for a pastor "who pleases the people." But he also preached sermons resembling the exuberant, hopeful, sometimes lyrical tone of his forthcoming book on Paul's letter to the Romans.[41]

Barth's *Römerbrief* was published in December 1918 with no thought of acclaim or a wide audience; he later recalled, "I had no inkling of the repercussions which would follow." In Barth's telling, Paul taught that true history is made only through the in-breaking power of the Spirit. This spiritual truth could not be grasped by historical criticism or cutting Paul's theology to fit the worldview of modern culture. Liberal theology contrasted the Christ myth of Paul to the social gospel of Jesus. It criticized Paul's Christology, doctrine of blood redemption, typology of Christ and Adam, disregard of the historical Jesus, devotion to scriptural authority, and nonhistorical exegesis. Barth's early sermons recycled Harnack, Herrmann, and Marburg New Testament scholar Adolf Jülicher on these points. He had entered the ministry believing that Luther was superior to Paul and Schleiermacher was superior to everyone. From the pulpit he had confessed that it was hard for him to preach about contrived and mythological Pauline texts.[42]

Now he proclaimed that Paul's mythical gospel of redemption and resurrection was the true gospel of Christ. This was the source of the book's exuberant spirit, Barth's joyful discovery that Paul was greater than Luther, Calvin, and even Schleiermacher. According to Barth, Paul's religious message was a history-changing and history-transcending theology of salvation, grace, and glory. The core of this message was that Christ, through his redeeming death and resurrection, inaugurated a new aeon of the Spirit that is the world's true salvation. The gospel is the proclamation of a new creation. As the redeeming "hinge of history," Jesus inaugurated a new aeon of real history overcoming the old, unreal aeon of sin and death. In the old aeon, Barth explained, God was hidden to the "old Adam" because of humankind's bondage to sin. In the new aeon of Christ's triumph over sin, God's sovereign grace worked upon all unbelief, sin, faith, and righteousness to bring about God's purpose.[43]

Paul was an apostle of the kingdom of God who speaks to people of every age. The differences between his age and the modern age were unimportant. Modern biblical criticism, Barth allowed, had a rightful place as a preparatory discipline, but otherwise it did very little to help readers apprehend the Bible's meaning. Barth declared that if he were compelled to choose between biblical criticism and the old doctrine of biblical inspiration, "I should without hesitation adopt the latter, which has a broader, deeper, more important justification." Biblical criticism, by itself, had little value, unlike the doctrine of inspiration. Liberal theology was weak because it historicized and psychologized the gospel. Barth preferred "to see through and beyond history into the spirit of the Bible, which is the Eternal Spirit."[44]

That was an echo of Plato's theory of forms and Kant's thing-in-itself. To Barth, as to Plato and Paul, salvation was about the restoration of a broken ideal and the hunger for a new age. To Barth, as to Plato and Kant, there was a "real reality" that lies beyond the world of appearance. In the new aeon of Christ's triumph over sin, God's grace worked upon faith *and* unbelief and sin to bring about God's purpose. Like the expressionist writers and painters Barth admired at the time, he distinguished between the surface appearances of the so-called real world and the real reality that lies beneath the world of appearances. He embraced the expressionist idea that true reality can be glimpsed only by disrupting or breaking up the world of appearances that empirical disciplines treat as "real." In Barth's telling, this was precisely what Paul's message of salvation accomplished. Paul's letter to the Romans offered an idol-breaking critique of every merely human strategy of salvation.[45]

Paul did not believe, Barth said, that ordinary history contains no sign of God's better world. Paul believed the presence of the Law contains the promise of a world in which sin and death do not prevail. To Paul, the existence of the Law was "the highpoint of *so-called* history." But this Law, Barth explained, can only judge and point. It cannot save, since it cannot generate a human capacity to fulfill its demands. Salvation comes only from the better world the Law promises but cannot deliver. It comes through the world of God, where no complete repudiation ever took place. God's concern is always the entire world. God works through belief and unbelief to save the entire world.[46]

This was still a version of liberal theology, replacing historicist liberalisms with spiritual idealism. It emphasized experiences of value and treated the gospel message as a progress report, placing Moses, Plato, Kant, and Fichte in the same kingdom-bringing line as prophets of God's righteousness. On redemption, Barth was closer to Andreas Osiander than to Luther and Calvin. Osiander, a mid-sixteenth-century Lutheran theologian, opposed Luther's doctrine of imputed righteousness, contending that salvation triggers a substantial transference of Christ's righteousness to the believer. Barth's idea of salvation as the disclosure of a transforming "true world" of God, to the extent it had a Reformation basis, was a page from Osiander. His first-edition *Römerbrief* lumped religious socialism with liberal theology, Pietism, and conventional church religion as faulty vehicles of salvation, but he still spoke of the kingdom in Christian socialist terms as the hidden "motor" that drives "so-called history" through its own "real history." In essence, Barth's first edition registered his joyful discovery of the supernatural kingdom, which breaks into human life as a world-transforming divine Word to create a new age of the Spirit.[47]

The book got a smattering of mixed reviews, all of which commented on its spiritual passion and torrential flow of metaphor, and it found a small group of appreciative readers, whom Barth had to caution against enthusiasm. He conceived the book as an exercise in theological scholarship, not a source of religious enthusiasm. The first stirrings of the crisis theology movement took place in the postwar debates over Barth's perspective. Jülicher played a leading role, albeit as a liberal foil. It appalled him that Barth, a graduate of Marburg, lifted biblical inspiration over historical criticism. Jülicher admonished that denigrating "scientific exegesis" was not the way forward in theology. He lamented that for Barth and young Lutheran theologian Friedrich Gogarten, it was axiomatic "that there is no more progress in history, that development is forever at an end, and that no optimism in the interest of culture moves us anymore." Gogarten did not try to make sense of history, and Barth was only slightly less extreme. Jülicher noted that Barth dressed up his book with often-mistaken scholarly glosses on textual and exegetical problems, which showed, at least, his recognition that interpreting a difficult text from ancient times in a foreign language requires critical expertise. But critical knowledge was a source of conflict for Barth because he believed the true meaning of scripture is spiritual, not historical. Barth tried to pass through historical understanding to the spiritual world of the Bible.[48]

This was not a new idea, Jülicher observed. In the mid-second century Marcion developed the very theological position Barth now advanced as original to himself via Paul's letter to the Romans. The Marcionite Gnostics espoused the antihistorical spiritualism that Barth read into Paul, teaching that others attained merely a historical understanding, not a spiritual understanding. They proceeded with the same disdain for culture, tradition, and the real world that Barth purveyed "and never tired of tossing a few pet ideas in front of us." Jülicher allowed that Marcion was not a pure Gnostic and neither was Barth; so far, Gogarten was the Valentinus of the new Gnosticism, soaring completely out of history.[49]

Barth's first edition got similar reviews from Karl Ludwig Schmidt, who compared Barth to Marcion, and young Rudolf Bultmann, who dismissed the book as "enthusiastic revivalism" that interpreted history as myth. Barth took them in stride, at first. He told Thurneysen that Jülicher's critique felt more like a "gentle evening rain" than a "fearful thunderstorm." It intrigued him that scholars pinned a heretic's hat on him. Later he mused that Paul teetered on heresy too, and Paul was interesting and strange, unlike the boring books on him that scholars wrote. Barth vowed to avoid the spectacle of a youthful rebellion against an aging establishment: "In the presence of these scholars who know twenty-five times as much as we do we shall in the future lift our hats more respectfully, even though it seems to us quite idolatrous."[50]

Then he gave a sensational address at Tambach that showed where theology was going. The occasion was a social Christian conference entitled "Religion and Social Relations" in September 1919. Two German pastors affiliated with the USPD organized it, and most of the one hundred attendees were USPD clerics or professors, along with a quiet sprinkling of SPD supporters and Evangelical Congress veterans. To most of this crowd, as theologian Günther Dehn later recalled, the SPD was a reactionary sellout. Ragaz and Kutter were invited to speak as a token of respect for the older and stronger Swiss movement, but both declined. The organizers invited Barth to substitute for Ragaz, believing he belonged to the Ragaz camp.

Barth swiftly disabused them, dispensing with ingratiating prefatory repartee. He came to Tambach fully imbued with his discovery of Pauline theology. He brushed aside Ragaz, a purveyor of hyphenated Christianity. Barth chided the organizers for asking him to address how the teaching of Jesus should be applied to the postwar economic, racial, national, and international order. This was the wrong question, he said, always yielding a bad answer. What mattered was to ask what it means to be indwelt by Christ. The wrong question yielded hyphenated Christianities—social Christian, social evangelical, religious socialist, and the like. All produced "dangerous short circuits." To be sure, serving God entails serving humankind, but even the "purest love" does not necessarily make the opposite true. Admittedly, the seed is the word and the world is the field, as the gospel maxim went. But who had a sure grasp of the word? Who could live through the Great War and come out more confident than Moses or Isaiah that one planted divine seeds? Barth told the social Christians to stop asking wrong questions that begged for presumptuous answers: "The Divine is something whole, complete in itself, a kind of new and different something in contrast to the world. It does not permit of being applied, stuck on, and fitted in. It does not permit of being divided and distributed, for the very reason that it is more than religion. It does not passively permit itself to be used: it overthrows and builds up as it wills. It is complete or it is nothing."[51]

It was a perilous thing, Barth warned, to take "the shortest step with Christ into society." Social Democracy and pacifism were popular, now that liberal culture and nationalism were unpopular. Barth feared a revival of Ragaz idealism, declaring that if social Christians succeeded with their old theology, Christ would be betrayed once again. He mocked their enthusiasms, the kind of thing that Ragaz would have said: "Let us establish a new church with democratic manners and socialistic motives! Let us build community houses, push our young people's program, organize discussion groups, plan special services of music!" Next they would want lay sermons, Barth chided, adding that Naumann showed what came of secularizing Christ. First, Naumann secularized Christ for progressive reasons; then he dropped Christ for nationalistic liberalism. Barth implored that Christians had to learn to wait upon God "in a wholly new way," relearning from Jeremiah and Paul that God alone saves the world.[52]

He had no answer, except God, and he had no theological standpoint because speaking theologically was like trying to paint a bird in flight. Every position, Barth cautioned, is an instant in a movement. The movement that matters came from above, "the movement whose power and import are revealed in the resurrection of Jesus Christ from the dead." Barth took for granted that this group realized he was not a conservative. He took one swipe at this topic, observing that a faithful church courted danger. The German Revolution had come and ended, Social Democrats took power, Protestants were aghast, they feared Social Democrats and the godless Weimar Constitution, and nothing happened to the church. As Barth put it, the revolution did not touch the gate of religion. Religion still had the status in Germany of being intrinsically valuable to the social order. Barth knew very well that his audience of pastors and religious academics, no matter how radically socialist, had to be anxious about the future of Christianity under the new order. They belonged to denominations in which most ministers and congregants could not imagine how Protestantism would survive without the protection of princes. Barth suggested that Christians needed to disturb the one thing that worked for them in this situation—the assumption that the church earned its keep by undergirding the social order.[53]

He electrified the ministers and academics gathered at Tambach. Some were ready to drop social Christianity, and some had preached prowar sermons they regretted. Wilhelm Wibbeling, an attending pastor, later recalled, "The impact was colossal." Barth's message and commanding performance spoke powerfully to ministers grappling with the problem of the sermon in a time of crisis. Many said they had never heard anything like it, although Wilhelm Pauck later recalled that some "fled from the scene in despair." Pauck was a precocious gymnasium student in Berlin destined for the University of Berlin and an American academic career. Barth met Gogarten for the first time at Tambach, absorbing Gogarten's aggressive, cheeky, high-powered persona. He made other new friends who agreed with him that Harnack and Naumann led German Protestantism to bankruptcy. During the war Barth argued with Naumann about their diverging trajectories. After the war Barth said Naumann kept up with church affairs "with a certain mild superiority, as one who has looked behind the scenes and no longer lets himself be taken in." Naumann remembered his social gospel days with a sad smile. Barth's reaction was, "All these things will I give thee, if thou wilt fall down and worship me."[54]

Tambach made Barth a figure to be reckoned with in German theology. The doors of German universities and church groups opened to him. Politically he situated himself between German Social Democracy and Bolshevism, much like Blumhardt and, less comfortably, Ragaz. In December 1919 Barth told a Social Democratic gathering that good socialism was a "sentinel" (*Wächterpost*) between two sorry paths: "We should take neither the path of the German majoritarian social democracy nor the path of Russian Soviet-socialism. Both paths are bourgeois paths: foul peace agreements, practical methods which are too facile, a desire to reach the goal too quickly, to be right." If socialists took either option, Barth warned, "there is a tremendous danger that we might forget what we are in fact all about." By his lights he was doing the same thing in theology, taking the narrow path of the sentinel.[55]

In the early going Barth was delighted to have Gogarten as an ally. Prone to sharp replies, Gogarten gave many on behalf of himself and Barth, emphasizing the nonreligious worldliness of biblical piety and contending that time and history made no difference to faith. Gogarten said Jülicher's "superior mockery" backfired because the age of liberal theology was over: "It is the destiny of our generation to stand between the times." He chastised liberal theologians for replacing God's Word with biblical criticism: "Your concepts were strange to us, always strange. . . . You do not know how it tormented us that we could hear nothing more. . . . You left us empty. . . . We received much that was scholarly, much that was interesting, but nothing that would have been worthy of this word." According to Gogarten, the old liberals were responsible for Germany's war catastrophe and its empty churches: "We never belonged to your period." He observed that to his teachers he and Barth were somehow radical and reactionary at the same time. Though trained on a diet of Schleiermacher, Ritschl, Harnack, and Jülicher, they turned to Nietzsche and Kierkegaard: "Today we are witnessing the demise of your world. We can be calm about all that concerns this decline as if we were seeing the extinction of something with which we had no connection at all." In the crisis of European civilization, Gogarten urged, the only worthy response was to be open to God's creative activity and endure the divine judgment.[56]

"Here is a dreadnought on our side and against our opponents," Barth enthused to Thurneysen. "I have great expectations concerning him." Barth admired Gogarten's intellectual energy and his zeal for battle against the theological establishment. He took great satisfaction, for a while, in having such a tenacious ally, ignoring that both of them relied on arguments about faith, history, and Luther they got from Herrmann, a pillar of the discredited establishment. By 1920 Barth could see the idol tottering. At a student conference at Aarau he ridiculed the idea of an objective approach to theology, adding that biblical piety is against religion too. In Barth's telling, biblical piety held fast to a peculiar kind of worldliness that refuses to regard anything as sacred. Only

God is sacred, and in the scriptural witness God is holy, incomparable, and unattainable: "He is not a thing among other things, but the *Wholly Other*, the infinite aggregate of all merely relative others. He is not the form of religious history but is the Lord of our life, the eternal Lord of the world."[57]

One bewildered listener, Harnack, was appalled. He told a friend, "The effect of Barth's lecture was just staggering. Not one word, not one sentence could I have said or thought. I saw the sincerity of Barth's speech, but its theology frightened me." Harnack compared Barth's thinking to a meteor "rushing toward its disintegration." He allowed to Barth that perhaps the church needed to be shaken up "a bit" but urged him to keep his opinion to himself, not making an "export article" of it. In Barth's telling of their encounter, "Finally I was branded a Calvinist and intellectualist and let go with the prophecy that according to all the experiences of church history I will found a sect and receive inspirations." Elsewhere he recalled: "Things now began to snowball."[58]

To Harnack, Barth's approach to theology was apocalyptic and self-negating. If Barth was the future, modern theology was finished as a rational enterprise worthy of academic respect. The worst aspect of Barth's theology was its eschatological mania. Barth, however, decided the opposite. To really break from liberalism he had to heighten his eschatological alternative. He had written the *Romans* book in the fresh excitement of a conversion experience. Then he read uncomprehending reviews, plus Kierkegaard, Fyodor Dostoyevsky, and Swiss antitheologian Franz Overbeck, and completely rewrote the book.[59]

FIRE ALARM OF A COMING NEW WORLD

The exuberant mood of the first edition gave way to the angry, sharp-edged, and prophetic spirit of the book's immediately famous second edition of 1921. The first edition was long on repetition, exaggeration, hyperbole, dashes, exclamation points, and other expressionist techniques. The second edition was loaded with them. Both editions showed Barth's affection for Christoph Blumhardt and his father, who gave Barth what he needed above all else: compelling examples of living in the reality of the resurrected Jesus. Barth owed more to his friendship with the younger Blumhardt than he owed to Kierkegaard, Dostoyevsky, or Overbeck. On the other hand, Blumhardt was a Christian witness, not a theorist, and Barth was determined to accentuate his independence from Ragaz and Kutter. To overhaul his book he needed different concepts, which he got from Kierkegaard, Dostoyevsky, and Overbeck.[60]

The immediate problem was the governing schema. Barth's first edition *Romans* featured a sacred history (*Heilsgeschichte*) scheme in which the stream of God's "real history" made episodic appearances in the everyday history of Israel (especially the prophets) and in figures such as Socrates and Plato before it broke fully into the world in the fullness of time (the new age) in Jesus Christ. The second edition dropped the organic metaphors of the kingdom, overhauled the age-of-Adam/age-of-Christ scheme, and appropriated the attacks on Christendom by Overbeck and Kierkegaard. Overbeck was an atheist who taught New Testament and early church history from 1870 to 1897 at Basel and whose best friend was Friedrich Nietzsche. He taught that original Christianity was an intensely eschatological movement that expected an imminent apocalyptic intervention from above. All subsequent Christianity was a corrupted adjustment. Overbeck believed that German cultural Protestantism under Bismarck represented the final stage of Christian degeneration. With Overbeck and Kierkegaard, Barth said Christian churches were hopelessly corrupt. With Kierkegaard, Barth affirmed that Christianity is about the invasion of the eternal into time in the moment. With Dostoyevsky, he said the church replaced the freedom of Christ with mystery, authority, and miracle. With Christoph Blumhardt, Barth conceived Christianity as a kingdom faith that proclaims the transformation of the present from beyond.[61]

These witnesses helped Barth declare his break from liberal theology. He retained the Pauline dialectic of Adam and Christ but stopped describing the new creation under Christ as a new world that becomes a life process in human history. The new world cannot be born until the old world has died, he said. All human history stands under the sign of sin, death, and judgment, including Christian history. Liberal theology taught that history has an inner capacity for renewal because God is an aspect of the temporal order. Barth's reply was a version of Kierkegaard's Religiousness B and the sickness unto death: History is not a life process brought to fulfillment by a divine indwelling. History is the life of the old world existing under the judgment of death.

Barth realized that his negative dialecticism stood in danger of losing any basis for making positive affirmations. With Blumhardt in mind he declared, "There *must still* be a way from there to here." Theology is possible, Barth reasoned, only as inner waiting for and openness to God's revelation: "However much the holy may frighten us back from its unattainable elevation, no less are we impelled to venture our lives upon it immediately and completely." To be a faithful Christian is to live, like Blumhardt, in the fullness of what exists while waiting inwardly "for that which seeks to be through the power from on high."[62]

Blumhardt lived in the fullness of the present historical crisis. He had no use for compromised socialism, compromised Christianity, or compromised fusions of them. He did not lure workers away from Social Democracy or accommodate the gospel to modern sensibilities. He joined the SPD outright and refused to trim his socialism or his Christianity. Barth treasured him for these reasons: "No world war and no revolution could make him a liar." Although Blumhardt lost his pastorate and most of his followers, he was joyful in anticipating God's kingdom. Barth remarked: "The unique element, and I say it quite deliberately, the prophetic, in Blumhardt's message and mission consists in the way in which the hurrying and the waiting, the worldly and the divine, the present and the coming, again and again meet, were united, supplemented one another, sought and found one another."[63]

That was the ideal, something Barth had to have if he was going to dance so perilously with Overbeck and Kierkegaard. Blumhardt's radical socialism was sustained by his Christian hope, which he never reduced to his politics. He saw the idol in Christianity, socialism, and Christian socialism. Barth described all religions as monuments to the "no-God." The only basis for a nonidolatrous affirmation of God and the world, he contended, is "the possibility of a new order absolutely beyond human thought." Only a kingdom-oriented eschatological Christianity bears any true relation to Christ. But for the kingdom to become an actual possibility for theology "there must come a crisis that denies all human thought."[64]

Barth's second-edition *Romans* announced that the death rattle of Christendom presented such a possibility. The gospel message is "the fire alarm of a coming new world." He used nearly all of Kierkegaard's concepts to explicate Pauline theology: the divine incognito of the incarnation, the scandal of faith, the sickness unto death, the dialectic of revelatory unveiling, the leap, the paradoxical character of the gospel, and the "Moment," the transhistorical divine act through which God breaks into history from beyond. The only Kierkegaardian trope Barth left behind was his preoccupation with how one becomes a Christian, which was too self-absorbed for Barth's purpose. Like Kierkegaard, Barth insisted that faith is "always a leap into the darkness of the unknown." Faith cannot be communicated to oneself or to one from another; it must be revealed. Just as Kierkegaard said true Christianity is destroyed when it becomes a form of direct communication, losing its capacity to shock, Barth said in Jesus "the communication of God begins with a rebuff, with the exposure of a vast chasm, with the clear revelation of a great stumbling block." To have faith in Jesus is to call upon God in God's utter incomprehensibility. To live faithfully is not to seek rational stability or religious comfort, but to embrace "the absolute scandal of His death upon the cross."[65]

The second edition thrived upon paradox as the language of faith, abounding with metaphors of disruption and cleavage. To Barth, as for Kierkegaard,

God was an impossibility whose possibility cannot be avoided. "God is pure negation," Barth declared. "He is both 'here' and 'there.' He is the negation of the negation in which the other world contradicts this world and this world the other world. He is the death of our death and the non-existence of our non-existence." Barth likened the grace of God to an explosion that blasts everything away without leaving a trace. Divine grace is not a religious possibility standing alongside sin. It is a "shattering disturbance, an assault which brings everything into question." Then how does the new world of the Spirit make contact with the existing world of Adam? In a striking image Barth said it touches the old world "as a tangent touches a circle, that is, without touching it." Because the new creation does not touch the old world, "it touches it as its frontier—as the new world." Christianity is true only as eschatology.[66]

That eliminated the possibility of systematic theology, which was fine with Barth, until he became a theology professor: "If I have a system, it is limited to a recognition of what Kierkegaard called the 'infinite qualitative distinction' between time and eternity, and to my regarding this as possessing negative as well as positive significance: 'God is in heaven, and thou on earth.'" Within time, the receiver of grace experiences eternity in the absolute moment of revelation and anticipates the complete overcoming of time by eternity.[67]

Barth's existentialist phase put Kierkegaard on the map of modern theology, yielding a profusion of existential theologies that Barth did not like. Every major theologian who came out of the crisis theology circle or was influenced by it adopted Kierkegaard's theory of religious truth as existential encounter. Gogarten and Emil Brunner stuck with Kierkegaard's tropes long after Barth relinquished most of them. Rudolf Bultmann, Paul Tillich, and Jewish theologian Martin Buber were similarly indebted to Kierkegaard without being Barthians. Existentialism had a long run in theology on the strength of these figures. All regretted that Barth opted for dogmatic theology after he began teaching it, and some exaggerated his abandonment of dialectical method. In 1921 Barth began his academic career as Honorary Professor of Reformed Theology at Göttingen, a position for which he felt grossly unqualified. He had no doctorate, he had never read the Reformed confessions, and Calvin overwhelmed him. For years Barth struggled to fill the gaps, immersing himself in the history of Christian dogmatics, whereby he became a dogmatic theologian.

The later Barth turned to Luther and Calvin to get his bearings, but first he had to read them. The early Barth set theology in a new direction by stressing the infinite qualitative difference between God and humankind. In the Hegelian and Marxist traditions, dialectic is a critical process, the dynamic of history that makes history move. Barth, explicating Paul's theology via

Kierkegaard, affirmed the movement but also its dissolution. Crisis theology was an explosion of Kierkegaardian cleavages between God and world, existence and essence, and faith and reason. Against liberal theology, Barth asserted the priority of the Word of God for theology; but against Protestant orthodoxy, he rejected any identification of the divine Word with the biblical text. Barth took his doctrine of revelation from Herrmann, who got it from Hegel and Schleiermacher: Revelation is divine *self*-revealing, not the disclosure of propositional truths about God or anything else. Barth never acknowledged that the linchpin of his theology was a liberal idea. He did say that any human apprehension of revelation is limited by the incomprehensible otherness of God and the impossibility of extricating oneself from the revelatory act. Theology makes progress only as a dialectical process of question and answer, answer and question, in faithful anticipation of the Spirit's movement, through which an always-fallible discernment of the ineffable divine mystery takes place.[68]

As long as Barth believed that Gogarten, Brunner, Bultmann, and other crisis theologians shared Barth's Pauline rendering of faith, he held back on his disagreements with them. There is no way to faith, for faith is its own presupposition. Faith is a form of daring, a leap into the unknown, not a possession or the end of an argument. The early Barth put it in self-dramatizing, Kierkegaardian fashion, boasting about leaping into the dark. The later Barth dropped his wild Expressionist tropes and reliance on Kierkegaard, expounding traditional doctrines that he interpreted as analogies of faith; otherwise he could not have written twelve volumes of *Church Dogmatics*. But in both cases Barth pressed the Pauline theme that faith is a gift of the Holy Spirit, and he did it dialectically, stressing that God remains hidden even when disclosed in revelation. Faith is not a matter of grasping a revelation that cannot be held. Faith is a matter of being open to being held in God's ever-gracious hands.

At every step of the way Barth was keenly aware of who was with him and who was against him. His letters to Thurneysen, which circulated to their Swiss friends, were filled with competitive jockeying. In 1923 Barth founded a journal with Gogarten, Thurneysen, and Georg Merz to which Tillich and Brunner contributed. Gogarten wanted to call it *The Word*, which was "unbearably pretentious" to Barth, so it became *Zwischen den Zeiten* (Between the times), not lacking presumption. Bultmann surprised Barth by befriending him, defending him, and writing for the journal. Kutter had barely tolerated Barth's early crisis theology writings because they abounded with the battle of concepts that Kutter abhorred. Then Barth launched a journal, and Kutter renounced him for becoming a conceited theology professor. Barth said good riddance; he had no patience for a debate with Kutter about who served God or merely a concept of

God. Neither would he indulge Kutter's ploy to lump him with Ragaz. Barth soon tired of Gogarten's cocksure aggressiveness and Brunner's cocksure popularity, struggling for years not to say so, as they were allies and he wanted the journal to succeed. He taught a course on Schleiermacher that proved to be "shattering" to him, telling his students, "I was prepared for something bad," but Schleiermacher was much worse than he remembered, fatally corrupting modern theology. Barth noted that Ragaz won applause for what he said about socialism, militarism, and the League of Nations, all of which was fine on its own terms, and not for what he said about God, even though what he said about God was not bad. God got lost to Ragaz's audience in the political activism. This perception played a role in Barth's decision to stop assuring audiences that he had the same politics as Ragaz and Blumhardt, even though he did.[69]

Barth worried from the early days of the journal that Gogarten, Brunner, and Bultmann went overboard with existentialism, in Bultmann's case by relying on Martin Heidegger. Rade told Barth perceptively that Bultmann fell into Barth's camp only because his extreme historical skepticism left him nowhere to go. Bultmann pressed Barth for a debate about philosophy, which Barth put off, but Barth grudgingly debated Tillich, who was sufficiently different from him not to be threatening to him. Tillich, in the early going, was more generous to Barth than Barth was to Tillich. Playing the friendly outsider to Barth's camp, Tillich commended Barth's critique of Positivist dogmatism and liberal intellectualism, gently pressing two points of criticism: Barth ran roughshod over historical criticism, and he was not dialectical about his own standpoint. This was an invitation to Tillich's method of mutual appropriation, but Barth disliked how Tillich approached theology. They were opposite kinds of crisis theologians, united only by generational experience and Pauline radicalism about faith. Tillich drew deeply on philosophical and cultural analysis, while Barth immersed himself in doctrinal arguments about the Trinity, the Incarnation, and the Reformed confessions. Barth sharply accused Tillich of playing "hide-and-seek with the frosty monster 'the unconditioned.'" To Barth, Tillich's emerging perspective smacked of Schleiermacher and Hegel, rolling everything and nothing into a Hegel-like dialectic of strife and peace, far from the spirit of Luther and Calvin.[70]

More fatefully, Barth jousted with his Göttingen colleague Emanuel Hirsch, who blended modern Lutheranism, Kierkegaard, hot nationalism, and bitter tirades against Germany's enemies. The son of a Prussian Lutheran pastor, Hirsch studied under Harnack and church historian Karl Holl at Berlin, absorbing Holl's case for a politically relevant Luther and the importance of justification by faith. Hirsch was Holl's prize protégé. He completed his first theological degree under Holl in 1911 and his dissertation on Fichte in 1914, just as Holl developed his signature thesis on Lutheranism as a religion of conscience (*Gewissensreligion*). Holl's celebrated lecture in 1917 on Luther's understanding of religion, delivered on the four hundredth anniversary of the Reformation, sparked a "Luther Renaissance" at Berlin, Göttingen, and Erlangen that rolled on for the rest of the twentieth century. In 1914 Hirsch flunked the army's physical exam, very sadly for him, and began his teaching career at the University of Bonn. He learned Danish to read Kierkegaard, becoming Germany's leading expert on Kierkegaard, and moved to Göttingen in 1921, where he taught until 1945. Hirsch did his fighting at the typewriter, compensating for missing the war. He weighed barely one hundred pounds and could barely see anything, having been nicked in his one good eye by a barber's razor. He and Barth had brilliance and high intellectual ambition in common, two things they shared only with each other at Göttingen. They sparred over Lutheran versus Reformed and stab-in-the-back nationalism. Each had just written a blockbuster book that spoke dramatically to the postwar crisis.

Hirsch's book was a manifesto of what became the Political Theology movement, *Deutschlands Schicksal: Staat, Volk, und Menschkeit im Lichte einer ethischen Geschichtsansicht* (Germany's destiny: State, *Volk*, and humanity in the light of an ethical point of view, 1920). The book traded on the historic German mythology of a German-Aryan soul transcending class and partisan politics, employing the entire bundle of Volk terms specifying Germanness: *Volkstum* (German identity), *Volksgeist* (German feeling/thinking), *Volksseele* (German soul), and so on. As such, Political Theology was open to Catholics, Reformed, and other German-Aryans, but its Lutheran version had special advantages owing to Luther's status as a national hero, his two-kingdom doctrine, his polemics against Jews, and his concept of the orders of creation. Hirsch worked all these tropes, building to a dramatic conclusion. A great people had become a denigrated colony, he declared: "We were a world Volk, a noble Volk, perhaps the most flourishing and best of all. We now stand in danger of being humiliated or even destroyed as a Volk, so that only a formless mass of workers in the service of foreign interests remains." It would not have happened, he said, had Germany prevented its internal aliens from establishing political parties and holding forth in the Reichstag, poisoning German society with lies about the humanity and legitimate interests of Germany's external enemies.[71]

Deutschlands Schicksal ran through three editions in five years, making Hirsch a major player in German theology. He teamed with Erlangen theologian Paul Althaus to found Political Theology as a Lutheran enterprise, independently from legal theorist Carl Schmitt, putatively a Catholic, who opted for a secular version of fascist theology in the late 1920s. Hirsch and Althaus emphasized the Lutheran doctrine that God acts continually through the orders of creation. Marriage, the family, work, the economy, the people (*das Volk*), the state, the church, and society are orders of creation through which God moves the world toward the kingdom. The state, as conceived in Luther's doctrine of the two kingdoms, is the means by which God orders and preserves society. The state has divine work to do in rightly ordering society, the first need of all. It is divine precisely as the instrument of God's law in the world, commanding obedience. Speaking to the crisis of the 1920s, Hirsch and Althaus lifted *das Volk* above other orders of creation, insisting that will, not fate, rules history. To them, the Weimar Republic was an affront to Germany's spiritual character and a crisis for the church. In his second edition of *Deutschlands Schicksal* (1922), Hirsch explained why dialectical theology was not the answer to the crisis. Barth's attempt to separate Christianity from the concepts of religion and culture was a failure of nerve and conviction, abandoning a sinking ship. Tillich's religious socialism was the same thing flipped over, abandoning the real world for an ideological-religious fantasy. Gogarten was a variation on Barth, somehow expecting people to believe in an unknown God. Hirsch ascended in the church and academy by aggressively playing the Barth role in a very different movement.[72]

Barth got his fill of it listening to Hirsch. In the early going Barth wilted under Hirsch's domineering treatment, very uncharacteristically for Barth. He told Thurneysen that Hirsch filled the air with rants about war guilt lies, conveying a "sinister passion" for this subject. In May 1922 he said Hirsch had realized only recently "that I am 'seriously bad.'" Barth reproached himself for allowing Hirsch to bully him for months. The following month Barth recoiled when Hirsch publicly defended the August 1921 murder of Catholic politician Matthias Erzberger, a right-wing political assassination. Göttingen went badly for Barth, aside from providing his doorway to the German academy. Hirsch had a bumpy beginning at Göttingen too, but nothing like the frosty treatment Barth got. The faculty loathed Barth's politics and derided his honorary appointment to a marginal position funded by American Presbyterian churches. Althaus blasted him publicly in Hirsch's journal, treating Barth's theology as a bizarre offshoot of religious socialism fixed on a wholly unavailable God and a narrow Christocentrism abstracted from the real world. Barth accentuated his Christocentrism in response, deciding that a revelatory anything outside Christ is corrupting for Christianity. His own previous appeals to the voice of conscience began to embarrass him. He went to faculty meetings where colleagues sneered at his scholarly inadequacies, resented his growing fame, and looked down on his subject, Reformed dogmatics. Barth's bitter experience at Göttingen stuck with him for the rest of his life. In March 1924 he told Thurneysen, "All of them are now outspokenly unfriendly to me. But that is mutual." The following year he got out, accepting a chair in dogmatics and New Testament exegesis in the Protestant faculty of theology at Münster, where Barth taught for five years.[73]

That took him from a Lutheran stronghold to a Catholic stronghold, where Barth published the first volume of a projected dogmatics, *Christliche Dogmatik*, and decided his chief opponent was Roman Catholicism. Münster was slightly better than Göttingen as far as his collegiality was concerned, and Barth grew estranged during his Münster years from the entire *Zwischen den Zeiten* group, his anger rising. Increasingly he complained that Protestant theology was tedious and thin, lacking any real conviction in the Word of God. Protestant theologians lurched from one pitiful stopgap to another. At least Catholics took their dogmatic tradition seriously. On the other hand, Catholicism smothered Christianity in pagan tropes long before Luther came along, just as Luther famously argued in *The Babylonian Captivity of the Church*, and nationalistic gore made deep inroads in Catholic Germany. Barth railed against Protestant and Catholic paganism, taking a hard line against theological dependence on philosophy. The first volume of his projected dogmatics, *Christliche Dogmatik*, published in 1927, tried to throw off the existential and expressionist influences that lit up his books on Romans. If he believed his own argument about how theology should proceed, he had to listen, as much as possible, to the Word in its own voice, not read existential philosophy or his politics into it. Barth argued that philosophy got in the way of allowing the Word to express itself, and in really bad cases it became a substitute for the Word, negating what theology was supposed to be about. *Christliche Dogmatik* made a strenuous case for this position while retaining some existential elements. Then Barth decided that the existential retentions ruined the book, so he had to start over, rewriting it under a new series title, *Die Kirchliche Dogmatik* (Church dogmatics).[74]

Barth welcomed the controversy that his dogmatic turn and his stricture against philosophy stirred in Protestant theology. The opposition from his group, however, was another matter. Merz urged Barth not to publish *Christliche Dogmatik*, lamenting that Barth's teaching labors were turning him into an orthodox scholastic. Gogarten, Brunner, and Bultmann variously dissented from Barth's *sola Scriptura* straightjacket. Gogarten organized his theology of reconciliation around the I-and-Thou motif, Brunner developed a modest theology of natural revelation, and Bultmann pressed Barth to defend his impossible antiphilosophy position. Every theology, Bultmann argued, is guided by implicit or explicit philosophical assumptions about the knower and the known. The choice is between using philosophy intelligently or badly. Bultmann pressed for a public debate of the issue, Barth put him off, Bultmann persisted, and Barth gave some ground. If Barth had to defend himself, his point was that theology should not depend on a *single* philosophical perspective. He used philosophical concepts in an eclectic fashion whenever they helped him explicate his meaning. Barth contended that theology needed to be free to do its own work, which was not possible if it was chained to a philosophical system or ideology. He held off, for a long as he could stand, from saying that his friends accommodated the gospel to alien philosophies. Then in 1930 he began to say it angrily.[75]

He could not read *Zwischen den Zeiten* without getting angry, which isolated him, even as he soared to the top of the field as the leading exponent of dialectical theology. Barth admonished Bultmann that the entire group of dialectical theologians undertook "a large-scale return to the fleshpots of Egypt." Even so-called Barthians were committing the liberal mistake of understanding faith as a human possibility and thus surrendering theology to philosophy. The *Zwischen den Zeiten* theologians were no better than the old liberals, Barth protested. In fact, the old religious socialism was better than Bultmann's Heideggerian phenomenology, Brunner's natural revelation, Gogarten's theo-philosophy about states of life, and Tillich's existential/ontological refashioning of religious socialism. To Barth, the faith itself was at stake in the battle of theologies, whether or not the Nazis won power.[76]

The Weimar Republic went through fifteen governments and three distinct phases during its brief history. The founding phase ran from February 1919 to Hitler's failed Beer Hall putsch in Munich in November 1923. The second phase, comparatively stable, ran from 1924 to the global economic collapse of 1929. The third phase was the sorry end that came after Hermann Müller's Great Coalition folded in March 1930. Securing a regular appointment at Münster qualified Barth for dual citizenship. He voted for the Social Democrats in 1928 and was relieved when they beat the nationalistic second-place German National People's Party by 29.8 percent to 14.2 percent, forming a coalition government with the third-place Centre Party, fifth-place German People's Party, and sixth-place German Democratic Party. It looked like the Republic would survive.

Instead the economy fell into a recession, which worsened after the American stock market crashed in October 1929. Barth taught an ethics class at Münster in which he defended democracy, supported the right of women to vote, opposed imperialism, and opposed racial and class discrimination, all against the grain of a seething German academy replete with Nazi students. Universities showed their contempt for the Weimar Republic by conducting formal celebrations of the founding of the Reich on January 19, 1871. Every university had a variety of nationalists on the faculty, plus rows of middle-class, male, right-wing students raised on stab-in-the-back mythology. Numerous right-nationalist groups spewed the *Völkish* ideology glorifying the German spirit and people. The Nazis stood out only by featuring a cult demigod and a huge youth brigade operating outside the Reichstag. According to the *Völkish* worldview, true Germans were incorporated into a corporate will, the German Volk, and called to selfless devotion to the Fatherland. In the theological versions propounded by Hirsch and Althaus, corporate racial identity was a sacred order of creation to be cherished, protected, and served obediently.[77]

Althaus came to respectable Lutheran conservatism by family and academic tradition, following in the footsteps of his father, a Lutheran pastor and theologian at Göttingen. Educated at Erlangen and Tübingen, Althaus taught briefly at Göttingen before the war, served as an orderly and pastor in Poland during the war, and resumed his academic career at Rostock in 1919. He was pious, sincere, scholarly, a bit stodgy, and a winsome teacher, long on religious feeling, which he conveyed with no hint of irony. He was determinedly orthodox in a conventional conservative fashion, opposing liberal theology and orthodox rigidity. From the beginning of his career, he taught that Lutheran orthodoxy blended readily with *Völkish* spirituality and stab-in-the-back nationalism. Althaus told his church audiences the German church needed to rebuke the crimes of Germany's enemies at Versailles and the crimes of the Germans who signed the Versailles treaty. In 1921 he blasted religious socialism, contending it violated Luther's doctrine of the two kingdoms. Althaus said Luther regarded the state as an ultimate entity in history. Under God's rule, the state operated by the law and the sword, and the church by the gospel and the Spirit. Religious socialists violated God's dual ordering of the world by espousing religious politics and internationalist fantasies such as the League of Nations and a Christian league of nations. Only Luther's steely doctrine of two kingdoms united under the sovereignty of God made sense of the unwieldy problem of religion and society.[78]

Althaus and Hirsch facilitated Luther's rightwing cooptation in Germany, in Althaus's case without Hirsch's biting sarcasm or modernizing willingness to depart from Lutheran orthodoxy. In 1925 Althaus was called to the chair of systematic theology at Erlangen, already recognized as a leading authority on Luther via the Luther Renaissance. Holl died in 1926 and Althaus succeeded him as president of the Luther Society, a post he served until 1964. Althaus accepted the Nazi myth that Nazism was a spiritual and moral movement transcending politics, not merely a party. He prized and defended the Nazi movement on these terms, without joining the party, lauding National Socialism as a bulwark of moral, spiritual, and national renewal. In 1927 he declared to the Königsburg *Kirchentag* that the mission of the German church was to serve "the *Volk as Volk*," a "truly German proclamation of the gospel" that immersed the church "into the organic forms of life and living customs of *Volkstum*." Althaus said the time had come to "sanctify" *Völkish* ideology for the sake of the kingdom of God. The following year there was a book version: *Kirche und Volkstum: Der völkische Wille im Lichte des Evangeliums* (Church and nationality: The national will in the light of the gospel, 1928).[79]

Althaus was averse to conflict and being challenged, believing his immense goodwill and scholarship should shield him from unpleasantness. He got precious little resistance from the academy, which was swamped by right-wing students, academics fanning the flames, and churches desperate not to be left behind by its youth. Liberals who dissented from the upsurge of nationalism were hooted down and threatened. Rade observed dolefully in December 1930 that approximately 90 percent of the Protestant theologians at North German universities "appear at lectures with the National Socialist Party badge." Erlangen was the epicenter of theological fascism, where Althaus drew huge crowds to his lectures. Outright anti-Semitism, though tolerated in the churches and universities, had usually been downplayed as a fever swamp crudity. Even the Nazis employed it only selectively in the 1920s, in areas where it played especially well. Church leaders echoed right-wing politicians in churchly diction, condemning the enemies of the German Volk—the Bolsheviks above all, followed closely by all secularists, materialists, internationalists, and pacifists, and all socialists who were any of the above.[80]

The enemy was everything that diminished or impeded German nationalism. The great struggle was between the true Germans and their many enemies, a sloppy list that begged for a special enemy. Anti-Semitism had an ample German heritage in Stöcker's organizations and the writings of Göttingen scholar Paul Lagarde, the founder of the history of religions school. A powerful, original, and prolific scholar and active in the Prussian Conservative Party, Lagarde played a major role in legitimizing anti-Jewish racism in the German academy. He supplemented his scholarly tomes with vile screeds describing Jews as vermin needing to be exterminated as soon as possible. His *Schriften für das deutsche Volk* (1878) was a classic of anti-Semitic bigotry that the Nazis canonized. Althaus was decorous by comparison, which made him all the more effective when he broke the taboo on anti-Semitism in polite society Lutheranism. Germany had 525,000 Jews in a nation of 65 million. Althaus declared that the church was compelled to "have an eye and word for the Jewish threat to our *Volkstum*."[81]

From there it was a short step to full-blown German Christianity. Jews stood in the way of Germany's racial destiny, Jesus was Aryan, and true Christianity had to be rescued from the superstitions of Hebrew scripture and Paul. Althaus never quite joined the German Christian movement for the same reason he never quite joined the Nazi Party. He was loyal to orthodox Lutheranism as he understood it and wary of the Nazi/German Christian proclivity to jettison conventional orthodoxy. But he provided influential service to the Nazi and German Christian movements and supported Hirsch's formal involvement in both. Harnack fueled the German Christian fire in 1921 by venturing his long-held conviction that the Christian Bible should consist only of the New Testament. Otherwise he played a mostly constructive role in the early Weimar period, reluctantly accepting the new Constitution and counseling friends to relinquish their nostalgia for the monarchy and the Reich. Harnack's idea of seizing the moment, however, was to expunge the Bible of the so-called Old Testament because Hebrew religion was supposedly inferior to Christianity. In his telling, the Reformers recovered the gospel faith only halfway because they failed to solve the Bible problem. The real Christian Bible was the New Testament and nothing else. Harnack told Holl he taught his children to regard the Old Testament as the "law and history of the Jews." Althaus and Hirsch, stumping for German Christianity—which they called "Positive" Christianity— enlisted Harnack's immense cultural authority on behalf of a purified Aryan religion stripped of Jewish everything.[82]

Althaus and Hirsch won adoring crowds for promoting German Christianity. By the academic year 1929–1930 Nazi students constituted an absolute majority at Erlangen and Greifswald. The Nazis had by far the youngest average age of all political parties, twenty-five, while less than 8 percent of Social Democrats were under twenty-five. In 1933 Althaus heralded the Nazi takeover: "Our Protestant churches have greeted the German change of 1933 as a gift and as God's miracle." He and theologian Werner Elert drafted the Aryan paragraph for the German Evangelical Church, which prohibited non-Aryans and those married to non-Aryans from employment in the church. Althaus boasted that German Christians were purifying Christianity by recovering the German soul and the ancient Germanic religion: "There is a mutual penetration of Christianity and the German soul. What we call German has actually come into being through the effectiveness of Christianity." He kept it up through 1937, lauding the Nazis heartily, and never recanted doing so. In 1937 Althaus was still mythologizing the Volk in full-Nazi mode, describing it as a holy and absolute obligation that added immeasurably to the Bible and Lutheran Confessions, which unfortunately lacked consciousness of Volk: "Whatever I am and have, God has given me out of the wellspring of my Volk: the inheritance of blood, the corporeality, the soul, the Spirit. . . . Our life in our Volk is not our eternal life; but we have no eternal life if we do not live for our Volk." After the war began he went quiet about politics and grew his reputation as a Luther scholar. The American military government sidelined Althaus briefly in 1947, but he was teaching again at Erlangen in 1948 and taught there until 1966, also serving from 1932 to 1964 as university preacher, lauded for his Luther scholarship, meaty sermons, Bavarian loyalty, and being such a nice man. American scholar Robert Ericksen stressed that Althaus was very nice, "the perfect gentleman," plus perfectly reasonable, albeit for a losing team: "He was a good man. He was a good German, a good professor, a good theologian, a good churchman."[83]

Barth resisted the tide of nationalist idolatry everywhere he taught. In 1930 he joined the Protestant faculty at Bonn, succeeding Otto Ritschl, Albrecht Ritschl's son, just as the Müller cabinet resigned. Bonn had a distinguished faculty and a growing student body including foreign students, women, and Roman Catholics. Barth caught the university at the height of its heyday, boosting its international reputation. He came with his love partner and secretary, Charlotte von Kirschbaum, and his wife, Nelly Barth, and three youngest children, uncomfortably for all. At Münster von Kirschbaum became indispensable to Barth's work and happiness, conducting theological research. She remained with him for the rest of her life. Catholic Münster was not a good place for Barth to deal with the marital spectacle he created there or with colleagues who spurned his theology, politics, and demeanor. His growing fame did not wear well, and he was glad to leave. At Bonn he clashed with two pro-Nazi colleagues, pastoral theologian Emil Pfennigsdorf and systematic theologian Wilhelm Schmidt-Japing, but otherwise felt supported by colleagues. Barth taught many Nazi students at Bonn, plus others in steel helmets, without incident. He also acquired his first batch of ardent Barthian protégés, notably Georg Eichholz, Helmut Gollwitzer, Heinz Kloppenburg, Walter Kreck, and Karl Gerhard Steck. Barth enthused that life was just beginning for him, at age forty-four.[84]

His happiness at Bonn was a factor in his slowness to fathom what was coming. Barth later said the same thing as Tillich about why he failed to take the Nazi threat seriously: Nazi ideology was too absurd to take seriously, and he respected Germans too much to believe they would fall for it. The Müller coalition gave way in March 1930 to Heinrich Brüning's Centre Party government. Chancellor Brüning threatened to invoke Article 48 of the Weimar Constitution, granting emergency power to the president (Paul von Hindenburg) to enact policy by decree. Brüning submitted a budget to parliament, which was rejected; he submitted an emergency budget, also rejected; then he dissolved the Reichstag, calling for a new election in September 1930. That was a colossal blunder, effectively ending the Republic. The Nazis had won only 12 seats in parliament in the 1928 election. In the run-up to the new election they clashed with Communists in the streets, sowing fear and gratitude, which helped them win 107 seats in 1930. In two years the Nazi vote skyrocketed from 810,127 (2.6 percent) to 6,379,672 (18.25 percent), placing second between the SPD and KPD. Brüning, having angled for a more compliant parliament, got a Nazi parliament that sabotaged the government with walkouts and street theater. Barth voted for the SPD in September 1930 and joined the party the following May. He explained to Lutheran pastor Hans Asmussen that he took a nearly ten-year moratorium from politics after he began his teaching career: "But early last year, in view of the fact that right-wing terror was gaining the upper hand, I thought it right to make it clear with whom I would like to be imprisoned and hanged."[85]

That put it dramatically but did not speak well for the moratorium. After Hitler gained total power in 1933, he vengefully attacked the SPD, which tried to avoid a bloodbath by self-liquidating. Officeholders resigned from the party and destroyed their party cards. Tillich, following party discipline, resigned from the party and tried to persuade Barth that resigning was the socialist thing to do. Barth replied that he and Tillich, as usual, saw things differently. Barth said he had four reasons for joining the SPD: It was the party of the working class, of democracy, of antimilitarism, and of judicious patriotism. He stressed that these were concrete reasons. He did not claim any intrinsic affinity to Marxism as such. Neither did he profess socialism as a religious worldview, the mistake of religious socialists like Tillich: "As an idea and worldview, I can bring to it neither fear nor love nor trust. Membership in the SPD means for me simply a practical political decision." Because the SPD cared about the working class and democracy, stood against militarism, and stood for decency on the national issue, Barth felt obligated to join it as an exercise of his God-given freedom to make political decisions.[86]

This freedom to make purely political decisions, and his obligation to employ it with integrity, were crucial to Barth. He was a socialist because the concrete goals of socialism had strong affinities to the kingdom of God, not because he embraced socialist ideology and therefore submitted to the discipline of the SPD. Barth had not known the SPD wanted its members to resign; then he rebuffed Tillich's counsel to follow party discipline. He did not think in terms of party discipline or ideology, so party directives did not apply to him. American theologian George Hunsinger aptly observes that for Barth the crucial relationship was between the gospel and socialism, not between theology and socialism. Put differently, it was "between the freedom and love of the living God and socialism." Barth disclaimed any interest in proving that theology and socialism were logically related, just as he opposed all attempts to prove the existence of God, the deity of Christ, or any other Christian doctrine. Theology is the explication of revelation—secondary reflection on God's concrete reality as proclaimed in the gospel. Socialism is relevant to theology only to the extent that its goals conform to God's goals for the world. As Hunsinger says, to Barth, theology was "the conceptual clarification, not the logical deduction, of those goals." Theology does not relate to socialism as theory to theory, but as theory to praxis.[87]

Many of Barth's students implored him to permit classroom discussion of the political crisis engulfing them. Barth disappointed them, assiduously invoking the disciplinary boundary between theology and politics. His political awakening did not change how he dealt with politics in the classroom. Although his courses on ethics, which Barth taught in 1930 and 1933, strayed occasionally into dangerous territory, his courses on doctrinal topics forbade all discussion of politics. Much of the relevant lore about Barth as a teacher comes from this period, when he repeatedly admonished students that his sole concern was to teach Christian theology. Meanwhile the German Christians launched their first house organ in October 1932, *Evangelium im Dritten Reich*, bestowing a halo on Hitler.[88]

Barth was a popular teacher, long on snarky humor that students enjoyed. Helmut Thielicke studied under Barth in 1932 before earning his doctorate at Erlangen under Althaus. Barth's fiery polemics against bad theology enthralled him. Thielicke could not get enough of Barth's powerful, cheeky classroom performances: "And woe betide the person upon whom he hurled his firebrands!" Althaus was a favorite target, especially in seminars. Barth told students that Althaus's theology resounded with the sound of his childhood family harmonium. He had a story about how Althaus became the kind of theologian he turned out to be. It was Christmas at the Althaus home, the Christmas tree was adorned with candles, a model train set rattled, the harmonium hummed solemnly, when suddenly little Paul Althaus cried out, "Mommy, I can feel my religious consciousness awakening!" This story got back to Althaus, who couldn't fathom why students found it uproariously funny. Barth shared with Hegel a fiercely humorous penchant for ridiculing theologians who talked about their feelings.[89]

He was more careful in public, on this topic and others, but Barth risked an occasional controversy. In 1930, in *Zwischen den Zeiten,* he criticized Protestant church leaders (Prussian superintendent Otto Dibelius epitomized the type) for stoking Germany's idolatrous appetite for flattery about the soul of the German people. The following year a right-wing smear campaign started up against Barth's friend Günther Dehn, a left-socialist theologian at Halle. Barth defended Dehn's right to his antimilitaristic views, protesting that the campaign against Dehn threatened the right to academic freedom. He wrote a petition that only four others were willing to sign: Karl Ludwig Schmidt, Martin Dibelius, Otto Piper, and Georg Wünsch. Gogarten and Bultmann refused to sign, a bitter omen for Barth. Hirsch replied that no university should employ anyone that did not share "the passionate will for freedom in our Volk, enslaved and violated by power-hungry and avaricious enemies." To Barth personally, Hirsch said that being Swiss disqualified him from the right to an opinion. Barth's being as a human being was not fused with the Volk and state, so his opinion was mere chatter at best. Barth heard a lot of that in the run-up to the Third Reich.[90]

The pleading from students got more intense as the nation hurtled toward fascism. Barth stuck to his insistence that political topics were "not a subject for theology." His opinions about such things were for private conversation. Thielicke later contributed mightily to stereotypes about Barth during this period, contending that Barth had no theological ethic because he was smitten with Trinitarian speculation and he had no anthropology. Thielicke puzzled with fellow Lutherans over Barth's insistence that the Word of God creates its own audience. Any attempt to find common ground with an audience showed that one did not believe the Word possesses a self-authenticating power of its own. Every attempt to ground theology in an ontology, anthropology, or anything else substituted a human word for the Word that God speaks in scripture and preaching. Thielicke reached for the word "magical" to describe this position: "At the basis of his position lay something like a magical understanding of the Word which robbed the Gospel of its concreteness and brought back the old heresy of Docetism in a new and extreme form. He thereby barred the way toward the development of a Christian ethics and left the human being with no theological guidance in life." Many others said similar things, most notably nearly everyone in Barth's own group, which fueled his anger about the situation in theology.[91]

Protestantism made itself pathetic by resting on pitiful substitutes for the Word, Catholicism was a sophisticated rationale for doing so, and German national idolatry offered a grotesque display of what came of doing so. Barth put it furiously in the opening pages of *Church Dogmatics*, published in August 1932. Thomas Aquinas taught that something in the being of human beings has its analogy in the being of God. Barth declared, "I regard the *analogia entis* as the invention of Antichrist, and think that because of it one cannot become Catholic." On the other hand, he said, there was no other serious reason not to become Catholic. Barth's respect for Catholic doctrine made him willing to bear the accusation that he had become a Catholic scholastic, although he insisted the charge was ridiculous. He enlisted Anselm to his side, contending that Anselm's ontological argument was not a foundation for a natural theology. Anselm presupposed that God is objectively given, then sought to understand what is given in faith. As for Protestantism, Barth wept over "the constantly increasing barbarism, tedium, and insignificance of modern Protestantism." Protestant theologians threw out the Trinity, the Virgin Birth, and mystery itself, "only to be punished with every possible worthless substitute." First they ran through "High Church, German Church, Christian Community, religious socialism, and similar miserable cliques and sects." Now they worshipped their German soul, discovering religious insight "in the intoxication of their Nordic blood and in their political *Führer.*"[92]

Reich president Hindenburg appointed a right-wing chancellor in June 1932, former Centre Party official Franz von Papen, who tried to co-opt the Nazis before and after they crushed all other parties in the July election. The Nazis won 13,745,680 votes (37 percent), beating the second-place SPD, which won 7,959,712 votes (21 percent), and the third-place KPD (14 percent). Hitler could have taken power in a coalition with the Centre Party and the right-wing National People's Party (DNVP), but he demanded to be chancellor, Hindenburg refused, and no party assembled a governing majority. Papen's minority government continued, lacking parliamentary support and relying on legislative decrees by Hindenburg. In September Hindenburg dissolved the parliament to preempt a no-confidence motion, yielding another inconclusive election in November in which the Nazis lost thirty-four seats and the KPD gained eleven seats. The following January Hindenburg briefly replaced Papen with Major General Kurt von Schleicher. Papen turned to Hitler, cutting a deal in which Hitler became chancellor of a Nazi/DNVP coalition government, Papen became vice chancellor in Hitler's cabinet, and Hindenburg approved. Hitler moved swiftly to attain absolute power. In February the Nazis burned the Reichstag and blamed the Communists. In the March election the Nazis fell short of winning a Reichstag majority, but an Enabling Act supported by the Centre Party and the Bavarian People's Party made Hitler dictator on March 23, 1933. The SPD was banned in June. By July the Nazis were Germany's only legal party.

The political parties floundered in confused disarray just before being outlawed. In April 1933 Hitler appointed naval chaplain Ludwig Müller to organize
the new German Evangelical Church. The following September Hitler signed a
concordat with the Catholic Church and imposed Müller on the new Evangelical
church as bishop. Hirsch worked hard for Müller as his assistant, but Müller was
grossly incompetent. In June Barth launched a pamphlet series titled *Theological
Existence Today!* He vowed to carry on his theological work "as if nothing had
happened," a statement inviting misinterpretation. Many took it to mean that
theology was above politics or Germans should roll over for Hitler or inward
resistance was the Christian answer—three leading misinterpretations that Barth
decried for the rest of his life. To him, it meant the gospel had not changed, so
the work of theology remained the same. To teach and preach the Word was to
deny that Hitler ruled the church. Theology stripped Nazism of its animating
passion and victorious presumption. It was a form of resistance not lacking a
political dimension, as Barth explained: "I regard the pursuit of theology as the
proper attitude to adopt: at any rate it is one befitting church-politics, and indirectly, even politics. And I expect that this communication, without 'particular
messages,' will be heard and interpreted by the students committed to my charge,
as well as may be, amidst the stirring happenings of our time."[93]

Barth desperately wanted to keep his job at Bonn, and he worked very hard
over the next two years to avoid being expelled from Germany. He also had an
exalted view of the importance of theology. As the explication of God's Word,
theology surpassed all intellectual endeavors and was more relevant than any
ideology. In that spirit Barth fought for the right of the church to be nonidola-
trously Christian. Hitler demanded support from the churches, which helped
the German Christians sweep over 70 percent of all seats in the presbyteries and
synods of the Evangelical church. Lutheran pastor Martin Niemöller, previously a National Conservative (DNVP) pro-Nazi who welcomed Hitler's ascen-
sion to power, balked at the Aryan Paragraph. Niemöller founded the Pastors'
Emergency League in September 1933 to support Protestant clergy of Jewish
descent. The group grew rapidly, expanding its original rationale to include
other forms of Nazi interference in church affairs. In October Barth told a
Reformation festival in Berlin the Reformation was a decision to recognize that
the rule of God is absolute. Alternatives to faith were always available, he said.
Morality, reason, humanity, and culture were perennial options; now *Volkstum*
and the state had supplanted them. To be true to the Reformation decision was
to resist every substitute for the faith of the Reformation. Barth's reference to
resistance got thunderous applause. Meanwhile German Christian rallies
demanded the expulsion of all anti-Nazi pastors and all members of Jewish

descent, churchwide implementation of the Aryan Paragraph, an Aryan Jesus, elimination of Hebrew scriptures from the Bible, and the abolition of all non-German elements in religious services.[94]

By the end of 1933 approximately one-third of the Protestant clergy in Germany supported the Pastors' Emergency League. The following May the dissident pastors convened an independent synod in Barmen, Wuppertal, to found a rival Evangelical Church of Germany, usually called the Confessing Church. It was not a new church, and it did not abolish the confessional status of its constitutive Lutheran, Reformed, and United churches. The Confessing movement defiantly took the same name as the pro-Nazi church, proclaiming that it was a visible sign of the unity of the true Evangelical Churches through the Word of God. Negatively, it existed to say that the pro-Nazi church bearing a noble name was heretical. Barth wrote the confessional statement of the Confessing Church, the Barmen Declaration. It rejected the subordination of the church to the state and the subordination of the Word and Spirit to the church, imploring, "Do not listen to the seducers who pervert our intentions, as if we wanted to break up the unity of the German Evangelical Church or to forsake the Confessions of the Fathers!" Barmen said nothing about the Nazi persecution of the Jews and nothing about Nazi ideology. It was purely a declaration of ecclesiastical independence and a claim of fidelity to the "one Lord of the one, holy, catholic, and apostolic Church."[95]

On that narrow ground Barmen staked a position that wrung concessions from Hitler, who replaced Muller with Westphalian superintendent William Zoellner, a smarter operative who negotiated with the Confessing Church. Gogarten moved from Jena to Göttingen in 1933 and was briefly infatuated with fascism, although he never joined the Nazi Party. Hirsch and Heidegger became Nazi apologists, as Barth expected, and Bultmann joined the Confessing Church, to Barth's surprise. Barth wounded Bultmann by acknowledging his surprise, conceding that he had misjudged Bultmann. Still, Barth puzzled that Bultmann's infatuation with Heidegger did not lead him to German Christianity, and he later chafed that Bultmann got through the Nazi period unscathed at Marburg. Brunner, egged on by friends, wrote a booklet expounding his idea of a point of contact between the divine giver and receiver of revelation. There had to be a point of contact; otherwise how did anyone recognize revelation? Barth's scorching reply, *Nein!*, began hilariously: "I am by nature a gentle being and entirely averse to all unnecessary disputes." Then he furiously denounced Brunner for opening the floodgate to natural theology. God needs no point of contact besides the point that God establishes. Barth said it was more important to repudiate Brunner than Hirsch because Brunner was closer to him and the Bible and thus "much more dangerous." He

blistered Brunner for abandoning Reformation theology, plus writing oily statements about his friendship with Barth. Many Confessing pastors choked on Barth's
harsh treatment of Brunner and Barth's extreme rendering of *sola Scriptura* purity.
Barth's clerical supporters, notably Niemöller, Hans Asmussen, Karl Immer, and
Heinrich Vogel, welcomed his theological leadership of the Confessing Church,
as did brilliant young theologian Dietrich Bonhoeffer, who fashioned a Lutheran
version of Barthian theology. But Bonhoeffer grieved that the Confessing Church
was an insular outfit that never outgrew its self-preoccupied origin, a failing that
played a role in Bonhoeffer's martyrdom.[96]

Some responsibility for the insularity fell on Barth, even as he begrudged
Confessing insularity. By 1935 Barth had worn out his welcome with Lutheran
bishop Hans Meiser and many other Confessing leaders. In July they excluded
Barth from the Third General Confessing Synod in Augsburg. Some had theo-
logical and/or political reasons for snubbing him, and some just didn't like him.
To Confessing pastor Hermann Hesse Barth raged against the Confessing
Church: "It still has no heart for the millions who suffer unjustly. It still has
nothing to say on the simplest questions of public honesty. When it speaks, it
speaks only about its own affairs." Barth thought he was done with the Confessing
Church, which turned out not to be true. He was done with it only in Germany.
After Hindenburg died in 1934, Hitler became president and compelled all state
officials to take the Hitler loyalty oath. Barth tried to take it, desperately endeav-
oring to keep his position. He would have taken the oath had he been allowed
to add, "so far as I can do so responsibly as an Evangelical Christian." His appeals
ran out in November 1935, and he was expelled the following month, replaced
at Bonn by a German Christian, Schmidt-Japing. Barth's departing words to his
students were, "Exegesis, exegesis, and again, exegesis! Then, certainly, take
care for systematics and dogmatics." To his regret, no other dialectical theologian of note believed that good theology rested entirely on exegesis. On his way
out of Germany, the Gestapo forbade him from making a public statement.[97]

Barth's censure of Nazi idolatry put him in danger in Nazi Germany, providing a brave witness to pastors who never managed to support the Weimar
Republic. For all his prophetic force at Bonn, however, Barth's legacy did not
compare to Tillich's for getting the big things right. Tillich had to leave Germany
as soon as Hitler took power because there was plenty of evidence to convict
him. Barth played it more carefully, covered by his political moratorium.
Though Barth was a religious socialist before Tillich had a clue about socialism
or the working class, Barth shucked it off just as Tillich converted to socialism,
in Barth's case buoyed by a private assurance that he was still more or less like
Blumhardt. Helmut Gollwitzer regretted that his teacher and friend dropped

political activism after World War I and admonished students against "squandering their energies" on Social Democracy or any kind of politics. Gollwitzer heard Barth implore students and friends to transform the church instead.⁹⁸

Those who interpreted Barth as claiming that theology had no political responsibilities had plenty of proof texts to cite from his years in Germany, especially at Bonn. His furious farewell from *Zwischen den Zeiten* in 1933 was a quotable classic on this theme. Barth blasted former friends who said his theological position had political underpinnings. Aiming at Tillich's band of religious socialists, he boasted dramatically of cutting down Ragaz: "I could damage the German religious socialists as badly as I did in 1919, as Ragaz bears witness." Barth took pride in eviscerating the old religious socialism, which was better, by his lights, than the new one. He denied he had any "theological and ecclesiastical affinity to Marxism, liberalism, etc." He ripped political allies and political enemies alike who talked about "my political background." This chatter, he insisted, was "unworthy of gentlemen."⁹⁹

That was extra snarky even for Barth. On his telling, the dialectical theologians betrayed the gospel with political and existential theologies that would not last, unlike him. But Barth stopped claiming after he left Germany that his theology had no political underpinnings and no affinity with socialism. In 1938 he said exactly the opposite in *Church and State*, a pamphlet widely distributed by SCM Press. The German annexation of Austria in March 1938 spurred Barth to develop a positive theology of the state, especially the church's responsibility to the state. He told friends that Blumhardt was still his model in this area, and in 1938 he told the *Christian Century* he never espoused an otherworldly theology, adding that he tended to alienate allies and lose them: "My lifework seems to be wanting in a certain accumulative power—even more, that a certain explosive, or in any case centrifugal, effect seems to inhere in it." He regretted losing so many friends, though he accumulated many new ones. He denied ever saying that theology was about eschatological waiting in an abstract church for an abstract God: "All that existed, *not* in *my* head, but only in the heads of many of my readers and *especially* in the heads of those who have written reviews and even whole books about me." Barth acknowledged some responsibility for being "surrounded by so much anger and confusion." As it was, he was not sure how to avoid sowing more of both.¹⁰⁰

Barth was the pioneer of an approach to politics that had impressive staying power among theologians. He floated above politics except when he did not, and he claimed not to be ideological when he made exceptions. In 1938 Barth declared that when Czech soldiers resisted Hitler's invasion, they fought for Christ and his church. The following year he defended Switzerland's military preparedness program, and two years later he implored British Christians to

remain steadfast in opposing Nazi Germany. Later he explained that World
War II was a supreme emergency for the world and German fascism endangered the soul of the church. Barth acquired a large school of followers who
said he destroyed political theologies of every stripe. On their view, which came
to be called neo-orthodoxy, Barth believed theology was too abstract and
divinely privileged to underwrite political radicalism or bear any political
responsibilities besides opposing Nazi fascism, a supreme emergency for the
church. A bit later many Barthians would have been happier with Barth had he
made another exception for anti-Communism or underwritten their own comfort with capitalism. Barth caustically opposed Christian anti-Communism and
was scathing about American capitalism.

Never a neo-orthodox Barthian, even in this area, Barth rankled at ostensible
followers who lacked his critical perspective on capitalism, militarism, bourgeois civilization, and political conservatism. He knew the finer points of socialist theory better than any major theologian of his time aside from Ragaz, Tillich,
and William Temple. Barth believed theology had radical political consequences precisely *as theology*. In his time the interpreters who grasped what
that meant were usually socialist theologians who mostly agreed with him, notably Gollwitzer, Paul Lehmann, and Frederick Herzog. Gollwitzer knew very
well that his friend was volatile, inconsistent, and complex, especially in this
area—"This man's spirit cannot be reduced to a simple or a single formula." He
also knew that Barth's anticapitalism and antimilitarism ran very deep. Shucking
off either was never an option for Barth. Gollwitzer explained that Barth came
from the generation for whom the language of democratic socialism became
"too shopworn, too discredited, too much fallen under the suspicion of ideology" to help him express his anticapitalism and political radicalism.[101]

Moreover, when Barth dropped religious socialism during World War I he
traded radical democratic socialism for Social Democracy, where pragmatism
reigned supreme in politics. This move reinforced Barth's predisposition to a
state-fixated conception of politics. He had no concept of politics that was not a
politics of government. Barth completely missed guild socialism and other
movements for economic democracy that developed alternatives to state fixation. Intellectually he was too German to take up any tradition of nonstatist
theory or practice. Socialism was a serious thing to him only as state socialism.
Moreover, the church was the only voluntary community that interested him,
notwithstanding that Barth's church existed mostly in his head. By relegating
his own socialism to an independent realm of pragmatic statist reform, Barth
walled himself off from the deepest insights of socialist theory. He did not apply
a socialist critique of the class struggle to the political issues he addressed. His

later political writings criticized Nazism, the Cold War, West German rearmament, American imperialism, and Christian complicity from a moral perspective, lacking a Marxian or even vaguely socialist account of structural economic
forces that drove the world to another world war and turned anti-Communism
into an obligatory Western religion.[102]

Today it is still true that the keenest interpreters of Barth's political theology
tend to be more-or-less Barthians who share his theological approach to left
politics. British theologian Timothy Gorringe says that Barth's opposition to
hegemony was a keynote of his theology *and* that Barth was "completely in earnest in denying that his theology is at the disposal of any political movement—
even the anti-Fascist movement." American theologian Kathryn Tanner says that
Barth rightly criticized the competitive logic of capitalism on theological
grounds, although he failed to do so on the Christological grounds that his theology ostensibly commended. Hunsinger says that Barth persistently accounted for
social justice politics in terms of Christian salvation, not the other way around:
"Salvation is conceptually prior to and independent of social action, and social
action is conceptually subsequent to and dependent on salvation."[103]

It is hard to say, however, what kind of politics should come from this kind
of theology. Hence the confusion never abated concerning Barth. He censured
Ragaz and Reinhold Niebuhr for plunging into social justice movements *and*
for marshaling Christian reasons for doing so. Barth's attacks on this theme
paved the way to two generations of Barthians who did not share Barth's politics
and who represented him as otherworldly or apolitical. To many, Barthian theology was a rationale for risking nothing for social justice and doing nothing
for it. Meanwhile it was not true that the theologians Barth attacked for
sticking with Christian socialism—Ragaz, Kutter, Brunner, Tillich, and, briefly,
Niebuhr—had a negligible legacy compared to his. Brunner influenced more
American Barthians than Barth and blasted Communism for the same democratic socialist reasons that motivated Ragaz. Niebuhr dominated American
Christian social ethics. Tillich provided the most sophisticated argument for
religious socialism of any twentieth-century theologian. Tillich said he was
prouder of *The Socialist Decision* than anything else he wrote. But his later
students and readers had trouble making sense of what that could mean.

TILLICH AND SOCIALIST THEOLOGY

Paul Tillich was a highly creative theorist of religious socialism long before
he won fame for his *Systematic Theology* and best-selling books on psychologized religion. He remained a religious socialist with a Marxist bent for the rest

of his life, although carefully not in a way that interfered with his spectacular later career. He became a socialist in 1918, put socialism at the center of his thought in the 1920s and 1930s, and pragmatically changed the subject afterward, girded with Marxist reasons for doing so. He had a keen sense of irony, which applied to his career. Thoroughly trained for an academic career in Germany, Tillich despaired when he had to take refuge in the United States, a place he dreaded but where he attained extraordinary fame by changing what he wrote about. Religious socialism was the key to everything that Tillich wrote in his pre-American career. Afterward it was still there for the discerning, but Tillich's contribution to political theology came early, as he knew. His profound debt to Friedrich Schelling carried into his American career more readily than his debt to Marx, although very few Americans understood what he owed to Schelling either.

He was born in 1886 in a parsonage in Starzeddel, a walled, feudal-like village in east-Elbian Prussia near Berlin, where Tillich's father, Johannes Tillich, was the first Lutheran pastor in a family of musicians and manufacturers. Johannes Tillich was a pillar of Prussian society. He exuded Prussian dignity and authority, prized Greek philosophy and things intellectual, rose to parish superintendent in Schönfliess when Tillich was five years old, and was gifted musically. A subsequent promotion in 1900 took the Tillich family to Berlin. In both places Tillich befriended children of the landed nobility, far above his family's modest economic status, and was tutored in Latin by his father. He later recalled that he was raised to regard the SPD as a criminal enterprise.

Though Tillich chafed at his father's drillmaster teaching, he later took pride in his command of Latin and Greek, often sprinkling his lectures with etymological points. He portrayed his father as strict and overbearing, notwithstanding that Johannes Tillich's letters to his son were kindly, sensitive, philosophically sophisticated, and sympathetic, plus parental and theologically orthodox. Tillich said very little about his rigidly Calvinist mother, Mathilde Tillich, except that he adored her and was crushed when she died of cancer at the age of forty-three. He said he lost her during his preadolescence, although he was seventeen when she died. Tillich exaggerated the time of his maternal loss and his father's severity for similar reasons. He was sensitive, deeply admired and loved his parents, and had to justify why he so desperately sought to overcome his father's influence over him. Tillich's closest friend, Richard Wegener, aptly judged—much like Barth—that the key to Tillich's theology was his consuming need to free himself from the Grand Inquisitor.[104]

As a teenager Tillich withdrew as often as possible into romantic reverie, preferring imaginary worlds. He pored over Kant and Fichte during his last year of

Gymnasium training before retracing his father's theological itinerary for a semester at Berlin, a semester at Tübingen, two years at Halle, and a year at Berlin. He
started at Berlin in 1904, plunging into Schelling's transcendental philosophy. At
Tübingen he tramped through hills and woods, giving himself to nature adora-
tion. Tillich was a nature mystic, enthralled by landscapes, cloud formations,
flowers, forests, and especially the sea, savoring experiences of the finite blurring
into the infinite. Schelling's nature romanticism caught Tillich before he noticed
Schelling's sense of the demonic. He also studied Schleiermacher's theology and
thrilled at the poets of German romanticism, Hölderlin, Novalis, and Rilke. To
Tillich, Goethe was too scientific to rank near Hölderlin. For the rest of his life
Tillich said he was a pagan as far as trees were concerned.

The great teacher for Tillich was Halle theologian Martin Kähler, then near
the end of his long battle against the nineteenth century. Young philosopher
Fritz Medicus, who specialized in German idealism, especially Fichte, also
influenced Tillich and remained a treasured friend. But Kähler got to him like
no other teacher. Kähler began his career as a Goethe enthusiast before converting to the Lutheran doctrine of justification. He taught that modern theology wrongly fixed on a pointless enterprise, the quest of the historical Jesus, and
that justification by grace through faith applies to doubters as well as sinners, a
godsend notion for Tillich. Historical criticism, Kähler said, yields no depend-
able knowledge of Jesus of Nazareth, so faith cannot be founded on so-called
historical facts. The New Testament gospels are testimonies of faith, not source
material for historical knowledge. The gospels present a picture of Jesus Christ
as a figure who made an impression of divinity on the apostles. What they experienced can be grasped only in faith.

These ideas linked Tillich to Barth and the crisis theologians in 1920. Another
Kähler principle was more important yet to Tillich: All serious doubt contains
faith in the truth as such. Tillich said he could not have become a theologian
lacking this teaching. Whoever doubts in good faith actually affirms God and is
justified. Kähler said God is not a being among other beings, as though God
were an object. To speak of God as the Supreme Being is stupid. Though Kähler
described himself as a lonely biblical theologian perched between liberal theology and orthodoxy, he sometimes referred to God as the unconditioned that
conditions everything else, borrowing a phrase from German idealism. Every
one of these ideas played a prominent role in Tillich's theology, and many readers thought he originated them. Tillich told his father that the theological titans
at Berlin were dwarfs compared to Kähler.[105]

Halle was also important to Tillich for his enrollment in the Wingolf fraternity. It was his father's fraternity and the first organization Tillich freely joined.

He loved everything about it, especially its muscular Christianity, nationalistic gore, and dramatic military uniforms. To Tillich, Wingolf was a refuge from the competitive individualism of the academy, a site of homey bonding. He was enthralled by the spirited talks that Kähler gave at Wingolf meetings and worked hard as a fraternity officer, supporting efforts to exclude liberal members. Tillich wanted the fraternity to take a stand against watered-down religion. In 1908 he befriended Hirsch at a Wingolf meeting in Berlin. They bonded deeply on the basis of mutual brilliance and intellectual similarity. Many said their thinking was identical, and their friendship strengthened after Hirsch fell in love with Tillich's sister Johanna, although she married another of Tillich's close friends, Alfred Fritz, wounding Hirsch. Tillich waxed nostalgic about Wingolf for the rest of his life, describing its midnight debates and bonds of friendship as the emotional high point of his life.

His course work completed in 1908, Tillich prepared for ordination exams while considering whether to become an academic. He earned his doctorate in philosophy in 1910 from the University of Breslau, where he never studied but submitted a dissertation on Schelling's philosophy of religion, and his licentiate in theology in 1912 from Halle, where he wrote a dissertation on Schelling's mysticism and guilt consciousness. Schelling expressed Tillich's sense of nature as the finite expression of the infinite ground of all things. The 1910 dissertation combined Schelling's metaphysic of potencies with a Schelling-like survey of the history of religion. The 1912 dissertation mapped out the differences between grounding religion in mystical experience of God and the experience of guilt.

Schelling scholars have long debated how many phases Schelling went through. In Tillich's view there were only two: The early Schelling was a philosopher of nature and identity, and the later Schelling from 1809 onward was a positive philosopher of existence, freedom, myth, and the demonic. Tillich reasoned that his expertise in Schelling qualified him to teach philosophy; at the same time, Schelling's metaphysical idealism provided ballast for Tillich's theological imagination and vocation. After the war Tillich did not feel compelled to put down his teachers in the manner of Barth or Gogarten. He prized his training in German idealism and theology, reasoning that every generation has to find its own path. Shortly before Germany went to war Tillich applied to Halle for a faculty position and served as a pastor in the Evangelical Church of the Prussian Union. He married his first love, Margarethe Wever, who had two children with Wegener after Tillich went off to war as an army chaplain. Tillich characteristically never held it against either of them. He had befriended Wegener in 1909 and looked up to him, as Wegener was gregarious, intellectual, and three years older than Tillich. When the war began Tillich was a shy intellectual, a monarchist, a churchy Lutheran, and a typical German patriot, steeped in the authoritarian ethos of Wilhelmine Prussia. He knew almost nothing about the working class, women, or himself. He preached nationalistic war theology throughout the war, later recalling that he was thirty years old before he lost "my enthusiasm for uniforms, parades, maneuvers, history of battles and ideas of strategy."[106]

The war burned a hole in Tillich's psyche that showed for the rest of his life. For four years he endured bayonet charges, battle fatigue, nervous waiting, the disfigurement and death of friends, and mass burials at the western front with the Seventh Division. He also endured two nervous breakdowns. For two years Tillich teamed with a Catholic chaplain at the front lines, conducting worship services under trees, in caves, and in trenches, all under fire. His first exposure to heavy fire occurred at the end of October 1915 at the battle of Tahure in north-eastern France. The invading Germans sustained heavy losses. Tillich preached about patriotic self-sacrifice, courage, loyalty, eternal life, and divine sovereignty. He surprised himself by winning the trust of working-class soldiers. He devoured art books at the front and toured art museums on leaves, craving beauty. The battle of Champagne in 1915 seared him permanently. Tillich ministered all night to the wounded and dying as they were brought in, "many of them my close friends. All that horrible, long night I walked along the rows of dying men, and much of my German classical philosophy broke down that night."[107]

It seemed to him that the world was ending. The battle of Verdun in May 1916 was the worst of the war, with slaughter on both sides totaling seven hundred thousand deaths. Tillich wrote to his father that unimaginable hell raged all around him. Verdun caused his first nervous breakdown. A friend sent a picture of herself sitting on a lawn, clothed in a white dress. Tillich said it was inconceivable to him that something like that still existed. He had a break-through in the French forest, reading Nietzsche's *Thus Spoke Zarathustra*. Nietzsche's ecstatic affirmation of life and his searing assault on Christian morality were intoxicating to the traumatized chaplain. Inspired by Nietzsche, Tillich allowed himself to imagine a life after the hell and death of war. Afterward he partied and caroused on leaves like a typical soldier, enduring the "turnip winter" of 1917, when Germans survived on turnips. In April 1918 he had a second breakdown after a bloodbath and asked to be relieved from service. The army turned him down, and Tillich rallied again near the end, grateful not to have missed it. In August 1918 he was assigned to the Spandau military base in Berlin, where he witnessed the German Revolution. Tillich was still a militaristic nationalist when he arrived at Spandau, but he sympathized with the rebelling workers, believing that Germany needed a social revolution. He studied political theory, careening rapidly to USPD socialism, not pausing at liberalism or the SPD. For the rest of his life Tillich said Germany needed a social revolution after the war, but its aborted revolution was killed off "by interferences of the victors." He discarded his churchy sexual code, later recalling that he entered the forest a dreaming innocent and emerged from it a wild man.[108]

The only kind of theology that deserved to be written had to address the abyss in human existence. The later Schelling glimpsed the abyss; Tillich felt engulfed by it. He told Hirsch in 1918 that the "gloomy power" of the later Schelling spoke to him far more powerfully than the early Schelling's nature romanticism. Later Tillich recalled, "The experience of the four years of war tore this chasm open for me and for my entire generation to such an extent, that it was impossible ever to cover it up." Elsewhere he said the war caused a "personal *kairos*" for him. Tillich threw himself into Berlin's sprawling café society of musicians, actors, painters, writers, and intellectuals. Halle shut down the theological seminary that Tillich expected to head, so he transferred his record of qualification to the University of Berlin, hung out with bohemians, and stopped going to church. Released from army service on January 1, 1919, Tillich taught his first class that month as a *Privatdozent* at Berlin, still dressed in his army grays and Iron Cross. He assigned Troeltsch's *Social Teaching of the Christian Churches* in a course called "Christianity and the Social Problems of the Present," declaring that Troeltsch's work ranked with Harnack's *History of Dogma* as a theological classic.[109]

For the rest of his career Tillich drew upon Troeltsch's categories and historical analyses. He taught at Berlin for five years, ranging over theology, philosophy, philosophy of religion, politics, art, depth psychology, and sociology. He read voraciously, keenly interested in intellectual and cultural trends, compiling the knowledge base on which he drew for decades, as Tillich pretty much stopped reading in the late 1930s. His first published speech, "On the Idea of a Theology of Culture," expounded what became his signature thesis: Religion is the substance of culture, and culture is the form of religion.

Fast upon changing his politics Tillich identified with the USPD. He befriended party members, voted for USPD candidates, and spoke at a USPD gathering in May 1919 on Christianity and socialism. But he never formally joined the party or spoke at another party meeting. Political activism was never the point for Tillich, and he got in trouble with the church for speaking to the USPD. He tried to avoid trouble by working a typical dialectic. On the one hand, Tillich opposed all attempts to identify Christianity with a favored ideology or social order. On the other hand, Christians were compelled to support struggles for justice and liberty. The Protestant Consistory of Brandenburg reprimanded Tillich for speaking at a radical socialist gathering, so he sent the text to the consistory superintendent, who replied that Tillich had no business mixing politics with religion or consorting with radical socialists. He added that Tillich wrote in a vague manner that seemed sneaky. The war had not changed the church's identification with the feudal–capitalist order, its idea of how respectable clergy should behave, or the superintendent's revulsion at radical socialism.

Tillich pulled back, stressing that he did not belong to the USPD and had no intention of joining. He did not like its emphasis on agitation, and religious socialism was what mattered to him, not party politics. Tillich and Wegener coauthored a pamphlet calling religious socialists to come together, prefiguring a union of Christianity and socialism. "We stand in a period of dissolution," they declared. A wholly new social order was needed. Religious socialism was not something piecemeal, such as a strategy to lure workers to the church or church members to a party. The point of religious socialism was to imagine and inspire a new social order, born of a fusion of Christianity and socialism that broke the power of nationalism and capitalism and recovered a premodern sense of the sacred.[110]

Finding like-minded intellectuals for this project was crucial to Tillich. He found them in a tiny group that morphed out of a social worker association in Berlin in 1919. Karl Mennicke, a minister and social worker in an East Berlin settlement house, Soziale Arbeitsgemeinschaft, was the catalyst. Mennicke, Tillich, and Günther Dehn launched a religious socialist discussion group, although Dehn drifted away in 1923, as the discussions were too theoretical for him. The group's core figures confirmed Tillich's feeling that Bolshevik Communism was a dead end, the SPD was rigid and excessively calculating, and socialism needed new answers. Eduard Heimann was the key figure for Tillich. An economist from Berlin whose father was a prominent publisher and SPD official, Heimann belonged to the Bernstein wing of the SPD, sharing Bernstein's ambiguous relationship to Marxism. He opposed ethical socialists who dropped Marxian dialecticism but embraced Bernstein's view that catastrophe thinking was central to Marx and gravely problematic for socialist theory. Heimann ran the Socialization Commission of the provisional government, introduced Tillich to SPD bigwigs, and taught at Hamburg from 1925 to 1933. Tillich formed a similarly close and enduring friendship with economist Adolf Löwe, who schooled Tillich on economic theory. Heimann and Löwe played down their Jewish heritages, as Heimann identified more with progressive Christianity and Löwe was religiously non-Orthodox, but Tillich took pride that his closest comrades were Jews. Alexander Rüstow and Arnold Wolfers, both Protestants, also played leading roles in the group. Rüstow, an atheist free-thinker, economist, and historian from a military background, had a dogmatic style that offended everyone in the group. Even the legendarily peaceable Tillich clashed with him. Wolfers, a Swiss lawyer, directed the Deutsche Hochschule für Politik (German academy of politics) and later taught at Yale University. Heimann said Tillich was the head of the group and Mennicke was its heart. In later life Heimann was sometimes more doleful about the group, reacting to Tillich's exaggerations about it. Heimann described the group as "naive, optimistic, esoteric, eccentric academicians." Tillich, dissenting about naïve, esoteric, and eccentric, said all were "explicitly concerned with theory" but not lacking political smarts.[111]

The Berlin group had no real name until Tillich provided one, "the *Kairos* Circle," placing his stamp upon it. In later life Tillich conveyed to American audiences that the *Kairos* Circle had been a major player in German society. In fact it never exceeded a dozen members, although it published a sophisticated journal, *Blätter für religiösen Sozialismus* (Leaves for religious socialism), in which Tillich developed most of his signature ideas. The group met every two weeks until 1924, after which Tillich remained close to Heimann, Löwe, and Mennicke. They were intellectuals and thus not easily dominated by anyone's thinking. Most considered themselves to be realists who began with given polit-ical realities and spurned utopian fantasies. All believed the German socialist parties were stuck in dogmatic ideologies and bygone battles, plus compro-mised by parliamentary maneuvering. Some members operated on the edges of the SPD or the USPD, but most felt that customary socialist irreligion impover-ished both parties. Relatedly, the religious socialists believed that both socialist parties overidentified socialism with economic policies and politics. Uniting the existing churches and socialist parties was not the point because all were deeply flawed. Something new had to break through. Tillich made a Kähler move to express what it was, renewing a biblical term with rich connotations and no recent history: *kairos*.

Kairos, in Greek, is literally the "right time," distinguished from formal time, *chronos*. Tillich loved the Greek recognition that time as the richly significant moment—kairos—needed its own word, distinct from time as temporal succes-sion. This recognition enabled the Greek language to express the dynamism of Hebrew religion and early Christianity, as in the gospel idea that the kairos of the *Logos* Incarnate did not come until the moment of the fullness of time (kai-ros). The kairos, in Tillich's appropriation, was the moment in time when the eternal breaks into the ambiguous relativity of existence and creates something new. Schelling (and Hegel) taught that every living thing contains in its deep essence the conflict between a present and a becoming form. The conflict between our intuition of a becoming form and the existing form moves life forward, although never without dangers and risks. The kairos, Tillich reasoned, has an ultimate sense and a special sense, plus a twofold sense as the right time of a becoming form and a break against treating any envisaged possibility as an absolute. In its ultimate sense the kairos is the center of history, the interpretive key to the whole of history and its parts. In its special sense it is a decisive force in a given situation, the coming of a new "theonomy" that fuses the sacred with critical rationality. Some things are possible only in particular times; all great turning points in history reflect the one eternal kairos that confers meaning on the whole of history; and all possibilities contain idolatrous dangers.

Thus the doctrine of the kairos was tightly linked with Tillich's ideas of the religious nature of culture, the demonic, the "Protestant principle," the Unconditioned, and the dialectic of heteronomy and autonomy, all of which he developed in his early writings and first major work, *Das System der Wissenschaften* (1923). Religion is the substance of culture in the sense of signifying the incarnation of faith in a given culture. The sacred is the life *in* the profane, for nothing can live outside the sacred power of its origin. But everything in life is subject to idolatrous corruption—the demonic attribution of absoluteness to something finite, relative, and corruptible. The glory of Protestantism is the Protestant Principle that legitimizes rigorous criticism of everything and thereby serves as a brake against idolatry. The Unconditioned is the meaning that is the foundation of all meaning-fulfillment. It cannot be proved and does not "exist," for it would no longer be the Unconditioned if it were something established in the temporal order. It can only be pointed to. Tillich never wrote a systematic essay on the Unconditioned, but he sprinkled his early writings with it, especially *Das System der Wissenschaften*, and wrote systematic essays on his other signature concepts. He argued that bold new directions were suddenly possible in Germany, plus new forms of idolatry. The old order was gone and discredited, and bourgeois culture went down with it. The socialist and Communist movements were products of the same spiritually bankrupt culture that these movements opposed. Europe needed a liberating religious socialism that synthesized and transcended the heteronomous consciousness of the authoritarian theocratic past and the autonomous consciousness of individualistic bourgeois modernity.[112]

Early Weimar, for Tillich, was a moment bursting with kairos possibilities. The SPD rode high in the early going, winning nearly twice as many votes as the second-place Centre Party in the national election of 1919. A year later the left-socialist and right-nationalist movements surged at the expense of the two moderate parties, as the USPD won nearly as many votes as the SPD. The enmity between the two Social Democratic parties, bitter from the beginning, got worse in January 1920, when government troops killed forty-two demonstrators outside the Reichstag. Tillich and the kairos socialists sought to play a mediating role between socialist adversaries, clinging to realistic idealism as they conceived it and deeply disappointed when the majority half of the USPD opted for Communism in December 1920. The kairos socialists were for radical change without revolutionary romanticism or utopianism. They were realists who dared to imagine a completely different world. In 1923, defining the basic principles of religious socialism, Tillich said dialectical mediation is a spiritual necessity, not merely a political one.

The sacramental consciousness has a sense of the holy, it consecrates matter or concepts as divine, and it conceives history as myth, construing everything in life in relationship to sacred symbols of faith. Its power radiates through sacred myths that confer meaning upon past and present, humankind and nature, and individual and community, the latter through family, soil, tribe, cult, class, nation, and/or political system. The rational consciousness, by contrast, is based on form and law as directed toward the right (*das Richtige*), not the holy. Tillich observed that rationality judges even the holy according to critical standards of right, demystifying the world with relentless criticism, as in Kantian criticism. Religious socialism, to him, was inherently dialectical and prophetic, uniting the mythological and critical interpretations of history: "It has the holy, but only as it permeates law and form; it is free from sacramental indifference, but it does not succumb to rational purgation."[113]

Religious socialism warded off the demonic elements of mythic sacramentalism by embracing rational, liberal, and democratic elements. At the same time it opposed the sterile materialism and soulless autonomy of the bourgeoisie that socialist movements strangely borrowed. This did not mean, to Tillich, that heteronomy and autonomy were equally problematic. Religious socialism began as a struggle against injustice, dehumanization, inequality, and authoritarianism. As such, it was never less than ethical and prophetic. When religious socialists confronted a choice between defending liberal democracy and upholding their religious traditions, they had to defend liberal democracy. Tillich hated that church leaders sneered at the Weimar Republic for reactionary reasons. He had a similar feeling about left-wing antiliberalism, which destroyed Germany's best political hope, the USPD. By 1922 the only political vehicle for democratic socialists was the SPD, which welcomed the rump-USPD leftovers. Tillich insisted that the road to religious socialism ran through liberal democracy. Illiberal socialism, even for an interim, did not tempt him.

Bad forms of Marxism treated democracy and liberal rights as superfluous. Tillich said that Marx's critique of commodity fetishism was the best part of Marxism, which Tillich theologized as a critique of spiritual death. Capitalism strips nature of its sacramental power by commodifying all existence: "The more a thing becomes a commodity, the less it exists in an eros-relation to the possessor and the less intrinsic power it possesses. In this inner emptiness, however, the thing becomes the object of the subjective eros and of the subjective will to power." The sacramental relationship to nature provides a brake on natural human desires for pleasure and domination. Capitalism, Tillich argued, eliminates the brake. Anything that the subjective will to power or desire for dominance takes from nature, it loses for itself.[114]

Tillich conceived the class struggle as an expression of the demonic character of capitalism, not as a given of human nature to be tolerated. He faulted the socialist parties for treating socialism as a counter-concept to capitalist economics. Socialists had to stop saying that socializing the economy was the essence of socialism. To Tillich, the goal of socialism was theonomy, replacing the subjective will to power with a liberating religious ethos. Socialism as mere counter-capitalism rationalized alternative forms of hubris, power worship, and dehumanization. Religious socialism applied the antiauthoritarian principle of radical democracy to everything, accepting the democratic constitutional state "as a universal form" and filling this form with the divine good. Tillich said that socialism is essentially and emphatically a struggle for justice. As such, it cannot be absolutely pacifist or anarchist because gains toward justice must be defended against the enemies of justice. Neither does true socialism romanticize the proletariat because every working-class community abounds with vulgar tastes and prejudices that socialism must overcome.[115]

Religious socialism might have gained some traction as a religious caucus within the SPD, but Tillich had no interest in combating Erfurt Marxists over a caucus. He had the customary professorial aversion to party politics, although his later tendency to exaggerate the impact of his group implied a greater ambition. In his telling, religious socialism was too important to attach itself to a political party. Tillich's Berlin period exemplified the personal as the political, an experience of personal liberation that fired his hope of social transformation and inspired his signature ideas. He studied art, literature, psychoanalysis, and politics, immersed himself in the culture of bohemian cafés and dance clubs, and indulged himself sexually, even after remarrying. He thrived on his new friendships and interests, sexual and otherwise, rationalizing that he could not fulfill his potential if he did not satisfy himself erotically. Hirsch pleaded with Tillich to curtail his promiscuity or, failing that, to choose philosophy over theology, before his lifestyle became a scandal for theology. Tillich appreciated Hirsch's friendly candor but liked his new life. In 1924 he wrote in *Blätter für Religiösen Sozialismus*, "I have come to know the Bohème; I went through the war; I got involved in politics; I became fascinated by the art of painting, and, in the course of this winter, with greatest passion by music." Tillich's second wife, Hannah Gottschow, shared his sexual lifestyle during their years in Germany, but not after they were exiled to the United States. For the rest of his life Tillich was sexually promiscuous, a fact that, after they moved to America, Hannah Tillich bitterly regretted and he assiduously kept secret.[116]

In 1924, lacking any chance of promotion at Berlin, he made a career move to Marburg. Tillich felt stifled at Marburg, where Rudolf Otto was ailing, Heidegger was frosty, Tillich barely knew Bultmann, and the community reeked of quaint, small-town provincialism. The following year he moved to Dresden Institute of Technology, rescued by his friend Richard Kroner, a wealthy post-Kantian idealist who admired Tillich's thought while believing it was too close to Schelling to be Christian. The Dresden Institute lacked accredited university status but was in a city, a necessity for Tillich. He published a breakthrough book, *The Religious Situation* (1926), calling for a "faithful realist" revolt against bourgeois civilization. In much of European art, philosophy, and science, Tillich said, the revolt was happening. The expressionist and postexpressionist movements in painting, the Nietzschean and Bergsonian philosophies of life, the Freudian discovery of the unconscious, and the Einsteinian revolution in physics exuded a fundamental openness to the Unconditioned, Tillich's God term. He favored expressionist painting for the rest of his life, commending its subversive disruption of appearances. *The Religious Situation* lamented that theology was not similarly creative. Tillich felt increasingly alienated from the church, bristling at Barth's popularity among church theologians. He protested that Barth didn't even try to address modern cultural developments.[117]

Tillich was nice to Barth in their first back-and-forth, which yielded Barth's riposte that the Unconditioned was a "frosty monster" rolling over everything in the spirit of Hegel and Schleiermacher. Tillich subsequently replied that Barth's theology, for all its influence, was merely a sophisticated form of other-worldliness. In essence, Barth offered the God of Pauline supernaturalism as the answer to modern religious needs. This prescription, Tillich said, even in Barth's able rendering of it, was neither credible nor even cognizant of its religious elements. Barth's religion of faith was still religion, notwithstanding his polemics against religion, and its otherworldly appeal to revelation brushed aside modern challenges to belief. If theologians wanted to say something worthwhile, they had to become philosophers of culture as well as theologians.

Tillich put it sharply in 1929: "Revelation is revelation to me in my conscious situation, in my historical reality."[118]

He won a following for this message in the Hofgeismar Circle, a group of young socialists who challenged the SPD's statism from the left. In 1928 Tillich, Heimann, Löwe, and Mennicke joined eighty religious socialists and young socialists for a three-day conference at Heppenheim-on-the-Bergstrasse, near Heidelberg, to discuss the political situation. Ragaz, Martin Buber, and Hendrik de Man participated. De Man, a popular ethical socialist writer, urged the group to make a clean break from Marxism. Socialism and religious social-ism, he said, would never attract many followers as long as socialism bore the albatross of Marxist materialism, determinism, and atheism. Heimann and Tillich countered that this seemingly attractive position lacked something indispensable, Marxian dialectic. Did the gathered socialists see the coming of the Gestalt in the seething tensions of the proletarian situation? Did they believe the new order was struggling to emerge in the existing proletarian movement? That was Marxian dialectic. Heimann and Tillich said it was far superior to nondialectical morality *and* the mechanical dialecticism of vulgar Marxism. This argument inspired the religious socialists to revive the journal of the defunct Kairos Circle, renamed *Neue Blätter für den Sozialismus*, adding "new" and dropping "religious." Tillich assumed editorial responsibility for it, persuading a young Hofgeismar socialist, August Rathmann, to be managing editor. The first issue appeared in January 1930, four months after Tillich began teaching at the University of Frankfurt. He kept it going for three and a half years, on a monthly basis, reaching a circulation of three thousand, until the Nazis shut it down in June 1933.[119]

Winning the philosophy chair at Frankfurt was Tillich's academic break-through, at the age of forty-three. It thrilled him to land at Frankfurt. Founded in a bustling, historic banking and industrial city in 1914, the university had scientific institutes and a growing reputation for progressiveness and faculty stars. One of its semi-independent institutes, the Institute for Social Research, grew out of a symposium in 1922 featuring Hungarian Communist theorist Georg Lukács, German Communist philosopher Karl Korsch, German social-ist sociologist Friedrich Pollock, and other Marxist theorists. All sought to overcome the mechanistic Marxism of the Engels–Kautsky tradition, chiefly through historical, philosophical, and sociological studies. All were critical of the Bolshevik imposition of Leninist rigidity on the KPD and other Communist parties. The following year Carl Grünberg and Felix Weil founded the institute as the first Marxist research center affiliated with a German university. Grünberg, an Austrian Marxist legal scholar, led the institute in its early years;

Weil, an independent scholar and wealthy protégé of Korsch, financed the institute; Pollock and Max Horkheimer, young Marxists trained by Frankfurt Kantian philosopher Hans Cornelius, played active roles in it from the beginning.[120]

The founding of the institute in 1923 was indelibly associated with two books of the same year signaling a generational turn in Marxist theory: Lukács's *History and Class Consciousness* and Korsch's *Marxism and Philosophy*. Both emphasized Marx's intellectual debts to Hegel and the subjective preconditions of a successful revolution. Both sought to alleviate Marxist orthodoxy of mechanistic scholasticism by interpreting Hegelian dialectics from a materialist standpoint. Both offended Kautsky-style Social Democrats and Soviet Communist leaders by doing so, generating controversies in both movements. Lukács, a former commissar in the Hungarian Soviet Republic now living in exile in Vienna, said orthodoxy in Marxism referred exclusively to the *method* of dialectical materialism as the "road to truth," not to Marx's opinions about anything else. Korsch's heresies alarmed Comintern leader Grigory Zinoviev, a Bolshevik revolutionary founder, because Korsch was a prominent figure in the KPD, the world's major Communist party outside the Soviet Union. Korsch earned a law degree from Jena in 1910, studied political philosophy in London, became a Fabian, and entered the wartime German army as a lieutenant, despite opposing the war. He refused to carry a gun or to live in officers' quarters yet won the Iron Cross. He joined the USPD in 1917, kept moving leftward, and organized a soldiers' soviet in 1918, becoming a theorist of the Berlin Workers' Councils and Revolutionary Shop Stewards.[121]

Korsch was already a leading Communist theorist in the spring of 1919 when he began to study Marx and Engels. He became a self-styled Leninist by conceiving Leninism as revolutionary activism on all fronts of the class struggle, not as vanguard dictatorship. This reading soon threw him into conflict with actual Leninists. In the early 1920s Korsch taught at Jena and was deeply involved in the KPD's attempt to seize power in Thuringia and Saxony. He served in 1923 as minister of justice in the short-lived SPD–KPD coalition government in Thuringia, just before *Marxism and Philosophy* made him famous. Then he served as a Communist delegate in the Reichstag and took over the KPD theoretical journal, only to be denounced by Zinoviev at the 1924 Comintern for deviationism. Zinoviev said Communism would not survive if it had to tolerate opinionated intellectuals like Korsch and Lukács. Korsch was expelled from the KPD in 1926, the same year Zinoviev lost his contest for leadership power with Joseph Stalin. Lukács recanted in 1930 and remained loyal to the Communist Party until his death in 1971, surviving various purges and party turbulence.

Tillich came to Frankfurt during the intense ideological drama over these events. French philosopher Maurice Merleau-Ponty later hung the name "Western Marxism" on the turn in Marxist theory that dissented from Soviet dogmatism, downplayed economic analysis, and variously favored Hegelian philosophy, social theory, cultural theory, ideology critique, humanism, and/or structuralism.[122]

Kurt Riezler, formerly a high government official in the imperial and SPD governments, took over as *Kurator* of the university the year before Tillich got there. He took pride and delight in bringing Tillich to Frankfurt. Tillich succeeded Cornelius on the faculty, although he usually said he succeeded Max Scheler, an existential personalist closer to Tillich's style, who fell ill and retired. Tillich risked being marginalized in the academy by identifying with the institute Marxists. Three early institute stalwarts—Karl August Wittfogel, Franz Borkenau, and Julian Gumperz—belonged to the KPD, and Korsch participated in institute seminars during and after his stormy leadership years in the KPD. Most of the institute Marxists quietly sympathized with the Soviet revolution, hoping it would turn democratic; Pollock's frank skepticism in this area made him exceptional. Tillich befriended the two cornerstones of the institute, Horkheimer and Pollock, identifying with their work and lending his academic prestige to it. In 1929, with Tillich's help, Horkheimer won a university chair in social philosophy and Löwe won a chair in economics, both in new positions funded by Weil. Horkheimer and Pollock, during their student days in Munich in 1919, had provided refuge for revolutionaries persecuted by the white terror, although neither joined the KPD. Horkheimer said Rosa Luxemburg was the last socialist leader he followed, after which he opted for intellectual independence. He also said he quietly cheered for a Soviet turnaround in the same way that a cancer victim cheered for a cure. Horkheimer was extroverted and prolific, and Pollock was introverted, less prolific, and fiercely loyal to Horkheimer. Together they built a powerhouse of neo-Marxist social theory that Horkheimer took over as director in 1930. Later it was called the Frankfurt School.[123]

Tillich's friendships with two other Frankfurt School up-and-comers, sociologist Leo Lowenthal and cultural philosopher Theodor Adorno, were equally vital to him. Lowenthal, the son of a Frankfurt physician, moved in the same radical student circles as Horkheimer, Pollock, and Weil and bonded with two subsequently prominent protégés of Rabbi Nehemiah Nobel—Buber and Franz Rosenzweig. Like Adorno, Lowenthal mixed philosophy, cultural studies, and aesthetics, protesting that orthodox Marxists wrote shallow drivel about culture. Lowenthal dared to go low, writing about popular culture. Adorno was severely intellectual by comparison, combining his training in music theory and post-Kantian philosophy to range over issues in aesthetics, epistemology, and cultural theory. He began his doctoral work under Cornelius at Frankfurt, but Cornelius retired and Adorno became Tillich's first doctoral advisee. Under Tillich, Adorno wrote a thesis on Kierkegaard's aesthetics; like Tillich, he cheered that Horkheimer steered the institute away from the idea of social philosophy as a single *Wissenschaft* pursuing an immutable truth. Horkheimer welcomed psychoanalytic thinkers Erich Fromm and Karl Landauer to the institute, contending that critical social philosophy needed to enrich materialist theory with empirical studies in the same way that natural philosophy drew upon chemistry, biology, and other scientific disciplines.[124]

Critical theory, on this telling, was still a form of orthodox Marxian analysis. It began with the idea of the simple exchange of commodities and refined this idea by employing what Horkheimer called "relatively universal concepts." It kept the language of strict deduction and necessity, claiming that Marxian analysis deduced the same kind of necessity as the study of electricity. But Horkheimer opened the door to neo-Marxian cultural theory, recognizing that orthodox Marxists overrelied on a base–superstructure reductionism that screened out existential and cultural factors. Moreover, Kautsky Marxists refused to acknowledge the hypothetical character of scientific endeavor. Horkheimer affirmed with Marx that the entire global capitalist society derives from the basic relation of exchange but stressed that this was an existential judgment. In its totality, Marxian critical theory unfolded a single existential judgment: "The theory says that the basic form of the historically given commodity economy on which modern history rests contains in itself the internal and external tensions of the modern era; it generates these tensions over and over again in an increasingly heightened form; and after a period of progress, development of human powers, and emancipation for the individual, after an enormous extension of human control over nature, it finally hinders further development and drives humanity into a new barbarism." Marxism, on this telling, was a magnificent tradition of social criticism needing to be saved from scholastics determined to make it small and manageable.[125]

On Horkheimer's watch the institute surveyed the attitudes of German workers on economic, political, and social issues. These surveys gathered troubling data, for nearly every member of the institute was of Jewish lineage. In 1932 Horkheimer established a research office in Geneva and hired young philosopher Herbert Marcuse for it. Marcuse came from a prosperous family in Berlin, fought in the war, joined the SPD in 1917, and quit two years later, appalled that the SPD betrayed the revolution. He studied under Heidegger and Edmund Husserl at Freiburg, deeply impressed by their phenomenological methods, but

Heidegger's politics repelled him, which put Marcuse's career in jeopardy just before the Nazis took over. The Geneva office saved the institute after Hitler came to power, yielding a new moniker, the Frankfurt School. Horkheimer was fired from the university along with Tillich, Löwe, and sociologist Karl Mannheim. The entire institute staff in Frankfurt fled the city, except Wittfogel, who was thrown into a concentration camp. Horkheimer and Lowenthal followed Marcuse to Geneva, Adorno enrolled at Oxford, and the highly assimilated Frankfurt Marxists struggled to absorb that Germany had capitulated to Nazi anti-Semitism.[126]

With the partial exceptions of Lowenthal and Fromm, none of the Frankfurt Marxists had any attachment to Judaism. Literary theorist Walter Benjamin later became another half exception, and Löwe was not a Frankfurt School insider. Being Jewish meant nothing to the Frankfurt Marxists, in their telling. Weil later insisted that Jewishness of any kind—religious, ethnic, or cultural— played no role whatsoever in the group's thinking or membership policy. The Frankfurt Marxists were like Marx in believing that Judaism was a closed book, or at least it should be. Pollock put it categorically: "All of us, up to the years before Hitler, had no feeling of insecurity originating from our ethnic descent. Unless we were ready to undergo baptism, certain positions in public service and business were closed to us, but that never bothered us. And under the Weimar republic many of these barriers had been moved away." In their later careers the Frankfurt School founders seethed at reading that socialism must have been their answer to being ethnically oppressed. They had not needed to be Jews to be socialists. They were against making an issue of religion or ethnicity, and they felt safe under the Weimar governments. It was Hitler who turned them into Jews and punished them for it. In their case they made it easy for Hitler by espousing radical socialism or communism. Often they said they had a much harder time assimilating to American society than they felt in Wilhelmian Germany or Weimar Germany.[127]

Historian Martin Jay thought the Frankfurt School founders protested too much when he interviewed them in 1970. How could they have felt safe with so much anti-Semitic invective in the air? But Jay allowed that historians only guess at the truth. Jürgen Habermas, an eminent Frankfurt School theorist of a later generation, noted that Jewish cultural tradition and German idealism had much in common, both believing that speech, not picture thinking, is the way to approach God. Jews distrusted the profane speech of the Diaspora much as post-Kantians looked down on empirical reality. The chasm between the sacred language of Hebrew and the grubby realities of Diaspora existence drove assimilated Jews to idealism. Tillich's theology resounded with these ideas, but

Tillich did not share the feeling of Paul Massing, one of the few gentiles at the institute, who said he always felt somewhat removed from his colleagues because he was not a Jew. Tillich, despite being far more conscious of the Jewish factor than most of his Jewish-lineage colleagues, felt no estrangement on this count. Horkheimer and Adorno called him "Paulus among the Jews." Tillich said the Jewish factor mattered because there would have been no socialism or religious socialism without it. On occasion, when provoked, he said Germany had no more Christians; the only Christians were Jews.[128]

He thrived in Frankfurt. Tillich loved his overflowing classes and sophisticated company, especially the invitations to high-society salons. He was enthralled by the Taunus hills, the Rhine and Main Rivers, the quaint nearby villages, and his first car, a Mercedes. He loved the fancy-dress winter balls and the costume parties he threw at his apartment; Adorno once showed up as Napoleon. Tillich enjoyed all of it too much to take seriously that it might vanish overnight, although he remained politically engaged in his style, producing articles and lectures. He joined the SPD in 1929, holding his nose, because he wanted to reach the existing socialist audience, and the Nazis were gaining. He implored that religion has to do with God's dealing with the world, and God apparently chose to work through "a profane, even anti-Christian phenomenon like socialism." He tracked and appropriated the neo-Marxism of Lukács, Korsch, Gramsci, and the Frankfurt School. "Western Marxism" nudged aside the Marxian focus on economic alienation, the class struggle, and revolutionary organization. Horkheimer, Adorno, Pollock, Lowenthal, Marcuse, and Fromm—the core of the Frankfurt School—focused on psychology, aesthetics, social manipulation, and the forms and transmission of cultural evil, theorizing about undertheorized superstructures. The new Marxism was more sociological than epistemological, more concerned with the function of ideas within social life than with the truth/reality or falsity/unreality of ideas.[129]

Horkheimer teased that Tillich could not help sounding like a theologian, which kept Tillich off the "A" list of Frankfurt institute insiders. It didn't help that Tillich prized Heidegger and Scheler for taking up perennial questions about the nature of human existence. To Horkheimer, existential phenomenology was a distraction from philosophy that mattered. It smacked of backward religious hankerings and legitimized reactionary myths of origin. Most of the Frankfurt Marxists did not care for Tillich's trope that nearly all people are religious by virtue of having ultimate concerns. They wanted to keep religion where it belonged, in museums.

Horkheimer said it was "a vain hope" to think that an upsurge of progressive religion might make religion vital again. Religion commendably provided hope and norms for people crushed by the world, but the world moved forward, enough that "good will, solidarity with wretchedness, and the struggle for a better world have now thrown off their religious garb." Tillich heard a lot of that at conferences. Yet he was more fully a Frankfurt Marxist than scholarly gatekeepers of the Frankfurt legacy acknowledged, having anticipated signature Frankfurt themes before he got there. Tillich perceived Hegel's under-recognized influence on Marx before it became fashionable to say that Marx was not a dogmatic materialist and empiricist. He caught Marx's Hegelian humanism long before J. P. Mayer and Siegfried Landshut, in 1932, published Marx's previously unknown *Economic and Philosophic Manuscripts of 1844*. Mayer and Landshut were contributors to *Neue Blätter*. Tillich believed throughout his career that Marx was a secular prophet and existentialist, albeit with a problematic utopian impulse. He taught that Marx's dialectical and humanist tropes were more important than the economic arguments in *Capital* and the *Contribution to the Critique of Political Economy*. As it was, Tillich never learned much economic theory and did not believe that a socialist theologian needed to do so.[130]

For the generation of orthodox Marxists who knew little of Marx's early work, "ideology" meant false consciousness or illusion, the opposite of scientific Marxism. Tillich came of age intellectually just as Marxists recognized that ideology was complex and elusive regardless of what Marx said about it and that Marx said contrary things about it. In his Frankfurt years Tillich took from Marx primarily the claim of the centrality of the proletarian struggle, the critique of commodity fetishism, the suspicion of ideological taint in bourgeois thought, the unmasking of ideological distortion, and the prophetic condemnation of exploitation and oppression. His rendering of Marxism was essentially political. Later, upon landing in the United States, Tillich drew more deeply from critical theory, largely as compensation for having lost even an imagined political context, and he relied more heavily on ontological and psychoanalytic arguments. The influence of Marx on Tillich's thought can be exaggerated, and is by some scholars, because he took barely a pass at *Capital*, and Schelling was a greater influence upon him. But Tillich's thought was indebted to Marx throughout his career.[131]

The most deeply Marxist piece he ever wrote appeared in 1929. Tillich declared in "The Class Struggle and Religious Socialism" that religious socialism does not rest on a repudiation of Marxian materialism because "Marxism is primarily a reality and only secondarily an idea." What is real is the raising of the proletariat from abjection and oppression "to a powerful consciousness of meaning." The existential reality of proletarian uplift outstrips every intellectual rendering of it. Marxism as an idea, whatever it is, is much less important than the Marxian reality. To Tillich, the reality of the proletarian revolution was a religious achievement, not merely a struggle for political power. It marked a breakthrough toward universal human dignity, not merely a regime featuring a socialized economy. To conceive socialism as a religious phenomenon is to view socialism "as a genuine revelation of the human situation of our time." Radical versions of the social gospel, whatever their faults in other areas, were profoundly right to theologize the proletarian movement as a struggle for the kingdom of God. Tillich put it plainly: "The struggle of the proletariat takes on the form of a struggle for the Kingdom of God. It is a struggle to overcome the demonic, whose destructive power is particularly evident to the proletariat. Hence the proletariat feels that its struggle is a struggle for the Kingdom of God; it senses a kind of messianic mission for itself and for the whole of society."[132]

In 1950, when American social ethicist James Luther Adams assembled Tillich's early essays for the book *The Protestant Era*, he included this article on the class struggle. Tillich was aghast, imploring Adams not to include it because it would ruin him in America: "You can't publish that! Oh, no, no, it's too Marxist." Adams obligingly eliminated the article from a reader that otherwise richly reflected Tillich's early thought. Near the end of his life, when Tillich published the third volume of his *Systematic Theology*, his section on the kingdom of God rambled with faint echoes of religious socialism minus any reference to the proletariat, for which he substituted a depoliticized euphemism, "the bearers of history." Tillich knew his early writings said it better, and he never stopped believing that the kingdom idea compels Christians to struggle for radical social justice. In 1929 he spelled out why Christian theology needed Marxism to avoid turning the kingdom ethic into mere utopianism, notwithstanding that Marxism had its own utopia problem: "Religious socialism must recognize the inevitability of the class struggle and disclose its demonic character. Its task cannot be to call for socialism without a class struggle. To do so would be to betray the real situation of the proletariat, to withdraw from reality. Religious socialism would then become utopianism, a utopianism that would be no better for its religious sanction."[133]

He felt the ambiguity of his situation before he suddenly lost everything that mattered to him. If his rendering of religion and socialism was right, why was he so isolated in it? If Protestantism rarely espoused anything resembling religious socialism, why did he hang on to it? Tillich's best writings usually pressed his existential questions. In 1931 he said Protestantism was only Protestant when it transcended its religious and confessional character and socialism was not identical with the proletarian situation. Since Protestantism and socialism might have developed differently, the enmity between them was not inevitable. However, to the extent that socialism expressed the proletarian situation, it challenged Protestantism to discover its true nature in the Protestant principle, which sanctifies the spirit of criticism. The Protestant principle is the source of everything creative and life giving in Protestantism, but it is not identical with anything in Protestantism, and it cannot be confined to a definition. It is not like the Being of Greek philosophy or the Absolute of German idealism, which derive an ultimate ontological concept from an analysis of being. Tillich described the Protestant principle as the theological expression of the true relation between the Unconditioned and the conditioned or, in religious terms, between the divine and the human. Thus its great concern is faith, "the state of mind in which we are grasped by the power of something unconditional which manifests itself to us as the ground and judge of our existence."[134]

This power that grasps us in the state of faith is not an object among objects or even the greatest whatever-object. Tillich said it tirelessly throughout his career, urging audiences to break free of idolatry. The power that grasps us "is a quality of all beings and objects, the quality of pointing beyond themselves and their finite existence to the infinite, inexhaustible, and unapproachable depth of their being and meaning." The Protestant principle, as he conceived it, expressed this relationship. It opposed and refuted all attempts to treat something finite as infinite. It criticized every form of religious pride, ecclesiastical arrogance, and secular self-sufficiency and their ravages. It said the human situation is basically distorted because human beings arrogantly make gods of themselves, their desires, and their products. The Protestant Reformation, Tillich said, recovered the biblical doctrine that human beings are unities of body and soul. As such, the Reformation was a protest against dualistic corruptions in the Catholic Church: "But in Protestantism itself this idea has become only partially effective for individual ethics and not at all for social ethics." Protestantism only half-recovered the biblical critique of idolatry and the biblical unity of body and soul. The churches were so cut off from biblical prophecy they had to learn social ethics from the socialist movement. So far, Tillich judged, little had changed: "The proletarian situation, in forcing Protestantism to bring to the fore the critical element of its own principle, creates the constant suspicion that Protestantism has itself become an ideology, the worship of a man-made God." The socialist movement, merely by caring about the right things, vindicated the Protestant principle and shamed the Protestant churches.[135]

Tillich granted that liberal Protestantism was generally better than nonliberal varieties. Liberal Protestantism respected science and modern criticism, and it upheld a humanistic ideal of personality. But it rarely recognized the idolatrous elements in the Protestant emphasis on the cognition and morality of an individual self. Cartesian philosophy led to Schleiermacher in Protestant theology, yielding a religion of consciousness that only middle-class churchgoers found edifying. Tillich said religious feeling does not belong solely to the sphere of consciousness, so liberal Protestantism would never unite Protestantism with the proletariat. Depth psychology was like socialism in recovering lost worlds of meaning and vitality. It was no coincidence that psychoanalysis spread in the very Protestant nations that suffered massive breakdowns of the conscious personality through war, trauma, loss, and destruction. Depth psychology became a social necessity: "A religion that does not appeal to the subconscious basis of all decisions is untenable in the long run and can never become a religion for the masses." Liberal Protestantism was too rationalistic, leaving the religious individual isolated, and it made specious claims about its political neutrality that managed to be sincere only because middle-class Protestants did not recognize their biases. For example, they routinely said they were neutral about the farm labor issue, which was pure ideology in the Marxist sense of the term—outright false consciousness. Farm laborers readily grasped that churches sided with the landowners. Then the church lost the farm laborers when they joined the urban proletariat. Tillich said one sign of hope existed in this grim situation, the rise of religious socialism: "The religious socialists have set for themselves the goal of freeing Protestantism from the sociological attachments resulting from its antiproletarian past."[136]

Socialism, understood as the self-expression of the oppressed, provides meaning for the subjected in a brutally meaningless world, and meaning is ultimately religious, pointing to the Unconditioned that transcends all specific contexts. Tillich knew his neo-Marxian friends did not want to hear about the indispensability of faith and the religious character of their ultimate concerns, but he labored these themes anyway because socialism was incomprehensible without its religious dimension. A person's religion is whatever concerns her ultimately. Nobody fights for justice lacking faith and ultimate concerns. Many heard this only as backward religiosity and/or political naiveté. Even Tillich's friends attested that he lived in his head. Harold Poelchau claimed that Tillich sustained a childlike optimism right up to his firing. Riezler said Tillich was a sophomore in politics. Dehn was stunned in 1932 when Tillich gave a lecture never mentioning the political crisis, enraptured by his own ideas. All of this entered the lore about Tillich, notwithstanding that precious few academics had more on their record to convict them when the Nazis took over. In October 1931 Tillich lectured on socialism at Wolfers's German Academy of Politics, feeling his way toward a book. The following July he witnessed a right-wing riot on the Frankfurt campus, replete with storm troopers and Nazi students beating up leftist and Jewish students. By then Tillich was dean of the philosophy faculty. He flushed with anger, dragged the injured students to safety, and made an outraged speech against the Nazi students, demanding their expulsion. This reaction sealed his fate in Germany, although Tillich had no inkling of it, still believing that cultured Germany would not turn fascist. Later that summer, vacationing in the mountains of Sils Maria, Switzerland, along with Hannah Tillich, Löwe, Karl Mannheim, and Adolf Grimme, Tillich wrote *The Socialist Decision*.[137]

The socialist decision was *of* and *for* socialism, and there were two sides of the latter. Tillich implored socialists to make a new decision for socialism that searched for new answers, and he told antisocialists they had a future in the socialism that was coming. These were the two sides of the decision *for* socialism. The decision *of* socialism, on the other hand, applied only to the parties and groups that smeared the socialist name by claiming it for hateful nationalistic ideologies. Tillich shuddered that the Nazis called themselves socialists, a calamity for true socialism and mere decency. He vowed to show that true socialism was the salvation of Europe and that Marxism made an important contribution to it. The Nazis were gaining, and Tillich had joined the SPD as a sign of his political seriousness. He placed himself between the older generation of crusty SPD politicos and the younger generation of socialists who quoted Hendrik de Man, wrote for *Neue Blätter*, and made Tillich feel middle-aged. The older generation still dominated the socialist movement, stuck in mechanistic materialism, while the younger generation renounced nineteenth-century positivism and the grotesque socialism of the Soviet Union. Tillich said there was a case to be made for progressive Marxian socialism: "It holds fast to Marxism and defends it against the activism of the younger generation; but it rejects the form in which the older generation took it over from the nineteenth century. It goes back to the real Marx and to a concept of dialectic in which necessity and freedom are conjoined."[138]

This confident statement exuded Tillich's excitement at the recent publication of the *Economic and Philosophic Manuscripts of 1844*, which gave ballast to his Marx-the-secular-prophet interpretation. But he cautioned that he did not throw out the old Engels–Kautsky orthodoxy. The real Marx was a unity of the younger humanist and older materialist: "Only if the one is interpreted by the other is a true understanding of Marx possible." Marx the prophetic humanist got the crucial things right: the class struggle, socialism as the self-expression of the proletariat, and the dialectic of transformation. Thus Tillich inveighed against facile forms of ethical socialism that appealed to middle-class anxieties by throwing Marx overboard.[139]

Swiftly he plunged readers into an existential phenomenology of the two roots of political thought in human being itself, although Tillich told readers that if abstract philosophy scared them, feel free to skip chapter one. To Tillich, existential phenomenology was distinctly enabling because it disclosed the existential realities of estrangement, despair, the void, the demonic, and death. His conversion to religious socialism had begun in the French forest, reading Nietzsche. His experience of the abyss in existence was more real to him than nature love or anything else. Thus he admired and relied upon Nietzsche, Scheler, Kierkegaard, and especially Heidegger. Tillich was deeply influenced by Heidegger's *Being and Time* phase. He savored Heidegger's description of human beings as the unique type of being through whom Being (the primordial ground) presents itself to be known. He absorbed Heidegger's vivid theorizing of the "thrown" character of human "being-there" (*Dasein*) and the perils that attend the self's coming-to-awareness of its arbitrarily given ("thrown") existence. Heidegger's account of the choice between authentic and inauthentic existence impressed Tillich, no less than Bultmann, as a powerful, modern, existential way of expressing the truths of Pauline theology. Like Bultmann, Tillich theologized Heidegger's description of the inauthentic self falling into anxiety, or replacing its first (infantile) totalized form of life with a substitute, or giving up caring ("fallenness"). He took over Heidegger's notion that the authentic self faces up to one's nothingness and becomes a caretaking "being-toward-death" by changing the form of one's totalized givenness. Authentic existence, Heidegger argued, is the way of death-accepting courage and care for the world.[140]

Tillich recognized that he and Heidegger had similar debts to German Pietism, which mediated Pauline theology to them. Heidegger's atheism, in some ways, made him easier to trust, much like Tillich felt about Marx and Nietzsche. He stayed off the topic of Heidegger's politics, not sure to what extent Heidegger identified with fascism. He absolved Heidegger of needing to answer the problem of existence, since any philosophical answer would have to be idealism, not existentialism. Existentialism, however, asked the question of existence in a fresh and radical way. To Tillich, existential analysis clarified and developed the ontological problem to which faith and theology were the answer. It did not replace idealism or theology; it supplemented the philosophical account of reality that undergirds theology.[141]

All of that was in Tillich's head, not in the book. Tillich did not explicate how he appropriated Schelling, Marx, Kierkegaard, Nietzsche, Heidegger, and the rest of his canon until he wrote *The Interpretation of History* in 1936. *The Socialist Decision*, however, began with a Heideggerian excavation of the powers and tensions of human nature that lay behind all political thinking. Some account of human nature had to underlie any serious attempt to reason about political possibilities and tendencies. Tillich said Marxists usually waved off the problem of anthropology. They felt justified in doing so whether or not they knew Marx's early writings because Marx dismissed anthropology when he renounced Feuerbach's theorizing about humanity in general. Marx became a Marxist when he focused relentlessly on actual human beings determined by class and society. Tillich countered that these class-determined beings were still human. They were selves with a history who lived in societies, could be split into classes, fell into dehumanization and objectification, struggled for a social order worthy of their humanity, and so on. The entire Marxist argument had an implied account of what human beings are like and what is possible for them. But Marxists were not good at talking about any of it, unlike their enemies.

Every human being, Tillich said, has an internal duality, and every element of human and social being is shaped by consciousness. There is a constitutively human consciousness that does not correspond to being. The very idea of a "false consciousness" is possible or knowable only if there is a true consciousness, but Marxists habitually invoked false consciousness as an accusation to shut down any consideration of the human unity of being and consciousness. Tillich believed German idealism was enabling for what Marx wanted to say, contrary to orthodox Marxism. There is a true consciousness. It arises out of being and simultaneously determines being. Human nature is the unity of consciousness arising out of and determining being. Human beings find themselves in existence *and* they find themselves as they find their environment, which finds them and itself. Tillich could have invoked Schelling or Hegel on this idea of finding oneself in something that does not originate with oneself. But he opted for Heidegger's "pregnant phrase" about being thrown into the world, stressing that philosophy is a latecomer to the question of the whence of existence. Like Schelling, Tillich said the first normative answer comes in myths that express the eruption of something new into being. Myths express the experience of being thrown into existence and independent of it, bearing a creative origin that grounds human existence despite no longer existing. The subject of myth is the dialectic of dependence and independence—the mystery of birth involving the self in having to die.[142]

As far as we know, philosophy began there; Anaximander ruminated that it was apparently the nature of things that things must pass away into that from which they are born. Every myth is a myth of origin that tries to explain the whence of existence *and* that expresses the dependence of human beings on the origin and its power. Tillich reasoned that all political thinking grows out of this unity in duality, yielding two kinds of politics. Conservative and romantic varieties of political thought fix on a myth of origin. Liberal, democratic, and (authentically) socialist thinking is always about breaking the myth of origin through criticism. Since the true origin of existence is ambiguous, it is wrong to simply oppose the two kinds of political thinking. Both kinds of politics are rooted in something deeply human. But only one side recognizes that justice is the true power of being. The demand for justice breaks free of every person's ambiguous origin, recognizing the equal dignity of every human being.

Two kinds of right-wing political romanticism vied for power and sporadically worked together in Germany. Tillich described classic German conservatism as organic, monarchical, and conservative in the literal sense of the term. Classic conservatism was a powerful force in the landowning aristocracy, certain elements of the peasantry and churches, and the older generation of military officers, seeking to preserve Germany's myths of origin in traditional forms. The second type of political romanticism was newer, revolutionary, surging, and more conflicted about its relationship to the myths of origin. The Nazi movement and its allies proposed to restore posited myths of origin by overthrowing the bourgeois order. Nazi fascism resounded with mythic appeals to soil, blood, and national solidarity, despite being wildly anticonservative and deracinated, demanding revolutionary upheaval. Organic traditionalist tropes did not work for fascist ideologues, so they ransacked Nietzsche, French revolutionary syndicalist Georges Sorel, German philosophical historian Oswald Spengler, and others to dress up their propaganda. As a worldview, Tillich observed, Nazi romanticism was too novel and hypocritical not to be cut off from the historic meanings of its myths. It gloried in the fantasy of a Third Reich linking Hitler to Bismarck and Charlemagne. Thus it was dangerously prone to violence.[143]

The Socialist Decision assembled Tillich's customary case for religious socialism, adding a chapter on economic policy on which Tillich took guidance from Löwe. Religious socialism, he explained, embraced the liberal, democratic, and critical elements of the bourgeois revolution and rejected its autonomous elements. It was critical of modernist antireligion, affirming the sacramental values of the myths of origin in critically interpreted forms. It was the antithesis of National Socialism because it embraced the Protestant principle, the humanistic values of the Enlightenment, and the social gains of nineteenth-century liberalism. Religious socialists, he allowed, had a hard time convincing socialists to give up their entrenched antireligious animus. In Germany the early socialist movement naturally allied itself with the bourgeois parties that opposed the state church. Plus, socialists truly believed that scientific socialism abolished the need for religion. Then the bourgeois parties made their peace with religion, but the socialist movement never did. All of this had to be overcome, beginning with confessions of sin by churches that had staunchly opposed social justice for centuries. As usual, Tillich insisted he was not being idealistic. Socialism was pointless as idealism; it had to emerge from existing liberation movements. Thus he saw no hope for religious socialism in the Catholic Church, although he said that some Centre Party unionists were open to it. The Vatican crushed every wellspring of the critical spirit within theological education and the clergy, and official Catholicism was unremittingly clerical. Tillich assumed that as long as dogmatic clericalism dominated the Catholic Church there would be no Catholic socialism anywhere. Catholic socialism had to begin with unionists demanding freedom and justice, but they could only get so far in the existing Catholic Church.[144]

At every key turn in the book Tillich addressed the questions of what he took from Marx and whether religious socialism worked better without Marxism. The first question was always complicated for him and the second was not: no. In his lecture podium experience one objection far outstripped all others: Marxism is materialism, and materialism is economism. Tillich acknowledged that Engels–Kautsky orthodoxy was very problematic on this issue, and Marx contributed mightily to the problem. There was no denying that orthodox Marxism denigrated all ideas, artistic and literary creations, spiritual values, moral intuitions, and love and feeling as superstructural rationalizations of economic interests. But Tillich said orthodox Marxism was never an adequate summary of Marx's complex thought, and the recent publication of Marx's early grappling with Feuerbach and Hegel clarified the purpose and meaning of his teaching. Marx was routinely interpreted as teaching that spirit (*Geist*) is causally dependent on economics. Tillich countered that spirit is not a thing, and neither is economics. Economics is infinitely complex and multifaceted, involving the direction and quality of needs, modes of production and social relationships, scales of enterprise, and virtually every aspect of human being. Economics cannot be isolated and made the cause of something intrinsic to it, spirit.

Neither is spirit anything in itself. Spirit is always the spirit of something, "the spirit of a being that, through spirit, achieves self-understanding." Tillich said Marx grasped this connection between being and consciousness and even emphasized it, like Hegel. Marx took from Hegel that the unity of being and consciousness is lost when being is conceived as a discrete cause from which spirit follows as a discrete effect. Tillich put it bluntly: "There is no such being and no such spirit." Human being is always a twofold unity of being and consciousness in which the positing of subject or object as a discrete factor is nonsensical. This did not mean that false consciousness did not exist. Tillich steered clear of scholarly debates about Marx's polemics against ideology, except to say the idea of a false consciousness makes sense only in connection with the idea of a true consciousness—a consciousness united with the new being: "A false consciousness is nothing other than the willful self-affirmation of old social structures that are being threatened and destroyed by new ones." False consciousness willfully thwarts the movement toward liberation. The upshot for religion was terribly important for religious socialism, whatever Marx believed about ideology. Religious false consciousness is false for being reactionary, not for being religious.[145]

Tillich had no interest in the religion described by the Erfurt Program—a private matter belonging to a discrete sphere of thought and action. Religion, for Tillich, was the depth dimension of life, the living out of the deepest well-spring of human being, the "power supporting and determining all spheres." Social Democracy congratulated itself for officially adopting the liberal view of religion, but religious socialists were too religious to settle for cheap tolerance. Tillich sympathized with the Social Democratic predicament on this issue, just as he sympathized with SPD leaders who tried to hold the nation together and got pilloried for doing so. The churches demonized Social Democracy at its founding, so the Social Democratic movement had to fight to survive. Then liberalism made its peace with the German churches, and the SPD became the only group still holding the liberal view of religion. Tillich said the socialist movement was overdue to stop repelling religious people with shopworn polemics from another era. Socialism itself is religious in the sense of religion that is not trivializing and compartmentalized.[146]

In the category of socialism needing new answers, Tillich highlighted the problems of community and economics. The religion issue exemplified the dilemmas in the former area. Historically, he said, liberalism played the leading role in dissolving the communal bonds to land, social rank, ethnicity, race, religion, and patriarchy, but in every case the socialist movement became the executor of the dissolving powers of liberalism. It was Social Democracy that carried through the liberal attack on privilege and inequality, even as socialism defined itself fundamentally against the bourgeois principle of class rule. Tillich acknowledged that socialism had special problems concerning the politics of community, beginning with its deeply contradictory relationship to liberalism. Socialism was the greatest ally of liberalism and its greatest enemy, a contradiction plaguing every socialist electoral party. Moreover, socialists had huge disadvantages to overcome in the electoral arena. They could not compete with the right-nationalist parties in appealing to the bonds of soil, race, memory, and nation, and they had no apparent substitute for the liberal belief that unfettered capitalism created social harmony and prosperity.

In fact, Tillich said, socialism was more deeply opposed to liberalism than to right-nationalist conservatism, paradoxical as that sounded, as the politics usually played out differently. Socialists rejected both parts of the liberal view that capitalism creates social harmony because free markets conform to natural law. Tillich implored that socialists could not give ground on this twofold principle and still be socialist. The concessions had to tilt the other way, conceiving socialism as a politics of community, with all its perils. Even to lean in this direction was to ensnare the socialist movement in feudal ideologies that buttressed the class rule of aristocrats by appealing to the powers of origin. Tillich moved straight to the issue of national community, urging that socialism had to get its bearings by beginning there. Traditional socialist internationalism was liberalism taken seriously, transcending national limitations in the name of an international ideal of humanity. Tillich agreed that internationalism was the ideal, "in the last analysis." Socialism had to put humankind above the nation and be a champion of international law. But socialists could not afford to ignore that socialism depends for its realization "on national powers of origin." He implied that the SPD ignored it for too long. To suggest that Social Democrats flunked the patriotism test before 1914 or during the war or in 1919 or in the 1920s was perilous and wrong, but Tillich went there anyway, grasping at straws in a desperate situation. He could have faulted the SPD for exalting its partisan self-interest above the cause of democracy but opted for a larger concession. German Social Democracy, he said, belatedly learned its lesson about protecting the nation: "It has learned that the concrete community of place, race, and culture, is, in spite of the opposition of classes, stronger than the abstract identity of its destiny to that of the proletariat in other countries."[147]

Finally the socialist movement recognized that it could not actualize itself if it did not actualize itself nationally. Socialists had never believed in the free market rationale for liberal internationalism, and now "the bourgeois belief in harmony is shattered for socialism on this point also." Dissolving the bonds of origin did not lead to a united humanity. It led to permanent economic warfare and wars of empire. Tillich said socialists had to accept the nation as a power of origin, much as it pained them to do so. They needed to do it emphatically as socialists, recognizing that the nation is the most important and powerful weapon of domination ever placed in the hands of capital. Socialism had no future if it did not embrace this contradiction. It had to be internationalist in opposition to national imperialism and nationalist in opposition to the liberal and previously socialist ideology of international citizenship. The SPD, Tillich said, had rightly moved in this direction. The SPD put the nation first in the German Revolution and the civil war, in the battle against inflation, and in the coal industry battle against France in the Ruhr valley in the early 1920s. These patriotic policies tore the party apart and nearly killed it, even as the party was constantly accused of betraying the nation. Tillich bitterly noted that the right-wing parties never demonstrated similar self-denial for the nation. He reached for the strongest way of saying it, charging that right-wing demagoguery on this point was "demonic in the most negative sense of the word."[148]

Economics was nearly as problematic as the problem of national community. Tillich said it was slightly less so only because socialism was clear about disbelieving in capitalist salvation. Still, even at the point of the deepest opposition between liberalism and socialism, Social Democracy assumed responsibility for saving capitalism. Tillich stressed that every reformist measure championed by socialists concerning labor issues, social insurance, and the like had the effect of strengthening capitalism. When landholders, artisans, and the peasantry clashed with liberals, Social Democracy usually sided with liberalism. Above all, the socialist movement rarely opposed market laws flowing from nationalism. It championed free trade against import duties and entrepreneurs against government protectionism. It dismissed national autarky as a throwback to agrarian premodernity. Tillich was describing, not criticizing. He did not censure Social Democracy for saving capitalism, but it had to be said—this was a large part of the socialist legacy. He accepted the ironies of socialist politics but declared that socialists had to stand for state ownership of the means of production and centralized economic planning: "Socialism places itself on the side of the antiliberal position in economics: central control instead of *laissez faire*, leadership from above instead of faith in harmony from below." That is, socialism favored the democratic aspect of the bourgeois worldview over the liberal aspect, placing the economy in the hands of rational human beings to accomplish what unfettered markets could not, "the best supply of economic goods for all."[149]

Tillich took no interest in debating whether nationalization was the best form of socialization. Marx's rhetoric about the withering away of the state fell under the category of baleful utopianism, and the German tradition of straightforward state socialism was the corrective. Tillich did acknowledge, however, the chief problem with this prescription. Where would the state find these geniuses who reasoned with pure reason and extraordinary goodwill for the sake of all? How would they know what society needed? He raised the question with a shrug, moved to other topics, and swung back to economic planning at the end, declaring, "Positions of economic power held by private enterprise must be placed in the hands of society as a whole, and that means in the hands of the leading groups in the social structure." Every field had a band of experts who knew more than everyone else about its specialty. The key areas were the landed estates, heavy industry, major manufacturing concerns, banking, and international trade. If the government hired the best experts in these fields to manage the economy, the process of production could be socialized without bureaucratic overreaching. This was the commanding heights strategy, although Tillich did not name it, eschewing his usual historiography lesson. He explained that he favored this model because it preserved the free market, which registered needs on macro levels, regulated the direction of production, and got prices right—"all, to be sure, within the perimeters of central planning." There was no need to socialize everything. A free economy was desirable in secondary areas, and socialists had to avoid "the bureaucratization of the whole economy." Only the market calibrated needs and got prices right. Tillich said bureaucracy was a defining feature of advanced capitalism, not socialism. Socialists did not own the bureaucratic idea, did not prize it, and realized that too much of it was bad for society. If socialists got control of the commanding economic forces, they would use bureaucratic tools judiciously.[150]

Tillich finished *The Socialist Decision* in November 1932, a month after he attended one of Hitler's rallies, which he found terrifying and disgusting. Hannah Tillich said Tillich saw the demon in Hitler's eyes. This experience drove him to complete the book, which he ended by imploring that proletarians could not succeed by themselves. There had to be a coalition of proletarian, religious, and liberal forces; otherwise the right-nationalists would prevail. Even right-nationalists were not beyond the pale, if approached correctly. Right-romanticism expressed a legitimate protest against the bourgeois evisceration of the powers of origin. Religious socialists sympathized with this reaction and channeled it to better ends. Tillich later admitted that he grasped the emotional power of Nazi mythology because he felt it personally. One reason he wrote the book was to overcome the mythical romantic element in himself. *The Socialist Decision* came off the press just as Hitler became chancellor in January 1933. The following month Horkheimer began warning Tillich to find a job outside Germany. In March, after Hitler became dictator, Nazi propaganda minister Joseph Goebbels organized the first purges of cultural institutions. *The Socialist Decision* was suppressed along with all other socialist books issued by Tillich's publisher, Alfred Protte. No review was published, but nasty articles impugning Tillich's loyalty appeared. On April 6 the German Student Association announced a nationwide campaign to purify universities as centers of German nationalism. Nationalist students marched in torchlight parades opposing toleration of the un-German spirit, rehearsing for the book burnings that began on May 10. On April 13 the government issued its first list of enemies of the state, under two categories. The first category consisted of Communists, socialists, other left-wing intellectuals, and others deemed politically suspect. The second consisted of Jews.[151]

Tillich, Horkheimer, Löwe, Mannheim, and two legal scholars, Hermann Heller and Hugo Sinzheimer, were purged from Frankfurt immediately. Dehn and Berlin economist Emil Lederer were among others purged on April 13. Every week there were new dismissals. On April 26 Mennicke was fired from Frankfurt and expressionist painter Paul Klee was fired from Berlin. The roll of famous Jewish intellectuals and artists was staggering, headed by Bertholt Brecht, Ernst Cassirer, Albert Einstein, Wassily Kandinsky, Wolfgang Köhler, Thomas Mann, Erwin Panofsky, Max Reinhardt, Karl Ludwig Schmidt, and Bruno Walter. Most were purged for being Jews, although Tillich was less singular as a gentile than he sometimes claimed, being joined by Dehn, Mennicke, Klee, and sociologist Alfred Weber. Frankfurt law professor Karl Reinhardt resigned in May 1933, protesting that German humanism had been abolished in the universities. Meanwhile most of Frankfurt's ostensibly humanist professors swiftly made their peace with fascism. Within a year 1,684 scholars were banished from university circles. Tillich was stunned to be fired, having refused to believe it was coming. On May 10 he witnessed a Nazi rally in Frankfurt at which his books were burned among hundreds of others. He watched from a window of the Römer, where German emperors were crowned, reflecting incredulously that Germany re-created the Spanish Inquisition. For months he traveled through the country, conferring with friends about what he should do, not quite absorbing that he was as vulnerable as the hundreds of Communists, socialists, liberals, Catholics, gays, Gypsies, and pacifists being arrested, beaten, tortured, imprisoned, and murdered.[152]

In May Union Theological Seminary president Henry Sloane Coffin attended a meeting at Columbia University that discussed the fate of the purged academics. Coffin knew hardly anything of Tillich, but Reinhold Niebuhr's brother, H. Richard Niebuhr, had translated *The Religious Situation*. Reinhold Niebuhr urged the Union faculty to offer refuge to Tillich; that summer every Union faculty member agreed to a 5 percent salary reduction to fund a position. Tillich balked and grieved at the thought of leaving Germany to teach anywhere in America, much less a seminary. Adorno pleaded with him that staying in Germany was not worth getting killed. Tillich endeavored to get his job back, until the secret police tried to arrest him at a friend's home in Dresden in October. Then he relented to being rescued by Union, at the age of forty-seven, for many years later identifying with Abraham in Genesis 12:1: "Now the Lord said to Abram, 'Go from your country and your kindred and your father's house to the land that I will show you.'" He also described Niebuhr as "my savior."[153]

Tillich knew almost nothing about American theology. He dreaded that American culture was provincial and superficial, opined that America had no theological tradition, and told friends that leaving cultured Germany was a kind of death for him. Though grateful to be rescued, he doubted he could continue his theological and philosophical work anywhere outside Germany; American academe was especially unpromising. American philosophy was pragmatic and empiricist, and American students bantered with professors practically as equals, which shocked Tillich. Many of his faculty colleagues at Union could not see Christianity anywhere in Tillich's stew of Schelling, Hegel, Marx, Nietzsche, and Heidegger. Tillich joined Niebuhr's Fellowship of Socialist Christians, at first enthusing that Niebuhr's neo-Marxist realism was his kind of socialism. But that soon became a reason to stop espousing religious socialism in Tillich's new context. Long before Niebuhr said it, Tillich had insisted that idealistic socialism is pointless. Lacking a proletarian movement base, socialism is nothing but middle-class ethical idealism. By Tillich's lights, America lacked a serious trade union movement, even at the depth of the Depression. Moreover, Tillich never entirely overcame the feeling that it was unseemly for him to stump for socialism in the colossal bastion of capitalism that saved his life. In his early years at Union he stewed over this misgiving. Then the Cold War confirmed his feeling that he had made the right choice in pulling back from political activism.

For years Tillich struggled with the English language, finding it easy to read but hard to understand and extremely difficult to speak. He never became more than a passable English speaker, and he waved off understanding American politics, deferring to his friends James Luther Adams and Wilhelm Pauck on things political and social. He reunited in New York with Horkheimer and Adorno, who taught at Columbia, and with Heimann and Löwe, who taught at the New School for Social Research. Tillich worked hard for years at helping other émigrés from Nazi Germany find work and accommodations. He loved the bustle and internationalism of New York City, and he missed Germany desperately. In 1934 he pleaded to be reinstated at Frankfurt, telling the Nazi government, "As the theoretician of Religious Socialism I have fought throughout the years against the dogmatic Marxism of the German labor movement, and thereby I have supplied a number of concepts to the National Socialist theoreticians." This pathetic boast was true, but fortunately Tillich stopped taking credit for Hirsch after his appeal was brusquely denied.[154]

Tillich distinguished between the obligations and limits of religious engagement in political life, reasoning that striving for justice is obligatory, but so is

acknowledging one's interpretive fallibility and the transcendent mystery
of faith. In 1934 Hirsch offended him by appropriating Tillich's key concepts
without mentioning Tillich's name or his distinction between obligation and
reservation. Hirsch refashioned Tillich's ideas of the kairos, the demonic, the
boundary, the myths of origin, and the religious interpretation of history, con-
flating the Christian and Nazi faiths. He argued that the Christian's freedom
of conscience from the law unconditionally sanctifies one's faithful attempt
to fulfill the law. He reversed Tillich's insistence that nothing earthly can be
holy without reservation, contending that anything earthly can become holy.
Equating the German nation with a blood-bond, Hirsch interpreted the
Eucharistic sacrament as a reinforcement of the blood-bond and celebrated the
triumph of fascism as a religious event closely approximating, in significance,
the death and resurrection of Jesus. Tillich protested that Hirsch distorted his
concepts and discarded the religious reservation, failing to uphold the integrity
of religion against ideological and utopian enthusiasms: "Your book shows me
that you have neither seen it nor fulfilled it." He implored Hirsch to confess his
blasphemy and his totalitarian crime against the spirit. Blood-bond theology
betrayed the gospel and colluded in Nazi idolatry. Tillich's open letter to Hirsch
infuriated Hirsch, ending their direct communication for eleven years. Hirsch
replied with an open letter to his publisher, Wilhelm Stapel, declaring that 1934
was a moment for an ecstatic unconditional yes, not presumptuous criticism.[155]

Tillich's clash with Hirsch helped him accept his American fate. In 1936
Tillich tried to introduce himself to Americans by explaining that Barth was an
authoritarian theologian and he was a theologian in the liberal tradition.
Barthian theology played a prophetic role in the Confessional Church's resistance to fascism, Tillich allowed, "but it created at the same time a new heteronomy, an anti-autonomous and anti-humanistic feeling, which I must regard
as an abnegation of the Protestant principle." Tillich's occasional broadsides
against liberal theology always held in mind Ritschlian Culture Protestantism,
not the Kant, Schleiermacher, and Schelling line to which he belonged: "It was
and is impossible for me to associate myself with the all too-common criticism
of 'liberal thinking.' I would rather be accused of being 'liberalistic' myself, than
aid in discounting the great and truly human element in the liberal idea."[156]

German idealism was bread and life to Tillich, and Kähler provided theological foundations: The Pauline/Lutheran doctrine of justification is the central doctrine of Christianity. It relativizes all orthodoxies while affirming that
the burden of human sin is overcome by the paradoxical judgment that the sin-
ner is just before God. The foundation of Christian belief is the biblical picture
of Christ. The center of Christianity is the picture of Christ that thrives in

human experience and is preached by the church. Tillich fused these Kähler arguments to German idealism. To him, idealism was essentially the principle of identity, the point where subject and object come together. It was an assertion of the identity of thought and being as the principle of truth.[157]

With Kant and Schelling, Tillich conceived idealism as a philosophy of freedom and creativity—asking questions, recognizing absolute demands, and perceiving meaningful forms in nature, art, and society. Post-Kantian idealism looked for the correspondence between reality and the human spirit in the concept of meaning. Tillich agreed with Hegel that the task of philosophy is to give meaning to the various realms of existence, finding the unity of objective and subjective spirit. But Tillich had no stake in Hegel's system or even Schelling's. Tillich reveled in Kierkegaard's attacks on Hegel and Schelling, not minding that Kierkegaard distorted both thinkers. Kierkegaard polemicized brilliantly on behalf of subjectivity, reflecting profoundly on anxiety and despair. Tillich came to Kierkegaard through Hirsch, he returned to Kierkegaard through Barth's second-edition *Romans*, and he had a third go-round with Kierkegaard through Heidegger. To Tillich, Kierkegaard and Marx fit together as a dialectical synthesis. Kierkegaard attacked essentialism within the idealistic framework, emphasizing the situation of the individual. Marx skewered the ideological taint in bourgeois thought, emphasizing the social situation, though Tillich judged that Marx wrongly confined this taint to the economic realm. Kierkegaard and Marx belonged together because both bonded truth to the situation of the knower. To them, knowledge of pure essence had to wait for contradictions within existence to be recognized and overcome.[158]

During his early career at Union Tillich helped streams of refugees who knew nothing of his philosophy. In 1942 he began to serve in another way, delivering weekly radio addresses for the Voice of America broadcast into Germany. Beginning at an Allied low point in the war and concluding just before D-Day 1944, Tillich wrote 112 speeches, each beginning with the salutation, "My German friends!" Passionately he condemned the Nazi annihilation of the Jews and called for the defeat of fascism. His first address described Jews as "the people of history, the people of the prophetic, future-judging spirit," declaring that the blood of the Jews was "upon us and our children." In December 1942 Tillich began to give detailed descriptions of the death trains and the machine-gun executions of Jews: "Today they are being hauled away to mass death by German hangmen, by those who are trash and the disgrace of the German people, and you are standing by! Can you stand by any longer, German officers, when you still have a sword to use and an honor to lose? . . . Do you know that the cattle cars that roll through the German cities with this burden of wretchedness are bolted up for days; that no bread and water is let in, no dying or dead are let out; and that at the end of the journey, frequently over half of the deportees are lying dead on the ice-cold floor of the car? And you want to be spectators of that, German clergy, you who are praying for German victory?"[159]

Bitterly he pronounced that the hope of a unified Europe led by Germany had been forfeited by the spectacular evil of the Nazi torturers and executioners: "I believe that National Socialism was the outbreak and the concentration of nearly all that was diseased within the German soul. Long have these poisons accumulated within it." At Advent he warned, "You can't have it both ways. Whoever follows National Socialism must persecute the child in the manger." He reached for the term "prehuman" to describe German life, contending that Germans needed to be reborn into the human race: "Two thousand years of German education out of barbarity into humanity have been taken back. The chivalry of the Middle Ages toward the enemy is forgotten, but the cruelty of the Middle Ages has arisen again and has brutalized the hearts and trampled all nobility underfoot. The humanity of the classical age of Germans is being made contemptuous, but the warlike instincts of the German past have become intensified beyond all boundaries." The Nazi regime was based on "the desire for human degradation, abuse and elimination of the enemy. . . . National Socialism is brutality coupled with lust for revenge and a deep inner weakness." With a hopeful spirit he added: "Everything that is creative in the German people demands a return to the human race. . . . For all nations—but particularly for Germany, the country of Middle Europe—everything will depend on the fact that the national remains subordinated to the human race as a whole."[160]

In the last months of the war Tillich chaired the Council for a Democratic Germany, a national German émigré organization calling for a disarmed Germany without economic or political dismemberment. It was a bruising experience that eviscerated his desire to play a role in American politics. Members of the council fiercely debated the group's exclusion of Communists, among other disagreements, and Tillich was blacklisted by the U.S. Army under the mistaken assumption that his chairmanship proved he was pro-German and pro-Communist. This taste of early anti-Communist hysteria repelled him from risking more of it. He carefully avoided contacts with activists in the orbit of the pro-Communist Old Left, which cut him off from most white activists who risked something for racial justice.

In 1948 Tillich returned to Germany, gave numerous lectures, and was warmly received, as long as he stayed off the topic of German guilt. He recoiled at the self-pity of his German friends and their refusal to count themselves guilty for the fate of European Jews. Tillich reasoned that their feeling of guilt was so great they were forced to repress it. He had an unexpectedly jovial reunion with Barth in Basel and a poignant reunion with Hirsch, who was blind, impoverished, bitter, and unapologetic. Offered teaching positions at numerous German universities, Tillich carefully considered each one but returned to the United States. He no longer worried that he could not write theology outside Germany. A collection of his articles, *The Protestant Era*, was published to great acclaim in 1948, as was a collection of his sermons, *The Shaking of the Foundations*. To a friend Tillich wrote, "Harvest time is here; indeed I am now gathering in my harvest!"[161]

Unlike Niebuhr, Tillich remained a socialist for the rest of his life. From 1933 to 1965 he wrote fourteen essays that were explicitly Marxist, usually after being invited by a magazine editor to explain his perspective. Tillich explained that neo-Marxian religious socialism remained central to his thinking. He had not really changed, although he became famous for writing about other things. He struggled to formulate a "system of existential truth," which consumed his American years. In 1945 Tillich remarked at a public discussion with Horkheimer, Löwe, and Pollock that he had to make a major adjustment upon moving to the United States: "I once believed that with the categories of religious socialism I could lead a fundamental change in Christian theology. But since then my hopes are confined to giving the American people a well-worked-out theology which they have never had. In 1920 it was different, then I wanted to inaugurate a new period of Christianity."[162]

Depth psychology took over the role that politics played in Tillich's previous work. He made a spectacular success but bristled when Americans misconstrued his shift in approach as a change of mind. In 1949 the *Christian Century* published an autobiographical essay by Tillich under the title "Beyond Religious Socialism." Tillich hated the title, correcting its mistaken impression. In 1952 he declared, "If the prophetic message is true, there is nothing 'beyond religious socialism.'" Even his view of Marx had not changed, hard as it was to say at the height of McCarthyism and the Cold War. Tillich said he still admired the "prophetic, humanistic and realistic elements in Marx's passionate style and profound thought," and he still rejected the "calculating, materialistic, and resentful elements in Marx's analysis, polemics, and propaganda." The Cold War, he allowed, snuffed out his guilty feeling that he should involve himself in political issues. It created a bipolar world that crushed any possibility of a theonomous third way between capitalism and Communism, making politics small and depressing. The tragedy of the fascist catastrophe gave way to the tragedy of Cold War dualism: "I lost the inspiration for, and the contact with, active politics."[163]

This was the Tillich who wrote psychologized best sellers on religious themes, especially *The Courage to Be,* and a massive three-volume *Systematic Theology.* He retired from Union in 1955, taught at Harvard University from 1955 to 1962, and taught at the University of Chicago Divinity School from 1962 until his death in 1965, lecturing across the nation and world to vast audiences. Many puzzled at his debt to Nietzsche and Heidegger. How could a theologian sympathize with Nietzsche's anti-Christian atheism? Part of the answer was that Tillich's idealist wellspring freed him to take daring excursions into the realms of radical doubt and criticism. He did not worry that he would lose his idealist language and inspiration—analytic philosophy had nothing to tempt him. He had an idealistic concept of what philosophy and theology should try to do. Moreover, Nietzschean disbelief aggressively stated the negative side of what Tillich believed. The God that Nietzsche and Heidegger rejected was the God that is bound to the structural dichotomy of subject and object. Tillich said that if God is an object for human subjects, and human beings are objects for God as a subject, God deprives every subject of her subjectivity by reducing her to an object of God's all-consuming power. The human subject, if merely an object, revolts, trying to make God into an object, "but the revolt fails and becomes desperate." If God is a being among other beings, God inevitably becomes the enemy of freedom and subjectivity: "This is the God Nietzsche said had to be killed because nobody can tolerate being made into a mere object of absolute knowledge and absolute control."[164]

Religious socialism was the political theology that went with Tillich's religious existentialism. He found that the audience for religious existentialism was far bigger, but religious socialism remained precious to him. Heimann drew out Tillich's feeling about it by publicly airing his long-running debate with Tillich about Marxism. Heimann taught at the New School and still admired the bold attempt of religious socialism to find a place for social struggle without pulling God to earth or raising humanity to heaven. He lauded Tillich for emphasizing the religious dignity of the proletarian movement as it was, refusing to wink at readers about the vices of the oppressed. He believed that Tillich improved upon Kutter and Ragaz in theorizing religious socialism. He still believed in 1952 that Tillich's conception of socialist theonomy was magnificent, even "immaculate." But Heimann changed his mind in the 1940s about the way he and Tillich had used Marxism. Heimann had always shared the Bernstein critique of Marxism, and later he wished that he and Tillich had not said that Marxian dialectic was what mattered. Tillich correctly perceived that Marx's utopianism was the key to everything that Marx got wrong, so Tillich conceived religious socialism as a realistic neo-Marxist corrective to

Marx's mistaken vision of the future. But Tillich wrongly believed that Marxism could be logically dissociated from utopianism. Heimann said the real conflict between Marxism and religious socialism was anthropological, not a disagreement about catastrophe thinking: "Tillich's error is in associating Marxist utopianism with its doctrine of revolution rather than with its doctrine of man, which, in an atheist system, occupies the place of theology."[165]

Neo-Marxists wrongly shucked off Soviet Communism as not Marx's fault and not their problem. In truth, Heimann argued, Marxism was deeply implicated in the Russian catastrophe, as all Marxists once knew. Heimann remembered that Tillich commended the Soviet Union in the early 1930s for cultivating a critical, antiauthoritarian, collective consciousness among the people. He recalled that Tillich employed the word "critical" almost synonymously with "creative" in pressing this argument, contending that the goal of Marxism was to produce creative people. He cited Tillich's repeated claim that Marxism and Tillich shared the same doctrine of the human person as a creative being constantly threatened by demonization, plus Tillich's emphasis that the utopian aspects of Marxism and Christianity had to be stripped out. Tillich had a vision of a purified Marxism that fit his vision of a purified Christianity. In fact, Heimann said, Tillich conceived religious socialism as an aid to the "kind of miracle" that Marx assumed would facilitate a utopian future. *The Socialist Decision* described the transition as a leap forward, a dramatic breakthrough that defied present circumstances and seemed impossible within them. Religious socialism, as Heimann keenly remembered it, was about helping Marxism recover its "scientific purity and religious profundity," making the breakthrough possible.[166]

Heimann was so embarrassed at having embraced this argument that he failed to say he had done so. He left himself out of it and said that Tillich seriously misinterpreted Marx's scientific message. Everything that Marx wrote as an economic analyst, Heimann observed, was directed toward the goal of proving "that the decline and beginning catastrophe of capitalism is, by the same token, the ascendancy of socialism, in the sense of making socialism the logically necessary effect of that cause." Bernstein did not exaggerate the extent of catastrophe utopianism in Marxism. Heimann still believed that Tillich's critique of capitalism was profound and compelling. Socialism was compelling as a moral and critical response to the dehumanization of the working class under capitalism and the periodic crashes of the capitalist system. But that was not Marxism, Heimann judged, no matter what academics like Tillich made of Marx.[167]

Marx taught that the institutional transformation of industrial existence by capitalism led logically and inevitably to a homogenous proletarian society.

To Marx and Lenin, it was an essential claim, "not just an accidental utopian whim," to say that communism would abolish the capitalist state while some-how enabling workers to take turns in various jobs in production and govern-ment. In Marxism, Heimann stressed, the transition to socialism is logical and inevitable, not a miracle. Since Tillich never believed that, he shucked it off as one of Marx's mistakes. Heimann admonished that Marx did not labor for the modest commanding heights model outlined in *The Socialist Decision*. More important, Christianity cannot be combined with dialectical materialism. Tillich was wrong to claim that Marx preserved the creative meaning of Hegel's dialectic because a specific Marxist end of the dialectic meant everything to Marx. On that count Marx was far more essentialist than Hegel. Heimann put it dramatically, wishing that Marx had been as Hegelian as neo-Marxists like Tillich claimed. Marxism, Heimann said, degraded "the noblest instrument of thought" to a mere means of establishing a universal mechanism of production and exchange. Marxism was a vision of human beings dialectically becoming cogs in a mechanism, "which on the one hand cannot sin because on the other it can no longer create."[168]

That set the template for Tillich scholars who wrote off Tillich's Marxism, ranging from ethical socialists to Niebuhrian realists to antisocialist conserva-tives. Many said Tillich would have done better to leave Marx out of it. Robert Fitch claimed that Tillich's interpretation of Marxism was "naïve, contradic-tory, and badly muddled," and Tillich never grasped "why Marxism in practice must lead to the Soviet Communist pattern." Alistair MacLeod agreed that Tillich was vague, intellectually sloppy, and incoherent on politics and theol-ogy. Clark Kucheman contended that Tillich failed to demonstrate any contra-dictions in the nature of capitalism because he based his analysis on Marx, who also failed. Eberhard Amelung judged that Tillich's religious socialism was an ideology in the sense of the term condemned by Marx—a mistaken and con-torted view of reality. Dennis McCann said Tillich commendably tried to be ontological and historical at the same time, and he commendably defied politi-cal convention by imagining an unlikely coalition of antifascist forces. But McCann judged that Tillich led much of modern theology astray by expound-ing kairos religious socialism as something more than a personal religious vision of a passing moment, which it was not. Tillich's writing in this area was highly oracular and intuitive, McCann noted—too much so to be commendable.[169]

Other Tillich scholars debated if and why Tillich dropped his commitment to religious socialism in 1934 or at some point afterward, usually 1948. Terence O'Keeffe said that Tillich's emigration to the United States marked "the end of his overt espousal of the socialist cause," and his subsequent work contained "little trace" of his previous debt to Marxism. Walter Weisskopf said Tillich's socialist writing stopped in 1934, and he never explained afterward why religious and Marxian socialism failed. Wilhelm Pauck and James Luther Adams, the two Tillich scholars closest to Tillich personally, said Tillich felt compelled in his American career to express his enduring Marxian socialist convictions in alternative ways. Both told stories about Tillich avoiding involvements that might have gotten messy. Pauck said Tillich had an extreme case of career ambition, and Adams said Tillich folded on the Communist issue, spurning fellow travelers. Ronald Stone and Guy Hammond documented that Tillich sustained his debt to Marxism, at least intellectually. James Champion adeptly noted that Tillich's theological imagination was sufficiently broad to be taken in other directions, yet his later books had religious socialist resonances. Brian Donnelly documented the implicit Marxism in Tillich's later books, superbly.[170]

My reading is that Tillich marshaled his signature ideas in his early career and refashioned them in different ways throughout his career. He remained the same kind of neo-Marxian religious socialist just as he remained the same kind of post-Kantian idealist and existentialist. He wrote about love, power, and justice in ways that reflected a religious socialist worldview without naming it. His politics were always there, which he never denied when pressed on the subject, even as Union students passed through his classroom with no clue he had ever been a Marxist or even politically active. He said as much in replying to Heimann, contending that a faithful church always inspires prophetic criticism, and he did not give up the kairos idea after World War II yielded the void of the Cold War.

The kairos idea, Tillich said, enabled him to experience the present void as sacred. To take on the void as sacred is to interpret, once again, the moment in the light of the eternal. It is to proclaim the kairos in a very different context, one demanding patient waiting in a vacuum, not transformative action. Realizing whom that sounded like, Tillich said Barth wrongly gave up the very idea of a concrete kairos, viewing the relation of the eternal to the temporal as a permanent crisis. Tillich did not regret having risked something in the twenties and thirties, even as he railed against utopianism. Neither did he believe there was only one kairos, the mistake of supernaturalistic Lutheranism: "I myself am convinced that the prophetic spirit will not leave the churches and mankind forever, and that the venturing judgment of a concrete historical moment, in spite of its unavoidable errors, will prove more creative than an ecclesiastical conservatism which clings tenaciously to the past."[171]

As for Marxism, the interpretive options are profuse, and Tillich did not accept Heimann's unsympathetic reading of Marx. To be sure, Marx bore some responsibility for orthodox Marxism, which turned dialectical materialism into a doctrine of metaphysical materialism. But Tillich stressed that he had always said so, and still did. Mechanical Marxism did not explain or cohere with Marx's revolutionary call to the proletariat, his "moral aggression against the bourgeoisie," or his prophetic rage against capitalist alienation. That was "genuine dialectics," Tillich said—the real thing that drew him to Marx and made him some kind of Marxist. He allowed that some of Marx's statements undoubtedly smacked of mechanistic determinism, but determinism is no more defining or fatal in Marxism than it is in Christianity.[172]

My regret about Tillich goes back to the religious obligation to struggle for justice. He might have followed through on it had he not burdened his political theology with Marxist requirements and expectations. That is a charitable reading. Less charitably, being a Marxist provided him an excuse to eschew the obligation. The religious socialists of Tillich's time who persisted through failure and disappointment, refusing to give up, were the realistic idealists who rooted themselves in real world struggles for justice and accepted ridicule for being idealistic. Quitting the struggle was not an option for them, and thus not considered. In the United States that group included Rauschenbusch, Vida Scudder, Reverdy Ransom, Benjamin E. Mays, Norman Thomas, Walter Muelder, Pauli Murray, and Martin Luther King Jr. In this chapter, it described Ragaz.

5

BRITISH BREAKTHROUGH: GUILD SOCIALIST VISIONS AND SOCIAL DEMOCRATIC REALITIES

British socialism was distinct in combining a rich Christian socialist tradition and a powerful Social Democratic politics. One might call it British exceptionalism, allowing for a similar exception in Canada. In England, Christian socialism and socialism were ethical, pragmatic, liberal, non-Marxist, culturally British, not very ideological, and thus exceptional. Well into the twentieth century the radical democratic wing of the Liberal Party in Britain held on to working-class voters who would have belonged, on the Continent, to socialist parties. The British Labour Party at its founding in 1906 was late in coming and ideologically amorphous. It did not acquire an official ideology until 1918, and the one it belatedly adopted—Fabian Collectivism—was the epitome of pragmatic, minimally ideological, religion-friendly, big-government Progressivism. Even after Labour declared it was a socialist party it remained the party of a labor movement, not a Continental-style socialist party, and this kept in play—at least for many—the question of what it was supposed to be.

In 1893 Keir Hardie founded the Independent Labour Party (ILP) to provide an alternative to being used by Liberals. George Bernard Shaw attended the founding convention, and Eduard Bernstein offered a supportive greeting. Hardie's ethical Christian socialism provided the spark but no real basis of unity. Hardie had begun working in Scottish mines at the age of seven, led the failed Ayrshire miners' strike in 1881, espoused the Single Tax in the 1880s, and drifted to Fabian socialism. Formally he was a Congregationalist, but his Christianity was nontheological, much like his nonideological socialism; thus he felt at home in the Labour Church. The ILP created a working-class party with vaguely socialist rhetoric. It grew rapidly in the North but failed to forge alliances with top union officials and organizations; thus it failed to elect anyone in 1895 while hurting the Liberals. In 1900 Hardie scaled up by founding the Labour Representation Committee (LRC), the forerunner of the Labour Party.

The LRC gathered unionized and nonunionized workers from the mill towns, a handful of Fabian Society intellectuals, the Social Democratic Federation (SDF), and, most important, the ILP, the core of the LRC. The new group, like the ILP, pulled the Liberal Party to the left and ran its own candidates—unionists whom Liberals looked down on. In 1906 the Liberals swept into office in a landslide election, making Henry Campbell-Bannerman the new prime minister, while the LRC won twenty-nine seats and renamed itself the Labour Party, with Hardie as leader. A secret pact between ILP leader Ramsay MacDonald and Liberal chief whip Herbert Gladstone paid off for both parties, winning seats for Labour in races uncontested by Liberals. MacDonald had come from Scottish poverty, night school, and freelance journalism, joining the ILP in 1894. He cut his activist teeth in the ILP and Fabian Society, became the founding secretary of the LRC, and personified the role of the ILP in the Labour Party—the ILP was a ginger group pulling Labour to the socialist left.[1]

The Church Socialist League was born the same year as the Labour Party, 1906, riding the same wave of northern union activism. It had Headlam's radical spirit but emphasized economic socialism and spurned the High Church exclusivity of the Guild of Saint Matthew (GSM). It was Anglican with a Broad Church ethos like the Christian Social Union (CSU) but emphatically working class, leftist, and committed to political activism. It eschewed shorthand, proudly going by its full name, which conveyed that it was church based, socialist, and a coalition. The Church Socialist League straightforwardly contended that the community should own all land and capital collectively, using both cooperatively for the good of all. From the beginning it had able Anglo-Catholic clerical leaders—G. Algernon West, Conrad Noel, Percy Widdrington, F. L. Donaldson, Paul Bull, and Egerton Swann. West was its pioneer founder, having come from the working class, one year of missionary college education in Islington, the GSM, and the SDF. He appreciated Headlam but knew that Anglican socialism could do better. He found a brilliant partner in Noel, who served as organizing secretary and speaker for the organization that West and Widdrington built.[2]

Conrad Noel grew up loathing his privileges in one of the queen's houses at Kew Green, getting his temperament from his father, Roden Noel, who served as groom of the privy chamber. Roden Noel wrote "The Red Flag," the solidarity anthem of the British Labour Party, the Northern Irish Social Democratic and Labour Party, and the Irish Labour Party, and his son hated the snobbery, corruption, and militarism of British public schools. For the rest of his life Conrad Noel blamed British imperialism on the public schools. He found Christian socialist mentors along the way, notably Eton tutors Henry S. Salt and James L. Joynes. Salt graduated from the Single Tax to Christian socialism and animal rights, and Joynes was a coeditor of the *Christian Socialist* before getting fired from Eton for being arrested with Henry George in Ireland. The other Joynes brother, Herman Joynes, more anarchist than socialist, was another important mentor to Noel at Eton, tutoring him in classics. The latter Joynes got Noel into Chichester Theological College during the early 1890s upsurge of Christian socialism, where Noel was thrilled to discover that St. Ambrose, St. Gregory the Great, and other church fathers forcefully condemned economic oppression. Ordained in 1894, Noel struggled for several years to obtain or keep a curacy, much like Headlam. He befriended GSM cleric William A. Morris—the legendary "Brother Bob" of the London labor movement—while Noel lectured to Labour Churches and socialist clubs in the Manchester area. Eventually Charles Gore found a job for Noel at St. Phillip's, Salford, getting him started; later he landed as a curate at Newcastle-at-Tyne, during the Boer War. Like nearly all the Christian socialist leaders, including Noel's GSM rector W. E. Moll, Noel opposed the Boer War. He stuck out for speaking vehemently against it to gatherings of munitions workers. Noel also stuck out for protesting that Christian socialism was a milk-and-water phenomenon smacking too much of the sanctuary.[3]

This protest yielded the founding of the Church Socialist League at the Morecambe Conference of 1906. By 1909 the organization had one thousand members in twenty-five branches, including a strong branch in Bristol headed by Charles L. Marson, and a journal, *Church Socialist Quarterly*. By 1911 it had seventeen branches in London alone, which lessened its northern proletarian ethos. From the beginning the leaders battled over how they should relate to the Labour Party and how much intellectual theorizing they needed. West wanted the league to align with Labour and keep theological and social theorizing to a minimum. The Christian faith, he said, endured by adapting, assimilating, and permeating; so should the Church Socialist League. Widdrington countered that assimilating with the Labour Party would be disastrous and the league needed all the Christian sociology it could get. Both sides rehashed whether Headlam had been right to spurn the ILP and to publish so much High Church theology. MacDonald and newcomer Christian socialist George Lansbury weighed in, both urging the league to align with the Labour Party. The league decided, however, that to remain definitely Anglican, radically socialist, and committed to activism, it needed to make no formal alliance with Labour, disappointing West, and to eschew seminar intellectualism, disappointing Widdrington. Noel spoke for the league during its prewar peak years and held it together, more or less, in the early war years, though he chafed at its theological vagueness, believing that only Anglo-Catholicism provided the sturdy theological basis that Christian socialism needed.[4]

The Labour Party got off to a dismal start. At first it was merely a pressure group appendage of the Liberal Party that Liberals didn't need to get their way in Parliament. Labour operated independently while lacking a definite view about Irish home rule, the House of Lords, female suffrage, and socialism. In 1908 three watershed transitions occurred. H. H. Asquith took over as prime minister, Arthur Henderson succeeded Hardie as Labour leader, and Labour made its first formal commitment to nationalizing the railways. For twenty years Hardie had pulled the movement toward his advocacy of nationalizing the mines, railways, and land. Henderson, a Methodist lay preacher and Scottish unionist, continued this socializing trend, winning a policy commitment in 1910 to nationalizing the waterways. Two years later the Labour Party called for nationalizing the coal mines; by then the politics had changed dramatically. In 1909 Chancellor of the Exchequer David Lloyd George pushed through a land tax that enraged the aristocracy. Asquith, battling the unelected House of Lords, was forced to bargain for Labour and Irish votes. Labour became an unofficial junior partner to the Asquith government, the last Liberal administration without a formal coalition. MacDonald was Labour's strongest voice, forming a duo with Henderson. His socialism was ethical, Edwardian, progressive, flexible, and statist, in the Fabian mode, but also pacifist and anti-imperialist. Britain was comparatively short on radical socialism. Scottish Labour Party founder James Connolly and English firebrand Tom Mann tried to ignite syndical movements, but revolutionary unionism made little headway in proudly civilized Britain — or so it seemed.[5]

Then Edwardian England crashed ingloriously. Edwardian England was a brief and hollowed-out version of Victorian England. The Victorian expansion of the English Empire had waned. The Boer War drained the English economy and dominated English international affairs. The clash between corporate capitalism and a growing union movement made labor strife routine. The Victorian belief that England had a national mission waned along with the British Empire and economy. In 1910 nine kings rode in the funeral procession for Edward VII, a formal ending. Britain seethed with protest movements over economic oppression, union rights, imperial overreach, women's rights, Irish home rule, and political representation. Syndicalists won beachheads in the railway unions and among Welsh miners. It seemed to literary doyen Virginia Woolf that "human character changed" in approximately December 1910: "All human relations have shifted—those between masters and servants, husbands and wives, parents and children. And when human relations change there is at the same time a change in religion, conduct, politics, and literature."[6]

The Labour Party, despite failing to define its program, and despite receiving blistering criticism from the left for failing, benefited from the turmoil and the war. When World War I began, Labour had 1.6 million members, the ILP had 30,000 members, and the Fabian Society had 3,304 members. By 1917 the Labour Party had 2.5 million members, in 1919 it had 3.5 million, and in 1920 it had 4.4 million. Sidney and Beatrice Webb, shrewd observers of arithmetic and political trends, joined the Labour Party in 1914. Labour needed political guidance, and they were happy to provide it. It helped that MacDonald's opposition to World War I turned him into a pariah, and the Webbs had frosty relations with Liberal leaders dating back to their alliance with Prime Minister Balfour. If Liberals insisted on parading their anti-imperialism, the Webbs preferred Tory company. By 1914 the Webbs wanted to retire to the country to write big books, but the war came and they threw in with Labour. In 1918 Sidney Webb and Henderson co-authored Labour's first Constitution, *Labor and the New Social Order*. It was pure Fabian Collectivism. The Labour Party morphed from a federation acting through affiliated societies to a national party with local branches in every parliamentary constituency. The Constitution subordinated the party's socialist societies and unions to a twenty-three-member executive board and established the party's four ideological pillars: full employment and a living wage, public control of industry, progressive taxation, and surplus spending for the common good. Clause Four, demanding public ownership of industry, defined the party for decades.[7]

Unlike most of Europe Britain did not clash between 1914 and 1924 with revolutionary violence, and its Communist party was tiny compared to Germany, France, and Italy. In Britain the surging party of the workers proclaimed that a strong dose of centralized progressive governance should be enough to fix the nation, beginning with nationalized railroads and coal mines. The wartime Coalition government of Lloyd George—the last Liberal to serve as prime minister—proved to many that vigorous government leadership was good for employment, wages, social welfare, and restraining the market, an outcome that roiled and split Lloyd George's party. Sidney Webb's ideological guidance gave the Labour Party the appearance of knowing what it believed. It wanted government economic planning without worker control of industry. Social Democracy was conceived in England on that basis.

British Christian socialism played a sizable role in legitimizing Labour socialism and in challenging its centralizing bias. It gave rectors, bishops, theologians, and activists to the struggle for democratic socialism, both centralized and not. Christian socialists persistently conceived socialism in moral terms, regardless of their ideological differences as cooperative socialists, Fabians, unionists, social unionists, syndicalists, guild socialists, romantic medievalists, or, later, mixed-economy revisionists. Most of them were similarly antiwar for ethical reasons, right up to Germany's invasion of Belgium, after which the Church Socialist League and CSU struggled to hold together. The war was passionately divisive in the league. Lansbury, Dick Sheppard, and *Church Socialist* coeditor Mary Phelps led its pacifist wing, while Swann (boisterously) and R. H. Tawney (temperately) defended the British war effort. Noel and Maurice Reckitt sided with Tawney while contending that the more important war was the one at home — the socialist struggle to make England worth defending. The latter view became a trademark of guild socialism. Noel, Reckitt, Widdrington, Tawney, Paul Bull, and A. J. Penty pulled most of the league into the guild socialist movement, touting the moral-communitarian spirit of the guild idea. Other Christian socialists gravitated to state socialism, sometimes joining the Fabian Society. Scott Holland and the CSU, both fading when England went to war, commended the Fabians for compelling the state to accept its moral obligations. But Holland lived to see an outburst of decentralizing radicalism among Christian socialists and, more remarkably, the Fabian Society.

.   The idea of decentralized economic democracy had a history in every cooperative network and every union movement that strove for worker ownership. It fired the revolutionary unions that dreamed of running the nation on syndical terms. It permeated every version of cooperative socialism linked to Robert Owen, F. D. Maurice, John Ludlow, John Ruskin, William Morris, and French radicalism. In the United States the syndicalism of the Industrial Workers of the World and the Socialist Labor Party had a national or statewide focus, dreaming of One Big Union and one big strike. French and American syndicalism were both catastrophic, contending that capitalism had to be destroyed by many little strikes or one big one. In Britain syndicalism had a fervent but small union following. British guild socialism made a bold attempt to change this picture.

The founders of guild socialism were exiles from the Fabian Society or dissenters within it. They refashioned the syndicalist idea by invoking medieval and literary nostalgia, banking on the hope of no violence, and appealing to middle-class intellectuals. They said the nation's productive life should be organized and operated by self-governing democratic organizations, the National Guilds. These guilds would emerge from the existing trade union movement, embracing all workers in every industry and service. The guilds would organize industry but not own it. They would be owned by the state, which provided the capital, while the guilds produced the goods.

Guild socialism variously combined the best parts of state socialism, syndicalism, Christian socialism, romantic medievalism, and cooperative reformism. It had a backstory in the writings of Ruskin and Morris, but its twentieth-century history began with an Anglo-Catholic Fabian admirer of Ruskin and Morris, Arthur J. Penty. In 1906 Penty's book *The Restoration of the Guild System* registered the disgust he felt at Fabian meetings. A Church Socialist League architect, his turning point had occurred when Sidney Webb selected a utilitarian architect for the London School of Economics. Penty flushed with revulsion at the philistinism of the Fabian mind, realizing he could not work with Fabians. Fabian Collectivism was socialism without a soul. Penty reflected on why he treasured Ruskin and Morris; his book was the answer. Ruskin said trade unions should convert themselves into self-governing guilds, refashioning the medieval guilds. Morris imagined a decent, beautiful, civilized society in which people found happiness in equality. Penty said he no longer cared about the battle of existing socialisms because Fabian Collectivism had already won it, "owing to the superior logic of its position." He took for granted that Fabianism was the only existing form of socialism that made sense. He had gone to Fabian meetings until he couldn't take any more. He loved Ruskin's dream of worker self-governance, but it died with Ruskin and Morris. The time had come to revive their dream of a decent society.[8]

Somehow the medieval traditions of craftsmanship, self-regulation, and self-government had to be recovered. Penty said capitalism was corrupting and dehumanizing, while Fabian Collectivism was corrupting and balefully bureaucratic. The guilds could not be recovered by refashioning modern lines of development. Only social forces that opposed modern development could do it. He named three: trade unions, the arts and crafts movement, and religion. Religion was crucial because it always linked back to something; Penty declared that reverence for the past "is the hope of the future." His book inspired two Fabians, A. R. Orage and Holbrook Jackson, to revamp an old radical magazine, *The New Age*, in May 1907, with Bernard Shaw's money. Orage, a brilliant editor, turned *New Age* into a must-read sensation, the best politics-and-culture magazine of its time. He recruited a sparkling cast of writers featuring Shaw, Penty, Ezra Pound, Havelock Ellis, H. G. Wells, Belfort Bax, Hilaire Belloc, G. K. Chesterton, and, most important, S. G. Hobson.[9]

New Age blistered Labour as a total sellout, declaring in November 1908, "We sent the Labour Party to Parliament to make war on Toryism and Liberalism, not to make terms with them. The Labour Party is dead." The magazine had no party line, acquiring must-read status by being interesting, but Orage and Hobson got a movement going for guild socialism, eventually calling it "guild socialism" in 1912. *New Age* had a flank of writers who idealized medieval society in Penty's style, imagining a communal society lacking a division of labor. Orage and Hobson were more worldly, writing edgy, intellectually rigorous articles emphasizing that the guild idea was socialist. Political theorist G. D. H. Cole was a prominent convert, fighting for guild socialism in the Fabian Society and Labour Party, clashing with the Webbs in both places. Reckitt, Noel, Penty, and Widdrington persuaded most of the Church Socialist League that socialism was more Christian and radical when realized as a community of communities, not a central collective. Political philosopher John Neville Figgis provided crucial ballast for this idea in a stream of writings on political pluralism. Figgis, an Anglo-Catholic socialist cleric and monk in Gore's Community of the Resurrection at Mirfield, never quite joined the Church Socialist League, and his orthodox theology and antivoluntarism made him very different from Cole, Orage, and Hobson. But Figgis greatly influenced Cole and the Church Socialist League.[10]

Meanwhile Belloc and Chesterton popularized a Roman Catholic and Anglo-Catholic antimodernist version of the guild idea, "Distributism"—a return to the guild economics that prevailed in Europe for the thousand years it was Catholic. Distributism had a British tradition dating to William Cobbett's *History of the Protestant Reformation in England and Ireland*, serialized in 1823–1824, which contrasted an idealized medieval society with the poverty and degradation wrought by the Reformation. Belloc's *The Servile State* (1912) shrewdly reworked this story, contending that capitalism shaped the course of industrialization in England as a consequence of the destruction of English monasteries, not as a natural outgrowth of the industrial revolution. Belloc wrote as an orthodox Roman Catholic steeped in the teaching of *Rerum Novarum* that property ownership is a fundamental right that should be widely distributed in society. Chesterton wrote as an Anglo-Catholic on his way to Roman Catholicism, converting in 1922. Both were dazzling writers who reached mass audiences. Belloc repeated his church's condemnations of socialism, but guild socialists counted him as an ally.[11]

For a while guild socialists seriously challenged the centralizing impulse of modern politics and the Fabian movement, touting the ethical, humanizing, decentralized superiority of the guild idea. Noel split the Church Socialist League in 1916, forming a new organization in 1918, the Catholic Crusade, a name reflecting Noel's ardor: Ecumenism of any kind, either within or beyond Anglicanism, was too frothy to change the world. Guild socialism, a militant idea, needed a serious theological basis, which only Anglo-Catholicism provided. Others countered that Christian socialism had to be ecumenical to justify its rhetoric about being ethical, humanizing, and freedom loving. In both cases guild socialism and its theory of state pluralism were not mere theories. The Guildsmen, as they called themselves, were dead serious about transforming British society. They campaigned for guild socialism through the war years and into the 1920s, faltering in 1923 after the economy turned bad and the Labour Party funds for the National Guilds League dried up. Cole settled for a distinguished academic career at Oxford and a new role in the Labour Party as a state socialist. Tawney adjusted to what worked for the Labour Party, becoming its leading intellectual. Temple scaled the hierarchy of Anglican bishoprics and made a case for a modest guild socialism. Guild socialism became an academic theory and a defeated flank in the Labour Party and Christian socialist movements, an experimental enterprise that named what many preferred and still imagined. It stayed alive for many as an Anglo-Catholic or Roman Catholic protest against the modern age and an idea of economic life conforming to natural law.

It mattered that England's best young socialists preferred to see what was possible along guild socialist lines. Then they adjusted to the triumph of the Fabian idea in Labour Party politics. Temple, Tawney, and Cole were prolific, quintessentially English intellectuals of their generation, seeing the world through a British lens, plus too political not to be pragmatic about their favorite ideas. All were graduates of Balliol College, Oxford, and draped in the privileges that came with their training. All were deeply involved in the working-class movement for adult education, the Workers' Educational Association (WEA), deriving the greatest satisfaction of their careers from this work. Cole became a socialist upon learning as a college student that socialism and William Morris existed. Temple and Tawney joined the CSU on its way up. Cole was proletarian, temperamental, and atheistic, making radical socialism his religion. Temple was gregarious, jolly, and philosophical, radiating spiritual conviction. Tawney was legendarily modest and influential, although he bristled when friends called him a Christian socialist, since socialism was universal to Tawney. Everyone should be a socialist, he said, so socialism should not be qualified with sectarian labels.

GROWING UP EDWARDIAN: TEMPLE AND TAWNEY

William Temple was born in 1881 in the Palace at Exeter, Devon, England, as the second son of Frederick Temple, then bishop of Exeter. Temple's grandfather Octavius Temple was lieutenant governor of Sierra Leone before retiring to Devon, and Frederick Temple spent much of his career weathering a spectacular national controversy over a slightly liberal theological book, *Essays and Reviews* (1860), to which he contributed a mildly liberal chapter. Frederick Temple's success at church politics legitimized Broad Church liberalism in the Church of England, an achievement sealed by his enthronement as archbishop of Canterbury in 1896. He was a quintessential Victorian whose lifespan matched Queen Victoria's almost exactly and who presided at her Diamond Jubilee in 1897. He came late to marriage, having been a bishop for five years before marrying an aristocratic woman, Beatrice Lascelles, who grew up in two castles. Frederick Temple was nearly sixty years old when his second son was born. William Temple adored his parents and grew up wanting to be like them. He mused that his mother got most of her education by soaking up conversations with such guests as William Gladstone and Matthew Arnold.[12]

From an early age Temple wanted to be a cleric like his father, although he grew up to be exceedingly genial, unlike his father, and he dropped his father's colonial racism and Tory-leaning Liberal politics. Temple was schooled at Rugby, which Thomas Arnold built into a bastion of Broad Church refinement in the 1830s and where Frederick Temple served as headmaster from 1858 to 1869. Billy Temple was buoyant, friendly, self-confident, and expressive, making friends easily. At Rugby he befriended Harry Tawney, who was shy and withdrawn. The often-told story of their meeting is not true, as they did not meet at the railway station on their first day of school. Tawney began at Rugby a year ahead of Temple, and their friendship commenced during a summer holiday in 1896, when Temple was fifteen and Tawney was sixteen. Tawney recalled that Temple was reading Kant's *Critique of Pure Reason*, while Tawney splashed in the water and fished. Temple and Tawney were best friends before they became Christian socialists and remained both for the rest of their lives.[13]

Born in 1880 in Calcutta, India, Richard Henry Tawney rarely said anything about his family except that he chose a different path. His father, Charles H. Tawney, was a distinguished historian and Sanskrit scholar who mastered Hindi, Urdu, Persian, and numerous European classical and modern languages. Charles Tawney joined the Bengal Education Department in India in 1864 after graduating from Rugby and Trinity College, Cambridge. He taught history at the University of Calcutta and served as principal of the university's Presidency College, adding three stints as university registrar. Tawney biographers have clashed over Charles Tawney's ostensible sense of cultural superiority and his son's ostensible rebellion against it. Ross Terrill said both were real, and Tawney vowed from an early age not to carry on his father's work of ruling and enlightening Britain's colonial subjects. However, Tawney's nephew and literary executor, Michal Vyvyan, and Tawney biographer Lawrence Goldman vehemently disputed both assertions, claiming that Charles Tawney deeply respected Indian culture and his son became alienated from him over academic disappointment and socialism, not India and colonialism.[14]

Both interpretations make both Tawneys come out too much one way. Charles Tawney was never a member of the Indian Civil Service, and he devoted his scholarship to making Hindu epics available to Western audiences. Still, he had a missionary streak, and his milieu reeked of colonial snobbery. On occasion he made caustic remarks about British imperialism, much like his son, who was not outspoken on this issue and who said that British imperialism was inadvertent, not so bad, and not really imperialist. R. H. Tawney registered conventional progressive disdain of British colonialism and nothing more. He wrote almost nothing about India, refusing to go there, while writing hundreds of pages about China and going there twice. He wrote prolifically about England's industrial revolution but took no interest in his family's substantial role in it—the Oxford area Tawneys did very well in banking, beer, timber, and engineering, lifting the family to upper-middle-class status. At the age of five Tawney left India with his mother, Constance Tawney, and seven siblings. Constance Tawney had had enough of India, waiting seven years in England before her husband rejoined her and their children in 1892. Two years later Harry Tawney went to Rugby to prepare for Oxford. By all accounts he was keen for Rugby and Oxford, excelling at Rugby's regime of classics, the Bible, and religious formality, although Tawney later shuddered at being a child of privilege. He also recalled that Rugby religion conveyed the impression that the events of the gospels "all happened on a Sunday."[15]

Tawney and Temple enrolled at Balliol, respectively, in 1899 and 1900, versed in Balliol lore about T. H. Green, Arnold Toynbee, Benjamin Jowett, Scott Holland, and Charles Gore. They studied "Mods and Greats" (Classical Moderations followed by Literae Humaniores) and befriended classmate William Beveridge, later the architect of Britain's welfare state. Beveridge was born in 1879 in Rangpur, where his father was a judge in the Indian Civil Service. Schooled at Charterhouse in Surrey, Beveridge enrolled at Balliol in 1899 and became Tawney's closest friend except for Temple. He also had a sister, Jeanette Beveridge, through whom he became Tawney's brother-in-law.

Balliol's closed-club atmosphere produced privileged achievers who were comfortable with males and not with females. Tawney epitomized the type; Temple overcame it only through extroversion and becoming a cleric. In 1893 neo-Hegelian philosopher Edward Caird took the helm at Balliol, succeeding Jowett as master. Caird was the younger brother of theologian John Caird, a fellow Scottish Hegelian influenced by Green. Temple flourished at Balliol, serving as president of the Oxford Union and deeply imbibing Caird's idealism. Hegelian logic was second nature to Temple. He looked for the dialectic in everything, exuding Caird's rationalistic social idealism. Temple absorbed the Christian socialism of the Green-to-Gore tradition at Balliol and joined the protectionist Tariff Reform League, though he annoyed members by arguing that protectionism would make England poorer, in a good way, by forcing England to become more cooperative in its economic life. By his sophomore year he was fully himself. Upon graduating from Balliol in 1904 Temple was showered with thirty academic offers, accepting a philosophical Fellowship at Queen's College, Oxford. He moved leftward with the CSU during the phase that Christian socialism got serious about forging alliances with trade unions.[16]

Temple gave six years to an academic career, specializing in classical and English philosophy. He kept reading Hegel, surprised himself by developing an admiration for Spinoza, and took a study leave in Germany with Tawney. Temple alarmed faculty colleagues by plunging into socialist activism and laughing uproariously in the Oxford Senior Common Room. Some colleagues found his laughter unbearable. Evolutionary biologist Julian Huxley disagreed, later recalling, "It was laughter in the grand manner and on the largest scale, earth-shaking laughter that shook the laugher too. While it infected everybody who heard it with cheerfulness, it was a potent disinfectant against all meanness, prurience, and petty-mindedness. It was the intensely valuable complement of Temple's deep seriousness." In 1905 Temple joined the newly founded WEA, which taught courses in humanities and social science to workers, and later served as its president for sixteen years. In 1908 he declared at the Pan-Anglican Congress that he was a democratic socialist and a believer that the church needed to move in a socialist direction: "If Christianity is to be applied to the economic system, an organization which rests primarily on the principle of competition must give way to one which rests primarily on cooperation." The following year he was ordained to the priesthood by Archbishop of Canterbury Randall Davidson, putting him on a clerical track: headmaster of Repton School from 1910 to 1913 and rector of St. James, Piccadilly, London, from 1914 to 1919.[17]

The way was harder for Tawney. Balliol trained its students to be graciously superior gentlemen, a struggle for Tawney. He lacked Temple's outgoing confidence, despite winning the top classical entrance scholarship to Balliol in his class. Balliol gentlemen were supposed to make society better by lending their grace and intelligence to it. To express their self-confident seriousness they used their initials instead of their first names; thus Tawney became R. H. He also grew a moustache that remained for the rest of his life. Tawney did not join the

Arnold Society and was not asked to write for school papers. He recoiled at Caird's exhortation to heed the Call of India, although Caird had a related theme that stuck with Tawney: Find out why England had so much poverty alongside its riches and do something about it. Tawney and Beveridge founded their own little group, delivering papers on social issues, and Tawney joined the ILP, a harder-edged crowd than the CSU, which he also joined.

Some faculty perceived that Tawney was brilliant, and others were much less impressed. He won a First in Mods and was expected to excel in Greats (Greek philosophy, ancient history, logic, and moral and political philosophy). Later he had trouble admitting that Balliol noblesse oblige rubbed off on him, and he desperately wanted an academic career. In Tawney's telling, Oxford was a high school for gentlemen, not a real university, and he recoiled at Balliol's pretensions. Tawney, however, did not get the career he wanted because he earned a Second in Greats. The examiners determined that he bluffed and bloviated about books he never read. Privately they tagged him a "fraud." Charles Tawney was devastated, inquiring, "How do you propose to wipe out this disgrace?" Tawney tried to shrug it off, then and later. He told Beveridge at least it spared him from enduring more family expectations. Caird, perhaps not knowing why Tawney had done poorly, told Tawney's former teacher at Rugby, "I grant you his mind was chaotic: but his examiners ought to have seen that it was the chaos of a great mind."[18]

Tawney's chaotic brilliance needed the discipline of a field, regardless of what he read or faked. Suddenly he had to rethink what to do with his life. Beveridge graduated with Tawney in 1903, won a First and an Oxford fellowship at University College, and took his fellowship to Toynbee Hall, serving as Samuel Barnett's subwarden. Tawney vacationed with Temple in Germany, nursed his wounded ego, winced at the anti-English attitudes of Germans, ruled out the English civil service, and welcomed an invitation from Barnett: come to Toynbee Hall. Charles Tawney entreated his son not to waste his life doing social work. Tawney, however, had Caird, Gore, Holland, and Ruskin in his head just enough to hold off Charles Tawney.

He grew close to Barnett, who became a father figure to him, an exemplar of social Christianity. Tawney embraced Barnett's mission to share the benefits of university culture with working-class people. He taught classes on nineteenth-century writers and modern theology, which confirmed Tawney's resolve to leave theology, Hegel, and all things philosophical to Temple. The parts of Christianity that spoke to Tawney did not have to be theologized, notwithstanding that Tawney regarded Gore as his chief mentor. He began to disparage his education, opining that classics and scholarship were vain enterprises for snobs.

Tawney taught for three years at Toynbee Hall, developed a course on trade unions, and deepened his commitment to socialism. He and Beveridge cotaught a course on social institutions that proved to be formative for both of them. Tawney was finding his subject, plus his historical approach to it. In 1905 he and Beveridge met the Webbs, who were impressed with Beveridge and not with Tawney. Beatrice Webb sharply reproved Tawney for accidentally walking off with the hat of a Liberal minister, John Burns. Gradually Tawney and Beveridge chafed at the limitations of settlement work. Albert Mansbridge had founded the WEA in 1903 to reach larger numbers of workers. In 1905 Tawney joined the executive board of the WEA and recruited Temple to be its first president. To Temple, working for the WEA was transforming; to Tawney, it was transforming and the key to his entire career.

Mansbridge was an archetypal victim of England's class system. His father had refused a Grammar School scholarship for him because that would have been unfair to three older brothers who lacked an education. Mansbridge began as a clerk in the Co-operative Wholesale Society, networked assiduously, and developed a social Christian philosophy: Education was enriching for working-class people, not just the privileged. Oxford should justify its privileged existence by supporting educational opportunities for working people. The best reform work fostered institutions that allowed working people to fulfill their potential. Small tutorial classes that nurtured personal relationships were better than big lecture classes. Unionized and nonunion workers had to solve their own problems, mobilize their own forces, and create a cooperative social order. Spiritual character was more important than politics, and unions had to be kept from taking over the WEA.

Mansbridge recruited Gore, Tawney, Temple, Fabian neo-Hegelian philosopher A. D. Lindsay, and other Oxford friends to sponsor a joint committee governing board of Oxford and WEA representatives. He formed a close friendship with Tawney and instilled a spiritual ethos in the WEA, imploring tutors and staff not to politicize its mission. Mansbridge's religiosity sparked a factional divide in the organization that Temple and Tawney mediated, even as Tawney believed increasingly that adult education should empower workers for political struggle. Temple said the WEA invented him, providing the integral focus for his work. Tawney, though never emoting like Temple, said the same thing was truer for him. He enjoyed the assertive, spunky spirit of his students in the mill towns who created the Labour Party, a far cry from the beaten-down subservience of London's East End poor. Tawney's early Christian socialism was about mobilizing local communities to become self-determined, not about building a Fabian state.[19]

He came alive in the WEA classes at Rochdale, Longton, Littleborough, Wrexham, and Chesterfield. Tawney radiated moral seriousness and care, winning the affection of potters, spinners, loom operators, and velvet menders. He later recalled with typical ironic modesty that his "very improper conceit" helped him to succeed. Tawney assumed that workers would agree with him as soon as they were enlightened, so he "never felt tempted to engage in propaganda." His job was to promote enlightenment, taking the shortest way home. His classes set the gold standard for adult education in England. Tawney was a rigorous teacher who did not act like he belonged to a privileged class. He bantered with students and corrected their arguments. He was shabby and disheveled, always looking like he had slept in his clothes, which bemused his students and appalled his bride, Jeanette. He welcomed Marxists but skewered their slogans about abolishing profit and the state. He loved the work, appreciating that workers were desperate to learn about things that mattered, a far cry from the university. Tawney was fond of saying that many academics "make a darkness and call it research, while shrinking from the light of general ideas." He never forgot that he did not find his academic field in the academy.[20]

In 1906 Tawney began teaching part-time at Glasgow University and joined the Fabian Society, though he did not endorse state collectivism until 1919. In 1909 he persuaded Jeanette Beveridge to marry him, unhappily for her. She wanted romantic love, and he wanted a movement partner. He had very little experience with women or interest in them. Her mother adamantly opposed the marriage, pegging Tawney as a loser who would not make a good living, which helped Tawney win the argument. Barnett and Temple conducted the wedding, urging the young couple, in Jeanette's doleful telling, to make each other spiritually uncomfortable as a brake against smug contentment. They lived in Manchester for five years, suiting Tawney's commutes to WEA classes. Jeanette Beveridge came from privilege and liberal refinement. Her father supported Indian nationalism and the Congress Party, despite his job. She graduated from Somerville College, Oxford, in 1899 and was vibrant, playful, and a shrewd judge of Tawney's character. Though Jeanette was politically progressive and gave speeches on women's suffrage, social activism was not her life. She knew better than to marry someone lacking tenderness and wedded to activism, but she married him anyway, committing the mistake of her life. Tawney, in his way, was good to Jeanette Tawney, supporting her through decades of her many illnesses and disappointments. But his model of an ideal spouse was Beatrice Webb, who described her marriage as a movement partnership. Jeanette paid dearly for marrying the wrong person and then came off as an eccentric nuisance in literature about her husband.[21]

A few months after her wedding Jeanette Tawney fell seriously ill with swollen legs and colitis. She battled chronic illnesses for the rest of her life. In her telling, she and Tawney fought almost constantly from the beginning, at first about his uncleanly habits, although her habits were similarly chaotic. She spent long periods of their early marriage convalescing alone in Italian hospitals, while Tawney found his work and voice, writing articles for the WEA monthly magazine *Highway*. These articles yielded his first book in 1912, *The Agrarian Problem in the Sixteenth Century*. Tawney's historical passion was the seventeenth-century transition from feudalism to early capitalism. His first book backed up a century to account for it, examining the changing class relationships on the land in the Tudor period. He argued that the rural economy before the sixteenth century was not stagnant, allowing industrious peasants to develop small-scale enclosures. In the Tudor era the growth of the textile industry provided incentives for wool production that made sheep pasturing more productive than traditional tillage. Single proprietors consolidated large-scale enclosures and evicted customary tenants. Small farms were amalgamated into large leasehold forms for pasture, which facilitated the enclosure of common land in the seventeenth century. Tawney argued that the transition out of feudalism changed the concept of land itself, not merely the use of land and who owned it. Land became an income-yielding investment, not the basis of political functions and obligations. Contrary to Whig celebrations of the seventeenth century as a breakthrough for personal liberty against a corrupt crown, Tawney said that a predatory aristocracy savaged the rural economy, albeit with high-minded rhetoric about securing freedom from the crown.[22]

The Agrarian Problem in the Sixteenth Century was an academic treatise and a movement book, presenting English economic history as a subject worthy of respect on both counts. For the rest of his life Tawney stressed that much of his first book did not come from books. In 1914 he teamed with two fellow WEA tutors, Public Record Office researcher Alfred E. Bland and Durham University lecturer P. A. Brown, to publish a volume of primary documents, *English Economic History*. Tawney was already thinking like a scholar of an emerging field, building an audience by publishing source material in political and constitutional history. Sadly, however, all three coeditors were soon called to war, two were killed in battle and the other was very nearly killed.[23]

Although Tawney was quiet about his personal religion and averse to theology, he shared the same faith as Temple, who was eloquent about religion and a profound theologian. Giving up his career at Oxford was Temple's way of taking the path of humility. He was geared for big thoughts, big books, activism, and running things, yet he chose a parish ministry track for which he was less suited. Temple understood that he could not be a good pastor if he acted like an Oxford don, so he got by on humor and geniality and worked at small talk. On the side, he developed his ideas in small books. Temple said he was too Hegelian to be either inductive or deductive. He approached a group of facts, the facts suggested a theory, the theory gave him a fuller grasp of the facts, the fuller grasp led to modifications of the theory, and so on. He made sense of the problem of Christology by distinguishing between the human will and divine will in Jesus. Temple reasoned that the will of Christ was both human and divine simultaneously. It was human because that which willed was human, and it was divine because that which was willed was the divine will.

Orthodox Christology from the Council of Chalcedon onward committed Christianity to a two-natures doctrine. Temple argued that the concepts of spirit and will are more fluid and spiritual than the category of substance employed at Chalcedon. In a real sense it is possible for two persons to share the same mind or will. Form and content are inseparable in mind and identical in content. The identity of content affects the form. Temple took his belief about the superiority of subject over substance from Hegel and his emphasis on the subject as will from American neo-Hegelian philosopher Josiah Royce. Ecclesiastically he straddled the Anglo-Catholic and Modernist parties without belonging to either, disliking the Modernist emphasis on what it disbelieved. Temple said his ideal of the Church had no sharply defined boundaries. The unity of the Church was like a ray of light, bright at its center and shooting out in all directions without definite ending points. At the same time, Temple said, the teaching of Christ condemned selfishness and injustice, an obligatory matter for all Christians. His first social Christian book, *The Kingdom of God* (1913), blasted capitalist competition as "a thing that pervades our whole life. It is simply organized selfishness." If capitalism was right to make competition the rule of life, "Christ was wrong."[24]

When the war came Temple preached sermons that mentioned it as little as possible, believing the church needed to be a brake on jingoism. He played a leading role in the Church of England's wartime National Mission of Repentance and Hope, a campaign to uphold England's (fading) sense of itself as a Christian nation committed to Christian values. One National Mission report lamented that a "limitless desire for riches, for power, for pleasure, has run like a flame through the nations," taking possession of the relations between nations. One of Temple's maxims, "Keep clear the character of God," applied especially to wartime sermons. He urged parishioners not to enlist God as a partisan in the war or to speak of the war as God's judgment or will: "We can trace the actual causes of the war, and we know quite well that its causes were in human wills, and we are not at liberty to say that God intervened in the history of the world to inflict anguish and pain by means of the war." Temple allowed that "one nation" bore most of the blame for starting the war, "but the root is to be found among all peoples, and not only among those who are fighting, but neutral peoples just as much." There is a divine moral order, its violation by all individuals and nations leads to terrible wars, and God cares about the salvation of the world. Many said that Temple's joviality was a welcome tonic that helped them get through the war. For as long as the war returned dead and wounded soldiers to Britain, Temple played down the imperial factor. Then he risked public rebuke by insisting that liberal internationalism was the alternative to wars of empire.[25]

Tawney risked his life and very nearly lost it in the war. In 1912 he took a job writing for the *Manchester Guardian* and another job running the Ratan Tata Foundation at the London School of Economics, which paid him to conduct antipoverty research. He and Jeanette moved to Mecklenburgh Square in London, between Bloomsbury and Holborn, where they lived in various dwellings for the rest of their lives. Tawney was thirty-three years old when the war began. He stewed with guilt feelings for three months as soldiers drilled in the streets of London. Then he enlisted in November 1914 with the 7th City Battalion of the Manchester Regiment, as a private. He would not stay out of the war or take an army commission, although he wavered for months about accepting a commission since he and Jeanette needed the money. Finally he told Jeanette that staying in the ranks involved him as deeply in the army as he could stand. He detested the military in every way but one, never doubting that England had to thwart German aggression and militarism.[26]

By April 1915 he was a corporal in the Twenty-second Manchester Regiment, and five months later he was promoted to sergeant. Tawney felt his status incongruity, not belonging anywhere. He could not fraternize with officers, even if they were former classmates, and he had trouble relating to his fellow noncommissioned officers. He drilled in the streets of Manchester and at three army bases before landing in northern France, at Boulogne, in November 1915. Tawney surprised himself by liking France immensely. He had warm conversations with locals in French villages and worked at perfecting his French. He told Beveridge he felt better about fighting for France than for England. The French Revolution, he surmised, made the difference; the French were open and expansive in ways that Britons rarely managed. Tawney never changed his mind about France being the world's best nation. He entered the line of fighting in December 1915, thereafter rotating in and out of trenches. He loathed the lice, vermin, mud, and officers, complaining that idiots commanded brave

British troops. In 1916 he lucked into a welcome captain, his friend Alfred (Bill) Bland, who had turned down a chair at Melbourne University to enlist as an officer. Finally Tawney knew one officer he respected.

On June 30, 1916, his battalion received a Special Order at Fricourt in the battle of the Somme, absolutely forbidding any use of the word "retire." The following morning Tawney led his platoon across three lines of trenches and took cover in the fourth. They were hit with machine gun fire and fired back, killing many Germans. Tawney said that for a while he downed so many soldiers it felt like he could not miss. He didn't hate the Germans he killed: "That's the beastliest thing in war, the damnable frivolity. One's like a merry mischievous ape tearing up the image of God." His comrades were wounded and killed all around him. Trying to rally his company, Tawney threatened to shoot a soldier who buried his head in the ground and cried. The soldier resumed fighting, and Tawney crawled over corpses in search of survivors. He spotted a tiny group of survivors to his right, knelt upward and waved, and was shot by a machine gun through his chest and abdomen, crumpling to the ground. He thought, "This is death," hoping it would not take long. Later he recalled, "What I felt was that I had been hit by a tremendous iron hammer, swung by a giant of inconceivable strength, and then twisted with a sickening sort of wrench so that my head and back banged on the ground, and my feet struggled as though they didn't belong to me."[27]

Gasping for breath and writhing with pain in his stomach, Tawney found he could not move. All he could do was lie on his back and wait to die. He raised his knees to ease the pain, making him a target for sniper fire. He said he lost interest in living, just like Tolstoy's account of the death of Prince Andrew, although he wondered how Tolstoy knew. Tawney lay in the open throughout the day and evening, bleeding and lacking water. Finally a corporal in the Royal Army Medical Corps found him, summoning a medic, who bandaged Tawney and gave him morphine in the face of sniper fire, believing Tawney had no chance to survive. The following day Tawney was evacuated. His battalion of 20 officers and 754 soldiers no longer existed, as 241 were wounded, 120 were killed, and 111 were never found. A total of 20,000 British soldiers were killed in one day of battle, and 40,000 were wounded. Tawney was barely alive when the army got him out. He was sent to three makeshift military hospitals near Oxford, landing at Cuddeson, where Gore came to see him. Gore tracked down the hospital matron, imploring her: "Remember you have in your care one of the most valuable lives in England." The matron rushed to Tawney's bed to scold him: "Why ever didn't you *tell* us you were a *gentleman?*"[28]

Healing from his wounds, Tawney wrote an edgy article for the *Nation* contrasting the shabby mediocrity of British life and the stupidity of officers to the brave solidarity of the Tommies at the front. British soldiers did not hate the Germans, he said, unlike British editorialists. In an article for the *Welsh Outlook* that the WEA reprinted as a pamphlet, *Democracy or Defeat*, Tawney said patriots and pacifists both mistook the vehicle of war for its spirit. Patriotism nerved soldiers to fight only for a few weeks. Pacifists refused to take moral responsibility for creating a decent social order. Tawney contended that war drives soldiers to their common humanity, not to their national distinctiveness. Pacifists, seeing only the clash of nationalities, excused themselves from taking responsibility for what would happen if Germany won the war. Patriotism, however, did not provide enough reason to defend England, especially the England of 1914. Tawney implored that German militarism and oligarchy had to be defeated to make it possible for England to become a Social Democracy. He had fought for a new England, not the old one. As soon as he was physically able he joined the National Mission campaign to make a case for redeeming the war. Gore and Mansbridge served on the National Mission committee on Christianity and Industrial Problems, chaired by Bishop Edward Talbot, which issued a historic and controversial "Fifth Report." Tawney wrote most of it, calling for a family-sustaining living wage for every worker and declaring that a future age would view modern industrialism much as modern England viewed slavery.[29]

Tawney's moral authority to say so was a boon for the church and British socialism. He believed in human equality before he fought in the war, but fighting deepened his commitment to it. He was glad to have learned about his upper-middle-class biases in WEA classrooms before he went to the front because war taught the same lessons more brutally. Tawney had breakfast with Lloyd George on November 28, 1916, just before he replaced Asquith as prime minister. At the time, Lloyd George was secretary of state for war. Tawney wanted Lloyd George to say what Woodrow Wilson soon declared: This was a war for democracy. Only an enlightened peace would justify the sacrifices of the war. In early 1917 Tawney wrote a flurry of articles on this theme, still struggling to heal, and joined Temple in the Life and Liberty Movement, a new Church of England enterprise dedicated to carrying out the best parts of the National Mission reports. Then he recoiled at Lloyd George's anti-German demagoguery in the 1918 election, which carried Lloyd George's Coalition Liberal government to a landslide victory. That year Temple joined the Labour Party, and Tawney threw himself into electoral politics as a Labour candidate in Rochdale. Sidney and Beatrice Webb primed Tawney for a political career, overlooking that he was unsuited for it. Tawney loathed small talk and was too introverted to pretend otherwise, although he ran four times for office, never successfully.

Balliol made him a Fellow in 1918, relieving Tawney of financial anxiety, but he did not aspire to a career at Oxford, where dons would have said he didn't belong on the faculty. The London School of Economics, the pride and joy of the Webbs, suited Tawney better. He began teaching there in 1920, putting himself in the middle of Labour's campaign for national power, and stayed for thirty-two years. His life turned a corner in 1919, when Lloyd George asked Tawney to serve on the Royal Commission on the Coal Industry, chaired by Justice John Sankey. Tawney's intense involvement in the coal issue turned him into an ordinary Labour Party state socialist. He still supported guild socialism as one method among others, notably nationalization, but the movement for it faded just after Tawney won national renown on the coal commission. He bailed out of guild socialism without regret, cautioning that the guild movement burgeoned with political activists lacking any real experience of industrial management. To Tawney, it was imperative to build an achievable Social Democracy, not waste time on a movement ideal smacking of utopianism. Cole eventually agreed, with the difference that for Cole, the adjustment was initially heartbreaking.

G. D. H. COLE AND GUILD SOCIALISM

George Douglas Howard Cole, another Balliol graduate who opted for initials, was born in Cambridge in 1889 and raised in Ealing, where his father ran a real estate business. He had nothing against his family, rather liking his father, and nothing against his teachers at St. Paul's and Balliol. Yet he said he owed nothing important to any family member or teacher. Eccentric, brilliant, rebellious, and autodidactic but also devoted to factual evidence and being sensible, Cole fought energetically for the kind of socialism he preferred but later proved willing to stump for the kind that Labour sought and achieved.

He was twelve years old when he left home for Colet Court, a preparatory school, and thirteen when he started at St. Paul's in Hammersmith. Cole read English literature so voraciously that classmates believed he was writing a history of it. He especially favored Victorian fiction, before and after he became a socialist. In 1905, at the age of sixteen, Cole was still a Tory, like his father, until he read William Morris. Cole started with *The Defence of Guenevere*, which enthralled him, and moved to *News from Nowhere*, which converted him. Then he consumed *The Earthly Paradise*. Morris thrilled him with his vision of a decent, beautiful society. *News from Nowhere* "made me feel, suddenly and irrevocably, that there was nothing except a Socialist that it was possible for me to be." In Morris's utopia people found their work enriching, and equality made them happy. This idea defined and motivated Cole for the rest of his life. A good society enabled people to find meaningful work and express themselves through it. Cole caught Morris's catastrophe assumption that it would take a civil war to persuade people to cooperate — a realistic improvement on the rationalistic optimism of Robert Owen and Edward Bellamy. But Morris's socialism was deeply ethical and aesthetic. Socialism was about a new way of living, a transformation of personal and social relationships. That was the core for Cole, evermore. He loved to quote Morris's aphorism, "Fellowship is heaven, and lack of fellowship is hell."[30]

Cole hated anything smacking of domination, hierarchy, superiority, or exploitation. He was not merely antiwar; he hated and resented the existence of armies. He was not merely egalitarian; he resented any issue of an order by a determinate human authority. He took these feelings and selective Victorian literary tastes to Balliol in 1908, the only college he considered. Cole detested emotive coloring and eloquent phraseology. Therefore he loathed Burke, Gibbon, Macaulay, and Carlyle, he later grimaced at reading Tawney, and he later had the same problem with Margaret Cole, a stylish wordsmith who fortunately shared his politics. Among prose writers, Cole ranked Morris above everyone and also admired Defoe, Swift, Shaw, and Bertrand Russell. In poetry he loved Morris above others, followed by Wordsworth and Walt Whitman. Margaret Cole puzzled that her husband made an exception for the colorful Whitman, especially since Cole hated all things American; he never explained the Whitman exception. Cole disliked Shakespeare because the historical plays were imperialist, and he reviled D. H. Lawrence as the apotheosis of conceited depravity. He made no apology for being interested only in English literature, and it was not until World War II that Cole took any real interest in anything outside Britain. He also made no apology for saying he truly hated bad writers. Cole wrote one flat, dull, clear sentence after another, writing pages of them every day with disciplined moral passion, and battled with editors wanting color. He wrote hundreds of articles for the *New Statesman*, brilliantly edited by Kingsley Martin, who explained that his friend Cole was obsessed with Greek prose construction, so he began every sentence with a particle.[31]

At Balliol he sailed through Mods and Greats at the top of the class, finding plenty of time for independent reading. Cole dutifully attended compulsory chapel until his twenty-first birthday. Then he approached J. L. Strachan-Davidson, who succeeded Caird as master in 1907. Cole explained that he attended chapel out of respect for his parents, but now he was of age, plus an atheist, so he should not have to attend anymore. However, when the preacher was someone who interested him, he would be happy to attend. Strachan-Davidson forbade Cole from ever entering the chapel again. Cole also took little interest in his teachers, although he appreciated that Balliol medieval historian A. J. Carlyle supported the Labour Party. For a while A. D. Lindsay persuaded Cole that Plato, Aristotle, and Hegel were great thinkers, until Cole decided that great philosophers were worthless because they built baleful unitary systems to solve unsolvable problems. The only high theorist he liked was Rousseau, who provided the groundwork of Cole's political philosophy, albeit while contradicting what became Cole's pluralistic socialism. Rousseau said that will, not force, is the basis of social and political organization, and human beings must cooperate in associations to satisfy their needs. He distinguished between the interests an individual acquires as a personal self and a citizen. Only citizens are capable of forming the general will that builds a good society because conflicting claims between individual personalities are irresolvable. Individuals become social beings by forming associations, which Rousseau denigrated. They become political beings by becoming citizens, which Rousseau celebrated. Rousseau's emphasis on will and his focus on associations deeply influenced Cole, even as he rejected Rousseau's statist prescription.

The highlight of Cole's Balliol career came through Edward Pease, Sidney Webb's operative at the Fabian Society, who appointed Cole as editor of the Oxford Fabian paper *Fabian News*, later renamed the *Oxford Reformer*. Cole won the attention of all the Fabian bigwigs. He slanted the paper in favor of the ILP, which he also joined, and spoke for and to the Fabian Society, becoming a polished speaker. He embraced the Fabian strategy of permeating society and the Fabian emphasis on amassing factual evidence. For nearly two years Cole looked to the Webbs for guidance, while they treated him as their sonlike heir. This feeling of parental affinity mattered after Cole turned against the Webbs. Beatrice Webb never quite relinquished her feeling that Cole was her wayward son. She worried about his rebellious streak before he rebelled against her and Fabian Collectivism. Cole became the enfant terrible of the Fabian Society shortly after novelist H. G. Wells rocked it with a stormy exit. Wells was famous for his science fiction blockbusters *The Time Machine* (1895), *The Invisible Man* (1897), and *The War of the Worlds* (1898). By 1909 he had run through many mistresses and was married for a second time when he impregnated Amber Reeves, a writer whose parents, William and Maud Pember Reeves, were Fabian Society stalwarts. Sidney and Beatrice Webb, disapproving of Wells's creepy philandering, got their comeuppance in Wells's spectacle novel of 1911, *The New Machiavelli*, which portrayed Oscar and Altiora Bailey as oily opportunists lacking intellectual integrity and their organization as a hapless outfit cowed by its leaders. The Webbs were already reeling from Wells's ridicule when their ostensible heir began to spout similar things.[32]

Cole decided during his junior year at Balliol that Fabian Society socialism trusted far too much in government officials and nationalization. He read *New Age* and welcomed its challenge to the Fabian and Labour movements. He made two kinds of friends in the Fabian Society while converting to guild socialist activism. Some Oxford eminences warmed to him, especially Lindsay, classicist Gilbert Murray, and All Saints' Oxford rector A. J. Carlyle. A younger group of Oxford friends gathered around him, especially William Mellor, Ivor Brown, A. L. Bacharach, Raymond Postgate, and J. Alan Kaye. Cole also knew Tawney, but Tawney fell between these two groups in age and work-life. Equally important to Cole, he made friends and inroads in trade unions, deciding that socialism needed radicalized unions more than anything else. Cole began to say caustic things about the Webbs. They were not real socialists because the real thing was not a government bureaucracy headed by the likes of them. They were dishonest schemers who sold out socialism, bent the facts to suit their purposes, and were bad on imperialism. Plus they treated underlings like serfs.[33]

Cole took little interest in the Labour Party for the same reasons he turned against the Webbs. The older generation of union leaders, left-liberals, and state socialists had no feeling for worker-directed socialism because they looked down on workers. ILP leader Ramsay MacDonald was no better, in Cole's estimation, rising to the top on slickness. When Cole graduated from Balliol in 1912 he was a romantic syndicalist, consumed by the vision of revolutionary unionism. Guild socialism was just becoming a serious movement; Hobson's bellwether *New Age* articles on it were published in 1912. Hobson said workers needed the dignity of self-governing organizations, not Lloyd George's patronizing social insurance. Some guild socialists left the Fabian Society, but most stayed in it, including Cole. It helped that Beatrice Webb indulged them, more or less, trying not to lose the younger generation or give up on Cole. Cole got similar treatment from Oxford, despite his rants against stodgy Oxford. Shortly after he graduated from Balliol he won the Prize Fellowship at Magdalen College, Oxford, which provided seven years of income and cushy accommodations with no obligations. Cole soared to a leadership role in the socialist movement on the strength of his prodigious intellectual energy and lack of worldly responsibilities.

His first book, *The World of Labour* (1913), was a manifesto for radicalized unions. It was a smashing success, the biggest splash Cole ever made with a book. The standard text on unions, Sidney and Beatrice Webb's *History of Trade Unionism* (1894), was sympathetic, cool, and detached, asserting that unions existed to improve the conditions under which employees labored. Cole spurned detachment, passionately identifying with his subject. Unions existed, he said, to fight the employers. Unions combated the exploitation of workers, something the general public never did, so the public had no business compelling the state to intervene against workers. The presumption that the state should always try to stop strikes was repugnant. Good unions cultivated a fighting spirit, and goodwilled people realized that strikes were sometimes necessary. Cole pressed an idealistic question: "What is the Labour movement capable of making of itself?" He angled for a syndicalist answer without endorsing every syndicalist doctrine, contending that general strikes repelled reachable recruits and were too chaotic to get efficient results. In 1913 Cole granted more authority to the state than he did by 1917, declaring that expropriation was "the State's business" and the state needed to develop new forms of industrial control. Cole opposed the French syndical doctrine that unions should run the nation because pure syndicalism would institute a new form of tyranny in which a union-state exploited the community. The answer was to devise "some sort of division of functions, allowing both producer and consumer a say in the control of what is, after all, supremely important to both."[34]

This was the core of what became Cole's guild socialism, an argument about achieving maximal individual freedom. He did not apologize for giving advice from the sideline, since he wanted unions to be more demanding. Union officials were usually political types who had to be pushed. Moreover, in England they were too reliant on the Fabian Society. Cole's first edition thanked the Webbs and *New Age* for stimulating his thinking, especially in disagreement. *The World of Labour* gave the state a direct role in deciding what to produce, and Cole wobbled in explicating his differences with Orage and Hobson. Orage objected that Cole misconstrued the differences, failed to explain the Orage/Hobson line on remuneration, and wrongly made the state responsible for production. Cole made revisions in his second edition; later there were many more. He was a newcomer finding his way into guild socialism, who judged that Hobson was insufficiently democratic. The book ran through four editions during the war, after which there was a fifth edition in 1919 that dolefully updated the progress of the Webbs in colonizing Labour politics: "The first leaders of the Fabian Society, and in particular Mr. and Mrs. Sidney Webb, were able so completely, through the Independent Labour Party, to impose their conception of society on the Labour movement that it seemed unnecessary for any one to do any further thinking."[35]

As long as the Webbs defined means and ends the Labour movement had no intellectual life. It had only practical problems and tinkering. Cole conceded nothing on this point, imploring Labour to do better than "Sidneywebbicalism." He bristled that Fabians turned Rousseau's concepts of citizenship, the general will, and the state into bureaucratic tropes. In 1913 Cole published an English edition of Rousseau's *The Social Contract and Discourses*, contending that Rousseau was the "great forerunner" of modern idealism. Contrary to conventional readings, Rousseau was not primarily a theorist of the state. Cole said Rousseau's commitment to the general will compelled him to care about "the whole life of the community," not just the state. Rousseau was a champion of democracy who perceived that small associations and social feeling are crucial to democracy. In 1915 Cole historicized the major counterfactual to his interpretation. Admittedly, Rousseau treated the state as morally superior to smaller associations because the state is the most general association. Cole said Rousseau denigrated small associations only because they were bastions of privilege in prerevolutionary France. To promote democracy in his context, he had to subordinate small associations to the general will. To equate Rousseau with what he said in his context was to miss Rousseau himself—the champion of democratic idealism who did not equate lesser associations with provincial selfishness, at least universally. Cole battled for his version of Rousseau because Rousseau had the saving passion for justice, unlike the English liberals Cole read at Oxford. *The World of Labour* stressed that he was not a wrecker. Cole loved the traditions of socialism, the labor movement, and idealistic social theory, and he built upon the best of the past: "What is wanted is not annihilation and a new start, but revaluation and a new synthesis."[36]

The Fabians and guild socialists did not suffer the fate of the many Progressives the war crushed. Pacifists, internationalists, and idealists were devastated by the outbreak of war and war psychology. MacDonald was vilified for opposing the war, damaging his ability to speak for the Labour Party. The Fabians and guild socialists took no position on the war or played it down, in both cases contending it was a distraction from what mattered, abolishing capitalism. Foreign policy was not the business of the Fabian Society. Beatrice Webb founded the *New Statesman* in 1913 to press the argument about capitalism, shaking down Shaw for seed money. She wanted it to be her last contribution to movement politics before she retired to the country—a weekly voice for her middle-class anticapitalism. Instead the war came, she and Sidney Webb signed on with Labour, and the magazine became a fixture of left politics. In 1915 Cole wrote a book that similarly treated World War I as a distraction from the war that mattered. The Socialist International, he said, had no chance of regaining a common policy as long as it tried to apportion blame for the war: "Its only consistent course is to go on in war time demanding the reference to arbitration or to a conference of all the Powers which it urged when war threatened." Cole acknowledged that this would accomplish nothing except keep the movement's hands clean, the best that socialists could do under capitalism. He conceived the war as a threat to workers; what mattered was to limit the harm. Cole found a very receptive audience for this message among seething miners, builders, and railway workers.[37]

Samuel George Hobson was the major theorist of guild socialism until Cole surpassed him. He had grown up Quaker, joined the Fabians, led the tiny Socialist Quaker Society, cofounded the ILP in 1893, blistered Fabian leaders for looking down on the ILP, and written for the ILP paper *Labour Leader*. In 1906 he began writing about worker self-management after Penty published *The Restoration of the Guild System*. Four years later Hobson quit the Fabian Society, and in 1912 his articles in *New Age* catalyzed a movement for guild socialism; the book version was titled *National Guilds: An Inquiry into the Wage System and the Way Out*. Hobson wrote winsomely and strongly. He was eccentric and industrious, managing a banana plantation on the side, plus editing an investment journal. Beatrice Webb loathed him because Hobson said Fabianism was a terrible mistake — a form of socialism that didn't even try to replace the wage system, the basis of capitalism. Capitalists understood that nothing else really mattered. Only pretend socialists did not understand that everything depends on who holds the power to exact rent and interest. Hobson acknowledged that he didn't know exactly how to replace the wage system. Guild socialists, he wrote, had to pick their way carefully "through the thickets and morasses of an unknown and unmapped territory." But Fabian Collectivism was a road to ruin: "It has assumed that the transformation of capitalism means economic emancipation. We now know that it means nothing of the sort."[38]

Every guild socialist was anxious not to end up as a Fabian statist. Agreeing about how to do it was another matter. Hobson accepted the Fabian theory of state sovereignty and its corollary that the state represented consumers, but he argued that empowering consumers through the state would not achieve industrial democracy. If Fabians took seriously their own rhetoric of industrial democracy, they had to demand direct control by the producers over industries and services. To be sure, consumers had a right to decide what should be produced and how products should be distributed. Hobson said the Fabian doctrine of the state safeguarded the rights of consumers. His version of guild socialism was a two-track scheme requiring cooperation between the state and the National Guilds, at both the national and local levels. The state owned the means of production and exchange, and the National Guilds controlled the process of production and exchange. Working out the machinery of cooperation would be piecemeal and experimental; Hobson tried to resist the blueprint mentality, though sometimes he gave in to demands for it. He ripped the Webbs for dropping worker self-determination, the essence of socialism. Sometimes he said it tartly: "The more meliorist politics be tested the more certain it becomes that emancipation cannot be effected by patchwork."[39]

Unlike Hobson, Cole stayed to fight the older Fabians. Cole's ploy seemed to pay off in the winter of 1912–1913, as Sidney and Beatrice Webb tried to handle Cole and his Oxford sidekick William Mellor by commissioning busywork from them. The Fabian Society created a typically sprawling research project, the Committee of Enquiry into the Control of Industry. It spawned a section charged with investigating the control of industry by associations of wage earners, chaired by Cole, who stacked the section with his allies. Then Cole's group morphed into a Fabian Research Committee while Cole plotted to convert the Fabian Society.

The Fabian Research Committee reached out to radicals and Christian socialists not belonging to the Fabian Society, creating, in April 1915, the first national organization committed to guild socialism, the National Guilds League. Cole, Mellor, Reckitt, Noel, Ivor Brown, and *Herald* editor Will Dyson led the National Guilds League. Orage and Hobson opposed the new organization because Orage said it was premature, and Hobson said it would be too much like the Fabian Society. These reactions helped Cole become the movement ringleader. Fabian bigwigs took pride in being civil, reasonable, disciplined, and mannered. Cole's defiance toward them won a band of awestruck disciples. Reckitt later recalled, "I admired him enormously for his fierce devotion to the workers' cause as he understood it; for his lightning-like power to discern and formulate an issue; for his allusive wit; and for the less obvious but very real kindness which underlay a certain haughty ruthlessness towards many of those who were not his intellectual equals." Cole's future brother-in-law, Raymond Postgate, had a similar reaction, at first struck by Cole's air of patrician culture and his elegant rooms at Magdalen: "However, there was nothing arrogant about him, though he could be rude enough on occasion. He talked on a level of perfect equality to all his fellow Socialists, in meetings or outside. Only, none of us were his equal both in knowledge and intelligence."[40]

Beatrice Webb, in February 1915, could see the explosion coming: "I often speculate about G. D. H. Cole's future. He interests me because he shows remarkable intensity of purpose; is he as persistent as intense? He has a clear-cutting and sometimes subtle intellect. But he lacks humor and the *bonhomie* which springs from it, and he has an absurd habit of ruling out everybody and everything that he does not happen to like or find convenient." Cole, she observed, had a long list "of personal hatreds," an ominous defect in a movement leader: "The weak point of his outlook is that there is no one that he does like except as a temporary tool—he resents anyone who is not a follower and has a contempt for all leaders other than himself." She believed Cole was too brilliant and aristocratic to stick with his current fixation. He idealized the "manual working class," but only because he had never been subjected to its crude forms of democracy and behavior. Beatrice Webb was proudly bourgeois, benevolent, and bureaucratic. She and her husband had a fundamental faith in civil servants and trained bureaucrats, a far cry from Cole's arrogant anarchism, which she could not help seeing as aristocratic, having wrestled with her own aristocratic upbringing.[41]

By May 1915 Cole believed he had momentum, youth, organization, and the future on his side against the fusty Fabians. He made a power move, demanding the Fabian Society drop its commitment to collectivism in favor of guild social-ism. He said harsh things at the annual meeting about sellout middle-class bureaucrats pretending to be socialists. The Fabians rejected Cole's proposal, and he stormed out of the meeting and the Fabian Society. Beatrice Webb shuddered: "Cole disgraced himself and ruined his cause; first by ill-tempered and tactless argument, and then, when the vote went against him, by a silly display of temper." If Cole was not embarrassed by his childish behavior, she was embarrassed for him. Only one executive committee member resigned with Cole. The following March she chortled at Cole's strenuous attempt to dodge military conscription. Unlike his guild socialist friends Clifford Allen and Bertrand Russell, Cole did not make a pacifist claim about the sanctity of human life, which smacked of sanctimony to him, and he did not believe that war was always the greater evil, although he loathed uniforms, rank, militarism, killing, and chains of command. He and Mellor tried to avoid being conscripted without having to lie about their position, laughably to Beatrice Webb, who said they were too childish to take orders from anyone: "They are not conscientious objectors; they are professional rebels." Yet she cheered when Cole's union con-nections won a deferment for him. The government was anxious to keep peace with the unions, and she respected Cole's success at creating "an intellectual center for Trade Unionism."[42]

Planting a few Fabians on the Labour executive board was less impressive, even to Beatrice Webb. Cole poured out articles in the *Daily Herald*, seizing the moment. He took an unpaid job as a research adviser for the Amalgamated Society of Engineers (ASE), handling complex union business on wages and prices. His work for the ASE won the trust of union leaders, though Beatrice Webb chided that he drew too much attention to himself, unlike the quiet way her husband worked with unions. Cole eventually learned the value of quiet service, giving forty years of it to unions and the Labour Party. In 1914 he was eager to publish his major work, *Self-Government in Industry*, but the war came, and he threw himself into labor activism. Thus the book had to wait until 1917, after most of it appeared in *New Age*, the *Daily Herald*, the *Nation*, the *Church Socialist*, the *Highway*, and the *Labour Leader*. Cole spoke for the guild socialist movement as a whole *and* stumped for his semianarchist version of it. He clashed with Hobson, Orage, and other *New Age* critics about which parts of Fabianism had to be scuttled. He pulled the movement in his direction but also rethought his position constantly, sometimes apologizing for putting it too dogmatically in a previous polemic. His position was closer to Hobson than he acknowledged, but Cole did not like Hobson, viewing him as a rival, hence the polemics. It was easier to admit, as he did, that pressures of the moment got in the way of achieving a clear position.[43]

From the beginning he implored the movement to rely as little as possible on the Fabian doctrine of the state, unlike Hobson and Orage, except where the state was needed, which Hobson and Orage also failed to do. To Hobson and Orage, the sovereignty of the state was an essential foundation of guild socialist doctrine. The function of the state was to exercise its sovereignty as the ultimate representative of the civic viewpoint, something distinct from the viewpoint of the producer or consumer. The civic viewpoint lay behind and transcended the point of view held by the producer as producer and the consumer as consumer. Hobson and Orage said that producer guilds should control industry and could be trusted to protect the interests of consumers. Workers should work in the field of their highest competence, an issue for guilds to adjudicate. The state, meanwhile, was the ultimate authority, and as such it represented citizens as citizens. Cole countered that Hobson and Orage retained too much Fabianism even as they railed against it and undermined the part they retained. To Hobson and Orage, the state was still sovereign in the economic and other spheres but played no role in the conduct of industry and took no responsibility for representing the interests of consumers in relation to the organization of production. In theory Hobson-style guild socialism claimed unlimited authority for the state. In practice, Hobson's state did not intervene precisely where it was needed.[44]

Cole staked his guild socialist position on this two-sided critique. He wanted the industrial and civil guilds to represent workers as producers or providers of services, and the state (including local authorities) to represent consumers. Neither form of organization should be superior to the other, he argued. Rejecting state sovereignty, Cole conceived the state and the guilds as cosovereigns in the economic sphere and as possibly cosovereign in other spheres, although he struggled with unwieldy aspects of the latter point. In the early going he said the state was the final and only representative of consumers, without denying it had necessary functions outside the economic sphere. By 1919 he had backed off on the state as the sole representative of consumers and also regretted having claimed it was merely one neighborhood organization among others. Through all his shifts of position Cole conceived of guild socialism as an equal partnership between a socially responsible state and a network of guilds that limited the scope and authority of the state. The state and local authorities, being primarily geographical organizations, were suited to express the viewpoint of the consumer. The trade union guilds were industrial organizations and thus suited to select workers for given industries and services.[45]

Cole believed that large-scale organization and centralization in modern economies, societies, and politics was a capitalist phenomenon that would end as soon as capitalism was overthrown. A free and democratic society would have a localizing logic, something hard to imagine for anyone operating under capitalism. This was Cole's touchstone whenever he tried to define the optimum role of the state. Capitalism yielded only bad choices, making it hard to imagine a decent society lacking a powerful state. In his early career Cole sneered at cooperatives, fixed on achieving democratic control over production. By 1919 he had stopped sneering, having been forced by his debate with Hobson to think about the consumer side of political economics. The cooperative movement, Cole said, represented consumers better than any other form of organization. Expanding the cooperative sector was therefore an indispensable feature of guild socialism: "I want to see these industries of production and distribution organized in local Guilds working in the closest possible conjunction with the Cooperative Movement." In *Self-Government in Industry* Cole contended that producer versus consumer conflicts should be adjudicated by the state and the pertinent guild and, failing that, by the state and the Congress of Guilds. By 1919 he was more committed to keeping the state out of it, reasoning that conflicts should be resolved between the guild or guilds concerned and the appropriate cooperative, public utility, or consumer congress on the other side. Only if that failed should the state and the Congress of Guilds render a joint judgment.[46]

Always he argued that only constructive idealism is saving. Tyrants prevailed wherever idealistic will and spirit were lacking, but idealism had to be constructive. A union movement standing only for materialism did not deserve to be supported, and if it lacked constructive idealism it had no chance of becoming the revolutionary power of the future. Cole rebuked the Webbs when he warmed to this theme, usually citing their book on trade unionism. Admittedly, the Webbs were idealists of a sort, but it was purely political idealism, chaining the labor movement to a political program: "The result was inevitable: the Trade Unions did not become idealistic, and the composite political body in which the Socialists chose to merge their identity was not only utterly without ideals, but also very soon emasculated the idealism of its Socialist wing." What came of that was the dismal political situation of 1917: "It is a Labour Party of which Capitalism has long lost all fear." Cole spoke for the angry unionists and socialists who felt sold out by the Labour Party. They were passionately idealistic in a way the older Fabians did not fathom. They were determined to accomplish what should have been achieved at the London Dock Strike of 1889, "a synthesis of the twin idealisms of Socialism and Trade Unionism." Guild socialism, a new form of syndicalism claiming "everything for the organized workers," was the synthesis.[47]

The state should own the means of production and the guilds should control the work of production. The state and the guilds needed to be equal partners, and to make it real the guilds had to bargain on equal terms with the state. The guilds reserved the right and preserved the means to withdraw their labor, and the state checked unjust demands by representing the organized views of the community as a whole. Cole said that guild socialism thus conceived carried forward the best aspects of the Fourierist, Christian socialist, and Communist traditions, focusing on the producer but now with a real plan. Fabian socialism lost socialism by focusing on the consumer, conceiving the state as a supreme authority and jack-of-all-trades. Bureaucrats loved Fabianism because it offered them "a wide field for petty tyranny." Guild socialists were more creative, assigning control of industry to national guilds in the common interest of a democratic state. Cole recycled Marx on wage slavery without mentioning Marx, defining it as the abstraction of labor from the laborer. Guild socialism, on his terms, repudiated the idea that labor is a commodity worth only what it fetches in the so-called labor market.[48]

Keen to win allies, Cole was kinder to Distributists than to some guild socialists. He admired Belloc's biting critique of capitalism and enjoyed Belloc's polemics against sellout politicians in Parliament. But Belloc wanted to distribute property as widely as possible under the right of private ownership, redistributing land to the peasant and poor classes. Cole said Belloc's prescription was geared to an agrarian society long passed. It operated on the principle of diffusion and distribution, providing individual owners of labor with direct ownership of capital. Guild socialism, Cole argued, improved the old dream of diffused ownership by fusing worker control with the collective ownership of capital by the state. The aim was to achieve collective ownership and control of capital, as socialists had always said. Guild socialism was a strategy to finally do it. Cole faulted Belloc for failing to think about how the transition period would work. Even if a fantasy world combination of unionism and Catholic revival brought about an individual distribution of ownership, it would not abolish the wage system. The real problem was to clarify how trade unions should intervene in industry. Redistribution strategies, past and present, were willing to settle for less than the collective ownership of capital. Often they made a point of being traditional, not threatening. Cole admonished that only the demanding and threatening types made a difference in this struggle.[49]

Anarchists described the state as the protector of property. Utilitarians said the state exists to promote the greatest happiness for the greatest number of people. Fabian Collectivism was a species of utilitarian theory, organizing the entire national life in the common interest. Philosophic idealists described the state as the supreme expression of the national consciousness. Cole felt the lure of each theory but offered his own: The state is a machine that reflects the social structure of the community in which it exists. Feudal communities created feudal states in their image; capitalist society did the same thing; in both cases the real action of the state was determined by the distribution of power in the community. Political power in itself, Cole reasoned, is nothing. It matters only as the expression of social power, whether military, ecclesiastical, industrial, economic, or whatever. In the modern age social power was primarily economic and industrial, even at war. Since economic power was the key to political power in modern society, those who controlled the means of production quite naturally dominated the state.[50]

In Cole's scheme, guild socialism did not require separate guilds to obtain their charters from Parliament. The various guilds had to be unified in a central Guild Congress, the supreme industrial body, which held the same relationship to producers that Parliament held in relationship to consumers. Cole had a separation-of-powers theory that separated the powers vertically, not horizontally. Every internal act of government passed through successive stages of legislation and administration. Instead of separating the legislative stage from the administrative stage in a horizontal fashion, Cole divided things by their function. The nature of the problem determined which authority dealt with it, not the stage at which an issue had arrived. In the judiciary he envisioned two sets of laws to administer—state law and guild law, each valid within its sphere—without dividing the judiciary. Cole divided legislative and executive power between the state and the guilds on the principle of function, and he preserved the integrity of the judiciary by making it an appendage of the state and guilds combined.[51]

Guild socialism opened new lines of inquiry in social and political theory. Cole, Hobson, Reckitt, Orage, and Russell propounded varieties of the guild idea; Belloc amplified the corporatist tradition in Catholic social teaching by proposing to replace Parliament with committees representing various interests;

and Figgis made a similar splash in 1913 with a punchy lecture collection on the role of religion in society, *Churches in the Modern State*. Figgis had studied under Lord Acton (John E. E. Dalberg-Acton) at Cambridge University, joined Gore's Community of the Resurrection, and published seven previous books on religion and political philosophy when he struck a cultural nerve with *Churches in the Modern State*. He stressed that the state did not create the family, churches, religious orders, medieval guilds, unions, or even most universities. All arose out of the natural associative instincts of human beings and deserved to be treated as authorities outranking the state because they nurtured the powers of life. Figgis described the Church of England as a voluntary spiritual community saddled with a baleful legacy of compulsory state religion. His opening chapter, "A Free Church in a Free State," sharply criticized the state church tradition as corrupting. His combative second chapter, "The New Leviathan," described the modern doctrine of state sovereignty as a disaster for religious liberty and the freedom of religious communities. To Figgis, freedom was the great prize, but the freedom of a mere individual against an omnipotent state was hardly better than slavery: "More and more is it evident that the real question of freedom in our day is the freedom of smaller unions to live within the whole."[52]

Cole was an avid reader of Belloc and Figgis, especially *Churches in the Modern State*. He praised the book as a godsend contribution to cultural pluralism, the cause of freedom, and guild socialism, lauding Figgis as an important contributor to the demolition of England's suffocating authoritarianism. *New Age* highlighted the affinities between guild socialism and the new movements for Distributism, ecclesiastical disestablishment, cultural pluralism, and worker ownership. Many *New Age* writers belonged personally to two or more camps. To them, the new pluralistic socialism was a bulwark against the bureaucratic reformism of the Labour Party. Cole said everyone knew how guilds worked because churches were the quintessential guilds. His willingness to say it bonded him to Reckitt, Noel, Widdrington, and other Church Socialist League radicals sharing Cole's emphasis on value pluralistic institutions. British political theorist Marc Stears stresses that Cole and Figgis never persuaded the guild socialist movement as a whole to exalt value pluralism over social welfare and the rhetoric of efficiency. To most guild socialists, social welfare trumped everything else. To Cole, who was romantic about unions, and the Christian socialists, who were romantic about religion and spiritual freedom, the strongest argument for guild socialism was that it promoted individual freedom like nothing else.[53]

Guild socialism was like democracy, Cole argued; in fact, it *was* democracy extended to labor. In the eighteenth century nobody thought democracy might work on a large scale. Anything bigger than a city-state was too big for democratic governance; even Rousseau said so. Cole invoked this historical lesson when critics said guild socialism was too democratic to work, or workers were lazy good-for-nothings who had to be treated harshly, or guild leaders would become petty tyrants, or democracy was too messy for the industrial sphere. Cole said the guilds would need competent leaders, and abolishing exploitation would unleash the better side of human nature. To do good work for a capitalist employer was to "help a thief to steal more successfully." To do good work for a democratic guild was to make a valuable contribution to a society of equals, appealing to the highest human motive, the sense of fellowship. Cole believed every rational worker would want to work for a guild. More important, most people wanted to be good, not merely rational. Guild socialism appealed to the moral feelings of average workers who wanted to feel good about their contribution to society.[54]

Cole, Mellor, and Reckitt worked hard to build up the National Guilds League. To them, it was imperative not to hide behind vague phrases about "industrial democracy" and "abolishing the wage system." They wrote a stream of wonky articles and books about mining guilds, railway guilds, and the like, straining to be clear. Cole's *Self-Government in Industry* and Reckitt's coauthored *The Meaning of National Guilds* (1918) exemplified the genre. Reckitt, responding to the "petty tyrant" objection, said the guilds would be vested with full authority over employment decisions and the productive process. To get more personal freedom as an outcome, society had to create new authority-bearing organizations. To many, Cole's group seemed like socialist monks, cut off from ordinary people by their religious-like devotion to an idealistic cause. Cole, especially, seemed utterly monk-like to Beatrice Webb, even after Cole shocked the Fabian Society by finding a romantic partner at the Fabian Society.[55]

Margaret Postgate, the daughter of a Latin professor at the University of Liverpool, had converted to socialism, feminism, and atheism while studying at Girton College and the University of Cambridge from 1911 to 1914. She taught classics at St. Paul's Girls' School in 1914 and applied the following year for a job at the Fabian Society, where Beatrice Webb caught a glimmer of herself in the young writer with a strong personality. Webb assigned Postgate to the Labour Research Department, expecting a sexual entanglement. Cole was the last person Webb expected it to be. Cole had turned the Fabian Research Committee into a semi-independent outfit, the Labour Research Department, shortly before he stormed out of the Fabian Society. Thus he still had one foot in the Fabian Society, bringing workers into its orbit. His friends and relatives believed he was asexual; Margaret Cole later confirmed they were right.

Cole's entire group, Margaret Cole said, was "as unconscious of sex and its ramifications as any body of people I have ever known." They were "as nearly as possible sexless," and Cole was asexual except for the slight exception he made for her. Cole and Postgate bonded deeply as friends and comrades. In 1916 she joined him in the campaign against the Military Service Act, supporting England's sixteen thousand conscientious objectors, including her brother and Cole. In 1918 she married Cole, shocking his friends and family. The Coles formed a loving partnership based on affection, ideology, and constant writing, raising three children. She put up with his view that women made lousy socialists, with few exceptions, and were not great writers either, except Jane Austen. Beatrice Webb saw more of herself in Margaret after she became Margaret Cole. The Webbs reached out to the newlyweds, even as Cole blasted them for ruining socialism in England. Beatrice Webb, with customary acuity, said she expected Cole to get over his infatuation with a trade union fantasy because he was an intellectual and aristocrat "from the intricate convolutions of his subtle brain to the tips of his long fingers."[56]

Cole's Magdalen fellowship ran out in 1919 just after the Labour Party acquired Sidney Webb's Constitution. The Labour Party had been little more than a pressure group until the end of the war. For research it relied on the Labor Research Department of the Fabian Society (LRD), which Cole took over in 1916, never mind his stormy resignation from the Fabians. Now Labour vied for power, while radicals vied to influence Labour. Hobson recalled how radicals experienced the moment: "In this hectic atmosphere thousands of wage-earners had a new vision. They were not thinking of the cut of their clothes or the shape of their boots; they were dreaming of a new spirit, perhaps even a new regime, in the workshop." This heady call for reconstruction was actually the last burst of optimism that launched guild socialism. Henderson ramped up Labour's knowledge base by appointing Cole as its first research director, which brought the LRD into the party, however briefly. Cole founded what became the powerful Research and Information Bureau under Arthur Greenwood, but Cole had too many rivals to last as a Labour official. Some wailed that Bolsheviks were taking over. In the summer of 1920 Cole resigned as secretary to the party's advisory committees; the following summer the party expelled the LRD from its headquarters in Eccleston Square. Meanwhile Cole wrote a primer in industrial democracy, *Labour in the Commonwealth* (1919), which explained that labor was a collective name for human beings, not something confined to workplaces, and the industrial system was the test of whether England would become a democracy. Schoolmasters taught English children to personify the Commonwealth, but England depersonalized the human beings of which the Commonwealth consisted.[57]

Battling for guild socialism compelled Cole to address nuts-and-bolts issues about railway and mine guilds, theoretical questions about associations and the state, and midrange issues about politics. He tried to do it all because the movement was hot and there had never been a moment like 1919–1921, when everyone talked about reconstruction. He stressed in the early years of the Soviet revolution that Soviet Communism was very much like and unlike guild socialism. The Soviet idea was the guild idea, almost exactly. But this idea had nothing to do with the dictatorship of the proletariat, a doctrine that Bolsheviks imposed on the Soviet idea, hopefully only as a temporary expedient. Cole put off dealing with Marxism until his book *Social Theory* (1920). Since he supported the Soviet revolution, and Marxism made a contribution to social theory, he had to deal with Marxism, notwithstanding British aversion to Marx. Cole said he agreed with "a large part of the Marxian case," notably that the state under capitalism protected the dominant power of the capitalist class. But he disbelieved the state would wither away under socialism, plus Cole disliked Marx's anti-individualism, although he put the latter point mildly. To Cole, most of the social theory he learned at Oxford began at the wrong end of the subject. English theory conceived human society in terms of force and law, fixing on the coercion that applies to human agents in society. It was usually about the state as the embodiment and representative of social consciousness. From Hobbes to the British Hegelians, it treated the state as almost its sole subject, conceiving the actions of the state as the actions of human agents in society. To Cole, Rousseau offered the needed alternative by fixing on the motives that bind human agents in association. Rousseau focused on the will, not the English obsession with force and law, although Rousseau had no inkling of modern democracy or democratic socialism.[58]

Social theory, by Cole's definition, was a normative social analogue to ethics. Ethics theorizes individual conduct, and social theory is about social conduct. Cole took a pass at showing that English social theory was more social than it claimed, since it could not get anywhere lacking a notion of associative will and action. Even Hobbes's imaginary social contract bonded selves by will into a society before they fell into brutish rivalries calling forth the strong hand of the state. Cole did not linger, however, over Hobbes, Locke, and British Hegelianism. English social theory habitually revolved around the state and the individual, beginning with the state or a particular form of association. Rousseau rightly searched for the universal principles of association, reflecting on association as a whole. Rousseau discerned the values of sociality, a normative enterprise, not merely the facts of sociality, a positive enterprise, although Rousseau wrongly rebuked Montesquieu for gathering facts. Cole argued that social theory needed to be normative, expansive, and positive, grasping how associations and institutions actually work. Values are more important than facts, and paying attention to facts is necessary for understanding. In the end, "the facts drop away and only questions of right remain."[59]

Fabians taught that the state is an association of consumers rightly claiming supremacy in the economic sphere because everyone shares basically the same concern about consumption. Fabian Collectivism offered the collectivist state as the solution to the consumption problem, gutting socialism of its core concern with production. Cole said production is never less important than consumption. Moreover, the Fabian state was monstrously overgrown, defying essential facts of association. Fabian Collectivism made the state wholly responsible for the infinitely expansive activities of coordination among banks, companies, partnerships, unions, clubs, and religious communities. Orage and Hobson, taking the Fabian position, claimed that guild socialism was Fabian on the role of the state. It galled Cole that they had followers; he countered that no association should be the judge of its own case. To entrust the state with the function of social coordination is to make it the judge of its own conflicts with unions, churches, and other associations. In a just society, coordination must not belong to the function of the state. But neither does it belong to any other association.[60]

Fabian Collectivism was the logical upshot of modern state sovereignty, rendering the state as superior to other forms of association and as absolutely different in kind from other forms. Thus the state was supposedly justified in assuming unlimited authority over all associations and individuals. Cole said the march of the state in modern society had to be thwarted by redefining the proper functions of the state—a job for social theory. Appropriating Rousseau's critique of representation and his reflections on the functions of representation, which Cole applied to the internal organization of all associations, he argued that true representation never represents human beings as individual personalities. Representation is always specific and functional, not general and inclusive. It represents certain purposes common to groups of individuals, never the individual. Human persons are ultimate realities—centers of consciousness, reason, and will possessed of the power of self-determination. No person can be made to stand in place of many. One cannot be a self and many other people at the same time.

Britain needed a functional understanding of representation that demythologized the quasi-miraculous versions of English political theory. Functional representation, to Cole, was a cooperative scheme for getting something done. Put differently, representation itself is real, plus necessary, only in relation to some well-defined function. Despite the unavoidable element of distortion in it, functional representation does not negate the will of any individual. Democracy, "a coordinated system of functional representation," combines representation with constant give-and-take with constituents. It preserves democratic control without capitulating to demands for party-disciplined delegation. In Cole's activist context, defining democracy and representation in functional terms was an antidote to angry left-wingers and anarchists. Cole knew how they felt, being one of them. Still, he controlled himself at meetings and seethed when they misbehaved. The alienated types demanded direct control by the rank and file, usually through delegates lacking any discretion about how to vote. Cole said democracy works best with real leaders who sustain constant and substantial relationships with those they represent.[61]

Strangely, Cole did not distinguish between the performing character of a function and the believing/holding character of a purpose. A function is a performed task that qualifies as functional by virtue of its objective relation to other tasks or its perception as functional. A purpose is a held conviction that may or may not bear any relation to objective consequences. Functions are performing and utilitarian in ways that do not inherently define purposes. Cole, however, despite criticizing political philosophers for ignoring function, employed a vague concept of it. *Social Theory* and *Guild Socialism Restated* (1920) used "function" and "purpose" as interchangeable terms. In both books he apologized for belaboring social theory, which he said is boring compared to political economics. Then he implored that social theory matters nonetheless. Bad social theory held back English socialism for decades; guild socialism needed to use the best theories and inspire better social theory. Carefully, Cole said Marxist theory is valuable but must be corrected. Marx was basically correct about how the state operates under capitalism and wrong about economic determinism and the true function of the state. The behavior of the state under capitalism perverts the true function of the state. Marxism powerfully corrects all theories that play down the importance of economics and the class struggle, but Marxian theory "suffers from its persistent identification of the economic structure with Society as a whole." Cole said churches and other cultural institutions were more functional than Marx acknowledged. Marxian theory lacked sophistication about anything social, notably the state, except its economic component. Thus Marxism was a powerful aid to making Marxism irrelevant: "If economic classes and class-conflicts are done away with, the Marxian thesis will no longer hold good, and economic power will no longer be the dominant factor in Society."[62]

The goal was to fulfill the democratic socialist revolution by achieving complex equality along pluralistic lines. Cole took for granted that religion was the acid test of his cultural pluralism. Churches, he acknowledged, are not like school boards, railway unions, or small businesses. Churches are not professedly complementary, and they do not naturally cohere. Almost every church that Cole could think of compelled its members to believe it was the only true church. Moreover, churches had a more diffuse subject matter than most associations, concerning themselves with political, economic, and spiritual matters. Thus religious communities posed tricky problems of recognition. It was very hard to fit churches to a job description. Cole said it was important to try, and religious communities should confine themselves to spiritual power, something exercised upon the mind and not the body. Churches had no proper role in the coordinating function of society, which employed material forms of coercion that religion rightly gave up during the Enlightenment. The proper relation of religious communities to the political and economic forms of association was to cooperate with nonreligious associations without taking on formal coordination responsibilities: "Only through such separation can Churches be freed for the attainment of the fullest liberty and the proper performance of their spiritual function." Cole did not say that Reckitt should leave his Anglo-Catholicism at home when he stumped for guild socialism. He did say he loved how Figgis was changing the discussion about religion in society.[63]

Good social theory, to Cole, did not conceive society as a mechanism or an organism. Society cannot be assembled like a machine because human wills influence how it develops: "We cannot describe its processes of growth and change in terms of any other body of knowledge, natural or unnatural. It has a method and processes of its own." In 1922 he took a job at the WEA, directing its program at the University of London. His experience was similar to Tawney's. Cole thrived on his classroom contact with workers, teaching as much as his administrative duties permitted. He taught one session on railroads and another on the King's Road neighborhood in Chelsea, London, willing to get very practical. Like Tawney, he learned at the WEA how to teach, with the difference that Cole's ideological reputation preceded him. Cole tried to forge a friendly relationship between the WEA and the (Marxist) National Council of Labour Colleges. It helped that his brother-in-law Raymond Postgate chaired the executive committee of the Plebs League, the propaganda organ of the National Council. The National Council Marxists, however, loathed the WEA as a bastion of bourgeois idealism. Why did Cole not see that he taught fake history and false economics, perpetuating the conceit of Christian socialists that workers needed the benefits of university culture? Cole heard a lot of that from Postgate, a reminder that Marxists didn't know everything.[64]

Cole and Reckitt campaigned all out for guild socialism, pouring out words spoken and written, seizing England's kairos moment. Reckitt enthused that guild socialism spoke to craft workers, rekindled "the blazing democracy of William Morris," heeded Belloc's warning against the servile state, embraced Penty's critique of industrialism, appropriated the French syndical focus on the producer and the American industrial union emphasis on industrial organization, and included "something of Marxian socialism, with its unsparing analysis of the wage-system by which capitalism exalts itself and enslaves the mass of men." He and Cole implored guild socialists not to settle for typical vagueness. They had to show they knew what they were talking about.[65]

Every such call for a blueprint heightened Cole's anxiety to provide one. His writing and speaking got increasingly wonky on this account. A second reason took hold between the first (1917) and third (1919) editions of *Self-Government in Industry*. Upon realizing that his early thought was too biased against consumers and consumer cooperatives, Cole rethought his focus on producer associations. To pursue his fixation rightly—restoring the product to the producer—he had to pay more attention to the interests people hold as consumers. His early work expounded the customary guild socialist dictum that the state exists to protect consumers. By 1919 he believed the representation of citizens as consumers required "a multiplicity of associations dealing with the representation of different groups of purposes and interests." The simpler half of his model got messy and labyrinthine, as Cole designed a pyramid of territorial associations complementing the pyramid of producer associations, replete with plans linking the two pyramids. He apologized for burdening readers with intricate blueprints, but the movement needed them. Cole added a territorial factor of division, a federalist component resembling Proudhon's revision of anarchist theory. Proudhon fused a federal network of democratic communities to the classic anarchist vision of self-governing producer associations. Cole took a similar path just before the movement for guild socialism lost its basis in the labor movement.[66]

Guild socialism, in Cole's rendering, became a theory of active participatory citizenship in the determination of common ends, not merely a theory of self-government in industry. It was organized from the grassroots upward, both vertically and horizontally. It was participatory at all levels and in all aspects, featuring consumer cooperatives, utility councils for utilities, and civic guilds for health and education. It was deeply indebted to Rousseau notwithstanding Cole's pluralism and Rousseau's ostensible antipluralism. Cole declared in *Guild Socialism Restated*, "Guildsmen assume that the essential social values are human values, and that Society is to be regarded as a complex of associations held together by the wills of their members, whose well-being is its purpose." They further assumed that a healthy society had to be fully democratic and self-governing, providing the "greatest possible opportunity" for every citizen to exercise his or her right to influence the policy of the nation. Cole stressed that he did not refer only or even mainly to a discrete sphere called "politics." In his telling, this was Rousseau's fatal mistake, separating the political sphere from everything else, which confined citizenship to the political sphere. Rousseau believed the democratic principle would get nowhere if citizenship sprawled beyond politics. Cole said democracy is not democratic if confined to politics. Democracy applies to "any and every form of social action, and, in especial, to industrial and economic fully as much as to political affairs." He apologized for the "terrible and bewildering complexity of social organization" that his robust concept of democracy yielded but reminded readers that organizational complexity was already a fact of life in modern society. Guild socialism was actually less unwieldy than the sprawling "medley of conflicting and warring associations" existing under capitalism and capitalist government.[67]

Long after the movement for guild socialism crashed and Cole moved on to political history, ordinary Labour politics, middle-aged respectability, and training Oxford students, there were debates about Rousseau's paradoxical influence over him. How could someone as deeply political and pluralistic as Cole admire the archenemy of politics and pluralism? Cole provided a clue in his introduction to the *Social Contract and Discourses*. Seven years before Rousseau wrote the *Social Contract*, his essay on political economy affirmed for the nation what he denied to the city—a nation comprises a profusion of institutions, not all of which are harmful to the general will of the state. Cole seized on this statement as evidence that Rousseau believed there was no inherent opposition between levels of organized will. Cole believed it passionately for himself and Rousseau. Rousseau's moral urgency came through to Cole as an ethical principle of recognition and respect. Cole laced his books with secular sermons conveying a similar urgency, imploring that a true democracy cannot exist in a society that allows "vast inequalities of wealth, status, and power among its members." If one person is a master and another is a wage-slaver, no amount of "purely electoral machinery" will make them socially or politically equal. If England wanted democracy, "we must abolish class distinctions by doing away with the huge inequalities of wealth and economic power on which they really depend."[68]

Cole did not profess to know how many guilds might be desirable, which was a matter of convenience, not principle. He thought direct elections were best within factories, but in larger bodies functional representation worked best. He saw no reason why National Guilds and cooperatives would not get along, since they cared about the same things. He believed that managers in guild factories would develop the cooperative spirit, no longer needing to bully workers. He said guilds should be "loose and elastic enough" to admit many varieties of work into a single guild, and factories should be allowed to remain independent if they desired. He wanted small independent producers to be left alone, enjoying "the greatest possible freedom of development." He believed the state would wither away from lack of anything to do once guild socialism got rolling. He denied that his blueprinted National Commune would be the state with a name change. He preached the principle of subsidiarity without naming it, imploring that every problem should be solved at the most decentralized level possible: "If the Guilds are to revive craftsmanship and pleasure in work well done; it they are to produce quality as well as quantity, and to be ever keen to devise new methods and utilize every fresh discovery by science without loss of tradition; if they are to breed free men capable of being good citizens both in industry and in every aspect of communal life; if they are to keep alive the motive of free service—they must at all costs shun centralization."[69]

The same social and historical forces that propelled guild socialism during its heyday overwhelmed it in the early 1920s. Postwar Britain convulsed with demobilization riots, strikes by railway workers and police, demands for nationalized mines, and ideological battles over both Russian revolutions of 1917. Lloyd George's government tried to overthrow the Bolsheviks, which united Labour and the unions against Lloyd George on antiwar grounds, not pro-Bolshevik. Most guild socialists welcomed the Bolshevik revolution as a victory for syndicalism and direct action. Then Russian workers caused industrial chaos by taking over factories, the Bolsheviks imposed centralized discipline, and guild socialists were forced to explain that they opposed chaotic disarray and Leninist centralism. Mellor, R. Page Arnot, Raymond Postgate, Ellen Wilkinson, and a few other guild socialists joined the British Communist Party after it formed in 1920, although most did not sign up for taking orders from Moscow. Cole did not join the Communist Party and later claimed he never considered doing so.

Two by-products of the war—labor scarcity and government control of industry—had to continue if the guild socialist movement was to succeed. Both ended with the end of the postwar economic boom in November 1920. Wages plummeted, miners and transport workers went on strike, and union funds were depleted. Labour and the unions thwarted Lloyd George from destroying the Bolshevik revolution, but that was a negative victory and very taxing. The season for big, creative ideas in the labor movement ended. Unions had to struggle just to survive. Electing a Labour government became paramount;

guild socialism was an indulgence no longer deserving of union funds. Cole heard it constantly, unable to disagree publicly, although he grieved at resorting to vanilla Labour politics. Ramsay MacDonald, having served in Parliament from 1906 to 1918, won a glow of martyrdom for opposing the war. He rode a surge of antiwar feeling that swept him back to Parliament and the Labour leadership in 1922. The following year Labour won its first fling at power, forming a minority government aligned with Asquith's reunited, third-place Liberals. Stanley Baldwin's Conservative government won far more seats than Labour, 344 to 142, which doomed MacDonald's government to a short run, eleven months. Still, Labour showed it was capable of running the government, leaning on its 23 Fabian members of Parliament. That year, 1923, the National Guilds League went into liquidation, the formal ending of guild socialism as a national movement.[70]

Many guild socialists retreated to the "Social Credit" reformism of British engineer C. H. Douglas. A writer for *New Age*, Douglas said the true purpose of production is consumption, and production should serve the freely expressed interests of consumers. Producer-oriented versions of economic democracy fixed on the wrong end of the problem. Cultural inheritance, Douglas reasoned, is a more important factor of production than the three factors recognized by textbook economics—land, labor, and capital. Societies grow and become wealthy by accruing and transmitting knowledge, techniques, and processes. Creating value through labor and accumulating capital are less important than making a society's cultural inheritance available to everyone. These ideas were staples of WEA teaching, but Douglas provided a strategy for conceiving economic democracy as individual equality and democratic access to credit. More important, he minted a catchphrase for it that caught on: social credit. The key was to redistribute economic power to the broadest possible range of individual consumers. Simply issuing dividends to every citizen would do more for distributive justice and individual equality than anything else. In his book *Economic Democracy* (1920) Douglas put it laboriously: "It is simply hypocrisy, conscious or unconscious, to discuss freedom of any description which does not secure to the individual, that in return for effort exercised as a right, not as a concession, an average economic equivalent of the effort made shall be forthcoming." In his best-selling book *Social Credit* (1924) Douglas said democracies grow by ensuring that every citizen has full access to the consumer goods and communal capital of society.[71]

Unlike Sidney and Beatrice Webb at the time, Douglas was not hostile to Communism or British Communists. But anti-Communism was the driving force of the Douglas phenomenon. The violence of the Russian Communist experiment and the founding of the British Communist Party frightened many progressives into a soft version of economic democracy. Orage was a leading convert, swinging *New Age* and the right flank of the guild socialist movement to consumer reformism. S. G. Hobson angrily dissented, severing his connection to *New Age*. Douglas claimed to salvage the best parts of guild socialism after the movement for it faded. Ezra Pound, T. S. Eliot, Aldous Huxley, and other literary stars supported Social Credit reformism, which morphed into a still-going tradition of strategies and techniques. To Cole, however, Social Credit was a mockery of the real thing. He grieved that guild socialism was reduced to bromides about cultural progress and dividend payouts. For a while Cole protested that Communists cared about unemployed workers while the Labour Party cared about getting elected. As a Labour official in 1921 he accepted a subsidy from a Russian trading company, enraging Beatrice Webb: "Cole really is an idiot if he thinks he can take money from the Bolshevik government without upsetting the mind of his present supporters and ruining himself and the LRD in the eyes of all outsiders." She lamented that Cole turned one of her proudest inventions, the Fabian Research Department, into "a lunatic asylum."[72]

In 1922 the Fourth Conference of the Communist International decreed that democratic centralism applied to every Communist national party. It was not just for Russians, and all Communists had to obey orders from Moscow. Many British socialists fled the Communist movement, Cole floundered in political isolation, and Beatrice Webb derided both developments. She judged in 1924 that Cole was "a lost soul—the older men have ceased to fear him; the younger men no longer look up to him." Cole, she noted, still believed in workers' control, but he defended it despairingly. He had wasted his brilliance on doctrines that were stale from being untrue, not from being old. In her telling, Tawney and Arthur Greenwood no longer looked up to Cole. They said polite things about him but refused to work with him because Cole had failed, becoming an embarrassment. Even the pro-Communists who worked with him didn't trust him. She had a ready explanation: "He is too much of the aristocrat and the anarchist, too childish in his likes and dislikes—he is not an artist—to succeed with an Anglo-Saxon democracy."[73]

The Webbs, like Shaw, never doubted that guild socialism was a hopeless pairing of opposites that canceled each other out. Guilds were conceivable, but not with socialism, and vice versa. If guild production required self-controlled industries to pool their products, some central agency was needed to receive, check, and distribute them, protecting citizens as consumers, not as producers. For a socialist to attack the state was idiotic because the history of producer cooperative associations showed with devastating finality that they don't work. Beatrice Webb said it to Cole repeatedly, trying to save him from wasting his brainy passion. She judged that coping with the frailties, ambiguities, and peculiarities of Anglo-Saxon democracy required a mature democratic temperament that Cole lacked. Reckitt later acknowledged that Cole and the guild socialists attacked state socialism so ferociously their impact was antisocialist, fracturing the movement. But Cole adjusted to the coming political realities far better than Sidney and Beatrice Webb, who wrote pro-Stalinist embarrassments in the 1930s and 1940s that trashed their immense legacies. Cole poured out books in a ceaseless flow for the rest of his life. Nearly every year there was a new book on labor history, socialist history, or contemporary politics. In 1925 Oxford called him to an unexpected academic career, teaching economics at University College, Oxford. Cole became a legendary teacher at Oxford, eventually in England's most prestigious position in political theory, the Chichele chair. He gave diligent service to the Labour Party, served in MacDonald's second Labour government of 1929 to 1931, rejoined the Fabian Society, tacked back and forth over Marxism, and defended democratic socialism as a distinct moral and political tradition. Always he said that democratic socialism was culturally specific, requiring distinct political and moral values, although Cole changed his mind in the 1940s about the fit between Marxism and democratic socialism. In 1923 he wrote his first detective novel, needing to write something while switching gears politically. In 1925 he and Margaret Cole wrote their first coauthored detective novel, after which there were thirty-three more. They shrugged off all thirty-four as pleasantly frivolous diversions.

Margaret Cole said her husband was incapable of not writing constantly. By 1926 Beatrice Webb had softened about Cole. In her telling, Cole was still a fanatic who pronounced, "I hate him," but he no longer meant it, being an incurable rebel who had lost his faith. His enduring attachment to the working class puzzled her: "The desire *to raise the underdog and abuse the boss* is a religion with him, a deep-rooted emotion more than a conviction." Cole was still an aristocrat of an ascetic intellectual type, she judged. He sought to impress his peculiar mentality on ordinary people, although for what purpose exactly she could not tell. By the end of the 1920s Cole admitted that his guild socialist activism was utopian in the dreaded Marxist sense of the term, although he said there was a role for utopian visualizing of socialist principles. Since he believed that socialist principles could be realized, his utopianism was not pie-in-the-sky. He wrote a book in 1929 that might have been a platform for the next Labour government, if not for the Great Depression and the timorous MacDonald administration. As it was, *The Next Ten Years in British Social and*

Economic Policy (1929) was already outdated when it appeared and MacDonald took office.[74]

Cole tried to adjust, serving with Liberal doyen John Maynard Keynes on MacDonald's Economic Advisory Council. They urged MacDonald to fight the Depression with Keynesian spending, but MacDonald stuck with economic orthodoxy, floundered disastrously, terminated his government, and betrayed his party, cutting a deal with Conservatives. Many socialists believed that Keynes pedaled the worst possible prescription—deficit spending. To Cole, it was a distinctly confounding and frustrating period. He went along with Keynes because at least Keynes tried to stop the carnage, Cole felt his irrelevance and inadequacy, and he hated MacDonald for betraying Labour. This brew of feelings drove Cole to initiate new research programs to strengthen the party's policy competence. In 1931 he regained the policy platform he had lost in 1921 by founding the New Fabian Research Bureau. Meanwhile the Webbs, despairing at a second Labour failure, lurched to the pro-Stalinist left and mused at the irony of ending up to the left of Cole.

Cole spent the rest of his career fighting for his idea of democratic socialism, which he called "liberal socialism." In the 1930s he feared that Western civilization was being destroyed, but he spurned the apocalyptic warnings of Labour theorist Harold Laski and American social ethicist Reinhold Niebuhr that Western democracies faced a brutal choice between fascist barbarism and revolutionary state socialism. Cole insisted that a genuine third way still existed, a democratic form of socialism that ran through Western liberalism and assumed its bedrock of individual rights. He moved back and forth on the role of Marxism within it. In the 1930s Cole enlisted Marxism in the democratic socialist project, writing a popular book, *What Marx Really Meant* (1934). Many of Marx's conclusions were obviously wrong, Cole said, but Marx was commendably realistic and rightly emphasized the class struggle. Moreover, his dialectical method was "fully as important as his doctrine" because Marx taught socialists to constantly relate the changing facts of the social situation to changing factors of production. Cole said that was his model of proceeding.[75]

Many scholars thus counted him a Marxist. In 1963 American sociologist C. Wright Mills classified Cole as a "plain Marxist" who embraced core Marxian doctrines while approaching them critically. By that standard Cole was still a Marxist when he wrote *The Meaning of Marxism* in 1948, a revision of *What Marx Really Meant*. He declared, "I remain 'Marx-influenced' to a high degree." But Cole no longer considered himself a Marxist or saw any advantage in claiming it, also declaring: "In a good many respects my mind recoils from Marxism, as a system." *The Meaning of Marxism* highlighted the

recoiling points: Marx wrongly attributed reality to classes instead of individuals, he concocted a substitute metaphysics masquerading as science, he never
considered that something other than socialism might replace capitalism, he
did not anticipate the problems of proletarian dictatorship, and his economic
materialism was crude and fatefully wrong, not something revisable. By 1948
Cole no longer believed that democratic socialists should claim an affinity with
Marx. Asked for an article showing that *The Communist Manifesto* was a Social
Democratic classic, not a Communist classic, Cole declined "for the sufficient
reason that no such case could be even plausibly made out." He sprinkled his
writings with critical asides about Marx's legacy, lamenting that Marx denigrated socialist idealism. In *Socialist Economics* (1950) Cole ignored Marx completely until the final chapter, where he claimed there was "nothing in Marx's
writings that has any important bearing on the matters discussed in this book."
Cole was done with cleaning up Marx for British consumption. He had tired of
acknowledging what he owed to Marx because Marxology was not worth the
trouble.[76]

In the 1930s it was worth the trouble because Cole was a Popular Front
leftist. Claiming an affinity with Marxism helped him make the case that socialists should work with Communists to defeat fascism. In 1932 Cole cofounded
the Socialist League, a left organization in the Labour Party, but he resigned the
following year after Stafford Cripps took it over. Thus Cole had no part in
the Socialist League's disastrous campaign to mount a Popular Front battle
against the British government. Cripps got expelled from the Labour Party in
1939 for going too far. Cole, however, was deeply involved in nonconspiratorial
forms of Popular Front activism from 1936 on. He sought Communist help in
repelling fascist aggression, acknowledging in 1938 he was no longer a pacifist.
Unlike Laski, Cole did not defend Popular Front politics on the ground that
capitalism and democracy were incompatible anyway; Cole said Social
Democrats should suspend their principled opposition to working with
Communists in order to defeat the fascist enemy. In 1939 he told the Fabian
Society he was still a democratic socialist, "despite all its failures and vacilla-
tions of recent years," and not a pro-Communist, even though only Communists
stood up for oppressed people. That was the nadir of Social Democracy, the
climax of a decade in which Nazi fascism obliterated German Social
Democracy, forced its leaders into exile, and devoured the vulnerable.[77]

Cole had never taken much interest in international affairs. Then the struggle against fascism turned him into a zealously supernationalist internationalist.
In 1941 he argued that Western Europe should consolidate after World War II
as a single political union with a socialist economy, and Stalin should be

allowed to "clean the stables of Eastern and Southern Europe." Then he went for broke, declaring he would rather see the Soviet Union, "even with its policy unchanged, dominant over *all* Europe, including Great Britain, than see an attempt to restore the pre-war States to their futile and uncreative interdependence and their petty economic nationalism under capitalist domination." Better to be ruled by the loathsome Stalin than by capitalist cliques! When Cole got rolling on comparative loathsomeness, he couldn't stop himself. He topped his hyperbole by claiming he would rather be ruled by Stalin "than by a pack of half-hearted and half-witted Social Democrats who do not believe in Socialism, but do still believe in the 'independence' of their separate, obsolete national States." This obnoxious overthrow of Cole's usual defense of freedom and liberal decency got him enrolled in the government's "Black Book" of figures to be arrested in the event of a Nazi invasion of Britain. Cole had a filter, but not reliably. On that count he wielded less influence in the Labour Party than Tawney.[78]

TAWNEY, THE ACQUISITIVE SOCIETY, AND LABOUR SOCIALISM

Cole made heroic demands on unions and chastised union leaders for resembling politicians. When he scolded, it was usually over political selling out. When Tawney scolded, it was usually over acquisitive corruption, a by-product of capitalism, though Tawney made an exception after the MacDonald debacle. Tawney's aversion to more-radical-than-you made him more accepting than Cole of ordinary Labour politics. He worked for the Labour Party without coming off as a party activist and won the trust of more laborers than any British socialist intellectual of his time. Just before he fought in World War I Tawney sketched a book proposal with a guild socialist title, "The New Leviathan." His first draft emphasized his philosophical idealism, but when he resumed it in 1918 he focused on social principles and values. He started over with an article in the *Hibbert Journal* that the Fabian Society republished as a pamphlet, *The Sickness of an Acquisitive Society*.[79]

The title crystallized what Tawney cared about. Philosophy was not quite the point, and he was not a blueprint thinker. Tawney joined Temple's campaign for social Anglicanism in the Life and Liberty Movement, which called for ecclesiastical freedom without disestablishment. In March 1919, while working on his book, Tawney agreed to serve on the Royal Commission on the Coal Industry, a response to a threatened miners' strike. Led by High Court judge John Sankey, the commission had three mine owners, three miners, three business representatives not directly involved in coal mining, and three economists, counting Tawney and Sidney Webb as economists. It gathered thousands of pages of testimony showing that every aspect of England's coal industry was riddled with gross inefficiency and abusive labor practices. Tawney probed a parade of witnesses with incisive questions and commentary. He won national renown in the process and changed his politics. If nationalizing mines was the only solution to the coal crisis, he had to stop deriding state socialism. The commission split three ways; Sankey supported the miners and economists in urging the state to purchase the nation's mineral resources and collieries; and the government left the industry in chaotic disarray. Tawney was appalled although thrilled that Sankey sided with the pro-miner group. It galled Tawney that shallow claims about the rights of capitalists trumped the commission's painstaking accumulation of evidence about working conditions, the economics of mining, and the common good. His pique showed in *The Acquisitive Society* (1920).[80]

The Acquisitive Society ruefully recounted that the triumph of English liberalism in the early 1830s carried modern preindustrial ideas about private property and freedom of contract into the new capitalist society. In the United States these ideas were crystallized in a constitution and thus treated as sacrosanct. In both places something magnificent—a philosophy of freedom invented by a society of farmers and craft workers—became an instrument of bondage wielded by a business aristocracy. Tawney said it was not too late, at least in England, to create a society based on functions, not rights. Rights should be deducible from the discharge of functions. Acquiring wealth and enjoying property should be contingent on performing services that benefit society. Social policy should favor the good of society over the individual right to acquire wealth. Tawney said every reform movement concerning factories, housing, and consumer goods rejected the capitalist principle that private property rights trump the common good. The challenge was to move beyond the piecemeal efforts of reform movements, building a functional society.

The guild socialist language of functionality was already more important to Tawney than the schemes to build National Guilds. The crucial thing was to fix the attention of the public on the purpose of society, which was to provide "the material foundation of a good social life." Tawney said the primary test of every policy is whether it enhances a healthy, flourishing society. People of vast wealth distort the marketplace by creating a demand for yachts, expensive hotels, and other playthings of the rich, crowding out investments in things society needs. The idle rich double their harm to society by owning without working, distorting production and consumption. Tawney preached a bit on this theme: "It is foolish to maintain property rights for which no service is performed, for payment without service is waste. . . . It is foolish to leave the direction of industry in the hands of servants of private property-owners who themselves know nothing about it but its balance sheets." Certain kinds of property, he observed, are antisocial by definition. Mine owners levied a royalty on every ton of coal that miners brought to the surface and a wayleave on every ton of coal transported from an owner's property—taxes levied by antisocial power. Tawney said every form of private property not benefiting society should be abolished. A good society does not allow privileged dandies who never saw a coal mine to live in splendor off the labor of coal miners. Neither does it allow the landlord class to make fortunes for doing nothing for society, although Tawney acknowledged that some landlords contributed to economic development. John Stuart Mill's principle about the justification of property in land was good enough for Tawney. Every proprietor must be an improver, not a parasite quartered on so-called privately owned land.[81]

Tawney had a vision of industries organized as professions. Building a school and teaching in a school are not functionally disparate, even though capitalist society treats the former as something lowly and the latter as a profession. The same thing is true of the difference between providing food and providing health or making war munitions and firing them. A society based upon service to the public would confer dignity and respect on all work serving the public. It would also confer respect and social responsibility on the professional organizations in each line of work.

Socialization could mean five different things, and Tawney was pragmatic about all of them. The first method, expropriating property owners without compensation, has one colossal precedent in England and Scotland, the seizure of Roman Catholic ecclesiastical property by the Protestant ruling classes. The second method, voluntary surrender, has no significant history at all, unless one counts the abolition of feudalism by the National Assembly of the French Revolution on August 4, 1789. The third method freezes the private owner class out of action by allowing workers to assume responsibility for the process of production and exchange, as in guild socialism. The fourth method limits or attenuates the proprietary interest of private owners to such a degree that they became mere rentiers receiving fixed payments and no profits, with no responsibility for the organization of industry. Cooperatives and similar decentralized economic democracy schemes work on this model. The fifth method is to buy out the private owners, the approach usually taken by municipalities and occasionally by national governments. Tawney said each method has its place. Every attempt to prescribe one as the universal ideal is wrongheaded; the best method is the one that works best in a given situation. Too many socialists and antisocialists identified socialism with nationalization, and now guild socialists fought each other over guild blueprints. Tawney conceived nationalization as one of several means to an end, not an end in itself. The socialist objective was to remove the deadly hand of private ownership, not to nationalize the economy.[82]

Ownership is a bundle of rights, not something singular. To own capital is to claim the right to interest as the price of capital, the right to profits, and the right to control the process of production. In some circumstances, Tawney argued, it is best to strip off specific parts of the bundle. In other cases, the government needs to wipe out the whole bundle through nationalization. The coal crisis, for example, was too vast and vital to be remedied by anything less than nationalization. In the building industry, on the other hand, a serious movement for producer control had arisen. Tawney stressed that this movement teemed with workers and officials who cared "nothing for socialist theories." They did not employ socialist language or speak of an economic revolution. Yet they called for a new system of worker control, including a system of public service accountability within the industry. This was a call for economic revolution, Tawney said. Producer control was in some ways more radical than nationalization, and in England it would be truly revolutionary for builders to win professional status.[83]

Organizing society on the basis of function, to Tawney, meant three things. First, proprietary rights must be earned by public service and abolished when service is lacking. Second, producers must be transparently accountable to consumers, which does not happen under shareholders who care only about financial gains. Third, the responsibility for carrying out an enterprise's service to society rests with the pertinent professional organization of the producers and is subject to the criticism of consumers. Tawney acknowledged that English society was too sick with economic egotism to make the transition smoothly. To institute limits on income, ordinary people had to be weaned from the assiduously nurtured fantasy of becoming rich. People had to imagine a society not stoked by the corrupt luxury tastes of the rich. It would take a while to expel the poison of greed and insatiable acquisitiveness fueling British capitalism. He ended with a litany of moral imperatives for British society: "It must rearrange its scale of values. It must regard economic interests as one element in life, not as the whole of life. It must persuade its members to renounce the opportunity of gains which accrue without any corresponding service, because the struggle for them keeps the whole community in a fever. It must so organize industry that the instrumental character of economic activity is emphasized by its subordination to the social purpose for which it is carried on."[84]

The Acquisitive Society had perfect pitch for the reconstruction moment, just before the economy tanked. It eschewed jargon, wonky policy riffs, and sectarian ideology, pressing a moral argument pitched to a broad audience. It was soaked in Christian socialism and friendly to the Labour Party, although Tawney skirted both topics. The book ignored the problems of inefficiency and bloated bureaucracy that come with nationalizing almost anything, emphasizing moral imperatives. Two readers very close to Tawney cautioned that he exuded too much moralistic certainty. Temple said Tawney's attack on the acquisitive impulse was too scolding and one-sided, since nearly everyone has one, and it isn't necessarily bad. Tawney's colleague at the London School of Economics (LSE), Fabian Society cofounder Graham Wallas, said the same thing more broadly, urging Tawney to reconsider his enthusiasm for producer control. Wallas had served on the London School Board for thirteen years and did not believe that teachers should control education. Too many groups had a stake in education for producer control to be a good idea. Wallas said Tawney preached too zealously against acquisitive desire and vested too much faith in his thesis—borrowed from Morris—that self-government increases the public spirit of the producer. Wallas hoped for less scolding in Tawney's next book, which did not happen.[85]

Just before he joined Wallas on the faculty at LSE, in 1920, Tawney took his first trip to the United States. He spoke at Amherst College, Clark College, and other New England schools, got more invitations at home to speak on religious topics, and accepted them. He supported Temple's energetic efforts in the Life and Liberty Movement and the fledgling ecumenical movement, carrying on Gore's social ethical legacy while leaving the theologizing to Temple. His friendship with Temple caused some to wonder if he would be less religious lacking the Temple factor. As it was, the mutual influence between them was great. Some of the lore on this topic is fanciful, but not the mutton cutlets episode. On one occasion Temple visited Tawney at his home in Mecklenburgh Square when Jeannette Tawney was away. They talked for hours, losing track of time. It occurred to Tawney they should eat something, so he rummaged behind a shelf of books, coming up with two cold mutton cutlets. They ate the cutlets with no garnish, and Temple curled up for the night in two traveling rugs near a box window in the front room. In the wee hours a police officer, noticing Temple's crumpled figure, felt compelled to investigate. He was surprised to awaken a prince of the church. Every aspect of this story paints a true picture.

Scott Holland's friends endowed in his memory a lecture series on the religion of the Incarnation and its commitment to social justice. In 1922 they asked Tawney to give the Holland Lectures, and he obliged with the major scholarly work of his career, *Religion and the Rise of Capitalism*. It was Tawney's take on a sprawling subject, the development of religious thought on social and economic questions from the twelfth to the early eighteenth centuries. He acknowledged his debts to scholarly forerunners, especially Max Weber and Ernst Troeltsch, focusing on the same questions that Troeltsch asked: What has Christianity said about social organization and economic conduct? How sharply have Christian thinkers distinguished between personal and social morality, and how sharply should they do so? Should Christianity espouse any particular theory of social ethics? Troeltsch and Weber, however, did not share Tawney's socialist politics, he was less impressed by Protestantism than they were, he treated Roman Catholicism more respectfully, and he said the Reformed tradition was more complex than they said. So he had to find his own answers.[86]

According to Tawney, there were four ways to conceive the relationship between religion and society, and all had ample histories in Christianity. The way of asceticism stands apart from society as a sphere of unrighteousness. The way of indifference takes society for granted and tries to ignore it. The way of activism seeks to reform or transform society. The way of having it both ways is passive and aggressive simultaneously, accepting society while criticizing it, tolerating society while seeking to correct it. Tawney criticized scholarly renderings of these types that correlated Protestantism with progress and modernity, and he stressed that Catholic thought was unified from the twelfth to the sixteenth centuries on how to think of society. All Catholic thinkers accepted the organic idea of society as analogous to the human body. All accepted the brutal facts of feudal society with little objection—class privilege, class oppression, exploitation, and serfdom. In Catholic thought, equality was a necessity within classes. Between classes, inequality was necessary, otherwise a class could not perform its function. Catholic social thought was thus repressive and protective simultaneously, spiritualizing the world by incorporating it in a sacramental universe.

Tawney highlighted that Catholic theologians revised the theories of just price and usury before the Reformation occurred and Florence was a financial powerhouse long before capitalism existed. Thomas Aquinas taught that prices should correspond with the labor and costs of the producer; the just price was a safeguard against extortion. The schoolmen of the fourteenth century, Tawney noted, said Thomas overlooked the subjective element in getting prices right, and the essence of value is utility. The schoolmen judged that the best way to get a fair price is to allow both parties to engage in free bargaining. In the fifteenth century St. Antonino took a further step toward relativity and modern economics, showing that variances in place, time, and subjectivity cannot be codified and that market forces are impersonal.[87]

From both sides Tawney narrowed the gap between the Catholic and Protestant worlds. He offered long, expository discussions of Luther, Calvin, and the Church of England before getting to his climactic discussion of the Puritan movement, where he squared off with Weber. Luther, Calvin, John Knox, and Puritan Richard Baxter, in Tawney's telling, were deeply medieval in their own ways; the Protestant fashion of assigning medievalism exclusively to the Catholic Church was factually mistaken. Like Troeltsch, Tawney spent many pages demonstrating that Calvinists sought to build a Christian civilization no less than their Catholic counterparts. But Troeltsch had theologically liberal reasons for playing up the medieval elements in premodern Protestantism. Troeltsch wrote as a liberal Protestant partisan and a close friend and ally of Weber's. By the time Tawney got to English Puritanism he had marshaled a case for assigning less import than Weber to English Puritan theology.[88]

In *The Protestant Ethic and the Spirit of Capitalism* (1905) Weber said Puritan anxiety about personal salvation engendered an ethic of industrious work that created the social and political conditions under which capitalism emerged in England. Tawney acknowledged his debt to Weber's analysis. He lauded Weber for writing the indispensable work on this subject, liked Weber's emphasis on the Puritan idea of a calling, and did not dispute that Puritan theology underwrote an ethic of industrious activity and entrepreneurship. But Weber's argument was "one-sided and overstrained." He exaggerated the role of Puritan moral and intellectual influences in creating capitalism. He overlooked that Florence, Venice, south Germany, and Flanders abounded with capitalist spirit in the fifteenth century. These locales, all at least nominally Catholic, thrived with commercial and financial activity. Tawney said Holland and England became economic dynamos in the sixteenth and seventeenth centuries for economic reasons, not because they were Protestant: "Of course material and psychological changes went together, and of course the second reacted on the first. But it seems a little artificial to talk as though capitalist enterprise could not appear till religious changes had produced a capitalist spirit. It would be equally true, and equally one-sided, to say that the religious changes were purely the result of economic movements."[89]

Weber gave short shrift to intellectual movements that favored capitalist development that were not religious. To Tawney, this was a major failing, yielding Weber's exaggerations. Renaissance political thought played a major role in the development of capitalism; Machiavelli was at least as influential as Calvin. Early modern economic writers were nearly as important as Machiavelli, explaining how money and prices worked and extolling the miracles of pecuniary gain. Moreover, Weber oversimplified what he did talk about, Calvinism.

Weber drew a straight line from Calvin to the English Puritans, getting one side of his argument wrong. Sixteenth-century Calvinists—including English Puritans—did believe in rigorous discipline, but they would have been "horrified" by the individualism of their Calvinist descendants. Tawney said this transition was what mattered in Weber's subject. Weber should have lingered with the many Calvinisms that Cromwell confronted when he tried to unite aristocrats, Levellers, Diggers, landowners, merchants, and artisans to overthrow the government. Instead Weber brushed past the winners and losers in seventeenth-century Calvinism to press a too-influential argument about the spirit of Calvinism creating capitalist society. Weber rightly stressed that England's commercial classes fought for the social order they wanted against the peasants, craftsmen, and many of the landed gentry. Tawney further granted that they made religious and political arguments serving their interests. But the Protestant ethic was more complex than Weber's rendering of it, and so was the spirit of capitalism.[90]

Religion and the Rise of Capitalism was a Christian socialist lament for what happened. The religion–capitalism story that mattered was that capitalism corrupted and trivialized Christian ethics, stripping the church of "departments of economic conduct and social theory long claimed as their province." The human desire for pecuniary gain, a natural frailty, was transmuted by capitalism into the mainspring of society. Tawney said Christianity survived the onslaught by casting off its social ethical character. When the Reformation began, economics was still a branch of ethics, ethics was a branch of theology, moral philosophers appealed to natural law, not utility, economic transactions were judged by Christian moral norms, the Church itself was a society, and all human activities belonged to a divine order. The secularization of political thought abetted the loss of the rule of right and replaced it with economic expediency. Tawney was realistic about the Church of England, which resisted feebly because it was a department of state. He felt sharper regrets about the Nonconforming churches, where the Weberian thesis unfortunately explained a great deal. Calvinist anxiety about one's predestined salvation did play a major role in yielding the Protestant ethic of economic individualism, with catastrophic consequences for Christian ethics. Protestant ministers, incredibly to Tawney, preached vulgar individualism without acknowledging their own novelty.[91]

He took a pass at not being scolding. Economic ambitions make great servants, Tawney said, and economic efficiency is a good thing. But economic ambitions make bad masters, and to convert economic efficiency from an instrument into the primary good "is to destroy efficiency itself." Tawney cautioned that no complex society survives without cooperation, the condition of effective action. All previous ages of Western civilization understood what that meant. Christian theology taught for centuries that good living is the only true wealth. Only with the rise of capitalism did ministers say the attainment of material riches is the prize of human effort and final criterion of success. Tawney allowed that capitalist ideology was plausible, powerful, and backed by the power of repressive force. He was not certain that anticapitalist forces would be able to abolish an economic system so powerfully defended by the capitalist class: "What is certain is that it is the negation of any system of thought or morals which can, except by a metaphor, be described as Christian."[92]

This was a dispirited ending, but the audience who gathered to remember Scott Holland and hear Tawney's story did not feel powerless or defeated. They were the successors of Maurice and Ludlow, Headlam, the GSM, the Christian Socialist Society, Holland, the CSU, the Church Socialist League, and the better parts of the National Mission campaign. Their organizations, although less celebrated, were more substantial as activist agencies, being connected to rising Labour Party and ecumenical movements. The Industrial Christian Fellowship (ICF), a fusion of the CSU and the evangelistic Navvy Mission, packed outdoor venues throughout the 1920s under the energetic leadership of Geoffrey Studdert Kennedy, a bighearted cleric with a common touch. He blasted Lloyd George's jingoistic 1918 campaign as an unbearably shameful descent into demagoguery. The following year he founded the ICF. Its platform was the Fifth Report of the National Mission authored by Tawney, demanding a living wage in every industry.

Kennedy steered the ICF away from partisan commitments, conceiving it as a Christian ecumenical pressure group. He emphasized moral criticism and building a broad-based movement, studiously avoiding the fate of the Church Socialist League, which was too hard-edged, battle-weary, and identified with guild socialism to survive the 1920s. Noel mortally wounded the Church Socialist League by splitting it in 1916 and founding the Catholic Crusade in 1918. He believed the only true Christian socialism was Anglo-Catholic; thus he never learned the Headlam lesson, ending with a sect that mirrored his radical socialism and anti-Nonconforming Protestantism. Two new religious socialist organizations arose after the Church Socialist League folded in 1924: the League for the Kingdom of God and the Society for Socialist Christians. The league was Anglo-Catholic, strongly theological, and mostly guild socialist, operating an influential Summer School of Sociology. Widdrington was its ringleader, along with Reckitt and V. A. Demant, as Widdrington finally got the organization he wanted. The society mixed ecumenical Anglicans with religious socialists from other traditions, boasting significant Quaker and Free

Church flanks, Tawney, and non-Christians. The league was stronger than the society, but Christian socialism was entering a phase in which ecumenical activism trumped confessional identities.[93]

In 1921 Temple was consecrated as bishop of Manchester, never quite sure why Lloyd George appointed him to a notoriously conservative diocese. Temple vowed to make the most of it by bringing the ecumenical movement to Manchester, although he resigned from the Labour Party, reasoning that bishops should stay out of party politics. Tawney pleaded that the church had plenty of Tory bishops, to no avail. In 1924 Temple convened the milestone event of the early ecumenical movement, the Conference on Christian Politics, Economics, and Citizenship (COPEC), at Birmingham. It was the most ambitious gathering of its kind to that point, readying a British delegation for the world ecumenical conference at Stockholm the following year.

MacDonald sent a congratulatory greeting as the new prime minister. COPEC gathered fifteen hundred delegates, eighty from outside the British Isles. It discussed reports from twelve appointed commissions and Temple's opening speech decrying Machiavellian moral bankruptcy in statecraft. Gore gave a forceful address on economic democracy, declaring, "We need tremendous courage to ask ourselves frankly whether we are really prepared to accept these fundamental principles and to apply them whatever the effect upon our party politics." The answer was no, with or without the determination of Temple and conference secretary Charles Raven to include church moderates. Two kinds of reports came out of COPEC, Christian socialist and muddled. Disappointed socialists sneered that COPEC stood for "Conventional Official Platitudes Expressing Caution." John Kent, a later critic, sneered that many delegates supported Gore and Temple as a moral gesture. At the conference Temple played the role of consensus builder; afterward he worked with Reckitt, Tawney, Raven, and Ruth Kenyan to get a Christian socialist legacy out of it.[94]

COPEC established that a next generation of Christian socialists had taken over from Gore and Noel. It published pamphlets in Fabian style for five years, featuring writings by Temple, Tawney, Gore, Kennedy, Lindsay, and Harold Laski. It played a role in reforming the penal system, expanding secondary education, and creating housing assistance, and in 1929 it merged into a new ecumenical organization, the Council of Christian Churches for Social Questions, ably led by Demant. COPEC pushed for living wage legislation, believing it found the borderline between attacking the wage system and settling for too little. But that was wrongly optimistic, as the living wage was furiously denounced as anticapitalist and went nowhere. Meanwhile Labour's first shot at governing was brief—eleven months. COPEC, having begun with buoyant expectations of carrying forward the legacy of Holland, Gore, and Noel, became a symbol of something else. It was the climax of the idealistic phase of British Christian socialism, not a new phase of it.

The fix was in for the living wage before COPEC convened, as Lloyd George's government responded to the economic downturn of 1920 by deflating the currency by 40 percent. The government calculated that a wage of three pounds per week would set off a flood of imports, crush the gold standard, and wreck the economy. It pegged Britain's monetary policy to a calculation about how much pressure the industrial firms could bear—a judgment overriding anybody's belief in the principle of a living wage. The ensuing pain yielded the first Labour government, a minority enterprise with no chance of lasting. Reckitt, later recalling how the Church Socialist League implored progressives not to shrink from the "profounder changes" that living wage legislation necessitated, remembered his bitter disillusionment vividly: "The bishops had no more idea than the rest of the great mass of social idealists what such 'profounder changes' might be, since they knew little or nothing of the financial factors which had transformed the situation on which had been based their cherished 'principle.' It was all very bewildering, and it could only be hoped that trade would soon 'revive' again and permit moral demands to operate with the approval of orthodox economics."[95]

This grim equation sapped the socialist movement of its idealism just as the Labour Party became the established opposition. For a while Tawney got along without idealistic expectations. It was enough to help Labour move forward, as long as it did so. In the mid-1920s he was deeply involved in Labour politics, shuttling between miners' union offices during the General Strike of 1926. Tawney boasted that he started the strike in 1925 by taking a call at the miners' headquarters. Northern colliers asked if they should go into the pits the following night. Tawney, seeing no official at hand, said no. The ensuing stoppage, in his gleeful telling, led to others, leading to the General Strike. More accurately, the General Strike capped seven years of ferment in the coal industry. Temple and ICF secretary P. T. R. Kirk led a church group that mediated between the miners and owners, endorsing the 1926 Report of the Royal Commission on the Coal Industry. Archbishop of Canterbury Randall Davidson reluctantly agreed to broadcast the Temple group's report, but the BBC canceled Davidson's broadcast, Kirk sided with the miners, enraging Davidson, and a public furor ensued over the church's right to interfere in politics. Temple took a beating in the press for prolonging the strike. He denied having sided with the miners but said they negotiated in good faith, the owners did not, and the settlement amounted to creeping socialism: "Quite evidently we are all Socialists now."

Since the big firms never protected the public interest, the government had to do so: "If that is so, the case for a movement in the Collectivist direction seems to be proved, whether or not the whole journey is to be travelled to a complete Socialist State."[96]

The General Strike, however, yielded vindictive antiunion legislation demanded by Stanley Baldwin's Conservative government. The Trade Disputes and Trade Unions Act of 1927 outlawed all strikes extending beyond a single trade or industry *and* all strikes that inflicted "hardship upon the community," with courts interpreting the hardship standard. The strike also demonstrated that Davidson had no mettle whatsoever for a fight over social justice. As soon as the miners went on strike Davidson wailed in the House of Lords against the shocking "mischievousness" of the unions. The government demanded unconditional surrender by the miners, Davidson stayed in line with the government, and he caught some of the backlash against Temple despite doing nothing for the miners. By the end of the strike Tawney was disgusted with the church. He supported the call of Widdrington and Demant for a full-fledged Christian sociology, no longer banking on ethical idealism. Demant declared in 1929, "You cannot moralize a contradiction. But if you are ignorant that a social situation involves contradictory policies you are looking for wrong ethical *motives* to account for the disasters—and you will mistake for these the moral perversions and poisoned relationships that spring from the strains imposed by the social dilemma."[97]

The highlight of Tawney's early work in the Labour Party came in the 1929 election, when Labour ran for the first time as a national party, not a class party, pitching Labour socialism as the nation's best hope. MacDonald called for a new charter replacing *Labour and the New Social Order*. Tawney wrote the first draft of *Labour and the Nation*, declaring that socialism rests on a moral conviction: "Socialism is neither a sentimental aspiration for an impossible Utopia, nor a blind movement of revolt against poverty and oppression. It is a practical recognition of the familiar commonplace that 'morality is the nature of things,' and that men are all, in very truth, members one of another." The party strenuously debated Tawney's draft before running on it. The ILP wanted a socialist program for a socialist government, as expressed in its slogan, "Socialism in Our Time" or, better, "Socialism Now." Many ILP stalwarts still believed in guild socialism but were willing to settle for extensive nationalization. MacDonald lieutenant Herbert Morrison said Tawney's draft gave Labour what it needed— a vague statement of aims and principles undergirding the election campaign. There were disputes over nationalizing all banks, nationalizing some banks, or converting the Bank of England to a public corporation. Philip Snowden, however, said Labour had to fudge the entire issue. Snowden, a Methodist weaver's son who came up through the Free Church Socialist League and joined the ILP at its founding, was Labour's only financial expert, plus never in doubt. Thus he got his way on matters financial, fatefully. MacDonald played left and right against each other to keep Tawney's draft intact, resisting all attempts to bind him to a specific program; later he said that Tawney's draft was too radical, making his government look bad.[98]

Labour never agreed about why it advocated public ownership. Was achieving social justice the highest priority, or increasing economic efficiency? If social justice was paramount, should it be cast as a moral issue? Tawney's view prevailed in *Labour and the Nation,* declaring that the purpose of public ownership was to convert industry "from a sordid struggle for the private gain into a co-operative undertaking." The election of 1929 pitted Labour's promise to fight unemployment against the Tory promise to keep Britain safe from Communism. For the first time, Labour won the most seats, although MacDonald needed Liberal support to form a government. Tawney glowed at being on the winning team and playing the role he wanted. His academic career had stalled because of his political activism, but he did not write for academic laurels. *The Acquisitive Society* and *Religion and the Rise of Capitalism* garnered wide attention. In the heady days of Labour's march to power, Tawney wrote his third signature book, *Equality,* a masterpiece of the genre he preferred, principles-for-policies. By the time it appeared in 1931 he felt very differently about the Labour Party.[99]

Winning office as a minority government on the doorstep of the Great Depression was a dubious achievement. Twelve of MacDonald's nineteen cabinet members were veterans of his first government, notably Arthur Henderson (foreign secretary), Philip Snowden (chancellor of the exchequer), J. R. Clynes (home secretary), and Sidney Webb (dominions and colonial secretary). The left wing got two cabinet posts, in education (Charles Trevelyan) and public works (George Lansbury). Newcomers included Arthur Greenwood (minister of health) and Herbert Morrison (minister of transport, noncabinet). Morrison was a pure product of Fabian Labour politics, having dropped out of school at the age of fourteen to become an errand boy, joined the Labour Party as a conscientious objector to World War I, and won the mayoralty of Hackney in 1920. The second Labour government said nothing about Socialism Now. It pushed through a mining reform bill that owners ignored, as enforcement powers did not exist. It expanded pension coverage for widows and retirees, struck down restrictions on unemployment insurance and health insurance, and accelerated spending on public works.

But Snowden was a true believer in free trade, the gold standard, and balanced budgets, and MacDonald deferred to Snowden. Oswald Mosley, chancellor of the

Duchy of Lancaster, begged the cabinet to take public control of banking and exports and aggressively stimulate the economy. Keynes and Lloyd George made similar proposals, and Cole supported Keynes on MacDonald's Economic Advisory Council. They got nowhere with MacDonald, Snowden, and half the cabinet. Mosley resigned dramatically in May 1930 and went public, making his case to the House of Commons; his frustration soon turned him into a fascist. By the summer of 1931 the government reeled from a financial crisis fanned by Snowden's sky-is-falling alarms meant for domestic consumption. The New York Federal Reserve Bank and the Bank of France demanded austerity measures, yielding bitterly divisive cabinet meetings over austerity cuts. Keynes implored MacDonald to devalue the pound by 25 percent and stop trying to balance the budget. The cabinet roiled and split over MacDonald's strategy. In late August a proposal to reduce unemployment benefits sundered the government. Nine cabinet members opposed the reduction, led by Henderson, eleven voted in support, and on August 24 MacDonald formally resigned, lacking a functioning government.[100]

Traumatized Labour officials figured that King George V would ask Baldwin to form a new government. They had no idea that MacDonald would persuade the Tories to form a government keeping him as prime minister. The deal was to balance the budget and address the economic emergency while spurning any new legislation on which the parties disagreed. MacDonald threw his party overboard, skipping the Labour meetings at which his decision was announced. Labour furiously expelled MacDonald, Snowden, and Clynes as traitors. MacDonald launched a party vehicle, the National Labour Party, for his arrangement with the Tories and Liberals, winning a landslide victory in October 1931 that crushed the Labour Party, headed by Henderson. MacDonald was conflicted about routing Labour so badly. His National Government coalition won 554 seats, but 473 were Conservatives; meanwhile Labour fell to 52 seats and political oblivion. The only Labour leaders to keep their seats were Stafford Cripps, Clement Attlee, who became vice-chair, and George Lansbury, the new chair. Even Henderson lost his seat in Parliament. Labour loathing of MacDonald, already hot when he was expelled, reached a fever pitch after Labour became a spectator to the politics of the 1930s. MacDonald governed until 1935, fading badly near the end, and died in 1937. He got a terrible press for forty years until a revisionist trend began in the late 1970s, crediting MacDonald with getting England through the worst of the Depression. Historians sympathetic to Labour conveyed the Labour revulsion at being betrayed, until sufficient temporal distance existed for revisionist considerations.[101]

Cole and Tawney had a similar take on the MacDonald debacle. Cole said MacDonald loved to play with ideas but hated to make up his mind. He was capable of agreeing with anyone, except anyone to the left of him. Thus he was an easy mark for Snowden, who arrogantly dragged MacDonald to an abyss, after which MacDonald dragged Snowden into a so-called National Government that Snowden despised. Cole judged that MacDonald cared about his vanity more than anything else, so losing his place in the Labour Party did not compare to his desire to remain prime minister: "MacDonald had no policy, except a rejection of the programme which he had been elected to carry out." Cole and Keynes, Cole recalled, "tried to get MacDonald to understand the sheer necessity of adopting some definite policy for stopping the rot," but MacDonald dithered in uncertainty, relying on Snowden, and most of the Labour Party did not grasp the severity of the crisis until the summer of 1931. Cole did not mention that Keynesian medicine was new and disputed in 1930, most European Social Democrats did not believe in it, and his own support of it was halfhearted, not knowing what to believe.[102]

Tawney had always held a low view of MacDonald, an insecure plebeian who climbed high on guile and egotism. On every count MacDonald was Tawney's opposite, since Tawney knew who he was and what he believed, and he had reached down, not up. By Tawney's lights the only principled stand MacDonald ever took was against World War I, which he got wrong. Shortly after the National Government took over, Tawney said MacDonald's character defects and lack of conviction doomed the Labour government. To be sure, Labour was unlucky to walk into a global financial crisis, and it tried to pass some good legislation. But Tawney did not buy the excuse about minority government, and he said that MacDonald's government botched its historic choice: It could live dangerously or play for safety. The choice was between proceeding with honesty and conviction or assuming its primary duty was to remain in office. Had Labour acted on its professed principles, it would have lasted no more than a year in office. Tawney wished desperately that Labour had taken that option, which was not possible with MacDonald at the helm because most of the party wanted him to make the wrong choice.[103]

This was not a stab-in-the-back story, according to Tawney. MacDonald exemplified the collective shortcomings of Labour. To scapegoat MacDonald for them was to guarantee that the next Labour government would be equally bad: "What Labour most needs is not self-commiseration, but a little cold realism. These plaintive romancers would dry its tears with a tale of Red Riding Hood and the wicked wolf. They retard the recovery of the party by concealing its malady." The second Labour government, Tawney said, was a rerun of the first, under worse conditions. Labour acted indecisively in power because it was uncertain and divided about what it wanted: "It frets out of office and fumbles in it, because it lacks the assurance either to wait or to strike." There was no organizational fix to this problem, he warned. Admittedly, unions had too much influence at party conferences, but union parochialism was not the cause of Labour failure. Neither was the campaign program the problem, although programs were always defective: "They sweep together great things and small; nationalize land, mines, and banking in one sentence, and abolish fox-hunting in the next; and, by touching on everything, commit ministers to nothing." This was another symptom, not the disease. Bad programs could not be helped as long as the party lacked a defining creed, an ordered conception of its beliefs and tasks. Tawney wanted Labour to know what it wanted and to risk defeat on that basis. In his telling, the glamour of a single word, "socialism," concealed from Labour leaders their own confusion and disarray. Labour thought it solved the creedal problem in 1918 by declaring itself to be a socialist party. But this was merely an aspiration, Tawney said. It was never fulfilled, so Labour never became a party that stood for something definite. To become a socialist party, Labour had to discipline itself for an entire decade toward this goal.[104]

Tawney reasoned that socialism was like any other creed in combining a personal attitude and a collective effort. The quality of the effort depended on the sincerity of the attitude. Socialists in power had to promote socialist policies and love what they believed. British socialism, he judged, was undisciplined because Labour grew too rapidly and easily. The unions brought the first wave of members; World War I triggered the second; the election of 1923 drew the third wave; and the General Strike of 1926 brought the fourth wave. With each wave it got easier to say you were a socialist; by 1926 it was even fashionable. This march to political respectability corrupted Labour into treating votes as equivalent to convictions. The party acquired leaders who shirked the fundamental socialist question: Who is to be master? Should a few thousand bankers, industrialists, and landowners continue to rule England?

To shirk the question was to flunk the essential test of being a socialist leader. Here Tawney got personal, without mentioning MacDonald's name or his cabinet followers. England's ruling class did not consist of simpletons, he said. They respected achievement and success and despised all attempts to wheedle them with cajolery. They were entirely willing to brutalize wage earners and the poor to keep their privileges. Tawney dismissed the Labour slogan of the moment, "Never office again without a majority." A majority Labour government with bad leaders would be no different than the first two Labour governments. It galled him that so many Labour officials preferred the company of their rich friends: "Who will believe that the Labour Party means business as long as some of its stalwarts sit up and beg for social sugar-plums, like poodles in a drawing room?"[105]

This polemic, "The Choice Before Us," had a complex career in Labour politics. It was quoted and reprinted for decades, becoming the most influential critique of its kind. It defined the Socialist League, which Tawney, Attlee, Cripps, Cole, Margaret Cole, Laski, and Postgate founded in 1932 to demand that Labour stand for socialism. The Socialist League reprinted Tawney's article as a pamphlet in 1934 as its platform, which it remained until Popular Front drama and Cripps's ego defined the league and got Cripps expelled from the party. Many Labour officials resented that Tawney ridiculed them so publicly, albeit not by name. Some countered that he was chummy with Lloyd George, Lloyd George's sidekick Lord Richard Burton Haldane, and Baldwin's speechwriter Tom Jones, one of Tawney's best friends. Who was he to cast aspersions?

Tawney had toured in China as the MacDonald government floundered. When he returned to England his nation and party felt very different to him. Lansbury, Attlee, Morrison, Cripps, Greenwood, Ernest Bevin, and Aneurin Bevan kept the party alive. Lansbury had led the pacifist faction of the Church Socialist League through World War I and kept his friends through the worst of it because disliking him was impossible. His kindly personality made him a Labour unifier. He led the party from 1931 to 1935, until his pacifism was disqualifying. Lansbury's opposition to rearming Britain roiled Labour conferences, yielding his resignation in 1935. Cripps, a Christian socialist from a privileged background, long on factional ambition and administrative ability, turned the Socialist League into a vehicle of his ambitions. Tawney, despite his call to militancy, pulled back from party activism and quietly supported Attlee. In March 1933 Jones asked Tawney why he had retreated to writing about education. Tawney replied that Europe was in the grip of a war of "Economic Religion," capitalism versus Communism. It was hard to stand somewhere when that framed everything, so he went back to bridge-building activism in intermediate organizations, doubling down on WEA work, writing about education, and conducting historical research.[106]

Tawney's chief contributions to British socialism were his three signature books. He seemed more present in the mid-1930s than he was because *Equality* became the socialist Bible to many socialists, a classic that proved hard to revise. *Equality* began as the Halley Stewart Lectures of 1929, there were two editions in 1931, Tawney revised it substantially in 1938, and he revised it slightly in 1952, adding an epilogue. He tried to restrict his revisions to the book's policy and political sections, where statistics and contextual judgments had to be updated. Tawney despaired of updating his references to "today" and "now," since there were so many. In the last edition he asked readers to remember that the book reflected the world of 1931, with minimal revisions. He seemed to forget that his remaining "now" language came from the 1938 edition. In 1960 he took another pass at updating the book but gave up. *Equality* had never been as timeless as the title suggested, but it achieved classic status for expounding his basic moral principles and political tropes: All human beings possess divinely imprinted equal worth and dignity. Socialism is moral and democratic, freedom and equality go together, inequality curtails liberty, the twin drivers of inequality in England were inherited wealth and the public schools, and socialists needed to stand for socialism.[107]

Equality famously echoed Matthew Arnold's lament that inequality was almost a religion in England. Tawney did not mean that England was the worst nation in Europe or anything of the sort. He took pride that England was the only nation in which feudalism did not create a caste system. Every other feudal nation had to have an earthquake revolution to get rid of feudal caste. England incorporated liberal elements before it had a revolution, so English social structure was based on differences of wealth, not formal inequalities of legal status. To Tawney, this explained why *bourgeoisie* never caught on in England. On the Continent the term designated a definite class, distinct from the nobility and peasants. In England it made no sense, "for the *bourgeoisie* included all strata above the manual workers." The small role played by legal privilege in England made English society immune to the egalitarian passions of French radicalism. Tawney put the same metaphor differently, contending that English liberalism inoculated English society with doses of freedom "small enough to be harmless." The upshot was England's religion of inequality: "Inequality, if not embodied in laws which assigned a different status to different classes, found a hardly less effective expression in the control by the upper orders of administration, in their virtual monopoly of educational opportunity, in their exclusive exercise of political authority, and in the enjoyment of the profitable perquisites which political authority could be made to yield."[108]

Tawney had no inkling that British socialism needed to dismantle white privilege and gender privilege. *Equality* said almost nothing about racial and gender caste barriers in England, except to suggest they didn't exist. He devoted two sentences to this subject, observing that in various times and places the dominating mentality "has colored the relations between the sexes; at another, those between religions; at a third, those between members of different races." English society no longer did so; at least, these forms of injustice held little sway "in communities no longer divided by religion or race, and in which men and women are treated as political and economic equals." *Equality* was not about these things. Tawney had no feminist sensibility, and he believed that racism was a negligible issue in Britain. Believing in equality, he said, has nothing to do with trying to believe that all people are equal in character and intelligence.

Differences at the individual level are to be valued; a good society enables individual differences to flourish. The mark of a civilized society is to eliminate all inequalities rooted in society's own organization. In England one form of domination prevailed, class rule. Tawney said a good society has plenty of differences and inequalities to negotiate, many of them welcome, after it minimizes the economic factor. Class difference should be the least important factor in society. Instead, in England it was virtually the national religion.[109]

To Tawney, the worst thing about economic inequality was its exclusion of many people from social goods, not that some people earn or inherit more money than others. A good society makes public provisions that recognize the equal dignity and rights of all citizens. Persons should be entitled to basic social goods as citizens, not as consumers. He fixed on the class factor because it got in the way of what matters, the flourishing of human fellowship. Democratic socialism combats the two essential features of capitalism: privilege and tyranny. Privilege is a function of interrelated social and economic power, usually as a by-product of wealth converting to social power, whereas tyranny is a function of the distribution of power. Equality is the antidote to privilege, but democratizing power is the antidote to tyranny. Democratic socialism makes it possible for human fellowship to flourish by democratizing economic and social power. In a good society, Tawney argued, people respect one another for what they are, not for what they own. A good society abolishes the reverence for wealth that capitalism feeds upon by abolishing the existence of an upper class: "What is important is not that all men should receive the same pecuniary income. It is that the surplus resources of society should be so husbanded and applied that it is a matter of minor significance whether they receive it or not."[110]

Health care and education topped Tawney's list. On health care he kept his cool; on education, his great passion, he raged. English citizens who lacked the means to pay for decent health care were grossly mistreated, he said, but not as a dogmatic principle. The religion of inequality was a bit squeamish about leaving the poor to suffer and die. On education, however, the religion of inequality was creedal and unapologetic, evoking Tawney's anger. He cut straight to a jeremiad: "The idea that differences of educational opportunity among children should depend upon differences of wealth among parents is a barbarity. It is as grotesque and repulsive as to suppose that the latter should result, as once they did, in differences of personal security and legal status." He protested that no nation in the world went as far as England to reserve special schools for children of the rich: "It is at once an educational monstrosity and a grave national misfortune." English education was "educationally vicious" for segregating the rich from all others, plus "socially disastrous" for reinforcing and perpetuating the capitalist division of classes. Tawney had a simple alternative, a parental version of the golden rule. A nation should provide for all children what good parents want for their children.[111]

A good society does not instill pride or fear in its people. It respects all people and feels awe toward none. It spurns all forms of authority that breed arrogance in a privileged class and subservience in a dominated class. Authority must rest on consent, and power is tolerable only to the extent it is accountable to the public. When Tawney revised *Equality* in 1938 he still believed the Labour governments failed from "exaggerated discretion," but he said it more gently than in 1932, having witnessed "an epidemic of the 'infantile disease of Left-wingism.'" More-radical-than-you was much in fashion, and Tawney had returned to his aversion to it. He gasped as Laski, an old friend, lurched into pro-Communism; meanwhile Labour's leader was an outright pacifist. To Tawney, freedom was not merely an escape from tyranny; it was the capacity to act independently or in association, an indispensable foundation of socialism. He said democratic socialists were more united than it seemed, and they needed to pull together now that Germany had descended "to a half-tribal conception of national unity" based on blood mythology, hero worship, the persecution of the alien, and the cult of force. The 1938 edition ripped Labour for retreating into private visions of socialism that did not speak to ordinary people, a resort of the bunker. Having retreated himself while the party trudged through dismal years of budget cuts for social services, Tawney implored others and himself to get in the game.[112]

THEOLOGIZING THE WORLD

Tawney's retreat coincided with Temple's emergence as a world figure. Baldwin placed Temple in charge of York as archbishop in 1929, reasoning that Temple towered above other candidates, his bad politics notwithstanding. Temple wrote and lectured prolifically, chaired the Council of the British Broadcasting Company, chaired the Lambeth Conference of Anglican Bishops in 1932, served on the Privy Council, supported the League of Nations, played leading roles in every major ecumenical conference of the 1930s, and delivered the Gifford Lectures of 1932–1933 and 1933–1934—in addition to visiting the 457 parishes in his diocese. It helped that he never needed a manuscript, even for his magnificent Gifford Lectures, and that Temple was constantly buoyant. Gore, believing his own grumpiness was a prophetic asset, puzzled that someone as happy as Temple did not shrink from social justice combat.

In 1931 Temple began to warn about another world war, calling for a foreign policy based on cooperation and international law. At a disarmament conference in Geneva in 1932 he blasted the War Guilt clause of the Versailles Treaty, contending it was historically wrong and morally offensive to blame Germany solely for World War I: "The voice of Christendom must be raised. . . . We have to ask not only who dropped the match but who strewed the ground with gunpowder." Temple ignored an outcry in the British press about attributing war guilt to England and criticizing England on foreign soil. He implored Davidson, who was like a second father to him, to sign a statement confessing that England shared in the guilt for the war. Davidson flatly refused. Temple's energetic support of the League of Nations sometimes romanticized it. The goal of history is to fulfill the Commonwealth of Value, he said; thus the founding of the league marked "an epoch of significance not only for our historical period but for History itself when viewed in relation to Eternity."[113]

No Anglican archbishop had ever given the Gifford Lectures. Temple's were conceived in off moments in trains and hotels. Most were written as he delivered them, from November 1932 to March 1934. The book version, *Nature, Man and God* (1934), recycled Temple's usual theological themes: Spirit is a *vera causa*, a real source and cause of process. Spirit is the nature of the Supreme Reality that created all things. The Will of Christ is one with the Will of God and expressive of it but not identical with it. Will and Personality are ideally interchangeable terms. To believe in God on the basis of experience and reason is to have an apprehension of universal import corresponding to the supreme claim of Truth. Love divine creates and calls out from created things the Love that all things were created to be and to express.[114]

Fifteen years after the Barthian revolt shook Continental theology, Temple had no trace of Barth's polemic against philosophical theology. "Crisis theology" did not suit his temperament or his reasoned faith. However, Temple felt deeply the crisis of capitalist civilization, which caused him to change his philosophical position. Marxism, he acknowledged, spoke powerfully to the Depression generation. It was so relevant that "only a Dialectic more comprehensive in its range of apprehension and more thorough in its appreciation of the inter-play of factors in the real world, can overthrow it or seriously modify it as a guide to action." Temple said the long reign of mind-centered idealism was over in theology and philosophy. A new dialectic was needed, which he called dialectical realism. To make his idealistic perspective make sense to a generation that no longer believed in progress or idealism, he had to find a realistic basis for it that drew upon "the inter-play of factors in the real world."[115]

He found it by appropriating the organic emergence theory of Alfred North Whitehead. Whitehead's career had three phases that corresponded with his teaching appointments at Trinity College, Cambridge; University College, London; and

Harvard University. From 1885 to 1914 he explored the logical foundations of mathematics; from 1914 to 1924 he worked on the philosophy of natural science, especially theoretical physics; from 1925 to his death in 1947 he concentrated on
metaphysics. His second and third phases built upon the organicism of University
of Manchester philosopher Samuel Alexander and University of Bristol philosopher C. Lloyd Morgan. Temple drew deeply on Whitehead's idea that becoming is
more elemental than being because reality is fundamentally temporal and creative.
Becoming, event, and relatedness are fundamental categories of understanding.
The world, from a commonsense standpoint, consists of material things that endure
in space and time, and events are occurrences that happen to things or that things
experience. Whitehead countered that events are the fundamental things, the
immanent movement of creativity itself.[116]

Methodologically, Whitehead's system had strong parallels to Heidegger's
phenomenology, taking immediate human experience as his point of departure,
in Whitehead's case as a pan-experiential belief that feeling is the essential clue
to being. Whitehead taught that perceiving, valuing, and remembering are
structural clues to the interpretation of experience. Like Alexander and Lloyd
Morgan, he was an emergent evolutionist in the tradition of Henri Bergson,
rejecting the mechanistic view of nature as a machinelike system of pushes and
pulls. Things are complexes of motions that possess within themselves their own
principle of motion. Evolution contains a *nisus* (striving) toward higher levels of
novel emergence, and each entity is related to all others in a living universe. In
the mid-1920s Whitehead disavowed his atheism, reasoning that God exists as
the source of cosmic order. In *Religion in the Making* (1926) he described God
as "the binding element in the world." In 1929, in *Process and Reality*, he developed this idea that human consciousness is universalized in God's being.[117]

Whitehead was deeply impressed by the mysterious fact that the evolving
universe, for all its chaotic randomness, possesses a high degree of order. The
universe consists of countless billions of droplets of experience that occur and
pass away. By themselves they possess nothing that stands in the way of chaos
and mutual destruction, and yet the universe is also orderly and pervaded by
examples of mutual adjustment. Each event strives toward the realization of
some value, and each event is succeeded by similar events. To account for the
existence of the creative process of life and the mutual support that makes the
creative process possible, Whitehead described creativity as "the creative
advance into novelty" and God as a concrete actual entity that envisages pure
potentials, "eternal objects." The world never reaches completion and neither
does God, for "both are in the grip of the ultimate metaphysical ground, the
creative advance into novelty." God and the world are necessary to each other,

for divine reality is always in process with creation. In Whitehead's system God's primordial nature is the universe of creative possibilities, the total potentiality of all existing entities at all moments of their actualization. God's consequent nature consists of the accumulated actualization of the choices of self-actualizing entities. Every self-actualizing entity is grounded in God's primordial nature and possesses the power to actualize or negate God's life-enhancing aim. But the reality of freedom makes it possible for self-actualizing entities to choose evil. God is the highest exemplification of all metaphysical principles, not an exception to them. As a primordial reality God is "the unlimited conceptual realization of the absolute wealth of potentiality." God lures God's subjects to make creative, life-enhancing choices, but God does not infringe upon the freedom of the moral agent to make choices. With a poetic flourish Whitehead described God as "the lure for feeling, the eternal urge of desire."[118]

Temple's appropriation of Whitehead was much like his appropriation of Hegel. Philosophically, these were the best modern resources for theology, but they had to be Christianized with a real Incarnation and a personal God. Temple believed that Barthian theology had no future in England because it ignored the real world described by science. Whiteheadian organicism was consistent with the modern understanding of evolution as a long, slow, gradual process of layered stages in which complex forms of life built upon simple ones, and Whitehead's expertise in relativity theory was a major strength of his system, conceiving the universe as dynamic and interconnected.

So Temple gave it two cheers, showing that his neo-Hegelian worldview folded into the Whiteheadian scheme. Both, after all, were temporal versions of Platonism. It seemed to Temple that a great dialectical movement of thought—Cartesianism—was finally passing away in the world-historical crisis of the 1930s. Modern thought, lured into a tunnel by Descartes, approached a phase of Hegelian antithesis, usually a briefer phase than thesis or synthesis. Every dominant thesis has inertia and the impression of common sense going for it; the antithesis is a protest against the limitations of the thesis; once the antithesis has been worked out and its shortcomings exposed, it gives way to a synthesis. The thesis, in the case of modern thought, was the Cartesian project of beginning with radical doubt, which Temple called mere "academic doubt," since Descartes did not really doubt the world was out there or that he was distinct from his kitchen.[119]

Descartes, pretending to doubt everything, set modern philosophy down the path in which Berkeley abolished the material world and Hume claimed he didn't have a mind, all he had was a flux of ideas caused by nothing, held by nothing, and merely happening. Hegel and English Hegelianism came close to uniting reason and experience, but the school of Hegel shared the customary philosophic sin of conceiving cognition as the original form of apprehension. Temple still believed in the real priority of Spirit, but he no longer believed in the metaphysical priority of the Subject in the subject–object relation of knowledge. He reasoned that one does not have to uphold the primacy of Spirit as Subject of knowledge to uphold a spiritual worldview. In fact, it is important not to say that the mind begins with itself and its ideas before apprehending the external world through construction and inference.[120]

Post-Kantian idealism had to be corrected by organic evolutionary theory. Temple took no position on the nature of the physical structure of reality; Whitehead's view that it was rudimentarily organic was a leading possibility. What mattered was that whatever it is, it preceded consciousness. Whether or not all existence is organic, the organic principle is the means by which all apprehensions of the world must be understood and placed. Experience precedes consciousness even if Whitehead overstretched in describing all actions and reactions of physical entities as experience. The mind discovers beauty and extension in the world, which are there in the initial datum. This is not naïve realism, Temple cautioned; an object apart from knowledge is not exactly what it is for knowledge. His view, dialectical realism, conceived the subject–object relation as ultimate in cognition; neither the subject nor the object is reducible to the other. All apprehension is of objects and is interpretive from the beginning: "Thus we are led to the view that thinking is grounded in the process of adjustment between organism and environment and is indeed an extension of that process." Thought expands by adjusting to wider environments: "Intellectual growth is a perpetually fuller responsiveness to the truth of the environment; aesthetic growth to its beauty; moral growth to its goodness; religious growth to its spiritual character expressed in all of these."[121]

The mind *emerges* through the process of apprehensions and adjustments it apprehends. The fact that the world gives rise to minds that apprehend the world, Temple argued, tells us something important about the world—there is a deep kinship between Mind and the world. The world has a relation of correspondence to Mind, something every rational being experiences in discovering oneself to be an occurrence within the natural process with which one recognizes kinship. But mind and matter are related dialectically, Temple said. Matter does not generate thought, nor does thought generate matter. The world of matter, always a relative flux of forms, lacks a self-explanatory principle, while mind has the principle of purpose or rational choice. Since there is no materialist explanation for the emergence of mind and because mind contains a self-explanatory principle of origination, it is reasonable to believe that Mind contains the explanation of the world-process: "The more completely we include Mind within Nature, the more inexplicable must Nature become except by reference to Mind." Put differently, if mind is part of nature, nature must be grounded in mind; otherwise nature could not contain it.[122]

The world-process as such stands in need of explanation. Here Temple took leave of Whitehead, whose proposed explanation—the primordial nature of God—did not explain anything. Whitehead said relevant novelty without God is impossible, but he did not explain how, *with* God, novelty is possible. The primordial nature of God is merely a name for something desired as essential, an explanation for the initiation of the flux. Temple argued that unless God is something other than the ground of possibility, it does not help to say, like Whitehead, that God is the ground of possibility. Such a statement has no more explanatory value than to say the ground of possibility is the ground of possibility. Temple acknowledged that Whitehead's rendering of God's consequent nature said beautifully poetic things sounding very much like Christian theology. But Whitehead excluded personality from his description of Organism in process, so it was hard to see how he justified his end-of-the-book description of God as "the great companion—the fellow-sufferer who understands."[123]

Temple conceived the world-process as the medium of God's personal action and God's active purpose as the determinant element in every actual cause. It is pointless to only half believe in God, he said. The concept of divine personality must be taken "in bitter earnest," conceiving God's purposive Mind as the immanent principle of the world-process. Temple drank deeply from Whitehead without giving up God's eternal perfections. God's saving purpose, Temple reasoned, is unchanging because it is perfectly good and persists through time. But God is neither changing nor unchanging because God does not persist through time; God eternally is.[124]

In the end Temple's dialectical realism was an adjustment, not a fundamental break. To his conflation of neo-Hegelian personal idealism and Christian Neoplatonism he added an organic evolutionary realist dimension. The world has an immanent reason, a Logos. If this principle is impersonal, it is a principle of logical coherence. If it is personal, it is purposive, moral, spiritual, and a principle of variation, for personality, whether human or divine, is immersed in the world-process at the level of immanent reason. Beyond the flux of the world-process, however, "there is the personality itself, transcendent, and, in proportion to its completeness of integration, unchangeable." God immanent is a principle of adjustment, but God transcendent "is the eternally self-identical—the I AM." This dialectic, Temple argued, not Whitehead's scheme of God and world, is at the heart of things. God transcendent is the eternal I AM, while in God immanent, God is self-expressed and the world is implicit.[125]

Revelation is the full actuality of the relationship between nature, humanity, and God. To Temple, everything was revelatory, but not everything was equally revelatory of the divine character. The principle of revelation is the "coincidence of event and appreciation," the apprehension by a mind arising out of the world-process of the process for what it is—the self-expression of the divine mind. Temple stressed, against centuries of church doctrine, that revelation is not the communication of doctrine. The church construed revelation as propositional because Greek and Scholastic theologians wrongly elevated conceptual thinking above revelatory experience. Temple countered, "There is no such thing as revealed truth." Revelation, although given primarily in objective events, is revelatory only when apprehended by discerning minds. Like beauty, it exists objectively but is subjectively conditioned.[126]

He could not renounce philosophical theology because too much was at stake in upholding a Christian worldview. The world was going to hell, propelled by nihilism, greed, cynicism, and militarism, but the answer was not in the swirl of redemption theologies propounded by neo-Reformation Protestants. Temple offered a theology of manifestation and explanation, preoccupied with reconstructing a Christian worldview. He took for granted that his Gifford audience was schooled in the Greats course and that philosophy should be employed across the entire range of theological topics. Reviewers of *Nature, Man and God* expressed astonishment that Temple managed to deliver a work of such magnitude while managing a large diocese, leading the ecumenical movement, immersing himself in social justice causes, and lecturing and writing on other topics. How did he do it? Temple gave the best clue to F. R. Barry, later bishop of Southwell, who arranged a mission at University Church, Oxford, in 1931 at which Temple spoke eight times: "When I book an engagement I spend a few minutes in thinking what line to take, and then I don't think about it anymore. When I get to the church I find it has done itself."[127]

In the 1930s Temple held out for international law, the League of Nations, economic planning, and Keynesian economic gas, in close tandem with his friends in the Liberal and Labour parties. He absorbed Keynes's emerging macroeconomic theory and joined the call for new socialist thinking as the second Labour government floundered. He tracked the developments in theory and policy that arose in the early 1930s, including the arguments over Keynes's versus Hobson's theories of underconsumption. He joined the socialist trend that lifted public control of finance above everything else but without giving up on guild socialism. Temple tried to believe that strengthening the League of Nations was the best way to stay out of war, even as doing so put at risk the frozen peace of the 1930s.

POLITICAL ECONOMY AND THE CLASH OF NATIONS

Three initiatives were crucial to the rethinking that occurred in British socialist economics in the 1930s. The first was the Keynesian revolution, which began with Keynes's *Treatise on Money* in 1930 and culminated with Keynes's *General Theory of Employment, Interest, and Money* in 1935. The second was the founding of the New Fabian Research Bureau (NFRB) in March 1931, an independent organization boasting the first brain trust of Labour economists, notably E. F. M. Durbin, James Meade, Colin Clark, and Hugh Gaitskell. Cole and Attlee were the founding organizers of the NFRB, fresh from Cole's bitter experience of being ignored by MacDonald. The third was the XYZ Club, a mishmash of financial experts founded in January 1932 for similar reasons, which was led by three socialist economists (Durbin, Gaitskell, and Douglas Jay) and three nonsocialists (Nicholas Davenport, Vaughan Berry, and Cecil Spriggs). A fourth initiative, another Cole organization called the Society for Socialist Inquiry and Propaganda (SSIP), organized lecture courses to educate the public and Labour Party about new research, theories, and policies in economics. Cole, Clark, E. F. Wise, and Ernest Bevin were the ringleaders of the SSIP. For a while in 1932 Cole tried to fuse the NFRB with the Socialist League but fortunately that failed, as Cole left the Socialist League, and the NFRB became an important independent research organization. Labour Party documents got more sophisticated shortly after Keynes revolutionized macroeconomic theory and these organizations were founded.[128]

Keynes's *Treatise on Money* distinguished between savings and investment, contending that recessions occur when savings exceed investment. When aggregate savings exceed aggregate investment, consumer spending falls short of the money spent on production, causing prices to fall and unemployment to rise. The excess of savings is used to cover the windfall losses, which diverts more savings into financing losses, resulting in less spending on capital goods and a cumulative contraction in economic activity. Textbook economics taught that imbalances self-correct like a seesaw. A glut of savings produces a lower interest rate, yielding more consumption. Recessions do not last if the economy is allowed to run its natural course. Keynes spent the early years of the Great Depression trying to figure out why economic orthodoxy was wrong. In the *General Theory* he provided an answer, arguing that the economy is more like an elevator than a seesaw. The economy can get stuck at any level because once it hits bottom, individuals have no excess income to save. The economy cannot save itself if individuals lack any savings to invest. Unemployment is caused by insufficient aggregate demand, not the price of labor and lack of competition.

The *General Theory* transformed economic theory by explaining how prolonged depressions are possible and even inevitable lacking effective government intervention. Keynes established the concepts of the multiplier, the consumption function, and the marginal efficiency of capital, and the principle of effective demand and liquidity preference. He changed the discussion about recessions before he fully developed his theory, as Meade and Jay swung a key sector of the Labour Party—its policy-making intelligentsia—toward Keynes's analysis shortly after the second Labour government crashed.[129]

J. A. Hobson had long been the touchstone thinker of the British left on these topics. His critique of the classical theory of rent anticipated the marginal productivity theory of distribution, and he originated the underconsumption theory of cyclical unemployment. His first book, *The Physiology of Industry* (1889), argued that capitalism creates imbalances between the production of capital goods and consumer goods. He developed this theory in two books, *The Problem of Poverty* (1891) and *The Problem of the Unemployed* (1896), became a lefty hero by opposing the Boer War, and became famous by writing *Imperialism* (1902), launching the entire field of economic imperialist criticism. In *The Industrial System* (1909) Hobson updated his argument that income maldistribution is caused by oversaving and underconsumption. If underconsumption is systemic and cyclical, he said, the remedy for unemployment is to redistribute income through taxation and nationalize all monopolies. Socialists told him he was already a socialist without admitting it. In 1917 Hobson conceded the point in *Democracy after the War*. Two years later he joined the ILP at the height of its campaign for guild socialism.

Hobson was a prize convert who exerted a huge influence in the ILP, challenging Labour to live up to its creed. To many others he came off as an autodidactic crank. In *The Economics of Unemployment* (1922) he restated his theory of underconsumption, which Keynes panned at the time and Cole lauded as definitive. In *The Evolution of Modern Capitalism* (1926) Hobson rejected the Fabian drive to collectivize everything, noting that ample sectors of industry were unlikely to become mechanized and standardized and thus had no inherent tendency to oligopoly or monopoly. Hobson wrote prolifically for *Socialist Review* and the *New Leader* and chaired Labour's Advisory Committee on Finance and Trade Policy. His comrades in the Labour left wing vehemently disputed that they should become Keynesians. To the extent that Keynes was right, Hobson had already said it better by their lights, from a socialist position. Every Labour platform of the 1930s had a backstory debate over Keynes, bridging different ideas about what it meant to say that Labour believed in economic planning and took seriously the fluctuations of capitalist economics.[130]

In July 1934 Labour issued a new platform titled *For Socialism and Peace*. It called for a planned national economy and closely paraphrased Keynes's arguments about underconsumption and unemployment. It supported the League of Nations, appealed for a global peace movement, and supported cooperation with the United States and the Soviet Union, just before Russia joined the league. It reaffirmed the party's commitment to parliamentary democracy, repelling a factional challenge from the Socialist League. It condemned "the private economic sovereignty of the trust and combine," calling for public control of banking and credit, transport, electricity, water, iron and steel, coal, gas, agriculture, textiles, shipping, shipbuilding, and engineering. It fudged bruising party debates about different kinds of public control and planning while assuring that dispossessed capitalist owners would be fairly compensated. *For Socialism and Peace* put a new emphasis on finance capitalism and gaining control over money and credit. A companion Labour paper, *Socialism and the Condition of the People* (1934), devoted eight of its twenty pages to banking, finance, and investment, suggesting that control of finance had become Labour's top priority. Reflecting the influence of Keynes, it said that a primary objective of securing public control of investment was to "make investment equal to savings." Three years later, in *Labour's Immediate Program*, the party declared outright that gaining control of finance was its top priority.[131]

These were the intellectual seeds of what became, twenty years later, a full-fledged movement for revisionist socialism that rocked the Labour Party, redefined what socialism was about, and bitterly divided the party. The key policy theorists in the 1930s were Dalton, Durbin, Jay, and Gaitskell. All said Labour had to incorporate Keynesian ideas about macroeconomic intervention and that Labour should emphasize the taxation of wealth and income, shifting away from the party's emphasis on public ownership. Jay pushed hardest in the latter direction, contending that Labour should never have identified socialism with public ownership of the means of production. The test of good socialism, he argued, revolved around the ownership of inherited property, not the socialization of as many industries as possible. Cole and Herbert Morrison served on National Executive policy subcommittees that legitimized the Keynesian trend in Labour policy without wholly endorsing it.

The Labour heavyweights of the 1930s had an early inkling of managerial theory—the argument that ownership of the means of production held declining importance in firms separating ownership from control, with control shifting to a "New Class" of managers. American economists Adolf Berle and Gardiner Means formulated a version of managerial theory in 1932 that was specifically geared to the American context. Modern corporations, they contended, severed the unity of ownership and control that previously defined property. Formally, a corporate person owned a corporate entity, but shareholders held shares in the entity and elected corporate directors. Berle and Means said the separation of ownership and control virtually defined what corporations were and how they operated, an arrangement codified in American corporate law. Over time managers dominated their boards, exercising real control. Berle and Means advocated transparency, accountability, and voting rights for all shareholders just before both economists played roles in Franklin Roosevelt's New Deal government. Their thesis about managerial control strengthened Labour's Keynesian wing, especially Jay. But managerial theory was too new and undeveloped in the early 1930s to be emphasized by Labour Keynesians. Twenty years later it took center stage in a boiling-hot controversy over social ownership and the meaning of socialism.[132]

Meanwhile British socialists watched with rueful envy as Roosevelt established the New Deal. Temple cheered FDR for administering Keynesian medicine, surprised that America somehow moved ahead of Britain, until 1935, when Temple fretted that FDR was already backing off. He told friends that FDR needed to keep his nerve and conviction, increasing employment spending. Then the world descended into four years of crisis heaped upon crisis. Italy invaded Abyssinia in October 1935, and Labour replaced Lansbury with Attlee, demanding sanctions against Italy. Attlee won the job by being stolid, modest, and unifying, unlike the aggressive Morrison, whom the left wing distrusted, and Greenwood, who struggled with alcoholism. Attlee's laconic temperament caused rivals to underestimate him throughout his career. Hitler invaded the Rhineland in March 1936, and the Spanish Civil War began three months later. In 1936 Attlee and Labour opposed Tory prime minister Neville Chamberlain's military expansion, but the following year Attlee swung Labour in support of rearmament, blasting Chamberlain for appeasing Hitler. In March 1938 Hitler invaded Austria. The following September Chamberlain joined France and Italy in granting the Sudetenland portions of Czechoslovakia to Hitler in the Munich Agreement, six months before Hitler invaded Czechoslovakia anyway. Attlee condemned the Munich Agreement as a shameful betrayal and capitulation: "We have seen today a gallant, civilized and democratic people betrayed and handed over to a ruthless despotism. We have seen something more. We have seen the cause of democracy, which is, in our view, the cause of civilization and humanity, receive a terrible defeat."[133]

Temple watched with mounting horror, clinging to the League of Nations, as did much of the Labour Party. Attlee, Tawney, Gaitskell, and Tory politicians Winston Churchill and Harold Macmillan were in the forefront of England's antifascist resistance. Tawney blasted Chamberlain in the *Manchester Guardian*, echoing Attlee's rebuke just as Chamberlain was showered with praise for averting war. In Tawney's view Britain should have united with France and the Soviet Union against aggression. Britain was wrong not to ally with the Soviets, and wrong again "to be frightened when gangsters brandish revolvers." Tawney openly admired Churchill on this subject, plus his powers of expression. Then the Nazi–Soviet pact of August 23, 1939, sealed the fate of Europe, clearing the way for Hitler to invade Poland on September 1, the beginning of World War II. Chamberlain formed a new government, adding National Liberal and National Labour members, but spurned the Labour Party and Liberal Party. Socialists and Liberals were still beyond the pale for Chamberlain, even in war. The following May Hitler invaded Holland and Belgium, and Chamberlain gave way to Churchill, who formed a unity government.[134]

Churchill brought Attlee, Bevin, Morrison, Greenwood, and Cripps into the top ranks of his government, appointing Attlee as Lord Privy Seal in 1940 and as deputy prime minister in 1942, a breakthrough for Labour. Equally significant, Bevin served as minister of labour and national service for Churchill's entire wartime government, and Morrison served as home secretary from 1942 to 1945. Cripps was forgiven his Popular Front excesses, as the government needed his skill at running things. To defeat Nazi Germany Britons followed an old-fashioned Tory imperialist, but to solve their domestic concerns they began to trust Labour officials. The memory of soldiers returning home from World War I to economic anarchy prodded Temple, the ICF, and Labour to think about the next postwar world. War production depended on the mobilization of the working class; Labour leaders and Christian socialists were determined to exact a price for wartime sacrifices, shaping a new social order. The breaking of the traumatizing peace of the 1930s unleashed a flood of moral imagining. Briefly, it had a hopeful spirit, before the horrors of colossal battleground killing, carpet bombing, Auschwitz, and Hiroshima occurred. This determination to imagine a better world was symbolized by a name, Malvern. Meanwhile Attlee dispatched Tawney to the United States to help Churchill and him persuade Americans to join the war against fascism.

Tawney joined LSE's evacuation to Cambridge at the beginning of the war, mourned the fall of France in May 1940, and pined to make a contribution. In July he wrote a long letter to the *New York Times* entitled "Why Britain Fights." Soon there was a pamphlet version amplifying Tawney's paradoxes and "this, not that" aphorisms. Britons were fighting because they hated war, he said. They fought in obedience to their own democracy, not to a thuggish government. They did not fight for territory—"What on earth should we do with it?"—or economic advantage, knowing that war is ruinous. They did not rant, they cherished no theory of racial superiority, and they didn't hate Germans. They were so modest and chastened they rarely expressed any feeling at all. To be sure, Tawney allowed, Britons had a "singularly un-imperial institution—part alliance, part investment—called, or miscalled, the British Empire." But World War II was not about that. Every British dominion knew it could secede "at any moment they please, without a finger being lifted in Great Britain to stop them." Tawney assured that India and Northern Ireland were not exceptions, however it looked from the United States. If Britons were able to express their feelings, he said, they would say they fought "to preserve a way of life which is still far from fully realized, but which, imperfect as it is, we value above life. We mean to leave it to our children, even if, in order to save it for them, we ourselves must be knocked out." To put it negatively, Britons fought to stop a criminal war machine from obliterating their villages, brutalizing their children, and leaving them no choice "but to submit to a soul-destroying despotism, or to lose their lives in resisting it." Tawney told Americans that Britain finally had a prime minister and unity government worth supporting. "Why Britain Fights" mixed standard howlers about Britain's global innocence with echoes of Churchill's galvanizing speeches of the same summer.[135]

The British Information Service in New York took note, asking Tawney to conduct public relations work with American labor officials and politicians. The British War cabinet took note, asking Tawney to set up shop at the British embassy in Washington, DC, to influence New Deal officials. Tawney didn't want to go, and not only because he was not a schmoozer. He deeply disliked the United States. Tawney said many Americans were fine as individuals, and he admired what he called America's "social equality and freedom from a caste system," somehow looking past America's racial and gender caste system. But America epitomized, to Tawney, what capitalism did to societies. American society was vulgar, obnoxious, and unhealthy because it was hypercapitalist. He departed for America anyway in 1941 to help the war effort, telling Beatrice Webb that American society had improved only slightly since 1920: "There is so much self-righteousness, so much criticism of other countries and so little criticism of America, so much advertising and publicity, so much pretence that fourth-rate work is first rate." Twenty years later he summarized to American philosopher Dorothy Emmet: "In the lump they are bad." Tawney held his nose for his country, lecturing in American cities before and after Pearl Harbor, all in the manner of "Why Britain Fights." On the stump he spoke of high ideals threatened by fascist aggressors. To Temple he was more reflective, writing in March 1942, "With Asia at last coming into its own, the British Empire of the past dissolving, and the British governing classes—exceptions apart—pretty badly discredited—one has the sensation of watching the world being turned before our eyes."[136]

Meanwhile Temple convened the historic ICF conference in Malvern, a spa town in Worcestershire, in January 1941, during the darkest days of the German air raids in England. Malvern resembled COPEC, except for being smaller and solely Anglican. Kirk stocked it with members of the Christendom Group, an Anglo-Catholic offshoot of the League for the Kingdom of God led by Reckitt, Widdrington, and Swann on its left flank and by literary luminaries T. S. Eliot and Dorothy Sayers on its right flank. The Christendom speakers helped to generate enormous publicity for Malvern, albeit at the expense of coherence. Radical Christian socialists Richard Acland and Kenneth Ingram, shortly before they founded the Common Wealth Party, pressed for socialist programs. Eliot entreated the conference to focus on education, and Sayers said the church needed to stay out of politics. Reckitt and Demant provided counterpoint to Sayers, stressing the theological underpinnings of their politics. Temple and Bishop of Chichester George Bell wrangled a consensus document out of the conference, declaring that private ownership of the major means of production "may be a stumbling block" to building a good society. That was weak even by COPEC standards, but Malvern became historic for trying, under air raid terror. Britain had to think now, not later, about the kind of society it wanted to be.[137]

Malvern was additionally significant for prodding Temple to spell out what he believed, relieved of moderator responsibilities. Thus he wrote his most important social-ethical work, *Christianity and the Social Order* (1942). It pressed an argument for economic democracy on natural law grounds, reflecting Temple's recent studies of Catholic philosopher Jacques Maritain. Three years later, addressing the Aquinas Society, Temple acknowledged he was not an expert on Thomas, unlike his father; nonetheless, he had come to believe that Thomas had much to teach the modern world about the proper relation of means and ends: "In his conception of property and in the principles which underlie the doctrines of the Just Price and the Prohibition of Usury, I am convinced that St. Thomas offers exactly what the world needs." *Christianity and the Social Order*, defining natural law as "the proper function of a human activity as apprehended by a consideration of its own nature," applied this Aristotelian/Thomist concept to modern political economy.[138]

Certain goods are produced, Temple said, because consuming them satisfies certain needs. In natural law theory, the natural law of production is that it exists for consumption. An economic system conforms to natural law insofar as the needs of consumers determine and regulate the extent of production. But any system that allows profit or a similar factor to regulate production defies the natural order of things. Unless an economic system is regulated in conformity with its own natural laws, it will not generate just wages and prices. When private profit is lifted above common need as the regulative principle, the economy naturally generates a widening gap between rich and poor. Temple stressed that there is nothing wrong with profits as such. The Christian natural law tradition recognizes the rights of producers and traders to earn a profit, which is deserved if it is earned by one's service to the community. Natural law theory preceded Kant in teaching that a person is never to be treated as a means to an end but always as the true end or end-in-itself. The consumer is a person whose interest is the true end of the economic system. Capitalism, however, violated the natural order by regarding the person "only as an indispensable condition of success in an essentially profit-seeking enterprise." Temple said capitalism reversed the true order of things by making consumption dependent on production and production dependent on finance.[139]

Even in its heyday capitalism featured unemployed workers and unmet human needs coexisting side by side, while economic resources were wasted in speculation and corporate mergers. Then the Depression yielded staggering rates of unemployment and unmet need. Temple called for a decentralized democratic socialism that democratized the factors of production, especially the investment process: "It is important to remember that the class-war was not first proclaimed as a crusade by Marx and Engels; it was first announced as a fact by Adam Smith. Nothing can securely end it except the acquisition by Labour of a share in the control of industry. Capital gets its dividends; Labour gets its wages; there is no reason why Capital should also get control and Labour have no share in it."[140]

His program featured a fixed rate on the distribution of profit to private shareholders, a wage-equalization fund to maintain wages in bad times, mutual export trade, a socialized monetary system, social use of land, and an excess profits tax to retire the capital debts of corporations and build up economic democracy. Temple wanted to gradually eliminate capitalists from existing corporations, though not from the system as a whole. In *The Hope of a New World* (1941) he called for an excess profits tax payable in the form of shares to worker funds that gradually gained democratic control over enterprises. Forty years later this scheme became the gold standard of economic democracy in the German and Swedish union movements, with no mention of Temple. In 1941 Temple said his scheme would be a type of guild socialism, though he cautioned against a blueprint mentality. Cole had succumbed to blueprint scholasticism, after which Social Credit proponents reduced the guild idea to frothy rhetoric and micro-schemes. In *Christianity and the Social Order*, Temple advocated a "withering capital" scheme in which, once the interest paid on an investment was equal to the amount invested, the principal was reduced by a specified amount each year until the claim to interest on dividends was eliminated. To facilitate the conversion to a capital investment policy based on human and economic need, he said the state should take over existing securities on a redemption basis, and big private banks should be turned into public utility corporations.[141]

Temple was incredulous that citizens of modern democracies tolerated private banks. If society had advanced beyond private currency, why should it allow private banks to make money by charging interest on credit? Money has three functions, he observed: to facilitate exchange, to measure value, and to facilitate claims to goods and services. In each case money is merely an intermediary, a means to wealth, not wealth itself, since wealth is the true end of economic activity. Following Thomas Aquinas, Temple argued that the true goal of enterprise is to create prosperity for the sake of human need. Thus one should not be able to make a living, much less a fortune, out of lending money. Temple allowed that charging interest on the loan of currency is morally legitimate because the lender transfers a real claim. But when credit is created and loaned by a book entry, no charge beyond the cost of administration is justifiable. This was an argument for converting all big private banks into public utility corporations or, when necessary, state enterprises.[142]

Temple said the worst thing about capitalism was its structural and historic connection with imperialism. He didn't mean just old-fashioned colonialism. All major capitalist powers unfairly used their leverage to exploit the resources and vulnerable economic position of poorer nations. The remedy cut very deep, renouncing the very goal of a favorable trade balance. Temple argued that striving for a favorable trade balance is morally indefensible, gaining advantage at a loss to others. The natural law of commerce is that commerce should aim for mutual gains among all trading concerns. As far as possible, international commerce should be organized as a negotiated volume of trade, "so planned as to utilize to the utmost the productive capacity of all parties to the transaction."[143]

Last, he restored the land issue to its former primacy in Christian socialism, advocating the socialization of land. Temple was fond of saying the primary requisites of life are air, light, land, and water, and thankfully no one claimed to own the first two. In *The Church Looks Forward* (1944) he put it puckishly: "I suppose if it were possible to have established property rights in air, somebody would have done it by now, and then he would demand of us that we should pay him if we wanted to breathe what he called *his* air. Well, it couldn't be done, so it hasn't been done. But it could be done with land, and it has been done with land; and, it seems to me, we have been far too tender towards the claims that have been made by the owners of land and of water as compared with the interests of the public." Temple saw no reason why anyone should be paid large sums of money "for merely owning the land on which our cities are built." Henry George had never been refuted on this point, only defeated, whereupon Christian socialists agreed to change the subject. Private ownership of urban land served no public purpose and undermined public planning. Rural land, meanwhile, if used productively, should be privately owned on a leasehold basis.[144]

At the height of the war, in April 1942, Temple was enthroned archbishop of Canterbury, just as allied bombing began to turn the Battle of Britain and just after *Christianity and the Social Order* was published. Archbishop of Canterbury Cosmo Lang told friends he stepped down to make way for Temple, although Temple thought his politics would disqualify him from being selected, certainly by Winston Churchill. Tory cleric W. R. Inge, longtime dean of St. Paul's in London, wished Churchill had seen it that way, declaring that Temple's appointment was "a disastrous choice" for war-ravaged England. Churchill said Temple was the obvious choice. George Bernard Shaw was amazed nonetheless, later recalling, "To a man of my generation, an Archbishop of Temple's enlightenment was a realized impossibility."[145]

Christianity and the Social Order got a thorough scrubbing from Tawney and Keynes before it went to Penguin, which landed a best seller. Temple's radio addresses had long addressed the conscience of the nation; then his move to Canterbury showered attention on the book. In August 1939 he declared that although "no positive good" was achievable by force of arms, "evil can be checked and held back by force, and it is precisely for this that we may be called upon to use it." On October 3 he summoned the nation to fight with "deep determination, accompanied by no sort of exhilaration, but by a profound sadness. . . . Nazi tyranny and oppression are destroying the traditional excellencies of European civilization and must be eliminated for the good of mankind. Over against the deified nation of the Nazis our people have taken their stand as a dedicated nation." Temple lauded Christian pacifists for being faithful to the mind of Christ but argued that British Christians faced the necessity of stopping a Nazi enemy bent on oppression and annihilation: "Where the method of redemptive suffering is possible and the people concerned are capable of rising to it, it is no doubt the best of all; but there is no way that I can see in which we could redemptively suffer so as to change the heart of Germany and deliver Poles and Czechs; and if there is, our country is not yet anything like prepared to do it. So once again we have to do the best we can, being what we are, in the circumstances where we are—and then God be merciful to us sinners!"[146]

Thus he spent his last years speaking the language of tragedy, crisis, and lesser evils, all against his nature. Canterbury was badly damaged in the air raids. Temple and his wife, Frances Temple, a justice of the peace, lived in Canterbury through the worst of the raids, and Temple made a point of preaching in churches where the bombing was most severe. Repeatedly he entreated the government to accept Jewish refugees and rescue Jewish prisoners in Europe. George Bell, one of Temple's closest friends, waged a lonely campaign against carpet bombing, pleading that slaughtering civilians could not be justified. Temple did not support him, contending that Britons were morally responsible for whatever it took to defeat Nazi Germany. His radio sermons were broadcast to troops in Europe and Africa, while Bell's protests against carpet bombing disqualified him from succeeding Temple as archbishop of Canterbury.

In 1944 Temple died suddenly of pulmonary embolism, setting off a flood of stricken eulogies. Franklin Roosevelt hailed him as "an ardent advocate of international cooperation based on Christian principles [who] exercised profound influence throughout the world." Reinhold Niebuhr said Temple was the most intellectually distinguished churchman of his time and a faithful Christian whose life was "completely and successfully integrated around love for Christ." Niebuhr's colleague John Bennett, a year before Temple died, made an observation that entered many eulogies: "William Temple receives publicity for everything except the thing that he is most concerned about—personal religion." William Beveridge later said his friend unfailingly opposed nationalistic hubris, jingoism, greed, cynicism, and injustice, and as such, "William Temple seemed to many of us the ideal destined leader. He was greater than his office. His loss to the world in its untimeliness is second only to the loss of Franklin Roosevelt."[147]

Temple felt the turning of Britain's theological tide in his last years. When he gave the Gifford Lectures there were a handful of Barthians in England, but no neo-orthodox movement. Five years later neo-orthodox condemnations of liberal idealism, rationalism, and naturalism were commonplace in England. In November 1939 Temple observed that "the world of today is one of which no Christian map can be made." His generation of liberalizing theologians believed "a great deal too light-heartedly" in the sovereignty of the God of love. He had blanched at Gore's contention that only the resurrection of Christ provided a compelling reason to believe God was revealed in Christ, not in Nero. Near the end Temple had more sympathy with Gore's position.[148]

"There is a new task for theologians today," Temple acknowledged. "We cannot come to the men of today saying, 'You will find that all your experience fits together in a harmonious system if you will only look at it in the illumination of the Gospel.'" The generation that cut its teeth on the Great Depression, a collapsing empire, and now a terrible battle against Nazi tyranny was not interested in a religion of explanation. Even England was due for a theology of crisis, confronting the world with a message of redemption: "Its need can be met, not by the discovery of its own immanent principle in signal manifestation through Jesus Christ, but only by the shattering impact upon its self-sufficiency and arrogance of the Son of God, crucified, risen and ascended, pouring forth that explosive and disruptive energy which is the Holy Ghost." Temple anticipated years of warfare and postwar battles over social justice and postcolonialism. He assured that Christ was the source of all true fellowship. But to achieve true fellowship, he said, Christ had to "break up those fellowships with which we have been deluding ourselves. . . . We must expect the movement of His spirit among us to produce sharper divisions as well as deeper unity."[149]

Temple's generation had taken the church for granted. The new generation, he believed, took the church more seriously, both in criticism and as a source of hope in a dark time: "We must dig the foundations deeper than we did in pre-war years, or in the inter-war years when we developed our post-war thoughts." Someday theologians would have the luxury of reclaiming the "larger and serener task" of explaining the world in a religious philosophy. There would be another "Christian map of life" in another time; Temple even presumed it would be offered to "a new Christendom," not grasping how that would sound to a postcolonial world: "But that day can barely dawn while any who are now already concerned with theology are still alive." In that mood British Anglicans lauded Temple as the greatest in their line and the symbol of a passing age.[150]

WELFARE CAPITALISM AND FABIAN ACCOMPLISHMENT

Meanwhile British-style Social Democracy surged into favor, chiefly through the Labour Party. On June 10, 1941, Minister without Portfolio Arthur Greenwood and Minister of Health Ernest Brown announced the establishment of an interdepartmental committee to study Britain's system of social insurance and allied services. It consisted of civil servants from twelve government agencies and was chaired by Beveridge. At the time, Beveridge was master of University College, Oxford. He rose early to national prominence, having advised Lloyd George on pensions and national insurance from 1906 to 1914. Beveridge joined the U.K. Board of Trade in 1908, published a landmark book on labor markets, *Unemployment: A Problem of Industry,* in 1909, drafted the Labor Exchanges Act of 1909, and ran mobilization efforts for the government during World War

I. His policy expertise and close friendships with the Webbs took him to LSE in 1919, which he ran until 1937. Beveridge was usually counted a Fabian because he opposed efforts to divert LSE from its Fabian roots, though he was cagey about his politics. He supported the baleful eugenics wing of the Fabian tradition, attempting to create a Department of Social Biology at LSE; fortunately his historic Beveridge Report contained no hint of eugenics bigotry. In 1940 Beveridge returned to government service, conducting a manpower survey, which kept him away from Bevin in the Labour ministry. To Bevin, Beveridge was unbearably conceited and thus to be marginalized. Instead Beveridge became a major shaper of postwar British society.[151]

The Beveridge Report to Parliament of 1942, *Social Insurance and Allied Services*, proposed that all people of working age should make a weekly contribution to a national insurance fund from which benefits would be paid to retirees, the widowed, the ill, and the unemployed. Britain needed to provide a minimum standard of living for all citizens, fighting the social evils of want, disease, ignorance, squalor, and idleness. Beveridge conceived his system of social insurance as a complement to the system of national health insurance being developed by the Ministry of Health. He argued that national social insurance would make Britain more competitive by relieving businesses of pension and health care costs and by making British citizens more healthy, productive, and secure. His proposal was widely acclaimed, catching the public and Parliament in a moment of national solidarity. Sheer national survival had been at stake in 1940 and early 1941. By the summer of 1941 many were ready to talk about reconstruction, as Malvern had done.

The Beveridge Report contributed mightily to reconstruction sentiment in a politically complicated moment. In 1942 a coalition of disaffected Labour and Liberal radicals led by Richard Acland and J. B. Priestley founded the Common Wealth Party, demanding common ownership, morality in politics, and radical democracy. Acland donated his large estate in Killerton, Devon, to the National Trust, and Common Wealth contested by-elections in 1943, taunting Labour and Liberal politicians for selling out. It pushed for radical, ethical, mostly Christian, decentralized socialism, opposing the centralizing thrust of Labour politics, while Labour and the Liberals were immobilized by the wartime electoral truce. Acland's group won the enmity of Labour and Liberal leaders by doing so, but Cole, Greenwood, and Laski prepared for a postwar world, in Cole's case as director of the Nuffield College Social Reconstruction Survey. In 1942 the Labour Party Conference, led by Laski, issued an interim report, *The Old World and the New Society*, on winning the war and reconstructing British society. It took a stand on what should be done and what Labour would do.[152]

The Old World and the New Society declared that the war had already swept away the world of 1939. Allied forces had to win a complete victory over Hitlerism and "those other governments, European and Asiatic alike, which share its foul purposes." Any peace with Hitler or his allies "would be meaningless." New forms of international authority had to be devised because small nations could not defend themselves unaided against aggression. The Labour socialists hailed FDR's "Four Freedoms" message of January 1941 and the Atlantic Charter of August 1941, appending both documents to their own. They charged that Chamberlain appeased Hitler because Chamberlain catered to economic royalists: "They would not admit the moral degradation of Hitlerism until their own power was in jeopardy." Bitterly, Labour recalled that Tories accused Attlee and Labour of "war-mongering," a new low in British politics. To wit: "All the major evils of the appeasement period are directly traceable to the unregulated operation of our economic system." Labour promised to pursue "planned production for community consumption." It demanded planned production for a full employment economy and public ownership of essential means of production. It condemned racial discrimination, looking past Morrison's slur on black American soldiers. In 1942 Home Secretary Morrison told a cabinet meeting he worried that black American soldiers would impregnate white British women, leaving behind "half-caste children." In *The Old World and the New Society* Labour vaguely called for a policy of colonial trusteeship without saying what it meant. The party did not say any British colony should be granted outright independence. Rather, Britain should make good-faith efforts to create as much colonial self-government as possible. As for trade policy, soon a matter of huge importance, Labour was too bereft even to be vague. The party had not done its homework on the trade issue or thrashed out its internal disagreements.[153]

The Old World and the New Society got Labour through the war years. Like every Labour document of the time, it obscured the party's divide over the scope and nature of economic planning. To Attlee, Dalton, and usually Cole, economic planning was direct and usually physical, downplaying any reliance on the price mechanism. The state took direct control of the major means of production in order to carry out its social and economic goals, especially full employment. To Meade, Jay, and Durbin, economic planning meant macroeconomic management, using fiscal and monetary policies to manipulate aggregate demand. Positively, the goal was to achieve full employment on a noninflationary basis; negatively, it was to keep nationalization to a minimum. Neither side of the argument said the other was flat wrong. Each side appropriated aspects of the other approach, making it possible for every Labour document to offer a synthesis. Still, the differences between direct control and macroeconomic management were steep and fateful; it mattered which side got the upper hand. To advocates of direct control, the point was to supplant market forces by socializing the economy. Socialism itself was at stake. To advocates of macroeconomic management, what mattered was to achieve socialist ends, something attainable by supplementing market forces and holding back inflation.[154]

Every Labour player took a position on the right mixture of strategies. Cole backed the Attlee–Morrison nationalizing mainstream of the party, supporting state socialism for Keynesian and non-Keynesian reasons. Having long put his guild socialism in storage, he argued for militant democratic socialism and a strong-as-possible program of state ownership. To many in Cole's wing of the party, the Depression provided all the more reason to enact Clause Four. Meade, Jay, and Durbin, on the other hand, chastened by the MacDonald fiasco, said Labour overrelied on Clause Four to define socialism and itself because nationalization was a very limited tool. In the early 1940s they welcomed a surprising ally to their wing of the party, former Communist author John Strachey.

Strachey had a colorful career on the British left. He dropped out of Oxford in 1922, joined the Labour Party in 1923, was elected to Parliament in 1929, briefly joined Mosley's New Party in 1931 before switching to the Communist Party, and wrote popular pro-Communist books, notably *The Coming Struggle for Power* (1933). For a while he was Britain's leading Marxist, and he helped found the Popular Front in 1936. Strachey said Marxism offered the West its best chance to save Western civilization. This was not a very Marxist argument, but it helped him win a large audience. Two things triggered Strachey's return to the Labour Party in 1940: His sustained argument with Keynes, which turned him into a Keynesian, and the Nazi–Soviet pact of August 1939, which paved the way for Stalin to invade Finland three months later. Many appalled Communists fled the party after Foreign Ministers Joachim von Ribbentrop and Vyacheslav Molotov signed the Nazi–Soviet pact. Strachey was a dramatic example, joining the Royal Air Force as a squadron leader. Meanwhile Strachey had grappled for years with a Keynesian problem—how to increase demand without increasing costs. He had already arrived at a Keynesian answer—a redistributive fiscal policy and an expansionary monetary policy, in both cases to build up a state capital investment program—before everything changed with the Nazi–Soviet pact. The crucial task was to increase the purchasing power of working-class consumers. This was a job for macroeconomic managers like Meade and Jay, never mind that they were professorial Keynesians and Strachey had just come from hardcore Marxist–Leninism.[155]

Labour said that some synthesis of its competing ideologies held the answer. In April 1945 the party issued a manifesto written by Morrison, *Let Us Face the Future*. It was not supposed to be an election platform, just before things moved very fast. The Nazis surrendered in May 1945. Churchill and Attlee wanted to keep the coalition government until Japan was defeated, but Labour was unwilling, especially Morrison, who hoped for a fall election. The Tories countered with a snap election in July, figuring Britons would reward Churchill. Labour ran on *Let Us Face the Future*, cautioning that after the last war "hard-faced men" and their political friends kept control of the government: "They controlled the banks, the mines, the big industries, largely the press and the cinema. They controlled the means by which the people got their living." This time, Morrison wrote, things were slightly better so far because Labour won the fight for a wartime excess profits tax, price controls, controls over industry and transport, and food rationing. Still, the profiteers and racketeers were poised to clean up as soon as the war ended: "They accuse the Labour Party of wishing to impose controls for the sake of control. That is not true, and they know it. What is true is that the anti-controllers and anti-planners desire to sweep away public controls, simply in order to give the profiteering interests and the privileged rich an entirely free hand to plunder the rest of the nation as shamelessly as they did in the nineteen-twenties."[156]

The Tories, in this telling, stood for inherited privilege, inequality, and another round of rapacious profiteering, while Labour stood for moral decency, efficient management, and common-good economics. Morrison put one promise ahead of the usual programmatic ones: Under the next Labour government the House of Lords would not be allowed to obstruct the will of the people. He did not explain how Labour planned to muzzle the Lords. The platform called for jobs for all; public ownership of coal, power, inland transport, iron, steel, and monopolies, plus the Bank of England; land for use; free secondary education for all; universal health insurance and national social insurance; and internationally protected peace. Labour cautioned it would need a successful economy and full employment to achieve its goals. It pushed hard for Beveridge Now, presenting itself as the only party with the will and ability to build a welfare state. Labour did not say that economic planning meant different things to rival wings of the party, and it made no pledge about which controls it might keep or forgo. It presented the usual fudge, adeptly, as Attlee was good at consensus. Labour said it would employ the National Investment Board to determine social priorities (a function of direct planning) *and* facilitate shrewd timing in public investment (a contra-cyclical macroeconomic strategy).[157]

British-style Social Democracy came of age in July 1945 when Labour swept into office in a landslide election comparable to the Liberal blowout of 1906.

Labour beat the Tories by 47 to 36 percent, winning 393 seats in the House of Commons and a working majority of 146. Attlee headed the third Labour government as prime minister and minister of defense; Morrison took over as lord president and leader of the House of Commons; Dalton became chancellor of the exchequer; Bevin, Greenwood, and Cripps became, respectively, foreign secretary, Lord Privy Seal, and president of the Board of Trade; and Aneurin Bevan took on the health ministry. Attlee inherited a nearly bankrupt economy, as Britain lost one-fourth of its wealth in the war. He steered Britain through a devastating trade deficit and, in August 1945, the sudden termination of American Lend-Lease aid. Peacetime economic transitions, the sale of overseas investments to pay for the war, and ongoing military spending turned the trade deficit into a major crisis, costing Dalton his job in 1947.

But Labour did not allow the cratered economy or financial crisis to thwart its campaign promises. In 1946 it pushed through a national social insurance program, providing pensions and unemployment benefits. In 1948 it created the publicly funded National Health System, offering medical treatment to all without charge at the point of use. Between 1945 and 1951 it built a million new homes and abolished a flock of antiunion laws, including the Trades Disputes Act of 1927. In 1946 it nationalized the Bank of England and civil aviation; in 1947 it nationalized the coal mines, railways, and natural monopolies; in 1948 it nationalized electricity and gas; in 1951 it nationalized the steel industry. By 1951 approximately 20 percent of Britain's economy had been socialized, mostly on Morrison's community board model, a type of public corporation modeled on the British Broadcasting Company, founded in 1927. Owners of corporate stock were given government bonds, and the government took full ownership of the companies, consolidating them into a national monopoly. Management of the companies and industries did not change, except the managers became public servants working for the government.[158]

In barely three years Labour enacted most of its historic policy commitments. Morrison said he found it easy to write *Let Us Face the Future* because he merely summarized what Labour had espoused for decades. It proved harder to write the 1949 platform, *Labour Believes in Britain*, because nearly every major domestic policy objective had been accomplished. The Attlee governments of 1945–1950 and 1950–1951 wracked up tremendous achievements. Labour significantly increased the incomes of wage earners, sustained the full employment economy the war created, established pensions and social insurance, instituted a steeply progressive income tax, abolished antiunion laws, instituted financial assistance for households, abolished restrictions on the rights of women to own property, dramatically expanded the housing stock and

educational opportunities, established a minimum wage for agricultural workers, and got colonial Britain out of India, Pakistan, Burma (Myanmar), Ceylon
(Sri Lanka), and Palestine. The Attlee governments made permanent changes
in British society and politics, democratizing both, lifting equality to a cardinal
social value, and breaking the stranglehold of British colonialism. They made
huge gains for equality of opportunity and condition in British society, carrying
out exactly what they promised, assuming the official fudge version and a basically Fabian idea of Labour aspiration.[159]

On the other hand, Labour tried and failed to break down Britain's concentration of wealth, as the House of Lords was a firewall against wealth equality,
and Labour did not even try to democratize the culture and management of
nationalized industries, boasting of doing nothing. In 1951 half of Britain's
wealth was still held by 1 percent of the population. The party's long-simmering
divide over direct control versus macroeconomic planning roiled Labour
through its glory years of governance and for a decade following. Morrison conducted a fabled "bonfire of controls" in 1948, terminating wartime controls over
industry, transport, and prices that many left-wing socialists wanted to keep.
The Labour government touted its achievements in technocratic terms that
obscured, for many, the party's ethical moorings as a vehicle of social justice
politics. Many Britons accused Labour of squandering the British Empire, an
emotional charge that compelled Labour leaders to rely on efficiency arguments, downplaying moral claims that cut no ice with accusers. Morrison and
U.S. ambassador Henry Grady proposed in 1946 to federalize Palestine under
overall British trusteeship, a technocratic solution roundly rejected in Palestine.
Morrison subsequently opposed Iran's nationalist prime minister Mohammed
Mosaddeq, approving his overthrow in 1953 during Morrison's brief run as foreign secretary, a disaster for the world that yielded the shah of Iran and subsequently the Khomeini Revolution of 1979. The party spent enormous energy
and political capital creating a welfare state, overbelieving the Fabian idea that
every act of collectivization was a worthy end in itself.[160]

Every variant of the "too technocratic" critique, ranging from libertarian
to communitarian to Tory to Marxist, registers something important about the
failure of Labour socialism to inspire the general public. Attlee's technocratic
style kept moral and ideological arguments to a minimum, and his success
exhausted Labour's agenda in remarkably short order. The nationalization list
shrank to nothing, and Labour was left with rearguard battles over its achievements. Attlee disappointed his left allies by curtailing the rush of socialization.
Left-wing partisans like Cole and Aneurin Bevan were caught between their
disappointment and the need to defend Attlee. Mostly they defended Attlee,

their ally who had carried out Labour's historic agenda. By 1950 the party's official shopping list was down to a handful of industries—water supply, cement, meat, sugar refining, and industrial insurance. The following year there was no list. Union leaders opposed nationalization, and the party seethed over its ideological disagreements. The left faction, led by health minister Bevan, demanded no retreat from the party's historic nationalizing agenda. The center faction, led by Morrison, urged the party to defend its historic achievement, the welfare state. The upstart right faction, led by treasury minister Gaitskell, said Labour had no future if it did not revise its mission. In 1951 the party split wide open. The sundering issue was how Britain should pay for budget-busting military spending, just as the Korean War began.

Hugh Gaitskell, the son of a British Supreme Court judge for China and Japan, had studied under Cole at New College in the mid-1920s, supported the General Strike of 1926, helped Cole run the New Fabian Research Bureau in 1931, and joined Dalton and Jay in the XYZ Club in 1934, forming a protégé relationship with Dalton. He assisted Dalton in Churchill's wartime government and briefly ran the Board of Trade. Later he supported Dalton's nationalization of the Bank of England as a Labour member of Parliament. Gaitskell ascended too quickly not to incur resentment from older officials he passed, especially Bevan. Plus, Gaitskell was prone to confrontation and smarter-than-you, and he was decidedly a Keynesian manager. In 1946 he was selected over Harold Wilson to serve as parliamentary under-secretary for fuel and power, where Gaitskell steered coal nationalization through the House of Commons. The following year he was appointed minister of fuel and power.

Gaitskell worried that high interest rates impeded Labour from implementing its socialist program. He shared the commitment of Cripps and Dalton to cheap money and financial exchange controls, remembering the wreckage of the deflationary policies of the 1920s. Then Britain suffered a massive capital drain in the summer of 1949, and Gaitskell persuaded Cripps and Attlee to devalue Britain's currency from $4.03 to $2.80. The following year he succeeded an ailing Cripps as chancellor of the exchequer, enraging Bevan, who hated Gaitskell. Cabinet meetings turned into Gaitskell versus Bevan slugfests. In 1951 Bevan erupted over Gaitskell's proposal to institute charges for prescription glasses and dentures. A tiny issue sparked a party schism, as Gaitskell's budget passed, and Bevan accused Gaitskell of betraying Labour and the public. Bevan resigned from the cabinet, along with Harold Wilson, and blew up his chance to become party leader, inadvertently boosting Gaitskell's career.

Right versus left became a very public feature of Labour politics, especially after Labour fell from power in 1951. Labour had won the 1950 election with a slim majority of five seats, so it angled for a bigger margin the following year, winning the popular vote but losing twenty seats and the election. Churchill regained power by charging that Labour ministers could not be trusted to oppose Communism. Always there was unavoidable political drama about that. Red-baiting that should not have succeeded against anti-Communist Labour officials succeeded anyway. In power, near the end, Labour had quarreled over small-bore issues like spectacles and dentures, subsidies, and raw material supplies. Out of power, stunned at losing the election, Labour fought over the real issue: What was democratic socialism in the new situation?

In 1952 two up-and-coming Labour intellectuals and members of Parliament, R. H. S. (Richard) Crossman and C. A. R. (Anthony) Crosland, made a powerful case for rethinking socialist politics and ideology. They took for granted that Labour was and needed to be a socialist party. The issue was what socialism needed to become, not whether Labour should squirm out of its identification with it. A Fabian Society reader edited by Crossman, *New Fabian Essays* (1952), announced that the world had changed too much for British socialism not to change. What came to be called the revisionist party, an echo of Bernstein, had four defining planks: (1) Fabian ideology was too technocratic and centralizing to be inspiring. (2) Nationalizing industries was not the essence of socialism. (3) British socialism needed to stand for mixed-economy pluralism. (4) The essence of socialism was moral protest for freedom and social justice. Usually there was a fifth argument, which gave ballast to the others: Managerial theory was essentially correct. Since managerial elitism and managerial control were the main problems for contemporary socialism, socialists had to change how they conceived socialism and addressed the British public.[161]

In the beginning there were two revisionist groups. One clustered around Gaitskell in the Parliament, and the other was an independent organization, Socialist Union, and its magazine, *Socialist Commentary*. A third group calling itself Friends of *Socialist Commentary* forged links between the parliamentary and periodical groups; it helped that Gaitskell was prominent in the third group. Gaitskell became the leader of the revisionist party, imploring that Labour had to move beyond Morrison versus Bevan because the tug-of-war between "consolidators" and "fundamentalists" was backward-looking and self-defeating. Labour needed to prove it had a compelling vision of Britain's future. Crosland and Crossman were powerful exponents of this argument. In 1955 the seventy-two-year-old Attlee refused to step aside, so Labour endured another campaign in which it won the popular vote and lost the election, this time to Conservatives led by Anthony Eden. Belatedly, Labour got a new party leader, Gaitskell, who crushed Bevan and Morrison in the party election of December 1955. Being smart and aggressive lifted Gaitskell to the top. He promised to lead in consensus fashion, hold the party together, and focus on the future. Then Labour lost the national election of 1959, and Gaitskell decided that consensus politics wasn't working because Britons believed that Labour still wanted to nationalize near-everything. By then Crossman had gone back to old-style socialism, believing Gaitskell misread the politics.[162]

Two issues transcended everything else: the Cold War and the revisionist critique of Labour socialism. Both loomed too large for Tawney to avoid, although he tried to keep a low profile. In 1948, just as anti-Communism heated up in the United States, Tawney told lecture audiences in Chicago that Britons did well to vote socialists into power, and Americans needed to keep their heads concerning the Soviet Union. British democratic culture, in his telling, rested on four pillars: a respect for consensus taking the form of parliamentary government, a passion for compromise, a deep belief in the rights of individual freedom, and a corollary belief that political opinions are private matters. In Britain, he explained, fascists and Communists had a right to say whatever they wanted, and Tory governments funded the WEA despite the socialist opinions of WEA teachers. Tawney prodded Americans to think about how different their society was becoming. The West had to coexist with the Soviet Union, and saying so did not make him a neutralist. Tawney disliked having to rattle on about why socialists opposed Communism — "too obvious to need emphasis," he pleaded. But audiences demanded it, and he obliged them. Communism repulsed him, he described the Soviet Union as a police state, and he praised the Labour Party for excluding Communists, denying that Communists had any right to the dignity of the socialist name. Tawney admired Soviet dams and bridges, but human rights were vastly more important; moreover, Communism was incompatible with British culture.[163]

Tawney felt the smallness and meanness of the postwar period, when much of his beloved party was reduced to defending the welfare state and pleading "me, too" on Cold War anticommunism. He accented the positive as a response to the climate of fear and reaction that enveloped British politics. Until 1939, Tawney said, the British economy ran on hunger and fear. In York 31 percent of the population lived in poverty. Then England went to war, the Coalition and Labour governments passed social legislation, and by 1950 3 percent of York's population lived in poverty. Lacking the social legislation, the poverty rate in 1950 would have been over 20 percent and growing. Serious people, Tawney implored, focused on these things — welcoming the tremendous social gains of the Attlee years, working to defend and extend the gains, and spurning the fearful politics of reaction.[164]

Tawney was philosophical when Churchill regained power, believing certain gains were permanent, assuming minimal democratic diligence. The Tories would undoubtedly tear holes in Labour's greatest achievement, postwar full employment, but that would yield another Labour government. Tawney wanted Labour socialism to go all out on two things, correcting the "indefensible inequalities" in wealth and education. Britain needed to establish a low maximum of inheritable wealth, taxing the rest at 100 percent, and to spend money on comprehensive education as though it believed in democracy. This was the core of the Gaitskell–Crosland agenda. Perhaps Labour would need to socialize a few more industries, but Tawney had no candidates in mind, and he shook his head at those who identified socialism with nationalization. Was there no getting through to these people? By 1952 he was willing to admit he may have underestimated the dangers of top-heavy bureaucracy and remoteness in nationalized enterprises. If nationalization left workers feeling indifferent or alienated, socialism needed better schemes. The socialists of his generation, he judged, focused too much on curing social evils and not enough on increasing the joy in living. Labour socialism came off as too technocratic, exactly as voters complained.[165]

Three years later he rejoiced when Gaitskell was elected to succeed Attlee as party leader. Tawney said Gaitskell was exactly what the party needed—a really smart and courageous leader with creative ideas. But Tawney wrote little about the policy arguments that roiled Labour politics in his last years. He was not up to adjudicating the debates over Gaitskell's leadership or Crosland's analysis. Gaitskell worked hard at unifying the party, and in 1959 he ran a moderate electoral campaign based on the slogan "Britain belongs to you." Labour seemed to be on the verge of regaining power. But Gaitskell vowed to increase spending without raising taxes, which seemed dubious to voters, and Labour lost by almost six percentage points to the Conservatives, now led by Harold Macmillan. The loss stunned Gaitskell into a dramatic gesture. The problem, he said, was the party's radical image. Gaitskell proposed to eliminate Clause Four, deeply grieving Tawney, although Gaitskell lost the battle to an infuriated left wing. Tawney shook his head that Gaitskell wanted to disown Sidney Webb and decades of Labour policy. Programs changed all the time, but why change the Constitution? Tawney told friends that Clause Four had never meant *all* enterprises; moreover, Labour no longer had a nationalization list. How hard could it be to explain that to voters? Tawney, however, said nothing in public about the Clause Four controversy. His time had passed, and he ended much like he started—imploring that the real mission of socialism is to fight the idolatry of money and success. He realized that Maurice–Morris ethical socialism would be relevant long after Gaitskell and Crosland were forgotten.[166]

When Tawney died in 1962 he was buried in the chapel at Highgate Cemetery, where Gaitskell gave the eulogy. Gaitskell said he did not deserve the honor, unlike many others in the gathering; then he gave a beautiful, simple remembrance, focusing on Tawney's books. Tawney was a scholarly writer who moved his readers, Gaitskell observed; his books made a huge impact because they distinctly combined scholarly learning and moral passion: "In exposing the contrast between the Christian ethic and the actual condition of society, Tawney was drawing aside the veil and showing us what existed behind it. He was not inventing things, but simply showing them to us—things we had failed to appreciate before, but which we recognized immediately after he wrote about them." Tawney had no neuroses, he wrote beautiful prose, "he hated servility and arrogance in any form," and he lived simply. Gaitskell spoke for many by sharing his opinion: "I always think of him as *the* Democratic Socialist par excellence—an idealist who was rationalist, a believer in liberty and equality—a man who loved his faith." He said Cole, who died in 1959, once told him that Tawney was the greatest man he knew. Cole said he admired Tawney's ruthlessness above everything else; Gaitskell held the same opinion of Tawney for a different reason. To be sure, Tawney had some faults. He was too uncompromising to be a team player, he could not bear small talk or social gatherings, he could be irritable, and he was "abominably untidy." But Gaitskell admired him above all others because "the quality of his goodness was such that it never embarrassed you. You just accepted it as you accept genius."[167]

No one said that about Cole, yet Cole humbly devoted himself to Labour causes and thankless Labour tasks, he lived with Tawney-like simplicity and integrity, and he never held his Oxford chair above others. Cole was not lauded as the soul of the party or the greatest anything, and most of his books stuck too close to current events to outlast a season. He hated that Gaitskell deradicalized the party, yet he was close to Gaitskell personally, having mentored him at Oxford. Moreover, the pluralizing turn in Labour socialism owed something to Cole's early stumping for guild socialism. Politically, Cole felt cast aside by Gaitskell's party; personally, he was conflicted.

A decade later, when the social revolutions of the 1960s yielded demands for participatory democracy, Cole was ripe for rediscovery, at least by academics. Feminist theorist Carole Pateman retrieved Cole as a founder of participatory democratic theory, along with Rousseau, Marx, and John Stuart Mill. Pateman said Cole's plan for guild socialism was of "minor importance" by comparison. She and Maure L. Goldschmidt revived Cole's interpretation of Rousseau, contending that Rousseau's call for the extinction of factions and privileged groups did not mean all partial associations had to be extinguished. Neither did it mean that all partial associations militated against the common good. Rousseau, they argued, believed that some civil associations might participate in the general will. In that case Rousseau's deep influence on Cole became less paradoxical. Another band of academics led by British social theorist Paul Q. Hirst and American political theorist Robert Dahl renewed the pluralist theory of the state, sometimes citing Cole, Figgis, and Laski.[168]

To Cole, all such consolations would have been cold comfort, as he had not come to provide grist for academic mills. He had begun as a William Morris socialist and remained one through all his twisting and turning to be useful to Labour. Cole's chance to change the world came in a rush, and it ended abruptly, all before he became an Oxford don, to his regret. He knew he made his mark early. Then he gave himself to conventional Labour duties, acknowledging the irony of doing so, and coined paradoxical concepts that mirrored his inner paradoxes and career. "Sensible extremism" was a self-description. "Scientific utopianism" described his temperament and approach. "Libertarian socialism" was his ideal, an impossibility naturally lacking a home, so Cole made a home in the Labour Party and ushered Oxford students into it. Another of his protégés, Harold Wilson, symbolized even more than Gaitskell the irony of Cole's legacy. Wilson opportunistically supported the Bevan left wing in the early 1950s, opportunistically backed Gaitskell in 1955, and opportunistically posed as a left-wing leader after Gaitskell died in 1963. He governed as prime minister from 1964 to 1970 and from 1974 to 1976, in both cases proving that Labour was quite capable of governing without disrupting business as usual. Like Gaitskell, Wilson was devoted to Cole and grateful for his mentorship. Labour became undeniably respectable and pedestrian under Wilson. That was emphatically not the legacy that Cole wanted.[169]

6

DEMOCRATIC SOCIALISM AS PLURALISTIC
SOCIAL DEMOCRACY

Our story ends with democratic socialism being reimagined and Social Democracy being substantially realized, just before the social movements of the late 1960s birthed new forms of radical politics and theology. Two world wars heightened the vast differences between British and German socialism, yet Social Democracy in both places morphed into a very similar form of revisionism. Labour fell out of power in 1931, floundered in the 1930s, regained power in 1945, and achieved almost its entire agenda, which proved oddly deflating, triggering a revisionist trend in the 1950s. The SPD fell out of power in 1930 with the end of Herman Müller's government, did not rule again until 1969, lost its East German wing during the Cold War, and went through a revisionist phase at the same time as Britain. In Britain revisionists said that Labour's postwar success demanded a new democratic socialist ideal. In Germany revisionists said the SPD would never win another election if it did not revise socialism.

In both cases, as in much of Europe, the gap between democratic socialist aspiration and Social Democratic politics became an argument for revising the socialist idea. The fact that Social Democracy developed in Britain through a pluralistic labor movement party, not a Continental-style Social Democratic party, made Britain more hospitable to religious socialists than in the Continental parties, but the logic of Social Democratic revision worked very similarly across this difference. It prevailed in the platform of the reestablished Socialist International, which declared in 1951 that socialists did not espouse all-out nationalization or any dogmatic scheme. Social Democracy after World War II was about adjusting to a resurgent capitalism, enacting social welfare programs, building international institutions, and thwarting Communism.

Thus it seemed stodgy and enfranchised when the antiwar and social movements of the late 1960s created new forms of political radicalism.

Soviet Russia was primarily responsible for destroying the Nazi war
machine, and it paid a horrific price for doing so. Russia lost more war dead—
approximately twenty million—than the other warring nations combined. It
emerged from the war as a major world power but deeply battered. The Red
Army, touting itself as an antifascist liberating force, conquered territories of
East and Central Europe that had long loathed Russia and Communism. Very
briefly, European Social Democrats hoped the historic enmity between Social
Democracy and Communism might be left behind. They admired the heroic
struggle of the Russian people, believed that Russians wanted democratic
socialism, and tried to believe the future belonged to it. Many were veterans of
the popular front organizations of 1935 to 1939, when socialists and Communists
joined forces against Fascism. But Social Democrats did not get the future they
wanted. In divided Germany the enmity between the KPD (the Communist
Party) and SPD worsened dramatically. Twice-conquered resentment prevailed
in most of what became the East Bloc, with few exceptions. Whatever chance
Russia may have had to work out decent relationships with the governments on
its western borders was erased by the Cold War. To Russian leaders, the searing
lesson of history was that unfriendly neighbors were highways for invaders. To
American leaders, Western-style democratic regimes had to be elected in East
and Central Europe, and Communism had to be prevented from expanding.
The Cold War overshadowed everything else in postwar Europe. It was fueled
by Russia's colossal suffering, sense of vulnerability, and overcompensating
belief in its messianic Communist mission and America's determination to
keep Russia as weak and constrained as possible.[1]

European Social Democrats, the original anti-Communists, came naturally
to the claim that Communism was a terrible perversion of a good idea. Some
West European nations, notably France and Italy, had strong Communist parties after World War II, plus multiparty systems in which patchwork coalitions
were the norm. But even in nations with complex political relationships
between socialists and Communists, socialists nursed bitter memories of the
early 1930s, when Communists said Social Democracy was the real enemy, and
of the 1939–1941 period, when Russia's pact with Nazi Germany allowed
both nations to invade Poland. The SPD's postwar leaders remembered how it
felt to be ridiculed by Moscow and accused of treason by the KPD: Fascism
was just the last gasp of a dying capitalism, while the real enemy, Social
Democracy, was better called "social fascism." Then the Nazi-Soviet pact
exploded the popular fronts of the late 1930s. After the war, Stalin treated his

neighbors brutally, and the Russian occupiers in East Germany drove the SPD into a new party. Meanwhile, Russia acquired a rival for the leadership of world Communism in China, the world's most populous nation. The Cold War demanded hyperbolic condemnations of Communism, causing Social Democrats to splinter over hard versus soft anti-Communism and what, exactly, the good idea was.

Upon refounding the Socialist International in 1951, Social Democrats said the usual socialist things about opposing racism and imperialism. But unlike Soviet Communism, no European Social Democratic party was known for caring about nonwhite peoples in the so-called Third World. European Social Democracy had no record of reaching out to Africans and Asians that compared to the Communist International, just as American socialists had no record of solidarity outreach to African Americans that compared to the Communist Party. The Communist movement energetically organized workers of every color everywhere. The contrast played out badly for Social Democratic parties long implicated in the colonial policies of their nations and tainted by national debates over good versus bad imperialism. European Social Democracy, always affected by the fate of Europe as a whole, became more so after World War II. Moreover, Christian traditions of democratic socialism faded almost everywhere except Britain and its colonial offshoots, reflecting the cultural conformism of the postwar period. Britain made little contribution to the liberation theologies of the 1970s that rebelled against racial, gender, and colonial oppression, notwithstanding that British Christian socialism had better traditions of anticapitalist criticism than the Marxist–Leninist rhetoric recycled by many liberationists. Christian socialism in Britain had a substantial ongoing tradition, a welcome role in Labour politics, and a similar entrée in churches. It did not rely on star theologians, and British theologians rarely became international stars anyway. British Christian socialism, for better and for worse, was like British socialism in moving far by staying close to the ground occupied by its unions, party officials, activists, and clergy.

Continental socialists routinely judged that British socialism was woefully undertheorized and pragmatic. By the standards of German and French Marxists, British socialism had little history of imagining the real thing. German Social Democracy began with Lassallean visions of state democratic socialism and was transformed by the powerful dialectics of a commanding thinker, Karl Marx. It struggled to square Marx's vision of revolutionary deliverance with ordinary German nationalism and an expanding bourgeoisie, yielding the strenuous theorizing of Friedrich Engels, Eduard Bernstein, Karl Kautsky, Rosa Luxemburg, Georg Lukács, Karl Korsch, and Max Horkheimer. By contrast,

Sidney Webb, Beatrice Webb, and R. H. Tawney gave pride of place to empirical research and practical politics, keeping theory to a minimum; the Christian socialist and ethical socialist traditions as a whole were short on theory *and* empiricism; G. D. H. Cole made an exception for social theory but not philosophy; and even the philosophical William Temple usually cut straight to politics when he wrote about things political.

On this basis the British tradition surpassed its Social Democratic counterparts up to the mid-1960s endpoint of this book. Nearly everything that made British socialism distinctive worked in its favor toward this outcome: The liberty heritage of British law and political liberalism produced a nation of individualists who were taught in school that their individuality depended on the success of the Commonwealth in sustaining Britain's civilized island. Christianity backstopped both parts of this equation as a spiritual worldview valorizing the God-given spiritual dignity of every human soul. Every form of British Christian socialism expounded some version of this trinity of Christianity/Commonwealth/freedom. British Christian socialism variously envisioned the Commonwealth as the ethical commonwealth of God, growing into something hard to imagine elsewhere—a vital religious component of a powerful Social Democratic politics.

The founders of British Christian socialism will always be hard to appreciate because they were so tame and quirky. F. D. Maurice was personally conservative, a monarchist, and averse to conflict. Charles Kingsley wrote novels laced with demagoguery, maudlin self-righteousness, and racist asides. John Ludlow, the best socialist of the group, deferred to Maurice. Moreover, Ludlow sowed the seeds of the debilitating socialist prejudice against consumer cooperatives. To later readers, the early Christian socialist preoccupation with producer cooperatives and worker education came off as precious or trivializing. To Christian socialists of the 1880s, however, the Maurice group deserved unstinting praise for championing the principle of cooperation as the centerpiece of Christian ethics and religion. Stewart Headlam put it frankly: "You, ladies and gentlemen, probably do not know what it is to have been delivered in the world of thought, emotion, imagination, from the belief that a large proportion of the human race are doomed to endless misery. You are freeborn—mainly through Maurice's work and courage. For myself I say that at a great price I obtained this freedom."[2]

Headlam's freedom cost him his right to earn a living as a cleric. His brilliant advocacy of a strangely insular idea—exclusive Anglo-Catholic socialism, with room for humanistic atheists—renewed a Christian socialist tradition that sprawled to every corner of the Anglican world. Ecumenical socialism sprouted at the same time as Headlam's Guild of Saint Matthew (GSM), through the *Christian Socialist*, but England's religious market operated through denominational channels, to the advantage of Anglo-Catholics. The Nonconforming Protestant fellowships gave individual leaders to the socialist movement, but their weakness as organizational vehicles confirmed to many that Anglo-Catholic theology and sacraments were essential to Christian socialism.

British Christian socialism began with producer cooperatives in 1848, moved up to land socialization in the socialist revival of the 1880s, and debated in the 1880s and 1890s how much nationalizing was compatible with its communitarian ethos. It was very much a product of middle-class, Victorian, clerical guilt consciousness, led by ministers to the urban poor. It was slow to develop a proletarian consciousness for the unavoidable reason that Britain had no workers' party until 1893. By then it was so middle-class that its own history and ethos stood in the way of growing a proletarian wing. Christian socialists had every reason to contend with each other over how much socialism was needed and how socialism should be defined. That, to me, was one of its most commendable features, outranked only by the fact that Christian socialists did not fall for militarism, imperialism, racism, or eugenics.

Christianity should have been enough to repel these evils but was not. The same thing was true of socialism. It took the two things fused together in England, in alliance with ethical socialists, to produce the nation's best anti-imperialist tradition. With very few exceptions Christian socialist leaders took for granted their ethical obligation to oppose all that went into British imperialism and came of it. Mirfield monk Paul Bull, a veteran of the Boer War, was the leading exception, and some yielded inevitably to nationalistic gore during World War I, notably Egerton Swann. But mostly there was determined agreement that Britain had to abolish the militaristic snobbery purveyed in public schools. The church had blood on its hands for blessing the empire and its brutality. Christian socialism was a late attempt to redeem the church for imperial sins that much of the church celebrated.[3]

CHRISTIAN SOCIALISM AND SOCIAL DARWINISM

Much of the literature on British Christian socialism derides its leaders as woolly-minded Victorian moralists who embarrassed themselves and the church without realizing it. I take a more appreciative view, having first unlearned similarly denigrating conventions about the American social gospel. Christian socialists played a leavening role in the political movements they joined, especially in Britain. They were in the forefront of movements for peace, social justice, dismantling the empire, and women's suffrage. Their supposedly pitiable moralism was a bulwark against Marxist cynicism about morality and a patchy counterweight to Social Darwinist bigotries about white supremacy. Later it was a bulwark against the eugenic bigotry that won a foothold in mainstream British politics, pervaded U.S. American racial politics, and escalated to levels of apocalyptic evil in Nazi Germany.[4]

Eugenics was a by-product of Social Darwinist anxiety and a throwback to ancient infanticide. It had a patina of scientific respectability as an outgrowth of eighteenth- and nineteenth-century scientific racism and the rise of Darwinian theory. Eighteenth- and nineteenth-century naturalists generally followed the father of modern taxonomy, Swedish zoologist Carl Linnaeus (1707–1778), in dividing *Homo sapiens* into four categories: American (described by Linnaeus as copper-colored, choleric, and regulated by custom), Asiatic (sooty, melancholic, and governed by opinions), African (black, languid, and governed by caprice), and European (fair, sanguine, and governed by laws). They disagreed about monogenesis versus polygenesis. The leading theorists of polygenic origins — Georges Cuvier, Charles White, George Morton, and Louis Agassiz — believed that anatomical and intellectual differences between African blacks and European whites were too great for them to belong to the same species.[5]

Polygenic theory was gaining in social respectability and scientific acceptance when Charles Darwin refuted it in 1859. *On the Origin of Species* discredited the enterprise of determining how many distinct races of human beings existed. Now the question shifted to the evolution of different racial groups within the human species and the scientific basis of distinguishing between them. Darwin argued in *The Descent of Man* (1874) that changes occur through natural selection, where slight differences in strength, attractiveness, and body type yield advantages in mating and propagation. His statements about sexual selection were sketchy, but he straightforwardly believed in white supremacy and male supremacy. Darwin ranked human groups hierarchically from the "savage" to the "civilized," giving ballast to an already thriving measuring industry. English evolutionist T. H. Huxley and French anthropologist Paul Broca focused on skin color to find a measurable determinant of race, getting nowhere. Broca and other phrenologists studied skull sizes and angles, finding that Caucasians alone included every possible head shape. If racial hierarchy was as real and important as scientists believed, there had to be a way of accounting for it.[6]

The staying power of Social Darwinism and especially its eugenic offspring owed much to the undeniable eminence of leading Social Darwinists. All aspiring intellectuals of the 1880s had to deal with Herbert Spencer. Ernst Haeckel, equally eminent in Germany, coined the terms "anthropogeny," "ecology," "phylum," and "phylogeny," teaching that every individual's biological development (ontogeny) recapitulates the entire evolutionary development (phylogeny) of its species. Francis Galton, another Social Darwinist heavy-weight, espoused hard heredity selection, rejected the leftover Lamarckianism of Spencer and Haeckel on the inheritability of acquired characteristics, and invented the essential tools of biometry—correlation, regression, and regression to the mean.[7]

The turn against biological determinism in early twentieth-century science fell hard on the reputation of Spencer, less hard on Haeckel—depending on how he was interpreted—and lesser yet on Galton and his protégé, Karl Pearson. Lamarckian theory was discredited, Spencer was too mechanistic and dogmatic to be revisable, and Haeckel was usually interpreted, wrongly, as espousing a strong version of recapitulation theory. The strong version—there is a one-to-one correspondence between phylogeny and ontogeny, such that ontogeny repeats forms of the ancestors—was refuted in early twentieth-century biology. The weak version—phylogeny and ontogeny are interconnected, such that recapitulation builds upon the ancestral embryonic process of development—is still in play as a theory explaining the similarities between all vertebrate embryos at early stages of development. Galton's pioneering advocacy of hard heredity and his development of biometrics conferred respectability on the prejudices underlying eugenics. He and Pearson had to fight off criticism from one wing of the eugenics movement that their approach was too mathematical and insufficiently biological, but the eugenic enterprise itself, as a movement, only benefited from this factional sparring. Eugenics kept growing long after anyone felt obligated to read Spencer.

Galton stayed respectable because he advanced the understanding of heredity and he launched a social movement suiting the self-interests of a rising middle class. Appeals to the heredity factor were sloppy and anecdotal before Galton systematized its study. Middle-class professionals used heredity to justify their belief that females were passive. Moralists moralized against social deviance by appealing to the supposed inheritance of acquired characteristics. Galton took over from Social Darwinism the ideology that society is atomistic and individualistic, biological unfitness causes social failure, and social progress depends on eliminating the unfit. His program outlasted mere Social Darwinism by correcting its Lamarckian mistakes and providing a stronger basis for its biological view of society. Eugenics was Social Darwinism plus aggressive government intervention. Spencer and Haeckel just wanted governments to stop aiding the poor and vulnerable. The natural laws of development would eliminate the "undesirables" if government did nothing for them. Galton said there was no reason not to accelerate the ruthless process of nature now that heredity was understood. Being the most toxic form of Social Darwinism played to the advantage of the eugenics movement because laissez faire took too long. Eugenics was a job for people who believed in using government to get big things done—progressives, Tories, nationalistic Liberals, and Fabian technocrats. Positive eugenics (ramping up the high end) and negative eugenics (eliminating the low end) were both needed to produce a society of superior Anglo-Saxon and Teutonic achievers.[8]

In Britain the eugenics movement focused on class and targeted the working class. Galton taught that the upper class had the highest genetic worth, the upper middle class was next highest, the respectable working class had middling genetic worth, the poor and lowly had little genetic worth, and the underclass of "undesirables" had almost no genetic worth. Galton stayed out of politics and believed only the lowest group should be prevented from bearing offspring. Thus he left the hard part to others. In 1907 Britain established a Eugenics Eradication Society, chaired by Darwin's son Leonard Darwin, which won a milestone victory in 1913 with Parliament's passage of the Mentally Deficient Act, a Trojan horse for breeding out the "feebleminded." Eugenic bigotry was rife among intellectuals and technocrats, notably Pearson, Sidney Webb, Beatrice Webb, George Bernard Shaw, H. G. Wells, Winston Churchill, Arthur Balfour, William Beveridge, Havelock Ellis, and John Maynard Keynes. Keynes served as director of the British Eugenics Society and opined that eugenics was the most important branch of sociology. Both Webbs were keen to institutionalize eugenics in social science and government policy, although eugenics never received significant state funding in Britain, and only University College London and Liverpool University taught it. Eminent eugenicists usually did not push for forced sterilization laws. Ellis was typical, exhorting the "feebleminded" to volunteer for sterilization as a civic duty. No Christian socialist or radical ethical socialist of any note endorsed eugenics bigotry. The fact that eugenics targeted working-class people impeded it politically in Britain, since they were the majority, and they voted. The Labour Party joined the Catholic Church and Christian socialists in opposing compulsory sterilization laws, and none were passed in England, even though the eugenics movement grew throughout the 1920s and made a lot of noise.[9]

In Germany eugenics was mostly a colonial project tied to *Lebensraum*—the idea that Germans had a mandate to create "living space" for overcrowded but racially superior Germans—until Nazi Germany used it to justify its conquest of Eastern Europe and its extermination of European Jewry. Germany colonized Togoland, the Cameroons, Tanganyika, and modern Namibia in the mid-1880s, establishing brutal regimes of labor enslavement and mass rape. In Southwest Africa—Namibia—German colonizers went further. From 1904 to 1908 German forces conducted the first genocide of the twentieth century, wiping out anticolonial rebels, building death camps for local civilians, issuing extermination orders against the Herero and Nama tribes, and slaughtering approximately ninety thousand tribespeople. Lieutenant General Lothar von Trotha and other military officers were showered with acclaim and coveted medals for exterminating the Hereros, replete with heroic soldier statues in Germany and Africa. All of it was shamelessly justified as serving the cause of *Lebensraum,* a term coined by German geographer Friedrich Ratzel at the end of the nineteenth century. If Germans needed more room to live comfortably, they were justified in slaughtering inferior beings who got in the way. German medical professor Eugen Fischer made his early renown by conducting unethical medical experiments on the Herero and Nama tribes. Fischer's eugenic writings influenced Hitler during his imprisonment in 1923 and later informed the Nuremberg Laws of 1935, two years after Hitler appointed Fischer as rector of the Friedrich Wilhelm University of Berlin.[10]

In the United States eugenics targeted black Americans and all non–Anglo Saxon immigrants, it was vengefully racist and nativist, and it provided models for the eugenic programs of Nazi Germany. Eugenic practices were widespread in the United States long before Galton coined the term and started a movement. Laws prohibiting interracial sexual relations and interracial marriage were enacted in colonial Virginia and Maryland in the 1660s, providing a template for state laws until 1967. Seven of the thirteen colonies that founded the United States in 1776 had laws prohibiting racial intermarriage, and in 1883 the U.S. Supreme Court upheld antimiscegenation laws (*Pace v. Alabama*). Between 1913 and 1948 thirty of the forty-eight states enforced antimiscegenation laws. America's first Galton-style eugenic organization was the American Breeders' Association, founded in 1906 by biologist Charles B. Davenport; its members included inventor Alexander Graham Bell and Stanford president David Starr Jordan. Eugenicists Lothrop Stoddard and Harry Laughlin played leading roles in the passage of the Immigration Act of 1924; Stoddard, in *The Rising Tide of Color Against White-World Supremacy* (1920), said race and heredity were the chief determinants of civilization, and Jews, a racially "Asiatic" people, threatened America's Nordic racial purity. Eugenic policies were widely propagated by scientists and extensively funded by the Carnegie Institution, Rockefeller Foundation, Harriman trust, Kellogg Foundation, and other foundations. Margaret Sanger, the founder of the modern birth control movement, was deeply involved in negative eugenic activism after World War I and also supported Anglo-Saxonist immigration policies, although Sanger opposed racial discrimination against middle-class blacks. Eugenic activism in the United

States was most aggressive when race and class combined to make someone "unfit," but race was by far the trump category in American weeding out.[11]

The authority of Social Darwinism was so powerful that leading black intellectuals subscribed to it, either to limit the damage or include black Americans in Manifest Destiny or both. Black social gospel pioneer Reverdy C. Ransom implored his white readers not to leave black Americans out of Manifest Destiny because black Americans contributed mightily to building up the American colossus. Ransom had a dream of white and black Americans marching together to spread American democracy, progress, and Christianity throughout the world. He clung desperately to this dream through a mania of racial lynching and decades of relentless white hostility, until he couldn't say the words, in the 1920s. The early W. E. B. Du Bois similarly took Social Darwinism for granted in stumping for what he called the "Talented Tenth." His book *The Philadelphia Negro* (1899) contended that black Americans had a right to freedom of self-development and no right to any government programs that violated the Social Darwinist conventions of American civilization. Du Bois did not begin to shed his elitism and Social Darwinist assumptions until he started on the path to democratic socialism in 1905, when he was already famous. Many black intellectuals contended that weeding out did not apply to them because they belonged to an educated, usually light-colored elite.[12]

The Christian socialists who defied Social Darwinism stood out for opposing it, despite knowing they were outgunned intellectually. Nobody on their side had the intellectual standing to say that Spencer, Haeckel, Galton, and Yale sociologist William Graham Sumner were terribly wrong. Yet they said it anyway. Nearly every British and American Christian socialist leader said it emphatically, and the best American Christian socialists stressed that this was an anti-racist position that had to combat a national culture of racism. Albion Tourgée, George Herron, George W. Woodbey, George A. Gates, and the later Ransom were prominent in the latter group. Walter Rauschenbusch, by contrast, caved on anti-racism for most of his career, even as he inveighed against Social Darwinism, which also perplexed him and his social gospel allies. Christian socialists of the late nineteenth century believed that Social Darwinism was bad without knowing how to prove it was false. Many relied on American polymath John Fiske to explain Darwinism to them while resisting Fiske's contention that Social Darwinism was true, truly Darwinian, progressive, and anti-imperialist. Christian socialists did not know how to draw the line between good and bad Darwinism. They only knew they were compelled to try, because Social Darwinism was the antithesis of biblical teaching about seeing Christ in the poor and oppressed; it denigrated the creative role of cooperation; and its political implications were brutal.[13]

Even the squishy forms of social Christianity in Britain, the United States, and Germany got their bearings by opposing Social Darwinism or at least trying to do so. Social Darwinism was popular for justifying why society should do little or nothing to help the underclass. The doyens of secular British progressivism admired Spencer and consorted amiably with him. Haeckel got similar treatment in Germany. Sumner assured his privileged students at Yale that Social Darwinism was the only scientific way to understand society, and they should expunge whatever tender feelings they held toward the poor. Late nineteenth-century Christian socialists did not have time for science to correct its mechanistic and racist assumptions. They built organizations without knowing exactly where bad Darwinism began. When union leaders said the churches had no record of caring about the poor and vulnerable, Christian socialists were embarrassed for the church.

Christian socialists shared the social Christian devotion to progress, democracy, rationality, goodwill, and the peaceable way of Christ. They played down power politics until an upsurge of radical unionism in the 1890s pulled British and American social Christianity to the political left, just as German social Christianity turned nationalist. The coming of fully political Christian socialism meant that confronting the structural problem of power could not be put off. Christian socialists fused progressive idealism with a socialist understanding of the locus of power in a capitalist society. Some construed power in Marxian terms as a bought, exchanged, or stolen commodity, usually without citing Marx. Some were more Marxian than they realized. The *Christian Socialist* and Christian Socialist Society purveyed both tendencies; later, the Church Socialist League and the guild socialist movement introduced harder-edged forms of economic socialism that still mentioned Marx as little as possible. Until 1914 the dividing issue in social Christianity pitted progressive reformers, who emphasized moral idealism, against Christian socialists, who fixed on democratizing power. To embrace socialism was to accept that the class issue could not be moralized away. One could not settle for sermons or liberal politics after Marx and Morris taught Christian socialists to see the class struggle in every crevice and turn of history.[14]

The leading Christian socialists of the early twentieth century did not say that middle-class idealism would transform society. They said that idealists alone never achieved *any* social justice cause. Charles Marson, W. Howard Paul Campbell, Conrad Noel, Maurice Reckitt, P. E. T. Widdrington, Charles Gore, Hermann Kutter, Leonhard Ragaz, Christoph Blumhardt, Walter Rauschenbusch, George Herron, Vida Scudder, W. D. P. Bliss, Albion Tourgée, George W. Woodbey, Harry Ward, and even Scott Holland said it plainly. Class is made when exploited people feel and articulate their interests in distinction from other classes, and justice is made when they fight for their rights. The early Christian socialists were the last believers that the church might truly atone for slavery, tyranny, capitalism, and imperialism. Ernst Troeltsch said Christian socialism, despite being wrong, represented a greater possibility: the third Christian philosophy.[15]

ERNST TROELTSCH AND GERMAN SOCIAL CHRISTIANITY

Troeltsch understood Christian socialism in historic terms and epitomized what happened to German social Christianity, two things that went together in his case. A major figure in modern theology, he established the history of religions approach to theology before he became famous for interpreting Christian social teaching. He was born in 1865 in Haunstetten near Augsburg, the city of the Augsburg Confession, where a Protestant minority and a Catholic majority had a long history of trying to get along. Troeltsch's father, also named Ernst, was a studious medical doctor, politically conservative and conventionally Lutheran. The elder Ernst Troeltsch favored the monarchy and a single German state and was consumed with his work, dispositions he passed to his son. At an early age Troeltsch adopted his father's scientific bent, but as a student at Erlangen in the early 1880s he opted for theology because it combined his two chief interests, metaphysics and history. Transferring to Berlin, Troeltsch respected Julius Kaftan's able Ritschlian teaching, admired Bismarck intensely, and detested Adolf Stöcker's crude speech making. He would have stayed in Berlin, but Albrecht Ritschl was still teaching at Göttingen, so Troeltsch and his friend Wilhelm Bousset decided to get their Ritschlian theology firsthand.[16]

From 1886 to 1888 Troeltsch studied under Ritschl and Orientalist scholar Paul de Lagarde, the founder of the history of religions school. He played a careful hand with Lagarde's anti-Semitism, saying nothing about it in public. Privately he said that Germany's rising anti-Semitism reeked of political opportunism and religious rivalry. Troeltsch began his teaching career in 1890, at Göttingen, moved to Bonn in 1892 and Heidelberg in 1894, and made his early name as the pioneer theologian of the history of religions approach. Ritschlian theology truncated its historicism by privileging Christianity as an independent entity grounded in faith. Troeltsch said theology had to begin with religion, not Christianity, which was one religion among others. Theology needed to take historical relativity fully seriously without being devoured by it. His early work in this field drew deeply on Kant, Hegel, Schleiermacher, post-Kantian philosopher Wilhelm Dilthey, and neo-Hegelian philosopher Rudolf Hermann Lotze.

To Troeltsch, metaphysics and history were consuming, and social issues were of little consequence. Politically he was conservative, bourgeois in temperament, and averse to the mild social Christianity of Harnack and the Evangelical Social Congress. But in 1897 Troeltsch befriended his Heidelberg colleague Max Weber, who scolded him for ignoring the social crisis of the 1890s, and Harnack prodded Troeltsch to join the congress. That was just enough to nudge Troeltsch into social Christianity. Weber's wife, Marianne Weber, urged him to reconsider democracy and feminism, but Troeltsch never warmed to feminism.[17]

With typical industry he plunged into his new subject, approaching it historically and prescriptively, forming his position. In 1904 Troeltsch unveiled his perspective in a speech to the Evangelical Social Congress in Breslau, declaring that Kantian and Hegelian cultural goals of the state were passé because realism had triumphed in German thought about state and society. His generation was schooled in the ascendancy of Germany under Bismarck. Politics was about power, power was the essence of the state, and a strong army was the backbone of the state. Marxism, in its own way, taught a similar lesson: All political, philosophical, and ethical theories are by-products of given configurations of power. But even hardcore realists had to sort out the relation of Christianity to modern society. Assuming that some kind of political ethic was needed, which forces in modern life yielded the best political ethic?[18]

Troeltsch said the four key forces are liberalism, nationalism, democracy, and conservatism, and democracy and conservatism are slightly more important than liberalism and nationalism. Liberalism, the ethic of a constitutional state (*Rechtsstaat*) serving a free culture, limits the role of the state to maintaining order and protecting high culture. Troeltsch lauded liberalism for making historic gains for individual freedom but said the merely negative liberty of a limited state was no place to rest, and Germany had not done so. In German life, nationalism was a stronger and more creative force. No state becomes a nation until the individuals in it identify with the state, and if one identifies with the state, "one no longer needs to fear any superior power, except possibly God." Troeltsch took for granted that any state with growing power is aggressive and devoted to conquest. However, once expansion is no longer possible, governments aim for stability and preserving the status quo. Friedrich Naumann was Troeltsch's exemplary nationalist, despite being a socialist, because Naumann was smart, calculating, and consumed with Germany's national interest.[19]

Troeltsch cautioned that patriotism is not the "last word" in a political ethic. The ethical value of a state rests on the spirit of its political institutions, the richness and depth of its culture, and the ethical ideas permeating its society, plus nationalistic feeling. From a political ethical standpoint, Switzerland had great value despite being tiny and low on nationalistic fervor, while Turkey, though large and nationalistic, "has none at all." Troeltsch argued that a strong, ethically valuable state must have ethical principles that penetrate the inner structures of its institutions and define the social good. Democracy and conservatism have this capacity to ascribe an intrinsic ethical value to the state; liberalism and nationalism do not.[20]

Unfortunately, Germans identified democracy with the proletarian movement, which had to change. Troeltsch implored that socialists did not own democracy. The democratic principle stood for transcending the class struggle, "its ideal is social peace." At its root, he argued, democracy is an ethical idea, "the great idea of human rights," which holds that every person has a moral right to independent value. The democratic idea of human rights stands against "exploitative colonialism" and "absolute male domination," although the qualifiers were important to Troeltsch, since he believed in good imperialism and opposed feminism: "The human rights of alien races would be protected in a program of peaceful colonization." Troeltsch stressed that modern democracy differed from ancient democracy because it was Protestant, springing from the Reformed ideal of popular sovereignty, not aristocratic or revolutionary. Even in an age of socialist movements, the strongest ally of democracy was "the Christian feeling that the poor and humble must be supported in their aspirations."[21]

But democracy had to be chastened by the aristocratic impulse; otherwise it was stupid and self-devouring. Troeltsch described modern conservatism as essentially aristocratic, understood in the political sense as the power of privileged individuals and groups to pass on the power to rule. Conservatism, so understood, rested on a profound truism, "the presupposition of the inequality of human nature, which is fundamental and can never be eliminated." Without this vast inequality in "native endowment," it would not be possible for human beings to form communities and societies, sort out divisions of labor, and instill habits of loyalty, modesty, piety, trust, and responsibility. Even the modern state depends on inequality because the state did not arise on liberal terms as a contract among atomistic individuals. Aristocratic conservatism, resting on the wisdom of the ages and confirmed by everyday experience, proclaims a "genuine and legitimate" fundamental principle: "Authority, not majority!" Human beings need authority desperately because they are vastly unequal in intelligence, competence, goodness, and power. To recognize this "indisputable fact" and its moral wisdom is to "appreciate the moral values that are destined to grow from these inequalities and power-based relations."[22]

Democracy and conservatism need each other, nationalism has an important role, and liberal liberties must be safeguarded. Troeltsch said the United States was not an exception to needing a conservative tradition. To be sure, the United States was too young and liberal to have an aristocratic tradition, but that would change as it got older: "For everything historical is aristocratic, and all aristocracy entails conservatism." In foreign policy he admired modern conservatism for its nationalistic realism and Kantian liberalism for its dream of a cooperative federation of nations. Troeltsch said conservatism was nearly always nationalistic, not shy about going to war, and always dedicated to preserving its privileges: "It will sanction the domination of small states by large ones and the subjection of inferior races by those more capable of rule and richer in culture; it will regard the idea of rule by the white race as the natural consequence of the place the white race has won for itself in history." A certain amount of white rule was merited and commendable; Troeltsch declined to say how far it should go.[23]

However that sorted out, Christianity needed to be part of the mix but didn't settle anything. Troeltsch explained that Christianity had no political ideas at its birth, and after it got into politics it had to borrow from Aristotle and Roman law. In modern times its political significance was indirect. The chief Christian contribution to political ethics was its religious and ethical personalism, which challenged individuals to fulfill their God-given capacities for love, creativity, and faithfulness. Christianity idealizes Adam, the primordial man of paradise free from sin and structures of dominion, but it lives in the real world of sin, guilt, proprietary distinctions, and violence. It commands moral feeling and works of mercy for the dispossessed but has no politics: "Today we know with certainty that the gospel contains no direct political and social instructions; it is fundamentally non-political."[24]

The heart of Christian ethics is the love ethic of Jesus, which has no place in a political ethic. Troeltsch said the best contributions of Christianity to political ethics came from its secondary ideas of personhood and submission to natural orders. The former idea is a bulwark of democracy, the latter idea goes with conservatism, and Christianity needed to help fuse them politically. But he cautioned that these ideas are never enough for a state, which has a moral idea of its own, nationalism. Every state needs the nationalist idea for its identity and self-preservation, something it does not get from Christianity. Since the nationalist idea is purely political, Christianity has never been able to do "anything directly" with it. The political role of Christianity is to press its ideas of personality and obedience on the state: "Christianity introduces something new and vital into political ethics, namely, an unconditional appreciation of the person and a respectful modesty." That left the question whether democracy or conservatism was more important in 1904. Troeltsch said neither was more important than the other; the crucial thing was to bring them together. Democrats and conservatives had to stop inveighing against each other with spiteful polemics. Perhaps the Evangelical Social Congress could help: "The two ideas must find each other and reach an accommodation."[25]

Like Weber, Troeltsch was restless, skeptical, prone to nervousness and melancholy, and fretted about losing his capacity for scholarly productivity. He was a loner but leaned on his friends and craved discussion. To some colleagues he seemed extroverted; to others he seemed passive and resigned; in reality he oscillated as a mixture of both, except at the lecture podium, where the extrovert prevailed. He could write a punchy sentence but favored long, winding sentences that piled up clauses, abstractions, and many-sided descriptions. He did not have clear positions before he embarked on his research or even started writing; he found his answers along the way. Like Weber, he was tremendously productive and gifted with rare analytical power, writing vast works on broad themes crammed with detail. His friend Friedrich Meinecke compared him to a thundering mountain stream whisking huge loads downriver as though at play. Harnack, with customary vividness, captured Troeltsch at the lecture podium: "His manner was unique and at the same time captivating. He did not aim to formulate his ideas sharply and concisely but with repeated efforts and with an overflowing eloquence which was amply, even overabundantly at his command, he tossed an observation to and fro, assailing it from all sides and putting it in different contexts until it appeared purified and clear. His mind acted like a powerful centrifugal machine or like a rotating drum which shook and tossed about the subject until it was cleansed from all foreign parts and loomed up in its own individuality."[26]

In 1904 Troeltsch was asked to review a new edition of a book by Greifswald theologian Martin von Nathusius on the church and the social question. The book was terrible, he judged; it showed that modern theologians had a pathetic understanding of social Christianity despite talking about it constantly. Nathusius confused two understandings of the "social" in social Christianity, failing to distinguish between the social character of the gospel and its sociological effects, and he made a mess of the relationships between state and society. Troeltsch began to think about a major work that paralleled Harnack's *History of Dogma*—featuring the notion of a self-unfolding of the religious idea and surveying the development of Christian social thought to the modern age, although Harnack stopped at the Reformation.[27]

But Troeltsch believed that Harnack was insufficiently sociological, treating ideas as continuous realities, and Harnack underemphasized the social factors shaping Christian doctrine. Troeltsch rejected the idea of a dogmatic subject that stays identical with itself through the permutations of history, for

"Christianity" is as various as the many historical groups and traditions claiming the name. A new model was needed, one built on historical sociology and the history of religions. In that spirit Troeltsch labored for many years on *The Social Teaching of the Christian Churches* (1912), later recalling, "This time I dispensed with any programmatic preliminary work and instead of all the mere spitting I devoted myself with indescribable toil to piping." On occasion he boasted that his magnum opus created a new discipline.[28]

For several years he played down that his research was leading to a big book. Characteristically, Troeltsch claimed he had no unifying argument. The massive articles he published between 1908 and 1910 did not defend a thesis; he merely sought to uncover what happened. But his studies of Christian social teaching elicited favorable comparisons to Harnack and Weber, which Troeltsch monitored closely. He cared intensely about his academic reputation and intended all along to produce a massive book.[29]

Meanwhile he found a bigger audience by accident, in 1906, after Weber begged off from addressing the Ninth Congress of German Historians and sent Troeltsch in his place. Weber was asked to speak on the significance of Protestantism in the rise of the modern world, a topic pegged to his new book, *The Protestant Ethic and the Spirit of Capitalism* (1905). Troeltsch filled in with a typical excursus, "The Significance of Protestantism for the Rise of the Modern World," taking aim at the cult of Martin Luther. On the one hand, he argued, Protestantism surely contributed to modern progress in law, government, economics, and high culture, and it accommodated the modern world very well. On the other hand, liberal Protestants needed to stop kidding themselves about their proximity to Luther. A chasm separated the premodern and modern worlds, and the Reformers belonged to the other side.[30]

This did not mean what Troeltsch's offended critics charged for decades afterward—that he wrote off Luther and Calvin as medieval. Troeltsch said the Reformation of Luther and Calvin was a momentous phase of transition from the old world of feudal authoritarianism to the new world of freedom and modernity. It broke the Catholic monopoly on religious authority and set the stage for new possibilities. But Luther and Calvin, Troeltsch insisted, did not cross into the new world, even with one foot. They gave a Protestant twist to Catholic problems, modifying medieval religion. Politically, socially, and religiously, Calvinism was more progressive than Lutheranism, and some elements of the Anabaptist and mystical movements were more progressive than Calvinism. But the transformation occurred in the eighteenth century, driven by Enlightenment criticism, the rise of capitalism, and the modern state. Protestantism contributed the ideas of freedom and personality to it, but

Protestantism became modern by being transformed by modernity, not by fulfilling something in its nature.

Troeltsch ended with a cautionary Weberian flourish. By his lights,
Protestantism made one important contribution to modern Western civilization, "an extraordinarily strong religious and metaphysical foundation, which,
moreover, exists independently of it." Liberal Protestantism helped to create a
civilization that prized individual freedom, generated vast new wealth, supported scholarship and high culture, and fostered a culture of material and
spiritual progress. However, Troeltsch warned, all this enlightened progress had
a destructive underside — powerful social trends that threatened to stop progress
cold, if not extinguish it: "Our economic development is rather tending in the
direction of a new bondage, and the great military and bureaucratic States, in
spite of all their parliaments, are not wholly favorable to the spirit of liberty."[31]

Science was falling into the hands of technocratic specialists, philosophy was
exhausted, and the arts produced frivolous aesthetes. These trends spelled trouble for the cause of freedom. Progressive optimism notwithstanding, the West
seemed to be heading toward an era of oppression by giant corporations, governments, and unions. In that case, Troeltsch said, it was more important than
ever for liberal Protestants to uphold their distinct contribution to modern civilization, their freedom-loving metaphysic of religious personalism. This religious worldview established freedom on "a foundation which an all-too-human
humanism cannot destroy." The best hope of Western civilization rested on
"faith in God as the power whence freedom and personality come to us; namely,
Protestantism." Troeltsch implored the German historians and his readers to
hold fast to it: "Otherwise the cause of freedom and personality may well be lost
in the very moment when we are boasting most loudly of our allegiance to it,
and of our progress in this direction."[32]

This was the burning social and religious concern underlying Troeltsch's
research for *The Social Teaching of the Christian Churches*. He poured out
lecture monographs and pamphlets on the way to producing it, always seeking
to interpret human history as a flow of events operating within complex webs of
interacting social, historical, and natural factors. His writings leading up to his
masterwork registered a conviction he dramatically expressed to a conference of
Ritschlian theologians: Everything was tottering.[33]

The Social Teaching of the Christian Churches, published in 1912 as the first
volume of Troeltsch's collected works, ran one thousand pages and conveyed a
strong sense of tottering. He said he once held Ritschl's twofold concept of how
theology should proceed, relating a distinct concept of traditional doctrine to a
critical understanding of the modern intellectual and religious situation. But

Troeltsch came to doubt that Ritschl got either part right. The Ritschlian strategy assimilated a dubious rendering of the Christian story to an equally questionable interpretation of the modern situation, covering up the actual contrasts between them. Troeltsch recalled, "Thus I found myself confronted by a double task: to make clear to myself both the ecclesiastical dogmatic tradition of Protestantism in its own historical sense, and the intellectual and practical situation of the present day in its true fundamental tendencies."[34]

This explained his twofold fixation on the history of Protestantism and the emergence of the modern world. Troeltsch told himself he was laying the historical groundwork for his systematic theology and philosophy of religion. But the more he studied modern problems, the more he found himself pulled into social ethics. If Christianity was "first and foremost a matter of practice," its chief problems belonged to the sphere of practical life, the very area in which modern churches were most confused and out of date. Theology in the modern age had to grapple, above all, with the social problem.[35]

Troeltsch offered long, thick, penetrating descriptions of social teaching in the early Christian movement, early Catholicism, medieval Catholicism, and numerous varieties of European Protestantism. Adopting Weber's concept of ideal types, he argued that the Christian community, from its beginning as an independent movement, developed three types of Christianity rooted in three distinct models of social organization. The gospel of Jesus was a religion of free piety, strong on spiritual intimacy, and lacking any concern with organizing a cult or creating a religious community, much less prescribing a political ideology. Thus it had gaping sociological deficits, which gave rise to the three kinds of Christianity: an institutional church model dispensing objective means of grace and redemption, a sectarian model of true believers living apart from the world, and a mystical faith emphasizing inward spirituality and playing down external forms of worship, doctrine, and organization.

Each of these ideal types produced a distinct theology, he argued. The church type, epitomized by medieval Catholicism, played down subjective holiness, conceiving Christ as the Redeemer whose saving work is mediated to believers through the sacraments of the church. The sect type was a voluntary society of born-again believers, lower class and strongly eschatological, conceiving Christ as a law-giving Lord of history destined to complete his work of redemption in the Second Coming. Troeltsch said the "very varied sect-movement" originated as a complement to Catholicism and was almost vanquished within Catholicism until it exploded in the Anabaptist and radical movements of the sixteenth century. The mystical type, being inward and individual, was the most various, so Troeltsch settled for capsule descriptions of prominent individuals and their communities, notably George Fox and the Society of Friends. The Christ of mystical Christianity was an inward spiritual principle, "the Divine Spark which lies hidden in every mind and soul, stifled by sin and by the finite, yet capable of being quickened into vitality by the touch of the Divine Spirit working on and in our souls."[36]

Ideal types, he allowed, are ideal constructs. Medieval Catholicism housed and sanctioned mystical theologies; Magisterial Calvinism had sectarian elements; and the Quakers would have been forgotten had they not adopted Anabaptist ecclesiology and accommodated the real world. Troeltsch let on that he favored the mystical type, which had a later history in German idealism and liberal theology. Moreover, he respected sectarian Christianity for standing for something. But the mystics and sectarians never produced a major social philosophy. Neither had a solution to the problem of how to relate a gospel of "infinite sublimity and childlike intimacy" to the world of culture, politics, nationalism, and other religions. The sectarian movements took a stab at the Sermon on the Mount as countercultural communities cut off from the world, sometimes flipping to apocalyptic vengeance. The mystics took refuge in spiritual religion, which was too private to change anything. These approaches, besides having no answer to the original problem, were useless in addressing out-of-control capitalism, labor unrest, urbanization, nationalism, militarism, and technology; Troeltsch described the modern social problem as "all this distress which weighs on our hearts and minds like a perpetual menace."[37]

Only the church type, he argued, had the capacity to be creative and expansive. Nineteen centuries of Christianity produced only two major social philosophies: medieval Catholicism and Calvinism. The first was built on the spiritual unity of a feudal, patriarchal civilization featuring a supreme church. The second created a covenantal Protestant Christendom by combining asceticism, pietism, Free Church ecclesiology, state church governance, democracy, liberalism, vocational diligence, and the "glorification of work for its own sake." Troeltsch said both models had an impressive history, having applied the "inner impulse of Christian thought" to the worlds of their time. And both were spent forces by the nineteenth century. The Catholic doctrine of the Catholic state was as laughable as the Vatican's opposition to evolution and historical criticism, and Calvinism fared little better under modern criticism. No serious Christian social philosophy existed. There was only the glimmer of one in the Christian socialist movement.[38]

Troeltsch's treatment of Christian socialism was odd, surprisingly appreciative, and truncated. Formally his study ended with the eighteenth century, but he peeked ahead on occasion, as in his long section on varieties of sectarianism, and he ended the book with an excursus on the current situation, which required some understanding of the century just passed. Christian socialism got a brief mention near the end of his discussion of Protestant sectarianism. It was obviously a form of sectarianism, he said, recycling "the familiar characteristics of the primitive Christian tendency, the characteristics of the aggressive sect which believes in an actual transformation of conditions in this world." Troeltsch explained that Christian socialists got to be socialists by listening to Social Democratic speeches, which helped them see things in the Bible they hadn't noticed previously. Once they did so, they joined the sectarian tradition, without putting it that way, and modernized its usual tropes: "The Kingdom of God and reason, the Kingdom of God realized *on earth*, the invincible faith in the victory of goodness and in the possibility of overcoming every human institution which is based upon the mere struggle for existence, the Christian Revolution: this is the primitive, splendid ideal of the sect."[39]

Troeltsch forgot to ask himself if this described the biggest piece of the story, Anglo-Catholic socialism. He generalized from his memories of Stöcker's rallies, Blumhardt's sermons, and early Naumann, trying not to sneer. It surprised him that Christian socialists, having been educated in modern universities, believed they grasped the original gospel faith. But Troeltsch allowed that Christian socialists had something valuable: an understanding of Christianity that harmonized traditional Christian norms with modern social views. Moreover, they were the first Christian movement to reject centuries of authoritarianism and conformism in ethics: "Christian Socialism alone has broken through these theories, and forced men to think out afresh the social ethic of Christianity and its relation to the actual changes in the social order. It has laid bare the worm-eaten condition of the previous conventional Christian ethic, which, at its best, offered something for the ethics of the family and the individual, but which, on the other hand, had no message for social ethics save that of acceptance of all existing institutions and conditions, much to the satisfaction of all in authority. Christian Socialism has regained for the Christian ethic its Utopian and revolutionary character; once more it has brought upon its heralds the reproach of Christ, which officials of Church and State are always ready to hurl at all who indulge humanitarian sentiment or in idealistic dreams."[40]

So Troeltsch lauded the Christian socialists for making a real advance, even as he judged them doubly naïve. Theologically they were innocents, invoking words of Jesus as though they blazed through the centuries. Politically they were innocent and dangerous, fantasizing about an international proletariat that refused all calls to war except perhaps class war. Even if Christian socialism became the third great Christian social philosophy, the church needed something else—a truly modern, critical, effective, and inspiring way of engaging the world. But Troeltsch admitted he didn't know what it was: "If the present social situation is to be controlled by Christian principles, thoughts will be necessary which have not yet been thought."[41]

All he could say was what he always said about upholding a Christian personalist worldview. Only Christianity provides a strong basis for personality and individuality. Through its concept of Divine Love, only Christianity embraces and unites all human souls. Ethically, only Christianity solves the problem of inequality, by viewing all people as children of God loved by God, without denying the "patent fact" that people vary greatly in intelligence and competence. Last, Christianity, being the consummate religion of love and personality, promotes charity as the fruit of the Christian Spirit, although Troeltsch stopped short of claiming that only Christianity promoted charity.[42]

Beyond that he was chastened about the relevance of modern Christianity: "Every idea is still faced by brutal facts, and all upward movement is checked and hindered by interior and exterior difficulties." Once the church lost its doctrinal certainties and social power, there was no answer. There was only the search for a new one: "Nowhere does there exist an absolute Christian ethic, which only awaits discovery; all that we can do is to learn to control the world-situation in its successive phases just as the earlier Christian ethic did in its own way."[43]

The Social Teaching of the Christian Churches made Troeltsch famous, dominated its field for decades, and eased his transition to philosophy of religion. Generations of theologians and social ethicists who rejected his theology taught his historical account as definitive. His typology of church, sect, and mysticism was canonical for decades, inspiring H. Richard Niebuhr's equally famous typology of religion and culture models in *Christ and Culture*. In 1915 Troeltsch accepted a chair in philosophy at Berlin, claiming not to have left theology behind, despite what theologians said. He had seized on the history of religions approach as soon as it arose, believing it marked an advance in the study of religion. But every time he taught systematic theology, he realized that history of religions scholarship was a very limited tool for theology.[44]

On doctrine after doctrine Troeltsch found himself refashioning Schleiermacher and scolding that the Mediating and Ritschlian schools did not improve on Schleiermacher. In 1913 he professed to disagree with Schleiermacher on only one important point, Schleiermacher's failed monism: "Schleiermacher's dogmatics is everywhere saturated with pantheistic thinking, shot through and through with an atmosphere that breathes heavily of Spinoza and Goethe—an atmosphere to which our own present day also stands very close, albeit more as a caricature." Troeltsch had moved from neo-Hegelian metaphysics to neo-Kantian value theory to avoid this fate, but he was still an idealist who held fast to the personalizing impulse in life. Neo-Kantian idealism, he believed, was better than Schleiermacher's monism because it gave free rein to personality, ethics, and will and the reality of a pluralistic external world.[45]

Sometimes he added that Schleiermacher's subjectivism bolstered Herrmann's disastrous mistake of setting faith against knowledge. Schleiermacher taught that to feel the spiritual power of Jesus's personality as mediated by the church and the gospel picture of Jesus is to be convinced of his divinity; doubt is an outsiders' problem. Troeltsch, appalled that Herrmann took this argument all the way to a fideist blind alley, urged liberals to keep their heads, avoiding blind alleys. It matters, for knowledge and faith, whether Jesus really existed. It matters whether the gospel picture of Jesus is more or less reliable. No particular detail or even hundreds of them together are crucial for Christian faith, but the "general results of the research" do matter for faith. Troeltsch implored liberals to stick with history and a more or less reliable gospel picture. He liked to think that Schleiermacher was on his side and would have said so had he read Herrmann. In any case, Schleiermacher otherwise got the main things right. The right strategy is to begin with religious feeling and uphold Christianity "as the highest living power."[46]

When the war came Troeltsch's first reaction was Augustinian, grieving at the terrible "antithesis of the wicked earthly world and the blessed heavenly world." He lamented the savage destruction and hatred of the war but gave patriotic speeches urging Germans to vanquish their enemies. Troeltsch's willingness to fire up crowds at rallies and conferences brought him public renown far beyond his academic base. Once he emoted, "Oh! If only the speaker this hour could turn every word into a bayonet, if only he could transform them into rifles, into cannon!" He enlisted God and history in support of Germany, lauding the army as an instrument of salvation. He implored audiences, "*Be German, remain German, become German!*" Sometimes he stooped to racist appeals. In Troeltsch's telling, the German boys on the western front fought for the lofty values expressed in the song "Deutschland, Deutschland, über Alles," while fighting a motley horde of "Asiatic Indians, Negroes, Frenchmen, Englishmen, and Belgians" united by nothing but "slanders and lies about German barbarians." Troeltsch extolled the German virtues of bravery, duty, and seriousness and called for a federation of central European powers.[47]

After the war he gamely entreated Germans to support democracy and ward off despair. Troeltsch won election to the Prussian State Assembly in 1919 as a member of the German Democratic Party, a centrist party cofounded by Weber.

He also served for two years as parliamentary undersecretary of state in the Prussian Ministry of Culture. To the end of his life Troeltsch said that philosophy of religion was his first love and he planned to write a major work on it. But his life was cut short by heart failure in 1923, leaving a major two-volume work on historicism only half completed and no philosophy of religion, and he let go of his anchor, the idea of personality as a universal principle. In *Der Historismus und seine Probleme* (1922) Troeltsch still had a metaphysical substructure, a Leibniz-like monadology in which every individual finite spirit "participates intuitively" in the divine Spirit. He theorized that history consists fundamentally of individual totalities—*wholes* synthesizing psychical processes and natural conditions. Historical wholes such as families, social classes, states, cultural epochs, revolutions, and schools of thought are original, partly unconscious, integral unities of meaning and value. The universal history that Troeltsch wanted to write would have focused on them, but he concluded it was not possible or was possible only in a qualified way—he could be quoted either way.[48]

Sometimes he argued for a universal history leading to a modern cultural synthesis resting on the ancient Hebraic tradition, classical Greece, the Hellenistic–Roman period, and the Occidental Middle Ages. Non-Western history, to Troeltsch, had little to contribute to universal history; he barely glanced at non-Occidental philosophies of history. But elsewhere in *Der Historismus und seine Probleme* and emphatically in his last book, *Der Historismus und seine Überwindung* (1924), Troeltsch said the dream of a universal history had to be given up. On occasion, in the former mode, he argued that historical wholes possess a common spirit or mind that is properly the object of historical reason, theology, and the philosophy of history. In his last book he argued that we know nothing of "humanity" or a Common Spirit. All we know are particular groups, families, races, classes, schools, and sects from six thousand years of history, a tiny fraction of the human experience, and in his case all he really cared about was the background to the European story.[49]

In the latter mode Troeltsch gave up his idea of personality as a universal principle because the idea of personality is too Christian to be universal. In place of his vision of historical development as the shaping of community life in accordance with a universal norm epitomized in Christianity, he settled for "Europeanism." Christianity, he said, is the best religion for Europe. Troeltsch still made a strained appeal to universality: "For us there is only the universal history of European culture" (*Universalgeschichte der europäischen Kultur*) or, stressing Europeanism as an idea, "For us there is only a universal history of Europeanism" (*Weltgeschichte des Europäertums*). In both cases he accepted that any idea claiming universality is as thoroughly particular and historical as any other idea. No historically conscious European has an idea of universality or a concept of values that is not decidedly European.[50]

Putting it positively is important, he argued, because Europeanism is worth defending and renewing on its own terms. It deserved "-ism" status alongside capitalism, liberalism, Expressionism, and the like, if not above them. Europeanism had a vital, scientific, and emancipating historical individuality. It valorized individuality and critical rationality more than any other culture, and its carryover into the United States was a major point in its favor. Troeltsch took pride that Americans read German scholars and filled their museums with European art. America's ascendancy as a world power had a chance of expanding the reach and career of European culture. But Troeltsch cautioned that America was highly unpredictable, and it lacked a sense of history. Thus it made a questionable repository for European culture. If America turned out to be a "vacant possession" for Europeanism, something precious would be lost— the full blooming of European individuality.[51]

Troeltsch lived to see the great sweeping away of liberal theology, social Christianity, Culture Protestantism, history of religions theology, and everything else he treasured. Barth's leap into irrationalism and dogma repelled Troeltsch, and his influence was unfathomable. How could theology leap backward, as though historical criticism did not exist? Troeltsch shook his head that "logical and historical reasons" meant nothing to the youthful generation determined to repudiate its teachers: "Anti-historicism, irrationalism, intuitionism— things with which we older people have concerned ourselves passionately and scrupulously—have already become comfortable and pleasant dogmas for many of the young."[52]

That was a sad spectacle to Troeltsch, one that pushed aside his historicism and history of religions theology as bankrupt enterprises. His writings on the historical career of Christian social teaching stayed in play, but not his idea that theology should be historicist, cultural, and comparative. A decade after Troeltsch was gone Reinhold Niebuhr renewed Troeltsch's attempt to enlist Christian personalism as a resource for an ambiguous, synthetic, power-oriented ethical realism. Like Troeltsch, Niebuhr drew deeply on Weber's conception of politics as a realistic vocation. Like Troeltsch, Niebuhr denied that Christian ethics was directly relevant to political issues and affirmed that the Christian factor in political ethics was indirect, ambiguous, and crucially valuable. Principally through Niebuhr's influence, American Christian social ethics took a socialist turn in the 1930s on grounds that Troeltsch would have recognized: American Christian ethics needed the hard-edged realism of Marx's critique of capitalism and Marx's understanding that the capitalist system was sure to explode. But Niebuhr's debt to Marx overshadowed his affinities with Troeltsch, and later he leaned on Augustine when he was finished with Marx.

Niebuhr was a social gospel pacifist minister in the 1920s, shifted to Christian socialism in the late 1920s, and joined the faculty of Union Theological Seminary in 1928. Basically he joined the socialist wing of the social gospel that his friends Sherwood Eddy, Kirby Page, and Harry Ward sustained after World War I, until the Depression drove Niebuhr to Marx's catastrophe vision of proletarian revolution. There was no third way, Niebuhr contended. America would either move forward to radical socialism or backward to fascist barbarism because Marx was right about the sooner-or-later capitalist implosion that destroyed everything. Niebuhr said it forcefully in two blistering works, *Moral Man and Immoral Society* (1932) and *Reflections on the End of an Era* (1934). Politics is a struggle for power. Liberal Christians were stupid for believing that reason and goodwill are saving. The same idiocy hoped that progressive reforms would save the nation: "Recognizing, as liberal Christianity does not, that the world of politics is full of demonic forces, we have chosen on the whole to support the devil of vengeance against the devil of hypocrisy." Niebuhr chose to support Marxist vengeance, knowing there was a devil in it, rather than allow the devil of hypocrisy to avoid conflict and preserve the status quo. Only a "sublime madness in the soul" had any chance of defeating "malignant power," contrary to liberal sermons and FDR. On that ground Niebuhr vehemently opposed the New Deal—a liberal Band-Aid, in his telling—until the late 1930s, when he made another course correction.[53]

Why stay in the tiny and marginalized Socialist Party when FDR carried out much of the socialist platform? Then the Socialist Party balked at World War II, and Niebuhr resigned from the party in January 1940. By then he favored Augustine, not Marx, as the exemplary realist, although Niebuhr was still a democratic socialist when he wrote *The Children of Light and the Children of Darkness* in 1944. The following year he dropped socialism altogether, a sooner-or-later inevitability after he gave up Marxism. Niebuhr's rejection of ethical idealism, like Tillich's, made him averse to sticking with socialism after he no longer believed that Marx was right about capitalist self-destruction. Why carry on about socialism in a nation lacking a proletarian tradition? Niebuhr repented of opposing the New Deal, joined the mainstream of the Democratic Party, stopped writing about economic justice, and might have played up his affinities with Troeltsch had Troeltsch's prowar nationalism not gone overboard.

Niebuhr's polemic against social idealism did not explain what happened in Britain, where Christian socialism went by its right name, knew why it was socialist, and did not give up the battle to democratize economic power. He was aware of the difference, being a half-Anglophile with an English spouse and Labour Party friends. Had Niebuhr lived in England he would have been at home in the Labour Party. As it was, he was a deeply patriotic American who cut his Christian realism to fit the national interests of the American government and his own shifting ideas about the demands of justice. America, to Niebuhr as to Tillich, became a place to give up on democratic socialism at the very moment it surged in England.

ACCOMPLISHED MEDIOCRE BRITISH SOCIALISM

Social Democracy and a supportive Christian socialist tradition advanced distinctly in England, where Marxism was a latecomer and even Marxists did not espouse the dictatorship of the proletariat. Fabians fashioned a distinct British socialism by supporting the civilizing progress they said was happening anyway, Labour socialists fought for England to thwart an intolerable Nazi tyranny, the heirs of Maurice and Morris kept alive the language of ethical idealism and economic democracy, and revisionists prevented Labour socialism from ossifying into an outdated dogma.

Sidney Webb built a Fabian powerhouse on research, lectures, technocratic proficiency, Commonwealth feeling, and pamphleteering. He and George Bernard Shaw stripped socialism of its proletarian atmosphere, conceiving socialist salvation as a job for policy experts. Many Fabian stalwarts would have preferred to take over the Liberal Party and keep the unions in a subordinate position, permeating society with their vision of gradual Collectivism. But keeping the unions down proved impossible after Keir Hardie formed the ILP and the ground shifted. Fabian Collectivism was an Edwardian project, epitomizing Edwardian progressivism, gentility, and urbanity. The Fabian Society would have died with the Edwardian era had Sidney Webb not convinced Arthur Henderson and the fledgling Labour Party that Labour needed Fabian guidance and ideology. Webb taught Labour the immense importance of a Fabian specialty, empirical research. Labour needed to stand upon factual evidence supporting (Fabian) socialism, making Labour propaganda open to correction and accessible to ordinary readers. In this respect Cole exemplified true-believing Fabianism throughout his career, as did the revisionists he enabled and battled.

Fabian Collectivism, however, was short on moral feeling, even after it signed on with the Labour Party. Sidney and Beatrice Webb were Edwardian technocrats who cringed at ethical claims and social justice rhetoric. Inexorable state collectivism, to them, trumped anything moral. They wanted to win without fighting, prevailing on the truth of their ideas. By their lights, prophetic types were preachy and strident. Fabian socialism needed to be, and was, reasonable, civil, mannered, and urbane. Two generations of Webb protégés struggled through two MacDonald governments, making Labour socialism more or less respectable, until they succeeded under Clement Attlee and Herbert Morrison, two prototypes of Fabian technocracy. But the Webbs realized the movement needed ethical socialists who burned for social justice. Thus they cultivated friendships with Tawney and Cole even as Cole blasted them for ruining English socialism.

The movement needed intellectuals fired by an ethical passion for justice and able to express it without going churchy or maudlin or self-righteous or emotional. Social Christianity, the WEA, and the unions were training grounds for social justice intellectuals of this sort, notably Tawney, Cole, Temple, and Reckitt. The Webbs were also good at inspiring loyalty. Tawney, Cole, Margaret Cole, and Tony Crosland were fiercely loyal to the Webbs long after the Webbs embarrassed Labour with pro-Stalinist tripe. Tawney loved and admired Beatrice Webb to the end, unfailingly grateful for her role in his life and the socialist movement. He made caustic remarks about pro-Stalinists without bothering to mention that one of his dearest friends was foremost in defending the purges and death camps of the largest mass murder in history.

In 1945 the Labour socialists won real power, long after anyone believed in inevitable cultural progress. To defend their own achievements and build upon them, Labour socialists had to appeal to something deeper and more inspiring than economic efficiency. They had to say they were building the ethical Commonwealth of social justice, the dream of Morris and Ruskin. They did not need Marxism or any high theory to pull it off. Just as Christian socialists of the 1880s leaned on Henry George for guidance in political economy, Tawney stressed that Labour socialists of the 1940s leaned on two Liberals in political economy—Keynes and Beveridge. Tawney said he was grateful not to be German because German socialists had a history of "dogmatic petrification" before they rolled over for World War I. He was also grateful not to be French, despite loving France, because French socialism was intellectualistic too, plus alienated from working-class society.[54]

Tawney allowed that Labour's union basis had its drawbacks, but at least British socialism thereby stayed close to actual workers and conditions. If saying so made him a bourgeois Philistine, so be it: "I remain unrepentant." British socialism surpassed Marxian Social Democratic movements by bonding with unions and emphasizing its moral basis. Tawney put it bluntly, describing Labour socialism as an ethically based working-class phenomenon helped by intellectuals and officials, not the other way around: "The impulse behind the movement has been obstinately and unashamedly ethical. The revolt of ordinary men against Capitalism has had its source neither in its obvious deficiencies as an economic engine, nor in the conviction that it represents a stage of social evolution now outgrown, but in the straightforward hatred of a system which stunts personality and corrupts human relations by permitting the use of man by man as an instrument of pecuniary gain." British socialism, he boasted, resounded with ordinary people "working without fear in comradeship for common ends." They conceived the state as a servant of the common good, their literature was empirical, not dogmatic, and they conceived economic interests as second-order priorities well below "sentiments of human dignity, justice, and equality."[55]

This ethically fired pragmatism paid off; in 1952 Tawney marveled at how fast it happened. Labour socialized the civil aviation and long-distance communication industries almost without notice. It nationalized gas and electricity with no public protests and only token opposition in the House of Commons. Socializing the railways and canals was naturally more complicated, but most of the debate focused on alternative structures, not the legitimacy of public ownership. Tawney worked up to his favorite example, recalling the outcry over nationalized coal mines in 1919. When it finally happened in 1946, "not a dog barked." He recognized the danger that nationalized enterprises might become too bureaucratic and lethargic, but he also knew energetic bureaucrats who were determined not to fail, so he took little pause in this area. Tawney worried more that government do-gooders would "pander to popular tastes, instead of instructing them," and spend too much on things the masses wanted instead of things society needed. He spun a variation on one of his favorite aphorisms. The state is quite capable of making a desert and calling it efficiency. Here was the real challenge for Labour socialism, he said. The state was capable of negating the moral values that legitimized Social Democracy. The challenge for ethical socialists was to prevent socialism from gaining the world but losing its soul.[56]

Tawney gave no quarter to objections that he made socialism too Christian. Historically, he said, individual dignity and human rights are Christian ideas. They did not come from anywhere else, which is very different from saying that only Christianity upholds them. No Christian socialist believed that. Austrian economist Friedrich von Hayek claimed that socialism created a tyrannical god, a modern Leviathan subjecting individuals to serfdom. Tawney said this was a lurid fantasy because there was no state bearing uniform characteristics. There were only particular states produced by various historical traditions, economic environments, constitutional arrangements, and social psychologies. The state was an important instrument, so socialists struggled to get hold of it, but it was nothing more than an instrument, "a serviceable drudge." Fools used it for foolish ends, criminals used it for criminal ends, and sensible people used it for sensible ends. Tawney boasted that England had to elect a socialist government to enact the best liberal ideas. It was entirely to Labour's credit that its two most important theorists were Liberals. Tawney did not share the anguish of left-wing socialists that Labour spent the Attlee years carrying out the ideas of Keynes and Beveridge. Attlee found the sweet spot between socialist aspiration and political reality. Six years of successful Labour governments proved that Social Democracy was a force for radical change without being scary, achieving the best kind of liberal democracy. Britons, Tawney observed, had a long history of remaking the state. Now they were doing it again: "Why, in heaven's name, should we be afraid of it?"[57]

Tawney's sanguine attitude about the achievements of Labour socialism rankled left-wing socialists, who said he let them down. Young political philosopher Alasdair MacIntyre, during his leftist phase in 1964, was one of them. MacIntyre said Gaitskell and Crosland had it too easy in the 1950s, remaking the party with relative ease because very few Labour intellectuals had the standing to hold off the triumph of Labour Keynesianism. Sidney and Beatrice Webb might have done it, but they defected to Stalinism, being elitists who never stopped believing in the imposition of socialism from above. John Strachey might have done it, but he defected from Marxism just when Britain desperately needed a Marxist perspective. Cole might have done it, but he twisted himself into a tangle by subordinating his Marxist position to the rules of the Labour right wing. MacIntyre exaggerated Cole's Marxism, not that it mattered. According to MacIntyre, Cole's failure left Tawney standing alone as the only Labour intellectual who might have saved Labour from selling out. And he failed miserably.[58]

MacIntyre said Tawney specialized in "banal earnestness" about the moral failings of capitalism, not a radical vision of socialism. Tawney thought it was a great moral achievement when Britain finally nationalized the coal mines and railways, never mind that it was the only solution to a practical and banal problem; even Tories said so. According to MacIntyre, Tawney impressed his British audience as an important voice only because the politicians of his time—MacDonald, Snowden, Baldwin, and Chamberlain—were "tiny and impotent figures." Compared to them, he seemed high-minded, ethical, sensible, and intelligent. In reality Tawney was insular and mediocre, like them, only slightly less so. Tawney had a two-level understanding of socialism that was superficial on both levels. First, socialism was about realizing the moral values of fellowship and equality; second, it replaced private ownership with public ownership and the welfare state. Everything Tawney said on level one was too vague and mushy to be of any political value. Moreover, Tawney never absorbed that corporate capitalism changed the picture, so he kept saying the same banal things about private ownership after the big corporations made their peace with trade unionism, accepted the welfare state, and even accepted a certain amount of state intervention and public ownership.[59]

Incredibly, to MacIntyre, Tawney never grasped that Keynesian policies strengthened the capitalist system and worked best under a capitalist ethos. MacIntyre mocked Tawney for celebrating the accomplishments of the Attlee governments as landmark socialist achievements. When Tawney wrote in this vein, he put his mediocrity on naked display, an embarrassment. Labour simply carried out the policy trajectory of the wartime Coalition government. The Education Act passed in 1944, a year before Labour took over. Attlee let go of India and built the National Health Service, but any intelligent pragmatist would have done both. The same could be said of everything else the Attlee governments pushed through. Moreover, Labour did not abolish the class system in education after it took power; Labour contributed mightily to a new class system favoring middle-class children. MacIntyre put it grandly, sweeping Labour's entire history into his indictment: The socialism espoused by Tawney and Labour "has always been managerial and meritocratic," lacking any belief in the real thing or gut-level sense of it. The real thing existed *in* the Labour Party, MacIntyre allowed. It was there in every rank-and-file local demanding worker control. But Labour Party orthodoxy, thanks to Sidney Webb, had always conspired against workers demanding self-determination.[60]

To MacIntyre, Labour was Britain's other conservative party. He reasoned that Tawney managed to conceal this fact from himself and his British readers because he was as insularly British as they were. Tawney restricted himself geographically and ideologically, never bothering to assemble an argument against Marxist theory. He treated the idea of economic expertise as a bad joke, and his theoretical range was confined to the House of Commons. Thus he had no concept of politics beyond the things debated at Parliament, and he did not join the cranky types in protesting that Parliament needed more democracy. In sum, MacIntyre judged, "however radical he may be about the economic activities of private capitalism, he is a true member of the Labour Party in being completely complacent about British political institutions."[61]

Young MacIntyre attacking Tawney was like young Cole attacking the Webbs and young Niebuhr attacking a generation of social gospel idealists. He made a name for himself by doing so, struck his target forcefully and harshly, and perfectly summarized a school of thought. Tawney had done the same thing to MacDonald, which set up Tawney for similar treatment after he stopped writing in the mode of "The Choice Before Us." Tawney's blistering attack on the second MacDonald government and his demand that Labour seriously choose socialism for the first time suggested a radical course he did not take. Instead he pulled back from party activism and quietly cheered Attlee's grinding, managerial, pragmatic, and eventually hawkish brand of Social Democratic leadership. Tawney's writings in the 1940s and 1950s were almost as pedestrian as MacIntyre scathingly said. He had no stomach for the infighting that consumed the Labour Party, whether personal, factional, ideological, or theoretical. He let Gaitskell patronize him as the saint of British socialism and floated above the fray, just as Gaitskell and Crosland redefined Labour socialism.

REVISIONIST SOCIALISM IN QUESTION

Revisionism had been coming for twenty years when it bloomed into a movement and overtook the Labour Party. It began with the Labour economists of the 1930s—Jay, Dalton, Durbin, and Gaitskell—who took Keynes more seriously than Sidney Webb's Constitution. It bloomed in the early 1950s as an alternative to the impasse between Morrison consolidationists and Bevan radicals. The Gaitskell revisionists said Labour needed to be forward-looking and creative, not fixed on a recent achievement or an outdated ideology. The way forward was to espouse pluralistic Social Democracy as an ethical politics of social justice. It was enough, plus good politics, to manage a mixed economy, emphasize equality of opportunity and condition, experiment with various kinds of social ownership, and support decolonization movements, all on moral grounds. Labour needed to speak the ethical language of freedom and play down its historic emphasis on nationalization, although Gaitskell eventually offended Tawney by disavowing nationalization.

Revisionism, a term resounding of the Bernstein episode, swept through the strongest European Social Democratic parties after World War II: Labour, the SPD, and Sweden's Social Democratic Party. In Sweden it defined a proficient welfare state party that ruled the nation for four decades without interruption. In France and Italy the revisionist impulse took longer to play out because the Section Française de l'Internationale Ouvrière and Partito Socialista Italiano had little governing experience, and when they governed it was in coalition with other (usually larger) parties. But the trend in European Social Democracy toward Keynesian management and mixed-economy pluralism was pronounced. Every Social Democratic party had a history of blaming private ownership of the means of production and the existence of social classes for everything that ailed modern nations. Now they said the world was more complicated than that. Social Democrats projected an image of openness, conscientious moral concern, democratic faith, pragmatism, and, above all, principled non-Communism. They had nothing to do with Stalin's tyranny in Russia and the East Bloc. They said these things plainly in 1951 upon reorganizing the Socialist International in Frankfurt.

The Second International folded in 1916, three years before the Communist parties founded the Comintern in Moscow. Three attempts were made to resurrect the Second International before World War II. Social Democrats founded the International Socialist Commission in 1919 at Berne and the International Working Union of Socialist Parties in 1921 at Vienna, otherwise known as the Berne International and the Vienna International. In 1923 the two organizations merged at Hamburg to form the Labor and Socialist International (LSI), a plucky throwback to the Second International, which died in 1940 amid World War II. The next refounding of international Social Democracy occurred in June–July 1951 in Frankfurt, at the founding Congress of the Socialist International.[62]

At Frankfurt the Social Democrats called for "a system of social justice, better living, freedom, and world peace." The Frankfurt Declaration affirmed the universal right to freedom of thought, expression, education, organization, and religion and the right "of every human being to a private life, protected from arbitrary invasion by the state." It called for democratic control of economic systems, declaring that various forms of public ownership are adaptable means of serving the welfare of the community. It supported "private ownership in agriculture, handicraft, retail trade, and small and middle-sized industries," confirming that pluralism applied to these areas. It affirmed that trade unions and organizations of producers and consumers are indispensable to a democratic society, but not as tools of a central bureaucracy or a corporative system. It supported the universal rights to work, health care, child care, leisure, education, economic security, and housing. On internationalism, the Frankfurt Declaration reaffirmed traditional socialist anti-imperialism in a new postcolonial context: Democratic socialism is inherently international and transnational; every form of imperialism is anathema to democratic socialism; no nation can solve its economic and social problems in isolation; peace and freedom go together. Moreover, democratic socialists supported liberation struggles throughout the world for self-determination, freedom, and justice.[63]

Democratic socialism thus conceived was and is an acceptance of the mixed economy of the welfare state on terms established by traditional socialist values. It insisted that breaking down concentrations of wealth and privilege was essential to creating a just society, and socialization was a means to an end, not an end in itself. Welfare capitalism did not democratize economic power, and its bureaucratic ethos was inimical to freedom and moral idealism. Thus democratic socialism was needed more than ever. But public ownership did not democratize economic power either, and it contained its own threat to freedom. Thus democratic socialism had to be reinvented. These arguments stood at the center of the British revisionist movement championed by Gaitskell, Crosland, Richard Crossman, Roy Jenkins, and Denis Healey.

Crosland won his first seat in Parliament in 1950 as a Dalton protégé, representing Gloucestershire South. He lost an election in 1955, which freed him to write the bible of revisionism, *The Future of Socialism*, in 1956, and returned to Parliament in 1959, representing Great Grimsby, which he served until his death in 1977. In his later career he held seven ministry or cabinet positions in the Labour governments of Harold Wilson, plus secretary of state for foreign and Commonwealth affairs under Labour prime minister James Callahan.

Crosland made a landmark contribution to the revisionist insurgency in his essay of 1952, "The Transition from Capitalism," published in *New Fabian Essays*. The old socialism was irrelevant, he said, because economic and social power no longer rested on individual property rights. Active ownership had converted to passive shareholding, through which control passed to a managerial class of directors. The welfare state, a major advance for social decency, had become an independent intermediate power sustaining low unemployment. Something had already replaced capitalism, although Crosland puzzled about what to call it since it was not socialism and James Burnham had already tainted the name "managerial state." Crosland called it "Statism," despite allowing that this name was ugly and misleading; it smacked too much of things he disliked in Burnham. Later he disavowed it as "a bad choice." By whatever name, Crosland said, the new something diffused economic power among the old capitalists in small-scale industry, the new class of corporate managers, the state machine, shareholders, executives of public boards, and organized workers, sometimes with gains in worker ownership. In some ways this new order was much better than the old capitalism. But Crosland gave it only one cheer because the new order subjected human beings and their rights to the power of a managerial class that would never deliver social justice.[64]

Crossman said the same thing more sharply and expansively in the same venue, *New Fabian Essays*. He represented Coventry East, having won his seat in 1945, which he held until his death in 1974. In his later career he served in the Wilson governments as housing minister, later as Lord President of the Council, and finally as secretary of state for health and social security. In his early career he was a pillar of the Bevan left wing and a gatekeeper of its slogan, "Keep Left." Crossman sailed through New College, Oxford, in 1931 at the top of his class, taught philosophy at New College until the war, and produced anti-Nazi broadcasts for the Special Operations Executive during the war. He whisked into Labour politics with the same brash brilliance that marked his careers at New College and Special Operations. In 1946 Crossman added pro-Zionism to his ideology, urging Britain to allow one hundred thousand displaced European Jews to enter Palestine. In 1950 he published a famous anti-Communist reader, *The God That Failed.* In 1952 he and Crosland said that Clause Four no longer defined what socialism needed to be.[65]

Crossman granted that until approximately 1950 England's disinterest in socialist theory was a blessing. Britain had no Marxist tradition worth mentioning until the 1930s, when a few socialists tried to adopt Marxism and the Left Book Club replaced the Fabian Society as the home of vanguard intellectuals. But British Marxism never quite materialized. The Webbs and Harold Laski, imposing it as a theoretical superstructure on their utilitarian principles, produced pro-Stalinist blundering and contradictory incoherence, respectively. John Strachey, the only Briton to intelligibly formulate Marxism in Anglo-Saxon terms, disavowed doing so after the Nazi–Soviet pact. Tawney appropriated bits of Marxism, but Tawney's socialism was fundamentally Christian. British Marxism imploded during World War II, the Labour victory of 1945 yielded a season of Fabian triumph and accomplishment, and Crossman did not begrudge the Fabians their moment of glory. Nobody was better suited than the Fabians to create the welfare state and turn the empire into a commonwealth. But neither of these achievements, he cautioned, was uniquely socialist. The welfare state fulfilled the promises of liberalism and demands of the labor movement, and Liberals championed anti-imperialism before Labour existed. In Britain, Crossman said, reconciling capitalism to the principles of democracy was a singular achievement of the Labour Party. But now Labour lacked a compelling agenda because its leaders knew only the pragmatic politics of the welfare state, which already existed. Labour was the party of the postwar status quo, a deadly impasse for socialists.[66]

Fabian pragmatism had run its course; meanwhile Crossman said nobody believed anymore that the world was progressing steadily toward unity and freedom or that democratic socialism would eventually become the basis of a world government. H. G. Wells won fame and fortune by contending that the expansion of scientific knowledge necessarily increases freedom, but even Wells didn't believe it when he died, despairingly, in 1946. Until the 1930s virtually all progressives and Marxists accepted the materialist concept of progress.

Crossman hedged only slightly on the empirical evidence refuting progress: "There is neither a natural identity of interests nor yet an inherent contradiction in the economic system." He stressed the negative and did not linger over "yet." The growth of science and education does not necessarily yield democratic, productive, or even morally decent results: "Judging by the facts, there is far more to be said for the Christian doctrine of original sin than for Rousseau's fantasy of the noble savage, or Marx's vision of a classless society."[67]

That smacked of Niebuhr, as Crossman confirmed. There is no such thing as moral progress because morality consists in the decision to do good; growing up in a modern civilization does not increase the odds of a good decision. Modern societies enlarge the area of free choice, but they do not *make* morally better people. A free society is like a garden, producing either a wilderness of weeds or an arid patch of ground. Left to itself, a garden runs wild; under a gardener's care, more time has to be spent rooting out weeds than planting flowers. Crossman said one kind of cultivation is like another. No law of economics or politics produces freedom, equality, or social morality. Exploitation, tyranny, and disorder are the normal state of things, and only with assiduous cultivation does anything get better. All groups become increasingly greedy and exploitative unless they are policed by a strong social morality, exactly as Niebuhr contended.

Crossman said it self-consciously as a political leader: Freedom is always in danger of being lost or usurped. Most human beings will acquiesce in its loss rather than fight for their freedom. Only a resolute minority ever challenges the wealth and privileges of the elite and the apathy of the masses. In the nineteenth century liberals were the party of freedom that fought against tyranny and subservience. In the twentieth century this responsibility fell to democratic socialists. Crossman lamented that most Labour socialists did not realize what it meant to relinquish the notion of inevitable progress, even though they didn't believe in it. Now they were overdue to recognize that material progress does not *make* human beings free, equal, or willing to be moral. The kind of determinism that socialists found hardest to relinquish was economic determinism. It had to be done because otherwise Labour made an idol of its historic achievement for economic justice, the welfare state, and it allowed conservatives to usurp the language of freedom.[68]

Nothing was going to carry England to becoming a socialist society because socialism is not a norm that evolving material conditions achieve. Crossman argued that a socialist society would be an exception to human nature and history, "imposed on immoral society by human will and social conscience." He still believed in Niebuhr's rationale for a democratic socialist society, at least for England, even though Niebuhr pulled back from it in the United States. Crossman wanted British socialists to stop pretending that history was on their side or that structural forces outside their control would carry them to victory. They needed to recognize that only human will and social conscience hold the power to liberate human beings from slavery, tyranny, exploitation, and war. To Soviet Communists, the test of their success was whether they achieved their Five Year Plans and expanded the Soviet Empire. To democratic socialists, the test was whether they shaped social institutions to the moral standards of freedom—"even at the cost of a lower standard of living or the surrender of an empire."[69]

Materialism and imperialism, to Crossman, were antithetical to socialist values, although he had materialistic comrades who grieved at losing colonies. His anticommunism did not stretch to global containment; Crossman implored Britons to stop supporting American containment, a newfangled overreach begging for disaster. He pointed to the French trauma in Vietnam, warning that there were worse things than the spread of Communism. In 1952 Crossman held more hope for freedom in Communist Yugoslavia, where Marshal Josip Broz Tito broke away from Soviet hegemony, than in Greece, where vast sums of anticommunist economic aid propped up a corrupt parliamentary democracy. He was more hopeful about Turkey than about Iran, Iraq, or Egypt, notwithstanding that Kemal Atatürk led a revolutionary war of liberation against Britain and Greece, with Soviet aid. By winning its independence Turkey was in a position to develop a friendly relationship with Britain. Meanwhile Britain and the United States conspired to retain British control of oil production in Iran, so Iran was a disaster waiting to happen. Crossman warned that Iran, Iraq, and Egypt seethed "with suppressed revolution and overt xenophobia." The world needed Labour to regain power in Britain, and Labour needed a better policy in the Middle East. Crossman had clashed with Attlee's foreign secretary, Ernest Bevin, over Palestine and anticolonial revolutions, which disqualified him for a ministerial post. Now he urged Labour to support Israel and stop thwarting anticolonial revolutions with "military force and political fraud." Labour needed to be the party that did not suppress national and social revolutions in the name of combating communism.[70]

On domestic policy, Crossman argued, Labour had two governing principles. The state is responsible to make every citizen secure against unemployment, illness, and old age. And the state is responsible for achieving a reasonable degree of economic equality through progressive taxation and full employment. He stressed that the "true aim" of the Labour Party was not and never had been for the working class to capture power. It was to convert the nation "to the socialist pattern of rights and values." This work rested on the two governing principles of the welfare state, but welfare capitalism—Crossman's name for the new something—fell short of the socialist goal. Welfare capitalism did not change the concentration of capital and economic privilege, it let the market determine wages and salaries, and it left the predominant power in the hands of a small managerial and civil service elite. The revisionists did not quite agree on how far they should take managerial theory. Crosland said capitalism was dead, and Jenkins said capitalism was dying but not quite dead. Crossman said the new something was still a form of capitalism, albeit fundamentally altered by the welfare state and full employment. Not to say so was to risk that Labour would not fight for a socialist transformation of the welfare state.[71]

The core idea of managerial theory was the "New Class," which had a colorful history. It originated in Mikhail Bakunin's charge in the 1870s that Marxian socialism would produce a class of rulers that established a new tyranny. In the 1890s Polish revolutionary Jan Wacław Machajski applied Bakunin's critique to Russian socialist intellectuals, charging that they schemed to replace the capitalist class by riding a proletarian revolution to power. In 1929, writing from internal Soviet exile, Bulgarian Trotskyist and Bolshevik politician Christian Rakovsky described the Soviet leadership as a new class of rulers wielding power on the basis of a new type of private property, the possession of state power. Rakovsky was a key player in developing the Trotskyist critique of Stalinism as "bureaucratic centralism," an argument popularized by Max Nomad's two books of the 1930s on the revolutionary tradition. Adolfe Berle and Gardner Means developed a liberal version of managerial theory in 1932, focusing on the peculiar legal status of the American corporation as a person, and in the late 1930s the Trotskyist movement conducted a tense debate over managerial theory, featuring Trotsky's opposition to it.[72]

Trotskyism was based on the premise that the Soviet regime would move forward to socialism or backward to capitalism. Two American Trotskyist intellectuals, James Burnham and Joseph Carter, challenged this assumption in 1937 at the founding congress of the Socialist Workers Party. The Trotskyists had just been expelled from the Socialist Party of Norman Thomas. Burnham and Carter, seeking to revise their group's position on the Soviet Union, questioned Trotsky's either/or. In their view, the Soviet Union, which Trotsky called a degenerated workers' state, had taken on a viable structure of its own. It wasn't degenerating into capitalism, but it wasn't moving toward socialism either. A third possibility not recognized in Marxist theory had emerged—a bureaucratic deformation of a workers' state. Trotsky fiercely replied that Burnham and Carter obscured the crucial issue. Certainly, something had gone wrong in the Soviet revolution; otherwise Trotsky would still be a leader in it. But Trotsky insisted that the Soviet state had not reverted to capitalism. A liver poisoned by malaria doesn't cease to be a liver, he reasoned. The Soviet Union had a nationalized economy, which made it a workers' state still worth defending, albeit a "partial and mutilated expression of a backward and isolated workers' state."[73]

Trotsky denied that he made a fetish of Marxist theory in this area, but Burnham, American Trotskyist Max Shachtman, and Italian Trotskyist fellow traveler Bruno Rizzi judged otherwise. Rizzi's book *La Bureaucratisation du Monde* (1939) described the Soviet regime as a new ruling class that converted the means of production into a new form of property: "The Soviet state, rather than becoming socialized, is becoming bureaucratized; instead of gradually dissolving into a society without classes, it is growing immeasurably." Burnham and Shachtman pressed the same argument within the Trotskyist camp, rejecting Trotsky's rationale that the Soviet bureaucracy was a caste, based on functions of control, not a class, based on ownership. Shachtman admonished Trotsky that his own prediction about the impossibility of establishing socialism in one nation, a belief he had shared with Lenin, came true under Stalin. The proletarian revolution stopped at the Russian border, the Bolsheviks were left on their own, and the workers' state *was* overthrown, although not by a bourgeois restoration. A new kind of counterrevolutionary class took over: "The old crap was revived in a new, unprecedented, hitherto unknown form, the rule of a new bureaucratic class."[74]

When the state owns the means of production, the crucial question becomes: Who owns the state? This question drove Shachtman out of the Socialist Workers Party in 1940, putting him on a winding sectarian journey that led to the right wing of the Socialist Party. There he had a bizarre legacy as a guru to prominent democratic socialists (Michael Harrington, Irving Howe, Bogdan Denitch), founders of the neoconservative movement (Emanuel Muravchik, Arnold Beichman, Arch Puddington), and a few who were both (Bayard Rustin, Tom Kahn, Rachelle Horowitz). Burnham, by contrast, raced headlong to the American political right after resigning in 1940 from the Socialist Workers Party. Burnham's brilliant idea was to generalize his sectarian experience. He may have plagiarized Rizzi, as Rizzi and many others alleged, but Burnham judged that Rizzi deserved no credit, perhaps because Rizzi extrapolated from Burnham's arguments with Trotsky. Burnham's book *The Managerial Revolution: What Is Happening in the World* (1941) said the theory of the New Class explained the entire global situation, not merely the Soviet experience. Control of the means of production—the basis of capitalist power—had passed to a new class of managers. World War II, though admittedly important in itself, was a secondary episode in the working out of the managerial revolution.[75]

Inexorable social forces were at work; the former Trotskyist still knew the story behind the newspaper stories. Newspapers went on about Germany's subjugation of France and Scandinavia, but Burnham said the war was merely a phase in the managerial revolution. The hegemonic power of the capitalist class had shifted to a managerial class of administrators, finance executives, finance capitalists, and major stockholders. The struggle of this New Class for power shaped the emerging world order. In the Soviet Union the worker councils gave way to Stalinism; in Germany the Weimar Republic was replaced by Nazi fascism; in the United States New Deal statism eviscerated a republican system. Burnham explained that industrial societies had an inner drive toward hierarchy and centralization. Neither capital nor labor matched the self-aggrandizing, partly unconscious drive for power of the New Class. Every revolution in the industrial world was a managerial revolution. Burnham took a German victory for granted, making no attempt to conceal his admiration for the imperial ambitions and efficiency of the Nazis. England, he said, was too decadent and declining to repel the Germans. Germany's managerial superiority guaranteed that Germans would control Europe whether they won or, somehow, lost the war. Elsewhere, Japan would control Manchuria and eastern China, and the United States would control the western remains of the British Empire. Burnham assumed that Germany would not attack the Soviet Union until Germany conquered Europe; then Germany would devour Russia. As late as the summer of 1944, after the Russians failed to crack, Burnham predicted they would soon form an alliance with Japan to prevent a Japanese defeat.[76]

The world's most advanced managerial society, Germany, was destined to rule over its weaker, decadent neighbors. Burnham denied he had any value judgments at stake; his job was to explain what was happening in the world. His theory assumed that possession of the means of production determines everything that matters. All power derives from economic power, just as he had thought when he was a Marxist. Economics inevitably swallows politics. Crossman and Crosland, ten years later, took comfort that Burnham got many things wrong. England bravely defended liberal democratic decency, Russia stopped Germany again, Burnham wrongly believed that low unemployment was impossible under peacetime capitalism, and economics did not swallow politics. Crosland added that Burnham underestimated the social complexity of the managerial class and its tangled political loyalties; Burnham's leftover Marxism caused him to isolate the managers too sharply from other groups. Still, Crossman and Crosland said Burnham was essentially right, finer points notwithstanding. Power had shifted from the owning to the managing class, a transformation of enormous significance, even if Burnham and managerial theorist Peter Drucker exaggerated it. The New Class was likely to grow stronger in every industrialized nation and everywhere that industrialism spread. It changed what socialism needed to be about. But the managerial revolution was hostile to freedom, and its triumph was not inevitable. Crossman put it hotter than Crosland because Crossman thrived on dramatic declamation. Every time he changed his politics he claimed to champion the left wing of his new group. But both said that democratic socialism, rightly conceived, was the only hope of averting the rule of the managers.[77]

Crossman put it sharply: "Today the enemy of human freedom is the managerial society and the central coercive power which goes with it." The old capitalism paled by comparison to the predatory reach of corporations and corporate-friendly governments. Moreover, as long as Labour carried on about nationalizing more industries and organizing a planned economy, Labour was doomed to look clueless and threatening, living off outworn slogans. He made a second banner statement: "The planned economy and the centralization of power are no longer socialist objectives." That meant two things. The managerial revolution was already planning and centralizing on its own terms, disastrously for freedom. And intelligent socialists no longer spoke this language, a remarkable verdict in 1952 since *New Fabian Essays* was a birth announcement. Outright revisionism, though rife with precedents in Labour policy committees, had no movement history. The book was an argument for starting a movement. Crossman implored that Labour had to be the party of democracy and freedom, demanding a choice between top-down, dictatorial, bureaucratic collectivism and a collectivizing strategy humanized by socialist rights and values: "The main task of socialism today is to prevent the concentration of power in the hands of *either* industrial management *or* the state bureaucracy—in brief, to distribute responsibility and so to enlarge freedom of choice."[78]

New Fabian Essays had a nice preface by Attlee, but Crossman blasted the Attlee governments for completely missing the main task of socialism. They nationalized industries without changing the old managements. They boasted of changing nothing when they appointed representatives to national, regional, and consultative boards. They took the same approach to planning, not even creating a mechanism for assessing resources and allocations. It took the convertibility crisis of 1947 to shock Labour into creating institutions that measured wealth, labor, and social needs. Just as the first Attlee government failed to socialize the management of the industries it nationalized, it left economic planning in the hands of the old Civil Service. Neither did it encourage Britons to participate in the new welfare state as though it belonged to them. Crossman recalled that before 1945 socialism was a way of life and a vocation for unionists, cooperative workers, and party officials. Then Labour created the welfare state and conveyed the impression that socialism was a job for the cabinet, acting through the Civil Service. The rest of the nation was not involved; life went on as before. Socialism, to all appearances, consisted of antisocialist managers and neutral civil servants carrying out a redistribution of benefits.[79]

Crossman countered that real socialism democratized the culture, especially in England, where the nation's oligarchic tradition made social responsibility the privilege of an educated elite. Too many British socialists and unionists distrusted democracy, preferring managerial efficiencies achieved by bureaucrats. In a world of ever-larger inhuman enterprises, Crossman argued, the task of socialism was to ensure that managerial responsibility did not degenerate into a form of class privilege. Citizens had to acquire and exercise their right to control the government, industries, political parties, and trade unions. For the highest aim of socialism was the enlargement of freedom, not the pursuit of happiness or efficiency.

Crossman's career as a movement revisionist was short lived. It was hard for him to defer to anyone; even his friends said he was an intellectual bully. More important, in the late 1950s Crossman decided that England was too corrupt and commercialized to care about the poor, provide for the national welfare, and fight Communism. He went back to saying that only a massive commitment to nationalization would save England, just as Gaitskell tried to eliminate Clause Four. Crossman nearly sabotaged his political career in the process. His illustrious later career was possible only because Gaitskell died prematurely. Crossman's last achievement occurred posthumously: His massive three-volume diary of the Wilson years broke open Britain's culture of secrecy about how government policy got made. In the early 1950s, however, when it mattered for revisionism, Crossman was a fire hydrant of opinions for it, forming a powerful duo with Crosland, whose masterwork, *The Future of Socialism*, bristled with to-the-dustbin statements.[80]

Karl Marx, Crosland declared, "has little or nothing to offer the contemporary socialist" concerning policy, analysis, concepts, or even framework: "His prophecies have been almost without exception falsified, and his conceptual tools are now quite inappropriate." To be sure, Marx was a genius like Freud and Keynes, "a towering giant among socialist thinkers." But Marx contributed mightily to the near-consensus of socialist thinkers that capitalism would self-destruct; even Britain was infected. Crosland said England's capitalist class no longer held the power of decision because Labour nationalized basic industries and real capitalism no longer existed anyway. The growth of the managerial corporation transferred decision-making power to salaried executives, "who suffer singularly little interference from the nominal owners." This new situation demanded a different kind of Labour Party.[81]

The Future of Socialism had respectful glosses on Christian socialism, especially Maurice, Tawney, and Temple, and the Morris tradition of radical ethical socialism, although Crosland let on that his background was secular and Fabian. Pointedly, unlike Crossman, he did not try to make revisionism sound militant or heroic. Crosland said that improving on Social Democratic success required a different temperament, one suited to the times. Since the capitalist class no longer got its way in basic industries, socialists had to adjust to their own achievements. Since Britons had full employment and social insurance, there was no reason to rail about capitalist oppression. Crosland sympathized with diehard Bevanites and young recruits who needed to battle and dream. He understood why they fulminated at Labour meetings; they had to fire themselves up because the meetings were boring: "That is why they resent revisionist thinkers who compel them to face the new reality." In his estimation, 90 percent of the resolutions at Annual Conference were "Quixotic tilts at objects still hopefully seen as 'outrageous giants of that detested race.'" Crosland cautioned that British socialism had not grown powerful on the basis of angry railing. Sidney and Beatrice Webb, the father and mother of Labour socialism, were gentle, kind, and humorous. They were also disciplined, productive, efficient, and abstinent, completely devoted to public duty. Crosland loved the Webbs for their virtues and legacy; every Labour socialist was indebted to them.[82]

But the Webbs, too, no longer exemplified what Labour needed. Permeation had occurred, and Fabian Labour had triumphed. Crosland put it with sweeping hyperbole: "Today we are all incipient bureaucrats and practical administrators." Every Labour official believed in hard work, guarded against romanticism and utopian foolishness, prized empirical research, and sounded like a graduate of the London School of Economics: "Posthumously, the Webbs have won their battle, and converted a generation to their standards." Crosland said it was time to cultivate very different values—"a greater emphasis on private life, on freedom and dissent, on culture, beauty, leisure, and even frivolity." He dared to put it personally: "Total abstinence and a good filing system are not now the right sign-posts to the socialist Utopia: or at least, if they are, some of us will fall by the wayside." Many who chortled knowingly knew only the public story. Crosland was suave, charming, handsome, and attractive to women. His first marriage was short lived, and he had affairs with numerous women before marrying, happily, a woman from Baltimore in 1964, Susan Catling. The deeper source of wayside falling was Crosland's bisexuality. During his student days at Oxford Crosland had an intense romantic relationship with Jenkins, his future revisionist ally and cabinet colleague. Both were Labour protégés of Dalton, who was secretly gay. The Labour Party was no friendlier to gays and lesbians than the Tories, and Crosland and Jenkins would not have qualified for their prominent political careers without seeming thoroughly heterosexual. For both of them, however, sexuality was a guilty secret, a reason to believe, without quite saying it, that Labour socialism was as bullying and repressive as its Tory rival.[83]

The weakest part of revisionist socialism was its conformity to the conformism of a peculiar historical moment. Crosland made socialism sound like a kinder refinement of managerial rule. He exaggerated the divorce between industrial ownership and control in Britain, although rigorous studies on this point did not exist until the late 1960s. Crosland believed that Keynesian theory solved the unemployment problem, another core conviction that did not survive the 1960s, and that economic issues had become as boring and secondary as they should be. His magnum opus on revisionist socialism paraded his lack of prophetic fire, reinforcing the shibboleth of its time: "You never had it so good." Crosland's next book, however, *The Conservative Enemy* (1962), shook off much of his complacent air, beginning with its aggressive title. He charged that Conservatives remained in power only because the nation succumbed to stagnation and insularity. He felt it constantly in parliamentary debates, chagrined that Conservatives paid no price for denigrating the poor and vulnerable. He contrasted Britain's regnant complacency to the struggles of trade unions for social decency. Crosland praised the unions for achieving "a remarkable degree of control" over the management decisions directly affecting unionized workers. He argued that British unions were powerful because they played an opposition role in British society, politics, and economics. The strength of the unions came from their oppositional independence and their willingness to strike for what they needed. To put it negatively, British unions did not acquiesce to a dismal time, and they refused to be co-opted into making management decisions. Neither worker control nor comanagement tempted them because British unionists were clear about what mattered: full employment, rising wages, good working conditions, and social insurance.[84]

He said it so strongly that he seemed to undercut his everything-is-related vision of pluralistic socialism. In *The Future of Socialism* Crosland said democracy, some degree of worker control, and individual freedom had highest priority: "What really matters is the degree to which management is autocratic or democratic, the extent of joint consultation and participation, and the freedom of the worker to strike or leave his job." His often-quoted conclusion put it vividly: "The ideal (or at least my ideal) is a society in which ownership is thoroughly mixed up — a society with a diverse, diffused, pluralist, and heterogeneous pattern of ownership, with the State, the nationalized industries, the Cooperatives, the Unions, government financial institutions, pension funds, foundations, and millions of private families all participating." Crosland did not say that retail trade and middle-sized industries remained private in his ideal society, since it was an ideal. Still, in the real world his pluralistic socialism left plenty of room for private firms. Crosland said Britain needed heavy taxes to limit profits and dividends, and he opposed the traditional socialist demand for more state monopolies. Britain, admittedly, probably needed to nationalize a few more industries: "But I at least do not want a steadily extending chain of State monopolies, believing this to be bad for liberty, and wholly irrelevant to socialism as defined in this book."[85]

The Future of Socialism contended that state ownership of industrial capital is not a condition of creating a socialist society or achieving social equality or increasing social welfare or abolishing class privilege. In Britain socialists needed to focus on redistributing private wealth, the essential remaining structural injustice in British society. Achieving this objective under a pluralistic economy was no harder than doing it under a state-owned economy, and doing it in a pluralistic fashion was better for society. Crosland's mixed-economy vision of socialism reflected and influenced similar proposals in German, French, Swedish, and Italian Social Democracy. He wrote *The Future of Socialism* just as Labour strenuously debated various forms of public ownership other than nationalization.

One proposal was for the state to run competitive public enterprises. Here the state took over individual enterprises instead of entire industries, or it created government-owned enterprises to compete with private companies. Another option was state shareholding, which established a form of partial public ownership without public control. Jay was the pioneer advocate of both proposals, although his case for state shareholding reworked Dalton's similar argument regarding landownership. Crosland, Crossman, and Jenkins took the lead in arguing for state enterprises, and Gaitskell enraged the left wing by pushing for state shareholding. The basic argument for competitive state enterprises was that socialism had to become more selective and efficient, bending the mixed economy to socialist purposes. Crosland said this policy, unfortunately, did very little to combat income inequality, but that made it politically palatable, something not to be derided. More important, competitive public enterprises significantly redistributed existing property, which was valuable in itself and a boon to equality when the enterprises increased in value. The party endorsed public enterprises on this basis, unhappily for the left wing, for which state enterprises sold out what mattered, nationalization.[86]

State shareholding, to old lefties, was much worse. In 1945 Jay began calling for the state to hold equity shares in private firms. In the 1950s he endorsed a national finance enterprise board on the French and Italian model. In 1957 he pushed for the state to buy shares of many firms, persuading Gaitskell that some public participation was better than total public ownership or no public ownership. Jay, Crosland, and Gaitskell argued that buying government shares offered a way to enhance the productive efficiency of a mixed economy and reduce wealth inequality. To Gaitskell, the redistributive potential was especially significant. The state could take death duties as equity shares or purchase equity shares from budget surpluses. In 1957 Gaitskell wrangled state shareholding into a party policy document, *Industry and Society*, and the left-wing erupted that shareholding was an outright capitulation to capitalism, turning Labour into a capitalist party. Any scheme that established partial public ownership without public control was a betrayal of socialism. Revisionists replied that the language of heresy was outdated, plus politically clueless. Labour had to prove it was ready to govern in the real world, which entailed caring about market efficiency.[87]

"Thoroughly mixed up," however, could be taken in ways that Crosland did not mean. His mixing ideal was a bulwark against Clause Four fundamentalism, the defining battle of his career. But Fabian nationalization had no monopoly on true socialism even in Britain, and Crosland admitted he felt a "nagging confusion" about the other great socialist orthodoxy, worker control. He said his friends shared his conflicted feelings about it: "We are emotionally in favour of the idea, but vague as to what should actually be done or even precisely why." Crosland knew what guild socialists, Marxists, and syndicalists meant when they said that worker control was the essence of socialism. Part of him even agreed or at least felt that he should. Sometimes he gave lip service to worker control as one of the three goals of socialism. But Crosland's judgment that British unions were better off without worker control or comanagement helped him clarify that his revisionism stood against the original socialist orthodoxy nearly as much as the Fabian one.[88]

The Future of Socialism put it carefully, declaring that he did not reject the ideal of an industrial fellowship in which all workers democratically shared control over their industries and fate. Crosland argued only that this right did not necessarily imply that workers should participate in management decisions through their unions. Democracy is a sufficiently ambiguous concept that the democratic rights of workers can be fulfilled in various ways. Workers and the community do not always have the same interests. There is nearly always a difference between workers in any one industry and workers generally. And every enterprise that is not a pure cooperative vests some managerial group with decisions about prices, market signals, capital costs for new machinery, shutting down plants, and the like. Crosland put the latter point bluntly: "The two sides exist, and must to a large extent remain two sides; and the workers' side must have an untrammeled Trade Union movement to defend its claims. These are harsh facts which cannot be spirited away by moral rearmament touring troupes, or luncheons of progressive businessmen, or syndicalist castles in the air." Even if Britain became a full-orbed Social Democracy, whatever that meant, the divergence of interests among various groups and the need for a union opposition would remain. Moreover, if workers were represented on industry boards, they needed to be chosen directly by the workers in each firm, not by the unions.[89]

The Conservative Enemy mostly targeted conservative foes, but Crosland added a critical word about Crossman and an amplifying word about German unionist "codetermination" (*Mithestimmung*). He blasted Crossman for retreating to nationalization fantasies and Burnham-like hyperbole: "There is the same cataclysmic view of history, dramatic shifts in power are always occurring, ineluctable choices have to be made, the oligopolists wield gigantic powers, freedom is threatened, democracy is being strangled, a new feudalism is emerging, nations and continents are rising and falling at bewildering speed." Crosland entreated readers to support the grinding, stubborn, prosaic work of unions, adding that German unionism was less different than it seemed. Worker councils existed through the Weimar years, the Nazis abolished them, the Allied powers restored them after World War II, and in 1951 German unions won a historic legislative victory that placed worker representatives on the supervisory boards of all enterprises exceeding one thousand workers. Crosland commended German unions for gaining real power—codetermination—in the coal and steel industries. He allowed that Germany's legacy of worker councils dating back to the nineteenth century was an advantage for the German left, and Germans were highly competent at codifying everything in legal terms. Thus it appeared that Germany had better unions than Britain. On closer inspection, however, Crosland noted that German unions rarely took part in general management. They stayed in their lane, defended the interests of workers, and suffered no divided loyalties. Most German enterprises had a supervisory board and a management board, and the latter, though chosen by the supervisors, did the daily managing. So codetermination was not quite what it sounded like, and Crosland denied it worked better than British unionism.

Union work was broadly similar across national borders, it was always a plus for democracy, even where unions were bad, and British unions were very good.[90]

To break through in England the revisionists had to be what they were constantly accused of being: irreverent, heretical, obnoxious, ungrateful, cheeky, and confrontational. They succeeded by finding a party leader, Gaitskell, who was long on cheek and self-confidence. For a while it helped to have Crossman on their side, until his proclivity for drama propelled him back to the left camp. The revisionists helped British socialism play a leading role in refashioning European Social Democracy. The mere fact that British socialists increasingly called themselves Social Democrats was telling. European Social Democracy opted for reforming capitalism, nationalizing a few companies, establishing social insurance, and opposing militarism, all by using the power of the state to achieve progressive ends. It became a politics of centralized state progressivism that projected an ambivalent attitude toward its own achievements, since old-style democratic socialism was never in play. In Britain Gaitskell's run as party leader (1955–1961) sealed the triumph of Keynesian Social Democracy, even as it pushed Wilson and Crossman to the left. The Labour left wing angrily defeated Gaitskell's proposal in 1959 to abolish Clause Four, but that was a symbolic victory at best.

Labour needed Britons to believe that Clause Four did not apply to all enterprises or big industries and never had. Gaitskell judged that Britons didn't believe it, so he sought to eliminate the offending statement. Losing the vote was less important than the fact that Gaitskell forced the party to fight about it. Many years later, in 1995, Labour under Tony Blair rewrote Clause Four in wordy, vague, aspiring fashion: "The Labour Party is a democratic socialist party. It believes that by the strength of our common endeavour we achieve more than we achieve alone, so as to create for each of us the means to realise our true potential and for all of us a community in which power, wealth and opportunity are in the hands of the many, not the few, where the rights we enjoy reflect the duties we owe, and where we live together, freely, in a spirit of solidarity, tolerance and respect."[91]

GERMAN SOCIAL DEMOCRACY REBORN

(West) German socialism got to a very similar outcome by a very different route. The Federal Republic of Germany, established in 1949, had many parties but only two strong ones: Konrad Adenauer's Christian Democratic Union (CDU) and Kurt Schumacher's SPD. All European Social Democratic parties believed in 1945 that a new dawn of democratic socialist freedom was coming across Europe. The old order was surely discredited by its complicity in fascism and the ravages of war. Socialists believed they knew how to rebuild Europe, and they cheered the Labour victory in Britain. But Soviet Russia rudely shattered the illusion of a Social Democratic future in East and Central Europe, and the winning idea in Germany, it turned out, was to bond with the capitalist, Cold War, triumphant United States.

Konrad Adenauer, a former Centre Party politician, mayor of Cologne, and president of the Prussian State Council in the Weimar Republic, survived the Nazi period mostly by keeping quiet and out of view. He was a Catholic Rhinelander who said that SPD socialism and Nazi socialism had the same taproot: vainglorious Prussian tyranny. The key to a better Germany was to purge the nation of Prussianism, a job for a strong Catholic leader who believed in market forces. The British, French, Russian, and U.S. American victors divided postwar Germany into occupied zones, and the American occupiers installed Adenauer as mayor of Cologne. But the British fired him for lack of deference, making his subsequent career possible. In 1946 Adenauer organized the CDU as an anti-Communist and antisocialist union of Catholics and Protestants, uniting the various prewar conservative factions. Meanwhile Communist hardliner Walter Ulbricht, freshly returned from Russian exile, played a leadership role in the Russian zone, where Russian authorities forcibly merged the KPD and SPD into a new party, the Socialist Unity Party. Economist Ludwig Erhard, advising U.S. zone military governor Lucius D. Clay, directed the bizonal Office of Economic Opportunity during the run-up to the founding of the Federal Republic. Erhard enacted a currency reform and decontrol of prices in 1948 that the fledgling SPD opposed, setting himself up for a major role in Adenauer's government.[92]

Kurt Schumacher was Adenauer's chief rival for political power. The son of a West Prussian small businessman, Schumacher lost an arm fighting in World War I, converted to Bernsteinian socialism in 1918, studied law and politics at Leipzig and Berlin, served as an SPD delegate in the Württemberg state legislature in the mid-1920s, and was elected in 1930 to the Reichstag, where he ferociously denounced the Nazis and KPD. Schumacher famously described Communists as "red-painted Nazis." When the Nazis took over, nine SPD leaders fled to Prague, forming an executive board in exile, and Philipp Scheidemann fled to Copenhagen, dying there in 1939. In 1938 the expropriated SPD kept itself alive by selling its Marx and Engels papers to the International Institute for Social History in Amsterdam, spurning a more generous offer from Moscow, which asked SPD leaders to name their price for the archive. Meanwhile Schumacher stayed in Germany and was nearly killed during ten years of harsh treatment in Flossenbürg, Dachau, and other concentration camps.[93]

In April 1945 Schumacher was liberated by the British from the Neuengamme camp and promptly began organizing the SPD in Hannover, before it was legal. He opposed the SPD leader in the Russian zone, Otto Grotewohl, who favored a KPD–SPD merger. The following January the British and American occupiers permitted the SPD to reorganize as a national party, and Schumacher was the obvious choice for leader, being the only SPD leader to spend the entire Nazi period in Germany, without collaborating. The SPD, having averaged one million members during the Weimar years, came back with remarkable resilience, numbering eight hundred thousand members despite losing its longtime strongholds in the Soviet zone. Schumacher wanted a new constitution with a strong presidency, assuming he would be the Federal Republic's first leader. He disbelieved that ordinary Germans would vote for the pro-American candidate because he misread the moment.

Schumacher invoked the historic self-understanding of the SPD as a workers' party representing the interests of the working class. Social Democracy, in his telling, was still dedicated to abolishing capitalism, and the SPD was still Marxist. It was also fiercely patriotic, like him, and averse to the capitalist class. Schumacher believed that middle-class Germans would vote for the SPD to purge their guilt for supporting the Nazis. Germany, he urged, should be united, socialist, and strongly anti-Communist but neutral in the Cold War. He got red-baited for insisting that Social Democrats were the true Marxists, but he gave as well as he got, charging that Adenauer was eager to sell out Germany. Fatefully, Schumacher was too self-confident and dogmatic to forge alliances with bourgeois parties, believing the Marxist logic of history would sweep the SPD into power. Moreover, his socialism was sufficiently old style that he scared church people, especially Catholics.

The Allies wrote off almost all of Germany's Nazi-era public debt, allowing West Germany to rebuild with minimal debt ratios in the 1950s, while England coped with devouring war debts. In 1948 the U.S. Congress passed the Marshall Plan to rebuild Western Europe, create European markets for American goods, and help West Europeans fight off Communism. Stalin blockaded West Berlin, bringing the United States to the brink of war with Russia, which spurred the Truman administration to get serious about collective security. Britain, France, Belgium, the Netherlands, Luxembourg, and the United States signed the Brussels Treaty in 1948. The following year Belgium, Britain, Canada, Denmark, France, Iceland, Italy, Luxembourg, the Netherlands, Norway, Portugal, and the United States formed the North Atlantic Treaty Organization (NATO), pledging to regard an attack on one as an attack on all. The Allies, especially the United States, wanted West Germany to have a federal system with a weak government, until Soviet aggression gave them second thoughts. Adenauer went along with the original Ally plan, unlike Schumacher; after Adenauer squeaked into power, he was glad the federal government of the new German state was dominant over the states.

Adenauer edged the SPD in 1949 by less than 2 percent of the vote, riding two key advantages to victory. One, the most conservative parts of the nation—Bavaria and the Rhineland—belonged to the Federal Republic, while the SPD's former strongholds were lost to the German Democratic Republic (GDR). Two, the United States and France went all out for Adenauer, while Britain's Labour government stayed neutral. Adenauer's alliance with the Christian Union of Bavaria helped him nose out the SPD, and he had to forge a coalition with the liberal Free Democratic Party and the right-wing German Party to form a government. In the early going the SPD had ample reason to believe its moment would come.

But Adenauer was cunning and strong, ruling with an iron hand, and he knew what he wanted. He supplicated the Allied victors and sometimes tweaked them. He played to capitalist interests, shook down reconstruction help, and made himself seemingly indispensable. He urged that rebuilding the economy and making friends with the Americans went together. He denounced the entire Allied denazification process, refused to accept the Oder–Neisse line as Germany's eastern frontier, acquiesced to the Allied dismantling of factories, and earned a bitter nickname from Schumacher, "Chancellor of the Allies." Adenauer's government was decidedly interventionist, absorbing 35 percent of GDP in taxes, which he used to influence aggregate demand and support select industries and firms. Nearly half of the Federal Republic's capital formation was financed directly or indirectly by the state. In 1952 Stalin proposed to create a united Germany that would be neutral in the Cold War and armed with its own national army. Adenauer risked a public furor by spurning Stalin's ostensible offer, but Schumacher didn't trust Stalin either, providing political cover. Adenauer needed SPD votes to push an unpopular reparations bill for Israel through the Bundestag, and he survived an assassination attempt—a bomb hidden in an encyclopedia—by Israeli Herut Party leader Menachem Begin, who opposed the reparations bill. Above all, Adenauer stood for integrating the Federal Republic into the Western alliance, no matter how Russia took it.[94]

Schumacher never grasped how the world had changed. His heroic story, truculent temperament, and dogmatic socialism made him a formidable party leader but unsuited for postwar politics. He commanded support from people he did not respect, not catching that they noticed. He castigated the Catholic Church as a fifth occupying power, never mind that the Federal Republic was

45 percent Catholic, a whopping 12 percent increase from prewar Germany. He opposed the Council of Europe, the European Defense Community, and other new organizations for European cooperation on the ground that they strengthened capitalism and Allied control of Germany. He wavered on French foreign minister Robert Schuman's proposal to control steel and coal production in France and the Federal Republic, but the British declined to join, and Schumacher detested the French, so he declined. He died in 1952 and was replaced by a moderate Social Democrat, Erich Ollenhauer, a stolid party functionary dedicated to keeping the party machinery running. Ollenhauer was not as viscerally anti-American as Schumacher, did not share Schumacher's passionate personality, and did not oppose America's military presence in Western Europe. But he sustained the party's opposition to German rearmament and joining NATO, warning that either or both would lose East Germany forever.

In 1953 the Red Army harshly repressed a rebellion in East Germany, and Adenauer seized the moment by calling an election. This time his CDU/CSU ticket crushed the SPD by 16 percent, although it still needed the Free Democrats and German Party to form a government. Nearly all the pertinent political variables pulled the SPD in a moderating direction: the reconstruction boom, getting crushed in an election, the mood of the era, Schumacher's death, growing prosperity, the Korean War boom that stoked a so-called economic miracle, the prospect of joining NATO, and the Hungarian uprising of 1956. The SPD was still calling for public ownership of basic industries, even as public ownership in the GDR floundered abysmally. The last hedge against moderating fell in 1956, when the Federal Constitutional Court banned the KPD. Now the SPD had no competition to its left, and all political debates took place to its right. The SPD campaigned with a softer ideological touch in 1957, but it didn't matter. Adenauer and the CDU/CSU won a landslide victory, defeating the SPD by 18 percent and winning an absolute majority in the Bundestag. This historic victory was a reward for prosperity, West Germany's full sovereignty in 1955, joining NATO the same year, securing a strong alliance with France, and joining the European Economic Community in 1957. Adenauer basked in Germany's economic miracle (*Wirtschaftswunder*), also known as the Miracle on the Rhine, which he attributed to his shrewd combination of free enterprise and government planning.[95]

The SPD was overdue for another revisionist adjustment. Party leaders Carlo Schmid, Herbert Wehner, and Fritz Erler said it was ridiculous to keep saying that middle-class people should vote for the Marxist party. The SPD had to stop claiming that a centrally planned economy would be better, which defied the common sense of West Germans about why they were better off than East Germans. Ever since the SPD was founded in 1875 it had debated the tension between its revolutionary vision and the demands of pragmatic reform. Bernstein revisionism conferred intellectual seriousness and respectability on reform socialism, but the SPD still said the goal was to create a classless society. The party officially declared otherwise at its Bad Godesberg conference in 1959. Revisionists wrote a new platform that scuttled the rhetoric of classless socialism and proletarian internationalism. They acknowledged that Erhard's social market policies had worked, more or less. Erhard said he combined as much competition as possible with as much planning as necessary. In truth, Erhard and Adenauer battled constantly over Erhard's market reverence versus Adenauer's Catholic social values, but the SPD agreed that getting the best mix of planning and competition was the right objective.

The Bad Godesberg Program announced that the SPD was a party of the German people as a whole, committed to reforming capitalism along revisionist socialist lines. It disavowed anticlericalism and the party's refusal to support West German defense policy, two hangovers from a century long past. The central objective of the SPD was to democratize economic power, not to overthrow private ownership. Public ownership was one legitimate form of public control among others, and it was no exception to the necessity of preventing concentrations of economic power. Thus "the principles of self-government and decentralization must be applied to the public sector." The SPD no longer considered nationalization to be the linchpin of a socialist economy. Nationalization was one of several ways to control economic concentration and power, "and then only the last." The party said it stood for freedom, justice, and solidarity—"the fundamental values of Socialism"—and it possessed no ultimate truths. Democratic socialism, rooted historically "in Christian ethics, humanism, and classical philosophy," respected the rights of individuals to form their own religious and philosophical beliefs. The Bad Godesberg Program declared that the aim of socialism is to enable outward-reaching individuality to flourish: "Socialists aim to establish a society in which every individual can develop his personality and as a responsible member of the community, take part in the political, economic, and cultural life of mankind."[96]

Sheri Berman drolly observes that if Bernstein witnessed his victory from a heavenly perch, he must have been slightly troubled at realizing that the SPD renounced Kautsky to "break out of a political ghetto," not because it had a bold new vision of the future. At one stroke, however, the SPD halted its electoral decline, making itself welcome to the middle-class progressives it had long wanted. The party's ideological adjustment coincided with the twilight of the fading, autocratic, elderly Adenauer, who stumbled while trying to sustain his dominance. Adenauer briefly campaigned for the federal presidency in 1959 but withdrew upon realizing he would be trading down for less power, plus rewarding his rival, Erhard. The same year Adenauer wanted to sign nonaggression pacts with Poland and Czechoslovakia but capitulated to the expellee lobby, which reviled both nations for expelling ethnic Germans during World War II. For six months Adenauer allowed a scandal over his minister of refugees, Theodor Oberländer, to drag on; Oberländer committed war crimes against Jews and Poles during World War II and subsequently became a leader of the expellee lobby. By the summer of 1961 Adenauer had lost much of his luster. Then the erection of the Berlin Wall in August made him look weak and clueless, especially to West Berliners. He compounded this impression by slandering the popular SPD mayor of West Berlin, Willy Brandt, declaring that Brandt's illegitimate birth disqualified him from holding any office. In September 1961 Adenauer eked out a coalition electoral victory over Brandt and the SPD, but the SPD became the largest individual party in the Bundestag, winning 203 of the 521 seats, an omen of its future.[97]

Now the SPD had a charismatic leader and an attractive agenda. Brandt, born Herbert E. K. Frahm, adopted a pseudonym during World War II as a leftist writer in Norway and Sweden, escaping detection by Nazi agents; in 1948 he formally adopted it. As mayor of West Berlin he built up vast tracts of the city, condemned the Soviet repression of Hungary, and supported the revisionist wing of the SPD. He won the favor of U.S. president John F. Kennedy, who snubbed Adenauer, just before Brandt blasted Kennedy for giving only lip service to anti-Communism. That played very well in West Berlin. In 1963 Adenauer resigned, Erhard became chancellor, and two years later Brandt ran against Erhard. The SPD increased its leading status in the Bundestag, winning 251 of 518 seats, but Erhard forged a coalition government, trading on his popularity as the father of the economic miracle, just before both evaporated. The miracle ended in 1966. Growth rates fell and unemployment ballooned; reactionary attacks on foreign workers escalated; the coalition government of Christian Democrats and Free Democrats fell apart over tax policy; and an outright neo-Nazi party, the National Democratic Party, made gains in Hesse and Bavaria. The echoes of the early 1930s were ominous. Erhard gave way to CDU/CSU leader Kurt Kiesinger, who reached out to Brandt and Wehner to save parliamentary democracy. Brandt's willingness to become vice-chancellor ended the SPD's exile—since 1930—from national governance. For three years the SPD sustained a Black–Red coalition that stabilized the nation and injected a strong dose of Keynesian medicine, cutting unemployment from five hundred thousand to two hundred thousand.[98]

The SPD grew strong on the reasonable proposition that Germany needed a progressive party with socialist values that didn't scare off middle-class voters. The Bad Godesberg Program adjusted to a demographic trend it sought to enhance. In 1952, 45 percent of the SPD membership consisted of manual workers, and 17 percent were white-collar employees. By 1968, the year before Brandt became chancellor, 34.5 percent were manual workers and 19 percent were white-collar employees. More important, the party began to attract young members after failing to do so through the 1950s, and the SPD's advocacy of codetermination boosted its constructive image. The broadly growing support for codetermination shaped German industry long before the SPD finally gained power in 1969 and enacted Germany's comprehensive codetermination law of 1976, the *Mitbestimmungsgesetz*.

Worker councils in Germany date back to four printing houses in Ellenburg, Saxony, in 1850. Germany had worker councils in scattered areas where unions were strong until 1920, when the SPD pushed through the first codetermination law, the Works Council Act (*Betriebsträtegesetz*). It mandated that all businesses employing more than twenty workers were required to recognize a consultative worker council that represented the social and economic interests of workers to the management. The Nazis abolished the worker councils and broke up the unions, but in 1946 the Allied Control Authority restored the councils in its *Kontrollratsgesetz* No. 22. After the Federal Republic was established, unions pushed hard for codetermination, threatening massive strikes. The payoff came in 1951 with the historic Coal, Steel, and Mining Codetermination Law (*Montan-Mitbestimmungsgesetz*), requiring codetermination in all businesses employing more than one thousand workers through worker representatives constituting one-half of supervisory company boards. The following year a follow-up law mandated that all workers at the shop-floor level had to be represented by a worker council. In 1955 the *Bundespersonalvertretungsgesetz* extended similar codetermination rights to all members of the civil services in the Federation and German states.[99]

Codetermination was and is like Social Democracy—humanizing capitalism with socialist reforms without abolishing capitalism. German unionists said that workers work more effectively when they are allowed to codetermine how their company operates. They turned out to be right, at least in Germany, where coal and steel producers employing more than one thousand workers had supervisory boards composed of eleven members: five from management, five representing workers, and the eleventh being neutral. Larger boards sustained the same proportion of representation. The shareholders and trade unions elected the supervisory board, while the supervisory board elected the management board. The chair of the supervisory board was always a shareholder representative, and the management board had one worker representative.

This was why Crosland judged that codetermination was less than it seemed, as the management boards still ran the daily operations. Workers still worked, and managers still managed. But Crosland doubted that German codetermination would move beyond shop-floor considerations—until he lived to see otherwise. German industries developed a cooperative culture that respected the input of workers on working conditions and industrial processes at the plant level. Many firms worked up to a consensus basis of decision making, creating sufficient trust to allow worker committees to contribute to higher management decisions about wage rates, layoffs, financial policies, and structural reforms. One degree of codetermination led to another, winning broadly popular support, a cultural achievement. Subsequently the Codetermination Act of 1976 expanded codetermination law to cover firms employing more than two thousand workers, eliminated the neutral eleventh board member, and mandated that workers and management have the same number of representatives.

The SPD grew with the fortunes of codetermination as soon as it stopped promising to abolish capitalism. It became a party that sought to fulfill democratic socialist values by progressively reforming capitalism. Brandt's dynamic leadership style and his bold advocacy of peaceful coexistence with the GDR played outsized roles in revitalizing the SPD between 1969 and 1974. Then the SPD grew stronger under Brandt's successor as chancellor, the professorial Helmut Schmidt, never described by anyone as charismatic. Schmidt served as minister of defense (1969–1972) and minister of finance (1972–1974) under Brandt, took over from Brandt in 1974, and was reelected chancellor in 1976 and 1980. He oozed gravitas and respectability, identifying his party with European cooperation and global economic coordination. Brandt and Schmidt put to rest the notion that Social Democrats were too radical to run the country, just as Harold Wilson and James Callahan played similar roles in Britain from 1964 to 1970 (Wilson), 1974 to 1976 (Wilson), and 1976 to 1979 (Callahan).[100]

Meanwhile Sweden built the model Social Democracy and then experimented with an innovative German version of Temple's guild socialist proposal. The Swedish Social Democratic Party (SAP), founded in 1889, faced the usual Social Democratic dilemma in 1920 between taking the insurrectionary road to power or winning power through elections. Many Social Democratic parties muddled indecisively between the two options, but the SAP decisively took the parliamentary approach, arguing that democratic socialism is like a good home—a place of community and togetherness in which caring and cooperation prevail. Per Albin Hansson, who became the SAP party chair in 1928, borrowed his homey imagery from the Swedish farm movement. In 1932 it paid off, sweeping Hansson and the SAP into power after six years in opposition, where the SAP remained for forty-four years of uninterrupted rule excepting a three-month quirk in 1936. SAP economist Ernst Wigforss persuaded Hansson and the party that Keynes was right about recessions and government intervention. The SAP needed to become something novel—a governing Social Democratic party that skillfully used Keynesian tools. It became the gold standard Social Democratic party on that basis.[101]

Building a rudimentary Keynesian Social Democracy was hard enough during the run-up to World War II. Building an advanced welfare state after the war posed additional political and economic challenges. Gösta Rehn, an economist for the Confederation of Swedish Trade Unions (LO) and SAP member trained at the University of Stockholm, teamed in the 1940s with LO economist Rudolf Meidner, a Jewish socialist from Breslau who fled Nazi Germany in 1933 at the age of nineteen and became a Swedish citizen ten years later. Together they devised the economic policy undergirding Sweden's advanced welfare state, the Rehn–Meidner Model. It was instituted in 1951, three years before Meidner earned his doctorate under Gunnar Myrdal at the Stockholm School of Economics.

Rehn–Meidner featured a centralized system of wage bargaining combining a solidarity wage policy and a state-run pension system built on collective savings, both in tandem with Sweden's high-tech, export-oriented focus on international trade. Wages were set to ensure approximately equal pay for equal work, assigning high rates to inefficient firms and low rates to productive, competitive firms. The model deliberately forced inefficient firms to improve or die, simultaneously promoting efficiency and equality. It committed the state to retrain and relocate displaced workers and promoted decommodification by eroding the connection between the marginal productivity of individual firms and wage rates. Rehn–Meidner helped to create the most egalitarian society in Europe, while Sweden's focus on high-tech exports avoided the inefficiency problems that plagued insular welfare states. Political historian Gøsta Esping-Andersen, putting it bluntly in *Politics Against Markets*, said that Sweden established universal solidarity by marginalizing the market "as the principal agent of distribution and the chief determinant of people's life chances." Swedish Social Democracy was so successful in the 1950s and 1960s that even Meidner felt no need to supplement the nation's wage policy with a profit-sharing scheme, although he studied Germany's ongoing debate over this idea.[102]

The German Trade Union Confederation (DGB) was the first to push for social funds because the German economic miracle yielded a highly unequal distribution of wealth. German unions grappled with this problem in the 1950s, and then the miracle ended. In the late 1960s the DGB advocated a scheme to create worker-controlled company funds by taxing major company profits. The SPD adopted this proposal just after it took power in 1969, but other issues engulfed the party, including the politics of strengthening codetermination. The Weimar inflation of 1923 stuck in West Germany's memory long after Germans shucked off the memory of being saved by Allied macroeconomic mercy after World War II. Weimar inflation ruined Germany's currency and middle class, paving the way to fascism. So went the story, a constant reminder to be efficient and prudent, although every West German government was highly interventionist by American standards. This situation left the social funds idea without a champion until Meidner picked it up in 1975, very near the end of the SAP's forty-four-year run in power, when it acquired a name: the Meidner Plan for Economic Democracy.

The Meidner Plan called for an annual 20 percent tax on major company profits to be paid in the form of stock to eight regional mutual funds. Worker, consumer, and government representatives controlled the funds. As their proportion of stock ownership grew, these groups were collectively entitled to representation on company boards. Locals and branch funds jointly held voting rights of the employee shares. In 1976 the LO embraced the Meidner Plan, and the Social Democrats had an anguished debate over it. Prime Minister Olof Palme pleaded that Sweden didn't need to socialize the economy; ordinary Social Democracy worked just fine. The SAP beat the second-place Centre Party in 1976 by 18 percent but lost the election, thwarted by campaign attacks on Meidner socialism. In 1982 the Social Democrats regained power and enacted a weak version of the Meidner Plan but downplayed it as much as possible, trying not to scare the investor class. A 40 percent ceiling was placed on the amount of stock the eight funds in total could own of any single firm, and the funds were managed conventionally. Still, even with a 40 percent ceiling the Meidner Plan would have eventually rendered effective control over Swedish companies to the worker and public organizations. Since the funds represented part of workers' compensation, the plan contained a built-in system of wage restraints and facilitated a new form of capital formation. It required no program of nationalization, and investors still sought the highest rate of return. Like most public bank models, the Meidner Plan separated risk in production from entrepreneurial risk, assigning production risks to worker-managed enterprises and entrepreneurial risks to the holding companies.[103]

The fate of the Meidner Plan, which unfolded long past the endpoint of our story, is a symbol of our time. Unionists and Social Democrats stressed that benefits from the capital fund accrued to all wage earners, and the plan traded wage restraint for greater control over investment capital. Big-business groups howled against it incessantly, determined to kill it. They protested that small businesses didn't have to pay the tax and charged that unions were consumed with power lust. The capitalist class inveighed against its loss of control. Stock markets are the home turf of financiers, a privilege that Swedish capitalists defended aggressively. Managers of the worker funds, trying to legitimize themselves to the financial class, managed like ordinary fund managers, but that made the whole enterprise abstract to the general population.

Palme did the minimum for the worker funds, and in 1986 he was assassinated. To stir popular support, Social Democrats needed to back up the plan with industrial policies targeting specific needs—things that citizens could see at work in their communities during the period that Sweden's shipbuilding industry and other pillars of the manufacturing base were restructured. Instead the charter for the Meidner Plan expired in 1990, and the SAP lost the 1991 election. The following year Conservatives wound up the social funds, which owned 7 percent of Sweden's stock market, using the proceeds to finance scientific research institutes. Sweden had a banking crisis in 1992, which it resolved by nationalizing the banks, and in 1994 the Social Democrats regained power as the party best suited to manage the turbulence of economic globalization and nationalized banks. They stabilized the currency, got the government's fiscal house in order, swore off economic democracy, and scaled back their historic achievement, the Swedish welfare state.[104]

That marked another sad ending for national-scale experiments in economic democracy of a guild socialist type. No comparable struggle for economic democracy has gotten this far at the national level anywhere since the abandonment of the Meidner Plan. The struggle for economic democracy has won important victories in many national contexts but always at lower levels of organization in which institutions that do not belong wholly to the capitalist market or the state are created. It begins by expanding the cooperative and social market sectors. Producer cooperatives take labor out of the market by removing corporate shares from the stock market and maintaining local worker ownership. Community land trusts take land out of the market and place it under local democratic controls to serve the needs of communities. Community finance corporations take democratic control over capital to finance cooperative firms, make investments in areas of social need, and fight the redlining policies of conventional banks.

These strategies counteract the manic capitalist logic of bigger is better. Economic democracy and ecologic survival are linked by the necessity of creating alternatives to the capitalist fantasy of unlimited growth and the capitalist fixation with purchasing commodities manufactured elsewhere. The economy is physical. There are limits to economic growth. The earth's ecosystem is not something external to us; it is everything bundled together with feedback loops and interconnected wholes. This ecosystem cannot sustain a U.S. American lifestyle for more than one-sixth of the world's population. Global warming is rapidly melting the Arctic ice cap and large areas of permafrost in Alaska, Canada, and Siberia and destroying wetlands and forests around the world.

Corporate giants like ExxonMobil succeed as businesses and investments while treating the destructive aspects of their behavior as someone else's problem. Technocratic advocates of sustainable development take the global economy for granted and try to sustain it ecologically. But the global market cannot be the model for a sustainable society because the global market destroys local cultures, substitutes commercial monocultures, generates ever-worsening inequality, and ravages the earth. The modern way of life itself is unsustainable. Lacking a fundamental course correction in our way of living, the earth is condemned to overheat, choke on its waste, exhaust its resources, and turn on its human destroyers. This ecological crisis was barely imagined at the mid-1960s endpoint of this book, but movements for economic democracy have always focused on the goal of creating healthy and sustainable communities. Today the link between economic democracy and the struggle for sustainable ecological communities is a matter of life and death for the entire planet.

Left–right debates about selling out, a staple of left politics, raged anew as the story of this book ended. When British and German socialists revised democratic socialism in the late 1950s, the story to many was that they betrayed socialism. Brandt's pro-American anti-Communism riled the SPD left wing throughout his twenty-three years as party leader, and Wilson broke through as a party leader by saying that Gaitskell sold out socialism. Then Gaitskell died, Wilson whisked into office, and he went on to epitomize the stodgy respectability of Labour socialism. The Labour Party and SPD went on to become so deeply integrated into welfare state capitalism that it was hard to see democratic socialist aspiration in either of them. Subsequently it was undeniably left behind in both party mainstreams. The struggle for it was left to the stubborn types in the back rows, pressing for economic democracy. The Meidner Plan, by whatever name, marks the difference between Social Democratic strategies that still fight for economic democracy and those that give up trying.

I am against giving up but also against identifying economic democracy exclusively with national-scale strategies. Economic democracy is the heart of democratic socialism and the test of its ambition for social justice. Historically, the guild socialist and revisionist traditions have been the most creative in exploring forms of socialization besides nationalization, with patchy records of stubborn persistence. Democratic socialism at its best expands the cooperative, public bank, and social market sectors, mixes various modes of social ownership, dismantles white privilege, male privilege, and heterosexual privilege, repudiates Eurocentric presumptions, and upholds ethical commitments to freedom, equality, community, and ecological flourishing. Thus described, it was not a new idea in the mid-1960s, but realizing it would have been a spectacular breakthrough and still would be.

TAWNEY, COLE, AND SOCIAL DEMOCRACY

Tawney shook his head when Cole and the Bevanites complained that the new socialism was too mushy to bite into. To Tawney, the struggle for Social Democracy had turned out remarkably well, as long as Labour socialists didn't sell their ethical souls for a politics of middle-class materialism. To Cole, the Labour Party fell pitifully short of creating a good society, so congratulations were not in order. Tawney and Cole agreed that creating a good society is the whole point of being a socialist. But Tawney never identified socialism-as-fellowship with a definite strategy or program, and his religious faith was a brake on making a religion of his politics. He did not clash with comrades over programs because he was not ideological in the sense of identifying his fellowship ideal with an ideological scheme. Tawney never had a blueprint mentality, and he did not expect the Labour Party or any faction of it to become some kind of church or a substitute for religion. Even the church to which he belonged did not model a righteous community, so Tawney was realistic about the limits of ethical fellowship in religious groups and the Labour Party. He did not make ethically heroic demands on institutions. He did not work out his religious issues in political organizations. And he did not expect the Labour Party to prefigure the ethical righteousness and solidarity of a socialist society.

These points distinguished him from Cole. Cole had no more use than Tawney for philosophy or high theory, and he said the same thing as Tawney about why he was glad not to be a Continental socialist: Continental Marxism and anarchism were obsessed with theory and correct doctrine, making socialism an esoteric affair of intellectuals. Sometimes Cole put it sharply, deriding philosophy as "all rubbish—failure to answer questions which are unanswerable because they are not real questions at all." Cole shook his head at Marxology even during the 1930s, when he had practical reasons to play up his Marxist credentials. Afterward he waved off editors asking for pro-Marxism articles.[105]

Reckitt captured the key to Cole early on, in 1919, when Reckitt and Cole tried to institute guild socialism in Britain. Reckitt said Cole had "a Bolshevik soul in a Fabian muzzle," making him surely "a bit of a puzzle." The muzzle was the compound of empirical and pragmatic commitments that Cole acquired during his early Fabian days and never relinquished. All of Cole's paradoxes were variations of the Bolshevik/Fabian puzzle. His socialism, like his personality, was a union of opposites, being simultaneously revolutionary and reformist, practical and utopian, romantic and rationalist, libertarian and collectivist, relativist and normative, Marxist and anti-Marxist, and nationalist and internationalist. A. W. Wright aptly described Cole's socialism as "full of internal tensions and ambiguities, as it struggled over time to erect and maintain balance, synthesis and compromise." Cole campaigned passionately against Fabian socialism before he campaigned ardently for it, without changing his mind. He was in the left wing of every group he joined but behaved as a sensible pragmatist, evoking puzzlement. He operated on two levels, writing books that oscillated uneasily between both.[106]

Level one was his North Star commitment to radical democratic socialism. Cole visualized a socialist ideal and elaborated principles for it. He puzzled that many of his comrades got along without a utopian goal, since he needed an end-state goal. He never doubted that the movement needed to visualize its ideal, and he said so repeatedly. But he immersed himself in everyday problems of strategy, policy, and organization — level two. Cole's left-wing critics despaired that he lost level-one clarity by plunging into level-two dickering. That was never how it seemed to him, however. From his standpoint, holding a North Star commitment allowed him to muck around in ordinary politics without losing his goal. Level two got the upper hand in his books because people were suffering, and there were always immediate problems to address. Cole never considered pulling back to theory-only, even in the Chichele chair.

In only one brief period did his dualism of theory–end and practice–means fuse together, compelling no choice of priority. Guild socialism was theory and practice folding together. Cole's guild activism offered an analysis of the existing situation and a program to address it that fit his concept of a theoretical ideal. Means and ends never really fused for him afterward because Cole remained a guild socialist at heart after leaving it behind. He stumped for Labour state socialism, then urged a Labour prime minister to implement Keynesian policies, then played up his Marxist credentials, then went back to ordinary Labour socialism, then disliked how it turned out, all without changing his mind. But this is not to say he changed only his strategy, not his goal, for Cole did change what he felt compelled to say about state socialism. His socialism changed on both levels.

Thus he was willing, during his purportedly Marxist phase in 1935, to define socialism in a vaguely inclusive fashion: "By Socialism I mean a form of society in which men and women are not divided into opposing economic classes, but live together under conditions of approximate social and economic equality, using in common the means that lie to their hands of promoting social welfare."[107]

What did not change were the moral principles of individuality, freedom, fellowship, and democracy underlying his socialism. Cole knew what was good. He plainly claimed his values were objective: "They are *good*, in a thoroughly and finally objective sense." His certainty that he held universally good values was the source of his confidence and socialist conviction. Everyone should be a socialist, and every society should uphold the values of individuality, freedom, fellowship, and democracy. The universal validity of democratic socialism is not diminished by the fact that democratic socialism is achievable only in societies that respect these values. It puzzled Cole that many of his comrades shied away from saying it. He loved Morris for radiating socialist conviction based on universal socialist values, he appreciated that a similar conviction was the source of Tawney's influence, and he would have appreciated the same thing in Rauschenbusch and Ragaz had he known them. There is such a thing as over-generalizing cultural relativism, Cole believed. The existence of universal moral truths is not disproven by the fact that some individuals and societies do not recognize them. Sometimes he put it harshly: "Anyone who denies their truth is blind, or mad, or wicked, or at least purblind."[108]

Cole refused to be shamed on this point. Socialists needed to say that individuality, freedom, fellowship, and democracy are always worth struggling for in every conceivable context. He implored democratic socialists to espouse what they believed, protesting that socialists retreated too readily to liberal relativism, the failure to take one's side in an argument. But Cole did not provide clear theoretical models of how to wage the argument. He spurned the hard work of precisely defining the relationships of socialism to individuality, liberty, and democracy; moreover, his fellowship ideal was his substitute religion. He found political philosophers hopelessly boring and pedantic on these topics. He ridiculed political philosophers for carving out an artificial discipline separate from social theory and for ignoring social institutions that were not the state. He disbelieved that socialist theory needed greater definitional precision, since that project smacked of Marxian scholasticism. He loathed the swing in economic theory toward ever more reliance on mathematical formulas, although Cole was adept at statistical analysis. He absorbed cultural relativism deeply enough to believe it undermined high theorizing of all kinds, especially in political philosophy. Thus he refused to critically analyze his concept of socialism.

These shortcomings and others were held against Cole before, during, and after he sat in the Chichele chair. Even his closest comrades said he might have left a better legacy by concentrating on theory or at least not disparaging it. Reckitt said Cole's devotion to "the lumbering army of official Labour" wiped out his chance "to make the contributions to social synthesis which he might have made if his mind had not been circumscribed by the obligations of such a loyalty." Mellor said Cole's mindset was more disabling in this area than his devotion to Labour. Cole was too devoted to reconciling irreconcilable things to be a successful theorist. Certainly, he was capable of lining out a coherent position, but he was incapable of settling on one thing. Cole's mind was far-reaching and never simple, constantly fusing opposing positions. Thus there was always the puzzle of utopian radicalism in a Fabian muzzle.[109]

Sympathetic academics agreed in the form of laments, while others said Cole had no business occupying the Chichele chair. Marxian economist Maurice Dobb said Cole's books usually left him feeling somewhat deflated: "One feels eminently informed yet insufficiently enlightened. One feels stimulated to thought yet left with concepts which are vague and imperfectly defined. One feels that the commentary has been, perhaps, too facile." Cole's body of work, Dobb lamented, was eclectic and unsystematic. The ironic upshot of trying to be relevant was that Cole never achieved clarity about what mattered. Wright concurred, noting that real Marxists didn't trust Cole and neither did Labour officials, as both found him slippery and eclectic. Wright pointed to Cole's "profound personal antipathy to philosophical niceties" and his cultural relativism, which gave him two reasons to spurn theoretical precision. Cole slipped back and forth between making logical-universal claims and cultural relativist claims; Wright wondered if he even noticed doing so. In any case, the result was a pluralist mishmash. Wright winced at Cole's assurance that state socialism in England would not replicate the Soviet record of tyranny and coercion because Britons were "reared in the traditions and practices of Western liberal democracy." That was "shabby" apologetics, Wright charged. Cole would have done more for socialism by offering a rigorous concept of it. Instead he tried to be relevant and resorted to relativistic apologetics for socialism.[110]

But Cole's belief that British culture was too *British* to fall into Stalinism ran deeper than apologetic spinning. He felt its truth in himself; *he* was too British to be a Communist, despite almost everything. Then Britain readily absorbed the sweeping transformation of 1945–1949 as though nothing happened, for better and worse. Wright caught that Cole's devotion to relevance aimed for something higher than theoretical accomplishment. Cole carried out what he sought to do—writing like Morris and upholding socialism as a distinct way of living.

L. P. Carpenter added that Cole tried to do many things well, just like his hero, Morris. It got harder for Cole's interpreters to convey what he accomplished because the audience for which he wrote mostly disappeared. Cole wrote for Labour militants, unionists, WEA and Ruskin College students, Christian socialists, intellectuals, and public-minded general readers. This was the audience that subscribed to *New Statesman* and the Left Book Club, turning the Labour Party's immediate program into practical politics. Informing this audience and keeping hope alive within it were Cole's everyday work. In the few books he wrote for academics he disappeared behind a mask of putative objectivity, showing he could do it, except when the topic was liberal arts versus specialization. Cole could not sustain a neutral pose on the mission of higher education. He despaired of the lust for specialization that rendered economics, political science, and sociology as separate disciplines. He ridiculed the attempt to make every discipline as mathematical as possible, protesting that in most fields putting a thought into a formula adds nothing to it. Losing this argument wore on Cole. He told a WEA Conference at Oxford in 1954, "The deepest insult you can offer me is to call me a 'social scientist.'"[111]

Fellowship, genuine community, was always the point for Cole, as it was for Tawney, as it was for Maurice/Morris ethical socialists. It began as something that could be realized in one's personal life. It generated the socialist principles of equality and social justice, but the order of derivation was crucial. The essential thing was to recognize each person as an individual. It did not faze him that the idea of personal individuality came from Christianity. Cole would have told the later Troeltsch that he should have deconstructed God, not Christian personality.

Cole never tired of saying that fellowship consists of treating human beings as ends in themselves and never as a means to an end: "Fellowship does not count heads, or, if it does, it counts everyone as more than one—in fact, as infinite." To him, this was mere idealistic chatter if he did not live by it. Reckitt said Cole worked at doing so throughout his life: "I have known him to cut a whole week out of a holiday to stay behind and look after an invalid, taken ill at a conference, towards whom he had no obligation whatsoever." Reckitt suggested, without naming it, that Cole internalized the Jesus ethic about caring for others. Cole took individual dignity as an absolute fact and command, quietly offering acts of mercy without drawing attention to them. But he was awkward, self-contained, and an Oxford eminence, so he appeared aloof to most people. Most who knew Cole only slightly saw only his awkwardness and not his surprising kindness, as he was never his best in a first meeting.[112]

Cole's hostility to spiritual everything left him with socialist fellowship as a religion, a bare ideal appealing to Kantian-like moral rationality stripped even of Kant's moral faith. Cole boasted of caring nothing about the state of his soul. He bridled at people who thought this was an issue; Gandhi repelled him on this count. Cole wailed in 1931, "Why could he not stop thinking of his own soul, and lose himself in the things he was striving for?" Cole somehow imagined that a secular Gandhi might have commanded the same following. Since Cole felt better off and morally purer without any religious faith, he wanted nothing less for the socialist movement, although he respected friends like Reckitt and Tawney who thought they got something from their faith. Cole recognized that much of the ILP tradition operated in a moral vacuum. Too many British socialists who cited Morris fixed on a bare moral ideal. They treated their socialism as a religion, making absolute demands and acting like guardians of a privileged faith. Cole believed he was somehow exempt from this outcome. The "somehow" was his willingness to negotiate political realities. His pragmatism saved him from moral vacuum radicalism. Actually, it didn't, but Cole was an exemplar of his ideal. Somebody had to show that democratic socialism was radical, compelling, realistic, and a real option, with or without religious compensations.[113]

NOTES

PREFACE

1. Socialist International, "The World Today: The Socialist Perspective," Socialist International Council Conference, Oslo, Norway (June 2–4, 1962), http://www. socialistinternational.org/viewArticle.cfm?ArticleID=2133.
2. See Gary Dorrien, *Economy, Difference, Empire: Social Ethics for Social Justice* (New York: Columbia University Press, 2010), 87–110.
3. Sheri Berman, *The Primacy of Politics: Social Democracy and the Making of Europe's Twentieth Century* (Cambridge: Cambridge University Press, 2006); Berman, *The Social Democratic Moment* (Cambridge: Harvard University Press, 1998).

1. CHRISTIAN SOCIALISM IN THE MAKING OF SOCIAL DEMOCRACY

1. Carl Schmitt, *Political Theology: Four Chapters on the Concept of Sovereignty*, trans. George Schwab (1st German ed., 1922; Chicago: University of Chicago Press, 1985); Schmitt, *Political Theology II*, trans. Michael Hoelzl and Graham Ward (Cambridge, UK: Polity Press, 2008); Schmitt, *The Concept of the Political*, trans. George Schwab (Chicago: University of Chicago Press, 2007); Chantal Mouffe, "Carl Schmitt and the Paradox of Liberal Democracy," in Mouffe, ed., *The Challenge of Carl Schmitt* (London: Verso, 1999); Michael Hollerich, "Carl Schmidt," in *The Blackwell Companion to Political Theology*, ed. Peter Scott and William T. Cavanaugh (Malden, MA: Blackwell, 2004), 107–122.
2. John Ruskin, *Fors Clavigera: Letters to the Workmen and Labourers of Great Britain*, 8 vols. (Orpington, Kent: G. Allen, 1871–1884); William Morris, *The Earthly Paradise* (1880; repr., New York: Routledge, 2002); Morris, *A Dream of John Ball; and, A King's Lesson* (London: Reeves and Turner, 1888); Morris, *Signs of Change; Seven Lectures Delivered on Various Occasions* (London: Reeves and Turner, 1888); Morris, *News from Nowhere, Or, An Epoch of Rest: Being Some Chapters from a Utopian Romance* (1890; repr., London: Routledge and Kegan Paul, 1970).

3. Hilaire Belloc, *The Servile State* (London: T. N. Foulis, 1912); Pope Leo XIII, *Rerum Novarum: The Condition of Labor* (1891), in *Catholic Social Thought: The Documentary Heritage*, ed. David J. O'Brien and Thomas A. Shannon (Maryknoll, NY: Orbis Books, 2004), 14–39; J. N. Figgis, *Churches in the Modern State* (London: Longmans, Green, 1913); Figgis, *The Fellowship of the Mystery* (London: Longmans, Green, 1915).

4. British Labour Party [Sidney Webb], *Labour and the New Social Order* (London: British Labour Party, 1918).

5. Karl Marx and Frederick Engels, "Manifesto of the Communist Party" (1848), in *The Marx–Engels Reader*, ed. Robert C. Tucker (New York: W. W. Norton, 1978), 469–500.

6. Karl Marx, "Critique of the Gotha Program" (1875), *The Marx–Engels Reader*, 525–41; Marx, *Capital: A Critique of Political Economy*, vol. 1, trans. Ben Fowkes (London: Penguin Books, 1990); Marx, *Capital: A Critique of Political Economy*, vol. 3, trans. David Fernbach (London: Penguin Books, 1991); Marx, "The Civil War in France," *The Marx–Engels Reader*, 618–652; Friedrich Engels, *Socialism: Utopian and Scientific* (1892), trans. Edward Aveling (New York: International Publishers, 2015).

7. Paul Tillich, *The Socialist Decision* (1933), trans. Franklin Sherman (New York: Harper and Row, 1977).

8. Gary Dorrien, *Social Ethics in the Making: Interpreting an American Tradition* (Oxford: Wiley-Blackwell, 2011), 6–225.

9. Gary Dorrien, *Kantian Reason and Hegelian Spirit: The Idealistic Logic of Modern Theology* (Oxford: Wiley-Blackwell, 2012), 378–415.

10. R. H. Tawney, *The Acquisitive Society* (New York: Harcourt, Brace, 1920); Tawney, *Equality* (1st ed., 1931; 5th ed., London: George Allen and Unwin, 1964).

2. BRITISH ORIGINS

1. Frederick Maurice, *The Life of Frederick Denison Maurice, Chiefly Told in His Letters*, 2 vols. (New York: Charles Scribner's Sons, 1884), 10–21; Florence Higham, *Frederick Denison Maurice* (London: SCM Press, 1947); Olive J. Brose, *Frederick Denison Maurice: Rebellious Conformist, 1805–1872* (Athens: Ohio University Press, 1971), 8–11; Chris Bryant, *Possible Dreams: A Personal History of the British Christian Socialists* (London: Hodder and Staughton, 1997), 29–30.

2. Samuel Taylor Coleridge, *Aids to Reflection: The Collected Works of Samuel Taylor Coleridge*, vol. 9, ed. John Beer (Princeton: Princeton University Press, 1993); Charles Merivale, *Autobiography and Letters*, ed. J. A. Merivale (Oxford: Oxford University Press, 1898), quote 98; see Peter Allen, *The Cambridge Apostles: The Early Years* (Cambridge: Cambridge University Press, 1978); Gary Dorrien, *Kantian Reason and Hegelian Spirit: The Idealistic Logic of Modern Theology* (Oxford: Wiley-Blackwell, 2012), 119–145.

3. Maurice, *The Life of Frederick Denison Maurice*, 1: 45–73, 102–138, quote 177; Maurice, editorial comments, *Athenaeum* (March 8, 1828), 289–290; (July 30, 1828), 623; (August 6, 1828), 641–642; William J. Wolf, "Frederick Denison Maurice," in *The Spirit of Anglicanism*, ed. Wolf (Harrisonburg, PA: Morehouse, 1979), 52–53; C. Brad Faught, *The*

Oxford Movement: A Thematic History of the Tractarians and Their Times (University Park: Pennsylvania State University Press, 2003); John Beer, "Coleridge's Religious Thought: The Search for a Medium," in *The Interpretation of Belief: Coleridge, Schleiermacher and Romanticism*, ed. D. Jasper (London: Macmillan, 1986), 47–50.

4. Frederick Denison Maurice, *Subscription no Bondage, or The practical advantages afforded by the Thirty-nine Articles as guides in all the branches of academical education* (Oxford: J. H. Parker, 1835), quote 79.

5. See Henry P. Liddon, *Life of Edward Bouverie Pusey, doctor of divinity, canon of Christ church; regius professor of Hebrew in the University of Oxford*, 4 vols. (London: Longmans, 1894–1898); John Henry Cardinal Newman, *Apologia Pro Vita Sua* (1863; repr. New York: Doubleday, 1956).

6. Frederick Denison Maurice, *Three Letters to the Rev. W. Palmer, fellow and tutor of Magdalene College Oxford, on the name "Protestant"; on the seemingly double character of the English church; and on the bishopric at Jerusalem* (London: J. W. Parker, 1842), 17.

7. Frederick Denison Maurice, *The Kingdom of Christ: or, Hints on the Principles, Ordinances, and Constitution of the Catholic Church in Letters to a Member of the Society of Friends*, 3 vols. (London: Darton and Clark, 1838; 2nd rev. ed., 1842); new ed., 2 vols., ed. Alec Vidler (London: SCM Press, 1958).

8. Maurice, *The Life of Frederick Denison Maurice*, 1: 174–175, "most grand" and "narrow" quotes 174; Maurice, *The Kingdom of Christ* (1958 ed.), "all its grand," "the old," and "that there is" quotes 1: 70.

9. See Maurice, *The Kingdom of Christ* (1958 ed.), 1: 258–288, 2: 17–185; Maurice, *Theological Essays* (New York: Harper and Brothers, 1957), 68–116.

10. Maurice, *The Kingdom of Christ*, 1958 ed., 2: 17–185.

11. Ibid., 2: 320–347, quotes 323.

12. Ibid., 2: 322–329, quotes 328.

13. Ibid., quotes 2: 328, 329, 331.

14. Ibid., quote 2: 331–332.

15. Ibid., 2: 333–334.

16. Ibid., 2: 332–342, quote 336.

17. Robert Owen, *The Life of Robert Owen, Written by Himself*, 2 vols. (1857; repr., London: G. Bell and Sons, 1920), 1: 1–23; B. L. Hutchins, *Robert Owen, Social Reformer*, Fabian Tract Number 166 (London: Fabian Society, 1912), 4–7; G. D. H. Cole, *The Life of Robert Owen* (London: Macmillan, 1930), 12–24.

18. Owen, *The Life of Robert Owen*, 1: 142–43; Robert Owen, *A New View of Society: Essays on the Principle of the Formation of Human Character* (1813; multiple reprints in various editions, London: Penguin Classics, 1991); Owen, *Observations on the Cotton Trade* (1815), repr. in Owen, Supplementary Appendix to *The Life of Robert Owen, Written by Himself*, 1: Appendix F, 60–62; J. F. C Harrison, *Robert Owen and the Owenites in Britain and America* (London: Routledge and Kegan Paul, 1969); I. Donnachie, *Robert Owen: Owen of New Lanark and New Harmony* (East Linton, Scotland: Tuckwell Press, 2000).

19. Owen, *The Life of Robert Owen*, 1: 156–80; Robert Owen, *The Book of the New Moral World: Containing the Rational System of Society Founded on Demonstrable Facts*

(London: E. Wilson, 1836); Frank Podmore, *Robert Owen: A Biography*, 2 vols. (London: Allen and Unwin, 1923), 1: 52–69; Arthur J. Booth, *Saint-Simon and Saint-Simonism: A Chapter in the History of Socialism in France* (London: Longmans, Green, Reader and Dyer, 1871); Charles Fourier, *Theory of Social Organization* (New York: C. P. Somerby, 1876); Richard T. Ely, *French and German Socialism* (New York: Harper Brothers, 1883).

20. Owen, *The Life of Robert Owen*, 1: 226–230, 290–335; 2: 1–95; Owen, *The Book of the New Moral World*, xx–xxi, 5–21.

21. Robert Owen, Speech to the Labour Exchange in Charlotte Street, May 1, 1833, *The Crisis* (May 11, 1833), in Gilbert C. Binyon, *The Christian Socialist Movement in England* (London: SPCK, 1931), 33; Max Beer, *History of British Socialism* (London: Bell, 1919), 325–330; George B. Lockwood, *The New Harmony Movement* (New York: Appleton, 1905); Harry W. Laidler, *A History of Socialist Thought* (New York: Thomas Y. Crowell, 1927), 119–120.

22. Karl Marx and Frederick Engels, *The Communist Manifesto* (1848), in *Karl Marx: Selected Writings* (Oxford: Oxford University Press, 1977), 221–246, "early," 243; "fantastic," 244; "castles" and "appeal," 245.

23. Armond Cuvillier, *P.-J.-B. Buchez et les Origines du Socialisme Chrétien* (Paris: Presses universitaires des France, 1948), 45–52; Maxime LeRoy, ed., *Les Précurseurs Français du Socialisme* (Paris: Éditions du Temps present, 1948), 325–326; L. Chevalier, *Classes laborieuses et classes dangereuses a Paris en 1848* (Paris: Presses universitaires de France, 1958); Jean Jaurés, ed., *Histoire socialiste, 1789–1900*, 13 vols. (Paris: J. Rouff, 1901–1908); Jaurés, *Histoire socialiste de la révolution française* (Paris: Editions de la Librairie de l'humanité, 1924); Annie Kriegel, *Le Pain et les roses: Jalons pour une histoire des socialismes* (Paris: Presses universitaires de France, 1968); John Plamenatz, *The Revolutionary Movement in France, 1815–1871* (London: Longmans, Green, 1952); Frank Deppe, *Verschwörung, Aufstand, und Revolution: Blanqui und das Problem der sozialen Revolution* (Frankfurt am Main: Europäische Verlaganst, 1970); Leo A. Loubére, *Louis Blanc: His Life and His Contribution to the Rise of French Jacobin Socialism* (Evanston: Northwestern University Press, 1961); Frank Manuel, *The New World of Henri Saint-Simon* (Cambridge: Harvard University Press, 1956).

24. Charles E. Raven, *Christian Socialism, 1848–1854* (London: Macmillan, 1920), 56–57, 72–73; N. C. Masterman, *John Malcolm Ludlow: The Builder of Christian Socialism* (Cambridge: Cambridge University Press, 1963), 8–20; John M. Ludlow, Letter to J. Carter, October 19, 1895, in Raven, *Christian Socialism*, "the only man," 73; Charles Kingsley, *Charles Kingsley: His Letters and Memories of His Life*, ed. Mrs. Charles Kingsley (New York: Scribner, 1877), "men who," 156; Frederick Denison Maurice, *The Prayer-book considered specially in reference to the Romish System* (1848; repr., Greenwood, SC: Attic Press, 1977), 331–447.

25. Torben Christensen, *Origin and History of Christian Socialism: 1848–54* (Copenhagen: Universtetsforlaget, 1962), quote 75; Masterman, *John Malcolm Ludlow*, 8–20; John C. Cort, *Christian Socialism: An Informal History* (Maryknoll, NY: Orbis Books, 1988), 141–143.

26. J. M. Ludlow, "The Great Partnership," *Politics for the People* (1848), 273–274; Ludlow, "The Laws: The Birthright of the People," ibid., 275; F. D. Maurice, "Is There Any Hope for Education in England?" ibid., 193–245; Maurice, "More Last Words," ibid., 283; Raven, *Christian Socialism*, 117–132; Christensen, *Origin and History of Christian Socialism*, 86; Maurice B. Reckitt, *Maurice to Temple: A Century of the Social Movement in the Church of England* (London: Faber and Faber, 1947), 70–74; Masterman, *John Malcolm Ludlow*, 15–20; Cort, *Christian Socialism*, 145.

27. Charles Kingsley, *Yeast: A Problem* (New York: Harper and Brothers, 1851); Charles Kingsley, *Alton Locke: Tailor and Poet*, 2 vols. (London: Chapman and Hall, 1849, 1850); Kingsley, *Works of Charles Kingsley*, 28 vols. (London: Macmillan, 1879), vol. 3: *Cheap Clothes and Nasty* (1850), "will weaken," lxxxvii.

28. Frederick Denison Maurice, *Dialogue between Somebody (a person of respectability) and Nobody (the writer): Tracts on Christian Socialism*, No. 1 (London: George Bell, 1850), 1–12; in Maurice, *Reconstructing Christian Ethics: Selected Writings*, ed. Ellen K. Wondra (Louisville: Westminster John Knox Press, 1995), quote 196.

29. Maurice, *Dialogue between*, "has a right" and "godly," 197.

30. Ibid., "if the," 199.

31. Ibid., "concerning" and become "mingled," 201.

32. Raven, *Christian Socialism*, "to the extent," 157; Masterman, *John Malcolm Ludlow*, "tracts full," 95; see Cort, *Christian Socialism*, 147–148; Christensen, *Origin and History of Christian Socialism*, 143–146.

33. Christensen, *Origin and History of Christian Socialism*, quote 145.

34. Sidney Webb and Beatrice Webb, *The Consumers' Cooperative Movement* (London: Longmans, Green, 1921), 5–6; Christensen, *Origin and History of Christian Socialism*, 257–263; Raven, *Christian Socialism*, 283–301; Alex Gourevitch, *From Slavery to the Cooperative Commonwealth: Labor and Republican Liberty in the Nineteenth Century* (Cambridge: Cambridge University Press, 2014).

35. Christensen, *Origin and History of Christian Socialism*, quote 364; J. F. C. Harrison, *A History of the Working Men's College (1854–1954)* (London: Routledge and Kegan Paul, 1954); Raven, *Christian Socialism*, 340–370; Binyon, *The Christian Socialist Movement in England*, 112–196.

36. Brenda Colloms, *Victorian Visionaries* (London: Constable, 1982), quotes 121.

37. Frederick Denison Maurice, *Theological Essays* (London: James Clarke, 1957), 302.

38. Ibid., quote 309.

39. Ibid., quote 316–317.

40. Ibid., quotes, 317, 319, 323.

41. Reckitt, *Maurice to Temple*, quote, 97; see Maurice, *The Kingdom of Christ*, 2: 302–305; Frederick Denison Maurice, *The Doctrine of Sacrifice Deduced from the Scriptures* (London: Macmillan, 1879), xx–xxii.

42. Charles F. G. Masterman, *Frederick Denison Maurice* (London: Mowbray), 1907), "the greatest," 1; Hallam Tennyson, *Alfred Lord Tennyson*, 2 vols. (London: Macmillan, 1897), 2: 168; Frederic Harrison, *Autobiographic Memoirs*, 2 vols. (London: Macmillan, 1911), 1: 151; *Letters and Diaries of John Henry Newman*, 2 vols., ed. Charles Dessain

and Edward Kelly (London: Thomas Nelson, 1971), 2: 504; John Stuart Mill, *Autobiography* (New York: Columbia University Press, 1944), 107; Raven, *Christian Socialism*, 75–76; Alec Vidler, *F. D. Maurice and Company* (London: SCM Press, 1966), 16–19.

43. Karl Marx, "The Difference Between Democritus' and Epicurus' Philosophy of Nature," Ph.D. diss., University of Jena, 1841, in *Karl Marx: Selected Writings*, ed. David McLellan (Oxford: Oxford University Press, 1977), 11–16; Marx, *Writings of the Young Marx on Philosophy and Society*, ed. L. Easton and K. Guddar (New York: Doubleday, 1967); Leszek Kolakowski, *Main Currents of Marxism: Its Rise, Growth and Dissolution*, 3 vols., vol. 1: *The Founders*, trans. P. S. Falla (Oxford: Clarendon Press, 1978), 81–146; Mary Gabriel, *Love and Capital: Karl and Jenny Marx and the Birth of a Revolution* (New York: Little, Brown, 2011), 11–69; Max Beer, *Life and Teaching of Karl Marx* (New York: International Publishers, 1929), 2–19.

44. David McLellan, *Karl Marx: His Life and Thought* (New York: Harper and Row, 1973), "my dark," 44; Karl Marx, "On the Freedom of the Press," *Rheinische Zweitung* (May 1842), *Karl Marx: Selected Writings*, 17–18; Marx, "The Leading Article of the *Kölnische Zeitung*," *Karl Marx: Selected Writings*, 18–20; Marx, "Communism and the *Augsburg Allgemeine Zeitung*," *Rheinische Zweitung* (October 16, 1842), in *The Karl Marx Library*, 7 vols., ed. Saul Padover, vol. 1: *On Revolution* (New York: McGraw-Hill, 1971–1977), 3–6; Heinrich Gemkow, *Friedrich Engels: A Biography* (Dresden: Verlag Zeit im Bild, 1972), 38–55; Tristram Hunt, *Marx's General: The Revolutionary Life of Friedrich Engels* (New York: Henry Holt, 2009), 19–24; Terrell Carver, *Friedrich Engels: His Life and Thought* (London: Macmillan, 1989), 16–22.

45. Karl Marx, *A Contribution to the Critique of Political Economy* (1859), trans. S. W. Ryazanskaya (New York: International Publishers, 1999), "arrived by," 22; Marx, "Contribution to the Critique of Hegel's *Philosophy of Right*" (1843), in *The Marx–Engels Reader*, 2nd ed., ed. Robert C. Tucker (New York: W. W. Norton, 1978), 16–25, "just as," 20.

46. Karl Marx, "Economic and Philosophic Manuscripts of 1844," *Karl Marx: Selected Writings*, "great achievement" and "nothing but," 97; Marx, "For a Ruthless Criticism of Everything Existing" (1843), in *The Marx–Engels Reader*, "I am speaking," "dogmatic abstraction," and "one-sided," 13; "new principles," 14; "from its dream" and "putting religious," 15; Friedrich Engels, *The Condition of the Working Class in England* (1845), in *Collected Works of Karl Marx and Friedrich Engels* (New York: International Publishers, 1975), 4: 295–596.

47. Karl Marx, "Theses on Feuerbach," in *Karl Marx: Selected Writings*, 157–158, and *The Marx–Engels Reader*, 144–145.

48. Karl Marx and Friedrich Engels, *The Holy Family* (1845), in *Karl Marx: Selected Writings*, 131–155, "all treatises," 132; "Critical Criticism," 133.

49. Karl Marx and Friedrich Engels, *The German Ideology* (1845), in *Karl Marx: Selected Writings*, 159–192, "the rule," 159; "the wretchedness," 160; "as individuals," 161.

50. Marx and Engels, *The German Ideology*, "life is not," 164; "of this" and "each can become," 169.

51. Marx and Engels, *The Communist Manifesto*, in *Karl Marx: Selected Writings*, "the specter," 221; Karl Marx, "Articles for the *Neue Rheinische Zeitung*," ibid., 271–276.

52. Marx and Engels, *The Communist Manifesto*, "prelude," 246; Karl Marx, "Address to the Communist League" (1850), in *Karl Marx: Selected Writings*, 277–285; Marx, "Speech to the Central Committee of the Communist League" (1850), ibid., 298–299; "Declaration of the World Society of Revolutionary Communists" (April 1850), in Christine Lattek, *Revolutionary Refugees: Socialism in Britain, 1840–1860* (London: Routledge, 2006), "the aim," 61.

53. Bertram D. Wolfe, *Marxism: One Hundred Years in the Life of a Doctrine* (New York: Dial Press, 1965), 165–182; Hal Draper, "Marx and the Dictatorship of the Proletariat," in *Etudes de Marxicologie* 6 (September 1962): 68–74, repr. in *New Politics* 1 (1962).

54. Sidney Hook, *Towards the Understanding of Karl Marx: A Revolutionary Interpretation* (New York: John Day, 1933), 300–314; Michael Harrington, *Socialism* (New York: Saturday Review Press, 1972), 50–52; Wolfe, *Marxism: One Hundred Years in the Life of a Doctrine*, 173–175.

55. Karl Marx to Joseph Weydemeyer, March 5, 1852, in *Karl Marx: Selected Writings*, 141; Marx, Preface to *A Critique of Political Economy*, ibid., 388–391; Marx, *Gundrisse*, ibid., 345–387.

56. Marx and Engels, *The Communist Manifesto*, "the history," 222.

57. William H. Dawson, *German Socialism and Ferdinand Lassalle* (London: Swan Sonnenschein, 1891), 114–132; Ferdinand Lassalle, *Gesammelte Reden und Schriften*, 12 vols., ed. Eduard Bernstein (Berlin: P. Cassirer, 1919–1920); Eduard Bernstein, *Ferdinand Lassalle as Social Reformer* (London: S. Sonnenschein, 1893), 18–19; Georges Brandes, *Ferdinand Lassalle* (New York: Bernard G. Richards, 1925); Roger Morgan, *The German Social Democrats and the First International, 1864–1872* (Cambridge: Cambridge University Press, 1965).

58. *Ferdinand Lassalles Reden und Schriften*, 3 vols., ed. Eduard Bernstein (Berlin: Vorwärts, 1893), 2: 443–445; Franz Mehring, *Zur Geschichte der deutschen Sozialdemokratie* (Magdeburg: Faber, 1877), 22–24; Saul K. Padover, ed., "Introduction: Marx's Role in the First International," in Karl Marx, *The Karl Marx Library*, vol. 3: *On the First International*, xiii–l, Julius Braunthal, *History of the International*, 3 vols. (New York: Praeger, 1967–1980), 1: 75–87.

59. Karl Marx, "Inaugural Address to the First International" (1864), in *Karl Marx: Selected Writings*, 531–537; "Policies and Programs," International Working Men's Association, *The Karl Marx Library*, vol. 3: *On the First International*, 82–156; Braunthal, *History of the International*, 1: 75–79; Albert S. Lindemann, *A History of European Socialism* (New Haven: Yale University Press, 1983), 120–125; Henry Collins and Chimen Abramsky, *Karl Marx and the British Labor Movement: Years of the First International* (London: Macmillan, 1965).

60. Karl Marx, "The Civil War in France" (1871), in *Karl Marx: Selected Writings*, 539–557; Samuel Bernstein, "The First International on the Eve of the Paris Commune," *Science and Society* 5 (Winter 1941): 24–42; Bernstein, "The First International and the Great Powers," *Science and Society* 16 (Summer 1952): 247–272; Collins and Abramsky,

Karl Marx and the British Labor Movement, 57–66; McLellan, *Karl Marx: His Life and Thought,* 400–403.

61. Mikhail Bakunin, *Statism and Anarchy* (1873), trans. Marshall Shatz (Cambridge: Cambridge University Press, 1990), "every German," 194; "they say" and "no dictatorship," 179; "if there is," 178; see *Bakunin on Anarchy,* trans. and ed., Sam Dolgoff (New York: Alfred A. Knopf, 1972); Rudolf Rocker, *Anarchosyndicalism* (London: Seeker and Warburg, 1938).

62. Bakunin, *Statism and Anarchy,* "I am," 192; "on the social-revolutionary," 197.

63. Karl Marx, "On Bakunin's *State and Anarchy,*" in *Karl Marx: Selected Writings,* 561–563, "schoolboy," 561; "he does not" and "with its," 562.

64. George Haw, *Christianity and the Working Classes* (London: Macmillan, 1906), 18–32; Richard Mudie-Smith, ed., *The Religious Life of London* (London: Hodder and Stoughton, 1904), 9–25; E. P. Thompson, *The Making of the English Working Class* (New York: Pantheon, 1963); Peter d'A. Jones, *The Christian Socialist Revival, 1877–1914: Religion, Class, and Social Conscience in Late-Victorian England* (Princeton: Princeton University Press, 1968), 58–79.

65. *Essays and Reviews* (London: John W. Parker and Son, 1860); *Essays and Reviews: The 1860 Text and Its Reading,* ed. Victor Shea and William Whitla (Charlottesville: University of Virginia Press, 2000); Ieuan Ellis, *Seven Against Christ: A Study of "Essays and Reviews"* (Leiden: E. J. Brill, 1980); Frederick Robertson, *Life and Letters of Frederick W. Robertson, M.A.,* ed. Stopford A. Brooke, 2 vols. (London: Smith, Elder, 1866); H. G. Wood, *F. D. Maurice* (Cambridge: Cambridge University Press, 1950), 160–161.

66. H. L. Beales, "The Great Depression in Industry and Trade," *Economic History Review* 5 (October 1934): 65–75; Charles Wilson, "Economy and Society in Late Victorian Britain," *Economic History Review* 18 (August 1965): 183–198.

67. Beatrice Webb, *My Apprenticeship* (London: Longmans, Green, 1926), "men" and "consciousness," 179; Arnold Toynbee, "Mr. George in England," lecture of June 18, 1883, in *Toynbee's Industrial Revolution* (1884; repr., New York: A. M. Kelley, 1969), "we," 318.

68. Samuel Augustus Barnett and Henrietta Barnett, *Practicable Socialism: Essays on Social Reform* (1888; repr., Freeport, NY: Books for Libraries, 1972); Barnett and Barnett, *Towards Social Reform* (New York: Macmillan, 1909); Jane Addams, *Twenty Years at Hull House, with Autobiographical Notes* (New York: Macmillan, 1910; Signet Classics Edition, New York: New American Library, 1961), 57–58.

69. Editorial, "Unconsidered Trifles," *Christian Socialist* (March 1884), 146; editorial, [Charles L. Marson], "The Coming Slavery," *Christian Socialist* (June 1884), 4; editorial, [Marson], "'The Christian Socialist' and Spread the Light!" *Christian Socialist* (June 1884), 10; editorial, [Marson], "Land Nationalization v. Land Monopoly," *Christian Socialist* (August 1884), 36; editorials, [Marson], "Depression of Trade" and untitled others, *Christian Socialist* (December 1884), 99–100; editorial, [Marson], "The Repression of Mendicity," *Christian Socialist* (May 1885), 178–179; editorial, [Marson], "Unconsidered Trifles," *Christian Socialist* (July 1885), 20; editorial, [Marson], "Social Horror," *Christian Socialist* (August 1885), 34; editorial, [Marson], "Unconsidered

Trifles," *Christian Socialist* (December 1885), 100–101; editorials, [Marson], "The Need of a Christian Socialist Society," and "Unconsidered Trifles," *Christian Socialist* (March 1886), 146–147, 148; [Marson], "Manifesto of the Christian Socialist Society," *Christian Socialist* (May 1886), "the good of" and "public control," 190.

70. W. Howard Paul Campbell, *The Robbery of the Poor* (London: Social Democratic Federation, 1884); Alfred Howard, "Socialism, Christian and Otherwise," *Christian Socialist* (January 1888), 9–11, "we hold," 11; editorial, [George W. Johnson], "To Our Readers," *Christian Socialist* (December 1891), "doomed," "all faith," "without," and "we aim," 7; editorial, [George W. Johnson], "Epilogue," *Christian Socialist* (December 1891), 129–130; Charles L. Marson, "The Pan-Anglican Synod," *To-Day* 10 (September 1888), 85–86; Marson, "Secular Education," *Commonwealth* 11 (August 1906): 233–236.

71. F. G. Bettany, *Stewart Headlam: A Biography* (London: John Murray, 1926), 4–13; John Richard Orens, *Stewart Headlam's Radical Anglicanism: The Mass, the Masses, and the Music Hall* (Urbana: University of Illinois Press, 2003), 2–9; Charles Kingsley, *His Letters and Memories of His Life*, ed. Fanny Kingsley, 2 vols. (London: C. Kegan Paul, 1877), "ghastly," 1: 203.

72. Stewart Headlam, *Priestcraft and Progress: Being Sermons and Lectures* (London: John Hodges, 1878); Orens, *Stewart Headlam's Radical Anglicanism*, 22–26; Edward R. Norman, *The Victorian Christian Socialists* (Cambridge: Cambridge University Press, 2002), 102–103; Trevor Beeson, *Priests and Politics: The Church Speaks Out* (London: SCM Press, 2013), 31–32.

73. Headlam, *Priestcraft and Progress*, "a horrid," 85; Headlam, *The Service of Humanity and Other Sermons* (London: John Hodges, 1882), "a monstrous," 131; "beautiful," 27; Headlam, *Theatres and Music Halls* (London: Women's Printing Society, 1878), "I should," 4. The phrase about a woman named Dull was an allusion to a figure in John Bunyan's Puritan masterpiece, *Pilgrim's Progress.*

74. Headlam, *Theatres and Music Halls*, v–vi, 396; Orens, *Stewart Headlam's Radical Anglicanism*, 30–31; Kenneth Leech, "Stewart Headlam," in *For Christ and the People*, ed. Maurice Reckitt (London: SPCK, 1968), 75.

75. Bettany, *Stewart Headlam*, 58–66; Orens, *Stewart Headlam's Radical Anglicanism*, 41–47.

76. Guild of Saint Matthew [Stewart Headlam], "Programme of the Guild of Saint Matthew," *Church Reformer* 3 (October 1884), "false," 1; Orens, *Stewart Headlam's Radical Anglicanism*, 36–44; Norman, *The Victorian Christian Socialists*, 104; Beeson, *Priests and Politics*, 32–33; Jones, *The Christian Socialist Revival*, 95–101; Stewart Headlam, *The Function of the Stage* (London: F. Verinder, 1889).

77. Henry George, *Progress and Poverty*, 2nd ed. (1879; New York: Robert Shalkenbach, 1919), "we may," 288.

78. Ibid., "from this," 240; Jones, *The Christian Socialist Revival*, 51–54; Peter d'A. Jones, *Henry George and British Socialism* (New York: Garland Press, 1991).

79. Henry M. Hyndman, *England for All: The Text-book of Democracy* (London: Gilbert and Rivington, 1881); Walter Kendall, *The Revolutionary Movement in Britain, 1900–21: The Origins of British Communism* (London: Weidenfeld and Nicolson, 1969), 3–8; John Callahan, *Socialism in Britain Since 1884* (Oxford: Blackwell, 1990),

12–17; H. Quelch, "H. M. Hyndman: An Interview," *The Comrade* (February 1902), 114.

80. Program of the Social Democratic Federation (1884), in Chushichi Tsuzuki, *H. M. Hyndman and British Socialism* (London: Oxford University Press, 1961), quote 40; Henry M. Hyndman, *The Historical Basis of Socialism in England* (London: Kegan, Paul, Trench, 1883); Hyndman, *The Record of an Adventurous Life* (London: Macmillan, 1911); Callahan, *Socialism in Britain Since 1884*, 17; Kendall, *The Revolutionary Movement*, 6–7; James D. Young, *Socialism and the English Working Class: A History of English Labour, 1883–1939* (Brighton: Harvester Wheatsheaf, 1989), 5–6; Norman Etherington, "Hyndman, the Social Democratic Federation and Imperialism," *Historical Studies* 16 (1974): 89–103.

81. "The Manifesto of the Socialist League," Signed by the Provisional Council at the Foundation of the League on 30 December 1884, and Adopted at the General Conference Held at Farringdon Hall, London, on July 5, 1885, A New Edition Annotated by William Morris and E. Belfort Bax (London: Socialist League Office, 1885); William Morris, *The Earthly Paradise* (1880; repr., New York: Routledge, 2002); Morris, *A Dream of John Ball; and, A King's Lesson* (London: Reeves and Turner, 1888); Morris, *Signs of Change; Seven Lectures Delivered on Various Occasions* (London: Reeves and Turner, 1888); Morris, *News from Nowhere, Or, An Epoch of Rest: Being Some Chapters from a Utopian Romance* (1890; repr., London: Routledge and Kegan Paul, 1970).

82. [Johnson], "To Our Readers," "there is a," 7; see H. H. Champion, "The Future of Socialism in England," and responding letters, *Common Sense* (September 15, 1887), 81–86.

83. Editor's Preface, *Fabian Essays in Socialism*, ed. George Bernard Shaw (London: W. Scot, 1889; repr., New York: Doubleday, 1967), "authoritative" and succeeding quotes, 6.

84. Edward R. Pease, *The History of the Fabian Society* (New York: E. P. Dutton, 1916), 4–10; Chushichi Tsuzuki, *Edward Carpenter, 1844–1929: Prophet of the Human Fellowship* (New York: Cambridge University Press, 1980).

85. Michael Holroyd, *Bernard Shaw*, 2 vols. (New York: Random House, 1988), 1: 28–55; Pease, *History of the Fabian Society*, 12–27; A. M. McBriar, *Fabian Socialism and English Politics, 1884–1918* (Cambridge: Cambridge University Press, 1966), 8–13; Margaret Cole, *The Story of Fabian Socialism* (Stanford: Stanford University Press, 1961); 3–25; Beatrice Webb, *The Diary of Beatrice Webb*, 4 vols., vol. 1, 1873–1892: *Glitter Around and Darkness Within*, ed. Norman and Jeanne MacKenzie (Cambridge: Harvard University Press, 1982), 1: 321–371.

86. G. Bernard Shaw, "The Basis of Socialism: 1. Economic," in *Fabian Essays in Socialism*, 15–45, "for since," 16.

87. Sidney Webb, "The Basis of Socialism: 2. Historic," in *Fabian Essays in Socialism*, 46–83, "a wave," 48; Hyndman, *The Historical Basis of Socialism*, 305; Sidney and Beatrice Webb, *Soviet Communism: A New Civilization?* (New York: Scribner's, 1935). The second and third editions of 1941 and 1944 dropped the question mark.

88. Webb, "The Basis of Socialism: 2. Historic," "slow," 51, "freaks," 83; John Stuart Mill, *Principles of Political Economy*, 2 vols. (1848; 7th ed., London: Longmans, Green, Reader, and Dyer, 1871).

89. Webb, "The Basis of Socialism: 2. Historic," "every shred" and "covered," 63; "Murdstones," 64; Jeremy Bentham, *An Introduction to the Principles of Morals and Legislation* (1789; repr., New York: Hafner, 1948); William Paley, *Natural Theology: or, Evidences of the Existence and Attributes of the Deity; Collected from the Appearances of Nature* (Philadelphia: John Morgan, 1802).

90. Webb, "The Basis of Socialism: 2. Historic," "local," 65; "the post office," 66.

91. Ibid., "such," 69.

92. Ibid., 63, 83, "we must," 79–80.

93. George Bernard Shaw, *Report on Fabian Policy and Resolutions* (London: Fabian Society, 1896), "on war," 3; Stewart Headlam, "The Sins That Cause Poverty," *Christian Socialist* 10 (March 1884), 149; Pease, *History of the Fabian Society*, 168; Orens, *Stewart Headlam's Radical Anglicanism*, 54.

94. Stewart Headlam, *The Guild of Saint Matthew: An Appeal to Churchmen* (London: Officers of the Guild of Saint Matthew, 1890), 1–2; Bettany, *Stewart Headlam*, "while showing," 143–144; Pease, *History of the Fabian Society*, 168.

95. Bettany, *Stewart Headlam*, 66–68; Orens, *Stewart Headlam's Radical Anglicanism*, 66–71; Frederick Temple, "The Education of the World," in *Essays and Reviews: The 1860 Text and Its Reading*, 137–164; Stewart Headlam, "Address to the Christian Socialist Society," *Christian Socialist* (February 1887), 29–30.

96. George, *Progress and Poverty*, "would ere," 469; "it is," 549; Stewart Headlam, *Fabianism and Land Values* (London: English League for the Taxation of Land Values, n.d.); Headlam, *The Socialist's Church* (London: George Allen, 1907), 60–62.

97. Stewart Headlam, "Christian Socialism, Fabian Tract No. 42" (London: Fabian Society, November 1892), "the righteous" and "secular," 2; "a monstrous" and "if you," 3.

98. Ibid., "so far as," 4; "if again," 6.

99. Ibid., "he deliberately" and "beautiful," 6; "doing on," 6–7; "tells you" and "but it," 7.

100. Ibid., quotes, 9.

101. Ibid., "to seize," 9.

102. Ibid., "we school," 10; "morality is," 13.

103. Ibid., quotes, 15.

104. Stewart Headlam, "Feeble Fabians," *Church Reformer* 12 (November 1893), "to advocate," 244–245; R. C. Robertson, "Our Aims and Objects," *The Miner* (January 1887), 2–3; Editorial, "Progress," *The Miner* (January 1887), 9; David Howell, *British Workers and the Independent Labour Party, 1888–1906* (Manchester: Manchester University Press, 1984), 447–490; Henry Pelling, *The Origins of the Labour Party* (London: Macmillan, 1954); Jones, *The Christian Socialist Revival*, 138–142.

105. Stewart Headlam, Editorial, *Church Reformer* 14 (May 1895), "to form," 99–100; Headlam, *The Guild of Saint Matthew: What It Is and Who Should Join It* (London: Officers of the Guild of Saint Matthew, 1895), 1–2; Jones, *The Christian Socialist Revival*, 143–144; James Keir Hardie, *From Serfdom to Socialism* (London: G. Allen, 1907), 95–96.

106. Bettany, *Stewart Headlam*, 125–130; Jones, *The Christian Socialist Revival*, 145–148; Stewart Headlam, "Socialism, Liberty, and the Church," *Church Reformer* 14 (October 1895), 221–222.

107. Reckitt, *Maurice to Temple*, "he had," 131; "Thomas Hancock," *Crockford's Clerical Dictionary* (Oxford: Oxford University Press, 1886, 1894), 514, 578; Jones, *The Christian Socialist Revival*, 107–108.

108. Thomas Hancock, "The Hymn of the Universal Social Revolution," *Church Reformer* (November 1886), 244–246; Hancock, "The Capitalist–Liberationist Press," *Church Reformer* (June 1885), 125–126; Hancock, "The Social Carcase and the Anti-Social Vultures," in Binyon, *The Christian Socialist Movement in England*, 131; Jones, *The Christian Socialist Revival*, 109–111.

109. H. C. Shuttleworth, *The English Church and the New Democracy* (London: Elliot Stock, 1885); Shuttleworth, *The Place of Music in Public Worship* (London: Elliot Stock, 1893); Shuttleworth, "The Parson, the Play, and the Ballet," *Universal Review* 1 (June 1888): 248–264; G. Bernard Shaw, *Plays Pleasant* (London: Penguin, 1946), "what he likes," 95; Reckitt, *Maurice to Temple*, 123.

110. [W. H. P. Campbell], editorial, *Christian Socialist* 5 (July 1887), 107; editorial, *Christian Socialist* (August 1887), 118–119; E. D. Girdlestone, "The What and Why of Christian Socialism," *Christian Socialist* 7 (September 1889), 133–135; [Stewart Headlam], editorial, *Church Reformer* (June 1887), 121–122; Orens, *Stewart Headlam's Radical Anglicanism*, 86–87; Jones, *The Christian Socialist Revival*, 318–319.

111. Thomas Hancock, *The Banner of Christ in the Hands of the Socialists* (London: Foulger, 1887), 3–10.

112. Shaw, *Plays Pleasant*, "religion," 8; Orens, *Stewart Headlam's Radical Anglicanism*, 95–96; Reckitt, *Maurice to Temple*, 134.

113. Edward Benson, *Christ and His Times: Addressed to the Diocese of Canterbury in His Second Visitation* (London: Macmillan, 1889), "there is," 58; "some," 79; A. C. Benson, *The Life of Edward White Benson*, 2 vols. (London: Macmillan, 1899).

114. *Lux Mundi: A Series of Studies in the Religion of the Incarnation*, ed. Charles Gore (1889; 5th ed., New York: John W. Lovell, n.d.). This section on *Lux Mundi* summarizes my discussion in Dorrien, *Kantian Reason and Hegelian Spirit*, 379–385.

115. G. L. Prestige, *The Life of Charles Gore, A Great Englishman* (London: Heinemann, 1935), 10–13; Charles Gore, Preface to *The Life and Work of John Richardson Illingworth*, ed. A. L. Illingworth (London: John Murray, 1917), xi; V. F. Storr, *The Development of English Theology in the Nineteenth Century* (London: Longmans, 1913), 429–430; James Carpenter, *Gore: A Study in Liberal Catholic Thought* (London: Faith Press, 1960), 27–29.

116. "Editor's Preface," *Lux Mundi*, quotes vii.

117. Ibid., ix.

118. T. H. Green, *Works of T. H. Green*, ed. R. L. Nettleship, 3 vols. (London: Longmans Green, 1885–1888); Green, *Prolegomena to Ethics*, ed. A. C. Bradley (Oxford: Clarendon, 1883).

119. S. C. Carpenter, *Church and People: 1789–1889* (London: SPCK, 1933), Holland quote, 482–483; C. C. J. Webb, *A Study of Religious Thought in England from 1850* (Oxford: Clarendon, 1933), 100–101.

120. J. R. Illingworth, "The Incarnation and Development," *Lux Mundi*, quotes 151; see Illingworth, *Personality, Human and Divine; the Bampton Lectures, 1894* (London: Macmillan, 1894); Illingworth, *Reason and Revelation: An Essay in Christian Apology* (London: Macmillan, 1906).

121. Illingworth, "The Incarnation and Development," quotes 153, 155, 156.

122. Ibid., quotes 162.

123. Ibid., quotes 167, 176.

124. Charles Gore, *The Reconstruction of Belief: Belief in God; Belief in Christ; The Holy Spirit and the Church*, 1-vol. ed. (New York: Scribner's, 1926), vii–viii; Carpenter, *Gore: A Study in Liberal Catholic Thought*, 23–30.

125. "I am profoundly" and "naturally" quotes, in Charles Gore, "The Nature of Faith and the Conditions of Its Exercise," printed privately by J. Parker, 1878, cited by Carpenter, *Gore: A Study in Liberal Catholic Thought*, 30; Gore, *The Reconstruction of Belief*, "I have," vi.

126. Charles Gore, "The Holy Spirit and Inspiration," *Lux Mundi*, 263–302, quotes 274, 294, 295; Heinrich Georg August Ewald, *The History of Israel*, 7 vols. (London: Longmans, Green, 1876–1888); Samuel R. Driver, *A Critical and Exegetical Commentary on Deuteronomy* (Edinburgh: T. and T. Clark, 1902); Driver, *Modern Research as Illustrating the Bible* (London: Henry Frowde, 1909).

127. Gore, "The Holy Spirit and Inspiration," quotes 271, 274.

128. Ibid., "a whole set," 282.

129. Ibid., quotes, 300, 301.

130. Ibid., 299.

131. Ibid., 301–302.

132. H. P. Liddon, *The Divinity of Our Lord and Savior Jesus Christ* (London: Rivingtons, 1867), 474; William Stubbs, *Ordination Addresses* (London: Longmans, 1901), 173–182; Arthur Michael Ramsey, *From Gore to Temple: The Development of Anglican Theology Between Lux Mundi and the Second World War, 1889–1930* (London: Longmans, Green, 1960), 7–8, 30–43; William Temple, *Christus Veritas* (London: Macmillan, 1924), 142; Charles Gore, *The Incarnation of the Son of God* (London: John Murray, 1891); Bernard M. G. Reardon, *Religious Thought in the Victorian Age* (London: Longman, 1995), 330–334; Henry Scott Holland to Bishop Copleston, October 1890, in *Henry Scott Holland: Memoir and Letters*, ed. Stephen Paget (New York: E. P. Dutton, 1921), 280.

133. Stewart Headlam, review of *Lux Mundi*, ed. Charles Gore, *Church Reformer* (June 1890), "Protestants," 128; Headlam, editorial, *Church Reformer* (November 1890), 245; Orens, *Stewart Headlam's Radical Anglicanism*, 104; Henry Scott Holland, "Faith," and W. J. H. Campion, "Christianity and Politics," in *Lux Mundi*, 3–44, 365–388.

134. On Gore's invocation of "liberal Catholicism," see Charles Gore, *The Basis of Anglican Fellowship in Faith and Organization* (London: Mowbray, 1914), 23; Gore,

Catholicism and Roman Catholicism (London: Mowbray, 1928), 47; Gore, *Dominant Ideals and Corrective Principles* (London: Mowbray, 1918), 93–94; Carpenter, *Gore: A Study in Liberal Catholic Thought*, 42–61.

135. Reckitt, *Maurice to Temple*, "we were," 120; "we woke," 121.

136. W. H. Fremantle, *The World as the Subject of Redemption* (London: Rivington, 1885; repr., London: Longmans, Green, 1895); Wilfrid Richmond, *Christian Economics* (London: Rivington, 1887); *Objects of the Christian Social Union* (London: Christian Social Union, 1889), pamphlet repr. in *Henry Scott Holland: Memoir and Letters*, 170; Binyon, *The Christian Socialist Movement in England*, 158; Arthur V. Woodworth, *Christian Socialism in England* (London: Sonnenschein, 1903), 140; Jones, *The Christian Socialist Revival*, 175–177.

137. *Objects of the Christian Social Union*, "ultimate" and "redemptive," 171; Henry Scott Holland, Preface to Wilfrid Richmond, *Economic Morals: Four Lectures* (London: W. H. Allen, 1890), "we live."

138. Stewart Headlam, *The Meaning of the Mass* (London: S. C. Brown, Langham, 1905), 7–12; "Program of the Christian Socialist Society," *Christian Socialist* (February 1, 1887), "public," 29; Orens, *Stewart Headlam's Radical Anglicanism*, 106; Reckitt, *Maurice to Temple*, 135.

139. Reckitt, *Maurice to Temple*, "here's," 138; Henry Scott Holland, *God's City and the Coming of the Kingdom* (London: Longmans, Green, 1894); Holland, "Is Socialism Christian?" *Commonwealth* 10 (November 1905): 329–332; Holland, *Memoir and Letters*, ed. Paget; Brook Foss Westcott, *Social Aspects of Christianity* (London: Macmillan, 1886); Westcott, *The Incarnation and Common Life* (London: Macmillan, 1893); Westcott, *Life and Letters of Brooke Foss Westcott*, 2 vols. (London: Macmillan, 1903).

140. Edgar Jepson, *Memories of an Edwardian and Neo-Georgian* (London: Richards, 1937), 16–17; Bettany, *Stewart Headlam*, 233–234; Orens, *Stewart Headlam's Radical Anglicanism*, 118–120.

141. Henry Scott Holland to Edward Talbot, September 1894, in *Henry Scott Holland: Memoir and Letters*, "partly," 204, "oppressively," 203; Reckitt, *Maurice to Temple*, "wage labour," 144.

142. Percy Dearmer, *The Beginnings of the Christian Social Union* (London: Commonwealth Press, 1912), 160–174; Dearmer, "The Christian Social Union," in *The Church and New Century Problems*, ed. W. J. Hocking (London: Wells, Gardner, Darton, 1901), 155–180; Jones, *The Christian Socialist Revival*, 182–186.

143. George Bernard Shaw, *Fabianism and Empire* (London: Grant Richards, 1900), "the fixed," 37; Beatrice Webb, *Our Partnership*, ed. Barbara Drake and Margaret I. Cole (New York: Longmans, Green, 1948), 131–132; Orens, *Stewart Headlam's Radical Anglicanism*, 126–127.

144. Sidney Webb, *Twentieth Century Politics: A Policy of National Efficiency* (London: Fabian Society, 1901), 3–18; H. G. Wells, *Experiment in Autobiography* (New York: Macmillan, 1934), 653–655.

145. Francis Galton, "Hereditary Talent and Character," *Macmillan's Magazine* 12 (1865), 157–166, 318–327; Galton, *Hereditary Genius: An Inquiry into its Laws and Consequences* (London: Macmillan, 1869); Galton, "Eugenics: Its Definition, Scope,

and Aims," *American Journal of Sociology* 10 (July 1904): 82–83; Mike Hawkins, *Social Darwinism in European and American Thought, 1860–1945: Nature as Model and Nature as Threat* (Cambridge: Cambridge University Press, 1997), 275–277; Michael Freeden, "Eugenics and Progressive Thought: A Study in Ideological Affinity," *Historical Journal* 22 (2009): 645–646.

146. Karl Pearson, *National Life from the Standpoint of Science* (London: Adam and Charles Black, 1901), 18–45, "my view," 43–44; "namely," 19–20; Sidney Webb, *The Decline in the Birth-Rate* (London: Fabian Society, 1907), "to the," 17; H. G. Wells, *A Modern Utopia* (London: Chapman and Hall, 1905), 141–143; Bernard Semmel, *Imperialism and Social Reform* (New York: Doubleday, 1968), 24–44; Raphael Patai and Jennifer Patai, *The Myth of the Jewish Race* (Detroit: Wayne State University Press, 1989), 146.

147. Margaret Cole, *The Story of Fabian Socialism*, 99; Stewart Headlam, *The Place of the Bible in Secular Education* (London: S. C. Brown, Langham, 1903), "grim" and "race," 25; Orens, *Stewart Headlam's Radical Anglicanism*, 128–130; Samuel Hynes, *The Edwardian Turn of Mind* (Princeton: Princeton University Press, 1968), 15–55.

148. Stewart Headlam, "Fabianism and Land Values" (October 1908), repr. as *Fabianism and Land Values* (London: English League for the Taxation of Land Values, n.d.), "from" and "the Fabian," 3–4; Conrad Noel, "The Church Socialist League," *Commonwealth* 11 (July 1906): 222–224; Noel, "What I Want to Get by My Vote: A Labour View," *Commonwealth* 11 (February 1906): 36–37; Noel, *An Autobiography*, ed. Sidney Dark (London: J. M. Dent, 1945).

149. Orens, *Stewart Headlam's Radical Anglicanism*, "Headlam never," 156.

150. Charles Gore, *The Incarnation of the Son of God* (London: John Murray, 1891), "its profound," 212; Gore, *The Reconstruction of Belief*, "why has it," 846; Gore, *The Social Doctrine of the Sermon on the Mount* (London: Percival, 1893); G. Prestige, *The Life of Charles Gore* (London: William Heinemann, 1935), 371–372.

151. Jones, *The Christian Socialist Revival*, "it was," 194; Donald MacKinnon, "Scott Holland and Contemporary Needs," in MacKinnon, *Borderlands of Theology and Other Essays*, ed. George W. Roberts and Donovan E. Schmucker (London: Lutterworth Press, 1968), 105–120, "he took," 116; *Henry Scott Holland: Memoir and Letters*, 174–175; Henry Scott Holland, "Is Socialism Christian?" *Commonwealth* 10 (November 1905): 329–332; Holland, "The Education Crisis," *Commonwealth* 7 (January 1902): 9–10; Holland, *Personal Studies* (London: Wells Gardner, Darton, 1895).

152. Henry Scott Holland to James Adderly, August 1895, in *Henry Scott Holland: Memoir and Letters*, quotes, 205.

153. Paul Kennedy, *The Rise and Fall of the Great Powers* (New York: Random House, 1987), 143–158; Niall Ferguson, *Empire: The Rise and Demise of the British World Order and the Lessons for Global Power* (New York: Basic Books, 2002); Adam Smith, *An Inquiry into the Nature and Causes of the Wealth of Nations* (1904 ed.; repr., Chicago: University of Chicago Press, 1976).

154. Richard Aldous, *The Lion and the Unicorn: Gladstone vs Disraeli* (New York: W. W. Norton, 2006), "climbed," 189; Christopher Hibbert, *Disraeli: A Personal History* (London: HarperCollins, 2004); Robert Blake, *Disraeli* (New York: St. Martin's Press, 1867).

155. W. E. B. Du Bois, "The African Roots of the War," *Atlantic Monthly* 115 (May 1915), 707–714, quotes 708; see Adam Hochschild, *King Leopold's Ghost: A Story of Greed, Terror, and Heroism in Colonial Africa* (Boston: Houghton Mifflin, 1998); Robert T. Edgerton, *The Troubled Heart of Africa* (New York: St. Martin's Press, 2002).

156. Du Bois, "The African Roots of the War," 708–709.

157. John A. Hobson and A. F. Mummery, *The Physiology of Industry: Being an Exposure of Certain Fallacies in Existing Theories of Economics* (London: John Murray, 1889); Hobson, *The Problem of the Unemployed: An Inquiry and an Economic Policy* (London: Methuen, 1896); Hobson, *The War in South Africa: Its Causes and Effects* (London: J. Nisbet, 1900); Jones, *The Christian Socialist Revival*, 199–200.

158. John A. Hobson, *Imperialism* (1902; repr., London: Allen and Unwin, 1948), quotes 35, 72.

159. Editorial [Charles H. Marson], "Unconsidered Trifles," *Christian Socialist* (September 1886), "stupid bullies" and "it is something," 36.

160. *Henry Scott Holland: Memoir and Letters*, "the War-party," "the savage," and "that we could fall," 215; Jones, *The Christian Socialist Revival*, "the worship," 203; Prestige, *The Life of Charles Gore*, 224–225.

161. Conrad Noel, *Socialism in Church History* (London: Frank Palmer, 1910), "a triumph," 238; Reckitt, *Maurice to Temple*, "made the rest," 147.

162. Charles Gore, *Christianity and Socialism*, CSU Pamphlet No. 24 (Oxford: Christian Social Union, 1908); repr. in Pan-Anglican Conference, *Official Proceedings* (London: SPCK, 1908), and Jones, *The Christian Socialist Revival*, quotes, 214–215.

163. *Henry Scott Holland: Memoir and Letters*, "horrible," 207; "my one," 312; Geoffrey Rowell, "Henry Scott Holland (1847–1918): Life and Context," *International Journal for the Study of the Christian Church* 15 (March 2015): 5.

3. GERMAN SOCIAL DEMOCRACY

1. W. H. Dawson, *German Socialism and Ferdinand Lassalle* (London: Swan Sonnenschein, 1891), 125–134; Eduard Bernstein, *Ferdinand Lassalle as a Social Reformer* (London: Swan Sonnenschein, 1893), 19–28; David Footman, *The Primrose Path: A Biography of Ferdinand Lassalle* (London: Cresset Press, 1994).

2. Franz Mehring, *Geschichte der deutschen Sozialdemokratie*, 5 vols. (Stuttgart: J. H. W. Dietz, 1919), 4: 35–54, 68–73; Mehring, *Zur Geschichte der deutschen Sozialdemokratie* (Magdeburg: Faber, 1877), 48–69; Eduard Bernstein, *Sozialdemokratische Lehrjahre* (Berlin: Bücherkreis, 1928), 15–24; August Bebel, *Aus meinem Leben*, 3 vols. (Stuttgart: J. H. W. Dietz, 1910–1914), 2: 308–329; *Handbuch der sozialdemokratischen Parteitage*, ed. Wilhelm Schröder (Munich: Birk, 1910), 458–469.

3. Karl Marx, "Critique of the Gotha Program: Marginal Notes to the Program of the German Workers' Party" (1875), in *On Revolution: The Karl Marx Library*, ed. and trans. Saul K. Padover (New York: McGraw-Hill, 1971), 488–506, "free state," "not even," "the present," and "civilized," 502. Other editions in *Karl Marx: Selected Writings*, ed. David McLellan (New York: Oxford University Press, 1977), 564–570; in *The Marx–Engels*

Reader, 2nd ed., ed. Robert C. Tucker (New York: W. W. Norton, 1978), 525–541; and in *Collected Works of Karl Marx and Friedrich Engels*, 50 vols., trans. Richard Dixon et al. (New York: International Publishers, 1975–2005), 24; Wilhelm Liebknecht, *Karl Marx, Biographical Memoirs*, trans. Ernest Untermann (Chicago: Charles H. Kerr, 1901), repr. in *Wilhelm Liebknecht and German Social Democracy: A Documentary History*, ed. William A. Pelz (Chicago: Haymarket Books, 2016), 93–94.

4. Mehring, *Zur Geschichte der deutschen Sozialdemokratie*, 55–58, 65–73; Mehring, *Geschichte der deutschen Sozialdemokratie*, 4: 5–12, 43–50; Bebel, *Aus meinem Leben*, 2: 311–316; *Handbuch der sozialdemokratischen Parteitage*, 463–469.

5. Karl Marx, *Capital: A Critique of Political Economy*, trans. from third German edition by Samuel Moore and Edward Aveling (Chicago: Charles H. Kerr, 1906), 1: 15–20, "they managed," 1: 20; "foreign," 1: 16. Marx completed essential portions of the second and third volumes before his death, but these volumes were completed and published by Engels. I use the Kerr edition of volume 1 out of longtime familiarity, and on occasion I will reference the same passages in the Penguin edition of volume 1 translated by Ben Fowkes, *Capital: A Critique of Political Economy*, vol. 1 (London: Penguin Books, 1990). For volumes 2 and 3 I will refer to the Penguin edition: *Capital*, vol. 2, trans. David Fernbach (London: Penguin Books, 1992), and *Capital*, vol. 3, trans. David Fernbach (London: Penguin Books, 1991).

6. Marx, *Capital*, 1: 24–25, "that mighty," "the demiurgos," and "the ideal," 1: 25. For the Penguin edition translated by Fowkes, see 1: 102–103.

7. Marx, *Capital*, 1: 25–26, "peevish" and "the rational," 1: 25; "is in its," 1: 26; Karl Marx, "Critique of Hegel's *Philosophy of Right*" (1843), in *Karl Marx: Early Texts*, trans. David McLellan (Oxford: Basil Blackwell, 1971), 61–72; Marx and Friedrich Engels, *The German Ideology* (1845), in *Karl Marx: Selected Writings*, 159–191.

8. Karl Marx, *A Contribution to the Critique of Political Economy* (1859), trans. S. W. Ryazanskaya (New York: International Publishers, 1999), 19–23, "to anticipate," "the real," and "on which arises," 20; "before all," 21.

9. Marx, *A Contribution to the Critique of Political Economy*, "natural relations" and "capital is," 213; Karl Marx, "Economic and Philosophical Manuscripts of 1844," in *Karl Marx: Selected Writings*, 75–112; Marx, *Grundrisse: Foundations of the Critique of Political Economy*, trans. Martin Nicolaus (London: Penguin Books, 1973), 83–111.

10. Friedrich Engels, review of *A Contribution to the Critique of Political Economy*, by Karl Marx, *Das Volk* 14 (Part 1: August 6, 1859), and *Das Volk* 16 (Part 2: August 20, 1859), appendix to *A Contribution to the Critique of Political Economy*, "the first," 222, and "anyone," 226–227.

11. David Ricardo, *On the Principles of Political Economy and Taxation: Works and Correspondence of David Ricardo*, ed. Piero Sraffa (Cambridge: Cambridge University Press, 1951), "depends on," 11; Marx, *Capital*, 1: 41–106.

12. Marx, *Capital*, 1: 80–83; "a very queer," 1: 81; "social things," "no connection," 1: 83.

13. Ibid., "the fantastic" and "this I call," 1: 83; "and this one," 1: 149.

14. Ibid., "strange," 1: 567; John Stuart Mill, *Principles of Political Economy*, 2 vols. (1848; 7th ed., London: Longmans, Green, Reader and Dyer, 1871), 1: 252–255.

15. Marx, *Capital*, 1: 567–590, "the materialization," 585; "habitually," 568; "phenome-nal," 588; "necessary" and "natural," 589; Adam Smith, *An Inquiry into the Nature and Causes of the Wealth of Nations* (1776), 2 vols. (Chicago: University of Chicago Press, 1976), 1: 450–473.

16. Marx, *Capital*, "this antagonism," 1: 533.

17. Marx, *Capital*, "vulgarizers," 1: 566; "imbecile," 568; Malthus, 675–676; "honest," 674; the Penguin Books translation by Fowkes is slightly less harsh, 1: 475–476; Thomas Malthus, *An Essay on the Principle of Population* (1798) (New York: Norton, 1976); Bernard de Mandeville, *The Fable of the Bees* (1714) (Harmondsworth: Penguin Books, 1970).

18. Marx, *Capital*, "first," "it is," and "by a few," 1: 837; "effrontery," 1: 701; "the despotism," 1: 702.

19. Marx, "Critique of the Gotha Program," "the proceeds" and "a fair," 493.

20. Ibid., "vulgar," 497; "ideological," 496.

21. Ibid., "the state" and "police-guarded," 503.

22. Ibid., "infinitely" and "the international," 498; "a certain," 500; "the social," "solution," and "Lasalle's imagination," 501; "equal elementary," 504.

23. Ibid., "freedom of," "should be," "awareness of," and "for all its," 505.

24. *Handbuch der sozialdemokratischen Parteitage*, 125–129; Mehring, *Zur Geschichte der deutschen Sozialdemokratie*, 77–87; Wilhelm Liebknecht, "The Battlefield—Not the Reichstag—Is the Final Court of Judgment," in *Wilhelm Liebknecht and German Social Democracy*, 43–44; Liebknecht, "No Funds for the War of Annexation" (November 26, 1870), ibid., 466–67; Arthur Rosenberg, *The Birth of the German Republic* (London: Oxford University Press, 1931), 1–13; Peter Gay, *The Dilemma of Democratic Socialism* (New York: Columbia University Press, 1952), 12–13.

25. Bebel, *Aus meinem Leben*, 2: 318–324; Wilhelm Liebknecht, "A Soldier of the Revolution," in *Wilhelm Liebknecht and German Social Democracy*, 44–46, "I am not," 44; Liebknecht, "The Paris Commune Has a Right to Self-Defense," *Der Volkstaat* (May 31, 1871), in *Wilhelm Liebknecht and German Social Democracy*, 313–315; *Handbuch der sozialdemokratischen Parteitage*, 466–467; Bernstein, *Sozialdemokratische Lehrjahre*, 46–47; Gay, *The Dilemma of Democratic Socialism*, 22; Fritz Stern, *Gold and Iron: Bismarck, Bleichröder, and the Building of the German Empire* (New York: Vintage Books, 1979), 145–175; Paul Kampffmeyer, *Changes in the Theory and Tactics of the German Social Democracy* (Chicago: Charles Kerr, 1908), 28–44; Harry W. Laidler, *A History of Socialist Thought* (New York: Thomas Y. Crowell, 1936), 286–289.

26. Bebel, *Aus meinem Leben*, 1: 130–135; Liebknecht, "A Soldier of the Revolution," 44–45; Liebknecht, "Liebknecht's First Speech in the German Reichstag" (November 21, 1874), in *Wilhelm Liebknecht and German Social Democracy*, 48–50; Wilhelm Liebknecht, "Preface to the London Edition of 1889: On the Political Position of Social Democracy, Particularly with Regard to the Reichstag," in *Wilhelm Liebknecht and German Social Democracy*," 151–153. Liebknecht republished his speech of 1869, "On the Political Position of Social Democracy," to prove to "some incorrigible block-heads" that he had not changed his ideological position.

27. Heinrich Heffter, *Die deutsch Selbstverwaltung im 19. Jahrhundert: Geschichte der Ideen und Institutionen* (Stuttgart: K. F. Koehler, 1950); 654–656; James J. Sheehan, *German Liberalism in the Nineteenth Century* (Chicago: University of Chicago Press, 1978), 181–183.

28. Heinrich von Treitschke, *Der Sozialismus und seine Gönner* (Berlin: G. Reimer, 1875), 45; Treitschke, *Deutsche Geschichte im neunzehnten Jahrhundert* (Leipzig: Hirzel, 1879); Rudolf Haym, *Ausgewählter Briefwechsel Rudolf Hayms*, ed. H. Rosenbert (Osnabrück: Biblio Verlag, 1967), 301–302; Walter Gagel, *Die Wahlrechtsfrage in der Geschichte der deutschen liberalen Parteien 1848–1918* (Düsseldorf: Droste Verlag, 1958), 87–89; Sheehan, *German Liberalism in the Nineteenth Century*, 155; Karl Hardach, *Die Bedeutung wirtschaftlicher Faktoren bei der Wiedereinfürung der Eisen-und Getreidezölle in Deutschland 1879* (Berlin: Duncker und Humblot, 1967), 185–189.

29. Bebel, *Aus meinem Leben*, 2: 274–280; August Bebel, *Women Under Socialism* (New York: New York Labor News, 1904); Wilhelm Liebknecht, "Preface to the London Edition of 1889," 151–154; Albert S. Lindemann, *A History of European Socialism* (New Haven: Yale University Press, 1983), 136–137; Thomas Kirkup, *A History of Socialism* (London: Adam and Charles Black, 1892), 218–224.

30. Wilhelm Liebknecht, *Socialism*, pamphlet repr. in *Wilhelm Liebknecht and German Social Democracy*, 218–254, "the Social Democracy," 250; David Goldstein and Martha Avery, *Socialism* (Boston: Flynn, 1911), "it is our," 95; "Christianity is," 148.

31. Eduard Bernstein, *Aus den Jahren meines Exils* (Berlin: Friedrich Reiss, 1917), English ed., Bernstein, *My Years of Exile: Reminiscences of a Socialist* (London: L. Parsons, 1921), 65–137; Roger Fletcher, "The Life and Work of Eduard Bernstein," in *Bernstein to Brandt: A Short History of German Social Democracy*, ed. Roger Fletcher (London: Edward Arnold, 1987), 45–52. Bernstein read Eugen Dühring, *Kritische Geschichte der Nationalökonomie und des Sozialismus*, 4th ed. (Leipzig: Naumann, 1900).

32. Pope Leo XIII, *Rerum Novarum: The Condition of Labor* (1891), in *Catholic Social Thought: The Documentary Heritage*, ed. David J. O'Brien and Thomas A. Shannon (Maryknoll, NY: Orbis Books, 1992), 14–39; Wilhelm Emmanuel von Ketteler, *Die Arbeiterfrage und das Christenthum* (Mainz: Kirchheim, 1864); Ketteler, *Deutschland nach dem Kriege von 1866* (Mainz: Kirchheim, 1867); Ketteler, *The Social Teachings of Wilhelm Emmanuel von Ketteler*, trans. Rupert J. Ederer (Washington, DC: Catholic University Press, 1981), 8–36, 83–121; William Hogan, *The Development of Bishop Wilhelm Emmanuel von Ketteler's Interpretation of the Social Problem* (Washington, DC: Catholic University Press, 1946), 145–172.

33. W. H. Dawson, *Bismarck and State Socialism* (London: Swan Sonnenschein, 1891), 107–113; Gustav Schmoller, "Die Arbeiterfrage," *Preussische Jahrbücher* 14 (1864): 393–422; Schmoller, *Zur Geschichte des deutschen Kleingewerbes im 19. Jahrhundert* (Halle: Bucchandlung des Waisenhauses, 1870), 680–684; Schmoller, *Zwanzig Jahre deutscher Politik (1897–1917)* (Leipzig: Duncker und Humblot, 1920).

34. Agnes von Zahn-Harnack, *Adolf von Harnack*, 2nd ed. (Berlin: Walter de Gruyter, 1951); Martin Rumscheidt, "Harnack's Liberalism in Theology: A Struggle for the Freedom of Theology," in *Adolf von Harnack: Liberal Theology at Its Height*,

ed. Martin Rumscheidt (Minneapolis: Fortress Press, 1991), 9–41; Wilhelm Pauck, "Adolf von Harnack," in *A Handbook of Christian Theologians*, ed. Dean G. Peerman and Martin E. Marty (Cleveland: World Publishing, 1965), 86–111; Kurt Nowak et al., eds., *Adolf von Harnack: Christentum, Wissenschaft und Gesellschaft* (Göttingen: Vandenboeck und Ruprecht, 2003); Gary Dorrien, *Kantian Reason and Hegelian Spirit: The Idealistic Logic of Modern Theology* (Oxford: Wiley-Blackwell, 2015), 321.

35. Adolf Stöcker, "Die Bedeutung der christlichen Weltanschauung für die brennenden Fragen den Gegenwart," in Stöcker, *Christlich-sozial, Reden und Aufsätze* (Berlin: Weigandt und Grieben, 1890), "their god," 267; Stöcker, *Sozialdemokratie und Sozialmonarchie* (Leipzig: Verlag von Fr. Wilh. Grunow, 1891); Stöcker, *Predigten von Stöcker* (Berlin: Buchhandlung der Berliner Stadmission, 1890); Stöcker, *Das moderne Judenthum in Deutschland, besonders in Berlin: zwei Reden in der christlich-sozialen Arbeiterpartei* (Berlin: Weigandt und Grieben, 1880); Friedrich Naumann, *Jesus als Volkmann* (Göttingen: Vandenhoeck und Ruprecht, 1894); Naumann, *Briefe über Religion* (Berlin: Buchverlag Die Hilfe, 1903), 41–48; Vernard Eller, ed., *Thy Kingdom Come: A Blumhardt Reader* (Grand Rapids: Eerdmans, 1980); James Bentley, *Between Marx and Christ: The Dialogue in German-Speaking Europe, 1870–1970* (London: New Left Books, 1982), 18–22; Ronald Lee Massanari, "True or False Socialism: Adolf Stoecker's Critique of Marxism from a Christian Socialist Perspective," *Church History* 41 (December 1972): 487–496; Asaf Kedar, "National Socialism Before Nazism: Friedrich Naumann and Theodor Fritsch, 1890–1914" (Ph.D. diss., University of California, Berkeley, 2010), 47–52.

36. Adolf Harnack, "The Evangelical Social Mission in the Light of the History of the Church," paper delivered at the Evangelical Social Congress, Frankfurt, May 17, 1894, published in Harnack and Wilhelm Herrmann, *Essays on the Social Gospel*, trans. G. M. Craik (New York: G. P. Putnam's Sons, 1907), 3–91, quotes 77–78.

37. Ibid., 80–81, 81.

38. Ibid., 83.

39. Ibid., "serious," 83; Zahn-Harnack, *Adolf von Harnack*, "on the soil," 301; see Rumscheidt, "Harnack's Liberalism in Theology," 23.

40. Frederick Engels, *Anti-Dühring: Herr Eugen Dühring's Revolution in Science* (1878), trans. Emile Burns (New York: Progress Publishers, 1947), 37–39; Eugen Dühring, *Capital und Arbeit* (Berlin: Eichoff, 1865); Dühring, *Due Verkkleinerer Careys und die Krisis der Nationalökonomie* (Breslau: Eduard Trewendt, 1867); Dühring, *Sache, Leben und Feinde*, 2nd ed. (Leipzig: Naumann, 1903); Marx, *Grundrisse*, 883–893.

41. Frederick Engels, *Socialism: Utopian and Scientific* (1880), in *The Marx–Engels Reader*, 683–717, "superstition" and "nothing more," 684; also in Engels, *Socialism: Utopian and Scientific*, trans. Edward Aveling (New York: International Publishers, 2015), 31–75.

42. Engels, *Socialism: Utopian and Scientific*, 684–698; Dorrien, *Kantian Reason and Hegelian Spirit*, 38–47, 165–173.

43. Engels, *Socialism: Utopian and Scientific*, "a colossal," 698.

44. Marx, *Capital*, 1: 331–353; Engels, *Socialism: Utopian and Scientific*, 700–702.

45. Engels, *Socialism: Utopian and Scientific*, "flunkeyism" and "a capitalist machine," 711; "by a small," 710; "social anarchy," 712.

46. Ibid., "all class," 713.

47. Karl Marx and Jules Guesde, "The Programme of the Parti Ouvrier" (1880), https://www.marxists.org/archive/marx/works/1880, "revolutionary" and "what is"; Boris Nicolaievsky and Otto Maenchen-Helfin, *Karl Marx: Man and Fighter* (New York: Penguin, 1975), 403.

48. Karl Marx, *The Poverty of Philosophy*, in *Karl Marx: Selected Writings*, 195–218, "he wants," 212; also in Marx, *The Poverty of Philosophy* (New York: International Publishers, 1963), 23–120.

49. Jules Guesde, "The Secularization Yet to Be Done," *La Socialiste* (October 22, 1887), https://www.marxists.org/archive/guesde/1887; Guesde, "May Day and the Public Authorities," *La Socialiste* (April 22, 1891), https://www.marxists.org/archive/guesde/1891; Samuel Bernstein, "Jules Guesde, Pioneer of Marxism in France," *Science and Society* 4 (Winter 1940): 29–56; Lindemann, *A History of European Socialism*, 135–143; Laidler, *A History of Socialist Thought*, 353–360.

50. Frank Kitz, "The Paris Congress: A Delegate's Report," *Commonweal* 5 (August 10, 1889), "in a useless," 291; William Morris, "Impressions of the Paris Conference," *Commonweal* 5 (July 27, 1889), "were very," 234; James Joll, *The Second International, 1889–1914* (New York: Harper and Row, 1966), 30–55.

51. Karl Marx, "On the Jewish Question" (1843), in *Karl Marx: Selected Writings*, 39–62, "the secret," 58; Igor Krivoguz, *The Second International, 1889–1914* (Moscow: Progress Publishers, 1989), 44–47; "The Second International: Social Democracy, 1880–1920," www.marxists.org/history/international/social-democracy; Lindemann, *A History of European Socialism*, 149; Joll, *The Second International*, 56–76; Julius Braunthal, *History of the International*, 3 vols. (New York: Praeger, 1967–1980), vol. 1: *1864–1914*; Morris, "Impressions of the Paris Conference," 234.

52. *Protokoll des Parteitages der Sozialdemokratischen Partei Deutschlands: Abgehalten zu Erfurt vom 14. bis 20. Oktober 1891* (Berlin: German Social Democratic Party, 1890–1913), 3–6, "the German," 6; Wilhelm Liebknecht, "On the Erfurt Program of 1891," in *Wilhelm Liebknecht and German Social Democracy*, 279–295.

53. Karl Kautsky, *Das Erfurter Program* (1892), English ed., *The Class Struggle (Erfurt Program)* (1892), trans. William E. Bohn (Chicago: Charles H. Kerr, 1910), "stampede" and "the more unbearable," 217; *Handbuch der sozialdemokratischen Parteitage*, 470–471.

54. Dieter Groh, *Negative Integration und revolutionärer Attentismus: Die deutsche Sozialdemokratie am Vorabend des Ersten Weltkrieges* (Berlin: Propyläen, 1973).

55. Bernstein, *My Years of Exile*, 56–58, 73–77, "less repugnant," 58.

56. Ibid., 85–113; Eduard Bernstein, *Sozialdemokratische Lehrjahre* (Berlin: J. H. W. Dietz, 1978), 71–72; Walter Betulius, *Friedrich Salomon Vögelin 1837–1888: Sein Beitrag zum schweizerischen Geistesleben in der zweiten Hälfte des 19. Jahrhunderts* (Winterthur: P. G. Keller, 1956); Alexander Isler, *Prof. Dr. Salomon Vögelin: Lebensbild eines Schweizerischen Volksmannes* (Winterthur: Geschwister Ziegler, 1892).

57. Bernstein, *Sozialdemokratische Lehrjahre*, "it converted," 72; Mehring, *Geschichte der deutschen Sozialdemokratie*, 4: 119–120; Anonymous [Karl Flesch], "Rückblicke auf die sozialistische Bewegung in Deutschland," *Jahrbuch für Sozial wissenschaft und Sozialpolitik* 1 (1879): 75–96; Gay, *The Dilemma of Democratic Socialism*, 30.

58. Bebel, *Aus meinem Leben*, 3: 58–59; Bernstein, *My Years of Exile*, 139–47; Mehring, *Geschichte der deutschen Sozialdemokratie*, 4: 168–169; Gustav Mayer, *Friedrich Engels*, 2 vols. (The Hague: Martinus Nijhoff, 1934), 333–334.

59. "LEO" [Eduard Bernstein], "Show Your Colors!" *Sozialdemokrat* (April 13, 1882), in *Marxism and Social Democracy: The Revisionist Debate, 1896–1898*, ed. and trans. H. Tudor and J. M. Tudor (Cambridge: Cambridge University Press, 1988), 38–43; "LEO" [Bernstein], "Socialism and the State," *Sozialdemokrat* (December 20, 1883), ibid., 43–47; Mehring, *Gescichte der deutschen Sozialdemokratie*, 4: 267–268; *Handbuch der sozialdemokratischen Parteitage*, 533–534; Mayer, *Friedrich Engels*, 2: 360–364.

60. "LEO" [Eduard Bernstein], "Producers' Co-operatives with State Credit," *Sozialdemokrat* (June 26, 1884), in *Marxism and Social Democracy*, 47–50, "a resolute," 49; "would emasculate," 50; Bernstein, *My Years of Exile*, 161–175.

61. Bernstein, *My Years of Exile*, 181–190; Rachel Holmes, *Eleanor Marx: A Life* (New York: Bloomsbury Press, 2015).

62. Bernstein, *My Years of Exile*, 205–209, 220–222.

63. Ibid., 211–217, "the admirable," 211; "peculiar," 216; Eduard Bernstein, *Sozialismus und Demokratie in der grossen englischen Revolution*, 2nd ed. (Stuttgart: J. H. W. Dietz, 1908).

64. Eduard Bernstein, "Der neueste Vernichter des Sozialismus," *Neue Zeit* 11 (1893): 502–508, 534–539; Bernstein, "Der Strike als politisches Kampfmittel," *Neue Zeit* 12 (1894): 689–695; Bernstein, "Carlyle und die sozialpolitische Entwicklung Englands," *Neue Zeit* 9 (1891): 665–673, 693–701, 729–736.

65. Eduard Bernstein, "Die preussischen Landtagswahlen," *Neue Zeit* 11 (1893): 774–78; Bernstein, "Der neueste Vernichter des Sozialismus" ["The Latest Destroyer of Socialism"], *Neue Zeit* 11 (1893): 502–508, 534–539; Bernstein, "Der dritte Band des 'Kapital,'" *Neue Zeit* 13 (1894–95): 333–338, 364–461; Bernstein, "German Social Democracy and the Turkish Troubles," *Neue Zeit* 15 (1896), in *Marxism and Social Democracy*, 51–61; Ernest Belfort Bax, "Our German Fabian Convert; or Socialism According to Bernstein," *Justice* (November 7, 1896), in *Marxism and Social Democracy*, 61–65; Bernstein, "Amongst the Philistines: A Rejoinder to Belfort Bax," *Justice* (November 14, 1896), in *Marxism and Social Democracy*, 65–69; Bernstein, "Probleme des Sozialismus: 2. Eine Theorie der Gebiete und Grenzen des Kollektivismus," *Neue Zeit* 15 (1896): 204–213; Bernstein, "Probleme des Sozialismus: 3. Der gegenwärtige Stand der industriellen Entwicklung in Deutschland," *Neue Zeit* 15 (1896): 303–311; Bernstein, "Probleme des Sozialismus: 4. Die neuere Entwicklung der Agrarverhältinisse in England," *Neue Zeit* 15 (1897): 772–783; Gay, *The Dilemma of Democratic Socialism*, 172–173; Tudor and Tudor, Introduction to *Marxism and Social Democracy*, 8–9; Gerhard Himmelmann, "Die Rolle der Werttheorie in Bernsteins Konzept der politischen Oekonomie des Zozialismus," in *Bernstein und der demokratische Sozialismus*, ed. Horst Heimann and Thomas Meyer (Berlin: Dietz, 1978), 97; Thomas Meyer, *Bernsteins konstruktiver Sozialismus* (Berlin: Dietz, 1977), 122–125.

66. Eduard Bernstein to August Bebel, October 20, 1898, in *Marxism and Social Democracy*, 325.

67. Eduard Bernstein, "The Social and Political Significance of Space and Number," *Neue Zeit* 16 (April 14 and 21, 1897), in *Marxism and Social Democracy*, 83–97, "there will always," 88; "whether this," 96–97.

68. Eduard Bernstein, *Zur Geschichte und Theorie des Sozialismus* (Berlin: Edelheim, 1901), 167–286; H. M. Hyndman, "Die Orientfrage und das Makedonien Europas" *Vorwärts* 5 (May 1897); Ernest Belfort Bax, "Colonial Policy and Chauvinism," *Neue Zeit* 16 (December 21, 1897), in *Marxism and Social Democracy*, 140–149, "too much," 148; Bernstein, "The Struggle of Social Democracy and the Social Revolution: 1. Polemical Aspects," *Neue Zeit* 16 (January 5, 1898), in *Marxism and Social Democracy*, 149–159, "one of the main," 151; Bernstein, "The Struggle of Social Democracy and the Social Revolution: 2. The Theory of Collapse and Colonial Policy," *Neue Zeit* 16 (January 19, 1898), in *Marxism and Social Democracy*, 159–173, "I frankly admit," 168–169, "the general movement," 169; Meyer, *Bernsteins konstruktiver Sozialismus*, 121–129.

69. *Protokoll über die Verhandlungen des Parteitages der Sozialdemokratischen Partei Deutschlands* (1898), 88–106; Parvus, "Soziale Revolution und Kolonialpolitik," *Sächsische Arbeiter-Zeitung* (January 27, 1898); Franz Mehring, "Sozialistische Selbstkritik," *Leipziger Volkszeitung* (February 9, 1898); Mehring, "In Sachen Bernstein," *Leipziger Volkszeitung* (March 10, 1898); Belfort Bax, "Der Sozialismus eines gewöhnlichen Menschenkindes gegenüber dem Sozialismus des Herrn Bernstein," *Neue Zeit* 16 (1898): 824–829; Eduard Bernstein, "Probleme des Sozialismus: 2. Das realistische und das ideologische Moment im Sozialismus," *Neue Zeit* 16 (1898): 225–232, 388–395; *Marxism and Social Democracy*, 19–22, 229–243.

70. Rosa Luxemburg to Leo Jogiches, April 19, 1899, in *The Rosa Luxemburg Reader*, ed. Peter Hudis and Kevin B. Anderson (New York: Monthly Review Press, 2004), "I want," 382; Rosa Luxemburg, "Sozialreform oder Revolution?: 1. Die Methode," *Leipziger Volkszeitung* (September 21, 1898); Luxemburg, "Sozialreform oder Revolution?: 2. Anpassung des Kapitalismus," *Leipziger Volkszeitung* (September 22 and 23, 1898); *Protokoll über die Verhadlungen des Parteitages der Sozialdemokratischen Partei Deutschlands, September 22–28, 1901* (Berlin: SPD, 1901), "guest," 191; J. P. Nettl, *Rosa Luxemburg* (London: Oxford University Press, 1966), 12–29; Raya Dunayevskaya, *Rosa Luxemburg, Women's Liberation, and Marx's Philosophy of Revolution* (Urbana: University of Illinois Press, 1991), 19–28.

71. "The Party Conference at Stuttgart," *Marxism and Social Democracy*, 276–304, "the bogey," 282; "I know quite," 281.

72. Ibid., 293–304, "exceedingly foolish" and "the final," 304.

73. Eduard Bernstein, "Erklärung," *Vorwärts* (February 7, 1898); Bernstein, "Prolmeme des Sozialismus: 2. Das realistische und das ideologische Moment im Sozialismus," *Neue Zeit* 16 (1898): 225–232, 388–395; Bernstein, "Eroberung der politischen Macht," *Vorwärts* (October 13, 1898); Karl Kautsky to Eduard Bernstein, October 1898, "you have decided," "completely lost," and "try to achieve," in Gay, *The Dilemma of Democratic Socialism*, 67–68; August Bebel to Eduard Bernstein, October 16, 1898, in *Marxism and Social Democracy*, 319–328, "the high," 320; "I think" and "you see," 321.

74. Bernstein to Bebel, October 20, 1898, in *Marxism and Social Democracy*, 323–28, "practiced," 322; Karl Kautsky, *Bernstein und das sozialdemokratische Programm*

(Stuttgart: J. H. W. Dietz, 1899), "the first sensational," 1; Eduard Bernstein, *Evolutionary Socialism: A Criticism and Affirmation*, trans. Edith C. Harvey (New York: Huebsch, 1909).

75. Eduard Bernstein, *The Preconditions of Socialism* (1899), trans. Henry Tudor (Cambridge: Cambridge University Press, 1993), "slow propaganda," 3; Karl Marx and Friedrich Engels, *The Communist Manifesto*, 1872 ed., in *Collected Works of Karl Marx and Friedrich Engels*, 18: 96; Engels, Preface to *The Class Struggles in France*, 1895 ed., *Collected Works of Marx and Engels*, "slow propaganda," 22: 523.

76. Bernstein, *The Preconditions of Socialism*, "the constant" and "the variable," 9.

77. Ibid., "nothing but," 14.

78. Ibid., "never completely," 32; Meyer, *Bernstein's konstruktiver Sozialismus*, 114–120.

79. Bernstein, *The Preconditions of Socialism*, "passing mood," 40; Marx and Engels, "Circular to the Communist League" (March 1850), in *Collected Works of Karl Marx and Friedrich Engels*, 10: 281.

80. Bernstein, *The Preconditions of Socialism*, "must certainly," 44, and Friedrich Engels, Preface (1857) to *Revelations on the Communist Trial*, in Karl Marx and Friedrich Engels, *Selected Works*, 3 vols. (Moscow: Progress Publishers, 1958), 2: 353; Karl Marx, *The Class Struggles in France* (1850), in *Karl Marx: Selected Writings*, 286–297.

81. Bernstein, *The Preconditions of Socialism*, 37–48.

82. Eduard Bernstein, "Arbeitswert oder Nutzwert?" *Neue Zeit* 17 (1899): 548–549; Bernstein, *The Preconditions of Socialism*, 47–54; Marx, *Capital*, 3: 1037–1051; Alfred Marshall, *Principles of Economics*, 8th ed. (London: Macmillan, 1947), 92–101; Erika Rikli, *Der Revisionismus* (Zurich: Girsberger, 1936), 68–74.

83. Bernstein, *The Preconditions of Socialism*, 54–56; Friedrich Engels, Preface to the first German ed. (1884) of Marx, *The Poverty of Philosophy*, 11.

84. Bernstein, *The Preconditions of Socialism*, 56–63, "a feather," 62; Marx, *Capital*, 1: 619–633, 834–837.

85. Bernstein, *The Preconditions of Socialism*, 64–65; Marx, *Capital*, 3: 318–319.

86. Bernstein, *The Preconditions of Socialism*, 83–88; Marx, *Capital*, 3: 572, 164; Luxemburg, "Sozialreform oder Revolution?: 2. Anpassung des Kapitalismus."

87. Karl Marx, *The Eighteenth Brumaire of Louis Bonaparte* (1851), in *Karl Marx: Selected Writings*, 316–320; Marx, *Capital*, 3: 572; Bernstein, *The Preconditions of Socialism*, 110–136; Beatrice Potter (Webb), *The Co-operative Movement in Great Britain* (London: George Allen and Unwin, 1891).

88. Bernstein, *The Preconditions of Socialism*, 136–141, "absolutely," "as we understand," and "the more democracy," 141.

89. Ibid., "in our times," 142.

90. Ibid., "it is a," 142; "have often offended," 145.

91. Ibid., "class dictatorship," "social democracy," and "it does not," 146.

92. Ferdinand Lassalle, *The Workers' Program*, in Lassalle, *Gesamtwerke*, ed. K. F. Pfau, 10 vols. (Leipzig: Pfau, 1899–1909), "it does not," 2: 27; Bernstein, *The Preconditions of Socialism*, "it does not" and "than we are," 147; "the aim," 147–148.

93. Bernstein, *The Preconditions of Socialism*, "socialism will" and "in this sense," 150.

94. Ibid., "my esteem," 164; "is no reason," 165.

95. Ibid., "German Social," 169; "It is not," 169–170.

96. Ibid., "an exchange," 170.

97. Marx, *The Civil War in France*, in Marx and Engels, *Collected Works*, "they have no," 22: 335; Bernstein, *The Preconditions of Socialism*, "to pure," 193; "an indisputable" and "the fact that," 194; Georg V. Plekhanov, Open Letter to Karl Kautsky, "What Should We Thank Him For?" in G. Plekhanov, *Selected Philosophical Works*, 2 vols. (London: Lawrence and Wishart, 1976), 2: 341–342.

98. Bernstein, *The Preconditions of Socialism*, "why should," 200; Bernstein, *Zur Geschichte und Theorie des Sozialismus*, 261–283; Karl Vorländer, *Kant und Marx* (Tübingen: J. C. B. Mohr, 1911), 156–171.

99. Wilhelm Liebknecht, *No Compromise—No Political Trading*, 1899 pamphlet, trans. A. M. Simons and Marcus Hitch (Chicago: Charles H. Kerr, 1919), repr. in *Wilhelm Liebknecht and German Social Democracy*, 178–215, "sentimental," 197.

100. *Protokoll über die Verhandlungen des Parteitages der SPD, 1901*, 99, 186–187; Gay, *The Dilemma of Democratic Socialism*, 252–253.

101. Theodor Cassau, *Die Gewerkschaftsbewegung* (Halberstadt: Meyer, 1925), 28–32, 153–155; Carl Legien, "Die Neutralisierung der Gewerkschaften," *Sozialistische Monatshefte* 4 (1900): 369–376; Theodor Leipart, *Carl Legien* (Berlin: Verlag des Allgemeinen Deutschen Gewerkschaftsbundes, 1929), 28–37; Carl E. Schorske, *German Social Democracy, 1905–1917: The Development of the Great Schism* (Cambridge: Harvard University Press, 1983), 12–13.

102. Gay, *The Politics of Democratic Socialism*, 122–129; Eduard David, *Sozialismus und Landwirtschaft* (Berlin: Sozialistische Monatshefte, 1903); Paul Kampffmeyer, "Die Lebensarbeit Conrad Schmidts," *Sozialistische Monatshefte* 76 (1932): 897–904.

103. Karl Kautsky, "Autobiographical Sketch" (1899), *The Social Democrat* (December 1902), in www.marxists.org/archive/kautsky; Gary P. Steenson, *Karl Kautsky, 1854–1938: Marxism in the Classical Years* (Pittsburgh: University of Pittsburgh Press, 1978); Massimo L. Salvadori, *Karl Kautsky and the Socialist Revolution, 1880–1938*, trans. Jon Rothschild (London: New Left Books, 1979); Paul Blackledge, "Karl Kautsky and Marxist Historiography," *Science and Society* 70 (July 2006): 338–339.

104. Luxemburg, *Sozialreform oder Revolution?*; English ed., *Reform or Revolution and Other Writings*, ed. Paul Buhle (Mineola, NY: Dover, 2006), 47–73, "a progressive" and "the real material," 160; "rigorously," 161; also in *The Rosa Luxemburg Reader*, 128–167.

105. Luxemburg, *Reform or Revolution*, "he began," 66; "a general," 67; "all the nice," 70.

106. Rosa Luxemburg to Leo Jogiches, May 1, 1899, in *The Rosa Luxemburg Reader*, "I am," 384, and in *The Letters of Rosa Luxemburg*, ed. Georg Adler, Peter Hudis, and Annelies Laschitza (London: Verso, 2011), 116–119, "I am," 118; Luxemburg, *Reform or Revolution*, "its feebleness," 72; "what," 72–73; "for only," 73.

107. Karl Kautsky, *Bernstein und das sozialdemokratische Programm* (Stuttgart: J. H. W. Dietz, 1899), 52–69, 111–128; English selections in *Karl Kautsky: Selected Political Writings*, trans. Patrick Goode (London: Macmillan, 1983), "The Revisionist Controversy," 16–19.

108. Kautsky, "The Revisionist Controversy," "for some years," 27–28; "his emphasis," 28; Karl Kautsky, "Bernstein's Old Articles and New Afflictions," *Justice* (July 20, 1901), www.marxists.org/kautsky/1901.

109. Kautsky, "The Revisionist Controversy," "they detest," 22; "proletarian," "what actually," and "that it is," 23; Karl Kautsky, "Bernstein über die Werttheorie und die Klassen," *Neue Zeit* 17 (1899): 68–81; Kautsky, "The Two Tendencies," *International Socialist Review* 3 (July 1902), www.marxists.org/kautsky/1902; Kautsky, "To What Extent Is the Communist Manifesto Obsolete?" *Social Democrat* 9 (1905): 155–164.

110. Karl Kautsky, *The Social Revolution*, trans. A. M. and May Wood Simons (Chicago: Charles H. Kerr, 1902), 65–73, "it is an attractive," 66; Kautsky, "The Revisionist Controversy," "both currents," 31; "the consummation," 30.

111. V. Lenin, *What Is to Be Done?* (1902) (New York: International Publishers, 1929), repr. in *Essential Works of Lenin*, ed. Henry M. Christman (New York: Bantam Books, 1966), "profoundly true," 81; "for humanity" and "to belittle," 82; Lenin, *The State and Revolution* (1917), in *Lenin: Selected Works* (New York: International Publishers, 1980), 339–340.

112. Jan Rehmann, *Theories of Ideology: The Powers of Alienation and Subjection* (Leiden: Brill, 2013), 64–66, 130–131.

113. Karl Kautsky, *Ethik und materialistische Geschichtsauffasung* (Stuttgart: J. H. W. Dietz, 1906), 127–144, in Kautsky, *Selected Political Writings*, 32–45, "but he is," 43.

114. Paul Frölich, *Rosa Luxemburg: Her Life and Work*, trans. Edward Fitzgerald (New York: Monthly Review Press, 1972), "determined," 216–217; Rosa Luxemburg, "Leninism or Marxism?" (1904), in Luxemburg, *Reform or Revolution*, 77–97, "pitiless," 79; "1. The blind," 82.

115. Luxemburg, "Leninism or Marxism?" "a regime," 83; "the ultra-centralism," 87; "military" and "a kind of," 88; Lenin, *What Is to Be Done?* 54–67.

116. Luxemburg, "Leninism or Marxism?" "it is by," 92.

117. Ibid., "despotic" and "as is," 92; "soon to" and "nothing will," 93.

118. Rosa Luxemburg, "The Mass Strike, the Political Party, and the Trade Union" (1906), trans. Patrick Lavan, in Luxemburg, *Reform or Revolution*, 101–180, "a grandiose," 103; "the most powerful," 105; same English translation in *The Rosa Luxemburg Reader*, 168–199; Dunayevskaya, *Rosa Luxemburg, Women's Liberation, and Marx's Philosophy of Liberation*, 91–93.

119. Luxemburg, "The Mass Strike, the Political Party, and the Trade Union," 134–152; Schorske, *German Social Democracy*, 36–58.

120. Steenson, *Karl Kautsky*, "tact and," 134; Nettl, *Rosa Luxemburg*, "heavy, dull," 255; Rosa Luxemburg, "Address to the Fifth Congress of the Russian Social-democratic Labor Party" (May 1907), in *The Rosa Luxemburg Reader*, 200–207, "in a stormy," 204; "without the slightest," 205; "a treacherous," 203; "the Russian," 207.

121. Rosa Luxemburg to Clara Zetkin, March 20, 1907, in *The Rosa Luxemburg Reader*, "I feel," 385; "because they," 386; Luxemburg to Konstantin Zetkin, September 24, 1907, *Letters of Rosa Luxemburg*, "complains to," 245; Luxemburg to Konstantin Zetkin, June 27, 1908, "Soon I," *The Rosa Luxemburg Reader*, 13.

122. Karl Kautsky, *The Road to Power* (Chicago: Bloch, 1909), "the power," 13; "I can say," 24; "we are," 47; "the growth," 29; "it is no," 47–48.

123. Ibid., "to be sure" and "the people," 112; "any natural," 113.

124. V. Lenin, "Dead Chauvinism and Living Socialism," *Collected Works* (London: International Publishers, 1964), 21: 94; Karl Kautsky, "Was nun?" *Neue Zeit* 38 (March 1910): 33–40, 68–80, English selections in Kautsky, *Selected Political Writings*, "not go," 56; "the conception," 60; Kautsky, "Das Neuestrategie," *Neue Zeit* 38 (June 1910): 332–341, 364–374.

125. Rosa Luxemburg, "Theory and Practice" (1910), in *The Rosa Luxemburg Reader*, 208–231, "Comrade Kautsky," 215; "these Russian," 217.

126. Karl Kautsky, "Der neue Liberalismus und der neue Mittelstand," *Vorwärts* (February 25, 1912); Schorske, *German Social Democracy*, 226–235.

127. Lindemann, *A History of European Socialism*, 181–182; Schorske, *German Social Democracy*, 224–256; Nettl, *Rosa Luxemburg*, 433.

128. Rosa Luxemburg, *The Accumulation of Capital* (1913), trans. Agnes Schwarzschild (New York: Monthly Review Press, 1968), "capitalism needs," 368; V. I. Lenin, "The International Socialist Congress in Stuttgart," *Proletary* 17 (October 20, 1907), "the chief," in Lenin, *Collected Works* (Moscow: Progress Publishers, 1972), 13: 75–81; E. Belfort Bax, "The International Congress and Colonial Policy," *Justice* (September 14, 1907), 3; J. C. Kennedy, "The Stuttgart Congress," *Journal of Political Economy* 15 (October 1907): 489–491. The German government expelled Quelch before the congress ended.

129. Karl Kautsky, "Der Imperialismus: Akkumulation und Imperialismus," *Neue Zeit* 32 (October 1914): 908–922, in Kautsky, *Selected Political Writings*, 82–89, "it is not," 88.

130. Eduard Bernstein, *Die englische Gefahr und das deutsche Volk* (Berlin: Vorwärts, 1911), 26–49; Fletcher, "The Life and Work of Eduard Bernstein," 46–48; Susanne Miller, "Bernstein's Political Position, 1914–1920," *Bernstein to Brandt*, 96–97.

131. Carl Grünberg, *Die Internationale und der Weltkrieg*, 2 vols. (Leipzig: Hirschfeld, 1916), "the class-conscious," 1: 51; Schorske, *German Social Democracy*, 286; Gay, *The Dilemma of Democratic Socialism*, 274; Edwyn Bevan, *German Social Democracy During the War* (London: G. Allen and Unwin, 1918), 8–9.

132. Paul Lensch, *Die deutsche Sozialdemokratie und der Weltkrieg* (Berlin: Vorwärts, 1915), 18–31; Schorske, *German Social Democracy*, 288; Gerald Feldman, *Army, Industry, and Labor in Germany, 1914–1918* (Princeton: Princeton University Press, 1968), 12–24; Lindemann, *A History of European Socialism*, 186–189; Evelyn Anderson, *Hammer or Anvil: The Story of the German Working Class Movement* (London: V. Gollancz, 1945), 19–25; William Maehl, "The Triumph of Nationalism in the German Socialist Party on the Eve of the First World War," *Journal of Modern History* 24 (1952): 40.

133. Eduard Bernstein, Karl Kautsky, and Hugo Haase, *The Demand of the Hour* (1915), in *Geschichte der U.S.P.D.*, 2nd ed., ed. Eugen Prager (Berlin: Verlag Freiheit, 1922), 72–74; Karl Liebknecht, *Klassenkampf gegen den Krieg* (Berlin: A. Hoffmans Verlag, 1919); Liebknecht, *Reden und Aufsätze*, ed. Julian Gumpers (Hamburg: Verlag der Kommunistischen Internationale Auslieferungsstelle für Deutschland, 1921);

Miller, "Bernstein's Political Position, 1914–1920," 98–99; Schorske, *German Social Democracy*, 301–302.

134. Gay, *The Dilemma of Democratic Socialism*, 284–285; Bevan, *German Social Democracy During the War*, 56–83; Schorske, *German Social Democracy*, 309–316; *Die Arbeiterschaft im neuen Deutschland*, ed. Friedrich Thimme and Carl Legien (Leipzig: Hirzel, 1915).

135. V. I. Lenin to A. G. Shlyapnikov, October 17, 1914, *Collected Works of Lenin*, "how dangerous" and "more harmful," 35: 161–162; Lenin, *Imperialism, The Highest Stage of Capitalism* (1916), in *Essential Works of Lenin*, 178–270; and *Lenin: Selected Works*, 171–263; Lindemann, *A History of European Socialism*, 192.

136. Lenin, *Imperialism, The Highest Stage of Capitalism*, in *Essential Works of Lenin*, 236–265, "utterly," 239.

137. Ibid., "a most," 261; "we have nothing," 256; "has nothing," 260; "Kautsky obscures," 264; Rudolf Hilferding, *Finance Capital: A Study of the Latest Phase of Capitalist Development*, ed. Tom Bottomore, trans. Morris Watnick and Sam Gordon (1910; English ed., London: Routledge, 2005).

138. "Junius" [Rosa Luxemburg], "The Junius Pamphlet: The Crisis in German Social Democracy" (1916), in *The Rosa Luxemburg Reader*, 312–341, "the show" and "shamed," 313; "jewel," "almost," and "the mightiest," 315.

139. Ibid., "our readiness," 320; "to the fate," 327.

140. Ibid., "they stuck" and "stood," 331; "imperialism," 336; "this madness," 341.

141. Eduard Bernstein, *Die deutsche Revolution* (Berlin: Gesellschaft und Erziehung, 1921), 126–157; A. Joseph Berlau, *The German Social Democratic Party, 1914–1921* (New York: Columbia University Press, 1950), 251–263; Gay, *The Dilemma of Democratic Socialism*, 288–289; Bertram D. Wolfe, *Three Who Made a Revolution* (New York: Stein and Day, 1984), 620–637; Leopold Haimson, *The Russian Marxists and the Origins of Bolshevism* (Cambridge: Harvard University Press, 1955), 87–111; Mikhail Heller and Aleksandr M. Nekrich, *Utopia in Power: The History of the Soviet Union from 1917 to the Present*, trans. Phyllis B. Carlos (New York: Summit Books, 1986), 50–110.

142. Bernstein, *Die deutsche Revolution*, 126–157; Berlau, *The German Social Democratic Party, 1914–1921*, 251–263; Gay, *The Dilemma of Democratic Socialism*, 288–289; Rosa Luxemburg, "Our Program and the Political Situation" (1918), *The Rosa Luxemburg Reader*, 357–378.

143. Rosa Luxemburg to Emanuel and Mathilde Wurm, December 28, 1916, *The Rosa Luxemburg Reader*, "the whole," 386; *"you* people," "the adorable," and "a creepy," 387; "Being a" and "the world," 388, and in *The Letters of Rosa Luxemburg*, 362–364; Luxemburg to Emanuel and Mathilde Wurm, February 16, 1917, "parliamentary," *The Rosa Luxemburg Reader*, 388, and *The Letters of Rosa Luxemburg*, 373–377.

144. Rosa Luxemburg to Sophie Liebknecht, mid-December 1917, in *The Rosa Luxemburg Reader*, "I am," 392; "I believe," 393; "Never mind," 395.

145. Rosa Luxemburg, "The Russian Revolution" (September 1918), in *The Rosa Luxemburg Reader*, 281–310, "parliamentary" and "that is," 289; "a dictatorship," 290.

146. Ibid., "but this," 308; "I have," 310.

147. Rosa Luxemburg, "The Beginning," *Die Rote Fahne* (November 18, 1918), in *The Rosa Luxemburg Reader*, 343–345, "this is," 343; Luxemburg, "The Socialization of Society," *Die Junge Garde* (December 1918), in *The Rosa Luxemburg Reader*, 346–348, "with lazy," 348.

148. Rosa Luxemburg, "What Does the Spartacus League Want?" *Die Rote Fahne* (December 14, 1918), in *The Rosa Luxemburg Reader*, 349–357, "acquire" and "can make," 351; "for the highest," 357.

149. Rosa Luxemburg, "Our Program and the Political Situation" (December 31, 1918), *The Rosa Luxemburg Reader*, 357–373, "the Preface," 362.

150. Ibid., "anarchism" and "the henchmen," 363; "for us," 365.

151. Rosa Luxemburg, "Order Reigns in Berlin," *Die Rote Fahne* (January 14, 1919), in *The Rosa Luxemburg Reader*, 373–378, "the political," 375; "you stupid," 378.

152. Bernstein, *My Years of Exile*, "true son" and "unbounded," 116; "the interest," 117; Bernstein, *Die deutsche Revolution*, 143–145, 158–160; Miller, "Bernstein's Political Position, 1914–1920," 99.

153. Philipp Scheidemann, "Bericht über den 9. November 1918," Deutsches Historisches Museum, https://web.archive.org/web/20140712054628/http://www.dhm.de/lemo/html/dokumente/scheidemann; *Biographisches Lexikon des Sozialismus: Verstorbene Persönlichkeiten*, ed. Franz Osterroth (Hannover: J. H. W. Dietz, 1960), 1: 262–263; Detlef Lehnert, "The SPD in German Politics and Society, 1919–1929," in *Bernstein to Brandt: A Short History of German Social Democracy*, ed. Roger Fletcher (London: Edward Arnold, 1987), 115–116.

154. Gay, *The Dilemma of Democratic Socialism*, 291–292, "our vote," 291; *Protokoll über die Verhandlungen der SPD*, 1919, 241; Berlau, *The German Social Democratic Party*, 285–318.

155. P. Broue, *The German Revolution, 1917–1923* (Chicago: Haymarket Books, 2006), 435–445; Lehnert, "The SPD in German Politics and Society, 1919–1929," 117–121; Heinrich August Winkler, "Eduard Bernstein as Critic of Weimar Social Democracy," *Bernstein to Brandt*, 174–176; Dieter Nohlen and Philip Stöver, *Elections in Europe: A Data Handbook* (Baden-Baden: Nomos, 2010), 762.

156. W. Smaldone, *Rudolf Hilferding: The Tragedy of a German Social Democrat* (DeKalb: Northern Illinois University Press, 1998), 32–44; E. P. Wagner, *Rudolf Hilferding: Theory and Politics of Democratic Socialism* (Atlantic Highlands, NJ: Humanities Press, 1996); Richard Evans, *The Coming of the Third Reich* (New York: Penguin, 2003), 106–110.

157. Eduard Bernstein, *Der Sozialismus einst und jetzt* (Stuttgart: J. H. W. Dietz, 1922), 113–125; *Verhandlungen des Reichstages* (March 3, 1921–March 19, 1921), 3094–3097, in Gay, *The Dilemma of Democratic Socialism*, 292; Eric D. Weitz, *Creating German Communism, 1890–1990* (Princeton: Princeton University Press, 1997).

158. Peter Fritzsche, "Did Weimar Fail?" *Journal of Modern History* 68 (1996): 629–656; Lehnert, "The SPD in German Politics and Society, 1919–1929," 120–121; Heinrich August Winkler, "Eduard Bernstein as Critic of Weimar Social Democracy," *Bernstein to Brandt*, 167–178; Ian Kershaw, *Weimar: Why Did German Democracy Fail?* (London: Weidenfeld and Nicolson, 1990), 29–34.

159. D. Evans and J. Jenkins, *Years of Weimar and the Third Reich* (London: Hodder and Stoughton, 1999), 82–89; Winkler, "Eduard Bernstein as Critic of Weimar Social Democracy," 177–178; Lehnert, "The SPD in German Politics and Society, 1919–1929), 122; M. Broszat, *Hitler and the Collapse of Weimar Germany* (Oxford: Berg Publishers, 1987), 43–47.

160. Gay, *The Dilemma of Democratic Socialism*, "helpful to," 295; Winkler, "Eduard Bernstein as Critic of Weimar Social Democracy," 178.

161. Eduard Bernstein to Karl Kautsky, July 26, 1924, and Bernstein to Kautsky, April 4, 1926, in Fletcher, "The Life and Work of Eduard Bernstein," 47, 52; Bernstein to Kautsky, January 23, 1932, in Gay, *The Dilemma of Democratic Socialism*, 295.

162. Sidney Hook, Introduction to Schocken Books edition of Bernstein, *Evolutionary Socialism: A Criticism and Affirmation*, trans. Edith C. Harvey (New York: Schocken Books, 1971), xvi; Tudor and Tudor, Introduction to *Marxism and Social Democracy*, "two incommensurate," 37.

163. Sidney Hook, *Marxism and Beyond* (Totowa, NJ: Rowman and Littlefield, 1983), 96–102; Henry Tudor, Introduction to Bernstein, *The Preconditions of Socialism*, xxxv.

164. Eberhard Kolb, *Die Arbeiterräte in der deutschen Innenpolitik* (Düsseldorf: Droste, 1962), 401–405; Susanne Miller, *Die Bürde der Macht: Die deutsche Sozialdemokratie 1918–1920* (Düsseldorf: Droste, 1974), 287–292; Heinrich Potthoff, *Die Sozialdemokratie von den Anfängen bis 1945* (Bonn-Bad Godesberg: Verlag Neue Gesellschaft, 1974), 74–77; Potthoff, *Gewerkschaften und Politik zwischen Revolution und Inflation* (Düsseldorf: Droste, 1979).

165. Thomas Meyer, *Bernsteins konstruktiver Sozialismus: Eduard Bernsteins Beitrag zur Theorie des Sozialismus* (Berlin: Dietz, 1977); Pierre Angel, *Eduard Bernstein et l'évolution du socialisme allemand* (Paris: Didier, 1961); Bo Gustafsson, *Marxismus und Revisionismus: Eduard Bernsteins Kritik des Marxismus und ihre ideengeschichtlichen Voraussetzungen*, 2 vols. (Frankfurt: Europäische Verlagsanstalt, 1972); Fletcher, "The Life and Work of Eduard Bernstein," "a man," 52.

166. Friedrich Engels, *On the History of Early Christianity* (1894), in Karl Marx and Friedrich Engels, *On Religion* (Atlanta: Scholars' Press, 1993), 316–359, "notable" and "Christianity," 316; Karl Kautsky, *Foundations of Christianity* (1908) (London: Socialist Resistance, 2008), "the crucifixion," 210.

4. GERMANIC POLITICAL THEOLOGY

1. Gary Dorrien, *Kantian Reason and Hegelian Spirit: The Idealistic Logic of Modern Theology* (Oxford: Wiley-Blackwell, 2012), 316–366; Ernst Troeltsch, "Political Ethics and Christianity," 1904 Address to the Evangelical Social Congress, trans. James Luther Adams, in Troeltsch, *Religion in History* (Minneapolis: Fortress Press, 1989), 173–209; Adolf Harnack and Wilhelm Herrmann, *Essays on the Social Gospel*, trans. G. M. Craik (New York: G. P. Putnam's, 1907), 3–21; Ernst Christian Helmreich, *The German Churches Under Hitler: Background, Struggle, and Epilogue* (Detroit: Wayne State University Press, 1979), 34–37; Klaus Scholder, *The Churches and the Third Reich*, 2 vols. (Philadelphia: Fortress Press, 1988), 1: 6–15; George Rupp, *Culture-*

Protestantism: German Liberal Theology at the Turn of the Twentieth Century (Atlanta: Scholars' Press, 1986), 9–11.

2. Karl Barth, "Autobiographical Sketch for the Faculty Album of the Faculty of Evangelical Theology at Münster, 1927," in *Karl Barth–Rudolf Bultmann Letters, 1922–1966*, ed. and trans. Geoffrey W. Bromiley (Grand Rapids: Eerdmans, 1971), 151–157, "absorbed Herrmann," 153; Hans-Anton Drewes, "Die Auseinandersetzung mit Adolf von Harnack," in *Karl Barth in Deutschland (1921–1935)*, ed. Michael Beintker, Christian Link, and Michael Trowitzsch (Zurich: TVZ, 2005), 191; Eberhard Busch, *Karl Barth: His Life from Letters and Autobiographical Texts* (London: SCM Press, 1976), 9–10; Gary Dorrien, *The Barthian Revolt in Modern Theology* (Louisville: Westminster John Knox Press, 2000), 27–32.

3. Busch, *Karl Barth*, 43–44.

4. Karl Barth, *Predigten 1913*, ed. Nelly Barth and Gerhard Sauter (Zurich: TVZ, 1976), 67–68, 166–168, 213–220; Karl Barth and Eduard Thurneysen, *Suchet Gott, so werdet ihr legen!* (Bern: G. A. Baschlin, 1917); Barth, "Autobiographical Sketch for the Faculty Album of the Faculty of Evangelical Theology at Münster," 154–155; Wilhelm Herrmann, "Religion und Sozialdemokratie," *Gesammelte Aufsätze*, ed. F. W. Schmidt (Tübingen: J. C. B. Mohr, 1923), 463–489; Friedrich Naumann, *Briefe über Religion* (Berlin: Buchverlag der Hilfe, 1903), 41–48; Jochen Fahler, *Der Ausbruch des 1. Weltkrieges in Karl Barths Predigten, 1913–1915* (Bern: Peter Lang, 1979), 17–21; Bruce L. McCormack, *Karl Barth's Critically Realistic Dialectical Theology: Its Genesis and Development, 1909–1936* (Oxford: Clarendon Press, 1995), 92–107.

5. Eduard Buess and Markus Mattmüller, *Prophetischer Sozialismus: Blumhardt–Ragaz–Barth* (Freiburg: Exodus, 1986), 5–22; Hermann Kutter Jr., *Hermann Kutters Lebenswerk* (Zurich: EVZ-Verlag, 1965); Markus Mattmüller, *Leonhard Ragaz und der religiöse Sozialismus* (Zollikon: Evangelischer Verlag, 1957), 11–19; Andreas Lindt, *Leonhard Ragaz: Eine Studie zur Geschichte und Theologie des religiösen Sozialismus* (Zollikon: Evangelischer Verlag, 1957), 12–15; János Pásztor, "Hermann Kutter: Pioneer Social Theologian, 1863–1931," *Princeton Seminary Bulletin* (1972): 80–81.

6. *Thy Kingdom Come: A Blumhardt Reader*, ed. Vernard Eller (Grand Rapids: Eerdmans, 1980), "God is now," 3; "the kingdom," i; Christoph Blumhardt, *Action in Waiting* (Rifton, NY: Plough, 2012), 1–22, 129–135; Buess and Mattmüller, *Prophetischer Sozialismus*, 8–13.

7. Hermann Kutter, *They Must; or, God and the Social Democracy* (Chicago: Co-operative Printing, 1908), "they all," 110, American ed. of 1904 German ed., Kutter, *Sie Müssen! Ein offenes Wort an die christliche Gesellschaft* (Berlin: Hermann Walther Verlagsbuchhandlung, 1904); see Kutter, *Social Democracy: Does It Mean Darkness or Light?* (Letchworth, UK: Garden City Press, 1910).

8. Kutter, *They Must*, "an entirely" and "either by," 15.

9. Ibid., "fettered," "thus we had," and "unthinkable," 16.

10. Ibid., "sad and," 16.

11. Ibid., "the Evangelical Socials" and "from the very," 19.

12. Ibid., "the radicalism" and "the Spirit," 21.

13. Ibid., "the Bible is," 25.

14. Ibid., "the despised," 27; "Christianity has lived," 29; see Lindt, *Leonhard Ragaz*, 236.
15. Kutter, *They Must*, 42–50, "has too much," 44; "the living God," 113; "the greatest," 114; Marx, *Capital*, "every old," 1: 916, Penguin ed.
16. Kutter, *They Must*, "the slightest," 126.
17. Ibid., "we cover," 195; "this must," 196; "leading lives," 199.
18. Ibid., "the holiest," 203; "knows," 205; "that no people" and "without," 207.
19. Leonhard Ragaz, "The Gospel and the Current Social Struggle" (1906), in *Signs of the Kingdom: A Ragaz Reader*, ed. and trans. Paul Bock (Grand Rapids: Eerdmans, 1984), 3–15, "the domineering" and "false," 8; "now an," 9.
20. Leonhard Ragaz, "Thy Kingdom Come" (1908), in *Signs of the Kingdom*, 18–21, "hope and future," 18; "we are," 21; "something," 22.
21. Editor's Introduction to *Signs of the Kingdom: A Ragaz Reader*, ed. and trans. Paul Bock (Grand Rapids: Eerdmans, 1984), "that was," xiv; Karl Barth, "Rückblick," in *Das Wort sie sollen lassen stahn: Festschrift für D. Albert Schädelin* (1950), repr. in *Karl Barth: Offene Briefe, 1945–1968* (Zurich: TVZ, 1984), "every young," 189.
22. Karl Barth, *The Theology of Schleiermacher*, trans. Geoffrey W. Bromiley (Grand Rapids: Eerdmans, 1982), "from Kutter" and "I had to read," 263; Barth, "Autobiographical Sketch for the Faculty Album of the Faculty of Evangelical Theology at Münster," "for the first," 154; see Karl Barth, "Jesus Christ and the Movement for Social Justice" (1911), Friedrich-Wilhelm Marquardt, "Socialism in the Theology of Karl Barth," and George Hunsinger, "Conclusion: Toward a Radical Barth," in George Hunsinger, trans. and ed., *Karl Barth and Radical Politics* (Philadelphia: Westminster Press, 1976), 19–46, 47–76, 181–233.
23. Barth, *The Theology of Schleiermacher*, "horrible" and "almost even," 263; "an entire," 264.
24. Dorrien, *The Barthian Revolt in Modern Theology*, 14–80.
25. Lindt, *Leonhard Ragaz*, 232–235; Hermann Kutter, *Wir Pfarrer* (Leipzig: H. Haessel Verlag, 1907); McCormack, *Karl Barth's Critically Realistic Dialectical Theology*, 117–119.
26. Karl Barth to Martin Rade, September 8, 1914, *Karl Barth–Martin Rade: Ein Briefwechsel*, ed. Christoph Schwöbel (Gütersloh: Gütersloher Verlagshaus Gerd Mohn, 1981), "simply with," 96; Barth to Rade, October 1, 1914, *Barth–Rade*, "German character," 101; Christoph Schwöbel, *Martin Rade, Der Verhältnis von Geschichte, Religion und Moral als Grundproblem seiner Theologie* (Gütersloh: Gerd Mohn, 1980), 182.
27. Martin Rade to Karl Barth, October 5, 1914, *Karl Barth–Martin Rade*, 110; Barth to Wilhelm Herrmann, November 4, 1914, 115; McCormack, *Karl Barth's Critically Realistic Dialectical Theology*, 113–120; Dorrien, *The Barthian Revolt in Modern Theology*, 37–40. Barth repeatedly told the manifesto story wrongly, claiming it came out on the same day as the call to war, which confused much of the literature on this subject, including the account of Barth's biographer Eberhard Busch, *Karl Barth*, 81.
28. Hermann Kutter, *Reden an die deutsche Nation* (Jena: Eugen Diederichs, 1916); Barth, *Predigten 1913*, 252; Karl Barth, *Action in Waiting* (Rifton, NY: Plough, 1969), "God is," 24; Karl Barth to Eduard Thurneysen, August 6, 1915, *Karl Barth–Eduard*

Thurneysen, Briefwechsel, 1913–1921, ed. Eduard Thurneysen (Zurich: TVZ, 1973), "you really," 70; Busch, *Karl Barth,* 97; Barth, "Autobiographical Sketch for the Faculty Album of the Faculty of Evangelical Theology at Münster," 154–155.

29. Leonhard Ragaz, "Not Religion but the Kingdom of God" (1917), in *Signs of the Kingdom,* 27–38, "this new" and "first of all," 27; "the kingdom of," 28; "Moses wanted" and "Jesus also," 29; McCormack, *Barth's Critically Realistic Dialectical Theology,* 123–125; Ingrid Spieckermann, *Gotteserkenntnis: Ein Beitrag zur Grundfrage der neuen Theologie Karl Barths* (Munich: Chr. Kaiser Verlag, 1985), 69–70.

30. Ragaz, "Not Religion but the Kingdom of God," "it is a whole," "we cannot think," and "what Jesus wants," 29; "he is the," 33.

31. Leonhard Ragaz, "The Battle Against Bolshevism" (November 1918), in *Signs of the Kingdom,* 43–46, "a perversion," 43; "on the one," 44; "everywhere," 45.

32. Leonhard Ragaz, *Sozialismus und Gewalt* (pamphlet, 1919), in *Signs of the Kingdom,* 49–63, "deep reverence," 49; "truth has," 54.

33. Ibid., "the wish," 57.

34. Leonhard Ragaz, *Von Christus zu Marx, von Marx zu Christus* (1929), in *Signs of the Kingdom,* 75–96, "the true child," 81; Ragaz, *Der Kampf um das Reich Gottes in Blumhardt Vater und Sonhund Weiter!* (Erlenbach-Zurich: Rotapfel Verlag, 1922); Ragaz, *Le Message revolutionaire* (Zurich: Neuchatel, 1941); Ragaz, *Israel, Judaism and Christianity* (London: Victor Gollancz, 1947); Busch, *Karl Barth,* 76; Karl Barth and Eduard Thurneysen, *Revolutionary Theology in the Making: Barth–Thurneysen Correspondence, 1914–1925,* trans. by James D. Smart (Richmond: John Knox Press, 1964), 27–32.

35. Karl Barth, "Biblical Questions, Insights, and Vistas," in *The Word of God and the Word of Man,* trans. Douglas Horton (Gloucester, MA: Peter Smith, 1978), "there must," 80; Barth, "The Strange New World Within the Bible," in *The Word of God and the Word of Man,* 28–50.

36. Karl Barth to Eduard Thurneysen, January 1, 1916, *Revolutionary Theology in the Making,* quotes 35–36; Busch, *Karl Barth,* 75, 87; *Karl Barth–Eduard Thurneysen, Briefwechsel, 1913–1921,* 103.

37. Karl Barth to Eduard Thurneysen, July 27, 1916, *Revolutionary Theology in the Making,* 38. On Beck's relation to Barth's family, see Eberhard Jüngel, *Karl Barth, a Theological Legacy,* trans. Garrett E. Paul (Philadelphia: Westminster Press, 1986), 23.

38. Barth, "The Strange New World Within the Bible," 33–34.

39. Ibid., 34, 37.

40. Ibid., 44–45.

41. Barth's sermon, "The Pastor Who Pleases the People," was published without his consent in *Die christliche Welt* 14 (1916): 262–265. See James D. Smart, *The Divided Mind of Modern Theology: Karl Barth and Rudolf Bultmann, 1908–1933* (Philadelphia: Westminster Press, 1957), 77–78; Arthur C. Cochrane, "The Sermons of 1913 and 1914," in *Karl Barth in Re-View: Posthumous Works Reviewed and Assessed,* ed. H. Martin Rumscheidt (Pittsburgh: Pickwick Press, 1981), 1–5; Karl Barth and William Willimon, *The Early Preaching of Karl Barth: Fourteen Sermons with Commentary by William H. Willimon* (Louisville: Westminster John Knox Press, 2009).

42. Barth, "Autobiographical Sketch for the Faculty Album of the Faculty of Evangelical Theology at Münster," "I had," 155; Karl Barth, *Der Römerbrief* (Bern: G. A. Baschlin, 1919).

43. Barth, *Der Römerbrief*, 1–22, 321–327.

44. Ibid., 1.

45. Ibid., 417–422; on Barth's early expressionism, see Hans Urs von Balthasar, *The Theology of Karl Barth*, trans. John Drury (New York: Holt, Rinehart and Winston, 1871), 70–71; Wilhelm Pauck, *Karl Barth: Prophet of a New Christianity?* (New York: Harper and Brothers, 1931), 19–20; Hans Frei, "An Afterword: Eberhard Busch's Biography of Karl Barth," in *Karl Barth in Re-View*, 98–102; Stephen H. Webb, *Re-Figuring Theology: The Rhetoric of Karl Barth* (Albany: State University of New York Press, 1991), 8–18.

46. Barth, *Der Römerbrief*, 48–49, 64–66, 76–86, 321–328. See Smart, *The Divided Mind of Modern Theology*, 83–84; McCormack, *Karl Barth's Critically Realistic Dialectical Theology*, 142–143.

47. Barth, *Der Römerbrief*, 105, 186, 308. Barth later characterized his shift away from the conceptuality of his first-edition *Romans* as a "shift from Osiander to Luther." See Barth to Thurneysen, December 3, 1920, *Revolutionary Theology in the Making*, 55. On Osiander, see David Steinmetz, *Reformers in the Wings* (Philadelphia: Westminster Press, 1971), 91–99.

48. Adolf Jülicher, "A Modern Interpreter of Paul," in *The Beginnings of Dialectic Theology*, ed. James M. Robinson, trans. Louis De Grazia and Keith R. Crim (Richmond: John Knox Press, 1968), quote 79; Philipp Bachmann, "Der Römerbrief verdeutscht und vergegenwärtigt: Ein Wort zu K. Barths Römerbrief," *Neue kirchliche Zeitschrift* 32 (1921): 518; Emil Brunner, "*The Epistle to the Romans*, by Karl Barth: An Up-to-Date, Unmodern Paraphrase," in *The Beginnings of Dialectic Theology*, 63.

49. Jülicher, "A Modern Interpreter of Paul," "and never tired," 79.

50. Rudolf Bultmann, "Ethical and Mystical Religion in Primitive Christianity," in *The Beginnings of Dialectic Theology*, 221–235, "enthusiastic," 230; Barth to Thurneysen, July 14, 1920, *Revolutionary Theology in the Making*, quotes 52–53; Karl Barth, "Preface to the Second Edition," in Barth, *The Epistle to the Romans*, 6th ed., trans. Edwyn C. Hoskyns (1935; repr. London: Oxford University Press, 1975), 13. Hereafter this is the text and edition signified by the title *The Epistle to the Romans*.

51. Karl Barth, "The Christian's Place in Society," in *The Word of God and the Word of Man*, 272–327, "dangerous" and "purest," 276; "the Divine is," 277; Günther Dehn, *Die alte Zeit, die vorigen Jahre: Lebenserinnerungen* (Munich: Christian Kaiser Verlag, 1964), 217.

52. Barth, "The Christian's Place in Society," "the shortest," 278; "let us establish," 280; "in a wholly," 281.

53. Ibid., "the movement," 283.

54. Wilhelm Wibbeling, *Evangelische Theologie* 24 (October 1964), "the impact," 556, in Jack Forstman, *Christian Faith in Dark Times: Theological Conflicts in the Shadow of Hitler* (Louisville: Westminster John Knox Press, 1992), 45; Wilhelm and Marion Pauck, *Paul Tillich: His Life and Thought* (New York: Harper and Row, 1989), "fled,"

70; Karl Barth, "Past and Future: Friedrich Naumann and Christoph Blumhardt," in *The Beginnings of Dialectic Theology*, "with a certain" and "all these," 38–39; Barth, "*Die Hilfe 1913*," *Die Christliche Welt* 28 (August 15, 1914), 776; Lindt, *Leonhard Ragaz*, 205–216.

55. Karl Barth, "Vom Rechthaben und Unrechthaben: Rede, gehaltn zu einer sozialde-mokratischen Volksversammlung," *Das neue Werk* (January 4, 1920), 640, in Christophe Chalamet, "Karl Barth and the Weimar Republic," *The Weimar Moment: Liberalism, Political Theology, and Law*, ed. Leonard V. Kaplan and Rudy Koshar (Lanham, MD: Lexington Books, 2012), "we should" and "there is," 259.

56. Friedrich Gogarten, "The Holy Egoism of the Christian: An Answer to Jülicher's Essay: 'A Modern Interpreter of Paul,'" *The Beginnings of Dialectic Theology*, 82–87, "superior," 87; Gogarten, "Between the Times," *The Beginnings of Dialectic Theology*, 277–282, "it is" and "your concepts," 277; "we never" and "today we," 278; Gogarten, "The Crisis of Our Culture," *The Beginnings of Dialectic Theology*, 283–300.

57. Barth to Thurneysen, October 27, 1920, *Revolutionary Theology in the Making*, "here is," 53; Barth, "Biblical Questions, Insights, and Vistas," "he is," 73–74.

58. Agnes zon Zahn-Harnack, *Adolf von Harnack* (Berlin: Walter de Gruyter, 1951), "not one" and "rushing," 415; Barth to Thurneysen, October 27, 1920, *Revolutionary Theology in the Making*, "a bit" and "finally," 50; Barth, "Autobiographical Sketch for the Faculty Album of the Faculty of Evangelical Theology at Münster, 1927," "things now," 156.

59. Barth to Thurneysen, October 27, 1920, 53; Karl Barth, "Preface to the Second Edition," Barth, *Epistle to the Romans*, 2–5.

60. Buess and Mattmüller, *Prophetischer Socialismus*, 9–15; Eduard Thurneysen, *Christoph Blumhardt* (Munich: Chr. Kaiser Verlag, 1926); *Karl Barth–Eduard Thurneysen: Briefwechsel*, 1: 29–33.

61. Franz Overbeck, *Christentum und Kultur: Gedanken und Anmerkungen zur modernen Theologie*, ed. Carl Albrecht Bernoulli (Basle: Benno Schwabe, 1919), 20–28, 52–68; Niklaus Peter, *Im Schatten der Modernität: Franz Overbecks Weg zur 'Christlichkeit unserer heutigen Theologie'* (Stuttgart: J. B. Metzler Verlag, 1992); Emil Brunner, "Der Römerbrief von Karl Barth," *Kirchenblatt für die Reformierte Schweiz* 34 (1919), 30–31; Karl Barth, "Unsettled Questions for Theology Today," in Barth, *Theology and Church: Shorter Writings 1920–1928*, trans. Louise Pettibone Smith (New York: Harper and Row, 1962), 57–68; Eduard Thurneysen, *Dostoiewski* (Munich: Chr. Kaiser Verlag, 1921).

62. Barth, "The Christian's Place in Society," "there must" and "however," 287; Barth, "Past and Future: Friedrich Naumann and Christoph Blumhardt," "fullness," 44; Blumhardt, *Action in Waiting*, 15–22.

63. Barth, "Past and Future: Friedrich Naumann and Christoph Blumhardt," 44–45.

64. Barth, "Biblical Questions, Insights, and Vistas," 80.

65. Barth, *Epistle to the Romans*, "fire alarm," 38; quotes 39, 42, 98–99, 105.

66. Ibid., quotes 141–142, 225 (108–109, 116, 100).

67. Barth, "Preface to the Second Edition," *Epistle to the Romans*, "if I have," 10.

68. On Herrmann's theology and Barth's appropriation of it, see Dorrien, *The Barthian Revolt in Modern Theology*, 15–32, 168–177.

69. Barth, *The Theology of Schleiermacher*, "shattering" and "I was," 259; Karl Barth to Eduard Thurneysen, October 16, 1922, *Revolutionary Theology*, 112–114, "unbearably," 114; Barth to Thurneysen, February 26, 1922, in *Revolutionary Theology*, 82–90; Barth to Thurneysen, March 20, 1922, *Revolutionary Theology*, 90–92; Barth to Thurneysen, April 2, 1922, *Revolutionary Theology*, 95–97; Barth to Thurneysen, January 23, 1923, *Revolutionary Theology*, 123–128; Barth to Thurneysen, December 20, 1923, *Revolutionary Theology*, 157–162; Barth to Thurneysen, February 1, 1924, *Revolutionary Theology*, 164–165; Barth to Thurneysen, March 1, 1925, *Revolutionary Theology*, 208–217; Dorrien, *The Barthian Revolt in Modern Theology*, 71–80.

70. Paul Tillich, "Critical and Positive Paradox: A Discussion with Karl Barth and Friedrich Gogarten," *Theologische Blätter* 2 (1923): 263–269, in *The Beginnings of Dialectic Theology*, 133–141; Karl Barth, "The Paradoxical Nature of the 'Positive Paradox': Answers and Questions to Paul Tillich," *Theologische Blätter* 2 (1923): 287–296, in *The Beginnings of Dialectic Theology*, 142–154, "this hide-and-seek," 147; Karl Barth to Eduard Thurneysen, March 4, 1924, *Revolutionary Theology*, 171.

71. Emanuel Hirsch, *Deutschlands Schicksal: Staat, Volk und Menschheit im Lichte einer ethischen Geschichtsansicht*, 2nd ed. (Göttingen: Vandenhoeck und Ruprecht, 1922), "we were," 142–143; Karl Holl, *Gesammelte Aufsätze zur Kirchengeschichte: Luther* (Tübingen: Mohr/Siebeck, 1948), 33–110; Robert P. Erickson, *Theologians Under Hitler: Gerhard Kittel, Paul Althaus, and Emanuel Hirsch* (New Haven: Yale University Press, 1985), 120–139; Friedrich Wilhelm Bautz, "Emanuel Hirsch," *Biographisch–Bibliographisches Kirchenlexikon*, ed. Friedrich Wilhelm Bautz (Hamm: Traugott 1990), 893–896; Peter Fritzsche, *Rehearsals for Fascism: Populism and Political Mobilization in Weimar Germany* (New York: Oxford University Press, 2012), 206–212.

72. Hirsch, *Deutschlands Schicksal*, 155–166; Emanuel Hirsch, *Die idealistische Philosophie und das Christentum* (Gütersloh: Bertelsmann, 1926); Carl Schmitt, *Political Theology: Four Chapters on the Concept of Sovereignty* (1922; rev. ed., Berlin: Duncker und Humblot, 1934), trans. George Schwab (Chicago: University of Chicago Press, 2005); Brian J. Fox, *Carl Schmitt and Political Catholicism: Friend or Foe?* (Ph.D. diss., City University of New York, Graduate Faculty in History, September 30, 2015), http://academicworks.cuny.edu/cgi/viewcontent.cgi?article.

73. Karl Barth to Eduard Thurneysen, January 22, 1922, *Revolutionary Theology*, "sinister," 88; Barth to Thurneysen, May 18, 1922, *Karl Barth–Eduard Thurneysen Briefwechsel, 1921–1930*, "that I am," 163; Barth to Thurneysen, March 4, 1924, *Revolutionary Theology*, 171–176, "all of them," 175; Barth to Thurneysen, June 28, 1922, *Barth–Thurneysen Briefwechsel, 1921–1930*, 88–89; Paul Althaus, "Theologie und Geschichte: Zur Auseinandersetzung mit der dialektischen Theologie," *Zeitschrift für systematische Theologie* 1 (1923–1924): 741–786.

74. Karl Barth, *Die christliche Dogmatik im Entwurf, I: Die Lehre vom Worte Gottes. Prolegomena zur christlichen Dogmatik* (Munich: Chr. Kaiser Verlag, 1927); Michael Hollerich, "Catholic Anti-Liberalism in Weimar," *The Weimar Moment*, 17–40.

75. Friedrich Gogarten, *Ich glaube an den dreieinigen Gott* (Jena: Eugen Diederichs Verlag, 1926); Gogarten, "Das Problem einer theologischen Anthropologie," *Zwischen den Zeiten* 7 (1929): 493–511; Emil Brunner, *Die Mystik und das Wort*, 2nd ed.

(Tübingen: J. C. B. Mohr, 1928), 297–299; Brunner, "Die andere Aufgabe der Theologie," *Zwischen den Zeiten* 7 (1929): 262–274; Rudolf Bultmann to Karl Barth, June 8, 1928, in *Karl Barth/Rudolf Bultmann Letters, 1922–1966,* trans. Bernd Jaspert, trans. and ed. Geoffrey W. Bromiley (Edinburgh: T. and T. Clark, 1982), 38–39; Karl Barth to Rudolf Bultmann, June 12, 1928, *Karl Barth/Rudolf Bultmann Letters,* 40–42.

76. Karl Barth to Rudolf Bultmann, February 5, 1930, *Karl Barth/Rudolf Bultmann Letters,* 49–50, "fleshpots," 49; Barth to Bultmann, June 20, 1931, *Karl Barth/Rudolf Bultmann Letters,* 65.

77. Angela Dienhart Hancock, *Karl Barth's Emergency Homiletic, 1932–1933* (Grand Rapids: Eerdmans, 2013), 70; McCormick, *Karl Barth's Critically Realistic Dialectical Theology,* 412; Gordon A. Craig, *Germany: 1866–1945* (Oxford: Oxford University Press, 1981), 522–524.

78. Paul Althaus, *Religiöser Sozialismus: Grundfragen der christlichen Sozialethic* (Gütersloh: C. Bertelsmann, 1921), 14–18, 39–41, 69–70; Ericksen, *Theologians Under Hitler,* 83–85.

79. Paul Althaus, *Kirche und Volkstum: Der völkische Wille im Lichte des Evangeliums* (Gütersloh: C. Bertelsmann, 1928), 22–46; Scholder, *The Churches and the Third Reich,* "the Volk," "a truly," and "into the organic," 1: 112; "sanctify," 1:113; Althaus, "Theologie und Geschichte: Zur Auseinandersetzung mit der dialektischen Theologie," *Zeitschrift für systematische Theologie* 1 (1923–1924): 741–786.

80. Martin Rade, editorial, *Christliche Welt* 44 (December 1930), "appear at," in Scholder, *Churches and the Third Reich,* 1: 131.

81. Paul Lagarde, *Schriften für das deutsche Volk* (1878; repr., Munich: J. F. Lehman, 1934); Lagarde, *Gesammeltze abhandlungen* (Leipzig: F. A. Brockhaus, 1866); Scholder, *The Churches and the Third Reich,* "an eye," 1: 113.

82. Adolf von Harnack, *Marcion, das Evangelium vom fremden Gott* (Leipzig: J. C. Hinrichs Verlag, 1921), 217–220; Hans-Joachim Kraus, *Geschichte der historisch-kritischen Erforschung des Alten Testaments* (Neukirchen-Vluyn: Neukirchener Verlag, 1969), 384–390.

83. Paul Althaus, *Die deutsche Stunde der Kirche,* 3rd ed. (Göttingen: Vandenhoeck und Ruprecht, 1934); "Our Protestant," 5; Althaus, *Christus und die deutsche Seele* (Gütersloh: C. Bertelsmann, 1934), "there is a," 16; Althaus, *Die Theologie Martin Luthers,* 2nd ed. (Gütersloh: Gütersloher Verlagshaus Gerd Mohn, 1963); Althaus, *Die Ethik Martin Luthers* (Gütersloh: G. V. Gerd Mohn, 1965); Ericksen, *Theologians Under Hitler,* "whatever I am" and "our life," 103; "the perfect," 79; Robert P. Ericksen, "The Political Theology of Paul Althaus: Nazi Supporter," *German Studies Review* 9 (October 1986): 547–567, "he was," 547; Hans Schwarz, "Paul Althaus (1888–1966)," in *Twentieth-Century Lutheran Theologians,* ed. Mark Mattes (Göttingen: Vandenhoeck und Ruprecht, 2013), 136–154.

84. Busch, *Karl Barth,* 199–207; Suzanne Selinger, *Charlotte von Kirschbaum and Karl Barth: A Study in Biography and the History of Theology* (University Park: Pennsylvania State University Press, 1998), 6–17, 78–87.

85. Karl Barth, "Zwischenzeit," *Kirchenblatt für die reformierte Schweiz* 118 (1962): 38; Karl Barth to Hans Asmussen, January 14, 1932, in McCormack, *Karl Barth's Critically Realistic Dialectical Theology,* 414.

86. Paul Tillich to Karl Barth, March 29, 1933, and Karl Barth to Paul Tillich, April 2, 1933, in *Evangelische Kommentar* 10 (1977): 111–115; Barth to Tillich letter in *Karl Barth and Radical Politics*, "as an idea," 116; Forstman, *Christian Faith in Dark Times*, 193–195.

87. George Hunsinger, Preface to *Karl Barth and Radical Politics*, "between the freedom" and "the conceptual," 8; see Friedrich-Wilhelm Marquardt, "Socialism in the Theology of Karl Barth," in *Karl Barth and Radical Politics*, 47–75.

88. McCormack, *Karl Barth's Critically Realistic Dialectical Theology*, 415–416; Helmut Thielicke, *Notes from a Wayfarer: The Autobiography of Helmut Thielicke*, trans. David R. Law (New York: Paragon House, 1995), 66–69; Timothy J. Gorringe, *Karl Barth: Against Hegemony* (Oxford: Oxford University Press, 1999), 119.

89. Thielicke, *Notes from a Wayfarer*, "and woe betide," 66; "Mommy," 70; on Hegel against feelings, see Dorrien, *Kantian Reason and Hegelian Spirit*, 212–213.

90. Karl Barth, "Quousque Tandem . . . ?" *Zwischen den Zeiten* 8 (1930): 1–6; Peter Matheson, *The Third Reich and the Christian Churches* (Edinburgh: T. and T. Clark, 1981), 2–5; Scholder, *Churches and the Third Reich*, "the passionate," 1: 175; Hancock, *Karl Barth's Emergency Homiletic*, 84–85; Frank J. Gordon, "Liberal German Churchmen and the First World War," *German Studies Review* 41 (1981): 59–60.

91. Thielicke, *Notes from a Wayfarer*, "not a subject," 67; "at the basis," 69.

92. Karl Barth, *Church Dogmatics: The Doctrine of the Word of God*, 14 vols., 1: 1, trans. G. T. Thomson (Edinburgh: T. and T. Clark, 1936), "I regard," x; "the constantly," "only to be," "High Church," and "in the intoxication," xi; Barth, *Anselm: Fides Quaerens Intellectum*, trans. Ian Robertson (London: SCM Press, 1961).

93. Peter Hoffmann, *The History of the German Resistance*, trans. Richard Barry (Cambridge: MIT Press, 1979), 6–7; Karl Barth, *Theological Existence Today! A Plea for Theological Freedom*, trans. R. Birch Hoyle (London: Hodder and Stoughton, 1933), "as if," 9; "I regard," 9–10.

94. Victoria Barnett, *For the Soul of the People: Protestant Protest Against Hitler* (New York: Oxford University Press, 1992), 32–55; Scholder, *The Churches and the Third Reich*, 1: 445–446, 580–581; Ian Kershaw, *Hitler, 1889–1936: Hubris* (New York: W. W. Norton, 1999), 485–487; Martin Niemöller, *Here Stand I!*, trans. Jane Lymburn (Chicago: Willett, Clark, 1937); Robert Michael, "Theological Myth, German Antisemitism, and the Holocaust: The Case of Martin Niemoeller," *Holocaust Genocide Studies* 2 (1987): 105–112; Hancock, *Karl Barth's Emergency Homiletic*, 132–136.

95. "The Theological Declaration of Barmen" (May 29–31, 1934), in *The Constitution of the Presbyterian Church (U.S.A.): Part 1, Book of Confessions* (Louisville: Office of the General Assembly, 1991), 8.01–8.28, and *The Church's Confession Under Hitler*, ed. Arthur C. Cochrane (Philadelphia: Westminster Press, 1962), 237–242, "do not listen," 8.03; "one Lord," 8.06.

96. Emil Brunner, "Nature and Grace," and Karl Barth, "No!" (1934), in Brunner and Barth, *Natural Theology*, trans. Peter Fraenkel (London: Centenary Press, 1946), "I am" and "much more," 67; Rudolf Bultmann to Karl Barth, July 7, 1934, in *Barth/Bultmann Letters*, 74–75; Barth to Bultmann, July 10, 1934, *Barth/Bultmann Letters*, 76–77; Dietrich Bonhoeffer, *Akt und Sein* (1931) (Munich: Christian Kaiser Verlag, 1956); Bonhoeffer, *A Testament to Freedom: The Essential Writings of Dietrich Bonhoeffer*, ed. Geffrey B. Kelly and F. Burton Nelson (New York: Harper Collins, 1995).

97. Karl Barth to Hermann Hesse, June 30, 1935, in Busch, *Karl Barth*, "it still has," 261; Karl Barth to Rudolf Bultmann, November 27, 1934, *Barth/Bultmann Letters*, "so far as," 78; Karl Barth, "Das Evangelium in der Gegenwart," *Theologische Existenz heute* 25 (1935), "exegesis" and "then," 17; Eberhard Jüngel, *Karl Barth: A Theological Legacy*, trans. Garrett E. Paul (Philadelphia: Westminster Press, 1986), 40.

98. Helmut Gollwitzer, "Kingdom of God and Socialism in the Theology of Karl Barth," in *Karl Barth and Radical Politics*, 77–120, "squandering," 82.

99. Karl Barth, "Abschied," *Zwischen den Zeiten* 11 (1933), "I could damage," "my political," and "unworthy," 542.

100. Karl Barth, "How I Changed My Mind," *Christian Century* (1938), repr. in Barth, *How I Changed My Mind*, ed. John D. Godsey (Richmond: John Knox Press, 1966), "my lifework," 41; "all that" and "surrounded by," 48; Barth, *Church and State*, trans. G. Ronald Howe (London: SCM Press, 1939).

101. Gollwitzer, "Kingdom of God and Socialism," "this man's," 100; "too shopworn," 83; Paul Lehmann, *The Transfiguration of Politics* (New York: Harper and Row, 1975), 43–47, 272–273.

102. Karl Barth, "The Christian Community and the Civil Community" (1946), trans. Stanley Godman, in Barth, *Against the Stream: Shorter Post-War Writings, 1946–52* (London: SCM Press, 1954), 15–50; Barth, "The Christian Community in the Midst of Political Change: Documents of a Hungarian Journey" (1948), in *Against the Stream*, 51–124; Barth, "The Christian Message in Europe Today" (1946), in *Against the Stream*, 165–180.

103. Gorringe, *Karl Barth: Against Hegemony*, "completely," 123; George Hunsinger, *How to Read Karl Barth* (Oxford: Oxford University Press, 1991), "salvation," 142; Kathryn Tanner, "Barth and the Economy of Grace," in *Commanding Grace: Studies in Karl Barth's Ethics*, ed. Daniel L. Migliore (Grand Rapids: Eerdmans, 2010), 176–197.

104. Paul Tillich, "Autobiographical Reflections of Paul Tillich," in *The Theology of Paul Tillich*, ed. Charles Kegley and Robert Bretall (New York: Macmillan, 1952), 7; Tillich, *The Interpretation of History*, trans. N. A. Rasetzki and Elsa Talmey (New York: Charles Scribner's Sons, 1936), 3–7; Pauck and Pauck, *Paul Tillich: His Life and Thought*, 1–14, reference to Grand Inquisitor, 30; Wilhelm Pauck, *From Luther to Tillich: The Reformers and Their Heirs* (New York: Harper and Row, 1984), 158–161. Near the end of his life Tillich published a revised edition of part 1 of *The Interpretation of History* under the title *On the Boundary: An Autobiographical Sketch* (New York: Charles Scribner's Sons, 1964).

105. Tillich, *The Interpretation of History*, 6–8; Pauck, *Paul Tillich*, 19–28; Paul Tillich, Foreword to Martin Kähler, *The So-Called Historical Jesus and the Historic Biblical Christ* (1896), trans. Carl E. Braaten (Philadelphia: Fortress Press, 1988), vii–viii; F. W. J. Schelling, *System of Transcendental Idealism* (1800), trans. Peter Heath (Charlottesville: University Press of Virginia, 1993); Schelling, *Ideas for a Philosophy of Nature* (2nd ed., 1803), trans. Errol E. Harris and Peter Heath (Cambridge: Cambridge University Press, 1988); Schelling, *Philosophical Investigations into the Essence of Human Freedom* (1809), trans. Jeff Love and Johannes Schmidt (Albany: State University of New York Press, 2006); Pauck, *From Luther to Tillich*, 168–173. On

Kähler, see Gary Dorrien, *The Word as True Myth: Interpreting Modern Theology* (Louisville: Westminster John Knox Press, 1997), 109–116.

106. Paul Tillich, *Die religionsgeschichtliche Konstruktion in Schellings positiver Philosophie, ihre Voraussetzungen und Prinzipien* (Breslau: Fleischmann, 1910); Tillich, *Mystik und Schuldbewusstein in Schellings philosophischer Entwicklung* (Gütersloh: Bertelsmann, 1912); Tillich, *Der Begriff des Uebernatürlichen, sein dialektischer Charakter und das Prinzip der Identät, dargestellt an der supranaturalistischen Theologie vor Schleiermacher* (Königsberg: Madrasch, 1915); Tillich, "Autobiographical Reflections of Paul Tillich," "my enthusiasm," 7; Tillich, *The New Being* (New York: Charles Scribner's Sons, 1955), 52; Jerome Stone, "Tillich and Schelling's Later Philosophy," in *Kairos and Logos*, ed. John Carey (Cambridge, MA: North American Paul Tillich Society, 1978), 11–44; Horst Fuhrmanns, *Schellings Philosophie der Weltalter: Schelling Philosophie in den Jahren 1806–1821* (Düsseldorf: L. Schwann, 1954), 75–82. This discussion of Tillich adapts material from Dorrien, *The Making of American Liberal Theology: Idealism, Realism, and Modernity* (Louisville: Westminster John Knox Press, 2003), 483–516.

107. [Cover story, no byline], "To Be or Not to Be?" *Time* 73 (March 16, 1959), "many of them," 47; Ronald Stone, *Politics and Faith: Reinhold Niebuhr and Paul Tillich at Union Theological Seminary in New York* (Macon, GA: Mercer University Press, 2012), 9–11.

108. Tillich, "Autobiographical Reflections of Paul Tillich," "by interferences," 12; Pauck, *Paul Tillich*, 46–54; Tillich, *My Search for Absolutes* (New York: Simon and Schuster, 1967), 39; Tillich, *On the Boundary*, 52.

109. Paul Tillich to Emanuel Hirsch, February 20, 1918, *E. Hirsch and P. Tillich–Briefwechsel 1917–18*, ed. Hans-Walter Schuette (Berlin: Die Spur, 1973), "gloomy," 21; Tillich, *The Interpretation of History*, "the experience," 35; *Ultimate Concern: Tillich in Dialogue*, ed. D. Mackenzie Brown (New York: Harper and Row, 1965), "personal," 153; Paul Tillich, "Über die Idee einer Theologie der Kultur," in *Religionsphilosophie der Kultur: zwei Entwürfe von Gustav Radbruch und Paul Tillich* (Berlin: Reuther and Reinhard, 1920), 27–52; Tillich, "Christentum und Sozialismus," *Das neue Deutschland* 8 (December 1919): 106–110; Ernst Troeltsch, *The Social Teaching of the Christian Churches* (1912), 2 vols., trans. Olive Wyon (Louisville: Westminster John Knox Press, 1992); Dorrien, *Kantian Reason and Hegelian Spirit*, 354–356.

110. Paul Tillich, "Christentum und Sozialismus," *Das neue Deutschland* 8 (December 1919): 106–110; Tillich and Richard Wegener, *Der Sozialismus als Kirchenfrage: Leitsätze von Paul Tillich und Richard Wegener* (Berlin: Gracht, 1919), in Tillich, *Gesammelte Werke*, 14 vols. (Stuttgart: Evangelisches Verlagswerk, 1962–1975), 2: 13–20, "we stand," 16; Tillich, "Revolution und Kirche," *Das neue Deutschland* 8 (July 1919): 394–397; Pauck and Pauck, *Paul Tillich*, 68–69.

111. Günther Dehn, *Die Alte Zeit, Die Vorigen Jahre: Lebenserinnerungen* (Munich: Chr. Kaiser Verlag, 1962), 212–213, 223; "Brief von Prof. Dr. Eduard Heimann an den Verfasser über die einzelnen Mitglieder des Kairos-Kreises," Appendix 1 in Eberhard Amelung, *Die gestalt der Liebe* (Gütersloh: Gerd Mohn, 1972), 215; Heimann, "naïve," in Pauck and Pauck, *Paul Tillich*, 70; Tillich, *On the Boundary*, 32–34, "explicitly," 33; Eduard Heimann, *Kapitalismus und Sozialismus* (Potsdam:

Alfred Protte, 1931); Heimann, *Die soziale Theorie des Kapitalismus* (Tübingen: J. C. B. Mohr, 1929); Adolf Löwe, *Economics and Sociology: A Plea for Cooperation in the Social Sciences* (1935; repr., New York: Routledge, 2003); Joan Campbell, *Joy in Work, German Work: The National Debate, 1800–1945* (Princeton: Princeton University Press, 2014), 306.

112. Paul Tillich, "Kairos," *Die Tat* 14 (August 1922): 330–350; Tillich, "Masse und Religion," *Blätter für religiösen Sozialismus* 2 (1921): 1–7, 9–12; Tillich, "Die Theologie als Wissenschaft," *Vossische Zeitung* 512 (October 30, 1921), 2–3; Tillich, "Religiöse Krisis," *Vivos voco* 11 (April–May 1922): 616–621; Tillich, *Das System der Wissenschaften nach Gegenständen und Methoden* (Göttingen: Vandenhoeck und Ruprecht, 1923), discussion of the Unconditioned, 129–130; Tillich, "Zur Klärung der religiösen Grundhaltung," *Blätter für religiösen Sozialismus* 3 (December 1922): 46–48; Tillich, *The Interpretation of History*, 123–175; Tillich, "Basic Principles of Religious Socialism" (1923), in *Political Expectation*, ed. James Luther Adams, trans. James Luther Adams and Victor Nuovo (New York: Harper and Row, 1971), 58–88.

113. Paul Tillich, "Basic Principles of Religious Socialism," "it has," 60.

114. Ibid., "the more," 74.

115. Ibid., "as a universal," 82.

116. Paul Tillich, "Die religiöse und philosophische Weiterbildung des Sozialismus," *Blätter für religiösen Sozialismus* 5 (May 1924): 18; Pauck and Pauck, *Paul Tillich*, "I have," 83; Hannah Tillich, *From Time to Time* (New York: Stein and Day, 1973).

117. Paul Tillich, *Die religiöse Lage der Gegenwart* (Berlin: Ullstein, 1926); English ed., *The Religious Situation*, trans. H. Richard Niebuhr (New York: Henry Holt, 1932).

118. Tillich, *Religiöse Verwirklichung* (Berlin: Furche Verlag, 1929), repr., Tillich, *The Protestant Era*, trans. James Luther Adams (London: Nisbet, 1951), 74–92, "revelation," 91; Tillich, "Kritisches und positives Paradox: eine Aufeinandersetzung mit Karl Barth und Friedrich Gogarten," *Theologische Blätter* 2 (November 1923): 263–269; Barth, "The Paradoxical Nature of the 'Positive Paradox': Answers and Questions to Paul Tillich," in *The Beginnings of Dialectic Theology*, 147.

119. [Heppenheim Conference contributors], *Sozialismus aus dem Glauben* (Zürich: Rotaphel-Verlag, 1929), 11–20, 102–106, 228–245; August Rathmann, "Tillich als religiöser Sozialist," in Tillich, *Gesammelte Werke*, 13: 566–567; John R. Stumme, Introduction to Paul Tillich, *The Socialist Decision*, trans. Franklin Sherman (1933; repr. New York: Harper and Row, 1977), xvii–xviii.

120. Martin Jay, *The Dialectical Imagination: A History of the Frankfurt School and the Institute of Social Research, 1923–1950* (Boston: Little, Brown, 1973), 5–12; *The Essential Frankfurt School Reader*, ed. Andrew Arato and Eike Gebhardt (New York: Continuum, 1988), ix–xiv.

121. Georg Lukács, *History and Class Consciousness: Studies in Marxist Dialectics* (1923), trans. Rodney Livingstone (Cambridge: MIT Press, 1972), 1–24, "road," 1; Karl Korsch, *Marxism and Philosophy*, trans. Fred Halliday (London: New Left Books, 1970); Korsch, "Why I Am a Marxist," *Modern Quarterly* 9 (April 1935): 88–95.

122. Karl Korsch, *Three Essays on Marxism* (New York: Monthly Review, 1971), 11–15; Paul Breines, Introduction to *Three Essays on Marxism*, 3–8; Maurice Merleau-Ponty,

Adventures of the Dialectic, trans. Joseph Bien (French ed., 1955; London: Heinemann, 1974), 30–58; Georg Lukács, *Marxism and Human Liberation: Essays on History, Culture, and Revolution* (New York: Delta, 1973), 267–276.

123. *The Essential Frankfurt School Reader,* 3–7; Jay, *The Dialectical Imagination,* 7–18; Max Horkheimer, "Materialism and Metaphysics," and Horkheimer, "Traditional and Critical Theory," in Horkheimer, *Critical Theory: Selected Essays,* trans. Matthew J. O'Connell et al. (New York: Continuum, 1992), 10–46, 188–243; Horkheimer and Theodor W. Adorno, *Dialectic of Enlightenment,* trans. John Cumming (New York: Continuum, 1988), 3–42.

124. Leo Lowenthal, *Literature and the Image of Man* (Boston: Beacon Press, 1957); Lowenthal, "German Popular Biographies: Culture's Bargain Counter," in *The Critical Spirit: Essays in Honor of Herbert Marcuse,* ed. Kurt H. Wolff and Barrington Moore Jr. (Boston: Beacon Press, 1967); Theodor Adorno, *Aesthetic Theory,* trans. C. Lenhardt (London: Routledge and Kegan Paul, 1984), 23–67; Adorno, *Negative Dialectics,* trans. E. B. Ashton (New York: Seabury, 1973), 300–360; Herbert Marcuse, "Philosophy and Critical Theory," in Marcuse, *Negations: Essays in Critical Theory,* trans. Jeremy J. Shapiro (Boston: Beacon Press, 1968), 134–158.

125. Horkheimer, "Traditional and Critical Theory," "relatively," 226; "the theory," 227.

126. Herbert Marcuse, *Hegels Ontologie und die Grundlegung einer Theorie der Geschichtlichkeit* (Frankfurt: V. Klostermann, 1932); Marcuse, *Reason and Revolution: Hegel and the Rise of Social Theory* (Boston: Beacon Press, 1960); Jay, *The Dialectical Imagination,* 26–32; Martin Jay, "The Metapolitics of Utopianism," *Dissent* 17 (July–August 1970); Marcuse, "Philosophy and Critical Theory," 135–136; Istvan Deak, *Weimar Germany's Left-Wing Intellectuals* (Berkeley: University of California Press, 1968), 29.

127. Friedrich Pollock to Martin Jay, March 24, 1970, in Jay, *The Dialectical Imagination,* "all of us," 33; Walter Benjamin, *Illuminations: Essays and Reflections,* trans. Harry Zohn (New York: Schocken Books, 1969); Erich Fromm, "The Method and Function of an Analytic Social Psychology," in *The Essential Frankfurt School Reader,* 477–496.

128. Jürgen Habermas, "Der deutsche Idealismus der jüdischen Philosophen," *Philosophisch-politische Profile* (Frankfurt: Suhrkamp, 1971), in Jay, *The Dialectical Imagination,* 34; Paul Massing interview with Martin Jay, November 25, 1970, in Jay, *The Dialectical Imagination,* 34; Pauck and Pauck, *Paul Tillich,* "Paul among," 118.

129. Paul Tillich, "Sozialismus: II. Religiöser Sozialismus," in *Die Religion in Geschichte und Gegenwart* (1930), repr. in Tillich, *Political Expectation,* 40–57, "a profane," 44; Tillich, "Sozialismus," *Neue Blätter für den Sozialismus* 1 (1930): 1–12. On Western Marxism, see Perry Anderson, *Considerations on Western Marxism* (London: New Left Books, 1976); Neil McInnes, *The Western Marxists* (New York: Library Press, 1972); Merleau-Ponty, *Adventures of the Dialectic,* 30–58; Martin Jay, *Marxism and Totality: The Adventures of a Concept from Lukács to Habermas* (Berkeley: University of California Press, 1984); Marcel Van der Linden, *Western Marxism and the Soviet Union* (Leiden: Brill, 2007).

130. Horkheimer, "Thoughts on Religion," in Horkheimer, *Critical Theory: Selected Essays,* "vain" and "good will," 130; David Held, *Introduction to Critical Theory:*

Horkheimer to Habermas (Berkeley: University of California Press, 1980); David Ingram, *Critical Theory and Philosophy* (New York: Paragon House, 1990); Zoltan Tar, *The Frankfurt School: The Critical Theories of Max Horkheimer and Theodor W. Adorno* (New York: Schocken Books, 1977); Raymond Geuss, *The Idea of Critical Theory* (Cambridge: Cambridge University Press, 1981); Seyla Benhabib, *Critique, Norm, and Utopia: A Study of the Foundations of Critical Theory* (New York: Columbia University Press, 1986).

131. On Tillich's Marxism, see John W. Murphy, "Paul Tillich and Western Marxism," *American Journal of Theology and Philosophy* 5 (January 1984): 13–24; Guy B. Hammond, *Conscience and Its Recovery: From the Frankfurt School to Feminism* (Charlottesville: University of Virginia Press, 1993), 44–57; Terence M. O'Keefe, "Paul Tillich and the Frankfurt School," in *Theonomy and Autonomy: Studies in Paul Tillich's Engagement with Modern Culture*, ed. John J. Carey (Macon, GA: Mercer University Press, 1982), 67–82; Ronald H. Stone, "Tillich's Critical Use of Marx and Freud in the Social Context of the Frankfurt School," *Union Seminary Quarterly Review* 32 (1977): 3–9; Stone, *Paul Tillich's Radical Social Thought* (Atlanta: John Knox Press, 1980); Dennis P. McCann, "Tillich's Religious Socialism: Creative Synthesis or Personal Statement?" in *The Thought of Paul Tillich*, ed. James Luther Adams, Wilhelm Pauck, and Roger L. Shinn (San Francisco: Harper and Row, 1985), 81–101; Brian Donnelly, *The Socialist Émigré: Marxism and the Later Tillich* (Macon, GA: Mercer University Press, 2003); Jean Richard, "The Socialist Tillich and Liberation Theology," in *Paul Tillich: A New Catholic Assessment*, ed. Raymond F. Bulman and Frederick J. Parrella (Minneapolis: Michael Glazier, 1994), 148–173; John R. Stumme, *Socialism in a Theological Perspective: A Study of Paul Tillich, 1918–1933* (Missoula, MT: Scholars' Press, 1978).

132. Paul Tillich, "The Class Struggle and Religious Socialism" (1929), trans. James Luther Adams, in *Paul Tillich on Creativity*, ed. Jacquelyn Ann Kegley (Lanham, MD: University Press of America, 1989), "Marxism is," "to a powerful," "as a genuine," 104; "the struggle of," 105.

133. James Luther Adams, "Reminiscences of Paul Tillich" (1987), in Adams, *An Examined Faith: Social Context and Religious Commitment*, ed. George W. Beach (Boston: Beacon Press, 1991), 125–133, "you can't," 127; Paul Tillich, *Systematic Theology*, 3 vols. (Chicago: University of Chicago Press, 1951, 1957, 1963), 3: 297–393; Tillich, "The Class Struggle and Religious Socialism," "religious socialism," 105; see James Luther Adams, "Theology and Modern Culture: Paul Tillich," in Adams, *On Being Human Religiously*, ed. Max L. Stackhouse (Boston: Beacon Press, 1976), 225–254; Adams, *Paul Tillich's Philosophy of Culture, Science, and Religion* (New York: Harper and Row, 1965), 203–204.

134. Paul Tillich, "The Protestant Principle and the Proletarian Situation" (1931 pamphlet), in Tillich, *The Protestant Era*, ed. and trans. James Luther Adams (London: Nisbet, 1951), "the state," 239.

135. Tillich, "The Protestant Principle and the Proletarian Situation," "is a quality," 242; "but in Protestantism," 243; "the proletarian," 247.

136. Ibid., "Protestantism in" and "a religion," 256; "the religious," 258.

137. Pauck and Pauck, *Paul Tillich*, 125–127; Hannah Tillich, *From Time to Time*, 147; Stumme, Introduction to *The Socialist Decision*, xxiii.

138. Tillich, *The Socialist Decision*, "it holds," xxxiv.

139. Ibid., "only if," 163.

140. See Martin Heidegger, *Being and Time*, trans. John Macquarrie and Edward Robinson (New York: Harper and Row, 1962); Heidegger, *The Basic Problems of Phenomenology*, trans. Albert Hofstadter (Bloomington: Indiana University Press, 1988); Paul Tillich, *Theology of Culture* (New York: Oxford University Press, 1959); Tillich, *The Courage to Be* (New Haven: Yale University Press, 1952).

141. Tillich, *The Interpretation of History*, 39–40; Tillich, *The Protestant Era*, 93; Tillich, *Theology of Culture*, 10–29, 112–126.

142. Tillich, *The Socialist Decision*, 2–6, "pregnant," 3.

143. Ibid., 27–44.

144. Ibid., 66–93, 127–150.

145. Ibid., "the spirit of" and "there is," 116; "a false," 117.

146. Ibid., "power," 80.

147. Ibid., "in the last," "on national," and "it has learned," 87.

148. Ibid., "the bourgeois," 87; "demonic," 173.

149. Ibid., "socialism places" and "the best," 90.

150. Ibid., "positions," 159; "all" and "the bureaucratization," 160.

151. Tillich, *On the Boundary*, 46; Hannah Tillich, *From Time to Time*, 147–156.

152. "Men of Learning, Jews and non-Jews, Fired by Nazis," *Manchester Guardian Weekly* (May 19, 1933); repr. by Jewish Telegraphic Agency, June 11, 1933, www.jta.org/1933/06/11; Paul Tillich, "The Ninth Anniversary of German Book Burning" (May 18, 1942), in Tillich, *Against the Third Reich: Paul Tillich's Wartime Addresses to Nazi Germany*, trans. Matthew Lon Weaver, ed. Ronald H. Stone and Matthew Lon Weaver (Louisville: Westminster John Knox Press, 1998), 32–35; Pauck and Pauck, *Paul Tillich*, 129–131; Stumme, Introduction to *The Socialist Decision*, xxiv.

153. Pauck and Pauck, *Paul Tillich*, 126–138; Hannah Tillich, *From Time to Time*, 151–156; Henry Sloane Coffin, *A Half Century of Union Theological Seminary, 1896–1945* (New York: Charles Scribner's Sons, 1954), 134–135, "my," 135.

154. Paul Tillich to the German Ministry for Science, Art, and Education, January 20, 1934, in Pauck and Pauck, *Paul Tillich*, 148–150, "as the theoretician," 149.

155. Paul Tillich, "Open Letter to Emanuel Hirsch," October 1, 1934, in *The Thought of Paul Tillich*, 353–388, "your book," 366; Emanuel Hirsch, *Die gegenwärtige geistige Lage im Spiegel philosophischer und theologischer Besinnung* (Göttingen: Vandenhoeck und Ruprecht, 1934); Hirsch, *Christliche Freiheit und politische Bindung: Ein Brief an Dr. Stapel und andere* (Hamburg: Hanseatische Verlagsanstalt, 1935), 38–39; Forstman, *Christian Faith in Dark Times*, 210–221; A. James Reimer, *The Emanuel Hirsch and Paul Tillich Debate: A Study in the Political Ramifications of Theology* (Lewiston, ME: Edwin Mellen Press, 1989).

156. Tillich, *The Interpretation of History*, 26–35, "but it created," 26; "it was and is," 29; Tillich, "The Protestant Principle and the Proletarian Situation," 237–259.

157. Martin Kähler, *Die Wissenschaft der christlichen Lehre* (Leipzig: A. Deichert, 1893); Kähler, *Dogmatische Zeitfragen: Angewandte Dogmen* (Leipzig: A. Deichert, 1908).

158. Tillich, *On the Boundary*, 83–86. This section is clearer in *On the Boundary* than in *The Interpretation of History*.

159. Tillich, *Against the Third Reich*, "The Question of the Jewish People," March 31, 1942, "the people," 14; "upon us," 16; "Dark Clouds are Gathering," December 1942, "today they are," 89.

160. Ibid., "Where Hope Lies This Advent Season," December 8, 1942, "I believe," 93; "The Tenth Anniversary of Hitler's Regime," February 1943, "pre-human" and "two thousand," 118; "The German Legacy," March 2, 1943, "the desire" and "National," 122; "Germany's Rebirth into the Human Race," March 23, 1943, "everything," 134.

161. Pauck and Pauck, *Paul Tillich*, 201–219, "harvest," 219; Paul Tillich, *The Shaking of the Foundations* (New York: Charles Scribner's Sons, 1948).

162. Paul Tillich, "Marx and the Prophetic Tradition," *Radical Religion* 1 (1935): 21–29; Tillich, "The Church and Communism," *Religion in Life* 6 (1937): 347–357; Tillich, "Marxism and Christian Socialism," *Christianity and Society* 7 (1942): 13–18; Tillich, "How Much Truth Is There in Karl Marx?" *Christian Century* 65 (September 1948): 906–908; Tillich, "Existentialism and Religious Socialism," *Christianity and Society* 15 (1949): 8–11; Tillich, "Autobiographical Reflections of Paul Tillich," "a system," 16; Tillich, Horkheimer, Löwe, and Pollock Discussion, "Theorie und Praxis," 1945, in Donnelly, *The Socialist Émigré*, "I once," 20.

163. Paul Tillich, "Beyond Religious Socialism," *Christian Century* 66 (June 15, 1949), 732–733; Tillich, "Autobiographical Reflections of Paul Tillich," "if the prophetic," "prophetic, humanistic," and "calculating," 13; "I lost," 19.

164. Tillich, *The Courage to Be*, quotes 184, 185.

165. Eduard Heimann, "Tillich's Doctrine of Religious Socialism," in *The Theology of Paul Tillich*, 312–325, "immaculate" and "Tillich's error," 320.

166. Ibid., "kind of" and "scientific," 321; see Tillich, "Marxism and Religious Socialism," *The Protestant Era*, 256–257; Tillich, "Kairos," *The Protestant Era*, 37–42; Tillich, *The Socialist Decision*, 106–112; Tillich, "Marx and the Prophetic Tradition," 28–29.

167. Heimann, "Tillich's Doctrine of Religious Socialism," "that the decline," 321.

168. Ibid., "not just," 323; "the noblest" and "which on," 324.

169. Robert Fitch, "The Social Philosophy of Paul Tillich," *Religion and Life* 27 (1958): 247–256, "naïve" and "why Marxism," 255; Alistair MacLeod, *Paul Tillich: An Essay on the Role of Ontology in His Philosophical Theology* (London: Allen and Unwin, 1973), 19; Clark Kucheman, "Justice and the Economic Order: A Critical and Constructive Study of the Economic Thought of Paul J. Tillich" (Ph.D. diss., University of Chicago, 1965); Stumme, *Socialism in Theological Perspective*, discussion of Amelung, 14; McCann, "Tillich's Religious Socialism: 'Creative Synthesis' or Personal Statement?" *The Thought of Paul Tillich*, 81–101.

170. Terence M. O'Keefe, "Paul Tillich's Marxism," *Social Research* 48 (1981): 472–499, "the end" and "little," 476; Walter A. Weisskopf, "Tillich and the Crisis of the West," *The Thought of Paul Tillich*, 63–78; Pauck and Pauck, *Paul Tillich*, 177–195; James

Luther Adams, "Introduction: The Storms of Our Times and *Starry Night*," in *The Thought of Paul Tillich*, 17–18; Ronald Stone, "Paul Tillich: On the Boundary Between Protestantism and Marxism," *Laval Théologique et Philosophie* 45 (October 1989): 393–401; Hammond, "Tillich and the Frankfurt Debates about Patriarchy and the Family," 89–110; James Champion, "Tillich and the Frankfurt School: Parallels and Differences in Prophetic Criticism," *Soundings* 69 (1986): 529; Donnelly, *The Socialist Émigré*.

171. Paul Tillich, "Reply to Interpretation and Criticism," *The Theology of Paul Tillich*, "void," 345; "I myself," 346; Paul Tillich, *Love, Power, and Justice: Ontological Analyses and Ethical Applications* (London: Oxford University Press, 1954).

172. Tillich, "Reply to Interpretation and Criticism," "moral" and "genuine," 346.

5. BRITISH BREAKTHROUGH

1. Frank Bealey and Henry M. Pelling, *Labour and Politics, 1900–1906: A History of the Labour Representation Committee* (London: Macmillan, 1958), 40–44, 284–295; Bealey, ed., *The Social and Political Thought of the British Labour Party* (London: Weidenfeld and Nicolson, 1970), 1–3; G. D. H. Cole, *A History of the Labour Party from 1914* (London: Routledge and Kegan Paul, 1948), 1–3; W. S. Adams, "Lloyd George and the Labour Movement," *Past and Present* 3 (February 1953): 55–64; Albert S. Lindemann, *A History of European Socialism* (New Haven: Yale University Press, 1983), 232–236; Ross I. McKibben, "James Ramsay MacDonald and the Problem of the Independence of the Labour Party, 1910–1914," *Journal of Modern History* 42 (1970): 216–235; John Shepherd, "The Lad from Lossiemouth," *History Today* 57 (November 2007): 31–33; T. L. Jarman, *Socialism in Britain* (New York: Littlehampton, 1972), 119–123.

2. Conrad Noel, "What I Want to Get by My Vote: A Labour View," *Commonwealth* 11 (February 1906): 36–37; Noel, "The Church Socialist League," *Commonwealth* 11 (July 1906): 222–224; Paul Bull, "Socialists and Education," *Commonwealth* 11 (October 1906): 290–293; Peter d'A. Jones, *The Christian Socialist Revival, 1877–1914: Religion, Class, and Social Conscience in Late-Victorian England* (Princeton: Princeton University Press, 1968), 225–281.

3. Conrad Noel, *An Autobiography*, ed. Sidney Dark (London: J. M. Dent, 1945), 1–26; Noel, "The Church Socialist League," 222–224; Noel, *Socialism in Church History* (London: Frank Palmer, 1910), 14–31; Jones, *The Christian Socialist Revival*, 238–248.

4. G. Algernon West, Address to the Church Socialist League Annual Conference, Leicester, May 1909, *Church Socialist Quarterly* 4 (July 1909): 181–189; A. T. B. Pinchard, editorial, *Church Socialist Quarterly* 4 (July 1909): 236–237; George Lansbury, *My Life* (London: Constable, 1928), 90–91; Jones, *The Christian Socialist Revival*, 259–266.

5. J. Ramsay MacDonald, "The Education Bill: The Secular Solution," *Fortnightly Review* 83 (April 1908): 707–716; Philip Snowden, *Autobiography*, 2 vols. (London: 1934), 1: 213–216; Ralph Miliband, *Parliamentary Socialism: A Study in the Politics of Labour* (London: Allen and Unwin, 1961), 19–31; A. M. McBriar, *Fabian Socialism and English Politics, 1884–1918* (London: Cambridge University Press, 1962), 315–320.

6. Virginia Woolf, "Mr. Bennett and Mrs. Brown," *The Hogarth Essays* (London: Hogarth Press, 1924), "human character" and "all human," 4–5; George Dangerfield, *The Strange Death of Liberal England* (London: Constable, 1936).

7. British Labour Party [Sidney Webb and Arthur Henderson], *Labour and the New Social Order* (London: British Labour Party, 1918); Sidney Webb, *Twentieth Century Politics: A Policy of National Efficiency* (London: Fabian Society, Fabian Tract No. 108, 1901); Cole, *A History of the Labour Party*, 9–64; Sidney Webb, *Socialism: True and False* (London: Fabian Society, Fabian Tract No. 51, 1894); Webb, *When Peace Comes: The Way of Industrial Reconstruction* (London: Fabian Society, Fabian Tract No. 181, 1916).

8. Arthur J. Penty, *The Restoration of the Guild System* (London: Swan Sonnenschein, 1906), "owing to," 1; Penty, *Towards a Christian Sociology* (London: G. Allen and Unwin, 1923), 189; Niles Carpenter, *Guild Socialism* (New York: D. Appleton, 1922), 82–84.

9. Penty, *The Restoration of the Guild System*, "is the hope," 35; Editorial [A. R. Orage and Holbrook Jackson], "The Outlook," *The New Age: An Independent Socialist Review of Politics, Literature, and Art* (May 2, 1907), 1; Hilaire Belloc, "The Economics of 'Cheap,'" *Dublin Review* 148 (January/April 1911): 296–297; Belloc, "The Taxation of Rent," *Dublin Review* 145 (July/October 1909), 290–291; Philip Mairet, *A. R. Orage* (London: Dent, 1936).

10. A. R. Orage, editorial, *New Age* (November 1908), "we sent," 23; Maurice Reckitt, "The Future of the Socialist Ideal," *Church Socialist* 2 (February 1913): 13–16; Reckitt, "The Future of the Socialist Ideal," *Church Socialist* 2 (August 1913): 8–15; J. N. Figgis, *Churches in the Modern State* (London: Longmans, Green, 1913); Cécile Laborde, *Pluralist Thought and the State in Britain and France, 1900–25* (Basingstoke: Macmillan, 2000), 45–98; Luke Bretherton, *Resurrecting Democracy: Faith, Citizenship, and the Politics of a Common Life* (Cambridge: Cambridge University Press, 2015), 393; Marc Stears, "Guild Socialism," in *Modern Pluralism: Anglo-American Debates Since 1880*, ed. Mark Bevir (Cambridge: Cambridge University Press, 2012), 40–59.

11. Hilaire Belloc, *The Servile State* (London: T. N. Foulis, 1912); William Cobbett, *History of the Protestant Reformation in England and Ireland* (1824; repr., New York: Benziger Brothers, 1930); Belloc and J. Ramsay MacDonald, *Socialism and the Servile State: A Debate Between Messrs. Hilaire Belloc and J. Ramsay MacDonald, M.P.* (London: West London Federation of the Independent Labour Party, 1911), 1–23; G. K. Chesterton, "Why I Am Not a Socialist," *New Age* (January 4, 1908), 189–190; Chesterton, "The Last of the Rationalists: A Reply to Mr. Bernard Shaw," *New Age* (February 29, 1908), 348; Chesterton, "What Is a Conservative?" *Dublin Review* 150 (January/April 1912): 349–356; A. J. Penty, *A Guildsman's Interpretation of History* (London: G. Allen and Unwin, 1921), 101–102; Maurice B. Reckitt, *As It Happened* (London: J. M. Dent, 1941), 244.

12. Frederick Temple, "The Education of the World," in *Essays and Reviews: The 1860 Text and Its Reading*, ed. Victor Shea and William Whitla (Charlottesville: University Press of Virginia, 2000), 137–164; Peter B. Hinchliff, *Frederick Temple, Archbishop of Canterbury: A Life* (Oxford: Clarendon Press, 1998), 11–25.

13. F. A. Iremonger, *William Temple, Archbishop of Canterbury: His Life and Letters* (London: Oxford University Press, 1948), 1–11; Joseph Fletcher, *William Temple:*

Twentieth-Century Christian (New York: Seabury Press, 1963), 234–242; Lawrence Goldman, *The Life of R. H. Tawney: Socialism and History* (London: Bloomsbury, 2014), 18. My discussion of Temple contains condensed summaries of my discussions in Gary Dorrien, *The Democratic Socialist Vision* (Totowa, NJ: Rowman and Littlefield, 1986), 18–45, and Dorrien, *Kantian Reason and Hegelian Spirit: The Idealistic Logic of Modern Theology* (Oxford: Wiley-Blackwell, 2012), 415–443.

14. Ross Terrill, *R. H. Tawney and His Times: Socialism as Fellowship* (Cambridge: Harvard University Press, 1973), 21–22; Goldman, *The Life of R. H. Tawney*, 13–15; A. W. Wright, *R. H. Tawney* (Manchester: University of Manchester Press, 1987), 7–12.

15. Frank Fletcher, *After Many Days* (London: R. Hale, 1937), 59, 90–91, "all happened," 91; L. S. Pressnell, *Country Banking in the Industrial Revolution* (Oxford: Oxford University Press, 1956), 34–36, 56; W. H. B. Court, *Scarcity and Choice in History* (London: Edward Arnold, 1970), 56.

16. Iremonger, *William Temple*, 12–59; Fletcher, *William Temple: Twentieth-Century Christian*, 245–246; Henry Jones and J. H. Muirhead, *The Life and Philosophy of Edward Caird* (Glasgow: Maclehose, Jackson, 1921), 30–37; William Beveridge, *India Called Them* (London: Macmillan, 1947); José Harris, *William Beveridge: A Biography* (Oxford: Oxford University Press, 1997), 11–19.

17. Iremonger, *William Temple*, 60–72, "it was laughter," 65; Pan-Anglican Congress, *General Report*, 2 vols. (London: SPCK, 1908), "if Christianity," 101; Fletcher, *William Temple: Twentieth-Century Christian*, 246–247.

18. Goldman, *The Life of R. H. Tawney*, "fraud" and "how do," 22; Terrill, *R. H. Tawney and His Times*, "I grant," 29; Fletcher, *After Many Days*, 69.

19. R. H. Tawney, "The Workers' Educational Association and Adult Education," lecture at University of London, May 8, 1933, in Tawney, *The Radical Tradition: Twelve Essays on Politics, Education and Literature*, ed. Rita Hinden (New York: Pantheon Books, 1964), 82–93; Tawney, *Poverty as an Industrial Problem* (London: Ratan Tata Foundation, 1913), 16; Tawney, "The Economics of Boy Labour," *Economics Journal* 19 (December 1909): 517–537; Iremonger, *William Temple*, 37–43; Mary Stocks, *The Workers' Educational Association* (London: Allen and Unwin, 1953), 37–43.

20. Tawney, "The Workers' Educational Association and Adult Education," "very improper" and "never felt," 89; R. H. Tawney, *The Agrarian Problem in the Sixteenth Century* (London: Longmans, Green, 1912); Terrill, *R. H. Tawney and His Times*, 36–41, "make," 41; Goldman, *The Life of R. H. Tawney*, 32–33; A. J. Davies, *To Build a New Jerusalem: The British Labour Party from Keir Hardie to Tony Blair* (London: Abacus, 1996), 176.

21. Terrill, *R. H. Tawney and His Times*, 108–111; Goldman, *The Life of R. H. Tawney*, 35–51; Beatrice Webb, *Our Partnership* (London: Longmans, Green, 1948). Goldman corrected decades of lore about the marital discord between Tawney and Jeanette Tawney.

22. Tawney, *The Agrarian Problem in the Sixteenth Century*, 13–22, 184–190; David Ormrod, "R. H. Tawney and the Origins of Capitalism," *History Workshop Journal* 18 (1984): 140–142.

23. A. E. Bland, P. A. Brown, and R. H. Tawney, eds., *English Economic History: Select Documents* (London: G. Bell and Sons, 1914).

24. William Temple, "The Divinity of Christ," *Foundations: A Statement of Christian Belief in Terms of Modern Thought, by Seven Oxford Men*, ed. B. H. Streeter (London: Macmillan, 1912), 213–259; William Temple, *The Kingdom of God* (London: Macmillan, 1913), "a thing" and "Christ was," 96; see Dorrien, *Kantian Reason and Hegelian Spirit*, 417–424.

25. *National Mission of Repentance and Hope*, Paper 3 (London: National Mission of Repentance and Hope, 1916), "limitless," cited in Chris Bryant, *Possible Dreams: A Personal History of the British Christian Socialists* (London: Hodder and Stoughton, 1997), 175; Iremonger, *William Temple*, "keep clear," 172; William Temple, "The War and Judgment," sermon of February 1916, in Iremonger, *William Temple*, 173–174, "we can," 173; "one nation" and "but the," 174.

26. R. H. Tawney, *Some Thoughts on Education and the War* (London: Workers' Educational Association, 1917), pamphlet republished as "A National College of All Souls," *Times Educational Supplement* (February 22, 1917) and repr. in Tawney, *The Attack and Other Papers* (London: Allen and Unwin, 1953), 29–34; Goldman, *The Life of R. H. Tawney*, 81–87.

27. R. H. Tawney, "The Attack," *Westminster Gazette* (August 1916), in Tawney, *The Attack and Other Papers*, 11–20, and Tawney, "The Attack," quotes, http://leoklein.com/itp/somme/texts/tawney_1916.html; Terrill, *R. H. Tawney and His Times*, 50; Goldman, *The Life of R. H. Tawney*, 94–100.

28. Terrill, *R. H. Tawney and His Times*, "remember" and "why ever," 51; Goldman, *The Life of R. H. Tawney*, 99–100.

29. R. H. Tawney, "Some Reflections of a Soldier," *The Nation* (October 1916), in Tawney, *The Attack and Other Papers*, 21–28; Tawney, *Democracy or Defeat* (London: Workers' Educational Association, 1917), 2–3; National Mission of Repentance and Hope, Fifth Report, *Christianity and Industrial Problems* (London: SPCK, 1918), 79–80; Maurice B. Reckitt, *Maurice to Temple: A Century of the Social Movement in the Church of England* (London: Faber and Faber, 1947), 162.

30. G. D. H. Cole, "The British Labour Movement—Retrospect and Prospect," *Fabian Special No. 8* (London: Fabian Society, 1952), "made me feel," 3; Cole, "The Inner Life of Socialism," *Aryan Path* 1 (February 1930), 7; Cole, "William Morris and the Modern World," in Cole, *Persons and Periods* (London: Macmillan, 1938), 293; William Morris, "A Dream of John Ball," in *William Morris: Prose, Verse, Lectures and Essays*, ed. G. D. H. Cole (London: Nonesuch Press, 1934), "fellowship is," 212; Margaret Cole, *The Life of G. D. H. Cole* (London: Macmillan, 1971), 21–35; A. W. Wright, *G. D. H. Cole and Socialist Democracy* (Oxford: Clarendon Press, 1979), 15–16; L. P. Carpenter, *G. D. H. Cole: An Intellectual Biography* (Cambridge: Cambridge University Press, 1973), 6–7.

31. Margaret Cole, *The Life of G. D. H. Cole*, 37–38; Margaret Cole, *Growing Up into Revolution* (London: Longmans Green, 1949), 77.

32. Cole, "The British Labour Movement—Retrospect and Prospect," 4; Margaret Cole, "H. G. Wells and the Fabian Society," in *Edwardian Radicalism, 1900–1914: Some Aspects of British Radicalism*, ed. A. J. Anthony Morris (London: Routledge, 1974), 97–114; Margaret Cole, *The Life of G. D. H. Cole*, 41–46; Carpenter, *G. D. H. Cole*, 19;

Andrea Lynn, *Shadow Lovers: The Last Affairs of H. G. Wells* (Boulder, CO: Westview Press, 2001), 10–14; David C. Smith, *H. G. Wells: Desperately Mortal, A Biography* (New Haven: Yale University Press, 1986), 43–55; H. G. Wells, *The New Machiavelli* (1911; repr. London: Penguin Classics, 2005).

33. G. D. H. Cole, *Socialism Now and Fifty Years Ago* (London: Athlone Press, 1958), 2; Carpenter, *G. D. H. Cole*, 16; Margaret Cole, *The Life of G. D. H. Cole*, 45–46.

34. G. D. H. Cole, *The World of Labour: A Discussion of the Present and Future of Trade Unionism* (1st ed., 1913; 4th ed., London: G. Bell and Sons, 1917; 5th ed., 1919), "the State's," 391; "some sort," 352. In 1928 Macmillan acquired the publication rights and brought out another edition of the book. Sidney Webb and Beatrice Webb, *The History of Trade Unionism* (London: self-published for the Amalgamated Society of Engineers, 1894; rev. ed., London: self-published for the Trade Unionists of the United Kingdom, 1919), 1–12. The Webbs defined the trade union as "a continuous association of wage-earners for the purpose of maintaining or improving the conditions of their employment," *The History of Trade Unionism*, 1. In later editions they replaced "their employment" with "their working lives" to clarify that their much-quoted definition did not imply that unions had always accepted capitalism as a system or the wage-system.

35. Cole, *The World of Labour*, 363–366, "the first," 2–3; A. R. Orage, "Survey and Strategy," *New Age* 14 (November 20, 1913), 71–72.

36. Cole, *The World of Labour*, "Sidneywebbicalism," 3; "what is wanted," 4; G. D. H. Cole, Introduction to J.-J. Rousseau, *The Social Contract and Discourses* (London: Dent, 1913), "great," vi; "the whole," xxvii; Cole, "Conflicting Social Obligations," *Proceedings of the Aristotelian Society* (1915): 149–150.

37. G. D. H. Cole, *Labour in War Time* (London: G. Bell and Sons, 1915), "its only consistent," 16.

38. S. G. Hobson, *National Guilds: An Enquiry into the Wage System and the Way Out*, 3rd ed. (London: G. Bell and Sons, 1919), "through the thickets," 10; "it has assumed," 10–11; Hobson, *National Guilds and the State* (London: G. Bell and Sons, 1920); Hobson, *Pilgrim to the Left: Memoirs of a Modern Revolutionist* (London: Longmans, Green, 1938).

39. Hobson, *National Guilds: An Enquiry into the Wage System and the Way Out*, 7–18, 132–151, 235–245, "the more," 1.

40. Reckitt, *As It Happened*, "I admired," 132; Margaret Cole, *The Life of G. D. H. Cole*, 84; Raymond Postgate to Margaret Cole, in *The Life of G. D. H. Cole*, "However, there was," 85.

41. Beatrice Webb, entry of February 14, 1915, in *The Diary of Beatrice Webb*, 4 vols., ed. Norman MacKenzie and Jeanne MacKenzie (Cambridge: Harvard University Press, 1982, 1983, 1984, 1985), "I often," "personal," "the weak," and "manual," 3: 222–223.

42. "Report by the Executive Committee," *Fabian News* 26 (May 1915), 40–41; Clifford Allen et al., "The Right Moment," *Fabian News* 26 (April 1915), 27–29; Margaret Cole, *The Story of Fabian Socialism* (Stanford: Stanford University Press, 1961), 153–154; Beatrice Webb, entry of May 15, 1915, *The Diary of Beatrice Webb*, "Cole disgraced," 3: 229; Margaret Cole, *The Life of G. D. H. Cole*, 87; Beatrice Webb, entry of March 9,

1916, "they are not" and "an intellectual," *The Diary of Beatrice Webb*, 3: 248; G. D. H. Cole, *Trade Unionism and Munitions* (Oxford: Clarendon Press, 1923), 145–147.

43. Sidney Webb and Beatrice Webb, *Industrial Democracy* (London: Longmans, Green, 1897); G. D. H. Cole, *Self-Government in Industry* (London: G. Bell and Sons, 1st ed., 1917; 3rd ed., 1919; 5th ed., 1920), 1.

44. S. G. Hobson, "Liberty Without Function," *New Age* 22 (May 1919), 69–70; Hobson, *National Guilds*, 12–33; A. R. Orage, *An Alphabet of Economics* (London: T. Fisher Unwin, 1917); R. D. Maeztu, "Beyond the Barriers of Liberty and Authority," *New Age* (September 2, 1915), 424–425.

45. Cole, *Self-Government in Industry*, 4–23.

46. Ibid., 14–22, 131–147, "I want," 14.

47. Ibid., "the result" and "it is," 27; "a synthesis," 28; "everything," 31.

48. Ibid., "a wide," 37.

49. Ibid., 83–85; G. D. H. Cole, *Social Theory* (New York: Frederick A. Stokes, 1920), 151–152.

50. Cole, *Self-Government in Industry*, 119–136.

51. Ibid., 132–148.

52. Figgis, *Churches in the Modern State*, 3–53, 54–98, "more and more," 52; John N. Figgis, *The Gospel and Human Needs* (London: Longmans, Green, 1911); Figgis, *The Fellowship of the Mystery* (London: Longmans, Green, 1915); Figgis, *The Will to Freedom: or, the Gospel of Nietzsche and the Gospel of Christ* (London: Longmans, Green, 1917); Hilaire Belloc and Cecil Chesterton, *The Party System* (London: H. Latimer, 1913); Bertrand Russell, *Proposed Roads to Freedom: Socialism, Anarchism, and Syndicalism* (New York: Henry Holt, 1919); M. Cohen, "Communal Ghosts and Other Perils in Social Philosophy," *Journal of Philosophy* 16 (1919): 673–690.

53. Marc Stears, *Progressives, Pluralists, and the Problems of the State* (Oxford: Oxford University Press, 2002) 90–123.

54. Cole, *Self-Government in Industry*, 180–193, "help," 189.

55. Maurice B. Reckitt and C. E. Bechhofer, *The Meaning of National Guilds* (London: Cecil Palmer and Hayward, 1918), 4–5.

56. Margaret Cole, *Growing Up into Revolution*, 75–79; Cole, *The Life of G. D. H. Cole*, "as unconscious," 89; "as nearly," 90; Beatrice Webb, entry of November 7, 1918, in *The Life of G. D. H. Cole*, "from the," 88, and *The Diary of Beatrice Webb*, 3: 317–318.

57. Hobson, *Pilgrim to the Left*, "in this hectic," 193; G. D. H. Cole, *Labour in the Commonwealth: A Book for the Younger Generation* (London: Headley Brothers, 1919), 15–40; Carpenter, *G. D. H. Cole*, 43; Margaret Cole, *The Story of Fabian Socialism*, 182.

58. Cole, *Social Theory*, 4–18, "a large," 149; Cole, *Self-Government in Industry*, 22–23.

59. Cole, *Social Theory*, "the facts," 21.

60. Ibid., 81–102.

61. Ibid., 103–116, "a coordinated," 109.

62. Ibid., 144–157, "suffers from," 156; "if economic," 153; G. D. H. Cole, *Guild Socialism Restated* (London: L. Parsons, 1920), 31–32; Richard Vernon, "Introduction," Transaction Books repr. of *Guild Socialism Restated* (New Brunswick, NJ: Transaction Books, 1980), xx–xxi; Carpenter, *G. D. H. Cole*, 59–66.

63. Cole, *Social Theory*, 172–179, "only through," 178.

64. Ibid., "we cannot," 204; Margaret Cole, *The Life of G. D. H. Cole*, 104–119.

65. Reckitt and Bechhofer, *The Meaning of National Guilds*, "blazing" and "something of," xiii–xiv.

66. Cole, *Self-Government in Industry*, "multiplicity," 148; P.-J. Proudhon, *On the Principle of Federation*, trans. and ed. Richard Vernon (Toronto: University of Toronto Press, 1979), 49; Vernon, "Introduction," Proudhon, *On the Principle of Federation*, xii.

67. Cole, *Guild Socialism Restated*, "Guildsmen," "greatest," "politics," and "any," 12; "terrible" and "medley," 159; Cole, Introduction to J.-J. Rousseau, *The Social Contract and Discourses*, xxvii.

68. Cole, Introduction to J.-J. Rousseau, *The Social Contract and Discourses*, xxxi; Cole, *Guild Socialism Restated*, "vast" and "purely," 15; "we must," 16.

69. Cole, *Guild Socialism Restated*, "loose and," 64; "the greatest," 65; "if the," 61.

70. Margaret Cole, *The Story of Fabian Socialism*, 193–194; Margaret Cole, *The Life of G. D. H. Cole*, 120–122.

71. C. H. Douglas, *Economic Democracy* (London: Cecil Palmer, 1920), "it is simply," 6; Douglas, *Social Credit* (London: Cecil Palmer, 1924).

72. Beatrice Webb, entry of October 1, 1921, *The Diary of Beatrice Webb*, "Cole really" and "a lunatic," 3: 388.

73. Beatrice Webb, entry of May 17, 1924, *The Diary of Beatrice Webb*, "a lost" and "he is," 4: 27.

74. G. D. H. Cole, *The Next Ten Years in British Social and Economic Policy* (London: Macmillan, 1929), 16–21; Beatrice Webb, entry of September 5, 1926, "I hate," *The Diary of Beatrice Webb*, 4: 97; "the desire," 4: 98; Beatrice Webb, entry of July 20, 1936, *The Diary of Beatrice Webb*, 4: 373; Reckitt, *Maurice to Temple*, 167; G. D. H. Cole, *Practical Economics* (London: Pelican Books, 1937); Cole, *Socialism in Evolution* (London: Pelican Books, 1938); Cole, *Fabian Socialism* (London: George Allen and Unwin, 1943); Cole, *A Century of Co-operation* (Oxford: George Allen and Unwin, 1944); Cole and Margaret Cole, *A Guide to Modern Politics* (New York: Alfred A. Knopf, 1934); Sidney and Beatrice Webb, *Soviet Communism: A New Civilization?* 2 vols. (New York: Charles Scribner's, 1935); the second and third editions of 1938 and 1941 dropped the question mark from the title.

75. Cole, *Fabian Socialism*, "liberal socialism," 114; Cole, *What Marx Really Meant* (New York: Alfred A. Knopf, 1934), "fully as important," 292.

76. C. Wright Mills, *The Marxists* (New York: Penguin Books, 1963), 153; G. D. H. Cole, *The Meaning of Marxism* (1948; repr. Ann Arbor: University of Michigan Press, 1964), "I remain," 12; "in a good," 11; Cole, "Marx and the Marxists," *Outlook* (1948), in Wright, *G. D. H. Cole and Socialist Democracy*, 232; Cole, *Socialist Economics* (London: V. Gollancz, 1950), "nothing in," 144.

77. G. D. H. Cole, "The Decline of Capitalism," 1939 lecture to the Fabian Society, in Wright, *G. D. H. Cole and Socialist Democracy*, "despite all," 226; Harold J. Laski, "Unity and the People's Front," *Labour Monthly* (March 1937); Cole, *The People's Front* (London: Victor Gollancz, 1937), 249–250.

78. G. D. H. Cole, *Europe, Russia, and the Future* (London: Victor Gollancz, 1941), "clean the stables," 15; "even with" and "better to be," 16; Wright, *G. D. H. Cole and Socialist Democracy*, 246; Carpenter, *G. D. H. Cole*, 192.

79. R. H. Tawney, *The Sickness of an Acquisitive Society* (London: Fabian Society/Allen and Unwin, 1920); Terrill, *R. H. Tawney and His Times*, 53.

80. R. H. Tawney, "The British Coal Industry and the Question of Nationalization," *Quarterly Journal of Economics* 35 (November 1920): 61–107; Tawney, "The Recent Proposals for the Nationalization of the British Coal Industry," *Clark College Record* 15 (October 1920): 233–256; Tawney, "The Coal Problem," *Contemporary Review* 119 (June 1921): 727–737; Tawney, *The Nationalization of the Coal Industry* (London: Labour Party, 1922); Goldman, *The Life of R. H. Tawney*, 114–119; Margaret Cole, *Beatrice Webb* (New York: Harcourt, Brace, 1946), 156.

81. R. H. Tawney, *The Acquisitive Society* (New York: Harcourt, Brace, 1920), "the material," 84; "it is foolish," 84–85.

82. Ibid., 91–105.

83. Ibid., "nothing for," 108; Building Trade Committee, "Scientific Management and the Reduction of Costs," *The Industrial Council for the Building Industry* (August 1919), in Tawney, *The Acquisitive Society*, 106–108.

84. Tawney, *The Acquisitive Society*, "it must," 184.

85. Graham Wallas, review of *The Acquisitive Society*, by R. H. Tawney, *The Nation* (June 11, 1921), 401; Matthew Grimley, *Citizenship, Community, and the Church of England: Liberal Anglican Theories of the State Between the Wars* (Oxford: Oxford University Press, 2004), 116; Bryant, *Possible Dreams*, 173–197; Arnold Toynbee, *Acquaintances* (London: Oxford University Press, 1967), 89–90; Terrill, *R. H. Tawney and His Times*, 58.

86. R. H. Tawney, *Religion and the Rise of Capitalism: A Historical Study*, Holland Memorial Lectures, 1922 (New York: Harcourt, Brace, 1926), ix, 14; Max Weber, *The Protestant Ethic and the Spirit of Capitalism*, trans. Peter Baehr and Gordon C. Wells (German ed., 1905; New York: Penguin, 2002); Ernst Troeltsch, *The Social Teaching of the Christian Churches*, 2 vols., trans. Olive Wyon (German ed., 1912; London: George Allen and Unwin, 1931).

87. Tawney, *Religion and the Rise of Capitalism*, 17–62.

88. Ibid., 63–194; Troeltsch, *The Social Teaching of the Christian Churches*, 2: 515–624; Ernst Troeltsch, *Protestantism and Progress: The Significance of Protestantism for the Rise of the Modern World* (1st English ed., 1912; repr., Philadelphia: Fortress Press, 1986), 41–69.

89. Tawney, *Religion and the Rise of Capitalism*, "one-sided" and "of course," 316.

90. Ibid., "horrified," 317.

91. Ibid., "departments," 277.

92. Ibid., "is to destroy," 283; "is the supreme" and "what is certain," 286.

93. Geoffrey Studdert Kennedy, *Democracy and the Dog Collar* (London: Hodder and Stoughton, 1921), 220–221; Bruce Wollenberg, *Christian Social Thought in Great Britain Between the Wars* (Lanham, MD: University Press of America, 1997), 43–44; Bryant, *Possible Dreams*, 177; Reckitt, *Maurice to Temple*, 170.

94. R. H. Tawney, "Industry and Property," *The Pilgrim* (October 1924); Tawney, "Protecting Our Churches," *Manchester Guardian* (December 4, 1925); Trevor Beeson, *Priests and Politics: The Church Speaks Out* (London: SCM Press, 2013), "we need," 93; Bryant, *Possible Dreams*, "conventional," 181; John Kent, *William Temple: Church, State and Society in Britain, 1880–1950* (Cambridge: Cambridge University Press, 1992), 122–125, 135–148; Wollenberg, *Christian Social Thought in Great Britain Between the Wars*, 38–40; Sidney Dark, *The People's Archbishop: The Man and His Message* (London: James Clarke, 1942), 30–31.

95. Reckitt, *Maurice to Temple*, "the bishops," 174.

96. William Temple, "Industry and the Community," *The Pilgrim* (1926), in Temple, *Essays in Christian Politics and Kindred Subjects* (London: Longmans, Green, 1927), 42–57, "quite evidently" and "if that is," 44; Temple, *Christianity and the State* (London: Macmillan, 1928), 78; R. H. Tawney, "How the Strike Came: A Day to Day Diary of the Negotiations," *Labour Magazine* (June 1926); Terrill, *R. H. Tawney and His Times*, 78; T. S. Ashton, "Richard Henry Tawney, 1880–1962," *Proceedings of the British Academy* (1962): 466; Bryant, *Possible Dreams*, 182–183; Edward Norman, *Church and Society in England, 1770–1970* (Oxford: Clarendon Press, 1976), 340.

97. Cole, *A History of the Labour Party from 1914*, "hardship," 193; Reckitt, *Maurice to Temple*, "mischievousness," 175; "you cannot," 177; V. A. Demant, *The Miners' Distress and the Coal Problem: An Outline for Christian Thought and Action* (London: SCM Press, 1929); R. H. Tawney, "God and Mammon," *Manchester Guardian* (July 23, 1931); Tawney, "Coal Industry Must Be Reorganized," *Manchester Guardian* (June 1, 1926).

98. *Labour and the Nation* (London: British Labour Party, 1928), "socialism is," 2; Cole, *A History of the Labour Party from 1914*, 196–217; Philip Snowden, *The Christ That Is to Be*, 3rd ed. (London: ILP pamphlet, 1905).

99. *Labour and the Nation*, "from a sordid," 14; Martin Francis, *Ideas and Policies Under Labour, 1945–1951* (Manchester: Manchester University Press, 1997), 71–73.

100. Ross McKibbin, "The Economic Policy of the Second Labour Government, 1929–1931," *Past and Present* 68 (August 1975): 95–123; Charles L. Mowat, "The Fall of the Labour Government in Great Britain, August 1931," *Huntington Library Quarterly* 7 (August 1944): 353–386; Phillip Williamson, *National Crisis and National Government: British Politics, the Economy, and the Empire, 1926–1932* (Cambridge: Cambridge University Press, 1992); Nicholas Owen, "MacDonald's Parties: The Labour Party and the 'Aristocratic Embrace,' 1922–31," *Twentieth-Century British History* 18 (2007): 1–53.

101. David Marquand's biography launched revisionist renderings of MacDonald; Marquand, *Ramsay MacDonald* (London: Jonathan Cape, 1977).

102. Cole, *A History of the Labour Party from 1914*, "MacDonald had," 258; "tried to get," 236.

103. R. H. Tawney, "The Choice Before the Labour Party," *Political Quarterly* 3 (July 1932): 323–345.

104. Ibid., "what Labour most," 326; "it frets," 327; "they sweep," 329.

105. Ibid., "never office," 340; "who will," 341.

106. Thomas Jones, *A Diary With Letters, 1931–1950* (London: Oxford University Press, 1954), "Economic," 102; Terrill, *R. H. Tawney and His Times*, 72; Goldman, *The Life of R. H. Tawney*, 157–161; John Shepherd, *George Lansbury: At the Heart of Old Labour* (Oxford: Oxford University Press, 2002), 320–329; George Lansbury, *My Life* (London: Constable, 1928); Bryant, *Possible Dreams*, 207–208.

107. R. H. Tawney, *Equality* (1st ed., New York: Harcourt, Brace, 1931; 4th ed., London: George Allen and Unwin, 1952; repr., London: George Allen and Unwin, 1964), 25–31.

108. Ibid., "for the" and "small enough," 93; "inequality," 94.

109. Ibid., "has colored" and "in communities," 57.

110. Ibid., "what is important," 113.

111. Ibid., "the idea," "it is," "educationally," and "socially," 145.

112. Ibid., 211–235, "exaggerated," 204; "an epidemic," 198; "to a half-tribal," 192.

113. Iremonger, *William Temple*, 363–386, "the voice," 376; Fletcher, *William Temple: Twentieth-Century Christian*, 266–268; William Temple, *Nature, Man and God* (London: Macmillan, 1934), quote, 448–449.

114. Temple, *Nature, Man and God*, 3–56.

115. Ibid., ix–x.

116. S. Alexander, *Space, Time, and Deity*, 2 vols. (London: Macmillan, 1920); C. Lloyd Morgan, *Emergent Evolution* (London: Williams and Norgate, 1923); Lloyd Morgan, *Life, Mind and Deity* (London: Williams and Norgate, 1925); J. F. Bethune-Baker, *The Way of Modernism and Other Essays* (Cambridge: Cambridge University Press, 1927), 50–91; Alfred North Whitehead, *Science and the Modern World* (New York: Macmillan, 1925).

117. Alfred North Whitehead, *Religion in the Making* (New York: Macmillan, 1926), "binding," 158; Henri Bergson, *Creative Evolution*, trans. Arthur Mitchell (New York: Henry Holt, 1911); Bergson, *The Creative Mind: An Introduction to Metaphysics*, trans. Mabelle L. Andison (New York: Philosophical Library, 1946); Lewis S. Ford, *The Emergence of Whitehead's Metaphysics, 1925–1929* (Albany: State University of New York Press, 1986); Martin Heidegger, *Being and Time*, trans. John Macquarrie and Edward Robinson (New York: Harper and Row, 1962); Heidegger, *The Basic Problems of Phenomenology*, trans. Albert Hofstadter (Bloomington: Indiana University Press, 1988); Gene Reeves and Delwin Brown, "The Development of Process Theology," in *Process Philosophy and Christian Thought*, ed. Delwin Brown, Ralph E. James Jr., and Gene Reeves (Indianapolis: Bobbs-Merrill, 1971), 22–23.

118. Alfred North Whitehead, *Process and Reality: An Essay in Cosmology* (New York: Macmillan, 1929), 27–54, "the creative" and "both are," 521; "the unlimited" and "the lure," 522; Whitehead, *Adventures of Ideas* (1933; repr., New York: Free Press, 1967), 175–190; William A. Christian, *An Interpretation of Whitehead's Metaphysics* (New Haven: Yale University Press, 1959), 11–13.

119. Temple, *Nature, Man and God*, quote 66.

120. Ibid., 57–81.

121. Ibid., quotes, 128.

122. Ibid., quote 133.

123. Ibid., 257–259; Whitehead, *Process and Reality*, "the great," 497.

124. Temple, *Nature, Man and God*, quote 269; see Jack F. Padgett, *The Christian Philosophy of William Temple* (The Hague: Martinus Nijhoff, 1974), 67–79.

125. Temple, *Nature, Man and God*, quotes 295.

126. Ibid., quotes 312, 315, 317.

127. F. R. Barry, Foreword to William Temple, *Christian Faith and Life* (1931; repr., London: SCM Press, 1963), quote 13.

128. E. F. M. Durbin, *Purchasing Power and Trade Depression: A Critique of Underconsumptionist Theories* (London: Jonathan Cape, 1933); Durbin, *The Power of Credit Policy* (London: Chapman and Hall, 1935); James Meade, *An Introduction to Economic Analysis and Policy*, 2nd ed. (Oxford: Oxford University Press, 1937); Noel Thompson, *Political Economy and the Labour Party: The Economics of Democratic Socialism, 1884–2005*, 2nd ed. (London: Routledge, 2006), 92–93; Cole, *A History of the Labour Party*, 280–284.

129. John Maynard Keynes, *A Treatise on Money: The Applied Theory of Money* (New York: Harcourt, Brace, 1930); Keynes, "The Pure Theory of Money: A Reply to Dr. Hayek," *Economica* 34 (November 1931): 387–397; Keynes, ["Mr. Keynes Theory of Money"]: A Rejoinder, *Economic Journal* 41 (1931): 412–423; Keynes, *The General Theory of Employment, Interest and Money* (New York: Harcourt, Brace, 1935), 245–254; F. A. von Hayek, "Reflections on the Pure Theory of Money of Mr. J. M. Keynes," *Economica* 33 (August 1931): 270–295.

130. J. A. Hobson, *Imperialism* (1902; repr., London: G. Allen and Unwin, 1938); Hobson, *The Industrial System: An Inquiry into Earned and Unearned Income* (London: Longmans, Green, 1910); Hobson, *Democracy after the War* (London: Macmillan, 1917); Hobson, *The Economics of Unemployment* (London: G. Allen and Unwin, 1922).

131. Labour Party, *For Socialism and Peace* (London: Labour Party, 1934), 8–22, "the private," 21; Labour Party, *Socialism and the Condition of the People* (London: Labour Party, 1934), 4–14, "make investment," 10; Labour Party, *Labour's Immediate Program* (London: Labour Party, 1937), 1; Cole, *A History of the Labour Party*, 291–299; Thompson, *Political Economy and the Labour Party*, 130–132; E. Durbin, *New Jerusalems: The Labour Party and the Economics of Democratic Socialism* (London: Routledge, 1985), 214–222; Hugh Dalton, *The Fateful Years, Memoirs 1931–45* (London: Muller, 1957).

132. Douglas Jay, *The Socialist Case* (London: Faber and Faber, 1937), 194–195; Adolf Berle and Gardiner Means, *The Modern Corporation and Private Property* (New York: Macmillan, 1932); Tudor Jones, *Remaking the Labour Party* (London: Routledge, 1996), 26–27.

133. Clement Attlee, response to Prime Minister's Statement, House of Commons, October 3, 1938, http://hansard.millbanksystems.com/commons/1938/oct/03/prime-ministers-statement, "we have seen"; Fletcher, *William Temple: Twentieth-Century Christian*, 274; Iremonger, *William Temple*, 384–385; Rhiannon Vickers, *The Labour Party and the World: The Evolution of Labour's Foreign Policy, 1900–51*, 2 vols. (Manchester: Manchester University Press, 2013), 1: 87–98.

134. R. H. Tawney, Letter to the Editor, *Manchester Guardian* (October 17, 1938), "to be frightened"; Goldman, *R. H. Tawney and His Times*, 163–165.

135. R. H. Tawney, "Why Britain Fights," *New York Times* (July 21, 1940), repr. in Tawney, *Why Britain Fights* (London: Macmillan, 1941), "what on earth," 4; "singularly" and "at any moment," 5; "to preserve," 6; "but to submit," 7.

136. R. H. Tawney to Beatrice Webb, December 6, 1942, "social equality" and "there is so"; Tawney to Dorothy Emmet, February 3, 1961, "in the lump"; Tawney to William Temple, March 23, 1942, in Goldman, *The Life of R. H. Tawney*, 145, 146, 260.

137. William Ebor [William Temple], ed., *Malvern, 1941: The Life of the Church and the Order of Society: Being the Proceedings of the Archbishop of York's Conference* (London: Longmans, Green, 1941), viii–ix, 58–69, 76–77, 89–94, 148–149, "may be," 65; Alan M. Suggate, *William Temple and Christian Social Ethics Today* (Edinburgh: T. and T. Clark, 1987), 98–125; Bryant, *Possible Dreams*, 193–194.

138. William Temple, "Thomism and Modern Needs," *Blackfriars* (March 1944), repr. in Temple, *Religious Experience and Other Essays and Addresses* (London: James Clarke, 1958), 229–236, "in his," 231; Temple, *Christianity and the Social Order* (Harmondsworth, Middlesex: Penguin Books, 1942), "the proper," 77; Kent, *William Temple: Church, State and Society in Britain*, 148–167.

139. Temple, *Christianity and the Social Order*, quote 78.

140. Ibid., quote 96.

141. Ibid., 110–114; William Temple, *The Hope of a New World* (New York: Macmillan, 1941), 54–62.

142. Temple, *Christianity and the Social Order*, 116.

143. Ibid., quote 115.

144. Ibid., 117; William Temple, *The Church Looks Forward* (New York: Macmillan, 1944), quote 116.

145. Fletcher, *William Temple: Twentieth-Century Christian*, 280; Adam Fox, *Dean Inge* (London: John Murray, 1950), Inge quote 157; Iremonger, *William Temple*, Shaw quote, 475.

146. Iremonger, *William Temple*, August 1939 excerpt of broadcast address, 540; excerpt of October 3, 1939, address, 540; "where the method," letter of November 1939, 543; see Temple, *William Temple's Teaching*, ed. A. E. Baker (London: James Clarke, 1949), 190–198.

147. Iremonger, *William Temple*, Roosevelt quote, 627; Beveridge quote, 631; W. R. Matthews et al., *William Temple: An Estimate and an Appreciation*, Niebuhr quote, 110; Bennett quote in *Anglican Theological Review* 25 (July 1943): 3, cited in Fletcher, *William Temple: Twentieth-Century Christian*, 269.

148. Ramsey, *From Gore to Temple*, 160–161, quote 160.

149. Ibid., 160–161.

150. Ibid., 161.

151. Harris, *William Beveridge*, 22–39; William Beveridge, *Unemployment: A Problem of Industry* (1909; repr., London: Longmans, Green, 1912); Paul Addison, *The Road to 1945* (London: Jonathan Cape, 1975), 168–171; Dennis Sewell, "How Eugenics Poisoned the Welfare State," *The Spectator* (November 2009), http://www.spectator.co.uk/2009/11/how-eugenics-poisoned-the-welfare-state.

152. [William Beveridge], *Social Insurance and Allied Services: Report by Sir William Beveridge, Presented to Parliament by Command of His Majesty*, November 1942, http://sourcebooks.fordham.edu/mod/1942beveridge.html; William Beveridge, *Full Employment in a Free Society* (London: Allen and Unwin, 1944); Common Wealth, *What Is Common Wealth?* (London: Common Wealth, 1943); Common Wealth, *We Answer Your Questions* (London: Common Wealth, 1943); Richard Acland, *Forward March* (London: Allen and Unwin, 1941); Acland, *What It Will Be Like in the New Britain* (London: Victor Gollancz, 1942).

153. National Executive Committee of the Labour Party, *The Old World and the New Society: A Report on the Problems of War and Peace Reconstruction* (London: British Labour Party, 1942), http://collections.mun.ca/PDFs/radical/TheOldWorldandtheNewSociety, "those other" and "would be," 6; "they would not" and "war-mongering," 9; "all the major" and "planned production," 10; Herbert Morrison, 1942 Cabinet memorandum, "half-caste" in "Marc Blitzstein, Roland Hayes, and the 'Negro Chorus' at the Royal Albert Hall in 1943," http://www.nickelinthemachine.com/2011/05/marc-blitzstein-roland-hayes-and-the-negro-chorus-at-the-royal-albert-hall-in-1943/.

154. Martin Francis, *Ideas and Policies Under Labour, 1945–51: Building a New Britain* (Manchester: Manchester University Press, 1997), 26–38; J. Tomlinson, "Mr. Attlee's 'Supply-Side Socialism,'" *Economic History Review* 46 (1993): 1–26; Thompson, *Political Economy and the Labour Party*, 137–138.

155. E. F. M. Durbin, *The Politics of Democratic Socialism: An Essay on Social Policy* (London: Routledge, 1940), 291–305; Jay, *The Socialist Case*, 189–215; G. D. H. Cole, *Economic Tracts for the Times* (London: Macmillan, 1932), 13–15; John Strachey, *A Programme for Progress* (London: V. Gollancz, 1940), 53–58, 151–155; Strachey, *The Coming Struggle for Power*, rev. ed. (New York: Modern Library, 1935); Larry Ceplair, *Under the Shadow of War: Fascism, Anti-Fascism, and Marxists, 1918–1939* (New York: Columbia University Press, 1987), 76–102, 163–165; Noel W. Thompson, *John Strachey: An Intellectual Biography* (Hampshire, UK: Macmillan, 1993), 35–41.

156. Labour Party, *Let Us Face the Future: A Declaration of Labour Policy for the Consideration of the Nation* (London: Labour Party, 1945), http://www.politicsresources.net/area/uk/man/lab45.htm., n.p.

157. Ibid., n.p.

158. Steven Fielding, "What Did 'the People' Want? The Meaning of the 1945 General Election," *Historical Journal* 35 (1992): 623–639; Francis, *Ideas and Policies Under Labour*, 34–39; Thompson, *Political Economy and the Labour Party*, 138–139.

159. Labour Party, *Labour Believes in Britain* (London: Labour Party, 1949), 2–5; Labour Party, *A Policy for Secondary Education* (London: Labour Party, 1951); Martin Francis, "Economics and Ethics: The Nature of Labour's Socialism, 1945–1951," *Twentieth-Century British History* 6 (1995): 223–224; Fielding, "What Did 'the People' Want?" 631–639.

160. Samuel H. Beer, *British Politics in the Collectivist Age* (New York: Knopf, 1965), 186–216; David S. Painter, *The United States, Great Britain, and Mossadeqh* (Washington, DC: Georgetown University Press, 1988); Miliband, *Parliamentary Socialism*, 272–

317; David Howell, *British Social Democracy: A Study in Development and Decay* (London: Croom Helm, 1980), 135–179.

161. R. H. S. Crossman, "Towards a Philosophy of Socialism," in *New Fabian Essays*, ed. R. H. S. Crossman (London: J. M. Dent, 1952), 1–32; C. A. R. Crosland, "The Transition from Capitalism," in *New Fabian Essays*, 33–68; Roy Jenkins, "Equality," in *New Fabian Essays*, 69–90; Denis Healey, "Power Politics and the Labour Party," in *New Fabian Essays*, 161–180; Edmund Dell, *The Chancellors: A History of the Chancellors of the Exchequer, 1945–90* (London: HarperCollins, 1997), 135–158; Philip M. Williams, *Hugh Gaitskell: A Political Biography* (Oxford: Oxford University Press, 1982), 22–46, 121–131; John Saville, "Hugh Gaitskell (1906–1963): An Assessment," *Socialist Register* (1980): 155–158; K. Jefferys, *The Churchill Coalition and Wartime Politics, 1940–1945* (Manchester: Manchester University Press, 1991); S. J. Brooke, *Labour's War* (Oxford: Oxford University Press, 1992); Paul Addison, *The Road to 1945: British Politics and the Second World War* (London: Pimlico, 1975).

162. Williams, *Hugh Gaitskell*, 320; Jones, *Remaking the Labour Party*, 26–28; Thompson, *Political Economy and the Labour Party*, 148–149.

163. Tawney lectures in late March and early April 1948, in Goldman, *The Life of R. H. Tawney*, 277–278; Tawney, "Social Democracy in Britain," 1949, in Tawney, *The Radical Tradition*, "too obvious," 158.

164. R. H. Tawney, "British Socialism Today," *Socialist Commentary* (June 1952), in Tawney, *The Radical Tradition*, 171; B. Seebohm Rountree and G. R. Lavers, *Poverty and the Welfare State* (London: Longmans, 1951).

165. Tawney, "British Socialism Today," "indefensible," 173.

166. Ibid., 178–179; Goldman, *The Life of R. H. Tawney*, 283; British Labour Party, "Britain Belongs to You: The Labour Party's Policy for Consideration by the British People," Labour Manifesto 1959, http://politicsresources.net/area/uk/man/lab59.htm.

167. Hugh Gaitskell, Eulogy for R. H. Tawney, February 8, 1962, in Tawney, *The Radical Tradition*, "in exposing" and "I always," 212; "he hated," 213; "abominably" and "the quality," 214.

168. Carole Pateman, *Participation and Democratic Theory* (Cambridge: Cambridge University Press, 1970), 22–27, "minor," 21; Maure L. Goldschmidt, "Rousseau on Intermediate Associations," in *Voluntary Associations*, ed. J. R. Pennock and J. W. Chapman (New York: Atherton, 1969), 119–137; Vernon, "Introduction," xxv.

169. Wright, *G. D. H. Cole and Socialist Democracy*, 264.

6. DEMOCRATIC SOCIALISM AS PLURALISTIC SOCIAL DEMOCRACY

1. Mikhail Heller and Aleksandr M. Nekrich, *Utopia in Power: The History of the Soviet Union from 1917 to the Present*, trans. Phyllis B. Carlos (New York: Summit Books, 1986), 370–511; Robert Leckie, *Delivered from Evil: The Saga of World War II* (New York: Harper and Row, 1987), 648–664; John Lewis Gaddis, *The United States and the Origins of the Cold War, 1941–1947* (New York: Columbia University Press, 1972), 230–243.

2. F. G. Bettany, *Stewart Duckworth Headlam: A Biography* (London: John Murray, 1926), "You," 20; Chris Bryant, *Possible Dreams: A Personal History of the British Christian Socialists* (London: Hodder and Staughton, 1997), 28–71.

3. Paul Bull, "Socialists and Education," *Commonwealth* 11 (October 1906): 290–293; Bull, *Urgent Church Reforms* (London: Mirfield Manuals for the Millions, No. 3, n.d.); N. E. Egerton Swann, "Christian Socialism Since Maurice and Kingsley," *Church Socialist* 6 (July 1917): 129–134.

4. See Edward R. Norman, *The Victorian Christian Socialists* (New York: Cambridge University Press, 1987); Paul Johnson, *Modern Times: The World from the Twenties to the Eighties* (New York: Harper and Row, 1983), 165–166.

5. Carolus Linnaeus, *Systema naturae per regna tria naturae, secundum classes, ordines, genera, species, cum characteribus, differentiis, synonymis, locis,* 3 vols. (Hale: Curt, 1760–1770), 1: 20–24; Georges Cuvier, *Le Régne animal,* 5 vols. (Paris: Deterville Librairie, 1829–1830), 1: 180; William Stanton, *The Leopard's Spots: Scientific Attitudes toward Race in America, 1815–1859* (Chicago: University of Chicago Press, 1960), 15–53; Thomas F. Gossett, *Race: The History of an Idea in America* (New York: Schocken Books, 1965), 54–64; George M. Fredrickson, *Racism: A Short History* (Princeton: Princeton University Press, 2002), 51–75.

6. Charles Darwin, *The Descent of Man* (New York: John Murray, 1874), 166–168; Gossett, *Race: The History of an Idea in America,* 63–83; M. Ruse, *The Darwinian Revolution* (Chicago: University of Chicago Press, 1979).

7. Ernst Haeckel, *The Riddle of the Universe at the Close of the Nineteenth Century* (1900; repr., Cambridge: Cambridge University Press, 2009); Haeckel, *Natürliche Schöpfungsgeschichte* (Berlin: Georg Reimer, 1868), 510–511; Haeckel, *The History of Creation,* 2 vols. (1876; 6th ed.: New York: D. Appleton, 1914), 2: 429; August Schleicher, *Über die Bedeutung der Sprache für die Naturgeschichte des Menschen* (Weimar: Hermann Böhlau, 1865), 16–19; Robert J. Richards, *The Tragic Sense of Life: Ernst Haeckel and the Struggle over Evolutionary Thought* (Chicago: University of Chicago Press, 2008), 255–261; M. K. Richardson and G. Keuck, "Haeckel's ABC of Evolution and Development," *Biological Reviews* 77 (2002): 495–528. Richardson and Keuck show that Haeckel did not argue for recapitulation theory in its strongest possible forms.

8. Jonathan M. Hess, *Germans, Jews, and the Claims of Modernity* (New Haven: Yale University Press, 2002); Michael Mack, *German Idealism and the Jew: The Inner Anti-Semitism of Philosophy and German Jewish Responses* (Chicago: University of Chicago Press, 2003). For the view that Haeckel was a violent anti-Semite and a chief forerunner of the Nazi movement, see Daniel Gasman, *Haeckel's Monism and the Birth of Fascist Ideology* (New York: Peter Lang, 1998). For a similar view, though more moderate about Haeckel's anti-Semitism, see Richard Weikart, *From Darwin to Hitler: Evolutionary Ethics, Eugenics, and Racism in Germany* (New York: Palgrave Macmillan, 2004). For a reading that views Haeckel's anti-Semitism as "behavioral," not racial, and as constitutive of his animus against all orthodox religions, see Richards, *The Tragic Sense of Life: Ernst Haeckel and the Struggle over Evolutionary Thought,* 273–275.

9. Francis Galton, *Essays in Eugenics* (London: Eugenics Education Society, 1909), 31–43; John Maynard Keynes, "Opening Remarks: The Galton Lecture," *Eugenics*

Review 38 (1946): 39–40; Dorothy Porter, "Eugenics and the Sterilization Debate in Sweden and Britain Before World War II," *Scandinavian Journal of History* 24 (1999): 145–162; Donald MacKenzie, "Eugenics in Britain," *Social Studies of Science* 6 (1976): 499–532; C. P. Blacker, *Eugenics: Galton and After* (London: Charles Duckworth, 1952); Victoria Brignell, "The Eugenics Movement Britain Wants to Forget," *New Statesman* (December 9, 2010), http://www.newstatesman.com/society/2010/12/british-eugenics-disabled.

10. Edwin Black, "In Germany's Extermination Program for Black Africans, a Template for the Holocaust," *Times of Israel* (May 5, 2016), http://www.timesofisrael.com/in-germanys-extermination-program-for-black-africans-a-template-for-the-holocaust; Black, *War Against the Weak: Eugenics and America's Campaign to Create a Master Race* (New York: Basic Books, 2003); P. Weindling, "Weimar Eugenics: The Kaiser Wilhelm Institute for Anthropology, Human Heredity and Eugenics in Social Context," *Annals of Science* 42 (1985): 303–318.

11. Ladelle McWhorter, *Racism and Sexual Oppression in Anglo-America: A Genealogy* (Bloomington: Indiana University Press, 2009), 201–207; Stefan Kühl, *The Nazi Connection: Eugenics, American Racism, and German National Socialism* (New York: Oxford University Press, 1994), 20–24, 33–88; Lothrop Stoddard, *The Rising Tide of Color Against White-World Supremacy* (New York: Charles Scribner's Sons, 1920), 9–20; Margaret Sanger, *Women and the New Race* (New York: Brentano, 1920), 91–102; Nancy Ordover, *American Eugenics: Race, Queer Anatomy, and the Science of Nationalism* (Minneapolis: University of Minnesota Press, 2003); Gossett, *Race: The History of an Idea*, 391; Erica B. Boudreau, " 'Yea, I Have a Goodly Heritage': Health Versus Heredity in the Fitter Family Contests, 1920–1928," *Journal of Family History* 30 (2005): 366–387.

12. Gary Dorrien, *The New Abolition: W. E. B. Du Bois and the Black Social Gospel* (New Haven: Yale University Press, 2015), 183–194, 312–313.

13. Albion Tourgée, *Undaunted Radical: The Selected Writings and Speeches of Albion W. Tourgée*, ed. Mark Elliott and John David Smith (Baton Rouge: Louisiana State University Press, 2010); George W. Woodbey, *Black Socialist Preacher*, ed. Philip S. Foner (San Francisco: Synthesis, 1983); John Fiske, "Manifest Destiny," *Harpers Monthly* (March 1885), 578–589; Fiske, *Through Nature to God* (Boston: Houghton Mifflin, 1899), 133–176; William Graham Sumner, *Social Darwinism: Selected Essays of William Graham Sumner* (Englewood Cliffs, NJ: Prentice-Hall, 1963).

14. George D. Herron, *The Christian Society* (Chicago: Fleming H. Revell, 1894); Albion Tourgée, *Murvale Eastman: Christian Socialist* (New York: Fords, Howard and Hulbert, 1890); W. D. P. Bliss, *What Is Christian Socialism?* (Boston: Society of Christian Socialists, 1890).

15. Charles L. Marson, *God's Co-operative Society* (London: Longmans, Green, 1914); W. Howard Paul Campbell, *The Robbery of the Poor* (London: Social Democratic Federation, 1884); Conrad Noel, *Socialism in Church History* (London: Frank Palmer, 1910); George D. Herron, *The Larger Christ* (Chicago: Revell, 1891); Walter Rauschenbusch, *Christianity and the Social Crisis* (1907; repr., Louisville: Westminster John Knox Press, 1991).

16. Ernst Troeltsch, *Gesammelte Schriften*, 4 vols.: 1. Bd. Die Soziallehren der christlichen kirchen und gruppen.–2. Bd. Zur religiösen lage, religionsphilosophie und ethik.–3. Bd. Der historismus und seine probleme. –4. Bd. Aufsätze zur geistesgeschichte und religionssoziologie (Tübingen: J. C. B. Mohr, 1912–1925); Troeltsch, *Meine Bücher* (1922), ibid., 4: 3–18; excerpt, "My Books," in Troeltsch, *Religion in History*, trans. James Luther Adams (Minneapolis: Fortress Press, 1989), 365–378.

17. Ernst Troeltsch, *Die Absolutheit des Christentums und die Religionsgeschichte* (Tübingen: J. C. B. Mohr, 1902), English ed., *The Absoluteness of Christianity and the History of Religions*, trans. David Reid (Louisville: Westminster John Knox Press, 2005), 46–47; Troeltsch, "Die 'kleine Göttinger Fakultät' von 1890," in Hans-Georg Drescher, *Ernst Troeltsch: His Life and Work*, trans. John Bowden (Minneapolis: Fortress Press, 1993), 8; Rudolf Hermann Lotze, *Metaphysik* (Leipzig: F. Meiner, 1912); Lotze, *Logik* (Leipzig: Weidmann'sche Buchhandlung, 1843); Lotze, *Grundzüge der Äesthetik* (Leipzig: S. Hirzel, 1884); Paul A. de Lagarde, *Gesammelte abhandlungen* (Leipzig: F. A. Brockhaus, 1866); Lagarde, *Librorum Veteris Testamenti canonicorum* (Göttingen: Prostat in aedibus Dieterichianus Arnoldi Hoyer, 1883); Wilhelm Bousset, *Jesu Predigt in ihrem Gegensatz zum Judentum: Ein religionsgeschichtlicher Vergleich* (Göttingen: Vandenhoeck und Ruprecht, 1892); Bousset, *Kyrios Christos* (Göttingen: Vandenhoeck und Ruprecht, 1913). This discussion of Troeltsch's social Christianity condenses my discussion in Dorrien, *Kantian Reason and Hegelian Spirit: The Idealistic Logic of Modern Theology* (Oxford: Wiley-Blackwell, 2012), 354–364.

18. Ernst Troeltsch, "Political Ethics and Christianity," 1904 Address to the Evangelical Social Congress, trans. James Luther Adams, in Troeltsch, *Religion in History*, 173–209.

19. Ibid., quote 179.

20. Ibid., quotes 179, 180.

21. Ibid., quotes 181, 182, 184.

22. Ibid., quotes 185.

23. Ibid., quotes 187, 188.

24. Ibid., quote 198–199.

25. Ibid., quotes 203, 208.

26. James Luther Adams, Foreword to Ernst Troeltsch, *The Social Teaching of the Christian Churches*, 2 vols., trans. Olive Wyon (first English ed., New York: Macmillan, 1931; first German ed., Troeltsch, *Die Soziallehren der christlichen Kirchen und Gruppen, Gesammelte Schriften* [Tübingen: J. C. B. Mohr, 1912]; Louisville: Westminster John Knox Press, 1992), Meinecke and Harnack quotes, 1: x.

27. Martin von Nathusius, *Die Mitarbeit der Kirche an der Lösung der sozialen Frage* (Leipzig: Hinrichs, 1893, 1894, 1904).

28. Drescher, *Ernst Troeltsch: His Life and Work*, 222–224, "this time," 222.

29. See Troeltsch, *The Social Teaching of the Christian Churches*, 1: ix–xx.

30. Max Weber, *The Protestant Ethic and the Spirit of Capitalism*, trans. Peter Baehr and Gordon C. Wells (German ed., 1905; New York: Penguin Books, 2002); Ernst Troeltsch, "Die Bedeutung des Protestantismus für die Enstehung der modernen Welt," April 1906 Address to the Ninth Congress of German Historians, Stuttgart; amplified edition

published under the same title in *Historische Zeitschrift* 97 (1906): 1–66; English ed., Troeltsch, *Protestantism and Progress: The Significance of Protestantism for the Rise of the Modern World*, trans. J. Montgomery (1912; Philadelphia: Fortress Press, 1986).

31. Troeltsch, *Protestantism and Progress*, 100–101.

32. Ibid., 101.

33. See Ernst Troeltsch, *Wesen der Religion und der Religionswissenschaft* (1906), in Troeltsch, *Gesammelte Schriften* 2: 452–499; Troeltsch, *Die Trennung von Staat und Kirche, ders Staatliche Religionsunterricht und die theologischen Fakultät* (Tübingen, 1907); Troeltsch, "Luther und die moderne Welt," in *Das Christentum*, ed. P. Herre (Leipzig), 69–101, and Troeltsch, *Gesammelte Schriften* 4: 202–254; Troeltsch, *Die Bedeutung der Geschichtlichkeit Jesu für den Glauben* (Tübingen: J. C. B. Mohr, 1911).

34. Troeltsch, *The Social Teaching of the Christian Churches*, 1: ix.

35. Ibid., 1: xx.

36. Ibid., 2: 688–784, quotes 700, 738.

37. Ibid., quotes 2: 999, 1011.

38. Ibid., 2: 1011, 1012.

39. Ibid., 2: 726–727.

40. Ibid., 2: 727–728.

41. Ibid., 2: 1012.

42. Ibid., 2: 1005.

43. Ibid., 2: 1013.

44. Ernst Troeltsch, *Glaubenslehre*, ed. Gertrud von le Fort (Berlin: Duncker und Humblot, 1925); English ed., *The Christian Faith*, trans. Garrett E. Paul (Minneapolis: Fortress Press, 1991), 16, 113; Ernst Troeltsch to Wilhelm Bousset, May 27, 1896, in Drescher, *Ernst Troeltsch: His Life and Work*, 57; H. Richard Niebuhr, *Christ and Culture* (New York: Harper and Row, 1951).

45. Troeltsch, *The Christian Faith*, quote 113.

46. Troeltsch, "The Significance of the Historical Jesus for Faith," 187–188; Troeltsch, *The Christian Faith*, quotes 92, 17; see Sarah Coakley, *Christ Without Absolutes: A Study of the Christology of Ernst Troeltsch* (Oxford: Oxford University Press, 1988); Walter E. Wyman Jr., *The Concept of Glaubensehre: Ernst Troeltsch and the Theological Heritage of Schleiermacher* (Chico, CA: Scholars' Press, 1983); *Ernst Troeltsch and the Future of Theology*, ed. John Powell Clayton (London: Cambridge University Press, 1976).

47. Ernst Troeltsch, "Friede auf Erden," *Die Hilfe* 51 (December 17, 1914), "antithesis," 833; Troeltsch, *Nach Erklürung der Mobilmachung* (Heidelberg: Carl Winters Universitätsbuchhandlung, 1914), "Oh!," 6; Troeltsch, *Das Wesen des Deutschen* (Heidelberg: Carl Winters Universitätsbuchhandlung, 1915), "Be German," 32; Troeltsch, *Unser Volksheer* (Heidelberg: Carl Winters Universitätsbuchhandlung, 1914), "Asiatic," 5; all cited in Robert J. Rubanowice, *Crisis in Consciousness: The Thought of Ernst Troeltsch* (Tallahassee: University Presses of Florida, 1982), 99–130, quotes on 101, 102, 103, 104; see Gustav Schmidt, *Deutscher Historismus und der Uebergang zur parlamentarischen Demokratie* (Hamburg: Matthiesen, 1964).

48. Ernst Troeltsch, *Der Historismus und seine Probleme* (Berlin: R. Heise, 1924), and Troeltsch, *Gesammelte Schriften*, quote 3: 677.

49. Troeltsch, *Der Historismus und seine Probleme*, 765–767; Ernst Troeltsch, *Der Historismus und seine Überwindung* (Berlin: Heise, 1924); English ed., Troeltsch, *Christian Thought: Its History and Application*, ed. F. von Hügel (1923; repr., New York: Meridian Books, 1957), 123–136, 218–222; see Rubanowice, *Crisis in Consciousness: The Thought of Ernst Troeltsch*, 62–98.

50. Troeltsch, *Der Historismus und seine Probleme*, *Gesammelte Schriften*, 3: 702–720, quotes 708, 710; see Troeltsch, *Christian Thought: Its History and Application*, 121–144.

51. Troeltsch, *Der Historismus und seine Probleme*, *Gesammelte Schriften*, 3: 728–729.

52. Ernst Troeltsch, "Ein Apfel von Baume Kierkegaards," *Christliche Welt* 35 (1921): 186–189; English ed., "An Apple from the Tree of Kierkegaard," in *The Beginnings of Dialectic Theology*, ed. James M. Robinson, trans. Louis De Grazia and Keith R. Crim (Richmond: John Knox Press, 1968), 311–316, quote 314.

53. Reinhold Niebuhr, *Moral Man and Immoral Society: A Study in Ethics and Politics* (New York: Scribner's, 1932), "a sublime" and "malignant," 277; Niebuhr, *Reflections on the End of an Era* (New York: Scribner's, 1934), 24–28; Niebuhr, "Why I Leave the F.O.R.," *Christian Century* 51 (January 3, 1934), in Niebuhr, *Love and Justice: Selections from the Shorter Writings of Reinhold Niebuhr*, ed. D. B. Robertson (Louisville: Westminster John Knox Press, 1992), "recognizing," 259; Niebuhr, "Dr. Niebuhr's Position," *Christian Century* 50 (January 18, 1933), 91–92; Niebuhr, "Ten Years That Shook My World," *Christian Century* 56 (April 26, 1939), 546; Niebuhr, "After Capitalism—What?" *The World Tomorrow* (March 1, 1933), 204; Niebuhr, "New Deal Medicine," *Radical Religion* 4 (Spring 1939): 1–2; Niebuhr, "Roosevelt's Merry-Go-Round," *Radical Religion* 3 (Spring 1938): 4; Niebuhr, *The Children of Light and the Children of Darkness: A Vindication of Democracy and a Critique of Its Traditional Defense* (New York: Scribner's, 1944), 113–114; Gary Dorrien, *Economy, Difference, Empire: Social Ethics for Social Justice* (New York: Columbia University Press, 2010), 30–37.

54. R. H. Tawney, "British Socialism Today," *Socialist Commentary* (June 1952), in Tawney, *The Radical Tradition: Twelve Essays on Politics, Education and Literature*, ed. Rita Hinden (New York: Pantheon Books, 1964), "dogmatic," 169.

55. Ibid., "I remain" and "sentiments," 169; "the impulse" and "working without," 168.

56. Tawney, "Social Democracy in Britain," 1949, in *The Radical Tradition*, "not a dog," 153; "pander to," 156.

57. Ibid., "a serviceable," 163; "Why, in heaven's," 164; Friedrich von Hayek, *The Road to Serfdom* (London: Routledge and Kegan Paul, 1944).

58. Alasdair MacIntyre, "The Socialism of R. H. Tawney," *New York Review of Books* (July 30, 1964), http://www.nybooks.com/articles/1964/07/30/the-socialism-of-r-h-tawney.

59. Ibid.

60. Ibid.

61. Ibid.

62. Peter Lamb and James Docherty, *Historical Dictionary of Socialism* (Lanham, MD: Scarecrow Press, 2006), 76–77, 177, 197.

63. I Congress of the Socialist International, Frankfurt, June 30–July 3, 1951, "Aims and Tasks of Democratic Socialism," http://www.socialistinternational.or/view/Article.

64. C. A. R. Crosland, "The Transition from Capitalism," in *New Fabian Essays*, ed. R. H. S. Crossman (London: J. M. Dent, 1952), 42–47; Crosland, *The Future of Socialism* (New York: Macmillan, 1956), "a bad," 67.

65. R. H. S. Crossman, Michael Foot, and Ian Markado, eds., *Keep Left* (London: New Statesman, 1947); Anthony Howard, *Crossman: The Pursuit of Power* (London: Jonathan Cape, 1990), 18–28; Tam Dalyell, *Dick Crossman: A Portrait* (London: Weidenfeld and Nicolson, 1989), 8–20; Crossman, *Palestine Mission: A Personal Record* (New York: Harper, 1947); Crossman, ed., *The God That Failed* (New York: Harper, 1950).

66. R. H. S. Crossman, "Towards a Philosophy of Socialism," in *New Fabian Essays*, 4–6.

67. Ibid., "there is" and "judging by," 8.

68. Ibid., 9–12.

69. Ibid., "imposed" and "even," 15.

70. Ibid., "with suppressed" and "military," 23.

71. Ibid., "true aim" and "to the socialist," 26; Roy Jenkins, *In Pursuit of Progress: A Critical Analysis of the Achievements and Prospects of the Labour Party* (London: Heinemann, 1953), 169; Jenkins, "Equality," in *New Fabian Essays*, 71–73.

72. Gary Dorrien, *The Neoconservative Mind: Politics, Culture, and the War of Ideology* (Philadelphia: Temple University Press, 1993), 30–31; Max Nomad, *Rebels and Renegades* (1932; repr., Freeport, NY: Books for Libraries Press, 1968); Nomad, *Apostles of Revolution* (1939; repr., New York: Collier Books, 1961).

73. Leon Trotsky, "Not a Workers' and Not a Bourgeois State?" in *Writings of Leon Trotsky* (1937–38) (New York: Pathfinder Press, 1970), 60–71, "partial," 67; Dorrien, *The Neoconservative Mind*, 31.

74. Leon Trotsky, "Once Again on the 'Crisis of Marxism,'" *Writings of Leon Trotsky* (1938–39) (New York: Pathfinder Press, 1974), 204–206; Trotsky, "Bureaucratism and the Revolution" and "Is the Bureaucracy a Ruling Class?" in *Basic Writings of Trotsky*, ed. Irving Howe (New York: Random House, 1963), 170–177, 216–222; Trotsky, "A Petty-Bourgeois Opposition in the Socialist Workers Party," in Trotsky, *In Defense of Marxism: Against the Petty-Bourgeois Opposition* (New York: Merit Publishers, 1965), 43–62; Bruno Rizzi, *The Bureaucratization of the World*, trans. Adam Westoby (1st Italian ed., 1939; English ed., New York: Free Press, 1985), "the Soviet," 50; Max Shachtman, untitled essay of 1940, in Shachtman, *The Bureaucratic Revolution: The Rise of the Stalinist State* (New York: Ronald Press, 1962), repr. as "Stalinism: A New Social Order" in *Essential Works of Socialism*, ed. Irving Howe (New Haven: Yale University Press, 1976), 526–546.

75. Daniel Bell, "The Strange Tale of Bruno R.," *New Leader* 42 (September 28, 1959), 19; Nomad, *Aspects of Revolt*, 15; James Burnham, "Letter of Resignation of James Burnham from the Workers Party," in Trotsky, *In Defense of Marxism*, 207–211; Burnham, *The Managerial Revolution: What Is Happening in the World?* (New York: John Day, 1941); Julius Jacobson, "The Two Deaths of Max Shachtman," *New Politics* 10 (Winter 1973): 96–99; Tom Kahn, "Max Shachtman: His Ideals and His Movement," *New America* 10 (November 16, 1972), 5; Irving Howe, *A Margin of Hope: An Intellectual Autobiography* (New York: Harcourt Brace Jovanovich, 1982), 40–55; Michael Harrington, *Fragments of the Century* (New York: Saturday Review Press, 1972), 67–75;

Maurice Isserman, *If I Had a Hammer . . . The Death of the Old Left and the Birth of the New Left* (New York: Basic Books, 1987), 37–75.

76. Burnham, *The Managerial Revolution*, 172–246; James Burnham, "The Sixth Turn of the Communist Screw," *Partisan Review* 11 (Summer 1944): 366; Dorrien, *The Neoconservative Mind*, 36–37.

77. Crossman, "The Philosophy of Socialism," 12, 27; Crosland, "The Transition from Capitalism," 38–39, 48–49.

78. Crossman, "The Philosophy of Socialism," "today the," 12; "the planned" and "the main," 27.

79. Ibid., 28–29.

80. R. H. S. Crossman, *Labour in the Affluent Society* (London: Fabian Society, 1960), 6–19; Crossman, "The Spectre of Revisionism," *Encounter* (April 1960), 24–28; Crossman, *The Diaries of a Cabinet Minister*, 3 vols. (New York: Holt, Rinehart and Winston, 1976–1978); Hugo Young, *The Crossman Affair* (London: Jonathan Cape, 1976), 11–29.

81. Crosland, *The Future of Socialism*, "has little" and "his prophecies," 20–21; "a towering," 21; "who suffer," 63.

82. Ibid., "that is why" and "Quixotic," 100.

83. Ibid., "today we," "posthumously," "a greater," and "total," 524; Keith Perry, "Roy Jenkins' Male Lover Tony Crosland Tried to Halt His Marriage," *Daily Telegraph* (March 10, 2014); Michael Bloch, "Daily Lives—A History of Sex and Secrecy at Westminster," *The Guardian* (May 16, 2015).

84. C. A. R. Crosland, *The Conservative Enemy: A Programme of Radical Reform for the 1960s* (New York: Schocken Books, 1962), "a remarkable," 218; T. Nicholls, *Ownership, Control and Ideology* (London: Allen and Unwin, 1969); Tudor Jones, *Remaking the Labour Party* (London: Routledge, 1996), 30–31; Noel Thompson, *Political Economy and the Labour Party: The Economics of Democratic Socialism, 1884–2005*, 2nd ed. (London: Routledge, 2006), 148–150; N. Abercrombie and A. Warde, *Contemporary British Society* (Oxford: Polity Press, 1988), 17–27.

85. Crosland, *The Future of Socialism*, "what really," 73; "the ideal" and "but I," 496.

86. Ibid., 486–490; Jenkins, *The Pursuit of Progress*, 107.

87. Douglas Jay, *The Socialist Case* (London: Faber and Faber, 1937), 277–278; Crosland, *The Future of Socialism*, 492–493; Hugh Gaitskell, *Socialism and Nationalization* (London: Fabian Society, 1956), 35–36.

88. Crosland, *The Conservative Enemy*, "nagging" and "we are," 217.

89. Crosland, *The Future of Socialism*, "the two," 346.

90. Crosland, *The Conservative Enemy*, 220–223, "there is," 133–134.

91. "Clause Four: The Original," and "Clause Four: Current Version," http://www.labourcounts.com/oldclausefour.htm, "The Labour Party is"; Aisha Gani, "Clause IV: A Brief History," *The Guardian* (August 9, 2015).

92. Horst Mendershausen, "Prices, Money and the Distribution of Goods in Postwar Germany," *American Economic Review* 39 (June 1949): 646–672; Walter Heller, "Tax and Monetary Reform in Occupied Germany," *National Tax Journal* 2 (1949): 215–231; Fred H. Klopstock, "Monetary Reform in Western Germany," *Journal of Political Economy* 57 (1949): 277–292; F. A. Lutz, "The German Currency Reform and the

Revival of the German Economy," *Economica* 16 (May 1949): 122–142; Walter Laqueur, *Europe Since Hitler* (Baltimore: Penguin, 1973), 222–223.

93. Mike Schmeitzner, *Totalitarismuskritik von links: Deutsche Diskurse im 20. Jahrhundert* (Göttingen: Vanderhoeck und Ruprecht, 2007), "red-painted," 255; Ulla Plener, "Kurt Schumacher, 1949–1952: Die innere Gestaltung der BRD im Schatten seines Antikommunismus," in *Jahrbuch für Forschungen zur Geschichte der Arbeiterbewegung* 111 (2002); Tony Judt, *Postwar: A History of Europe Since 1945* (New York: Penguin, 2006), 267–268; William Carr, "German Social Democracy Since 1945," in *Bernstein to Brandt: A Short History of German Social Democracy*, ed. Roger Fletcher (London: Edward Arnold, 1987), 194–195; Anthony Glees, "The SPD in Emigration and Resistance, 1933–45," *Bernstein to Brandt*, 183–192.

94. Gustav Stolper, *The German Economy, 1870 to the Present* (London: Weidenfeld and Nicolson, 1967); Sheri Berman, *The Primacy of Politics: Social Democracy and the Making of Europe's Twentieth Century* (Cambridge: Cambridge University Press, 2006), 183–184; André Fontaine, *History of the Cold War*, trans. Renaud Bruce (New York: Pantheon Books, 1969), 47–49; Jeffrey Herf, *Divided Memory: The Nazi Past in the Two Germanys* (Cambridge: Harvard University Press, 1997), 208–220, 280–294; Norbert Frei, *Adenauer's Germany and the Nazi Past: The Politics of Amnesty and Integration* (New York: Columbia University Press, 2002), 149–168; T. H. Tetens, *The New Germany and the Old Nazis* (New York: Random House, 1961), 32–43; Luke Harding, "Menachem Begin 'Plotted to Kill German Chancellor,'" *The Guardian* (June 15, 2006).

95. John Lewis Gaddis, *We Now Know: Rethinking Cold War History* (New York: Oxford University Press, 1998), 137–148; Fontaine, *History of the Cold War*, 72–73.

96. "Godesberg Program of the SPD" (November 1959), http://germanhistorydocs.ghi-dc .org/sub_document.cfm?document_id=3049, 1–9, "the principles" and "and then," 5; "the fundamental," "in Christian," and "Socialists aim," 1.

97. Berman, *The Primacy of Politics*, "break out," 191; Frederick Kempe, *Berlin 1961* (New York: Penguin, 2011), 93–104; Tetens, *The New Germany and the Old Nazis*, 185–197; Carr, "German Social Democracy Since 1945," 197.

98. Carr, "German Social Democracy Since 1945," 198.

99. Sarah Bormann, *Angriff auf die Mitbestimmung. Unternehmensstrategien gegen Betriebsräte—der Fall Schlecker* (Berlin: Sigma, 2007); *Mitbestimmung und Betriebsverfassung in Deutschland, Frankreich und Großbritannien seit dem 19. Jahrhundert'. Tagungsband zum 16. wissenschaftlichen Symposium auf Schloss Quint bei Trier 1993*, ed. Hans Pohl (Stuttgart: Steiner, 1996); Petra Junghans, *Mitwirkung und Mitbestimmung der Betriebsgewerkschaftsleitung in den Betrieben der DDR: Eine empirische Untersuchung in Ost-Berliner Industriebetrieben* (Berlin: WVB, 2004).

100. Kempe, *Berlin 1961*, 97–101, 162–170, 375; Ernest Mandel, "Willy Brandt and Petra Kelly," *New Left Review* 1 (November/December 1992): 125–128; Carr, "German Social Democracy Since 1945," 199; Peter Merseburger, *Willy Brandt, 1913–1992: Visionär und Realist* (Stuttgart: DVA, 2002); Helmut Schmidt, *Men and Powers: A Political Retrospective* (New York: Random House, 1989).

101. Timothy Tilton, *The Political Theory of Swedish Social Democracy* (Oxford: Oxford University Press, 1990), 125–126; Lars Trägärd, "Crisis and the Politics of National

Community," in *Culture and Crisis: The Case of Germany and Sweden*, ed. Nina Witoszek and Lars Trägärd (New York: Berghahn, 2003), 129–130; Berman, *The Primacy of Politics*, 162–175.

102. Magnus Ryner, *Capital Restructuring, Globalization and the Third Way* (London: Routledge, 2002), 85–86; Gosta Esping-Andersen, *Politics Against Markets: The Social Democratic Road to Power* (Princeton: Princeton University Press, 1985), "the principal," 245; Rudolf Meidner, "A Swedish Union Proposal for Collective Capital Sharing," in *Eurosocialism and America: Political Economy for the 1980s*, ed. Nancy Lieber (Philadelphia: Temple University Press, 1982), 27–33; Meidner, *Employee Investment Funds: An Approach to Collective Capital Formation* (London: George Allen and Unwin, 1978); Berman, *The Primacy of Politics*, 183–186; Jonas Pontusson, "Radicalization and Retreat in Swedish Social Democracy," *New Left Review*, 165 (September/October 1987): 5–33.

103. Meidner, "A Swedish Union Proposal for Collective Capital Sharing," 29–31; Jonas Pontusson, *The Limits of Social Democracy: Investment Politics in Sweden* (Ithaca: Cornell University Press, 1992), 237; Pontusson, *Public Pension Funds and the Politics of Capital Formation in Sweden* (Stockholm: Swedish Center for Working Life, 1984); Esping-Andersen, *Politics Against Markets*.

104. Rudolf Meidner, "Why Did the Swedish Model Fail?" *Socialist Register* (1993), 211–228; Jonas Pontusson, *Swedish Social Democracy and British Labour: Essays on the Nature and Conditions of Social Democratic Hegemony* (Ithaca: Cornell University Press, 1988); Robin Blackburn, "A Visionary Pragmatist," *Counterpunch* (December 22, 2005), http://www.counterpunch.org/2005/12/22/a-visonary-pragmatist.

105. G. D. H. Cole, "The New 'New Atlantis,'" *Fortnightly* (November 1942), "is all," n.p.

106. Maurice B. Reckitt, *The Guildsman* (June 1919), "a Bolshevik" and "a bit," 3, and in Reckitt, *As It Happened* (London: J. M. Dent, 1941), 123; A. W. Wright, *G. D. H. Cole and Socialist Democracy* (Oxford: Clarendon Press, 1979), "full of internal," 264.

107. Crosland, "The Transition from Capitalism," Cole quote, 61.

108. G. D. H. Cole, *Essays in Social Theory* (London: Macmillan, 1950), "they are," 250; "anyone who," 251.

109. Reckitt, *As It Happened*, "the lumbering" and "to make," 124; William Mellor, "A Critique of Guild Socialism," *Labour Monthly* (November 1921), n.p.

110. Maurice Dobb, *Economic Journal* 35 (June 1935): "one feels," 296; G. D. H. Cole, "The Soviet Polity," *Soviet Studies* 2 (1950): "reared," in Wright, *G. D. H. Cole and Socialist Democracy*, 265, and Wright, "profound," 264, and "shabby," 265.

111. G. D. H. Cole, "To-Day's Economists," *New Statesman* 11 (October 17, 1931), 488; L. P. Carpenter, *G. D. H. Cole: An Intellectual Biography* (Cambridge: Cambridge University Press, 1973), 222; Cole, "Bernard Shaw," lecture at WEA Conference, Oxford, August 1, 1954, in Wright, *G. D. H. Cole and Socialist Democracy*, 269.

112. G. D. H. Cole, *Economic Tracts for the Times* (London: Macmillan, 1932), "fellowship does," 323; Reckitt, *As It Happened*, "I have known," 122.

113. G. D. H. Cole, "Gandhi, the Man," *Aryan Path* (January 1931), "why could," in Wright, *G. D. H. Cole and Socialist Democracy*, 271.

INDEX